THE PEERS, THE PARTIES AND
THE PEOPLE

THE PEERS,
THE PARTIES AND
THE PEOPLE

The British General Elections of 1910

NEAL BLEWETT

UNIVERSITY OF TORONTO PRESS

First published 1972 by The Macmillan Press Ltd,
London and Basingstoke

First published in Canada and the United States 1972
by University of Toronto Press
Toronto and Buffalo

ISBN 0-8020-1838-6
ISBN (microfiche) 0-8020-0163-7

LC 73-185701

Printed in Great Britain

For Jill

Contents

APPENDIXES

Preface

The general elections of 1910 were among the most decisive of modern elections, for they resolved the most acute controversy over the functioning of the central political institutions in modern British history. They were at the same time terminal elections bringing to a close the electoral politics of pre-1914 Britain. And, as with all general elections in democratic or semi-democratic societies, the elections of 1910 provide a focal point for examining the political processes of the time. This book is organised around these three perspectives.

Lawrence Lowell in his *The Government of England* was perhaps the first political scientist to stress the need to examine electoral oscillations over time in order to interpret the outcome of any particular election. The acceptance of Lowell's dictum is reflected in Part I of this work, which traces the establishment, maintenance and ultimate destruction of the electoral hegemony of the Unionists between 1886 and 1906. From this emerges an explanation for the electoral ebb and flow in the generation preceding the 1910 elections.

But a theory of electoral oscillation does not obviate the necessity to examine the immediate context of a given election. Perhaps the most striking development in the Nuffield College studies of post-war British elections has been the growing attention paid to pre-campaign events and developments. Context is peculiarly important in a study of the elections of 1910, for the occasion of both elections was atypical. The January election was caused by the refusal of the House of Lords to pass the financial provisions for the year; the December election by the necessity of securing electoral sanction for the Parliament Bill so that the royal prerogative would be available to the Ministry if the Lords proved obstinate over veto limitation. Part II sets the elections in their immediate context by tracing events from the low point of the Liberal Government's fortunes in the winter of 1908–9 through to the third successive electoral triumph of the Liberal Party in December 1910.

Part III, in which the approach is topical, is concerned with the functioning of the parties, and, to a lesser extent, the press and the pressure groups in the two elections. In the electoral interplay between these structures, some of the more significant features of the Edwardian body politic are revealed. The inherently fragmented nature of an electoral study, reflecting the multi-faceted nature of a general election, is apparent in this section.

Finally, Part IV aims to integrate the results of 1910 into the theory of electoral oscillation developed earlier, and to relate the results to their immediate political context, to the imperfections of the electoral system, and to the forces operative in Edwardian society.

I am grateful to the Warden and Fellows of St Antony's College, Oxford, for giving me the opportunity to write the original thesis on which this book is based; to the Rhodes Trustees for support during the initial research; and to the University of Adelaide, whose generous study leave provisions enabled me to consult recently opened manuscript collections in Great Britain.

So many have contributed in so many different ways to the writing of this book that space forbids the catalogue of their contributions. I must, however, thank Mr P. M. Williams, Nuffield College, Oxford, whose enjoyment of historical research was contagious, and who first aroused my interest in Edwardian politics; Mr A. F. Thompson, Wadham College, Oxford, whose unfailing response to the constant demands of an exigent research student went far beyond the call of a supervisor's duty; and Mr Henry Pelling, St John's College, Cambridge, mentor and friend to the author, and midwife to this book. I am grateful, too, to Professor W. G. K. Duncan, Professor T. G. Wilson, Dr Peter Loveday, Mr Ross McKibbon, Dr Brian Dickey and Mr J. M. Main for reading and commenting on various drafts. What virtues this book may possess owes much to them; the defects are all my own.

I am most grateful to the following for granting me access to manuscript collections of which they are the owners or custodians, and for permission to quote from documents whose copyright they control: the First Beaverbrook Foundation; the Librarian, the University of Birmingham; the Curators of the Bodleian Library, Oxford; the Hon. Mark Bonham Carter; the Trustees of the British Museum; the Earl of Cromer; the Viscount Harcourt; the Lancashire and Cheshire Liberal Federation; the Liberal Central Association; Major J. H. Maxse and the West Sussex Record Office; the Trustees of the National Library of Scotland; the Trustees of the National Library of Wales;

the National Union of Conservative and Unionist Associations; the Warden and Fellows, New College, Oxford; the Northern Liberal Federation; the Passfield Trustees; Lord Primrose; Baron St Audries; the Scottish Liberal Association; the Librarian, Sheffield Public Library; the *Spectator*. I am indebted to Professor A. S. King of the University of Essex for allowing me to use his transcript of the Carrington Diary, and Dr R. Rempel of the University of South Carolina for permitting me to use his transcript of the Arthur Elliot Papers.

In addition I am grateful to the following for permission to quote from documents whose copyright they control: the Rt Hon. Julian Amery; the Earl of Balfour; Lord Balfour of Burleigh; Mrs Mary Bennett; Baron Carrington; the Viscount Chaplin; the Viscount Knollys; the Marquess of Lansdowne; the Viscount Long of Wraxall; Colonel A. T. Maxwell; the Marquess of Salisbury the Earl of Selborne. I have made every effort to clear and acknowledge all copyright material. I trust that anyone whose copyright has been infringed will accept sincere apologies.

The difficulties of writing on British history in the Antipodes were eased by the promptness and courtesy with which librarians have dealt with my requests. I would particularly like to thank the Keeper of Manuscripts, British Museum; the Superintendent, British Museum Newspaper Library, Colindale; Mr A. J. P. Taylor and staff of the Beaverbrook Library; Mr D. Wyn. Evans, University Library, Birmingham; Mr A. S. Bell, National Library of Scotland; and Mr G. D. M. Block of the Conservative Research Department. Transcontinental difficulties were also eased by competent research help from Miss Alison Priestley and Mr A. B. Cooke.

Early versions of some sections of this work have appeared in *Past and Present* and the *Historical Journal*, and I wish to thank the editors for permission to reprint material which first appeared in these journals.

The typing of this book has been an arduous task and for bearing the burdens I thank Mrs Edna Hawke, Mrs M. E. MacGillivray, Mrs Maureen Woodman and Mrs Linda Smyth.

To my children, Susan and Simon, whose whole lives have been lived in the shadow of this book, my apologies. My greatest debt is acknowledged in the dedication.

Adelaide,
August 1970

PART ONE

Electoral Politics 1885–1906

The Unionist Hegemony 1886–1902

The general elections of 1910 provided the first verdict on the Liberal renaissance ushered in by the great Liberal victory of 1906. They were also a final verdict, for by the time the electors were appealed to again the Liberal Party had broken asunder. As a result of this split, the Liberals forfeited for ever their entrenched electoral position as one of the two ruling parties in the system, a position they had possessed and exploited in 1910. But the elections of 1910 were not merely the last significant popular judgements on a united and dominant Liberal Party. They were also the last general elections of Edwardian England; the last general elections fought under the electoral system designed in 1884–5; and the last general elections fought within the party system moulded by the events of 1885–6, and only marginally modified by the intrusion of the Labour Party. As such they provide a final perspective on the politics of a generation.

It was a generation dominated by the Unionists, for from 1886 to 1906 they governed for all but three years. This period falls electorally into two distinct parts: first, the hegemony of the Unionists from 1886 to 1902; secondly, the disintegration and overthrow of that hegemony between 1902 and 1906. An understanding of this hegemony and its destruction is a necessary background to the elections of 1910.

The events of 1885–6 impressed themselves on British politics for decades. Gladstone's decision that winter to act upon Home Rule and his unbending determination to legislate in the light of this decision split the Liberal Party, already plagued by other disorders, and led to the parliamentary defeat of the third Gladstone Government. The general election that followed, in July 1886, shattered the electoral supremacy possessed by the anti-Conservative front since the disruption of the Conservatives in 1846, and opened a period of Tory dominance without parallel in the years since the 1832 Reform Bill.

The triumph of Disraeli and Tory reaction in 1846 had ended Peel's effort to adapt a predominantly aristocratic and rural party to a rapidly

changing socio-economic environment. In so doing it had postponed
for a generation that developing accommodation between the landed
interest and the urban bourgeoisie which had promised, in the first
years of Victoria's reign, to make the Conservative Party the majority
party in the nation. Instead, the realignment of 1846–7 had established
another national majority – the heterogeneous collection of Peelites,
Whigs, Liberals and Radicals eventually becoming the Gladstonian
Liberal Party – which was to endure until 1886.

Mid-Victorian prosperity had eased the internal tensions in the ranks
of the motley and fragile coalition that had constituted the mid-
Victorian majority and thus had contributed to its long imperium.
With relatively better economic conditions in the 1850s and 1860s
pressures for social reform were less obtrusive. In Palmerston's heyday
domestic questions, usually divisive, had been virtually put aside with
few electoral repercussions. True, personal and policy differences had
permitted Conservative minority governments in 1852, 1858–9, and
1866–8, but in the forty-year period 1846–86 the Conservatives had
secured a majority only once, in the general election of 1874. That this
was but a temporary deviation from the prevailing pattern was shown
by the resounding Liberal victory of 1880.

The general election of 1886 ended this supremacy. The realignment
of significant elements of electoral support in that election established a
new pattern which was to last for twenty years. The new ascendant
coalition resulting from these changes was the Unionist alliance. Forged
by the Home Rule crisis, this alliance was to win an absolute majority
of seats in Great Britain in 1886 and in the general elections of 1892,
1895 and 1900. Although in 1892 the Unionists failed to win either a
popular or a parliamentary majority in the United Kingdom as a whole,
their strength in both Houses allowed them to sabotage key measures
of the Gladstone–Rosebery régime. The thirty-four months of the
1892 Parliament were little more than a formal interregnum in the
Unionists' twenty-year monopoly of political power.

Unlike the events of 1846–7 which reversed critical electoral developments of the previous decade, the crisis of 1886 consummated movements foreshadowed in earlier elections. The years between 1868 and
1886 witnessed the gradual attachment of nationally significant sections
of the urban bourgeoisie to the Conservative Party.[1] Disraeli may have
'dished the Whigs' in 1867, but perhaps not quite in the way he
intended. The urban working classes, enfranchised by Disraeli, were a
source of temptation to the radical, and a cause of alarm to the con-

servative, elements in the Liberal Party. Fears that their own interests might be neglected in the pursuit of the working-class vote made cautious manufacturers and financiers, as well as Whigs, reluctant to remain beneath the Gladstonian umbrella, particularly once their own demands had been met. The banker George Goschen, a most successful representative of commercial Liberalism, complained in 1877 that 'political economy had been dethroned in [the House of Commons] and that philanthropy had been allowed to take its place. Political economy was the bugbear of the working classes, and philanthropy, he was sorry to say, was their idol. . . .'[2] By 1880 Goschen was little more than a nominal Liberal and in 1886 he was 'the most persistent lobbyist of potential Liberal Unionists'.[3] The apprehensions of the Whig oligarchy are well exemplified by the Marquess of Dufferin and Ava. '. . . the tendency of the extreme section of the Liberal party', he told the Whig Duke of Argyll in April 1881, 'is to buy the support of the masses by distributing among them the property of their own political opponents, and it is towards a social rather than a political revolution that we are tending. . . .'[4] The meteoric rise of Joseph Chamberlain from Mayor of Birmingham to Minister in Gladstone's second Cabinet in the brief space of five years provided a personal focus for such anxieties. Chamberlain's well-publicised programmes promised to become the future platform of the Liberal Party, while the rapidity of his advancement heralded the imminence of change.

Disquiet over the pliability of the Liberal Party was heightened by concern over developing social tensions, exacerbated by less buoyant economic conditions after 1875. Through the 1870s and early 1880s the defensively minded urban bourgeoisie and the Whig aristocrats turned more and more to the Conservative Party as the party of order, the party of resistance to radical change, and the best available defender of a desirable, but threatened, *status quo*. Disraelian rhetoric facilitated this movement to the right by investing the Conservative Party with the glamorous trappings of imperial duty, and with responsibility for the sober but morally uplifting task of serving the nation rather than the interests of oligarchy or class.

By 1874 a Conservative wedge had been established in the larger boroughs. Based partly on the consolidation and expansion of Tory support amongst the working classes, these Conservative gains also derived, paradoxically, from 'the defensive reaction [of the middle classes] against the challenge of Radicalism and labour'.[5] A. J. Mundella, the Nottingham lace manufacturer and Liberal M.P. for Sheffield, noted just before the 1874 election, when the by-election tide was already flowing strongly against the Liberals: '... numbers of the middle-class Liberals will join [the Tories] or refrain from voting out of dislike to the attitude of the artisan class. I think this distrust of the workmen has more to do with Liberal defeats than Toryism, Teetotalism or the 25th Clause [of the 1870 Education Bill].'[6] Few politicians were so well placed as Mundella to assess middle-class opinion.

Although the Conservatives were severely repulsed in 1880, their position in the very largest constituencies (mostly the great cities) remained, by contrast with the situation in nearly every other type of seat, a distinct improvement over that of 1868.[7] The middle-class trend to the Unionists between 1868 and 1880 was most noticeable in London and the surrounding suburban belt, where the middle classes were thick upon the ground. Between 1868 and 1880 Conservative representation from London rose from three to eight, while in the Home Counties it rose from twenty-two to thirty-five.[8] Here there was no Conservative recession between 1874 and 1880.

But the revival of Conservative electoral fortunes after 1867 was not due simply to the adding of segments of the urban bourgeoisie to the party's traditional rural base. In some regions the newly enfranchised working man gave substantial backing to the Conservative Party. Working-class Toryism plus middle-class desertions had increased Conservative strength in Lancashire, bringing the party a majority of seats in the County Palatine in 1868 and 1874. Not since the First Reform Bill had the party secured such triumphs in Lancashire. Thus, while the Reform Act of 1867 had indirectly benefited the Conservatives by enhancing their appeal to an uneasy bourgeoisie, the direct effect of the Act, the enfranchisement of the urban artisan, had not proved wholly detrimental to the Conservative Party.

This process of realignment promising a new majority party was confirmed and renewed in 1885. Chamberlain's aggressive rhetoric in the months before the 1885 election had done nothing to erase the middle-class sense of vulnerability. Rather the reverse. 'Chamberlain's language is very indiscreet', wrote Mundella to his ally, the Sheffield newspaper editor, Robert Leader, 'and unnecessarily alienates a number of *moderate and timid people*.'[9] The exasperated Liberal Whip Lord Richard Grosvenor was quite blunt with Chamberlain himself: 'I tell you frankly that *you* have frightened over shoals of what I call the "floating balance", the men who turn an election!'[10] Lord Richard's Whiggish sympathies may have led him to exaggerate the extent both of the 'shoals' and of Chamberlain's contribution to their fright. Never-theless the new electoral dispensation, ensuring the isolation in single constituencies of the middle-class pockets within the great cities, made obvious the growing disaffection of the well-to-do from Gladstonian Liberalism. In London the Conservatives won all but two of the eighteen predominantly middle-class constituencies. In the London conurbation, outside the County of London boundary, the Con-servatives won every predominantly middle-class seat.[11] In Leeds, Bristol and Wolverhampton modern patterns of electoral cleavage were apparent with the Conservatives winning the middle-class, their opponents the working-class, divisions. Not that the Conservatives were without successes amongst the working classes. In Lancashire they recovered their majority, lost in 1880, while in London consider-able working-class support allied with the middle-class drift gave the Conservatives their first electoral majority in the Metropolis. The overall result of these developments was that the Conservatives secured a majority in the English boroughs for the first time since 1832.

Yet the creation of a new electoral alignment was far from complete in England, and had scarcely begun in Scotland by the end of 1885. In the first place the significance of the Liberal rout in the boroughs is debatable. Gladstone for one recognized that this was due as much to the influence of short-term political forces as to any long-term socio-political trend. 'Fair Trade+Parnell+Church+Chamberlain have damaged us a good deal in the boroughs . . . I place the *causae damni* in what I think their order of importance.'[12] The long-run movement of the middle class away from the Liberal Party was apparent in 1885, and its expression was facilitated by the recent redistribution. But the dramatic shifts to the Conservatives in the towns in 1885 were more likely the result of potentially short-term transfers, arising from im-mediate and temporary political factors, rather than from any sig-nificant long-run changes in the basic pattern of partisan loyalties.[13]

When we examine the issues and conduct of the 1885 campaign we can see that the short-term forces operating were almost wholly disadvantageous to the Liberal Party, at least in the boroughs. Although the Conservatives had secured the dissolution, the electoral verdict was upon a Liberal Government that had floundered for five years at home and abroad. Wracked by internal dissension, plagued by Irish questions and by Irish Members, and inheriting imperial problems for which it showed a marked distaste, the second Gladstone Administration had angered its enemies and dismayed its friends. Apart from the Irish

measures of 1881-2 and the electoral enactments of 1883-5, its legislative record was unimpressive and did nothing to bring it votes in the
English cities. The Government's imperial misadventures had further
sullied its reputation, and Majuba and Khartoum had given the Conservatives emotive catchcries with the urban masses. In Ireland the
Government had vacillated between appeasement and coercion; at the
election the Irish voters in the English cities deserted to the Conservatives in the interests of Home Rule and the Catholic schools.[14] In
addition the economic climate was unfavourable. Unemployment was
worse than in any year since the 1879 depression and was continuing
to rise. Both Joseph Chamberlain in the Midlands and the Marquess of
Hartington in Lancashire noted that in such conditions the panacea of
Fair Trade, offered by many urban Conservatives, had made many
converts.[15]

Nor did the Liberal campaign offset the current difficulties of the
party. The party was blessed with 'a Pentecostian gift of tongues' as
the rival factions disputed with each other throughout the election
campaign as to future Liberal policy. While Chamberlain 'scandalised'
the Whigs with his 'Unauthorised Programme', his Cabinet colleague,
the Marquess of Hartington, made speeches which read, at least to
Chamberlain and his allies, like 'a declaration of war' on that programme and its author. Indeed the campaign rather gave the impression of a struggle between Chamberlain and Hartington for the
allegiance of Gladstone, with that wily politician eluding them both
behind a smokescreen of platitudes. As the *Annual Register* ironically
observed, 'the Liberals gained whatever advantage might be found in
stimulating discussion upon the aims and aspirations of their different
leaders'.[16]

Thus the immediate issues of the election and the conduct of the
campaign worked mostly to the disadvantage of the dominant party,
the Liberals, at least in the boroughs, and were likely to encourage a
deviation in voting patterns in favour of the minority party, the Conservatives. But as the factors were mostly short-run, at least in terms
of their anti-Liberal impact, such a deviation from the pattern that had
prevailed over the last forty years was likely to be short-lived. That
this potentially temporary oscillation in the cities was given features of
permanence was the result of the dramatic events of early 1886, which
did lead to fundamental changes in the patterns of partisan identification.

Moreover, if the division of votes in the cities was strongly influenced by short-term questions, suggesting that the more durable changes in the cities had still to take place, the overall picture indicated that the electoral pattern characteristic of the post-1886 decades was far from established in England and Scotland. The Liberals still possessed an English majority in seats and votes, something they were not to secure again until 1906. This was due mainly to the fact that the Liberal borough losses were offset by the Liberal landslide in the counties. It may be that a new Liberal majority alignment was in the making in 1885 with support from the miners, the agricultural labourers, and the small-holders offsetting losses amongst the bourgeoisie and the industrial workers, a development aborted by the events of 1886. However, it is more likely that the shift of the counties from their traditional allegiance was itself a temporary deviation, occasioned by short-term factors favouring the Liberals in the countryside. An immediate response to the enfranchisement of 1884 coinciding with the landlords' initial inability to handle the new electoral situation; the attractions of the 'Unauthorised Programme' with its promise of 'three acres and a cow', or at least the encouragement of anti-establishment tendencies among the agricultural labourers arising from Chamberlain's crusade for the programme and against the Lords; and a dislike of Fair Trade, were probably all elements in the success of the Liberals in the English counties in 1885. But whatever the cause in 1885, Liberal strength in rural England was not to be a feature of the post-1886 pattern.

Other features too of the 1885 result in England and Scotland were soon to disappear. The Liberals remained in control of the industrial region centred on Birmingham, and emerged as the predominant party in the West Country and East Anglia. Within the year their strength in these regions was to be successfully challenged, in some cases being destroyed, in others substantially impaired. In Scotland the Conservative Party remained an 'impotent minority'. In 1885 the party still could poll only one-third of the votes in Scotland, and win only ten out of the seventy-two Scottish seats.[17] This situation too was to be much changed by events in 1886.

But if in England and Scotland the electoral realignment remained tentative and uncertain, it had been completed by 1885 in Ireland and Wales. In Ireland the elections of 1874, 1880 and 1885 witnessed the elimination of the Liberals as an electoral force in Irish politics, and the establishment of a disciplined Nationalist Party committed to Home Rule.[18] Two geographically defined single-party systems resulted from this realignment. In the decades following 1885 the Nationalist writ ran virtually unchallenged in Connaught, Leinster and Munster; in Ulster the Unionists were almost equally unchallengeable. Savage factional disputes, the bane of non-totalitarian one-party systems, frequently disrupted the Nationalist Party, and occasionally milder ones the Unionists; but only in Dublin, West Belfast, and along the frontiers of Ulster was there inter-party conflict. This alignment was to last until world war and civil war destroyed both the Nationalist Party and the constitutional link with Great Britain.

By contrast the Liberal Party in Wales, by becoming the vehicle of Welsh nationalism, secured a monopoly of Welsh representation. The election of 1868 saw 'the age-old domination of many landed families . . . rudely interrupted'; 1880 witnessed 'something like an agrarian revolt' and Liberal representation increased by ten seats over 1874; 1885 was 'the *annus mirabilis* for Welsh Liberalism. . . . The Conservative Party was swept out almost completely, retaining only four of the thirty-four Welsh seats.'[19] Again the process was completed by 1885. Wales was to remain a Liberal bastion until the Liberal Party itself broke asunder in the Great War.

Thus by the close of 1885, while significant and durable realignments had taken place in Wales and Ireland, the electoral patterns in England and Scotland, though volatile, were still distinct from those that were to prevail in the next twenty years. But the causes of fundamental change were already in the making for by December 1885 Gladstone was committed to his fateful Irish policy. 'Mr G's scheme is death and damnation', wrote an alarmed Chamberlain to his ally Dilke on 17 December 1885.[20] And so it proved. The election of July 1886 disabled the Liberal Party, established the hegemony of the Unionists, and radically altered the lines of electoral cleavage in England and Scotland. Contemporaries were astounded. 'It is indeed', wrote Sir William Harcourt to his wife, 'a smash the like of which has not been known.'[21] The results swept like a flood across the landscape of the electoral order, utterly transforming some familiar landmarks, completing the erosion of others. As the election that opens the hegemony, 1886 is worth close attention.

II

The overall swing from the Liberals in Great Britain between 1885 and 1886 was 5·7 per cent,[22] by far the most substantial shift in opinion in the period until the Liberal landslide of 1906. With the situation in Ireland little changed from 1885, and with only a marginal movement against the Liberals in Wales, the Liberal Party's losses were confined almost entirely to England and Scotland. The extent of the Liberal losses – 143 seats – had had no parallel since 1832.

TABLE I.1 RESULTS UNITED KINGDOM 1886

	Swing (%)	Net Liberal Loss (seats)	Members Returned			
			C.	L.U.	Lib.	N.
England	5·8	119	282	56	122	1
Wales	1·9	5	5	3	26	–
Scotland	7·2	19	12	17	43	–
Great Britain	5·7	143	299	76	191	1
Ireland	*	†	17	2	–	84
United Kingdom		143	316	78	191	85

Notes: * Because of the large number of uncontested seats no swing calculations are possible for Ireland.

† In Ireland the Unionists won two seats from, and lost one seat to, the Nationalists.

The swing from the Liberals was most obvious in those seats in which the Liberal revolt was most overt, i.e. in those seats with Liberal Unionist candidates. All told, the Liberal Unionists put forward 157 candidates in 156 seats in Great Britain.[23] Twenty-nine of these were returned unopposed. In a further sixteen cases it is not possible to calculate swing because the seats were uncontested, or contested by two Liberals only, in 1885. In the remaining 111 seats fought by the Liberal Unionists the swing against the Liberals was 8·8 per cent, well above the average for Great Britain.

But this figure disguises the precise electoral impact of the overt Liberal secession. In those constituencies in which the Liberal M.P., usually supported by a significant segment of the élite of the local Liberal Party, was in revolt from Gladstonian policies the turnover of votes was spectacular – the swing where calculable averaging nearly three times the national figure – and the ratio of Liberal Unionist successes high. Of the eighty Liberal M.P.s who had 'ratted', and who now fought their seats as Liberal Unionists, twenty-nine were returned unopposed despite their alleged betrayal of the G.O.M., while a

TABLE I.2 LIBERAL UNIONISTS AND ELECTION RESULTS
GREAT BRITAIN 1886

Nature of L.U. candidate	No.	Type of Contest	Results Swing (%)	Won	Lost
Liberal Unionist candidate ex-Liberal M.P. for constituency	80	Returned Unopposed		29	–
		Opposed (But no swing calculation possible)		5	3
		Opposed	16·6	32	11
				66	14
Liberal Unionist candidate not ex-Liberal M.P. for constituency	77	Returned Unopposed		–	–
		Opposed (But no swing calculation possible)		–	8
		Opposed	3·9	10	59
				10	67

further thirty-seven emerged victorious from their contests. But in those constituences where the Liberal breakaway lacked a lead from the local M.P. and was confined mostly to elements of the rank and file, the Liberal Unionist candidate was usually a relatively unknown local Liberal or even a Conservative seeking to make his way under the new label. In these constituencies the swing against the Liberals was distinctly below the national average and Liberal Unionist successes were few.

Concentrations of secessionist Liberal Members produced marked regional variations. In those regions in England with large numbers of Liberal Unionist candidates, and where the majority of these were the ex-Liberal M.P.s, both the regional swing against the Liberals and the regional ratio of Liberal Unionist successes tended to be high. Thus in the Western Midlands the massive defection of the local Liberal leadership, led by the 'Judas of Birmingham', produced a significant switch of opinion away from Gladstone (underestimated by the swing figure because of the large number of unopposed Liberal Unionist returns) and thirteen Liberal Unionist successes from fourteen candidatures. Similarly, the revolt of Liberal M.P.s in the South-West Peninsula produced a spectacular turnover of votes and seven Liberal Unionist victories from ten contests. Numerically smaller but proportionally as successful mutinies took place along the Severn, in the

Western Marches and in East Anglia, with ex-Liberal M.P.s playing
leading roles in all three regions. On the other hand despite the size of
the Liberal Unionist offensive in the Eastern Midlands, the West
Riding and North-East England, an offensive mounted mainly by the
other ranks, successes were minimal and the turnover of votes below
the national average.

TABLE 1.3 LIBERAL UNIONIST INTERVENTION BY REGIONS 1886

Region*	Swing (%)	No.	Liberal Unionist Candidates		
			% total candidates	No. sitting M.P.s	No. successful
London	6·7	5	8	2	2
Outer London	12·9	1	6	1	–
S.E. England	6·8	1	4	1	1
Thames Valley – Essex	8·9	2	9	2	2
Wessex	5·9	3	16	2	2
East Anglia	5·1	7	25	4	5
S.W. Peninsula	15·4	10	59	8	7
Severn	6·7	7	26	5	5
Western Midlands	7·4	14	39	11	13
Western Marches	8·5	6	35	4	5
Eastern Midlands	3·9	11	41	3	2
Lincolnshire	7·9	1	8	1	1
Western Lancastria	–0·3†	1	4	–	–
Eastern Lancastria	1·7	3	8	3	3
West Riding	2·6	14	38	4	3
North-East Ridings	3·0	1	7	–	–
Cumbria	2·8	2	20	1	1
N.E. England	4·2	9	35	3	2
Industrial Wales	1·2	5	36	2	2
Rural Wales	2·4	7	35	3	2
Highlands	3·7	10	83	3	3
N.E. Scotland	7·5	6	50	2	1
Forth Valley	11·2	11	73	5	3
Clyde Valley	4·7	9	50	4	4
Southern Scotland	8·9	9	69	5	6

Notes: * See Appendix I for definition of regions.
       † Indicates a swing to the Liberals.

In Scotland, where the Queen noted with evident satisfaction if some
exaggeration, that 'the Scotch seem quite to have turned against Mr
Gladstone',[24] a widespread Liberal schism produced more erratic

regional patterns. This was perhaps due to the 'impotent minority' position occupied by the anti-Liberal forces in most parts of Scotland prior to 1886, which makes parallels with the English situation difficult. But there was one close parallel with the situation south of the border. Thirteen of the seventeen successful Liberal Unionists in Scotland were the ex-Liberal M.P.s for the seats.

But Table 1.3 suggests that significant popular shifts were not restricted simply to those regions where the provincial Liberal leaders broke with Gladstone. In England at least, most of the predominantly rural regions reveal above average movements away from the Liberal Party, while the very high swing, 12·9 per cent, in Outer London indicates the dimensions of the suburban disenchantment with Gladstone and his policies. These indications of the social bases of the geographical realignment of 1886 are confirmed by Table 1.4, which shows the average swing in varying types of constituency in England. The average swing in predominantly middle-class constituencies and in rural constituencies is distinctly above the national average; in all other

TABLE 1.4 TYPE OF CONSTITUENCY AND SWING ENGLAND 1886

Type of Constituency*	No.	Swing (%)	No. ex-Liberal M.P.s standing as L.U.s
URBAN			
Predominantly middle-class	48	7·9	5
Mixed-class composition	107	4·8	13
Predominantly working-class	124	4·0	11
MIXED URBAN/RURAL	51	5·2	5
RURAL	98	8·4	18
MINING	28	5·1	4
	456†		

Notes: * See Appendix II for basis of classification.
       † Does not include university constituencies. Double-member constituencies counted as two constituencies.

types of constituency the average swing is below the national figure. Given their numbers and distribution seceding Liberal M.P.s could have had but a marginal effect on these contrasts. Thus while the rebellion of the Liberals in the West Country, the Western Midlands, East Anglia and Scotland was the most obvious feature of the Liberal

disaster and the national political realignment of 1886, this was accompanied by a general acceleration in the rate of middle-class desertions
from Liberalism, and by the wholesale reversal of the Liberal rural
successes of 1885.

The middle-class exodus from the Liberal Party, gathering momentum during the 1880s, reached a new peak in 1886. The dramatic
nature of the Home Rule issue and the opportunity it provided for
men to break with Gladstone in defence of unity, empire and the
Protestant religion, were instrumental in severing the emotional and
traditional links that had inhibited many of the defensively-minded
bourgeoisie from breaking with the party, despite their mounting
dissatisfaction with its domestic policies. Without Home Rule the
rising stream of affluent seceders would have continued; with Home
Rule the stream became a torrent. Moreover the traumatic break was
eased for many by the existence of the Liberal Unionist Party, possess-
ing many of the symbols, some of the leaders, and even the name of the
party they were abandoning – indeed many were thus able to sustain
themselves with the belief that the Liberal Party was abandoning them.
Joseph Chamberlain was well aware of the symbolic value of Liberal
Unionism.

> No one [he told his son Austen in 1895] who has not worked among the electors
> can be aware how strong are old prejudices in connection with party names and
> colours and badges. A man may be a good Unionist at heart, and yet nothing can
> persuade him to vote 'blue' or give support to a 'Tory' candidate.[25]

Thus the Liberal Unionist Party acted as a stepping-stone to the right
for electors of conservative inclination but anti-Conservative prejudices.

No historian has paid detailed attention to the reversal of Liberal
fortunes in the English countryside between 1885 and 1886. Home
Rule as the decisive issue in itself is an inadequate explanation as rural
voters seemed little interested in the Irish question except in areas where
seasonal Irish labour impinged. Moreover, unlike the middle classes,
the rural voters had appeared to be moving in a Liberal direction, the
results of 1885 being seen by some as the beginning of a trend. Why
then the slump in 1886?

Liberalism in the countryside in 1886 was both leaderless and listless.
The Whigs' final parting with Gladstone united the rural hierarchy
as never before. The remarkable change in the political complexion
of Aylesbury resulting from the Rothschild secession, and of West
Derbyshire arising from the Cavendish defection, and the 'Harting-
tonian character' of electoral change in the Western Marches[26] are

merely the most obvious examples of the electoral repercussions of the secession of the Whigs and their country clientele. Furthermore, the split in the Liberal Party disillusioned and confused the rural voter. The erstwhile Liberal champions of the agricultural labourer, Chamberlain and Jesse Collings, now appealed for a Unionist vote, Collings charging that Gladstone had 'unjustly postponed' rural reforms in order to pursue Home Rule.[27] As in the towns, heavy abstentions in the countryside testified to the disarray of the Liberals. In these circumstances the landlords, having learnt the lessons of 1885, appeared better able to cope with rural Radicalism.

The electoral geography resulting from the changes of 1886 was maintained in the elections of 1892, 1895 and 1900. The critical nature of the 1886 realignment is well illustrated in Table 1.5, which relates the Unionist performance by regions in 1886 to the regional results in the next three elections. With few exceptions the results in 1886 are accurate predictors of regional performance in the next three elections. These durable patterns of party support in the last decade of the nineteenth century are shown on Map 1.1.

The territorial foundation of Unionist strength in this period was a great triangle, the apex of which lay in Western Lancastria and the base of which ran from the River Exe in the west to Margate in the east. Attached to the apex was an eastern extension comprising the rural Ridings of Yorkshire. The bastions of the Liberals were both fewer and more scattered. They comprised the Celtic fiefdoms of Wales and eastern Scotland and the industrial citadels of the West Riding and Northumberland-Durham. This left three geographical blocks in which the supremacy of neither party was clearly established: first, western and southern Scotland plus Cumbria; secondly, the regions in England to the east of the great triangle; thirdly, the South-West Peninsula.

Not of course that the situation was completely static. There was a small swing of 2 per cent to the Liberals in 1892 which, although it failed to give them a majority of the seats in Great Britain, enabled them with the aid of the Irish Nationalists to govern uneasily for almost three years. A bigger swing, 3·7 per cent, restored the Unionists in 1895, with a majority both larger and more united than in 1886. 1900 saw a marginal swing favouring the Unionists, 0·6 per cent, although they had a net loss of seats over 1895. While Professor Mackintosh's economic theory of the swing of the pendulum overrates the general influence of the trade cycle,[28] it is probable that the minor oscillations in this period were most influenced by economic fluctuations.

TABLE 1.5 RESULTS BY REGIONS 1886–1900

	Region	Unionist % of vote* 1886	1885	Majorities 1892–1900†
Safe	Outer London	68·4	55·5	Always Unionist
Unionist	S.E. England	64·4	57·6	,, ,,
1886	Thames Valley – Essex	61·5	52·6	,, ,,
	London	59·2	52·5	,, ,,
	S.W. Peninsula	59·2	43·8	Mostly Liberal
	Western Marches	58·3	49·8	Always Unionist
	Western Lancastria	57·9	58·2	,, ,,
↑	Wessex	57·2	51·3	,, ,,
	Lincolnshire	56·6	48·7	Mostly Unionist
	Severn	55·0	48·3	Always Unionist
	North and East Ridings	53·5	50·5	,, ,,
	Eastern Lancastria	52·0	50·3	Mostly Unionist
	Cumbria	51·8	49·0	,, ,,
	East Anglia	51·8	46·7	,, ,,
	Western Midlands	50·8‡	43·4	Always Unionist
	Clyde Valley	50·4	45·7	Mostly Unionist
	Southern Scotland	50·4	41·5	,, ,,
	Eastern Midlands	47·3	43·4	Mostly Liberal
↓	Rural Wales	43·8	41·2	Always Liberal
	West Riding	44·6	42·2	,, ,,
	N.E. England	42·6	38·4	,, ,,
	Forth Valley	41·7	30·5	,, ,,
Safe	Highlands	38·7	35·0	Mostly Liberal
Liberal	N.E. Scotland	35·6	28·1	Always Liberal
1886	Industrial Wales	31·6	30·4	,, ,,

Notes: *Adjusted for uncontested seats.
   † Seats, as well as votes, the basis for this classification.
   ‡ An underestimate because of the large number of unopposed Liberal Unionist returns in the region.

The Baring crisis of 1890 signalled the end of the late 1880s boom, and by 1892 flagging investment, slackening industrial activity, falling trade, rising unemployment and a further drastic slump in the price of wheat accompanied the downturn in the fortunes of the reigning Unionist Party. Under the Liberals the situation got worse before it

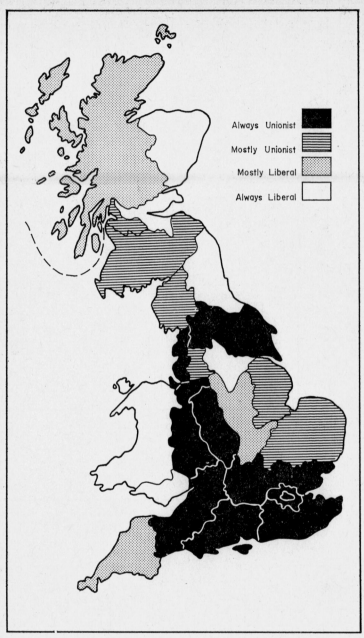

Map 1.1 RESULTS 1886–1900

Always Unionist

Mostly Unionist

Mostly Liberal

Always Liberal

got better. Unemployment rose until 1894 while, in Ensor's somewhat exaggerated phrase, agriculture was 'ruined a second time over',[29] wheat prices reaching a nadir in 1894. Although recovery was under way by 1895, it came too late to benefit the Liberals, Harcourt believing that 'this cry of "bad trade" has been the most potent of all our causes of defeat'.[30] On the other hand the 1900 election held under boom conditions artificially prolonged by the Boer War, and with signs of economic recovery at last in the countryside, saw no swing of the pendulum against the incumbents. Throughout, however, the imprint of 1886 remained firm, these swings producing only marginal modifications to the pattern of that year.

Certain trends were noticeable in the period, most of which favoured the Unionists. Overall their proportion of the vote rose from 52·2 per cent in 1886 to 54·3 per cent in 1900. Generally, the Unionists were weaker in the English rural regions in 1900 than in 1886, but this was more than offset by their increased strength in the urban and industrial regions and in Scotland. Nor were these advances simply Boer War phenomena, for the favourable trend to the Unionists was apparent in these regions in 1892 and 1895.

In Scotland attrition of Liberal support continued in the years after 1886, partly as a result of opposition to Church Disestablishment, which became part of the official programme of the Scottish Liberal Party in 1892. This proposal antagonised many erstwhile Liberal voters, particularly the Wee Frees in the Highlands.[31] Moreover, the Unionist identification with the current of imperialist sentiment in the 1890s culminating in the Boer War, appears to have struck a responsive chord amongst Scotsmen, perhaps because of the marked involvement of Scots in the armies and consulates of empire.

The consolidation of the Unionist position in the more urbanised regions of England in the last decade of the nineteenth century appears to have derived from Unionist successes in securing an increasing proportion of the working-class vote, or, at least, of working-class voters actually voting. Table 1.6 shows that while in the predominantly middle-class constituencies there was only a marginal Unionist advance between 1886 and 1900, in the mixed-class, and predominantly working-class, constituencies (including the mining constituencies) there were distinct Unionist gains. The demagogic Unionist appeal to working-class jingoism appears one reason for this advance. '[Chamberlain] has played it down low to the "man in the street"', observed the not unsympathetic Beatrice Webb of the campaign of 1900; 'the

TABLE 1.6 RESULTS BY TYPE OF CONSTITUENCY 1886-1900 ENGLAND

Type of Constituency	No.	Unionist %			
		1886	1892	1895	1900
URBAN					
Predominantly middle-class	48	65·0	60·3	64·3	65·8
Mixed-class	107	54·5	52·9	56·0	57·2
Predominantly working-class	124	50·2	48·5	52·9	54·1
MIXED URBAN/RURAL	51	56·2	53·2	56·5	55·3
RURAL	98	57·4	53·5	56·6	55·9
MINING	28	42·2	41·6	45·4	46·9

"street" has answered back with emphatic approval.'[32] Unionist association with the boom conditions at the end of the century, and the occasional, if meagre, instalments of Chamberlainite social reform were further positive elements in the Unionist success with the working-classes. But Liberal negativism was perhaps more important. Gladstone's preoccupation with Ireland, the parochial concerns of the Celtic fringe, and the specific fanaticisms of the Nonconformists, destroyed the prospects for social reforms despite the eclectic promises of the Newcastle Programme. Industrial distress accompanied legislative sterility between 1892-5 - hardly a combination likely to enthuse the working classes on behalf of Liberalism. At the grass roots the Liberals were much vexed by the difficulty of securing both middle-class money and working-class votes. Both were needed yet their pursuit gave rise to incompatible policies. While the party leaders were increasingly aware of the need for proletarian votes, the local Liberal caucuses tended to opt for middle-class money at the expense of working-class votes.[33]

III

Concentration on electoral geography and on changes in voting proportions alone can lead to neglect of the less positive aspects of the Unionist hegemony. For if the geographical imprint of 1886 was lasting, so was the negative element that was so crucial a feature of the 1886 results. While only twenty Members had been returned unopposed in Great Britain in 1885, in 1886 the figure rose to 153. The great bulk of these were Unionists. The Liberals indeed had difficulties in finding candidates to fight some of the secessionist Liberals, let alone to contest

Conservative seats.[34] The result was that nearly one-third of the Unionist M.P.s in Great Britain were returned unopposed.

TABLE I.7 UNOPPOSED RETURNS GREAT BRITAIN 1885–1906

[Figures in brackets no. of Unionists returned unopposed]

1885	1886	1892	1895	1900	1906
20 [6]	153 [116]	43 [30]	128 [117]	171 [149]	32 [5]

Having allowed 116 seats to go by default, the Liberals were overthrown completely by the fact that so many of their own voters then defected, not so much to Unionism, but rather into abstention. The polls in seats contested both in 1885 and 1886 fell in the latter year by nearly 10 per cent. Although the staleness of the register partly accounts for this fall, voluntary abstention by disillusioned Liberals seems the chief explanation. Chamberlain had warned his old ally Labouchere in April 1886: '. . . it is the men who stay away who turn elections, and there will be a larger abstention on this Irish question than we have ever had before in the history of the Liberal party.'[35] While the general theory is questionable, its applicability to 1886 seems inescapable. Surveying the débâcle Labouchere concluded that his former colleague's prediction had been correct: '. . . whilst the Conservatives voted, many Liberals and Radicals sulked, and did not come up to the poll.'[36]

If we examine voting figures in those 119 seats contested in both 1885 and 1886, and won by the Unionists from the Liberals at the latter election, we can see how profound was the influence of Liberal abstention. In these 119 seats the Liberal vote fell by 127,892 in 1886, yet the Unionist vote increased by only 45,735. Even allowing generously for involuntary abstention, it appears that the majority of these seats fell to the Unionists not as the result of Liberal switches, but through voluntary abstention. Thus the Unionist hegemony was ushered in by default rather than by conversion.

In the years that followed it was similarly maintained, not by positive enthusiasm for Unionism but by the inability of the Liberals to mobilise their resources and their potential voters. The inability of the Liberal machine to mount a wide-ranging election campaign was seen in the high level of uncontested seats that characterised the elections of the last decade of the nineteenth century. The number of unopposed returns was particularly high in 1895 and 1900, and the Unionist share of such returns greater than in 1886. In both these elections the Unionists were well on the way to victory before polling commenced. Even in 1892, the most favourable election for the Liberals in this period, and the election with the fewest unopposed returns, Unionist candidates returned without a contest outnumbered the Liberals by two to one. At the root lay lack of enthusiasm amongst Liberal Party members reflected in the poverty of party resources and the lack of party finance. Much of the wealth had gone with the Liberal Unionists, for as a contemporary noted 'the schism . . . had transferred to the Unionists the majority of the wealthy peers and county families'.[37] In some cases Liberal organisations crumbled away and, as Dunbabin has pointed out, in those constituencies where the Liberal Party was not able to compete regularly 'the balance tilted very sharply against it'.[38]

The general malaise affected Liberal voters as well as Liberal acti- vists. Turnout remained comparatively low until 1906, and seems to have resulted from a continuation of the Liberal abstention so notice- able in 1886. Cornford has shown for the period 1885–1906 that 'the Conservative percentage of the poll varied in inverse proportion to the size of the poll; in fact the smaller the poll the larger the Conservative share of it', and has argued convincingly from this that 'the chief factor in Conservative success was lack of enthusiasm among the Liberals'.[39] Although there are some difficulties with this thesis for 1906, it does support the contention that, in the period 1886–1900, the Unionist achievement was essentially a negative one, based on the failure of the Liberal leaders to arouse the party workers and to rally the Liberal voters.

Such a thesis is certainly plausible given the political events of the period. Throughout, the short-term forces distorting partisan allegiance were mostly anti-Liberal. Gladstone's obsession with Home Rule, the feuds amongst the Liberal leaders in the 1890s, the patriotic fervour of 1900 were all likely to drive otherwise Liberal voters to Unionism, or more often, given their party identification, to abstention. In retro- spect, the Liberals appear to have done their best to lose the elections of 1886, 1895 and 1900, while their Nationalist allies did their best to discredit the Home Rule cause in 1892. In 1886 Gladstone dissolved for a second election within six months, with his party rent by schism and with few of the prominent figures in the party sharing his suicidal en- thusiasm for Home Rule. In 1895 a leaderless party fought a peculiar campaign with each of the quarrelling triumvirs pushing his own pet project – Rosebery House of Lords reform, Harcourt Local Veto, and Morley Home Rule. It was difficult in 1900 to envisage the Liberal Party – outmanœuvred, split and despairing – as an alternative govern-

ment. If we omit the stress on 'Imperially' the magisterial verdict of
the *Annual Register* on the 1900 election could well serve as the epitaph
of the Unionist hegemony.

> The Ministerialists gained an immense victory, not because there was any
> popular enthusiasm either of approval for the past or of anticipation as to the
> future legislative or administrative achievements of the Unionist Government –
> for there was no such feeling – but because the Liberal party was recognised as
> being for the time Imperially impossible.[40]

The hegemony was founded and sustained not primarily because of
any positive enthusiasm for the Unionists, but because the Liberals
were considered 'impossible'. Unionist electoral supremacy rested not
so much on the conversion of Liberal voters, although there was an
element of this, but on the alienation of potential Liberal voters unable
for one reason or another to cast a vote for the party with which they
were identified. Thus the realignment of 1886 can be seen rather as a
negative restructuring of political patterns, sustained for two decades
more by antipathy to Liberalism than by enthusiasm for Unionism.

Of course the corollary of this thesis was that the Unionist majority
was really a minority, surviving in power simply because for varying
short-term reasons the potential Liberal majority could not be realised.
As Dunbabin has observed, 'there were many indications of the existence of a considerable body of radical feeling which might tip the
balance if it could be tapped', and he instances various Independent
Labour interventions which exploited this feeling, without at the same
time seriously diminishing the Liberal vote.[41] There were three ways
in which this vote could be tapped. First by the regeneration of the
Liberal Party; secondly by a powerful reaction against the dominant
Unionists; thirdly by the creation of a new party designed to secure
this untapped vote. All three were to play a role in the process which
brought about the ultimate downfall of the Unionists. But there is
perhaps a certain ironic justice in the fact that the Unionist hegemony
should have been destroyed above all by a revulsion against it, rather
than by any particular enthusiasm for its enemies. It is to this destruction that we must now turn.

The End of the Hegemony 1902–6

I

On 12 July 1902 Arthur Balfour succeeded his uncle Lord Salisbury as Prime Minister. For a decade at least Balfour had been the heir apparent. But what value the inheritance? A fortnight later the new Ministry suffered a severe and unexpected by-election reversal at North Leeds. The Unionist majority of 2517 at the general election of 1900 was turned into a deficit of 758, a swing of 13 per cent. 'One swallow does not make a summer', cautioned the Liberal *Review of Reviews*.[1] But North Leeds was to prove the harbinger of the Liberals' Indian summer. For July 1902 marks the beginning of the end of the Unionist hegemony and with it that resurgence of Liberalism that was to characterise the Edwardian age. It is perhaps not inappropriate that Balfour, whom his cousin Lord Hugh Cecil was one day to describe as 'the most unskilful leader (out of Parlt.) since Wellington',[2] should inherit the Prime Ministership in the very month that the great majority bequeathed him by his uncle began to disintegrate.

The Unionists had been almost totally unprepared for North Leeds. The Government's by-election record in the first eighteen months of the twentieth century had been a remarkably successful one, particularly given the Ministry's long tenure of power. The Unionists had retained their seats in nine contests up to May 1902 and, thanks to Labour intervention, had won North-East Lanark from the Liberals in September 1901. The small overall swing to the Liberals in these by-elections rightly occasioned no concern in the Unionist ranks. The first hint of trouble had come on 10 May, when the Liberals won Bury, Unionist since 1886, with an 8·3 per cent swing. This unforseen defeat was generally minimised on the grounds that the very recent conversion of the Unionist candidate to Unionism had damaged the party's chances.[3] No such excuse was available for the disaster at North Leeds. Comprising the 'villadom' of Leeds it had been a Unionist seat since its creation in 1885, and its fall shook the Unionist Party. But worse was to come. On 21 August the Liberals slashed the Unionist majority in Sevenoaks, a supposedly invulnerable seat in the Tory heartland, from 4812 in 1900 to a mere 891. 'The doom of Mr Balfour's Ministry pronounced at North Leeds has been countersigned at Sevenoaks', exulted the *Review of Reviews*,[4] while the near loss of this constituency is alleged, understandably, to have sent 'a shiver down the backs of Unionist organisers all over the country'.[5]

The formidable swing against the Government ushered in by these summer by-elections continued unabated for nearly twelve months, waned from mid-1903 to mid-1904, and then slowly gathered momentum again over the last eighteen months of the Government's life. Two general observations can be made about this by-election pattern set out in Figure 2.1. First, it suggests that the common

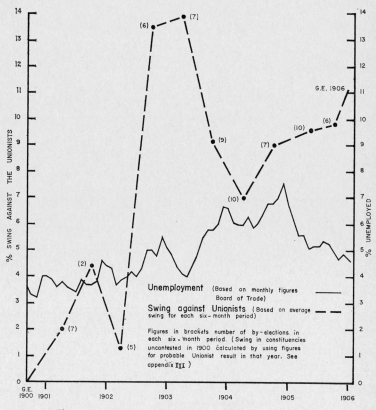

Figure 2.1   SWING AGAINST THE UNIONISTS 1900–6

emphasis on Joseph Chamberlain's role as the destroyer of the Unionist supremacy requires qualification. Secondly, economic fluctuations appear to have had little if anything to do with the Unionist decline.

It has frequently been argued that by defying his Cabinet colleagues and raising the issue of Tariff Reform in the momentous Birmingham speech of 15 May 1903, Chamberlain alienated the voters, split the Unionists and reunited the Liberals. Thus a principal architect of the hegemony becomes the chief agent of its disintegration. It is true that the internal dissensions provoked by Tariff Reform rendered the Unionists incapable of handling their electoral difficulties, although responsibility for the dissensions should perhaps be distributed between Chamberlain and his Cabinet colleagues. It is equally true that the threat to Free Trade restored the unity of the Liberals after a decade of internecine quarrels, although the Education Bill of 1902 had already made a signal contribution to this end. Nevertheless, the emphasis on Chamberlain's role obscures the extent of the electoral erosion prior to Chamberlain's Birmingham speech and ignores the distinct, though temporary, recovery that ensued. The by-elections ran more strongly against the Unionists in the twelve months preceding Chamberlain's *pronunciamento* than at any subsequent period while, in the months immediately following, the Unionists partially stemmed the tide that was running against them. Forces undermining the Unionist hegemony were well at work prior to May 1903, while it is at least arguable that the immediate effect of Tariff Reform was temporarily to arrest the Liberal resurgence.

The electoral slump of 1902 also occurred well in advance of the economic recession that followed the Boer War, while the gathering momentum of the anti-Unionist current in 1905 coincided with a rapidly improving economic climate. There are, paradoxically, some signs from 1903 on of an inverse relationship between the health of the economy and that of the Unionist Party, i.e. as the economy got worse the outlook for the Unionists improved, while as the economy improved the outlook for the Unionists got worse. This lends some weight to the argument that the 1903–4 recession abetted Chamberlain's crusade by confirming the need for fiscal change while, by contradicting Chamberlain's prophecies of woe, the 1905 recovery ruined whatever immediate chances his campaign might have had. But the relationship is by no means clear, and the thesis offers no explanation for the 1902 electoral collapse, nor for the persistently high level of Unionist unpopularity from 1902 on. While the trade cycle played but

a marginal role in the creation and preservation of the Unionist hegemony, so its role appears minimal in the collapse of that hegemony.

The critical nature of the electoral downturn between May 1902 and
May 1903 is further emphasised by the fact that the by-elections in these
months were already marked by the distinguishing characteristics of
the great débâcle of 1906. First, the reaction against the Unionists in
these by-elections had a universal quality, affecting apparently all types
of voters, certainly all types of constituency. The trend was obvious in
predominantly middle-class, as well as in predominantly working-
class seats, in rural seats and in Scottish seats. The loss of Orkney and
Shetland on 18–19 November 1902 opened the most inexorable trend
of all. Every Scottish Unionist seat contested at a by-election in the
next three years was lost.

Secondly, these early by-elections were characterised by turnout
figures unequalled since 1885. '. . . the figures of [the] by-elections',
noted the *Annual Register* in 1903, 'pointed . . . more to a rally of
Liberals at the polls than to a defection of Conservatives.'[6] That active
if primitive psephologist, W. T. Stead, editor of the *Review of Reviews*,
comparing the by-election results with the previous polls in the constituencies concerned, calculated that in these twelve months the total
Unionist vote fell by only 6 per cent while that of the Liberals rose by
50 per cent.[7] It appears that the Liberals were attracting former
abstainers, and thus undermining the vital negative support of the
Unionist supremacy.

This sudden crumbling of the Government's popularity at the very
moment of victory in South Africa, and with the economic climate
still fair, resulted apparently from the Education Bill of 1902. A comprehensive measure of administrative rationalisation and educational
reform, it was inevitably and deliberately entangled in the sectarian
question. Both to rally Anglican support for a measure assured of
Nonconformist hostility, and to render palatable to the Tory majority
a measure with broad bureaucratic, even collectivist, implications, the
Bill resolved a number of acrimonious sectarian issues in favour of the
Anglican establishment. In so doing it created the 'last great nonconformist political demonstration',[8] and with the protest of the
Dissenters came the revival of the Liberal Party.

Both at North Leeds and Sevenoaks the Liberal candidates were
Baptists and the Bill the main topic of the by-elections.[9] On 4 August
1902 an alarmed Chamberlain warned Balfour: '. . . I do not think that
any seat, where there is a strong Nonconformist electorate, can be

considered absolutely safe.'[10] The disasters at Newmarket and Rye in early 1903 confirmed Chamberlain's fears. The Newmarket constituency was full of Nonconformist villages, while Rye contained along the Weald some of the few significant pockets of Nonconformity in the rural Home Counties.[11] The Liberal Unionist wing of the alliance naturally suffered the most. The reports to the Liberal Unionist headquarters in Great George Street during the summer of 1902 were 'black as night'.[12] Facing a Nonconformist revolt in his own Duchy, Chamberlain wrote bitterly to Devonshire, the Minister nominally in charge of the Bill: 'I told you that your Education Bill would destroy your own party. It has done so. Our best friends are leaving us by scores and hundreds, and they will not come back.'[13]

Others blamed a second measure of the 1902 session – the corn duty – introduced as a war revenue measure in the 1902 Budget. Sandars, Balfour's influential private secretary, reported to his master that Captain Middleton, Chief Agent of the Conservative Party, 'takes a much more serious view of the Corn Tax [than of the Education Bill]. . . . He speaks of it as a millstone round our necks'.[14] The corn duty played an important role at Bury, the first by-election following its introduction, and the Woolwich by-election in March 1903 was 'largely fought on the "cheap loaf" '.[15] The question was prominent in the by-elections in the predominantly working-class constituencies; elsewhere it tended, at least in Liberal rhetoric, to play a secondary role. A study of the North Leeds campaign tends to confirm Chamberlain's surmise that the corn tax was 'only a convenient instrument used by the Nonconformist Party to support their own grievance'.[16]

But deeper currents sustained the reaction against Unionism. Although the secret concordat between Herbert Gladstone, Chief Whip of the Liberal Party, and Ramsay MacDonald, Secretary of the Labour Representation Committee, was not concluded until September 1903, a rapprochement between the Liberals and the forces of Labour was well under way in the previous eighteen months. The unopposed return of David Shackleton as Labour M.P. for Clitheroe in August 1902 in succession to the Liberal Kay-Shuttleworth, the official support given by the cotton operatives to the Liberal candidate at Bury, and the progressive alliance which won Woolwich under the nominal banner of the L.R.C. were indications of the developing accommodation, while the growth of the Liberal vote in working-class constituencies was its most significant manifestation. Disenchantment with the Unionist failure over social reform, and the obvious hostility of the

Unionist Party to any amendment, let alone reversal, of the Taff Vale Judgement, led Labour to pin its hopes increasingly on a Liberal victory. The growth of collectivist sentiment within the Liberal Party, the readiness of Liberals to take up cudgels against Taff Vale, and the active sympathy of the Liberal leaders, particularly Campbell-Bannerman and Herbert Gladstone, for Labour representation, engendered a revival of Lib-Labism. The secret Gladstone–MacDonald compact might ensure the independent representation of Labour; in the great majority of constituencies it would aid the channelling of Labour votes to the Liberal candidate.[17]

Nor is it perhaps accidental that the Unionist collapse followed so quickly after the Peace of Vereeniging. Once British soldiers were no longer dying on the Veldt British voters were no longer inhibited from expressing with their ballots their opinions on Unionist maladministration of the war. A Unionist journal was later to attribute the defeat of 1906 to the 'hideous mismanagement' of the war which it instanced as 'one prolonged object lesson in Ministerial incapacity'.[18] Nor were the Unionists allowed to forget their hollow claim, made in the general election of 1900, that the war then was all but won.

Moreover the Boer War had provided an opportunity to prolong the Unionist hegemony through the Khaki Election. In the late 1890s as domestic dissatisfaction with the Unionists grew, their electoral position had been threatened. For them the Boer War was a 'godsend'.[19] It enabled them to divert attention from the sterility of their domestic policy and to appeal for a renewal of their mandate in conditions totally favourable to themselves and totally unfavourable to their opponents. With the war out of the way, the pendulum, in a sense artificially reversed in 1900, resumed with all the violence of delay its swing against the Unionists.

II

Chamberlain's call at Birmingham in May 1903 for a revision of the Free Trade system arose from his conviction that the preservation of the Empire and of Britain's industrial supremacy demanded a scheme of imperial preference and a degree of industrial protection. But while Chamberlain's beliefs had long matured and were deeply held, the occasion of the speech was primarily tactical. It was first a riposte to those Cabinet colleagues who, in the spring of 1903, had permitted the Chancellor of the Exchequer, C. T. Ritchie, to abandon the corn

duty out of fear that it might be used as an instrument of preference.[20]
It was secondly a response to the gloomy electoral prospect, an effort
to revive the failing fortunes of the party by providing a great imperial
cause to which all classes in the nation might rally. 'You can burn all
your political leaflets and literature', Chamberlain told the Liberal
Chief Whip. 'We are going to talk about something else.'[21] If the
debate could be switched from education, war maladministration and
Taff Vale to fiscal reform, the electoral decline might yet be arrested.

For a while Chamberlain was allowed the illusion of success. By-
election results improved. In September 1903 Chamberlain pointed out
to Devonshire that 'Education and our War Office policy . . . gave us
[Woolwich] and Rye and Kent [Sevenoaks] – all before the fiscal
question was mentioned. Where have you had such a turnover of votes
since?'[22] The six Unionist seats contested in England in the last half of
1903 were all held, despite Liberal hopes in several cases. Although
these Liberal expectations were mostly exaggerated, the turnover of
votes suggested that the swing against the Government had eased.

The New Year brought two major defeats at Norwich and St Albans
which, with two less surprising losses, were widely regarded as having
broken the Tariff Reform boom. Certainly they appear to have knocked
the stuffing out of the Unionist Party. However, the swing at Norwich
and St Albans was not typical of the general pattern during the first
nine months of 1904. Balfour, although very ready to see the fiscal
divisions as the fount of all his troubles, admitted in September 1904
that 'the elections seem to have gone as much against us before, as after,
these divisions made themselves felt'.[23] The by-elections had, in fact,
been considerably worse in terms of votes, if not of seats, in the year
prior to Chamberlain's Birmingham call than in the year that followed.

This partial recovery is all the more remarkable in that other political
events in late 1903 and early 1904 were likely to tell against the Government electorally. The purging and reconstruction of the Cabinet in
September–October 1903 were hardly likely to restore confidence in
the Government, particularly as the two most influential figures in the
Ministry after Balfour, Joseph Chamberlain and the Duke of Devonshire, both left the Cabinet. Despite Balfour's expectation of June 1903
that 'the Education Bill fever will be allayed in twelve months',[24] it
showed little signs of abating. A massive campaign of passive resistance
was afoot in England, while by April 1904 the County Councils of
Wales were united in defiance of the Government. The Licensing Bill
of 1904 further aggravated the Nonconformist conscience, while the

employment of indentured Chinese labour in the Rand mines disturbed
the national conscience, confirmed for many the theory that the war
had been fought for the 'Randlords', and contributed to the mobilisation of Labour against the Government. Nor was Chinese labour the
only by-product of the war to trouble the Government in these
months. In August 1903 the report of the Elgin Commission was
published – a damning indictment of ministerial and military unpre-
paredness and incompetence.

Yes despite these developments the trend against the Government
was partially arrested. The *Annual Register* recognised that 'if it had
not been for the engrossing interest of the fiscal controversy, the position of the education question would have engaged a large measure of
public attention', while on the reception of the Elgin Report it opined:
'Anger against the Government as a whole might very possibly have
taken a menacing form if the public mind had not been . . . so markedly preoccupied by the fiscal question.'[25] Thus electorally damaging
issues were obscured by the smoke of the fiscal controversy. Perhaps,
too, the Government for a time benefited both from Chamberlain's
crusade and from the abolition of the corn duty. But it was soon to get
the worst of both worlds.

Chamberlain's campaign failed to save the Unionists, partly because
the current against the Government was already too strong, partly
because of the inherent difficulties of winning votes for Tariff Reform,
and partly because the fiscal issue destroyed the unity of the Unionist
Party. For many, Free Trade was an article of faith: it was un-English,
even un-Christian, to tamper with it. At a more mundane level the
taxation of food stuffs, a necessary aspect of imperial preference aroused
fears which Tariff Reform propaganda never overcame and most
of Chamberlain's dialectical efforts to do so were counter-productive.
On this point Balfour was clear. 'The prejudice of a small tax on food
is not the fad of a few imperfectly informed theorists: it is a deep-
rooted prejudice affecting the large mass of voters, especially of the
poorest class, which it will be a matter of extreme difficulty to overcome.'[26] Working-class fears of the 'stomach tax' were to outweigh
vague promises of 'employment for all' throughout the Edwardian
period. Again, while certain industries and regions, notably light
metals and the West Midlands, welcomed industrial protection, other
industries and regions, particularly cotton and Lancashire, were hostile,
while many in the world of finance and banking were also averse to a
protective policy. Moreover, the rapid development of boom conditions

after 1904 eradicated much of the protectionist sentiment fostered by recession. Thus while the working classes disliked the food duties, significant elements of the business community opposed industrial protection.[27]

Chamberlain's attack on Free Trade consolidated the growing unity of the Liberals, for all wings of the party rallied to the defence of the economic doctrine that lay at the heart of the traditional Liberal view of national and international society. The attack served too to strengthen the links between the Liberals and the L.R.C., for most of the Labour leaders were equally dedicated to the Free Trade faith. By 1904 the Unionists faced the most formidable and affluent Opposition they had encountered since their accession to power in 1886. As early as July 1903 the Liberals had candidates for nearly all winnable constituencies, while from 1903 on the party coffers were swollen by generous donations from the opponents of Tariff Reform.[28] Such conditions were in sharp contrast with the party's poverty and lack of candidates during most years of the Unionist hegemony.

The Unionists might still have escaped disaster, if not defeat, if they had been agreed on fiscal reform. But they were not.[29] Chamberlain was naturally supported by those in the party who had seen the light before he had, such as Henry Chaplin, the long-time proponent of agricultural protection, and Sir Howard Vincent, the able advocate of the Sheffield steel interests. Chamberlain secured widespread support within the party, particularly from the new men – shipowners such as R. P. Houston of Liverpool and George Renwick of Newcastle; ironmasters such as Andrew Bonar Law, H. Pike Pease, Sir John Randles and Sir Thomas Wrightson; retailers such as Sir John Maple. The Chamberlain faction, numbering at the most about 200 M.P.s, was based primarily upon urban Conservatism. Its chief industrial strongholds were Birmingham and the Black Country, 'the Chamberlain Duchy'; Merseyside where, reported Sandars in October 1903, 'Liverpool had gone Joe-mad . . . they won't look at anybody unless he swallows the whole of Joe's gospel . . .';[30] and Sheffield where the pioneering work of Vincent now paid dividends.[31] Chamberlain aroused, too, the devoted enthusiasm of a number of able young men, mostly at this time outside Parliament, who shared with Chamberlain his vision of an imperial order, sustained by national efficiency and economic interdependence. Among these were combative country gentlemen such as Edward Goulding, Henry Page Croft, Lord Winterton and Lord Willoughby de Broke, and intellectuals such as Halford Mackinder, W. A. S. Hewins and Leopold Amery.[32]

Both the young men and the new men shared with Chamberlain an awareness of the need to modernise both British economic policies and the Unionist Party. To make the Unionist Party the instrument for Tariff Reform was a means of securing both objectives. But the Whole Hoggers, as they were aptly nicknamed, commanded the support neither of a clear majority of the parliamentary party nor of the party leader.

Chamberlain's attempt to commit the Unionist Party to Tariff Reform met the uncompromising hostility of the leading Whig Unionists – Devonshire, Goschen, Balfour of Burleigh, James of Hereford; of prominent Cecilian Conservatives – Hicks Beach, Ritchie, and the younger members of the Cecil house itself; and of ambitious parliamentary *frondeurs* including Winston Churchill, Major J. E. Seely, and Thomas Gibson Bowles. This influential but small faction, numbering at most about sixty M.P.s, was dogmatic in its total rejection of Tariff Reform, 'an evil of the same class as Home Rule'.[33] The Unionist Free Traders or Free Fooders drew support particularly from Scotland and the West Country, centres of the Liberal revolt of 1886 yet relatively free from Birmingham influence; from cotton Lancashire wedded to Free Trade; from the Universities, wedded to economic orthodoxy; and from London where 'free foodism' was well entrenched in the City.

Between these contending factions stood Arthur Balfour and the Balfourites. The Balfourites were characterised more by a distaste for extremism than by any coherent view on the fiscal question. Moderation of temperament, dislike of the dogmatism of Free Fooder and Whole Hogger alike, and distrust of the political motives of the Chamberlainite crusade brought Unionists of all fiscal shades to Balfour. The social basis of the Balfourite faction was the landed interest, particularly the county gentlemen 'the cornerstone of the Hotel Cecil' during its long tenure of power.[34] The landed classes were not hostile to tariffs. Indeed they had an atavistic sympathy for the protectionist cause, although some feared that tariffs would alienate the mass of the agricultural population. But what they really disliked about the Tariff Reform campaign were its wider political implications. The landed interest had never really taken the screwmaker from Birmingham into the Tory fold, and it feared that the triumph of Tariff Reform would mean the victory of Birmingham within the party. It was the subversion of the existing power structure within the party, and the possible disruption of the party itself, that the landed interest feared, not tariffs *per se*.

Balfour himself had little sympathy for the dogmatism of either side, and even less sympathy for the political threat which he and his entourage saw implicit in the Chamberlain challenge. His prime, perhaps his sole, concern was the preservation of the party: in the short run in order to complete his ministerial projects – the creation of the Committee of Imperial Defence, naval reorganisation, the Entente with France, licensing legislation; in the long run as an organism to be maintained at virtually all costs, for without it the health of the body politic would be gravely, if not fatally, impaired. Another Peel he would never be.

Thus from the beginning Balfour sought to contain the explosive potential of the tariff controversy, insisting that fiscal differences 'shall not go beyond the question on which we differ, shall not strike at the root of party unity or party loyalty'.[35] Ignoring the incompatibility of the rival economic dogmas he justified their joint existence within the same party by a sophistical appeal to party traditions: '. . . our men were entitled by tradition to call themselves Protectionists, they were equally entitled to hold fast to the creed of Free Trade, as that had been the Party tradition for more than a generation.' Balfour thought it 'worth anything to try and reconcile these conflicting opinions'.[36]

Reconciliation was no easy task. While Balfour had close personal links with many of the Free Fooders, distrusted the political ambitions of the Tariff Reformers and abhorred the millennial aspects of the tariff crusade, intellectually his sympathies were closer to Chamberlain, although his sceptical mind was acutely aware of all sorts of difficulties. Moreover the Whole Hogger faction contained not only Joseph Chamberlain but also the bigger battalions. Thus Balfour's *via media*, whose signposts were Retaliation without Preference, and Preference after Colonial Conference and Election mandates, veered in the Tariff Reform direction, yet remained a path which at least some of the Free Fooders could tread. Moreover the signposts were obscure, for the Balfourite way was designed to secure unity through ambiguity. Throughout Balfour responded to the pressure of both wings and the exigencies of particular situations, clinging to compromise formulae, intentionally vague in order to prevent irremediable rupture.

In a formal sense the unity of the party was preserved, and in a real sense the premature fall of the Government was averted. But it could well be argued that Balfour's concern with the parliamentary situation blinded him to the long-run dangers to his party in the country. In the House of Commons his dialectical gymnastics and procedural dexterity enabled the Government to survive long beyond most expectations. Despite their growing exasperation with the party leader, the Whole Hoggers toed the party line in the Commons. A few Free Fooders, most notably Churchill, did cross the floor, and others on occasion cast their votes against Balfour or abstained, but never in sufficient numbers to endanger the Ministry.[37] But in the country Balfour's party tore itself apart, while its public support ebbed rapidly away.

Consumed by ideological passion, the Unionist Party, the great exemplar of political pragmatism, degenerated into a set of squabbling factions venting their invective on each other rather than on the Liberals. Doctrinal purity on the fiscal question became the supreme good of the extremists on both wings of the Unionist Party, and the necessities of political compromise were jettisoned. Rival fiscal leagues were formed, politicians were ostracised, party organisations purged. It was no coincidence that 'dissensions in the Unionist Party on policy . . . synchronised with a disintegration of the [party] organisation.'[38] For one thing the Balfourites at the Conservative Central Office were as much, if not more, concerned with keeping the Office out of the hands of the Whole Hoggers, as with running the party machine in the country. For another, the Whole Hogger purge of the Liberal Unionist organisation in 1904, which made it the Tariff Reform command post for the whole party, meant that the Liberal Unionist Council 'became a rival to the C.C.O. *within*, rather than in alliance with the Conservative Party, making the divisions at once more intimate and more acute'.[39]

Electorally the swing against the Government mounted again from the autumn of 1904. By now the fiscal question was an electoral incubus. The Unionist Party under Balfour could not be relied on to defend Free Trade, nor to amend it cautiously, nor to abandon it in favour of Tariff Reform. As the historian of the 1906 election has observed, 'A strong lead from Chamberlain, and a whole-hearted commitment to his policy, might have saved more seats than it lost, but so equally would a slower, less crusading but united evolution of the idea of fiscal reform under Balfour's leadership.'[40] By parading their differences in public the Unionists got the worst of both worlds, and lost whatever advantages might have accrued from the pursuit of a united fiscal policy.

By November 1905 Balfour could govern no longer. The National Union was in open revolt against the Balfourian compromise, while Chamberlain's hectoring tone in public presaged an immediate breach.[41]

Signs of Liberal disunity over Home Rule provided an inducement for resignation rather than dissolution, and on 4 December 1905 Balfour gave up the seals of office. This date marks the formal end of the Unionist hegemony, the election that followed in January 1906 its actual demise.

III

The magnitude of the Unionist disaster is the most striking feature of the election of 1906. The 402 Unionists returned for the United Kingdom in 1900 had by the dissolution been reduced through changes of party allegiance and by-election losses to 369. An unprecedented swing of 10·6 per cent against the Unionists now cut this representation by over half, leaving a rump of 157 Unionists in the new House of Commons. A Unionist majority in 1900 of 134 over all parties was transformed into an absolute Liberal majority of 130, and the Liberals in addition could generally rely on the support of the eighty-three Irish Nationalists and the thirty Labour M.P.s.[42] Balfour and all but four of his Cabinet colleagues from the Commons were amongst the defeated. Leader writers had to go back to 1832 for an adequate parallel.

A significant factor in the overwhelming defeat was the ability of the Liberals and the L.R.C. to mobilise previously untapped support. The turnout rose by 8 per cent over 1900 and was the highest since 1885. The overall Unionist vote in constituencies contested in both 1900 and 1906 remained remarkably stable, while the Liberal vote revealed extraordinary gains. In many cases Unionist polls sufficient to hold the seats in 1900 were overborne by the great increase in the Liberal vote. If we assume relative stability in the party allegiance of regular voters, then it would appear that the anti-Unionists secured the bulk of the former abstainers and new voters.[43] Thus with its negative prop removed, the hegemony collapsed.

Yet this is by no means an adequate explanation of the Unionist catastrophe. For one thing there is no clear correlation between the increase in the poll and the size of the swing,[44] which suggests the operation of other influential variables on the size of the swing. Moreover, it is very doubtful indeed whether party allegiances amongst regular Unionist voters were stable in 1906. In many constituencies particularly in London, Lancashire, Yorkshire, North-East England and Scotland, Unionist defections appear at least as important as increased turnout in explaining Unionist losses. It is likely too that in many other parts of the country Unionist defections were masked by the increase in turnout, i.e. Unionist switches to Liberals or to Labour or into abstention were hidden by substantial Unionist benefits from the turnout increase. The fresh register in 1906 by contrast with the stale register in 1900 undoubtedly helped to augment the Unionist as well as the Liberal vote in 1906, while there is no reason to assume that the Unionists did not secure a sizeable proportion of the half million additional new voters on the register.[45] Thus the stability of the Unionist poll probably hid a substantial decline in support amongst those who had voted Unionist in 1900.

Some fourteen Unionist M.P.s had brought themselves to cross the floor during the 1900 Parliament, mostly over Tariff Reform, and the influential Unionist Free Trade journal, the *Spectator*, advised Unionist electors to follow them and vote Liberal in 1906.[46] It is at least plausible to argue that many thousands of Unionist voters did so in 1906. Conversion to Liberalism as an explanation for Unionist losses seems applicable in those regions where Unionist opposition to Tariff Reform had been most apparent. Also, particularly in the industrial regions, the presence of Labour candidates served to bring former Tory working-class voters to both anti-Unionist parties.

Perhaps of even greater importance is the fact that the high turnout figures probably obscure a significant level of Unionist abstention. It seems likely that in an electoral landslide such as that of 1906, regarded by many historians as a rejection of Unionism rather than a positive vote for Liberalism, many Unionists, unable to support Balfour yet unwilling to vote for a Liberal, sought refuge in abstention. Others no doubt had simply been reduced to apathy. The low turn-out amongst London outvoters, mostly Unionist,[47] and the fact that the Unionist recovery in January 1910 is associated with the increased turnout in that election, lends weight to this supposition.[48] While the relative importance of each factor is impossible to determine it does seem that Unionist abstention, conversions from Unionism, and Liberal successes with new voters and former abstainers were each significant elements in the Liberal triumph.

Whatever the sources of the swing, the reaction it expressed was virtually universal, only Ireland remaining relatively unaffected by it. Elsewhere, at least in terms of regions, the swing was not only strikingly large but strikingly uniform. True it tended to be above average in the urban and industrial regions, and below average in the rural regions. But even this seems to be a hangover from the election of

1900, when rural England was already moving against the Unionists, while the Boer War appeal was swelling Unionist majorities in the cities. These contrary trends were compensated for in 1906. If we

TABLE 2.1 SWING 1900–1906: 1895–1906 GREAT BRITAIN

A. BY REGION
[Arranged in order of magnitude]

	1900–6	1895–1906
Outer London	21·1	19·3
N.E. Scotland	15·2	13·9
London	14·9	11·5
Western Lancastria	13·6	11·7
Eastern Lancastria	13·5	12·7
N.E. England	13·1	10·3
West Riding	12·8	12·5
Clyde Valley	12·5	11·0
Forth Valley	11·0	9·8
Highlands	10·9	7·7
Western Midlands	10·8	10·7
Rural Wales	10·2	11·7
Thames Valley – Essex	9·9	10·6
Western Marches	9·5	12·4
Severn	9·1	10·5
Eastern Midlands	9·1	10·5
Industrial Wales	8·7	11·2
Wessex	8·7	6·8
S.E. England	8·4	9·5
East Anglia	8·4	8·9
Southern Scotland	8·3	6·5
Cumbria	7·6	8·0
S.W. Peninsula	7·2	7·2
N. and E. Ridings	7·1	5·1
Lincolnshire	7·1	8·5

B. BY TYPE OF CONSTITUENCY (ENGLAND ONLY)

	1900–6	1895–1906
URBAN		
Predominantly middle-class	12·2	10·7
Mixed-class	11·7	10·5
Predominantly working-class	13·1	11·9
MIXED RURAL/URBAN	8·6	9·8
RURAL	8·3	9·0
MINING	11·0	10·5

compare regional movements between 1895, perhaps the most typical election of the hegemonic period, and 1906, the uniformity of the movement is more clearly underlined.

Labour's dramatic advent as the 'Fourth Party' in the system obscured the fact that electorally the party had functioned as part of the left wing of the Liberal Party. The impact of Labour candidates in working-class constituencies differed little from the impact of Liberals in similar constituencies. The average swing in the fifty-six seats contested by Labour candidates was 15·0 per cent, significantly above the national average.[49] This is partly explained by the fact that the sample is heavily weighted with constituencies from the industrial regions, where the swing tended to be above average. In addition there were Liberal rivals in nearly half the seats, and it appears that the presence of two anti-Unionist candidates increased the anti-Unionist swing.[50] A detailed examination of all official Labour candidatures suggests that only in Lancastria did Labour candidates do generally better than Liberal candidates in adjoining constituencies. Thus the presence of Labour candidates did little to disrupt the relative uniformity of the swing.

This is not to deny that the electoral concordat between the Liberal and Labour parties, and the similarity of their positions on the major electoral issues, helped generally to swell the anti-Unionist tide. Labour's role was most important in the former Tory working-class areas, where a Radical working-class tradition was weak. The breakthrough in working-class Lancastria, where the alliance was most extensive and operated most smoothly, was very much a joint anti-Unionist endeavour. Labour won eight, the Liberals seven predominantly working-class or mixed-class constituencies held in Lancastria by the Unionists since their creation in 1885. The co-operative nature of the enterprise is best seen in a number of the two-member seats in Lancastria. Preston had never before returned a Liberal, Bolton and Stockport never more than a single Liberal. In 1906 all three returned a Liberal and a Labour Member. In Lancastria the presence of Labour acted as a catalyst, accelerating the breakdown of the old Tory dominance. Without the presence there of Labour, traditional working-class antipathy to the Liberals might not have weakened so dramatically. But from Labour's imposition of the politics of class in an anti-Conservative form both the anti-Unionist parties benefited. In London, too, a considerable breach was established in working-class Toryism, although here Labour played a secondary role. Of the ten London predominantly working-class or mixed-class constituencies held by the Conservatives since 1885, but now captured by the anti-Unionists, the Liberals won eight, Labour two.

In retrospect these achievements in working-class Lancastria and London were to prove the critical inroads into the Unionist hegemony. But in 1906 their crucial nature was obscured by other equally dramatic ingresses into the Unionist heartland in constituencies of very different social complexion. In the residential areas of the Home Counties the Liberals won for the first time three predominantly middle-class constituencies and another nine with substantial numbers of middle-class voters. In the English rural seats the Liberals won fourteen constituencies for the first time, and a further fourteen won previously only in 1885.

Thus it was the resurgence of Liberalism among all classes and all major groups that underlay the Unionist rout. Russell concludes in his study of the 1906 election:

> On the Liberal side ... the election not only drew together – and amplified – all the elements which 'traditionally' supported the party – the Nonconformists, the Celtic fringes, the miners, and so on, but ... joined with these a number of new or enlarged elements that had never voted so solidly Liberal before, and almost certainly never did, to the same extent, again, – in particular the textile manufacturers; the manual workers of Lancashire, the East End and the West Riding; the agricultural labourers; the Irish and a large section of the middle classes, including a number of Free Trade, and other disgruntled Unionists.[51]

The swing was neither a middle-class, nor a working-class phenomenon; neither a rural nor an urban phenomenon; neither a Liberal nor a Labour phenomenon, but was, in fact, universal.

The general election of 1906 provides therefore a sharp contrast with the other critical election of this period, that of 1886. In 1906 around a much larger swing figure, the deviations from the average are much less noticeable than in 1886 and the distinctive asymmetrical regional swings characteristic of 1886 are rarely encountered in 1906. Thus the geographical distribution of relative party support remains virtually unchanged. The strongest Unionist areas in the past remain in 1906 the strongest Unionist areas, and the weakest Unionist areas in the past remain in 1906 the weakest Unionist areas. The Unionist majority has been overthrown but the geography of the hegemony persists [compare Map 1.1 (p.18) with Map 2.1].

Had the hegemony in fact been ended? Was 1906 merely a deviating election such as 1874, merely a temporary aberration from the prevailing pattern, or a realigning election such as 1886? Had the Unionists

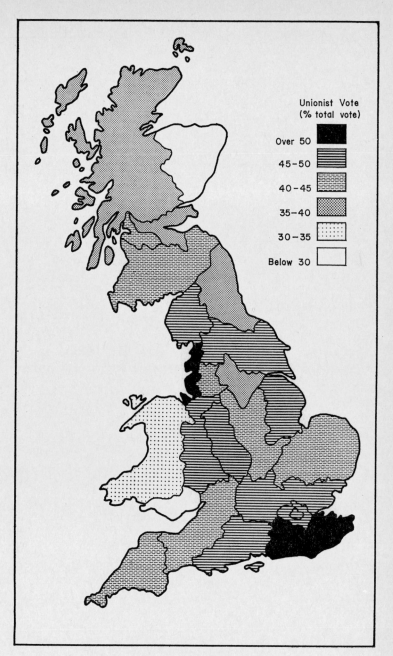

Map 2.1 RESULTS 1906

been overwhelmed by a powerful but temporary revulsion against their party, occasioned by essentially short-term forces, or by significant and lasting changes in the patterns of partisan identification? Undoubtedly there was present in 1906 a large number of factors, whose anti-Unionist implications were likely to be short-run. Moreover, there was no major national crisis, such as that over Home Rule, with which a more or less durable realignment of party loyalties is usually associated. In addition the universal nature of the Liberal resurgence raises doubts as to the permanence of change, for a degree of electoral polarisation is frequently an aspect of a realigning election.[52] On the other hand the magnitude of the swing and the advent of Labour suggest fundamental and durable changes in the patterns of partisan identification.

The resolution of this difficulty lies in the nature of a critical election as suggested by Pomper: 'Typically, the critical election represents a break in electoral continuity, but does not result in the immediate establishment of a new and persistent voter coalition. . . . Persistence comes after the critical election, and partially as a reaction to its upheavals.'[53] The more durable aspects of the electoral scene ushered in by 1906 become apparent in the general elections of 1910. The reaction to the upheaval of 1906 produces in 1910 a degree of polarisation along class and regional lines which serves to clarify the more persistent features of the new electoral order. That this new order itself was soon to pass away was but one result of the maelstrom into which all Europe was soon to descend.

PART TWO

Winter 1908—9 to Winter 1910—11

3

Winter 1908–9

I

The winter of 1908–9 found the Liberal Government at the nadir of its fortunes. The by-elections were running strongly against it. The Government's legislative programme had been mutilated by the Lords; powerful interests had been alienated by its attempts at reform; and a deepening trade recession gripped the country. Moreover this winter found the Liberal Party itself torn by a deep division over naval policy and expenditure. 1909 promised to be bleak indeed and the Liberals seemed hesitant as to how to combat the troubles that beset them. Thus, within three years of the Liberal *annus mirabilis*, it appeared that the party's tenure of power would be both short and rather barren.

The decline in Liberal popularity in the by-elections showed disturbing parallels with the post-1900 Unionist collapse. Throughout 1906 and 1907, there had been little evidence of any movement against the Government. (See Figure 3.1) Early in 1907 Liberals had been disturbed by a move to the right seen in the loss of Brigg – held in every general election since 1885 – and the rout of the Progressives in the L.C.C. elections, and by the unforeseen gains of the Left at Colne Valley and Jarrow. But the Unionist reaction petered out in the latter half of 1907 and the Left had no further successes.

The by-election at Mid-Devon on 17 January 1908 heralded a dramatic reversal. A Liberal majority of 1289 in 1906 was turned into a Unionist majority of 559, a swing of 10.1 per cent. The Liberals were stunned. 'The Mid-Devon smash, which was quite unexpected, spread gloom and dismay in Liberal ranks.'[1] Excuses were hastily proffered – that the Liberal candidate, C. R. Buxton, was a carpet-bagger; that his association with 'beer, high church, and socialism possibly didn't suit the Devonshire palate'; that while the Tory candidate had 'assiduously and lavishly nursed the constituency . . . [the sitting Liberal] has been conspicuous by his absence'; that the Tories had 'inundated the constituency with lying placards'; that dismissals at the Plymouth

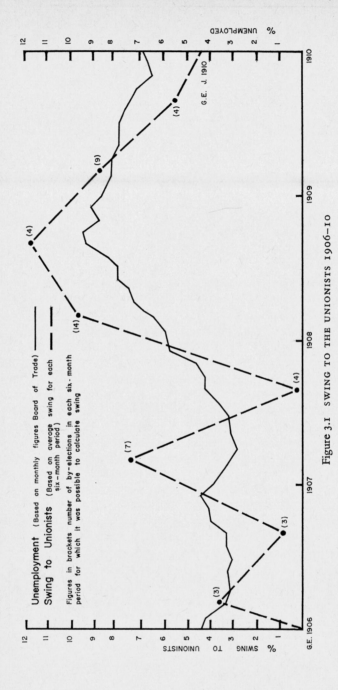

Figure 3.1 SWING TO THE UNIONISTS 1906–10

Unemployment (Based on monthly figures Board of Trade) ———

Swing to Unionists (Based on average swing for each six-month period) − − −

Figures in brackets number of by-elections in each six-month period for which it was possible to calculate swing dockyards had had unfortunate repercussions.[2] In Mid-Devon itself, the suffragettes were blamed, and Mrs Pankhurst barely escaped being rolled in a barrel through the streets of Newton Abbot.[3] But others saw the reversal as the turn in the tide. John Burns, ex-working-class agitator now Cabinet Minister, noted in his diary: 'A portent and a serious [one]. . . . I am . . . prepared for worse.'[4]

He was right. In the next eleven months the Liberals lost a further six seats and the swing against them in the 1908 by-elections averaged over 10 per cent. Socialist intervention contributed to Liberal defeats but the Unionist share of the poll rose significantly on nearly every occasion. The reaction was strong in middle-class, working-class and rural constituencies. Only the Celtic fringe appeared secure.

By the end of 1908, defeatism was rife in the Liberal camp. On 9 December when the Cabinet considered the electoral situation, Burns noted cryptically in his diary: 'Cabinet. Election now, beaten etc.'[5] Lord Fitzmaurice, Chancellor of the Duchy of Lancaster, reported to the Liberal editor, J. A. Spender, that nearly all his colleagues 'seem infected with a view that we are bound to look forward to defeat at the next election and to be willing to accept this with resignation, as a pre-ordained thing, intending no doubt in the interval to do as much good as they can, before we fall'.[6]

The New Year brought little to dispel the gloom. The illusion that Scotland was immune was shattered by the marked shift against the Government in by-elections at Central Glasgow, South Edinburgh and East Edinburgh. In England, by-elections at Taunton, Croydon, and Stratford-on-Avon testified to the continuing strength of the Unionist reaction. There seemed little doubt that, however long-delayed, the general election would be a débâcle for the Liberals.

The by-election results were merely the fever chart of the Government's decline. One cause of this decline was the Lords' success in emasculating the legislative programme of the Liberals, and governmental impotence before such success. A clash between the Houses had been inevitable. Never before had a House of Commons so overwhelmingly Liberal faced a House of Lords so overwhelmingly Conservative. Never before had a radical Government, desirous of great and sweeping changes, encountered an Opposition which, long used to power, believed that it had a divine right to govern. Yet few could have predicted the humiliation of the great Commons majority by the dominant faction in the Lords between 1906 and 1908.

In 1906 the peers had wrecked the Education Bill, the major item in that year's legislative programme, and had rejected the Plural Voting Bill. In 1907 they savaged a clutch of Liberal land bills, designed for the Celtic fringe. They began 1908 with the outright rejection of the reintroduced Scottish Smallholders Bill. They followed this by so defacing a second Scottish Land Values Bill that the Government had no alternative but to abandon it. On 27 November they climaxed their activities with the contemptuous second-reading rejection of the Licensing Bill. A few days later at a meeting of the Anglican Representative Church Council, a revolt of the laity led to the rejection of the compromise proposals embodied in the latest Education Bill. Aware that this would lead to the Bill's defeat in the House of Lords, the Government bowed before the inevitable and withdrew it. On 5 December 1908 Lord Carrington, President of the Board of Agriculture, summed up the position in his diary: '. . . the Session is spoilt and . . . Balfour and the Lords are masters of the situation'.[7]

The Liberal response to the actions of the Lords is best described as all bark but no bite. Hardly a month passed without a bitter attack on the Peers from a Liberal Minister, yet the years passed without any concrete action. Even the Campbell-Bannerman resolution of 1907, promising a limit on the veto of the Lords so as to secure that 'within the limits of a single Parliament the final decision of the Commons should prevail' which had momentarily cheered the party, now seemed but empty verbiage.

The Liberals appeared to have neglected their opportunities. In retrospect some of the Liberal leaders realised that the most propitious occasion for a dissolution had been December 1906, when the usurpation of the Lords might have been stopped at its beginning.[8] The Lords had given them little opportunity since. To have resigned on the Licensing Bill would have been suicidal, 'defeat inevitable and crushing',[9] and the Cabinet had quickly and unanimously decided against such action.

But why did the Cabinet not act upon the Campbell-Bannerman resolution in the 1908 session, possibly thereby forcing an election by a direct challenge to the Lords? Roy Jenkins has convincingly disposed of the suggestion that this failure was due to the change in Liberal leadership from Campbell-Bannerman to Asquith. He suggests that Campbell-Bannerman had not intended to take up the veto question in 1908, but proposed instead to give the Lords 'another year's trial before attempting to proceed any further'.[10] It is more likely that the Cabinet had less generous motives for not proceeding with veto legislation. First, it was clear to all that, unless coupled with truly popular reforms resisted by the Peers, a direct attack on the powers of the Lords would fail. The difficulty in 1908 was to find a truly popular measure that the Lords *would* resist, and which might accompany a veto bill in the legislative programme of the year.

Secondly, the Liberals hoped anyhow for a successful legislative year in 1908, and believed with reason that they could secure legislation on licensing and education. A compromise education measure did remain a real possibility throughout the year, while they believed that the sympathy of the bishops, the strong support of Labour, and 'the Trade's' fear of retaliatory licensing duties in a future budget, might ensure the passage of licensing legislation. Moreover, it was widely recognised that it was in the tactical interest of the Liberals to get these contentious and unrewarding items out of the way before joining battle with the Lords.[11]

Yet it was not to be. Liberal hopes were dashed, and many a Liberal no doubt saw not a prophecy, but a description of the existing situation in the words of the *Nation* on 28 November 1908. '[The Liberal Party] must admit that in a democracy nothing fails like failure, and that the cup that it fills by continuing to pass abortive Bills will be not the cup of wrath against the Lords, but the cup of ridicule for its own impotence.'

But impotence before the Lords was not the sole reason for the Liberal decline. Despite its abortive bills, the Government had managed to alienate important groups, while failing to satisfy many of the interests that had contributed to its overwhelming victory in 1906. 'We are', wrote Burns on 11 December 1908, 'knee deep in pledges we cannot keep; promises we must abandon; we have irritated nearly all the interests and subdued very few.'[12] The Government's education policy had antagonised Anglicans and Catholics alike, yet the 1902 Bill remained unamended, the Nonconformists unsatisfied. In 1906 the education controversy had been an asset; now it was, if anything, a handicap. The mass of Nonconformists had learnt to live with Balfour's Act; only the very militant continued to press for a measure that would probably lose more votes than it would gain.

Liberal land policies had merely confirmed the alienation of the landed interest from the Government in England and had had a divisive effect on the Liberal Party in Scotland. Farmers disliked the inadequate compensation provisions in the Small Holdings Act, while the policy itself did not produce a countervailing element in the countryside.[13] The vexed question of rural rates continued to embitter relations between landlords, farmers and Government, perpetuating the attitude of 'agin the Government' whatever its political complexion, that tended to characterise the agricultural interest throughout the Edwardian period.[14]

But the clearest example of the electoral repercussions of an outraged interest was the opposition of the liquor trade to the Licensing Bill of 1908. The brewers were determined to prevent any surrender by the Lords, and organised a costly and at times violent campaign against the measure. They poured money, propaganda and men into the by-elections, organised demonstrations, threatened to boycott charities and tradesmen, even warned the Conservative Party that they would withdraw their funds if the measure passed.[15] In March the Clerk of the House of Commons informed James Bryce, ex-Liberal Minister now Ambassador in Washington, that the opposition to the Licensing Bill 'is very formidable and very skilfully organised, and will doubtless cause the loss of many votes and seats to the Government. Already many Liberals are feeling very weak-kneed about it.'[16] And with good reason. At Peckham, where electioneering recalled the 'good old days', it was alleged that the Tory candidate was swept in on a sea of beer. At East Wolverhampton the Liberal candidate claimed he was saved by eight votes from a 'deluge of beer'.[17] The mobilisation of the brewery interests undoubtedly aided the Unionist recovery in 1908.

The contribution of each of these factors cannot be measured; they were probably secondary in the short run to the impact of the economic situation. The Government's performance in the by-elections seems closely related to economic trends, particularly the pattern of employment. The high correlation between the popularity of the Government as measured by the by-elections and the level of employment can be seen in Figure 3.1 on p. 46. The recovery in trade and employment dating from 1904 ended with the short lived boom of 1907.[18] The sudden slump in the Government's fortunes in 1908 coincided with a severe downturn in the trade cycle. Instead of diminishing with the summer, the 1908 unemployment figures climbed month by month. In June they stood at 7·9 per cent, the highest figure for a decade, in October at 9·5 per cent, while the annual average for 1908 – 7·8 per cent – was worse than for any year since the depression of the mid-1880s.

In October 1908 Churchill, now President of the Board of Trade, confronted an already beleaguered Cabinet with the grim facts of the economic situation:

... we have already entered upon a period of exceptional distress and industrial dislocation; and these conditions may be sensibly aggravated as the winter advances. ... Already the depression has been productive of a dislocation of industry more violent than that reached in 1904, after some years of gradually deepening depression.[19]

The general distress resulting had immediate political repercussions, with demonstrations over unemployment and bitter Labour criticism of the Government's remedial measures, particularly of the complacent and unimaginative response of the Local Government Board under John Burns.

But what really worried the Government was not the criticism from the Left, but whether, as by-elections in industrial centres suggested, these economic conditions would ensure the victory of the Unionists with their tariff propaganda. The electoral significance of the economic decline was due in great part to the excellent ammunition the slump provided for the Opposition's attack on Free Trade. For the Whole Hoggers the gloomy economic situation was highly propitious and the tariff gospel flourished both within and without the Unionist Party.

Governments in decline seem easy prey to internal squabbles. In the winter of 1908–9 the Liberal Government was no exception, and the issues at stake – the navy and future policy – were both momentous for the election barely a year away. In the week before Christmas 1908, Reginald McKenna, First Lord of the Admiralty, faced the Cabinet with evidence suggesting an acceleration in German naval building and the consequent demand of the Sea Lords for six Dreadnoughts, not the planned four, in the 1909–10 programme.[20] Within days, the old and disruptive Little England/Liberal Imperialist fissure had reappeared under the guise of Little Navy/Big Navy factions. The Little Navy men challenged the basic assumptions about German acceleration, distrusted Admiralty calculations based on them, and fought for a four-Dreadnought programme. The Big Navy men, alarmed by the evidence of German building and convinced by the resolution of the Sea Lords, urged the immediate construction of six Dreadnoughts.

If Churchill was the most belligerent, Lloyd George was the backbone of the opposition to the larger programme and, but for him, the admirals would probably have easily got their way. His resistance was based not simply on the principles involved nor on the immediate dispute over facts and forecasts. He feared the effects of increased naval expenditure on his already overburdened Budget. Even more, he feared the impact of such a programme on Liberal opinion in the country. This was the burden of his long letter to Asquith on 2 February 1909:

> There are millions of earnest Liberals in the country who are beginning rather to lose confidence in the Govt. for reasons we are not altogether responsible for. When the £38,000,000 navy estimates are announced the disaffection of these good Liberals will break into open sedition and the usefulness of this Parliament will be at an end.[21]

The dispute was resolved by a typical Asquithian compromise, that four Dreadnoughts should be laid down immediately and that the Government be empowered, with Parliament's concurrence, to lay down four more in the current financial year should this appear necessary. In reality this was a victory for the Big Navy men and, as expected, the construction of the four contingent Dreadnoughts was sanctioned in July.

The compromise had, however, unfortunate consequences for the Government. In order to silence their own supporters Asquith, Grey (the Foreign Secretary) and McKenna were forced to make a series of speeches stressing the seriousness of the naval situation. While these secured virtual Liberal unanimity on the compromise, they alarmed the nation and the Unionists. Fanned by the Machiavellian First Sea Lord Sir John Fisher, by a sensational press and by the Unionist Party, a major panic with distinctive anti-German undertones blew up. Campaigning under the slogan, 'We want eight and we won't wait,' the Tories increased their majority at Croydon in March by over 3,000, while in the Commons they moved a censure motion on the Government's naval policy. The panic soon subsided, but doubts about the Government's naval policy had been sown. The Government itself had helped forge a weapon whose potential did not escape astute Unionist publicists. H. A. Gwynne, editor of the *Standard*, told Sandars that by 'stumping' the nation on the naval issue Balfour could 'save the country from a great danger and secure for many years the supremacy of the party'.[22] Nine months later in more desperate circumstances the Tories were to try.

The second question dividing the Liberals during this unhappy winter was the Liberal programme for the coming year. It was useless to go on passing measures merely to have them done to death in the Upper House. J. A. Spender told the Mastermans that to include another Licensing Bill, Welsh Church Disestablishment, or even Insurance in the 1909 programme would merely 'put up the backs of all the vested interests, and the Lords would reject and the Government could do nothing but fulminate and then forget'.[23] As the *Nation* miserably but correctly observed: 'Wherever the purpose of Liberalism is vital, wherever it received a direct message from the people three years ago, its executive power has gone.'[24] What then was to be done?

Two policies were being widely canvassed in public; a third was being prepared by Lloyd George at the Treasury. The first of these policies was the heroic if suicidal one of an early encounter with the Lords. During the winter of 1908–9 the radical weekly the *Nation* urged the introduction of provocative measures, and a dissolution in the summer of 1909. The specific measures varied over the weeks, but the underlying principle was clearly enunciated on Boxing Day 1908. 'The Bills introduced next Session should, in our opinion, be limited to those which strike directly at the political and economic power of the Peers.' Any other policy was but 'creeping paralysis'.

But the bulk of the parliamentary party, and more surprisingly the party press, favoured a less dramatic and much less heroic policy. They rightly saw that the course proposed by the *Nation* led to legislative sterility and probably electoral disaster. They preferred that the next session, and perhaps even the life of the Parliament, be spent on social reforms, unlikely to bring them into conflict with the Lords, and on defending the Liberal features of the *status quo*. This policy was summed up by the Liberal *Review of Reviews* in February 1909:

> If we can reform the Poor Law, maintain the Navy, carry a democratic Budget, safeguard Free Trade and keep the Jingoes out of office, we shall have done enough for glory, even if on all other questions we have to bow the neck before the Balfourian yoke.

The *Nation*, appalled, attacked this course as pusillanimous, and when it appeared from the King's Speech in February that the Cabinet had adopted such a policy, it dismissed the year's programme as 'neutral and colourless', framed 'not with regard to the desires of [the Government's] friends and its own views of popular needs, but with a vigilant eye on what the hereditary House will accept or reject'.[25]

But if the Ministry had rejected the heroic policy of the *Nation*, it had embarked upon a course more adventurous than a cursory reading of the King's Speech would indicate. The real clue to ministerial intentions lay in a single sentence: '. . . the provision necessary for the services of the State in the ensuing year will require very serious consideration, and, in consequence, less time than usual will, I fear, be available for the consideration of other legislative measures.'[26] The Government had already decided that the nucleus of its programme should be a radical budget.

It is, however, most unlikely that the Cabinet intended to provoke a decisive conflict with the Lords over the Budget. Certainly it does not seem to have contemplated an election before, at the earliest, the autumn of 1910.[27] Indeed, it seems highly probably that the Cabinet hoped by means of the Budget to by-pass the Lords and thus restore the initiative to the Government. Sir Courtenay Ilbert, Clerk of the House of Commons and chief adviser to the Government on constitutional questions, described the Budget as 'a bold & ingenious manoeuvre' designed 'to circumvent the House of Lords. . . . The political . . . object of the Finance Bill is to turn the tables on the House of Lords by compelling them to accept the policy which they defeated by the rejection of the Scottish Land Bill & the Licensing Bill.'[28] The Budget might well be distasteful to the Lords, but the Cabinet appeared confident at this time that the Lords would pass it, however unpleasant it might be. The attitude of the Lords to the Old Age Pensions Bill indicated that even this House of Lords would respect the financial prerogatives of the House of Commons.[29] Strong confirmation for this view came from Churchill's sources within the Unionist Party. On 26 December 1908 he wrote to Asquith: 'I learn that Lansdowne in private utterly scouts the suggestion that the Lords will reject the Budget Bill.'[30]

Circumnavigation not confrontation was the order of the day. While to introduce legislation disliked by the Lords was to sow barren seed, within the frame of the Budget might be implanted measures disliked by the Peers yet which they would not, because they could not, reject. While merely to pass non-contentious legislation would reveal an unbecoming subservience to the Upper Chamber, a controversial budget might well restore the initiative to the Liberals. Such a policy avoided the sterility of one course, the humiliation of the other. Moreover, the very difficulties of the financial situation, a heavy deficit and increased expenditure, contributed to the key role of the Budget. On 26 January 1909 Asquith informed the King that 'the main business of the year must . . . be of necessity the Budget'.[31] It was a necessity not unwelcome to some of the Ministers.

This policy had already been heralded by major speeches during the winter recess from Asquith, Lloyd George and Churchill, in which the coming Budget was coupled with vigorous attacks on the Lords. These speeches confused contemporaries and have sometimes puzzled later historians.[32] Understandably, for the gap between rhetoric and reality was considerable. The three Ministers were carrying out a familiar political operation, dressing up a somewhat cautious policy in martial clothing. They were rallying those who desired an early confrontation with the Lords to a policy designed to avoid just this. There was, in the short run, little real link between the Budget policy now adopted by the Ministry, and the policy of securing an early conclusion with the Lords, but this the Ministers were unwilling to proclaim.

The *Nation* was fully aware that the midwinter operation of the three Ministers was an exercise in revivalist rhetoric. It was critical of all three speeches, particularly Churchill's, which had most explicitly linked the Budget with the Lords. 'Liberals wish to be led against the House of Lords, not to be fed with excuses for running away from it', was its comment on Churchill's speech, and it condemned Churchill's suggestion that the Lords could possibly reject the Budget as 'an almost unthinkable contingency'.[33] It realised that, despite their bravado and abuse of the Lords, the speeches implied the abandonment of a policy of early confrontation, and, rightly, from its point of view, was suspicious of all this talk about finance. On 19 December the *Nation* warned: 'A Government cannot live by finance alone.' Lloyd George was about to prove that it could.

II

The winter of 1908–9 found the Government's allies in, if anything, a worse condition. The Labour Party had not escaped the effects of the pro-Unionist tide in public opinion, and the resultant electoral slump had quickened the disillusionment in the Labour movement with the tactics and policy of the parliamentary party. If in Ireland the Nationalist Party remained, as ever, immune to the ebb and flow of the electoral tide, factionalism within the party bred on the spreading discontent over the sterility of the Liberal alliance.

Labour's expectations had foundered along with those of the Liberals. Apart from Pete Curran's victory in a four-cornered fight at Jarrow in July 1907, and the success of Victor Grayson, standing as an independent Socialist in defiance of the Labour Executive, at Colne Valley in the same month, Labour candidates had fared badly. In the four seats contested for the first time at the by-elections, only at Taunton, where there was no Liberal candidate, did Labour get a

third of the vote. In the seven seats Labour contested in the general
election and at the by-elections, Labour's percentage of the poll fell
in every case. 1908 saw a heavy drop in the Labour poll at South Leeds,
early 1909 a cataclysmic fall at Croydon, 'the most disastrous of all the
battlefields fought by the Labour Party'.[34]

Political disenchantment accompanied electoral disappointment.[35]
The opening session of the 1906 Parliament had fed Labour's illusions.
A party-sponsored measure for providing needy children with school
meals was passed, the Labour Trades Disputes Bill virtually replaced
the Government's measure, and the party secured substantial amendments to the Workers' Compensation Bill. But 1907 was a barren
year, and 1908 ominous for Labour.

In that year under the stimulus of Lloyd George and Churchill, the
Government's social programme began to get under way. Neither
Minister had a fully fledged social policy, neither was in any sense a
doctrinaire reformer. Their pragmatic stance was well summed up by
Churchill: 'We are all collectivists for some purposes and individualists
for others.'[36] Their inspiration was diverse – Bismarckian paternalism,
colonial collectivism and the Nonconformist social gospel. Their
motivation was to restore the dynamism of Liberalism and pre-empt
the appeal of Labour. As the programme developed, Liberals showed
an increasing reluctance to allow Labour a creative share in the legislation. Yet the Labour Party could do little else but support such
legislation even if it was not happy with the details.

It is difficult to see what other policy the parliamentary party could
have pursued. Captious opposition to Liberal social reforms, a dogmatic insistence on socialist measures, or the theatrical antics of Victor
Grayson were hardly viable substitutes. Yet frustration was equally
inevitable. Labour's much-vaunted independence appeared to have
been lost amidst 'the jiggery pokery of party government';[37] distinctive
party policies, let alone socialist policies, were neglected; and the
Labour parliamentarians seemed little more than the working-class
lackeys of the Liberal majority. This frustration was reflected in
growing criticism of the parliamentarians, and mounting suspicion
of the alliance between the Socialist societies and the trade unions.

These suspicions were heightened by the cautious, if realistic, electoral
tactics pursued by the party leaders. Unwilling to jeopardise unnecessarily their electoral understanding with the Liberal Party,
reluctant to waste spare resources, or to illustrate publicly Labour's
electoral weaknesses, the Labour leaders were not prepared to sanction

contests merely for propaganda purposes. As Ramsay MacDonald, the architect of the policy, warned the militants at the Labour Party conference in 1909, the Executive 'would not allow men and money to be frittered away in contests which could yield no benefit to the party as a whole'.[38] As the electoral prospect grew increasingly gloomy, the National Executive Committee became increasingly cautious.

The two-member constituencies posed peculiarly delicate problems. In these seats unless the local Liberal and Labour associations were each prepared to nominate only a single candidate, both seats would in all likelihood be lost to the Unionists. As luck would have it, between 1906 and 1909 three Liberal Members died or resigned in two-member constituencies shared with Labour. At Leicester in March 1906 the post-election euphoria enabled the N.E.C. to prevent a Labour nomination. But two years later in more troubled times candidates were brought forward at Newcastle and Dundee in defiance of the N.E.C. Both were soundly trounced but at Newcastle the Liberal loss was attributed to Socialist intervention, and in both constituencies Liberal–Labour relations were damaged, although not irreparably.[39]

In the single-member constituencies the N.E.C. was less constrained, but even here it was unwilling to sanction what is considered hopeless candidatures. Its refusal to support a contest at Pudsey in June 1908 led to an unofficial Labour candidate, defeat for both anti-Unionist candidates, further Liberal–Labour irritation, and increased suspicions of Executive motives among the rank and file of the Labour Party. By contrast the Labour leaders blamed the disaster that befell the official Labour candidate at Croydon on the 'grossly misleading' information supplied by the local militants.[40] Charges against the malcontents of irresponsibility, against the Executive of subservience to the Liberals, and of 'Lib-Labism', filled the air at the I.L.P. and Labour Party conferences in 1909.

This discontent with policy and tactics was fanned by those who had always suspected that the alliance with the trade unions would emasculate socialism – the left activists of the Independent Labour Party and the Socialist forces outside the Labour Party. The danger came from the I.L.P., for it was at this point within the party that discontent was rife. The dominant figures of the I.L.P. – Keir Hardie, MacDonald and Snowden – were also leading figures in the parliamentary party, but they used their positions not to bring the parliamentary party to socialism, but to discipline the I.L.P. to the needs of the parliamentary party. They conceived their role in maintaining the alliance as one of securing I.L.P. support for a cautious pragmatism both in Parliament and in the electorate.

The revolt within the I.L.P. against this policy was focused around Victor Grayson, the surprise victor at Colne Valley. From the outset the middle-aged leaders of the party had handled the young and un-stable Grayson with considerable ineptness, thus helping to create a dangerous if erratic rebel.[41] Grayson and his friends hoped to prise apart the I.L.P.–trade union alliance, thus freeing the I.L.P. from the taint of opportunism and 'Lib-Labism' and returning it to a pristine socialist path. It could well be argued, of course, that if such an operation were successful electoral nullity would be the price of purity. Grayson was supported by the Social Democratic Party on ideological grounds, and by Robert Blatchford, editor of the *Clarion*, and the vituperative Ben Tillett, the dockers' leader, personal antagonists of the dominant group in the Labour Party.

The decision in 1908 of the powerful and wealthy Miners' Federation to affiliate with the Labour Party, while adding to the party's numbers and affluence, was scarcely likely to contribute either to its unity or its independence. The strong strain of 'Lib-Labism' amongst the miners' leaders, which had so long delayed the affiliation, did little to recom-mend the miners to the purists in the party, while even Keir Hardie felt 'sore at seeing the fruits of our years of toil being garnered by men who were never of us, and who even now would trick us out'.[42]

The Labour Party's problems in this winter stemmed essentially from a crisis of identity exacerbated by the electoral doldrums. How could the Labour Party maintain itself as an independent third force in a two-party system, particularly when one of the two dominant parties was openly striving to pre-empt Labour's appeal? Labour had to live with this predicament through both elections, for Lloyd George's Budget served merely to sharpen it.

Across the Irish Sea the Nationalist Party's troubles also stemmed from disillusionment. The Liberal alliance re-established during 1905 by the Nationalist leaders and Campbell-Bannerman had been am-biguous. Even Campbell-Bannerman, more forthcoming on Home Rule than many of his colleagues, had been guarded in his pledges, while Asquith and others had, during the 1906 election, taken a self-denying ordinance on Home Rule for the lifetime of the new Parlia-ment.[43] This unpromising start was compounded by the struggle with the House of Lords, for the Liberal Ministry had no intention of allowing the Lords to pose again as the saviours of the Union before the question of their powers had been settled.

The result had been a meagre output of Irish legislation, and no advance towards Home Rule. The one measure in the so-called 'step by step' programme of Home Rule, the Irish Councils Bill of 1907, was rejected by the Nationalists themselves as quite inadequate. By the winter of 1908-9 the alliance was increasingly under strain. Early in 1909, T. P. O'Connor, one of its architects, warned that in Great Britain 'the time is fast approaching when we shall be able no longer to resist the trend for our people to vote for the Tory rather than support a Liberal who, by reducing Home Rule to a pious opinion, practically postpones it to the Greek Kalends'.[44]

In Ireland the discontent with the alliance encouraged the centrifugal forces that had long plagued the party. Paradoxically one of the first results of the reaction against the alliance was centripetal – the re-admission of William O'Brien, T. M. Healy and their followers to the official party after several years of isolation.[45] Yet the reunion was artificial, not only because of the deep personal animosities that remained, but because the exiles returned to the party with the aim of nullifying the official policy. Since 1903 O'Brien had been the advocate of a policy of conciliation and compromise with all moderate elements in Ireland, including Unionists, a policy quite contrary to that of working with the Liberals alone. O'Brien no doubt hoped that the growing discontent with the Liberal Government would give his alternative policy its chance. Thus it was merely a matter of time before this fundamental political difference revealed the artificiality of the reunion.

The rupture came over the Irish Land Bill of 1909, which raised in an acute form the underlying disagreement between O'Brien and the dominant faction. O'Brien wanted the land question settled as in 1903 by way of a conference of landlords and tenants, i.e. by a compromise with the moderate Unionist landowners. The party leaders, Redmond and Dillon, determined to settle the question by consultation between the Nationalists and the Liberal Ministry, i.e. by the policy of the Liberal alliance. When O'Brien tried to present his views to a party convention in Dublin in February 1909 he was howled down, and several of his supporters manhandled, in a scene which O'Brien characteristically described as one of 'unmitigated blackguardism'. Although some of the rowdyism may have been organised, there was clearly little sympathy for O'Brien amongst the convention delegates.[46]

O'Brien's first reaction was anger. He hastened immediately to his stronghold, County Cork, raised the banner of revolt, and was joined by a number of the Cork M.P.s. But anger soon changed to despair. He was not well, support from the Nationalist M.P.s had been disappointing, and the party leaders were preparing to stamp out the rebellion. The campaign would be arduous, the outcome unclear. The final blow was the desertion of his colleague in the Cork City seat, Augustine (Gussy) Roche, a long-time associate and supporter. In April O'Brien resigned his seat, not for the first or last time, and retired to Florence.

Hopes that O'Brien's departure might end the troubles were soon dashed. In the ensuing by-election at Cork City, the strength of the O'Brienite faction was revealed. In the poll on 1 May Maurice Healy, the independent candidate, comfortably defeated the official nominee. Moreover Lloyd George's Budget, introduced two days before, contained land and liquor taxes that were to prove highly unpopular in Ireland. They were to give further encouragement to criticism of the Liberal alliance, and a new impetus to the rebel faction. When the election came, the Nationalist Party was more seriously split than at any time since the 1890s.

III

The winter of 1908–9 was a time of satisfaction and hope for the Unionist Opposition: and with good cause. Throughout the preceding three years the Lords, led by Lansdowne and guided by Balfour, had acted with great tactical skill. Astute in their rejections, they had been equally clever in their concessions. The measures they had rejected had been primarily those commanding only sectional support within the Liberal Party, measures on which the Government would find it difficult to dissolve and fight an election. The rejection of the Education Bill in 1906 had been a gamble, but the Lords had rightly bargained on Liberal reluctance to dissolve twice in the one year. There was little likelihood that the Ministry would fight on Celtic land measures, plural voting bills, or in the conditions of 1908, the Licensing Bill.

At the same time, impressed by the extent of Liberal victories in working-class areas in 1906, and perhaps more by the dramatic emergence of the Labour Party, Balfour and the Lords were determined to avoid any open collision with working-class interests. If the Lords watched the divisions in the House of Commons for Balfour's signals, equally they watched the lobbies for Labour's reactions. Thus in 1906 they passed the Trades Disputes Bill; thus in 1908 they passed unamended, albeit with some protests, the Old Age Pensions Bill; thus in 1908 they passed the Eight Hours Bill for coal miners. In its comment on this last, the Unionist *Birmingham Daily Post* summarised the policy of the Lords on all measures directly beneficial to the working classes: 'The Peers yielded to the demand of Labour for the Bill, not because they liked the Bill, but because expediency dictated that the measure should not be rejected'.[47]

The policy pursued by Balfour and Lansdowne had been by no means easy, but they had carried it through with skill and aplomb. Among the Peers there were many who regarded as anathema such measures as the Trades Disputes Act and Old Age Pensions, and who would have sympathised with Strachey, editor of the *Spectator*, when he wrote: 'My quarrel with the House of Lords is not that they pass too few Liberal measures but that they pass too many.'[48] Such men were effectively if judiciously ignored. On the other hand there were influential moderates who feared the consequences of flouting the popular majority. On the Licensing Bill, prominent peers such as St Aldwyn objected 'to being dragged by the brewers into opposition to all reforms', or, such as Milner, feared that outright rejection 'would . . . check the tide which is flowing so strongly against the Government'.[49] Such figures were cleverly isolated and their opposition to the Balfour–Lansdowne policy nullified.

The Unionists were, however, dangerously complacent about the Lords and made little effort to take up defensive positions. In response to the Campbell-Bannerman resolution, the House of Lords in 1907 appointed a Select Committee under Lord Rosebery to consider reform proposals. This Committee recommended, in December 1908, a complete overhaul of the composition of the House, and a considerable reduction in the hereditary element. The proposals envisaged a chamber which, while still strongly Conservative, would have been much easier to defend. As Lansdowne observed later, the scheme aimed 'at preventing the indecent influx, upon great occasions, of inexperienced Peers, the facile prey of the caricaturist and platform orator'.[50]

Yet there was no follow up. The report was not even debated. Balfour and Lansdowne, unsympathetic to reform in principle, were reluctant to tamper with a chamber which had served their purposes so admirably and, as Jenkins has written, 'Leisurely unconcern was the attitude of most of the Unionist peers'.[51] In the electoral and constitutional struggles of the coming years, the Unionists were to be gravely handicapped by their lack of an agreed and publicised plan for constitutional reform. Yet in the winter of 1908-9 the day of reckoning seemed so remote that Unionist neglect is understandable.

In the country electoral recovery was well under way by the close of 1908. If the by-election trend were to be maintained in a general election the Unionists could expect a majority of approximately 150 over all other parties. Aware of the unreliability of estimates based on by-elections, the Unionist leaders were more cautious in their expectations, indeed quite modest. At the beginning of 1909 the Conservative Central Office expected a Unionist majority of twenty. Austen Chamberlain, admitting that he was more sanguine than his colleagues, anticipated a majority of fifty.[52] Near universal amongst Unionists and widespread among Liberals was the conviction that the Government was doomed. In a leading article on 28 January *The Times* expressed vividly the tolerant contempt in which Unionists held the dying Liberal Government.

> So long as the Navy and the Army are properly maintained, and Sir Edward Grey continues to direct our foreign policy, and the House of Lords remains as a check upon the wild schemes ... [of] the Government, the Government will be acquiesced in, as a thing inevitable though not welcome. The by-elections, and perhaps even more the general trend of opinion, show that the Government are making steady progress to extinction.

Yet this outward confidence, even complacency, marked a continuing deep and bitter division over the fiscal question. The shattered party had relapsed into internecine conflict even before the 1906 election was over. More than ever the conflict assumed the dimensions of a power struggle between the party establishment and the Chamberlainite Whole Hoggers, with the small band of Free Fooders impotent on the sidelines.[53]

When the electoral storm had passed, it was clear that the Balfourites still controlled the seats of power within the party. The Opposition front bench was mostly Balfourite, the Lords strongly so. The Conservative Party machine was in the hands of Alexander Acland-Hood, Chief Whip, and J. P. Hughes, Principal Agent, both loyal servants of Arthur Balfour.

If age and authority lay with the Balfourites, numbers, youth and energy lay with Birmingham. In the House of Commons the Whole Hoggers at least equalled the forces of the Balfourites and Free Fooders combined.[54] In the country, reported the Chief Whip, 'the local leaders are mostly in favour of whole hogging ...'.[55] Under the Tariff Reform

banner were gathered most of the young politicians of promise e.g.
F. E. Smith, Leopold Amery, Arthur Lee, and Arthur Steel-Maitland.
The next four leaders of the Conservative Party were all at this time
associated with the Whole Hogger wing.

In the years after 1906 the initiative lay with the Whole Hoggers.
The unfortunate Free Fooders were weak in numbers and found no
viable course of action. They were never able to resolve the dilemma
posed by Balfour of Burleigh: 'Shall we go to the Devil of Protection
with our friends, or the Deep Sea of Socialism with our political
adversaries?'[56] Imaginative efforts to evade this dilemma, such as the
formation of a Centre Party under Lord Rosebery, were little more
than the fantasies of desperate men.

The electoral disaster of 1906 had confirmed for the Balfourites their
belief in the wisdom of relegating the fiscal question to the background.
In the years after 1906 they shunned initiatives on the fiscal issue, hoping
to keep it under wraps. In so far as the issue could not be avoided,
Balfour desired to continue the pursuit of unity through ambiguity.
He would favour a statement of fiscal ideals, but a statement which
would 'make it as easy as possible for the varying elements of the Party
to fall into line': and he wished for the avoidance of 'everything which
induces people overtly to proclaim themselves in different camps'.[57]

Also militating against a Balfourite initiative was Balfour's negative
concept of the role of Opposition. Balfour believed that the task of an
Opposition was to oppose, not to provide targets by offering programmes of its own. Thus he deplored the presentation of positive
programmes which he feared would be both vulnerable and disruptive.
Liberal attacks on the Church, the Pubs, the Land and the Wealthy
were all foreshadowed. Ultimately even the Union might be endangered. In fighting these the Unionists would rediscover their unity.[58]

This left the running to the Whole Hoggers, who knew what they
wanted. 'Everything', wrote Joseph Chamberlain to Walter Long on
30 January 1906, 'seems to me to depend upon our being able to
arrange for a firm, definite and united policy as the foundation of the
new army we have to raise.'[59] Without such a policy electoral success
would be worthless. Many Whole Hoggers agreed with Leo Maxse,
Chamberlainite editor of the *National Review*, that the Balfourite policy
of negative Opposition was 'perilous nonsense'.[60] They pressed Balfour
for 'a definite constructive alternative to the wild-cat and predatory
schemes of the present Government', or, despairing of Balfour, talked
wildly of a new 'Unauthorised Programme'.[61] Impatient, determined

and with a positive programme, the Whole Hoggers set out to capture the party before the next election. For this three things were necessary: to convert Balfour to their way of thinking; to get control of the party organisation; to convert or expel the remaining Free Fooders.

Balfour's conversion was crucial, for particularly after Joseph Chamberlain's crippling stroke in July 1906 no other Unionist was *papabile*. By early 1909 Balfour was a convert of sorts to some sort of Tariff Reform; his public, if still ambiguous, acceptance of the faith his Birmingham National Union speech of November 1907. In this speech Balfour committed himself to small and widespread duties, both preferential and protective, and dealt with details to an extent never vouchsafed before. The speech followed Balfour's recognition during 1907 of the growing strength of the Whole Hoggers within the Unionist ranks, and no doubt the swing to Tariff Reform in the 1908 by-elections confirmed him in his decision. An increasingly narrow interpretation of his Birmingham speech became the party dogma and the test of loyalty for candidates, and Balfour made no move to repudiate such interpretations.

Yet it would be a mistake to think that by 1909 the Whole Hoggers were rallied firmly behind Balfour, or that he made a convincing Tariff Reform leader. The Tariff Reformers were never to be sure that Balfour was really theirs. Their mistrust of his intellectual fastidiousness, their doubts about his whole-hearted commitment to their cause, are revealed in a notably moderate letter to Bonar Law from Leo Maxse on 5 June 1908. 'He [Balfour] gets screwed up to a certain point, and we all imagine it is all right, and then he invariably plays into the hands of the enemy, and discourages his own friends by some piece of mental gymnastics.'[62] For a convert, Balfour displayed his Tariff Reform convictions shyly and rarely. Nevertheless at the end of 1909 this reluctant Tariff Reformer was to lead a Unionist Party, committed as never before to the fiscal policy of Birmingham, into a decisive electoral encounter.

The Whole Hogger attack on the party machine had been renewed in 1906. In that year an assault on the Central Office had been foiled by Balfour's organisational lieutenants.[63] Despite this, a growing accommodation developed between the Central Office and the Chamberlain faction, partly due to the success of the Whole Hoggers at other levels of the organisation. By 1908 the National Union was in the hands of the Whole Hoggers, and was publicly and unequivocally committed to the full tariff programme. At the same time their failure to get control of the Central Office was being minimised at the base by the subversion of the local organisations of the Conservative Party. The policy of non-interference in local constituency matters pursued by Conservative Party headquarters, the sympathy for the Chamberlain cause among local party leaders, the pressures from local Tariff Reform League committees, the often ill-defined local relations between Liberal Unionists and Conservatives, were all exploited in a masterly and successful operation.[64] At the beginning of 1909 the Free Fooder Lord George Hamilton sadly concluded that 'the extreme section of the Tariff Reformers are in possession of the Political Local Machinery of the Unionist Party'.[65]

The Central Office could not remain indifferent to these developments. Balfour's speeches were increasingly interpreted in a manner favourable to the Tariff Reformers by a Central Office which, unlike Balfour, was concerned not with intellectual integrity but with a straightforward and unambiguous platform. Acland-Hood, who had dreaded a split in 1906, now faced the prospect with equanimity. 'If there is a split in the end, we shall of course lose some good men, whom we can ill spare, but they now have little influence.'[66] The apparent electoral success of the fiscal nostrums of Birmingham in the depressed conditions of 1908 set the seal on the entente between the Whole Hoggers and the Central Office. The outcome was the public declaration by the Central Office in January 1909 that official support would be withheld from all candidates who did not accept unreservedly the fiscal policy laid down by Balfour at Birmingham in 1907.[67]

The third of the Whole Hogger objectives, the expulsion of the unrepentant Free Fooders from the party, was in one sense the most difficult to achieve. If any single idea had originally united the Balfourites, it had been their opposition to any form of political ostracism. 'If such a policy succeeded in making the party unanimous', Balfour warned Austen Chamberlain, 'it would be at the price of keeping it small.'[68] Nevertheless the very success of the Whole Hoggers with Balfour and within the party organisation facilitated ostracism and also reduced the size of the problem by encouraging the more weak-kneed of the Free Fooders to abandon their principles or their seats.

As the *rapprochement* between Balfour, his allies in the party machine and the Whole Hoggers developed, the Balfourite party leadership became increasingly reluctant to protect the Free Fooders from their enemies within the Unionist Party. Balfour himself was positively unhelpful. '. . . with what plausibility either I, or anybody else, can require an Association . . . to retain the services of even the most distinguished politician, with whom neither they nor I agree, puzzles me.'[69] Acland-Hood, at least from 1908 on, was quite unwilling to back the Free-Fooders. 'I cannot use our Central Office to return to Parliament a group of men who, when we get a majority, will either refuse to support or will oppose the chief measure on which a majority has been returned.'[70] Given this attitude the outlook for the Free Fooders was grim.

Their difficulties were aggravated by the formation early in 1907 of a secret society of extremist Whole Hoggers known as the Confederacy. Moving spirits in this organisation seem to have been Henry Page Croft, who had fought Lincoln as an independent Tariff Reformer in 1906; Edward (Paddy) Goulding, 'Joe's Man Friday'; and Lord Winterton, another 'completely in the pocket of the B'ham gang', and that secretive but ubiquitous right-winger, Thomas Comyn-Platt.[71] Bonar Law and Leo Maxse appear to have acted as mentors to this juvenile ginger group. The Confederacy, which saw itself as the inquisitorial arm of the Tariff Reform movement, aimed first at seeing that every new Unionist candidate was right on Tariff Reform, and secondly at evicting the incumbent Free Fooders.

The winter of 1908-9 saw the climax of Confederate activity. In January 1909 the Confederates determined on a final purge of the remaining Free Traders so that the coming Unionist majority should not be hamstrung by a handful of Free Food M.P.s. On 18 January the *Morning Post*, the chief Whole Hogger daily, issued, with the apparent connivance of the Central Office, a list of sixteen Free Food M.P.s, plus a few suspects.[72] The expulsion of the blacklisted was urged by the *Morning Post*, the *Daily Express*, and the *Globe*. At Norwood the sitting Free Fooder was thrown over by his association; at Hertford the Free Trade Member was disowned by his executive; at East Marylebone Lord Robert Cecil, the leader of the Free Fooders in the Commons, was faced with a local rebellion. Unionist Free Fooders at Wakefield, South-East Durham, and West Dorset all came under fire.

The moderate Unionist press was alarmed, because they feared that the violence unleashed might wreck the Unionist Party on the eve of electoral victory. The fears of the moderates were vividly expressed by a correspondent to *The Times* signing himself 'Fox-hunter'.

A beaten fox is in view, and the leading hounds instead of devoting themselves to the kill are savaging the stragglers with what appears the tacit concurrence of the whippers-in. Is it possible while this is going on ... to kill the fox? I doubt it.[73]

Such fears were heightened by the desperate response of the savaged 'stragglers'. Their previous efforts to find a workable strategy had foundered on their reluctance to face the difficulty of establishing a separate party, or had been wrecked by their distaste for any alliance with a Liberal Party increasingly collectivist in its policies. For the moment such doubts were swept aside. An appeal for funds to protect the black-listed was launched, and plans were prepared to run Free Fooders against the most obnoxious of the Confederates – Henry Page Croft at Bournemouth, Bonar Law at Dulwich, Goulding at Worcester.[74] Secret negotiations were opened with Asquith and Liberal headquarters.[75]

But these plans needed time to mature. This the Free Fooders believed they had. E. G. Brunker, the Secretary of the Unionist Free Trade Club, thought it unlikely that there would be a general election 'for a considerable time'.[76] Yet time was running out, the election less than a year away.

A more immediate danger, the coming Budget, was recognised. In a prophetic note, written on Christmas Day 1908, Cromer, President of the Unionist Free Trade Club, feared that it would 'rather tend to crystallise party lines' making *rapprochement* with the Liberals, already difficult, impossible.[77] Should party lines crystallise over the Government's fiscal policy, then the anomalous position of the Unionist Free Fooders would be impossible to maintain. The polarisation of parties that followed the Budget did indeed put an end to the ambitions and pretensions of the Free Fooders. It also undermined what little remained of the Balfourian *via media*, and clinched the triumph of the Whole Hoggers.

4

The Budget of Lloyd George

I

The Unionist Free Fooders were not the only group apprehensive about the coming Budget. Unionists generally regarded the Chancellor of the Exchequer with a mixture of distaste and distrust, while the novel and often extravagant tax schemes current among Radicals served merely to increase Unionist alarm and to worry cautious Liberals. All were aware that the Chancellor's financial difficulties were formidable. A current deficit, an expected lower tax yield in the coming year, increased expenditure on the navy and the cost of Old Age Pensions faced Lloyd George with a prospective deficit for 1909–10 of £16,000,000. In terms of modern public finance, this sum seems small, but to cover it demanded a larger increase in revenue than had ever before been required in times of peace.[1] It was Lloyd George's achievement to turn these fiscal debts into political assets.

Almost from the moment he became Chancellor, Lloyd George had determined to use his first Budget as the instrument for reviving the Liberal Party. Referring to his Budget plans in a letter to his brother in May 1908, Lloyd George wrote: 'It is time we did something that appealed straight to the people – it will, I think, help to stop the electoral rot, and that is most necessary.'[2] After an attempt to achieve his objectives by a return to one of the cardinal principles of Gladstonian finance – the reduction of defence expenditure – had been foiled by the Liberal Imperialists, Lloyd George turned his attention increasingly to a reconstruction of the tax system. From the autumn of 1909 on, he appears to have decided that Liberal morale would have to be restored not by reducing expenditure but, paradoxically, by increasing taxation. On 29 April 1909, in a speech of over four hours,[3] Lloyd George introduced a Budget which was to transform the political situation.

To cover his anticipated deficit, Lloyd George introduced seven entirely new taxes – a super-tax of 6d. on incomes of £5000 and over; a tax on motor vehicles ranging from £2 2s. to £40 according to horsepower; a duty of 3*d*. per gallon on petrol; and four new land taxes – a tax of 20 per cent on the unearned increment of land values, an annual duty of ½*d*. in the pound on the capital value of underdeveloped land, a similar duty on ungotten minerals (changed in committee to a 5 per cent duty on the rental value of the rights to work minerals), and a 10 per cent reversion duty on any benefit accruing to a lessor at the termination of a lease. In addition, the system of liquor licences was completely remodelled and a higher scale of duties laid down. The death duties and the related legacy and succession duties were all increased, as were the stamp duties. The general rate of income tax was raised from 1*s*. to 1*s*. 2*d*. in the pound, but only for unearned incomes and for earned incomes over £3000. Finally, the duties on spirits were raised by a third, those on tobacco by a quarter.

These taxes were as much designed to 'stop the electoral rot' as to meet the financial deficit faced by the Government. During the genesis of the Budget, Lloyd George appears to have been concerned with the political, rather than the financial, yield of these taxes. Initially he showed little understanding of the finer points of his measure, and while his grasp undoubtedly improved, he remained a politician who 'allows his mind to revolve round big questions, to disregard of details altogether'.[4] How to restore the morale of the Liberal Party, how to recapture the working-class electorate, these were the 'big questions' absorbing Lloyd George. Moreover Lloyd George seems to have pursued the extraordinary course of both exaggerating his deficit and minimising the yield of the taxes in order to justify the inclusion of some of his more novel items. To serve his political ends the Chancellor was apparently quite prepared to paint his financial troubles in the darkest colours.[5] But it is the taxes themselves that reveal most clearly the political nature of the Budget.

The licence duties and the land taxes were designed to restore the morale of the Liberal Party, for the taxes in themselves were popular with Liberals, as well as being measures of retaliation against the House of Lords. Following the rejection of the Licensing Bill, most Unionists seemed to have been resigned to higher licence duties but were staggered by the 'murderous increase' which occurred.[6] Lloyd George planned to increase the yield of the licence duties by £2,500,000, thereby more than doubling the total annual revenue from liquor licences. No tax could have been more surely designed to rally the Nonconformists to the Government.

The land taxes did even more to arouse party enthusiasm. They had little to do with the immediate financial situation for, although promising higher yields in future years, they were to contribute only £500,000 in 1909–10. Their objective was twofold – to raise the morale of the party and to enable the Government to outwit the Lords. Applauded in principle by the Radical wing of the party, they were welcomed too as an irritant to the Lords, for, as Morley observed, 'to talk about land to the House of Lords was like talking to a butcher about Lent'.[7] But they were more than an irritant, for they were designed to enable the Cabinet to evade the veto of the Lords.

> It is now clear [Lloyd George told his colleagues in March] that it would be impossible to secure the passage of a separate Valuation Bill during the existence of the present Parliament, owing to the opposition of the Lords, and therefore the only possible chance which the Government have of redeeming their pledges in this respect is by incorporating proposals involving land valuation in a Finance Bill.[8]

To justify the valuation proposals, land taxes as such would have to be included in the Budget. Here at last was a response to the Lords, well calculated to cheer dispirited Liberals frustrated by the constant mutilation of their land legislation by the Upper House.

But the Budget was designed not just to revive the spirits of good Liberals, but also to arouse the support of the working classes. On the principle that the broadest shoulders should bear the heavier load, the new tax burdens were mainly in the direct-tax field, i.e. in the sphere of taxes which fell most heavily or exclusively on the wealthier section of the community. With the exception of the duties on spirits and tobacco, the taxes were aimed at a limited segment of the population. In 1909, approximately 1,000,000 persons paid income tax, and of these only a relatively small proportion were affected by the income tax increases. The super-tax proposals affected at the most 12,000 tax payers. Only about 80,000 persons were liable to death duties, while stamp duties and land taxes fell almost exclusively on the income-tax-paying segment of the population.[9] Even the motor car and petrol taxes fell upon the same limited group, for the motor car was perhaps the most unpopular and omnipresent example of the conspicuous consumption of the wealthy classes in Edwardian society.

Approximately 75 per cent of the tax increase would be paid by the income-tax-paying class, approximately 10 per cent of the population; the rest by the other 90 per cent of the population.[10] In an era in which real wages were stationary if not declining and in which the working classes were well aware that 'the world's increasing riches were passing them by',[11] a Budget so conceived was likely to arouse their support, despite the increased spirit and tobacco taxes. 'The Government', observed one outraged Unionist, Professor A. V. Dicey, 'have in violation of all constitutional morality offered a huge bribe to the poorer part of the electorate. . . .'[12]

Nor of course was the popularity of the Budget dependent solely on its tax structure. Lloyd George was well aware that raising £14,000,000 in new taxation was an unorthodox and even uncertain method of reviving a party's electoral fortunes. Never perhaps has a Chancellor struggling to raise revenue been so prodigal in promises to distribute money. All the money raised by the motor and petrol taxes was to go on the building of roads in order to allay the traffic nuisance. A National Development Grant was to be established for improving the natural resources of the country – by afforestation schemes, experimental farms and the reclamation of land. This was clearly aimed at Labour, being in a sense a substitute for the party's Right to Work Bill.[13] The Budget speech was embellished, too, with promises of costly new welfare legislation, e.g. the removal of the pauper disqualification for old-age pensions, and health and unemployment insurance, this latter Churchillian in inspiration.[14]

Lloyd George closed his Budget speech with a ringing declaration: 'This . . . is a War Budget.' Few would have disagreed, for if through the Budget war was to be waged against the 'poverty and squalidness' of the masses, the cannon had been indubitably trained on the classes.

II

'. . . this Budget will be kill or cure!' so said Churchill to his wife on Budget eve.[15] The Chancellor himself was not unaware of the electoral dangers inherent in a policy based on increased taxation. 'If it failed it might react in the House and bring us down prematurely.'[16] Much would depend on the Budget's impact on the dispirited Liberals, even more perhaps on the reaction of the Unionists.

The Budget upset some of the old Gladstonians in the Liberal Party. One Cabinet member, the aged Lord Wolverhampton, was reported as 'hat[ing] the whole scheme as heartily as any Tory . . .'; the ship-owner Sir Walter Runciman thought the Budget 'hadn't the merit of being more than a concoction of loot', and was barely restrained from resigning the Chairmanship of the Northern Liberal Federation. Lord Rosebery condemned the Budget as 'inquisitorial, tyrannical and socialistic' and severed his few remaining links with the Liberal Party.[17] In the House a group of mostly elderly and wealthy M.P.s, labelled 'the troglodytes', was formed to fight the land taxes, but this resistance was ineffectual and soon petered out. Outside, Rosebery and his chief adjutant, the wealthy Nonconformist Sir Robert Perks, appear to have contemplated using the Liberal League as an anti-Budget instrument but soon abandoned both the idea and the League.[18] Throughout the country there was evidence of a shift away from the Government amongst elderly upper-middle-class Liberals. For these men, the Budget was merely the most dramatic evidence of modern Liberalism's growing breach with the Gladstonian tradition.

But among the mass of the Liberal Party the Budget achieved its objective – the restoration of party morale. Hilaire Belloc, the Liberal M.P. for South Salford, who rarely praised his leaders, found it 'difficult to imagine a better Budget'.[19] His enthusiasm was shared by the more orthodox, Lloyd George's 'audacious counter-attack'[20] heartening his party both in the House and the country. A month after the introduction of the Budget, Lloyd George wrote triumphantly to Spender: 'The reports I have from all parts of the country are not merely of a favourable but of a glowing character. Members tell me that it had put new heart into the Party. . . .'[21] Unquestionably by July 1909 the Liberal Party as a whole was in better spirit than at any time since 1906.

The parliamentary wing of the Labour Party, despite its criticism of the indirect taxes, also reacted favourably. If the *Labour Leader* was guarded in its welcome – 'the Budget is, on the whole, better than we expected'[22] – leading parliamentarians vied with each other in praising it.[23] But the leftward lurch implicit in the Budget compounded Labour's difficulties in promoting an image sharply distinct from the Radical wing of the Liberal Party.

The Government's Irish allies were not similarly enamoured of the Bill. They were bitterly hostile to the spirit duties as unfair to Ireland, while the land taxes were suspect amongst the rural Irish. Nevertheless although dislike of the Budget furthered factionalism in Ireland, and was ultimately to be a crucial factor in British politics, for the moment the Government's impregnable position in the Commons made it impervious to Irish criticism.

But what of the country at large, where at the beginning of 1909 the Liberals had been far from impregnable? Would those who had to pay more for their 'beer and baccy' be reconciled by the burdens imposed on the rich? Would a policy pleasing to the Liberal Party stalwarts be equally acceptable to the mass of the population? Might not the numerically small yet influential interests affected be again able to humble the Government? The Budget had revived the ardour of the Liberal Party; would it also revive its electoral fortunes?

Tentative evidence on public opinion was provided by a cluster of four by-elections in July. The constituencies – Cleveland, High Peak, Mid-Derby and Dumfries Burghs – were not particularly representative, since three of them were safe Liberal seats, and all were located in the North. Cleveland had not been contested in 1906, but in the other three seats the swing to the Unionists, though persisting, averaged only 4·6 per cent, well under half that prevailing against the Government over the past twelve months. High Peak the Unionists had confidently expected to capture, and their failure to do so left 'Tories depressed, Liberals and Labour jubilant'.[24]

Not that the Budget alone explained the Liberal recovery. Summer had brought other blessings to the Government after its bleak winter. The naval scare had died away, there had been a seasonal improvement in the unemployment figures, the South Africa Union Act had been well received, and Churchill had recently won praise in settling a coal industry dispute. But the Budget appeared the chief cause. High Peak '. . . the Conservative agents reported, would have been captured . . . but for the Budget'.[25]

The popularity of Lloyd George's measure had been enhanced by the inept performance of its critics in the previous three months. During the summer Balfour and Lansdowne played only a secondary role in the public agitation against the Budget. During the critical month of June, as the agitation in the country really got under way with the formation of the Budget League and the Budget Protest League, neither Balfour nor Lansdowne appeared on the public platform.[26] None of Balfour's scathing private denunciations of the Budget were repeated in his public utterances. Occasional speeches from the party leaders raised no enthusiasm in the party press, since they developed neither a comprehensive attack nor a viable alternative. The failure of the Unionist Party leaders to give an effective lead at this time was a handicap from which the anti-Budget agitation never fully recovered.

The reason for this hiatus in leadership lay no doubt in the reluctance of the party leaders to restrict their opportunities for manœuvre. Both Balfour and Lansdowne seemed fearful of over-committing the

Unionist Party to an attack on the Budget, for a bold public assault on the measure would be foolish and might be electorally disastrous if, after all, the Lords were finally to acquiesce in its passage. Thus until the party reached a decision on the Budget Balfour and Lansdowne were hesitant in attack for, if they aroused expectations they could not, or would not, fulfil, then they might find themselves at the head of a rout, or destroyed by a party schism.

In addition, the Unionist leaders may well have hoped that a spontaneous demand for drastic treatment of the Budget would develop. The successful resistance to the Education and Licensing Bills had been conducted under the cover of a popular agitation whipped up by the pressure groups immediately concerned. Might not the same strategy succeed again? It meant, however, waiting on, rather than leading, events. The danger of such a policy was that a strategy successful against particular sectarian or sectional measures might fail, with unfortunate repercussions, against the masterly operation of the Chancellor, conceived as it was on a very broad front.

But if it lacked leadership and coherence, the public opposition to the Budget did not want for vehemence. If the Budget had aroused the enthusiasm of most Liberals, it had aroused the anger of many on the right. The City protested by letters and meetings, wealthy landlords cut subscriptions to charities and football clubs, and threatened to dismiss employees. Several dukes were unwisely vituperative about Lloyd George, his Budget, and his socialist allies. 'They had', jeered Churchill, with alliterative profusion, 'the woeful wail of the wealthy wastrel, . . . the dismal dirge of the dilapidated duke. . . .'[27]

The licensed trade responded by raising the price of beer and spirits and the price of tobacco went up. Organisations protesting against the Budget, particularly against the land taxes, proliferated. On 14 June the Budget Protest League was founded, an early effort to base the attack on the Budget on an argument with a wider appeal than those touted by the dukes. Nevertheless, the League's original policy reflected the negative approach of the party leaders, and led to an acrimonious debate with the Whole Hoggers, for its speakers were instructed by the President, Walter Long, to avoid discussion of the fiscal alternative to the Budget.[28]

Much of this agitation was maladroit because conducted by the politically naïve. The protestations of the City magnates merely stressed the democratic structure of the Budget. 'Rich men have simply wept in public on rich men's shoulders' was the *Nation*'s description of one

City meeting.[29] Increases in liquor and tobacco prices, often said to be exorbitant, may well have led to resentment against the brewers and the tobacconists rather than against the Government. The plaints and petty retaliations of the dukes aroused derision rather than sympathy. 'What asses the Dukes are', the Liberal Earl Carrington noted in his diary.[30] Many Unionists would have agreed, one young M.P. wishing 'the Dukes had held their tongues, everyone of them'.[31] They certainly provided the Radicals with superb opportunities to pillory the whole aristocratic order.

The Whole Hoggers, who had a definitive anti-Budget programme, were highly critical of this undisciplined agitation which threatened to boomerang on its initiators. They were alarmed by the damage being done to the Unionist cause by the self-interested protests of landlords and City magnates. As early as 14 May at a meeting of the Whole Hogger-dominated National Union Council, several members urged that speakers 'should have definite instructions to attack the Budget as a whole, and not on behalf of any one section'.[32]

Their alarm seemed justified by the July by-elections, while the inadequacy and vulnerability of the anti-Budget campaign was dramatically revealed in Lloyd George's Limehouse speech. So far the Chancellor had been absent from the public debate, the defence of his measure being borne by his colleagues, particularly the Prime Minister and Churchill. But on 30 July before an East End audience at Limehouse he capitalised on the ineptitude of his critics, lambasting landlords, financiers and, above all, the dukes. More deliberately than ever before, he pitched his appeal at the working class, risking the alienation of middle-class Liberals. A speech like this from a Minister of the Crown had not been heard in the land since the Radical days of Joseph Chamberlain.

The combination of the by-elections and Limehouse shook the Unionist Party. A smattering of misguided retorts came from the Dukes, but the prevailing mood was one of panic. A Unionist M.P., who had just toured the North and Midlands found amongst the local party leaders 'an almost unanimous consensus of opinion to this effect – "Choose any battle ground rather than that of coronets and landowners against the Budget" '.[33] The wisdom of resisting the Budget was questioned in the Unionist press, particularly in the Northcliffe papers which in the early days of August showed a distinct inclination to trim.[34] Indeed the *Spectator* on 7 August accused the *Daily Mail* of writing 'what almost amounted to a panegyric of the

Budget. The greater part read like a speech of the Chancellor of the Exchequer in one of his more chastened moods.' But the panic was momentary, for it coincided with the determination of Arthur Balfour to steel himself to rejection.[35]

III

Balfour's late summer decision in favour of rejection was not forced upon him by any group in the party, nor was he required to exercise strong leadership to enforce it upon a reluctant party. The Budget was rejected in November 1909 not at the behest of any single powerful interest, but as the result of an overwhelming consensus within the Unionist Party in favour of such action, a consensus which developed in the autumn of 1909. Balfour anticipated this development and helped to foster it, but such a consensus seems to have been inevitable whatever Balfour's attitude. Powerful interests allied with the Unionist Party, the most dynamic of the party factions, and powerful institutional forces all demanded rejection.

First, the landed interest was implacably opposed to the passage of the Budget. The great landowners, particularly those with urban holdings, were incensed, and many had achieved a summer notoriety through their attacks on the Budget and its author. The smaller landowners seemed solidly behind them. In mid-May the *Nation* reported smugly that the country gentlemen 'are almost inarticulate with wrath'.[36] 'Go into any West End Club or almost any country house', wrote Ilbert, 'and you hear nothing but execration of Lloyd George and his budget.'[37] Not that most of the rural landowners were immediately affected by the land taxes, for by devious means agricultural land had been exempted from taxation, though not, of course, from valuation. It was the land valuation, and the future implications of the land taxes that alarmed the gentry. A leading Conservative peer was reported as saying: 'It is not the Licence Duties or the super-tax or the death duties that we mind so much, though these are bad enough. What we can't and won't stand is the general valuation of land.'[38] The agricultural interest was but slowly recovering from a protracted economic depression, its political power had been eroded, its social power was in decline. Nervous landowners saw in land valuation the threat of ultimate ruin.

It was an interest that could not be ignored. It was the core of the old Conservative Party, and in the Edwardian period the foundation of the Balfourian middle way within the Unionist Party. One-third of the Unionist Party in the House of Commons could be classified as country gentlemen, while in the House of Lords at least two-thirds of those voting for rejection owned 5,000 acres of land or more.[39]

A second strongly anti-Budget influence was the licensed trade, which loathed the Budget, seeing it as a measure of revenge for the defeat of the Licensing Bill. Indeed it was reported that 'the Trade would rather have had the Licensing Bill of last year than this Bill'.[40] Strachey, who had little sympathy with the licensed interest, was by September 'beginning to think that the brewers honestly believe themselves to be on the brink of ruin'.[41] Although more discreet in its activities than in 1908, the licensed trade worked relentlessly and spent handsomely to defeat the Budget. Important paymasters to the Conservative Party for a generation, generous providers of committee rooms and public house meeting places, 'the Trade' could not be disregarded.

Thirdly, the financial and commercial interests clustered in the City opposed a Budget which, in the words of their most active spokesman, Lord Rothschild, aimed 'to establish the principles of Socialism and collectivism'.[42] They had been early and articulate critics of the measure, and their great rally against the Budget at the Cannon Street Hotel on 23 June demonstrated the virtual unanimity of City opinion. Their opposition to the Budget, although as negative as that of landowners and brewers, was broader in scope for to dislike of the 'vicious' land taxes and 'vindictive' licensing duties they added hostility to the sinking fund proposals, to the super-tax, and to the increases in income-tax and death duties.[43]

The City interest had many intimate links with the Unionist Party hierarchy. It also provided the bulk of Balfour's own constituents, had able and prominent representatives in the Lords, and was closely allied to the Budget Protest League. But it derived its real influence from its position as spokesman for property interests in the country generally. And, in mid-November, one reluctant supporter of rejection confessed that 'the feeling against [the Budget] among owners of property has risen to a point which perhaps makes the rejection inevitable'.[44]

But the Tariff Reform wing was the brain of the resistance to the Budget, and it was under its banner that the battle was ultimately be to fought. Lloyd George's measure struck directly at the Tariff Reformers by repudiating their argument that the Free Trade system was virtually bankrupt and that Tariff Reform alone could provide the revenue for extensive social reform. Obsessed with the notion that the Budget had been deliberately designed to thwart them, they were also increasingly fearful that the success of the Budget policy might ruin their chances of electoral victory.

They had chafed under the inaction of the leadership throughout the summer, for they had early resolved that the Budget must be resisted to the end, and they had a full anti-Budget programme. To them the Budget representing the socialistic dead end of Free Trade finance which, by attacking wealth, would injure wages, employment and trade. The Budget and the Free Trade system should be condemned together, and Unionists should offer the Tariff Reform alternative which would raise the required revenue and at the same time encourage the growth and development of British trade and industry. '. . . by far the best weapon, indeed the only effective and permanently success-ful weapon with which to destroy Lloyd Georgism, is our alternative policy of tariff reform.'[45] This was the banner under which the whole party could fight, offering as it did a comprehensive criticism and a positive alternative.

It was the programme of the Tariff Reformers that gave them a crucial role in the developing consensus. The Free Fooder and Tory ex-Chancellor of the Exchequer, St Aldwyn, had recognised this early. Three days after the Budget was introduced he told his son: 'Generally I should say the Tariff Reformers will profit largely by the Budget, for all the rich people will be wild about it; and many bankers and such like who are Free Traders will be driven to their side by the pro-posed Income Tax and Death Duties.'[46] The drift was soon evident. Among businessmen in 1909 there appears to have been a definite revulsion against Free Trade, and one Lancashire businessman put down the resultant movement to Tariff Reform as 'a revolt of income-tax payers'.[47] The Free Trade financiers, the brewers, and the Balfourite landowners did not have a constructive anti-Budget programme. The Whole Hoggers did.

The interest groups within the party, whose opposition to the Budget was based on more limited and negative grounds, rallied to the Chamberlain programme. Balfour's own position was seriously eroded as the landed interest swung towards Highbury.[48] A series of letters from the Duke of Northumberland, one of the greatest of the English landowners, to Strachey in the autumn of 1909 vividly portrays this shift. Initially an 'economic agnostic', Northumberland had backed Balfour throughout. But now 'the only chance we have of success is to find a different way of raising the money to that proposed by the Govt., & as far as I know Tariff Reform is the only possible alternative'. And Northumberland revealed how effective Tariff Reform propaganda had been in structuring the debate. 'Protection cannot be worse than Socialism. . . . And as . . . Tariff Reform or Socialism are the only possible alternatives at this moment, I am quite prepared to swallow the former.'[49] Thus the consensus that developed was not only for rejection but also for Tariff Reform.

Supplementing the interests gathering under the Tariff Reform flag were two institutional forces which also desired rejection – the Unionist majority in the Lords and the party organisation. Apart from any involvement as landlords, Tariff Reformers, or financiers, the peers were also affected as members of an institution which had increasingly acted as a barrier to radical reforms. Many feared that if this Budget passed untouched the conservative rationale of the Second Chamber would be seriously weakened. In perhaps the most explicit statement of his own attitude, Lansdowne in a letter to Balfour of Burleigh argued that if the Budget passed 'the position of the H. of L. would have been gravely and permanently impaired. We could never in future, however outrageous the financial policy of a Radical Government might be, claim the right to stand in its way.'[50]

The danger that the Tory position might be outflanked by measures clothed in the financial prerogatives of the Commons was regarded as imminent. The eminent jurist Professor Dicey feared: 'It being known that the H.L. will not touch any budget it is probable that the Finance Bill for 1910 will contain some further bribes e.g. . . . . old age pensions at 60 or a reform of the poor law. . . .'[51] If the landlords saw ultimate ruination for their class in the Budget, the Tory peers saw the ruination of their institutional position in the same measure. By late June this was reflected in 'a strong feeling among the leaders of the Lords that if the Lords cannot throw out the land clauses on which the country has never been consulted, the House of Lords has practically ceased to be a second chamber'.[52]

The mood of the Lords was not unimportant. Success had bred recklessness. After the fierce if undisciplined resistance to the Budget any surrender would be seen as 'an ignominious capitulation'.[53] Had Lansdowne sought to escape the clash, and he vacillated longer than Balfour, he probably would not have been able to control his backwoodsmen. Nor was it simply the backwoodsmen who were set on a bold course. Cawdor, Milner, and Curzon constituted a formidable trio favouring rejection, and Milner and Curzon, as heroes of the imperial tradition, commanded wide support among the rank-and-file peers.

Many observers feared that at an election following upon rejection the issue would be, as Esher crudely and succinctly put it, 'not the Budget, or the "bloody Government", but the House of Lords'.[54] Not so the peers, who, rendered complacent by success, believed that their House was not immediately endangered by rejection. Lansdowne himself assumed that 'We shall not . . . get through the present crisis without two general elections' and that therefore 'by the time the H. of L. issue is ripe for treatment, the popularity of the Budget will . . . have greatly diminished'.[55] In one sense Lansdowne was proven right. There were to be two elections before 'the H. of L. issue [was] ripe for treatment'. But in his failure to see that rejection would fuel a constitutional revolution, he was to be proven disastrously wrong.

Finally, the weight of the Tory organisation was added to these other pressures. The campaign against the Budget had aroused the party workers throughout the country. By the third week in August over 7,500,000 anti-Budget leaflets had been issued, 70,000 posters and cartoons were out, and 1,873 anti-Budget meetings had been held.[56] The very demands made by this campaign on the faithful engendered an aggressive enthusiasm. In early September Acland-Hood reported: 'All our people are spoiling for a fight and will be disappointed if they don't get it'.[57] Even in Scotland where the local Unionist leaders 'are fully convinced of the danger run in taking a very violent course against the Budget in the Lords . . . on every other issue they are simply spoiling for a fight'.[58] During the autumn the campaign gathered momentum, intoxicating the party activists.

Such enthusiasm was naturally allied with confident predictions. Apart from the temporary and probably superficial depression of early August the Unionist organisation tended towards optimism. The Chief Whip anticipated that the Unionists would return from an election at least 300 strong, i.e. at the worst some thirty-six seats short of an absolute majority,[59] while Lichfield, one of the peers opposed to rejection, told Strachey at the end of September that '. . . the Party wirepullers (Conservatives and L.U.s) are telling the Leaders that with the help of Tariff Reform they will secure a majority at the next election'.[60] The forecasts originating from the organisation promised at least near victory, and undoubtedly Unionists were encouraged by evidence during the autumn that the summer popularity of the Budget was on the wane.[61]

Not that Unionists were greatly perturbed by the possibility of a small adverse majority. Any opportunity to reduce, if not to destroy, the abnormal majority of 1906 was bound to prove attractive to the party, eager to shake off the stigma of that disaster. Lansdowne thought it 'quite conceivable that we shall be defeated', but comforted himself with the thought that 'the Radical majority would be greatly decreased'.[62]

A second strand in Unionist thinking was even more important. Even the organisation's worst forecasts would, if realised, mean that the Liberal Government would be dependent on the Irish Nationalists. Unionists were hypnotised by the fateful analogy with 1892.

> If we are beaten [wrote one Unionist editor] we shall, at any rate, be much stronger in numbers than we are now and the Radicals with their diminished majority will be preyed upon by the Irish and by the Socialists. . . . It will be a Parliament not unlike the Parliament of 1892 and I believe with similar results – it will last two or three years and be followed by a period of great Unionist supremacy.[63]

This view was widely and uncritically held amongst influential Unionists and few seem to have questioned the relevance of the analogy to the circumstances of 1909.

Only one group did not share the prevailing view. The polarisation of opinion around the fiscal alternatives had paralysed the Free Fooders. A Unionist victory or a Unionist defeat alike filled them with despair. A Unionist defeat would mean the triumph of a Budget that they regarded as a perversion of Free Trade, and it would renew the threat to the Union. A Unionist victory in the circumstances would be the victory of Tariff Reform. It is not surprising therefore that the Free Fooders were the leading critics of the autumn consensus. The anguish of their position lent them a remarkable detachment, and they forecast with admirable prescience the results of rejection. But their advice was tainted because of their heresy and, anyhow, as Sandars assured Garvin, 'If we engage "in the imminent deadly breach", you make take it that the dissentient few on Tariff will sink their differences and join unreservedly with us'. Indeed, as Sandars pointed out, '. . . that is another advantage in doing the bold thing'.[64]

Balfour foresaw early the problems posed for his leadership by the factional realignment involved in the autumn consensus. In deciding for rejection in August he recognised that one mark of a leader's quality was to arrive before his followers at their ultimate destination. Not that he found the destination either politically or personally distasteful. He disliked the principles of the Budget as 'destructive of public morality',[65] and even more was repelled by the demagoguery with which the measure was defended. Lansdowne, always more timid and ever uneasy about extreme courses, required more prodding, and was slower than Balfour to support rejection. But his ultimate concurrence in Balfour's decision was hardly every in doubt, for over the past decade Balfour had been the dominating figure in this close personal and political relationship.

In a sense, of course, the strategy adopted was a triumph for the Whole Hoggers, who had urged this course in the months when the party leaders vacillated. Moreover the consensus was based on the acceptance of the Whole Hogger programme. For a few crucial months the strategy and policies of Highbury were accepted by the party. Yet this should not be allowed to disguise the fact that the strategy adopted was not one imposed by the Chamberlainites but one desired by the vast bulk of the party. In accepting the Tariff Reform programme the Balfourite element were merely seizing on the best available weapon to deal with the hated Budget. Their commitment was essentially opportunistic and if the programme failed in its task they would be quite willing to return to their old practices of modifying or even, if circumstances demanded, discarding Tariff Reform. It is only when the consensual and opportunistic nature of the Unionist decision in the autumn of 1909 is realised, that it becomes possible to understand why the victory of the Whole Hoggers was both temporary and pyrrhic.

IV

In mid-August 1909 these developments lay in the future, but a hardening of Unionist attitudes was already apparent both in the correspondence of the Unionist leaders and in the Unionist press. The loyalist *Daily Telegraph*, the Whole Hogger *Morning Post* and the *Standard*, and above all Garvin's *Observer*, were marked by a growing insistence on the need to repudiate the Budget in favour of Tariff Reform. The period of the amateurs was coming to an end; the professionals were taking over. One indication of this is the silencing of the dukes. On 4 August, in a letter to Balfour, Garvin urged: 'Our

Dukes should be warned to keep off the grass',[66] and on the next day *The Times* rebuked 'those unwise persons going about proclaiming that they will reduce their expenditure on wages and their charities in order to get even with the Government'. These warnings seem to have had some effect. From the end of August the dukes seem either to have been muzzled, or to have recognised the error of their ways, for despite considerable provocation there were no further public gaffes.

The hardening of Unionist attitudes is reflected in a new note that crept into Lloyd George's correspondence with his brother. On 17 August he mentioned the possibility of rejection for the first time. 'What will happen if they throw it out I can only conjecture and I rejoice at the prospect. Many a rotten institution, system and law will be submerged by the deluge.'[67] Intoxicated by the impact of his own rhetoric, assured by his friends that the country was 'aflame', Lloyd George from now on seems to have hoped, indeed even to have worked, for rejection. In the end perhaps he came to believe that he had plotted rejection all along.[68]

Rumours of rejection were given new impetus by Lord Rosebery's violent attack on the Budget at Glasgow on 10 September, in which he claimed the Budget was pure socialism, 'the end of all, the negation of faith, of family, of property, of monarchy, of Empire'.[69] Although he was deliberately ambiguous on rejection, many Unionists, not knowing his Lordship, hoped that he might take the lead in moving rejection in the Lords.[70] Ministers abandoned their tactic of publicly ignoring the whole subject and now stressed the impropriety of rejection. Speaking at the Bingley Hall, Birmingham, on 17 September, Asquith warned: 'Amendment by the House of Lords is out of the question. Rejection by the House of Lords is equally out of the question. . . . That way revolution lies. . . .'[71]

In the same hall a week later, Balfour revealed the restructuring of his own thinking on the Budget. It was his most trenchant and comprehensive attack to date on the Budget, and its theme was the contrast between 'judicious Tariff Reform' and 'the bottomless confusion of Socialistic legislation'. Although on rejection he was intentionally Delphic, and although he refused to allow a resolution requesting the Lords to throw out the Budget, the logic of his speech pointed to rejection. And he permitted the reading of a letter from Joseph Chamberlain which bluntly hoped that 'The House of Lords will see their way to force an election'.[72]

The Bingley Hall speech irrevocably committed the party to resistance to the end on the Budget. Although averse to any public signalling to the Lords, Balfour had privately declared before the speech that if the Lords did not reject the Bill, he could no longer lead the party.[73] In the circumstances he probably had few qualms about making such a pledge. Liberals, too, grasped the import of the speech. On the day after, Haldane wrote to his mother: 'I think the Birmingham meeting and Chamberlain's letter point to an election in November.'[74] One Liberal Minister's reaction was eminently practical. On 27 September Lewis Harcourt gave his election agent absolute discretion to take whatever steps he thought necessary in the constituency. 'I am beginning gradually to believe', he wrote, 'that there is more chance of a rejection by the Lords of the Finance Bill than I previously thought possible.'[75] He was soon to be followed by most of the politicians. Although the position remained clouded for some weeks, from the end of September both parties began manoeuvring for the best possible ground for a winter election.

5

The Coming of the First Election

Until the autumn the Ministers had been sustained in private, as well
as in public, by their belief in the constitutional enormity of rejection.
Although Lloyd George for one was now working to provoke the
Lords to rejection in the belief that if they did 'then never has there
been such a delivery of our enemies into our hands since the Syrian
Army was stricken with blindness,'[1] most of the Ministers frankly
recoiled from the tumult and turmoil of a constitutional revolution.
Thus when on 8 September the Cabinet discussed the possibility of
rejection for the first time it was not the deliverance up of their enemies
that concerned them, but the great difficulties arising from rejection.[2]

And with good reason. Asquith had circulated for summer reading a
memorandum from Sir Courtenay Ilbert on 'The Powers of the House
of Lords with respect to The Finance Bill.'[3] The first section of this
dealt with the powers of the Lords to interfere with the Budget. Of
his two conclusions one was distinctly encouraging. 'Any attempt to
amend could be effectively defeated.' The second was depressing and
was to hang like a pall over the Ministers for some months. 'Exercise
of the theoretical right to reject would give rise to difficulties of the most
serious nature . . .' The remainder of the memorandum was a somewhat
gloomy consideration of the courses open to the Government if the
Lords threw out the Budget. Although the Cabinet of 8 September
came to no decision, it did recognise the two immediate and interrelated problems posed by rejection, viz. the timing of the dissolution,
and the financial difficulties arising out of rejection.[4] These two practical questions were to absorb the Cabinet in the coming months to
the detriment of more significant, if less immediate, problems arising
from the crisis.

Ministers wished to dissolve on the new register, for it was generally
held that an election on a stale register handicapped the Liberal Party.
At the same time it was 'of the highest importance that dissolution and

pollings should follow rejection with all possible speed. Deferred indignation and a stale crisis may be incalculably injurious'.[5] Yet to avoid the hazard both of a stale register and a stale crisis was difficult, for the new register did not come into effect until the New Year, while the Budget was likely to reach the Lords towards the end of October.

The obvious answer was to accelerate the register, a course favoured by a majority of the Cabinet on 8 September. But the Local Government Board protested the difficulties of such acceleration, and even Churchill, champing for action, thought that it 'will probably be physically impossible to bring the new Register into force in time to finish the Elections before Christmas'. Moreover the Bill necessary to antedate the register could be delayed in the Lords, or if readily accepted by them might, as Churchill shrewdly noted 'giv[e] them the opportunity of investing a constitutional outrage with a specious air of fair play'.[6]

If acceleration was impossible, the alternative was to postpone the crisis and ensure that the Lords did not reject the Budget until December. This was the course proposed by Churchill in a powerful memorandum at the beginning of October. His key proposal was that the House of Commons adjourn for a month between the report stage and the third reading of the Budget, thus ensuring that the Budget would not reach the Lords until December.

> The advantages of this course ought not lightly to be dismissed by the Cabinet. It reduces the period of crisis to the narrowest minimum; it enables the Government to act decisively the moment the outrage is committed; it involves no bargaining or discussions with the Lords about the Register; it secures the new Register naturally.[7]

But this scheme was too bold and too calculating for the Cabinet. It was open to the charge that the Government was placing the interest of the party above the need of the State, and would be a virtual admission that the Ministry expected rejection. The Government seems to have dawdled, indeed from early September the tempo of business slowed in the Commons, but Ministers baulked at a month-long adjournment. Accordingly the Budget was read a third time on 4 November.

The Cabinet was now faced with the very dangers that Churchill had foreseen – an election on the stale register or a dangerously protracted crisis. From this dilemma it was rescued by the Unionists, who also wished for an election in the New Year.[8] The Upper Chamber's leisurely treatment of the Budget suited the Government and when

Lansdowne asked that the debate in the House of Lords be prolonged until the end of November, as so many peers wished to speak, Asquith smoothly informed the King that it was 'impossible in the circumstances to refuse such a request.'[9] The necessity was not unwelcome to the Cabinet, which by this time had decided to hold the Dissolution Council for the issuing of the election writs on Saturday, 8 January 1910, thus enabling first polls on the following Thursday.[10]

This was not quite the end of the story. When the Cabinet met on 16 December 1909 for the last time before the dissolution, it was under considerable pressure from Liberals in the country to change the Dissolution Council date so as to ensure first polls on a Saturday, a day supposedly favourable to the Liberals.[11] Unfortunately, owing to a private tragedy Asquith was absent from this Cabinet meeting,[12] and without his guidance the Cabinet dithered. Cabinet opinion favoured first polls on Saturday, 15 January, but the Ministers do not appear to have faced the corollary of this, a change of dates for the Dissolution Council from 8 to 10 January.[13] Probably Crewe, who presided, did not relish telling the King that his engagements would have to be altered, in effect at the behest of the Liberal wirepullers. The result was confusion. Sir Almeric Fitzroy, Clerk of the Privy Council, noted with annoyance on 20 December:

> It is a pity the Prime Minister is not strong enough to resist the pressure of intrigue from different quarters to manipulate the date of the first elections in the supposed interests of the Government. In the result, after a great deal of vacillation, I cannot obtain final instructions upon the date of the dissolution.[14]

A flurry of telegrams between Ministers scattered campaigning across the country brought a decision on Christmas Eve. Opposition to any change of dates from J. A. Pease, the Liberal Chief Whip, who was worried by the effects of cup-tie football matches on Saturday voting, was overridden. Probably decisive was the telegram from Lloyd George campaigning in Llanelly.

> Chancellor says strongly urge date should be altered he has made enquiries since interview with prime minister all agree as to prime importance of securing first polls on saturday mayors in liberal boroughs would choose that day chancellor says therefore the first results would favour us and have good effect on country.

Asquith accordingly ordered that the Dissolution Council be post-poned until 10 January, thus securing first polls on the Saturday, and incidentally following exactly the precedents of 1906.[15]

The King was annoyed,[16] the Tories furious. Sandars informed Balfour that 'this fraudulent change of dates . . . is little less than a public scandal and I am glad to say that Acland-Hood has written Jack Pease a scorcher'.[17] On the Saturday in dispute the *Daily Mail* reminded its readers that 'to use a cricket analogy not only did [the Liberals] choose the pitch, but also they watered it'. But if the timing of the first polls suited the Liberals, the seven-week gap between the rejection of the Budget and the first polls benefited the Unionists. The Liberals did not entirely escape the perils of 'deferred indignation and a stale crisis'.

If the Cabinet had happened upon a not unsatisfactory result in dissolution, its courageous solution to the financial question was deliberate, although achieved only after much vacillation. Should the Budget be rejected, the Government would either have to collect taxes without the authority of the law, or to introduce temporary legislation, acceptable to the Lords, to cover the period from prorogation to the assembly of a new Parliament and the passage of a new finance bill. For from the prorogation the resolutions under which the new, increased and annual taxes were collected would cease to have authority.

From early autumn the Cabinet was subject to conflicting advice from its advisers. On one side the cautious Treasury officials pressed for '. . . a new Finance Bill . . . introduced and passed this session after the Bill now before Parliament has been rejected'. Such advice was influential and ministerial fears were heightened by Sir George Murray's alarming and alarmist estimate of a £49,000,000 deficit if the Budget were rejected and no remedial action taken.[18] Sir Courtenay Ilbert, as concerned as any Minister for the prerogatives of the Commons, deprecated the Treasury proposals. He opposed a second Finance Bill 'modelled on the rejected Bill, but truncated of provisions distasteful to the Lords'. This would be in effect 'an admission of the right of the Lords to dictate the amendment of a Finance Bill'. Instead, he suggested a Taxes Continuance Bill confirming all the taxes in course of collection and continuing them for a limited period. 'The Lords could hardly reject such a Bill. It would merely continue the *status quo* during the interval between two legislative periods.'[19]

After several weeks of debate, the Cabinet on 3 November decided, albeit with misgivings, that to avoid 'absolute financial and administrative chaos . . . a short Act must at once, before the Prorogation or dissolution, be passed through both Houses to legalise the continued collection of necessary revenue'.[20] A Finance (No. 2) Bill was drafted, its object being primarily to secure payment of the tea duty and the income tax.[21] This was a compromise, embodying the Treasury's desire for a second Budget, yet by its limited scope, recognising Ilbert's objections.

But Ilbert now contemplated an even bolder course. On 4 November he wrote to Bryce:

> I am being gradually forced to the conclusion that the least objectionable course would be to continue collection of the taxes authorised by the resolutions, avoiding collision with the courts as far as possible and shortening as much as possible the period of anarchy. . . . The justification for this extra-legal action would be that the action of the House of Lords would be revolutionary.[22]

The Clerk of the House found allies in Lloyd George and Churchill, who favoured 'extra-legal action by the Executive' provided it could be done 'without inflicting great loss on the public and exposing revenue officials to unjustifiable risks'. Influential backing for such a tactic came from Sir Robert Chalmers, Chairman of the Board of Inland Revenue. Chalmers was prepared to accept the risk of Ilbert's policy, believing the loss 'though serious, not so serious as to outweigh corresponding advantages'.[23]

Encouraged by these allies, Ilbert now presented his views to the Cabinet in a persuasive memorandum in which he appealed to the prejudices as well as the reason of the Ministers. He argued that if it was the Ministers' responsibility to minimise the loss of revenue and administrative friction, it was also their duty to 'maintain unimpaired and unprejudiced the rights and powers of the Commons with respect to Finance', which the Finance (No. 2) Bill certainly would not do. Moreover the introduction of such a Bill 'would involve the Govt. in dialectical difficulties of which the Leader of the Opposition would not be slow to take advantage'. Ilbert went on to urge that 'the safest, the most dignified, and the most constitutional methods, of meeting the unconstitutional action of the Lords would be to collect, and continue to collect, by executive and extra-legal action, the taxes which have been granted by the Commons'. He closed with this advice: 'There are occasions when respect for the constitution must override respect for the law. This may be one of them.'[24]

Ministers were in a receptive mood, for this memorandum coincided with the publication of the Lords' decision to reject the Budget. Faced at last with the actuality of rejection the fibre of the Cabinet perceptibly stiffened – a mood well caught in Asquith's report to the King on 17 November:

> . . . the general opinion was that there would be no necessity to introduce and pass a new Bill . . . It is recognised by Your Majesty's advisers to be their duty to minimise these evils [the financial difficulties arising from rejection], but they cannot hold themselves in any way responsible for their occurrence, or for their necessary consequences.[25]

A week later, the Cabinet confirmed the decision that 'no immediate legislation either to validate past collections of the new taxation, or to authorise their temporary continuance is either necessary or expedient'.[26] Thanks as much to the mettle of its advisers as to its own corporate courage, the Ministry was able to begin its campaign not with the unheroic, difficult and dubious task of putting through a second finance bill, but with a note of defiance welcome to its supporters.

These satisfactory decisions had not been reached without cost, for other problems less immediate but ultimately more significant had been neglected. The two most pressing of these, policies on Ireland and on the House of Lords, required Cabinet decisions before the opening of the election campaign. So absorbed had the Cabinet been with the more immediate technical questions that these issues do not seem to have been considered at any length until the Cabinet meetings of 30 November and 1 December. Yet it was not only other distractions that explain this neglect. Asquith, always dilatory on internally controversial issues, probably hesitated to force such divisive questions on the Cabinet.

Home Rule had been shelved during the lifetime of the 1906 Parliament, partly out of respect for the self-denying ordinance on the subject taken by a number of the Ministers in the 1906 election, but chiefly because the great Liberal majority rendered the Government impervious to Irish pressure. Some Ministers probably hoped to keep Home Rule in limbo for a further period, justifying this by pleading the overwhelming importance of the dominating issue. Yet the party had a traditional commitment to Home Rule, and some statement of its attitude would be required during the campaign. The Irish would not tolerate in the new Parliament the present Ministerial *non possumus* and were pressing for a definite commitment to Home Rule. It might no longer be possible to govern without them, and the significant Irish vote particularly in Lancashire and Scotland could not be ignored.

When the Cabinet met on 30 November it was faced with an

ultimatum from Redmond, forwarded through Morley, the chief
intermediary between the Irish and the Cabinet:

> The political conditions in Ireland are such that, unless an official declaration
> on the question of Home Rule be made, not only will it be impossible for us to
> support Liberal candidates in England, but we will most unquestionably have
> to ask our friends to vote against them . . . I see that the Prime Minister is to
> make his first declaration on the 10th of December, and I would press very
> strongly that this statement about Home Rule should then be made.[27]

Redmond himself had little choice but to pursue a tough line, for the
Liberal alliance, eroded by recent events, could only survive if the
Liberals were to pledge themselves publicly to Home Rule. Faced with
a repetition of the Parnellite tactic of 1885 the Ministers swallowed
whatever doubts they may have had. On 1 December the Cabinet
reached complete agreement on the need for a public declaration, on
its inclusion in the Albert Hall speech, and on its wording.[28] But
this unanimity hardly denoted enthusiasm, as the course of the campaign was to reveal.

More complex, more divisive, and much more central to the coming
election was the question of Liberal policy towards the House of Lords.
Some Ministers favoured joint sittings to solve deadlocks, as proposed
by a Cabinet Committee in 1907; others supported the suspensory veto
plan which Campbell-Bannerman had successfully insisted on in 1907;
still others saw a solution in a reform of the composition of the House
of Lords. In 1907 several leading Ministers including Asquith and Crewe
had supported the Campbell-Bannerman scheme only with reluctance,
and a number of memoranda circulated in late 1909 revealed the persistence of disparate views within the Cabinet.[29]

In the difficult last days of the Parliament Asquith was inclined to
temporise. Not that he was unaware of the dangers of going into the
campaign with an ill-defined policy. For one thing they had been
forcibly presented to him in a long, cogent and prescient letter from
his parliamentary private secretary, Edwin Montagu.

> The history of all former attempts at coming to close quarters with the House
> of Lords question, shows a record of disorder, dissipation of energy, of words
> and solemn exhortation, of individual rhetoric and impressive *ipse dixits* without
> any definite scheme of action, nothing more substantial than dark hints of pre-
> conceived plans, nothing which could give the electorate reason to believe that
> they were safe in following the Liberal leaders into battle or in assuming that
> those leaders knew where they were going.

Montagu argued that on this occasion therefore it should be

stipulated exactly what Ministers were and were not to say. Moreover a public and definite scheme now for the House of Lords would undermine the Unionist case for two elections, one on the Budget, and one on the House of Lords.[30]

But the Ministers, strained and divided and on the eve of the election, were in no mood to resolve their differences on constitutional policy by advancing definite and detailed proposals for resolving institutional deadlocks. Instead they grabbed at a tactical lifeline offered by Churchill: 'I would . . . avoid if possible any showing of our hand in detail before the election and fight on the general phrase of "smash the veto" or any more sober variant of that.'[31] This was the policy adopted. In a memorandum circulated to his colleagues at the beginning of the election, in his Albert Hall speech and in his election address, Asquith, while carefully echoing Campbell-Bannerman's phraseology, deliberately avoided committing himself to the suspensory veto plan. In all three he declared that the absolute veto must go, but in none was he explicit about what should replace it.[32] Two Cabinet Ministers, Haldane and Grey, felt free during the elections to advocate reform of the composition of the Lords; others spoke in favour of the suspensory veto; yet others followed Asquith. Most Liberals believed they knew where they were going; the opening days of the 1910 Parliament were to demonstrate that the Cabinet did not.

But an even more misguided tactic originated in the last Cabinets. This Ministry was occasionally prone to acts of giddiness, to a preference for the dramatic and sensational over the sober and sensible. Having no agreed Second Chamber policy, they now took the extraordinary step of publicly pledging themselves to secure guarantees in order to implement one.

On 30 November Crewe declared in the Lords: 'We must . . . set ourselves to obtain guarantees . . . which will prevent the indiscriminate destruction of our legislation.' In the next fortnight similar pledges were made by Lloyd George and Churchill. None, however, was as explicit as Asquith's at the Albert Hall on 10 December: 'We shall not assume office, and we shall not hold office, unless we can secure the safeguards which experience shows us to be necessary for the legislative utility and honour of the party of progress.'[33] The number of the pledges and the deliberation with which they were made, suggest that they were not individual aberrations, but stemmed from a collective decision. Asquith's Albert Hall pledge was almost certainly a statement of Cabinet intentions, indeed as with the Home Rule declaration, the exact wording was probably decided on by the Cabinet.[34] Certainly both the content of the Albert Hall speech and the question of contingent guarantees were discussed at the Cabinets of 30 November and 1 December.[35]

To what were the Ministers binding themselves in these apparently calculated utterances? It was widely held that they had pledged themselves to secure a promise from the King for the contingent exercise of the royal prerogative of creating peers. Asquith later denied this interpretation, implying that he had simply promised to secure 'statutory safeguards.'[36] Yet by using the constitutionally dubious 'we shall not assume office' Asquith indicated he was going to get whatever he was going to get before the next Parliament met.[37] But he could not secure 'statutory safeguards' prior to the meeting of Parliament; what he could secure were guarantees from the King that his 'statutory safeguards' would become law. 'Certainly . . . the vast mass of people did take Asquith's Albert Hall declaration . . . to mean that the Liberal Party would not retain office if the power to destroy the Lords' Veto (i.e. creation of Peers) was withheld.'[38]

And what were the guarantees to secure? What particular statutory provisions did the Cabinet envisage? The most relevant piece of evidence is the entry in Carrington's diary for 1 December: 'At the Cabinet this morning it was decided if the Liberals are returned again, to bring in a Bill the first thing affirming by statute the right of the Commons as regards finance with support from the Crown. If this is refused no Liberal administration could be formed.' Although ambiguous, the entry suggests that the guarantees related to a measure affirming the financial supremacy of the Commons.

This notion is immediately attractive because all the groups in the Cabinet, vetoists, reformers and joint conference men, were agreed that whatever solution was adopted, the Upper Chamber could have no veto over finance. But the very unanimity suggests how feeble and unimaginative a policy this was, for it obtained simply because, until late 1909, all believed that this was the custom of the constitution. It was hardly a strong response to the Lords' challenge simply to reaffirm by statute the supremacy of the Commons in finance, a supremacy which until November 1909 most Liberals believed the Commons possessed. Moreover, the pledges do seem to have referred to much more than merely denying the Lords a financial veto.

It is of course possible that the Ministry was once again, as in the winter of 1908–9, cloaking a cautious and limited policy in flamboyant rhetoric. However, unless further evidence comes to light the point must remain somewhat speculative. Perhaps the most likely explanation is that the overburdened Ministers failed to clarify for themselves both what they meant by guarantees, and how they were to be used.

What seems beyond dispute is that Asquith did not request guarantees prior to the opening of the 1910 Parliament. This may have been because the Ministers always regarded the request for guarantees as conditional on a good election result. There is some *post facto* evidence for this. On 26 January 1910 Lewis Harcourt wrote to Asquith: 'We can hardly ask the King *now* for a promise of the creation of peers: if we did he would have *some* grounds for refusal at present and we might have to resign *as against him.*'[39] After a conversation with Haldane in February, Esher told his son that Asquith 'is *not* going to ask the King for any assurances at this stage, feeling he is not justified in doing so, with so small a majority'.[40] From the outset then the pledges may have been conditional upon a sufficient majority.

It is more likely that they took on this conditional character as a result of the intervention of the King. On 15 December the King's secretary, Lord Knollys, summoned Vaughan Nash, Asquith's private secretary, to the palace, and told him that '. . . the King had come to the conclusion that he would not be justified in creating new peers (say 300) until after a second general election'.[41] Unless the Liberal Party was returned in overwhelming strength it would prove very difficult to challenge the King. The King's declaration had a further interesting effect. Although intended solely for Asquith, it seems to have been privately conveyed to the Ministers, for after mid-December the guarantees pledge disappeared from ministerial lips if not from public controversy. Thus a month before the polls weakened their position *vis-à-vis* the King, Ministers knew that their 'dark hints of preconceived plans' were likely to land them in a mess.

But if in retrospect the guarantees pledge appears ambiguous and conditional, at the time it was widely understood to imply that no Liberal Ministry would hold office unless it had guarantees from the King to ensure the passage of its anti-veto legislation. In some well informed circles it was rumoured that the pledges had already been given.[42] Local speeches, pamphlets and election addresses all show a literal and pathetic acceptance of the guarantees pledge. Oblivious of the vacuum at the core of ministerial policy, and of course of the King's *démarche*, the mass of the Liberal Party and its allies moved forward to disillusion.

II

The Unionist leaders had not been deterred from their momentous step by its 'questionable constitutionality'. They were well aware that the House of Lords had rejected no money bill for fifty years, and that the control of the Commons over the general financial provisions for the year had been undisputed since the seventeenth century. They were aware too that their action would compel a dissolution, and thus could be construed as transforming the relationships between the Government and the two Houses of Parliament. But these were but one element in Unionist calculations, and their historic decision was taken in defiance of 'the *prima facie* view presented by text-books and what has been the general practice especially for the last half century'.[43] Lansdowne put the matter quite bluntly: '. . . the case is not one for elaborate arguments with regard to so-called constitutional precedents, . . . our line of action must be determined on broad grounds of policy.'[44]

In this approach they were backed by leading constitutional lawyers. A. V. Dicey, Vinerian Professor of Law at Oxford and a staunch Unionist, displayed a remarkable flexibility for one who had done so much to give the customs of the constitution the status of law.

> In constitutional as in international law it is often a question rather of power than of right. Where there is no distinct rule enforceable by the Courts what e.g. the King or the H.L. or the H.C. can effectively do, is what each has a right to do. . . . If you ask what I mean by 'can effectively do' I answer I mean 'that wh the electors will support e.g. the H.L. doing.'[45]

Another leading constitutional lawyer, the Unionist, Sir Frederick Pollock, who was to oppose rejection, nevertheless saw the question in a similar light: 'All things are lawful for me but all things are not expedient.'[46] Sir William Anson, jurist, Warden of All Souls, and Conservative M.P. for the University of Oxford, was busily depreciating the force of constitutional customs, as he publicly disentangled himself from some embarrassing statements in his textbook *Law and Custom of the Constitution*.[47]

Given this approach by the constitutional lawyers it was not surprising that the Unionists gave little consideration to the question, 'Is rejection constitutional?', but concentrated rather on the question, 'Is rejection politically desirable and if so can we get away with it?' Having concluded on broadly political grounds that it was desirable, and that the chances of getting away with it were not unfavourable, the Unionist Party then found itself ironically, but inevitably, faced with a series of tactical questions with constitutional implications.

Chronologically the first of these was exactly how the Budget was to be 'done in'. Although it was generally held that the Lords had no power to amend money bills, support for drastic amendment by the Lords was more widespread than most writers have recognised. Lords Lansdowne, Milner and St Aldwyn, Strachey, and the *Spectator* all at one time suggested or supported amendment, either from fears of financial chaos, or for tactical reasons. Dicey lent his magisterial authority: '. . . from a constitutional point of view, I consider amendment or rejection equally lawful, equally unusual, and in the circumstances equally legitimate or if people prefer the term, constitutional.'[48] In the *Spectator* and in his vast private correspondence, Strachey endeavoured to develop a constitutional defence for the policy of amendment, a defence Balfour found 'extremely ingenious and worthy of the most careful consideration'.[49]

Despite its ingenuity the course was rejected by the Unionist leaders, not primarily on constitutional grounds, but on grounds of its electoral unwisdom. Strachey had argued that it would be better to reject the bits that were 'purely socialistic' rather than the whole Budget, for if the latter occurred 'the Lords will seem . . . the revolutionaries rather than the Government'.[50] But the Unionist leaders, warned by the unfortunate reaction to the early undisciplined criticism of the Budget, felt it better to appear as revolutionaries rather than as the defenders of narrow class interests. The fear that if the Lords rejected merely the land clauses 'they will certainly be accused of looking after their own interests, while leaving the burdens thrown on other shoulders untouched' was stressed by Balfour.[51] When Sandars reported to Balfour in late August that Lansdowne, fearing financial chaos, 'still hankers after amendment', Sandars was silent on the constitutional issues and merely invoked 'the obvious party objection on electioneering grounds, and the handle it will give to the Govt. supporters'.[52] When Lansdowne himself finally gave up amendment, the decisive factor seems to have been that the policy was electorally unsound.[53]

In choosing rejection as the mode of destruction the Unionists faced certain problems closely akin to those encountered by the Liberal Government. This is not surprising, for in choosing to act as they did the Unionists could not but assume certain responsibilities usually borne by the executive. They could not neglect to consider the financial difficulties, while the timing of rejection would virtually determine the date of dissolution.

Lansdowne's apprehensions about financial chaos had been heightened by Murray's alarmist Treasury memorandum, which the King, acting as the ministerial postman, had passed on to the Unionist leaders when he met them to discuss the impending crisis on 12 October.[54] Lansdowne's fears were finally assuaged in early November first by Milner, who, in a long, skilful and soothing letter, used his Inland Revenue Board experience to deprecate Murray's exaggerated estimates of financial loss;[55] and secondly by Sandars, who was able to pass on to Lansdowne reliable information that the Government was preparing a stop-gap budget, 'clear evidence that the Govt. do not intend chaos to follow on rejection'.[56] Lansdowne and the Lords were clearly taken aback when the substitute budget did not materialise, but as we have seen, the Government too was now willing to take risks.

Rejection gave the Opposition an unusually influential voice in determining the date of the election. The leisurely approach to the Budget by the Lords, who allowed nearly three weeks to elapse between the Bill's leaving the Commons and the second reading debate in the Lords, and who spread the debate itself over nine days, prevented an election before the New Year. It has been seen how this result was not unwelcome to the Government. Why was it also desired by the Opposition?

While the Ministry was most concerned with the benefits of a fresh register, the Unionists were swayed primarily by the advantages of delay. Austen Chamberlain wrote in late October that 'the Budget, no longer very hot now, will be quite cold by [the New Year].' Moreover Unionists believed that the severity of winter unemployment would be felt more in January than in November. In addition Unionists expected that the new register would favour them, first because of the organisation's success in getting lodgers on to the register, and secondly because 'the class of voter who usually makes a new register unfavourable to us will on this occasion vote for Tariff Reform and more work'. If a further motive for delay was required it was found in the suspicion that the Liberals anticipated a November election.[57]

An argumentative defence for the Lords' unusual action was a further consideration. Plausible platform arguments were certainly available to the Unionists. The constitutional precedents were not as simple and clear cut as most Liberals believed and the able speaker could always add to the muddle. The Lords undoubtedly possessed the legal right to reject a money bill. They had last used this right in 1860 when they rejected Gladstone's Paper Duties Bill. Was it now a convention of the constitution that the Lords could not reject money bills? Was fifty years' disuse of a right sufficient to sanction a constitutional convention? These questions admitted of no simple answer.

To claim that the House of Lords had not rejected a Budget for 250 years,[58] thus establishing a more venerable tradition, is merely to befog an already murky issue. The Budget, i.e. an omnibus bill including all the revenue measures for the year, was a relatively modern innovation. The process of consolidating all the revenue measures into a single bill began at the end of the eighteenth century, but was not fully realised until 1861, when, to outwit the Lords, Gladstone included repeal of the paper duties along with all other taxation proposals in a single measure. This practice had been followed ever since. Thus strictly the convention that the Lords could not reject the Budget was scarcely of greater antiquity than the convention that the Lords could not reject a money bill. Of course, to reject the Budget was to challenge the control of the Commons over the general financial provisions of the year, and this certainly the Lords had not attempted since the seventeenth century.

Much, too, could be made of the argument on tacking, i.e. that the Budget contained matter extraneous to a finance bill, the most often quoted example being the land valuation clauses. A vigorous statement on tacking is included in Milner's important letter to Lansdowne on 2 November: 'Our case . . . will rest on the contention that the Finance Bill itself is a constitutional monstrosity . . . a gross instance of "tacking" . . . our adoption of an unprecedented course was necessitated by the unprecedented character of the measure submitted to us.'[59] Although experienced Unionists such as Sir Robert Finlay, an ex-Attorney-General, and St Aldwyn, an ex-Chancellor of the Exchequer, doubted whether the argument had substance, both Anson and Dicey were prepared to invest it with their authority and nourish it with their casuistry.[60]

But the basic Unionist defence was a demagogic appeal to the common man. To the accusation that rejection threatened the responsibility of the Cabinet to the Commons the Unionists retorted that the rights of the people came before Cabinet or Commons. Dicey, ever prodigal in the cause, underwrote this argument too: 'Any step might be rightly taken either by King or H. of L. wh. safeguarded the rights of the nation. No respect is due to any privilege of the H. of C. if opposed to the rights of the nation.'[61] The Unionists thus became the advocates of plebiscitary democracy: 'the one great function of the Lords', argued Finlay '[is] to secure that no new departure of capital importance is made until the country . . . has been consulted'.[62] It was as the defenders of this version of democracy that the Lords took their public stand against the Budget, and the Unionist Party fought the election.

This theory demanded a plain and neutral amendment to the Finance Bill in the Lords. So did the Unionist press. Leading editors urged an amendment of 'the simplest kind' not 'a reasoned statement reciting Constitutional rights or the invasion of precedents and the Lords' privileges and so forth. That might be most excellent argument and defence: but it would not help us in the country.'[63] The peers, however, needed a little judicious discipline, for the desire 'to put in one or two epithets' was strong. But pressure from Balfour and Lansdowne for 'the simple form' was successful, so that on 22 November Lansdowne moved in the House of Lords 'That this House is not justified in giving its consent to this Bill until it has been submitted to the judgement of the country'.[64]

III

This amendment, and the decisions taken by both sides in anticipation of it, produced the most dramatic parliamentary prelude to any election in modern times. This prelude had two parts – the six-day debate in the Lords and the one-day response of the Commons. The debate in the Lords was perhaps the finest on the constitution that the House had ever conducted.

Despite this the debate was hardly a success from the Unionist point of view. For one thing, as Garvin complained to Sandars, it went on 'too long for our interests; it had flat intervals'.[65] It illustrated all too well that Unionist numerical preponderance did not equate with a similar preponderance in talent. Unionist efforts to prolong the debate had to be abandoned because as Sandars reported 'it cd. not be in our favour . . . and . . . I doubt if it cd. be conducted with decency'.[66]

Again, some of the most powerful indictments of Unionist policy came from the Unionist benches and the cross-benches. Balfour of Burleigh, James of Hereford, Cromer and Lytton emphatically condemned rejection. Rosebery, in whom many Unionists had placed great hopes, damned this decision to stake the future of the House of Lords on 'the tumultuous hazards of a General Election'.[67] In a maiden speech from the cross-benches, Lang, the new Archbishop of York, repudiated rejection in a masterly exposition of the constitutional case. St Aldwyn was ostentatiously absent. 'I am glad', Lansdowne wrote him, 'your formidable batteries were not ranged against us in the debate which ended last night – our own side supplied quite enough "Long Toms" as it was.'[68]

Finally, the Peers had waited long for this day, and their expletives shattered the deliberate moderation of the amendment. The aged Lord Ashbourne found the Budget 'unwonted, abnormal, unclean'; Lord Galway found it 'fraught with grave risk and danger to the country'. Lord Curzon, who pitched the claims of the Peers higher than most, revealed too their partisan basis. He thought it best to force a dissolution rather than have 'two more years . . . of insufficient attention to the defences of the country, two more years of Socialist experiments, two more years of tampering with the Church . . .'.[69] After all this even Garvin was a little subdued. '. . . the peers have not helped us much . . . They have talked too much like persons apart, instead of as member of the nation claiming to be trustees for its interests. So when the end is reached tomorrow I shall be heartily glad.'[70]

The end came on the evening of 30 November. A few minutes after 11.30 the House of Lords divided on the Finance Bill. So great was the crush in the 'not content' lobby, that it was a further twenty minutes before the Lord Chancellor could announce the result to the packed House. By 350 to 75 votes their Lordships refused their consent to the Budget. A subdued hum greeting this inevitable result, while from the corner gallery reserved for the Commons came the sound of hisses. Outside, two red rockets, fired from the *Daily News* office, burst above the centre of London, informing those citizens still awake that the 'evil deed' had been consummated.[71]

Both the size of the total vote and the majority for rejection had been surpassed only once in the previous one hundred years.[72] The vote was almost entirely along party lines. Only four Liberals voted or paired against the Bill, only eight Unionists supported it. Most of the spiritual peers abstained, but five gave their votes for the Budget, and one voted against. Rosebery, Balfour of Burleigh, Cromer, Lytton, and St Aldwyn abstained.

The Cabinet was ready and resolute. 'We are all quietly determined here to take up Lord Lansdowne's challenge. There is no doubt or hesitation.'[73] Although too strongly worded for the King,[74] the Cabinet resolution 'That the action of the House of Lords in refusing to pass into law the financial provision made by this House for the service of the year is a breach of the Constitution and an usurpation of the rights of the Commons,' was tabled on 1 December and debated the next day.

In a crowded House, reminiscent of the Lords two nights before, but this time with the Peers as silent spectators, with some Ministers nursing their lighter colleagues, with the benches overflowing and the galleries packed, the second act was played out. When Asquith rose to speak he was cheered for several minutes. His speech, one of the finest of his parliamentary career, outlined clearly, simply, and with humour the Liberal case against the House of Lords. Apart from rejecting the humiliating suggestion of a 'pruned and trimmed and refurbished' Bill to tide over the interregnum he concentrated on the constitutional principles at stake.

His twin themes were the present affront to the Commons, 'the greatest indignity, and . . . the most arrogant usurpation, to which, for more than two centuries, [the House of Commons] has been asked to submit', and the constant disadvantage under which a Liberal Ministry and the country laboured with a Tory House of Lords, 'a system of false balances and loaded dice.' But he was at his most powerful and scathing on 'this new-fangled Caesarism which converts the House of Lords into a kind of plebiscitory organ', designed to protect the people against their elected representatives. In a passage of sustained irony he asserted that according to this new theory providence had endowed each peer with 'a kind of instinct of divination which enables him . . . to discern to a nicety . . . the occasions and the matters in regard to which the people's representatives are betraying the people's trust'. Switching from satire to denunciation, he condemned all such talk about the right or duty of the Lords to refer measures to the people as 'the hollowest outcry of political cant'. The Lords 'rejected the Finance Bill . . . not because they love the people, but because they hate the Budget.'[75] There were to be more effective demagogic assaults on the action of the Lords from the platform, and more erudite attacks in the press, but for sheer power and cogency no utterance was to equal this in the spate of words about to burst upon the nation.

The unhappy Balfour, handicapped already by the illness that was to keep him out of the campaign until the end of December, and subject to much hostile interruption, endeavoured to reply. While he failed to develop a coherent counter-argument, he did score isolated points which seem to have rallied his supporters, if they did not dampen the ardour of his opponents.[76]

He stressed the contradiction between Asquith's talk of 'chaos' and the Government's refusal to introduce remedial legislation injuring 'their own pet vanities'. He gibed at the Liberal passion for abstract resolutions; ridiculed the notion that the English constitution began in 1860; derided the argument that rare usage necessarily implied desuetude. But he was most effective on what was for his party the crux of the question, the right of the House of Lords to consult the people. Thus he ridiculed the Liberal effort 'to persuade the people . . . that they are suffering some wrong, some terrible indignity, by having their opinion asked about the Budget'.[77]

The duel ended, the debate was soon over. Henderson for Labour pledged full support to the Ministers, although his party preferred the ending of the Lords to any mending. The Nationalists took no part in the debate or the vote, an attitude indicative of their dislike of the Budget. They would reserve their views on the conflict until Asquith pledged the Liberals to Home Rule. The next day, 3 December, Parliament was prorogued.

All parties, except perhaps the Labour Party, welcomed the end of the 1906 Parliament; the Liberals for the manner of its dying; the Unionists simply because it was dead; and the Nationalists since with its death Home Rule was alive once more. Although John Burns' lament for 'the best Parliament for the people this country had seen'[78] found echoes in Liberal circles, the conviction that the Lords in destroying the Parliament had destroyed themselves overwhelmed all other emotions in the Liberal camp. In their comments the Unionists revealed their deep aversion for the 'Yellow Parliament', the child of the Chinese slavery lie, that was at the root of many of their recent actions. But the time was past for laments, jubilation or even second thoughts. Attention now turned to the hustings.

6

The First Campaign

I

These dramatic parliamentary events ushered in the longest election campaign in modern British history. The actual campaign commenced the day Parliament was prorogued, 3 December, with platform speeches from Lloyd George, Lansdowne, and Austen Chamberlain. The final pollings took place ten weeks later on 10 February, but active campaigning had come to an end a fortnight before.

This eight-week campaign began sporadically in the days immediately following prorogation, with the Liberals active, the Unionists sluggish. Asquith's Albert Hall speech and the issue of the bedridden Balfour's election address, both on 10 December, marked the formal opening of the election. From that date on the campaign rapidly gathered momentum, reaching a climax in the days immediately before Christmas. Night after night the leaders drew great audiences to the public halls, theatres and vast covered skating rinks. Frequently a leading campaigner was required to address additional overflow meetings in the same centre. In the boroughs the local campaigns now got under way although in the counties, polling later, most constituency campaigns did not begin in earnest until after Christmas.

Christmas brought a brief electoral truce, originally intended to last for a week, but truncated by rising partisan passions to a bare four days. By the New Year the campaign was again in full swing. In the days before Christmas it had seemed unlikely that campaign activities could be stepped up, but there seems little doubt that activity intensified in the New Year, particularly as the county fights now began. The number of speeches was 'unparalleled', and an 'unprecedented' volume of propaganda material poured forth.[1]

But the intensification of the campaign was accompanied by an increasingly frenetic note. Bitterness and even violence marred the last weeks of the campaign. Tariff Reform shops, displaying dumped foreign goods, were damaged and meetings were broken up by rowdyism.

The Peers seem to have been the principal victims but prominent
Unionist Commoners, e.g. Walter Long, Alfred Lyttelton and Henry
Chaplin were all shouted down in the New Year. In South-East
Durham, the Unionist F. E. Lambton complained: 'My wife and I were
most unmercifully snowballed, at once place *stoned*. . . .' The Unionist
M.P. for Hammersmith had a fist fight with a heckler, and at Battersea
John Burns's opponent was for an hour unable 'to make himself heard
or even to hear himself speak'.[2] Similar incidents occurred throughout
the country in the remaining weeks of the contest, and although
both sides suffered – Lloyd George had to flee a mob at Grimsby on
polling day – it seems clear that the Unionists suffered most from
hecklers. In Ireland rival Nationalist factions introduced a degree of
turbulence unmatched since the 1890s.

The pollings which began on 15 January did not end the campaign,
but they did change its nature. Now the campaign became increasingly
fragmented with the leading figures returning to their own seats and
with the accent on the individual constituency rather than on the
national contest. Once the leading politicians were released from their
own constituency fights, they hurried to regions where the voting
trends indicated they might be of most use. The most spectacular
example of this was the ministerial invasion of the West Country in
the fourth week of January. Borough losses there had led to a panic
among the local Liberal organisers and Churchill, Burns and Birrell
were rushed down to stem the tide. Austen Chamberlain attributed
several Devonshire county failures to the fact that 'we were overwhelmed at the last moment by the weight of oratory on the Government side'.[3] The campaign finally petered out in the fourth week of
January.

Yet while this formal structure of the campaign is useful for the
electoral historian, his interest lies rather in the ebb and flow of party
fortunes during the campaign. For him the election falls into two parts,
before and after the last week of December 1909. During that week,
if the tide did not actually turn, the Liberal campaign faltered and
lost momentum. Up until the last days of 1909 it was difficult to avoid
the impression that the Liberals were sweeping all before them; in
the New Year the contending forces seemed more evenly matched.

II

For each party the rejection of the Budget had opened up a wider and more significant issue, for the Liberals the constitutional question, for the Unionists the fiscal alternative to the Budget. The rivalry between these issues was to play a major role in party strategy, and the faltering in the Liberal campaign occurred when Tariff Reform began to replace the House of Lords in the forefront of the electoral debate.

From the outset it was obvious that the success of the Liberal campaign would depend, first, on the ability of the party to maintain the ardour of its followers, and thus to infect the country with something of their passion; secondly, on the capacity of the party leaders to rally all the elements of the anti-Unionist front to the Government; and thirdly, on their ability to keep the House of Lords issue paramount. This last was the crucial consideration, for it was the constitutional question that united all the various anti-Unionist forces, aroused the enthusiasm of the militants and made many Unionists uneasy. The manifestos of the complex of pressure groups gathered around the Government bore witness to the issue's significance. Even the Labour Party manifesto gave first place to the constitutional issue.[4]

The reaction of the party militants to the Lords' rejection of the Budget accounts for the impetus with which the Liberal campaign began. For many Liberals the defeat of the Budget was an apocalyptic event. The morning after rejection headlines in the Liberal press flared across half-pages dramatically proclaiming 'Revolution Begins'[5] or, with more optimism if equal drama, 'Suicide of the House of Lords.'[6] The profusion of atavistic Civil War images in the Liberal press and speeches at this time suggests the profound challenge to Liberal traditions occasioned by rejection.

There were also undertones of a Holy War. Watching the fatal division in the Lords John Burns observed: 'The first decisive act in either a great victory or a great tragedy for the British Race. Will present snobbery, past jobbery, ancient robbery unite with dogma and drink to fetter our hands and to chloroform our minds again?'[7] Here were all the evil forces against which the party of Gladstone had fought in the nineteenth century. The conflict between good and evil was implicit in the Free Church Council manifesto: 'Not as party politicians, but as Christians, we are compelled by the teaching of our Lord to seek to remove the obstacles that stand in the way of the moral and religious welfare of the people', and the manifesto left no doubt that the House of Lords was one of the most serious of such obstacles.[8] Thus the Liberal campaign was a crusade to protect English democracy, English liberties, and the moral and spiritual welfare of the people.

It was a crusade the Radicals did not contemplate losing, for they were convinced that the incredible folly of the Lords had delivered them into the hands of 'the people'. This was memorably expressed by Lloyd George at the National Liberal Club on 3 December: 'At last, with all their cunning, their greed has overborne their craft. We have got them at last, and we do not mean to let them go until all the accounts in the ledger have been settled.'[9] Rejection gave the Liberals an opportunity they had scarcely dared to hope for. 'What a text we have to preach from!' wrote an excited Scottish radical.[10]

In London the Radical mood was well captured in a massive protest against the Peers organised by the National Democratic League in Trafalgar Square on the afternoon of Saturday, 4 December. The protest, rated by a Conservative journal as one of the 'most notable and effective of all political demonstrations held there in recent years',[11] attracted about 15,000 Londoners who listened in bleak weather to some vigorous Hyde Park oratory from Radical M.P.s, L.C.C. Progressives and Nonconformist divines. A coroneted turnip on a stick caused considerable hilarity, and the resolution denouncing the peers was carried in a sea of waving hats and umbrellas.

The Unionists had no intention of engaging in a Holy War with a lot of fervent Roundheads. For the moment all they could do was to try to lower the political temperature and from the beginning Unionist understatement countered Liberal hyperbole. The reports in the Unionist press of the Budget's rejection typified this response. Headlines were normal and the newspapers recorded with restraint another parliamentary decision, important but not earth-shaking, exemplified in the euphemism of the *Morning Post*, 'Finance Bill Hung Up', or the bald headline of the *Daily Mail*, 'The Vote of the House of Lords'. There was much to be said for playing it cool, for allowing the flames to burn themselves out.

While Unionist strategy sought, in the interest of the conservative mood, to moderate the temperature of the debate, it also aimed to divert the debate from the constitutional issue. 'The great peril', Garvin had warned Maxse in late September, 'is that well-meaning Unionists will talk land taxes and Constitutionalism and Socialism and mere Budget again . . . and forget to keep tariff reform "the dominating issue".'[12] The guardians of the anti-Budget consensus, the

Whole Hoggers, had not destroyed the Budget merely to entangle themselves in constitutional dialectics. Theirs was the dominant strategy in the Unionist Party and from the outset Unionists exhibited a marked reluctance to discuss the constitutional question. On the morrow of rejection the London Unionist press, with the notable exception of *The Times*, side-stepped the constitutional implications of the act, and was content to commend the Lords for having, in the words of the *Daily Telegraph*, 'done their duty without flinching and without fear'. In so far as the action of the Lords was defended, it was done by reference to the demerits of the Budget, which was, according to the *Daily Mail*, 'an audacious attempt to force socialism upon the country without consulting the people'. The same paper warned against 'Byzantine discussions' on constitutional precedents, while the *Morning Post* blandly asserted: '. . . the constitutional issue is not the issue which the electors have to decide'.[13]

What was the issue? 'It is, and must be,' declared the *Daily Express*, 'the Socialism of the Budget . . . or Tariff Reform.'[14] Garvin, now chief propaganda adviser to the Unionists, urged: '. . . nothing but hammering upon tariff reform and social reform . . . will do our business thoroughly.'[15] But if desirable it was to prove difficult to be so single-minded.

The early impetus of the Liberal platform campaign reflected the Radical mood, and contrasts with the dearth of Unionist oratory in the opening fortnight. Even before Parliament was prorogued Lloyd George and Churchill had set out on their 'double Midlothian'[16] designed, as had been its predecessor thirty years before, to raise the political temperature. Having lambasted the Lords at the National Liberal Club as 'broken bottles stuck on a park wall to keep off Radical poachers from lordly preserves', Lloyd George hurried to Wales to initiate the campaign in his own constituency, Caernarvon Boroughs, and in the Principality at large. Meanwhile in a fortnight's intensive campaigning Churchill stumped Lancashire 'performing feats of physical endurance comparable with those of a candidate for the American Presidency'.[17]

The only Unionist platform event in the first fortnight to interrupt what one Unionist journalist called the 'falsetto shrieks of Limehouse or the pinchbeck moralities of the younger demagogue'[18] was the evening rally at the Liberal Unionist conference at Plymouth on 3 December. The rally heard a typically moderate defence of the Lords from Lansdowne, and with greater appreciation a promise from Austen

Chamberlain that Tariff Reform would increase employment, unify the Empire, and provide for social reform.[19]

This contrast with Liberal activity did not simply arise from the Unionist strategy of playing it cool. It stemmed partly from Balfour's illness, which kept him out of the campaign until after Christmas, thereby 'depressing our people to a very disadvantageous extent',[20] from a scarcity of Unionist orators, and from a lack of imagination and flexibility at Central Office. Moreover, for the first fortnight liaison between the Central Office and the press was inadequate and Unionist speeches were poorly reported.[21]

III

Asquith's Albert Hall speech, which officially opened the Liberal campaign on 10 December was the pivotal speech of the campaign, indeed of the two elections.[22] It was also perhaps the most impressive. Long-heralded, superbly staged, it deliberately recalled Campbell-Bannerman's overture to victory staged in the same building almost exactly four years before. Flanked by a platform which included nearly all his Cabinet and most of the Liberal M.P.s, beneath a single large banner inscribed, 'Shall the People be Ruled by the Peers?', Asquith addressed an audience of ten thousand men. The fear of suffragette interference had led the Liberal organisers to exclude all women from the meeting. The resulting masculinity and the sombre colours gave the meeting, in the words of The Times, 'a grim aspect of strength and resolution'.[23]

The speech was a masterly illustration of Liberal strategic considerations. Its purpose was twofold: to bring home the gravity and paramount importance of the constitutional issue and to rally all elements of the heterogeneous anti-Unionist front to the Government. Asquith had to maintain a delicate balance between these two objectives, for the legislative promises involved in the second could easily distract attention from the first. By presenting the Lords as the past barrier and future obstacle to the demands of all the interests in the anti-Unionist front, Asquith sought to unite his forces against the Lords.

To the Nonconformists he promised education reform, to the temperance advocates another Licensing Bill, and to the Radicals franchise reforms. To the Welsh he offered disestablishment, and to the Scots he held out plans for land and rent reform. The Irish were promised Home Rule, while for the working classes the Budget would

provide 'the sinews of war for the initiation and the prosecution of what
must be a long, a costly social campaign'. But blocking all these
measures was a fatal impediment, the veto of the House of Lords.

> . . . we have at this moment . . . a single task, a task which dominates and trans-
> cends, because it embraces and involves, every great and beneficent change
> upon which our hearts are set. That task is to vindicate and to establish upon
> an unshakeable foundation the principle of representative government.

To restore the challenged supremacy of the Commons Asquith
promised an act of Parliament giving statutory effect to 'the ancient
unwritten usage . . . that it is beyond the province of the House of
Lords to meddle in any way, to any degree, or for any purpose, with
our national finance'. But this alone was not sufficient to protect a
Liberal government from 'the rebuffs and humiliations of the past
four years'. So Asquith pledged that 'the absolute veto . . . must go . . .
The will of the people, as deliberately expressed by their elected
representatives, must, within the limits of the lifetime of a single
Parliament, be made effective.' And he assured his audience that he
would secure guarantees to make this pledge effective.

This speech, 'that orgy of promises made to all the fanatical and
disruptive forces in political life', as *The Times* described it,[24] aroused
the enthusiasm of the Radicals and assured the Liberals of Labour and
Irish support. They did not of course recognise that the speech was
soft-centred, for the Government had no definite Upper Chamber
scheme, and immediate guarantees were to prove a mirage.

In so far as Labour conducted a national campaign it was as a part
of the Radical wing of the Liberal Party. Labour speeches differed
little in content and tone from Radical ones; the majority of Labour
candidates were little more than surrogates for Radicals. Only in
twenty-seven constituencies did official Labour candidates infringe
upon the dualism characteristic of the election in Great Britain. Even
in these triangular contests, which were fewer than the Liberals had
feared, the Liberal press emphasised the unity of the progressive forces
by its assiduous pursuit of electoral bargains. Only in the Clyde Valley
and Northumberland–Durham, where there were concentrations of
triangular contests, did Labour establish a distinctive electoral identity,
and the price was electoral discomfiture.

The Irish leaders campaigned in Britain in the Liberal interest, and
the Irish vote in Great Britain was lined up behind the Liberal candidates. However, the factional revolt in Ireland, itself the offspring of

dissatisfaction with the Liberal alliance, led to dual Nationalist candidates in eighteen seats, and restricted the British activities of the Irish leaders.

The Liberals capitalised on the initiative they now possessed. They used their first-rate resources in a systematic and intelligent way in order to rally all parts of the country to the party. In contrast with the Unionist Commoners, the Liberal leaders were highly mobile, and their itineraries reveal awareness of crucial areas. No doubt the fact that half the Liberal Commoners in the Cabinet held seats in the Celtic fringe encouraged such mobility. Asquith himself spoke at two more major meetings before Christmas both on Merseyside on 21 December. Churchill completed his Lancashire campaign before returning to Scotland where, apart from a fleeting visit to Birmingham on 10 January, he remained for the rest of the campaign. Lloyd George meanwhile continued to alternate between London and Wales.

In these three Ministers, the dominant figures of the Liberal campaign, the Liberals possessed outstanding platform orators, who were, as well, figures of major stature in the party. This latter fact, as the Unionists found to their discomfort, was as important in securing publicity and attention as the former. They were a well-balanced team, the *gravitas* of Asquith offsetting the exuberance of his younger colleagues, the polish of Churchill's and Asquith's oratory contrasting with the colloquial spontaneity of the Chancellor, perhaps the key factor in understanding his extraordinary rapport with his audiences.

Lloyd George was almost an electoral issue in himself, each of his speeches sparking off an outburst of Tory indignation. He also annoyed some of his colleagues – and their wives. Margot Asquith told Strachey: 'Lloyd George's speeches have been a *disgrace*: vulgar, silly and infinitely bad for us . . . I have given up reading them they are so disgusting.'[25] Harcourt found 'all over the country that all Ll. G.'s speeches and Winston's earlier ones (not the Lancs. campaign) had done us much harm, even with the advanced men of the *lower* middle class'.[26]

Yet others, like the old Welsh Radical, Lord Rendel, considered it likely that on balance Lloyd George had won the party more votes than he lost.[27] The working classes had to be wooed and Lloyd George knew it. If the heavy desertions from the party amongst the middle classes can be attributed partly to Lloyd George, the fidelity of the working classes to the Liberal Party can equally be partly attributed to him. This class polarisation which characterised the results was partly reflected in a geographical contrast, which Spender, for one, ascribed to Lloyd George. '. . . while George's qualities have won the north, his defects have done much to alienate the south.'[28]

Churchill did not arouse the same antagonism among Liberals. Harcourt exempted Churchill's Lancashire speeches, and Mrs Asquith found them 'closest reasoned' and 'admirable'.[29] Her husband agreed, comparing Churchill's Lancashire campaign to Gladstone's Midlothian tour.[30] But the real balance to Lloyd George was provided by Asquith. While the rhetoric of Lloyd George lit 'the damp squibs of radicalism in a Tory people',[31] a firing necessary to Liberal success, the massive urbanity and moderation of the Prime Minister assured the nervous that the crackers would not get out of control. He was particularly adept at ridiculing Tory bogeys, as for example his sustained satire at Liverpool on 21 December on the theme that the Liberals had gone to Westminster in 1906 'to conspire in secret like a set of half-hearted modern Guy Fawkes how to best destroy the Second Chamber'.[32]

The three leading figures were well supported by the lesser platform talents in the party. In his London campaign Lloyd George was flanked by John Burns, fighting to retain Battersea 'in the meanest contest this district has ever seen',[33] and by Sydney Buxton, Charles Masterman, and T. J. MacNamara, all members of the Government sitting for metropolitan constituencies. Burns, who disliked both the Budget and its author – 'that wild ass from Wales'[34] – was at his best on the old Radical themes – drink, peace and Free Trade – and had a sturdily demagogic line on the House of Lords. But his most significant contribution was not a speech, but his widely publicised role in directing rescue operations during a fatal departmental store fire in Clapham on 20 December. It gave an undoubted fillip to the fortunes of London Liberalism as well as to Burns's personal contest in Battersea. Grey worked the North-East with a brief visit to Scotland. Herbert Samuel and Walter Runciman were active in Yorkshire, Harcourt in Lancashire, and Birrell and McKenna in the West Country.

Throughout, the issue of the House of Lords remained pre-eminent. It was tackled in different ways by the different leaders. At the N.L.C. Lloyd George stressed the social conflict, condemning 'an order of men, blessed with every fortune which providence can bestow on them, grudging a small pittance out of their superabundance in order to protect those who have built up their wealth against the haunting terror of misery and despair'. At Caernarvon he presented the Lords as the enemy of the Celtic peoples: 'Neither Ireland nor Wales can ever obtain its rights except by marching over the ruins of the House of

Lords.' In Cardiff he recalled agrarian strife in Wales and used it against landlords and peers.[35] Personal gibes against the peers were frequent, including anti-semitic innuendoes against Lords Rothschild and Revelstoke.[36]

On 16 December at the Queen's Hall he added to the Welsh and the London working class a third group, the Nonconformists, to whom it was his especial task to carry the message of Liberalism. His speech to a gathering of free churchmen could be described as an exaltation of the Nonconformists. They were praised for their honesty, industry, thrift, business acumen, and independence. It was also a savage philippic against their hereditary enemies, 'The Peers, those Philistines who are not all uncircumcised'; who had torn to shreds Birrell's 'temperate' Education Bill; who had thrown out the Licensing Bill at 'the behest of a greedy too powerful trade'; who on all Nonconformist issues were 'essentially biassed, one sided, prejudiced'. The meeting responded with a unanimous pledge to do all in its power to destroy the veto of the House of Lords.[37]

This open and unashamed appeal to Nonconformist sentiment appalled the Archbishop of Canterbury – for him it was, 'in the most literal sense, the work of the Devil';[38] annoyed some moderate Nonconformists; and provoked a howl of anger from the Tory press. Two days later in a single editorial the Daily Telegraph managed to describe it as a 'Hyde Park lorry address', an 'inculcation of the doctrine of hate', an 'iniquitous and wanton effort to stir up the fierce furies of religious strife', and 'a revolting medley of illustrations and analogy . . . trespassing far beyond the limits of irreverence'.

Churchill's approach was primarily historical: seeing the House of Lords as 'a lingering relic of the feudal order', he scorned the peers' current pose as 'the true apostles of democracy'.[39] Asquith stressed the institutional conflict and though less picturesque than his colleagues outlined clearly and realistically the immediate points at issue. 'The question is not between two Chambers and a single Chamber. It is . . . a question whether when the Liberals are in a majority, the House of Lords shall be supreme.'[40]

The constitutional issue was their pre-eminent but not their sole concern. Free Trade necessarily played as big a role in Churchill's Lancashire campaign as the House of Lords, indeed at times it overshadowed the constitutional question. And when Asquith went to Merseyside one speech was devoted mainly to the House of Lords, the other mainly to Tariff Reform. In London Lloyd George relied much on social reform promises, in Wales on the heady talismen of national-ism, the Welsh language, shared historic experiences, and a mystical communion with the Welsh soil. The Budget was not forgotten and he railed against those who would 'tax the food of the workmen's children in order to spare the acres of the landlord's child'.[41] But as Asquith has shown at the Albert Hall all issues could be subsumed in the constitutional. So Lloyd George to all his audiences promised a glowing future once 'this garrotting of Liberal bills' was over.[42]

The Unionists desperately wanted for platform talent. They had been handicapped in this respect in 1906 but now with Joseph Chamberlain absent and Balfour ill for much of the campaign, their plight was far more serious. 'Oh! for a week of Mr Chamberlain', lamented the young Whole Hogger propagandist F. S. Oliver, 'and the Gadarene swine would be hurtling over the steep places into the sea!'[43] No front-rank Unionist Commoner possessed platform qualities comparable to those of Lloyd George, Churchill or Asquith. Austen Chamberlain was pedestrian, George Wyndham obscure, while the best that could be said for Walter Long was that though he 'does not talk well . . . a talking squire is like a talking horse'.[44] True the Unionist Party had a not ineffective 'tub-thumper' in Sir George Doughty, 'the Demosthenes of Tariff Reform',[45] but he was a figure of secondary stature. Similarly, the two ablest platform orators in the party, Bonar Law and F. E. Smith, were not yet sufficiently prominent to command as much national publicity as the leading ministerial figures.

In addition, most of the Unionist Commoners were constituency-bound, at least until the New Year. Austen Chamberlain remained in the Birmingham country. Before Christmas Wyndham, Lyttelton and F. E. Smith remained mostly in or about their constituencies, except for occasional and rather wasteful one-day forays further afield. Walter Long did bob up all over the country in Manchester, in Pembroke, in remote West Country hamlets, even in Ireland, covering vast distances, but with an itinerary at once aimless and haphazard. A more successful venture was Bonar Law's carefully planned and impressive campaign through North-Eastern England in the days immediately before Christmas.

While the Unionists were hampered by a dearth of orators among their Commons Front Bench, the two chief events of the Unionist campaign before Christmas abetted Liberal electoral strategy. Balfour's election address was issued on 10 December to coincide with Asquith's Albert Hall speech. Academic in tone, and curiously perverse in content, it was much more personal and idiosyncratic than Asquith's speech. It was devoted almost exclusively to the constitutional question, the only other subject dealt with at length being a system of peasant proprietorships. His argument on the House of Lords was a refurbishing of his Commons remarks of 3 December. He countered the growing attack on the Upper House by a conservative appeal to bicameralism, again coupled with a most-unconservative exaltation of the role of the people in government. The House of Lords protected the people against the tyranny of the Commons by ensuring an appeal to the people on fundamental issues. For Balfour, unchecked representative government stood impeached, as a danger to those who elected the representatives – the people themselves.[46]

This plausible apologia may have gratified the Peers but it annoyed many in Balfour's party. Preoccupied with the House of Lords and giving only cursory treatment to Tariff Reform, it ran counter to Whole Hogger strategy, to the emphases of much of Unionist propaganda, and was in striking contrast to the election addresses of most of his followers.

The second major development in the Unionist campaign in this period more dramatically stressed the constitutional question. The Peers had been inhibited, if not always prevented, from intervening in elections by a sessional order of the Commons which forbade their participation. The order was of dubious authority, and the failure of the Committee of Privileges to treat the Duke of Norfolk's intervention by letter at the High Peak by-election in July 1909 as a breach of the order finally rendered the prohibition ineffectual.[47]

Short on talent and with 'our men worn out', Sandars was already 'arranging to enlist the services of discreet and competent peers' early in November.[48] Fifty-one peers finally answered the call to defend their order on the platform.[49] These peers tended to be drawn from the activist core of the House of Lords. Nearly half of them had sat in the House of Commons, and over a third had held Government office. Many had distinguished military, administrative, and local government records. But too many had for too long been insulated in the Upper Chamber against popular contacts, or had ruled as autocrats in Ireland, India, or Africa.[50] Neither the seclusion of the gilded chamber nor the viceroy's throne were ideal preparations for going on the stump.

Many peers wilted under the 'peer-baiting' they had to undergo. Not untypical was a meeting at Droitwich – 'a very stormy meeting', wrote a Unionist present, 'and each time Lord D[onoughmore] mentioned the H. of Lords – they boo-ed and hissed and cried "House of Fools" '.[51] Dogged by heckling, the peers' responses were often rather wild. The Liberal press blazoned their doings and their indiscretions across the front pages, and in the process, according to one activist peer, Lord Ampthill, were guilty of 'malicious and scandalous misrepresentations'.[52] But the Unionist press gave them somewhat furtive treatment, being condemned by the same irate peer for 'scandalous neglect'. There was truth in the *Nation*'s New Year's Day claim that 'Never have public utterances been so carefully advertised by opponents, or hurried by supporters into such hasty oblivion'.

In every election such collections of trivia are possible. Their importance in this election was the maximum publicity they received because of their relevance to a central issue. Such statements emanated from the most vocal of those who had rejected the Budget, and who claimed to arrogate to themselves extensive legislative functions.

Yet, even if they were often inept, they did give the Unionist Party a sorely needed touch of colour, and earned it headlines and coverage it would otherwise have missed. If too often they seemed the defenders of their own privilege, or targets too easily pilloried, their very appearance on the platforms did something to counteract the beery, money-bag-clutching, robed and coroneted image that flowered on hoardings everywhere. Lord Ampthill, for one, was satisfied that the campaign 'has done a great deal of good and removed an immense amount of prejudice'.[53]

Moreover some rose to the challenge to such an extent that in the weeks before Balfour's return three members of the House of Lords bore the burden of the Unionist campaign, capturing headlines space and attention to a degree unrivalled by any of their Commons colleagues. At Oldham on 15 December, Curzon broke the Liberal oratorical monopoly, and in the following days he, Milner and Cawdor ensured that the Liberal supremacy in the national debate was at last really challenged. Moreover, they went into regions where the Unionist case seemed in danger of defeat by default – Lancashire, the industrial North and Wales.

Yet whatever the advantages, one aspect of this intervention was clear. The peers personalised in a striking fashion the issue on which the Liberals wished to fight the election. This is well illustrated by Curzon, the most active and most able of the platform peers. 'George Curzon is working handsomely,' wrote Sandars, 'and I make Hughes apply the incense which George so much appreciates.'[54] Curzon was certainly 'working handsomely', mastering three great meetings at Oldham, Derby and Burnley in the week before Christmas. He emerged, particularly at Oldham, as the most arrogant and outspoken defender of the House of Lords. Phrases from the Oldham speech of 15 December, particularly the claim that the Lords represented the 'permanent sentiment and temper of the British people' while the Commons reflected 'passing gusts of popular passion', and his quotation from Renan: 'All civilisation has been the work of aristocracies',[55] reverberated through the election.

An uneasy *Times* thought much of the speech 'more courageous than politic',[56] but Liberals were delighted. At the Queen's Hall Lloyd George told the Nonconformists that 'the Carpenter's son of Nazareth' had more to do with civilisation that Renan's aristocracies,[57] to which piece of piety Curzon retorted that 'anything less like the Sermon on the Mount than a speech from Mr Lloyd George can scarcely be conceived'.[58] Churchill found the Oldham oration 'a prize essay on the Middle Ages', and, *pace* Renan, thought it truer to say: 'The upkeep of aristocracies has been the hard work of all civilisations.'[59] Even Curzon seemed a little chastened, and his speeches at Derby and Burnley were more circumspect. But the very presence of a peer on the platform, however able his defence, underlined what for Liberals the election was all about. Curzon merely added an arrogance and extravagance all his own.

The Liberal campaign and Liberal strategy reached its apogee with the celebration of Gladstone's centenary on 29 December. Liberal plans to exploit this occasion had been made well in advance. Gladstone's support of Free Trade, his pioneering budgets, his advocacy of Home Rule were all relevant to the present campaign. But it was as the opponent of the Lords that the Liberals presented him to the nation, and on 29 December most Liberal papers in the country quoted copiously from Gladstone's last speech in the Commons, in which he had declared that the fundamental differences between the Houses 'once raised, must go forward to an issue'. All over the country the spirit of Gladstone was summoned to do battle against the Lords.

IV

But at this point the Liberals began to lose command of the campaign. It was as if a runner well clear of the field suddenly found a rival at his elbow. The Unionists were at last making a race of it. The reasons for this are clear. First, the very length of the contest and the exhaustion of argument led to a growing flatness and staleness in the campaign which rebounded to the disadvantage of the Liberals whose strategy rested on maintaining a high level of popular excitement. Secondly, the Unionists succeeded in pushing Tariff Reform to the forefront of the debate. Finally, in the plethora of issues growing up around the main questions one, the naval agitation, stood out, to the advantage of the Unionists.

By the New Year there was some evidence that the Liberal movement had begun too soon. Asquith bore the brunt of the national campaign in January, criss-crossing Great Britain to speak at Haddington, Brighton, Bath, Ipswich, Salisbury and Bradford all in the space of ten days. But, burdened by personal worries, with an exhausting year behind him and difficulties ahead whatever the result, Asquith visibly flagged.[60]

Lloyd George was in fine form at meetings in Reading and London at the turn of the year, and rebutted with vigour attacks in the press on his Boer War activities.[61] But he too was beginning to tire. Occasional metaphors stirred new outbursts of indignation, such as his reference at Wolverhampton to the Peers as simply 'the first of the litter'.[62] But his imagery was increasingly hackneyed and his epithets stale.

On the other hand, Balfour entered the campaign speaking at Hanley, Ipswich, Aberdeen, Glasgow, York and Bradford in the first fortnight of the New Year, and engaging in a running verbal duel with Asquith. With few gifts and little inclination for the hustings, Balfour was nevertheless an ex-Prime Minister, leader of the Opposition, and a fresh figure in the campaign. He was the only Unionist Commoner who could command press attention comparable with Asquith, Lloyd George or Churchill. His presence undoubtedly helped to invigorate the Unionist campaign. In addition, the other Unionist Commoners began to get out from their constituencies. Wyndham left Dover to spend a week campaigning in Cheshire; Lyttelton ranged widely through the Home Counties, East Anglia and the Midlands; and F. E. Smith plunged into Wales with rowdy meetings at Llandudno, Caernarvon and Swansea. Walter Long even visited Ireland, the only leading British politician to do so. The Lords, now joined by Lansdowne, remained active.

But the achievement of an oratorical balance did not offset the increasing exhaustion of argument, reflected in mounting recklessness, vituperation and scurrility in debate. The growing aridity of argument is seen in the black-bread-and-horseflesh controversy, the most futile offshoot of the fiscal argument from Germany. Lloyd George was the leading Liberal to indulge in tales of the German working classes eking out an existence on 'vile black bread' and 'juicy horseflesh'. While Lloyd George recommended this as a diet for the Peers,[63] the Unionist press waxed ecstatic over the discovery that Queen Alexandra was in the habit of eating pumpernickel. Candidates all over the country carried on the argument by offering samples of black bread to their listeners. The Unionists usually offered their audiences the best-quality pumpernickel, the Liberals poor-quality rye bread, often exhibited for several days in Free Trade Union shops or Liberal committee rooms before being offered for public consumption.[64]

The staleness of the major controversies underlay the staleness of the campaign in the New Year. The long campaign saw no development in the three major issues – the House of Lords, the Budget, and Tariff Reform. This might have been tolerable in a shorter campaign. In January 1910 it robbed the Liberals of their early dynamism.

The trouble was the major questions had been well thrashed out before the campaign began. After eight months of verbal conflict on the Budget, the debate on its merits was hackneyed. The catalogue of its charms had been exhausted, the syllabus of its errors completed long before the election. The fiscal controversy had been debated continuously for the past seven years. It was virtually impossible to say anything new. Tariff Reform was presented as it had been for the past seven years as the panacea for all the country's economic ills from unemployment to the alleged flight of capital, and as it had been for the past eight months as the alternative to a detested Budget. Free Trade was defended as it had been for generations by a unique blending of economic facts and metaphysics for it was as much a faith as an economic system.

Faced at last with the constitutional crisis, the parties might have been expected to develop during the election constructive proposals on the House of Lords. Yet they did not. The explanation lies in the fact that the Liberals did not have an agreed solution, and that the Unionists were unwilling to develop one under the stress of an election.

The courageous words of the Prime Minister at the Albert Hall covered Cabinet indecision as to exactly what should be done with the House of Lords. While Grey announced that he preferred composition reforms, and 'a real second Chamber' with substantial powers,[65] most Ministers vaguely endorsed the suspensory veto scheme. The incompatibility of these solutions was hidden by the ambiguity of most ministerial utterances. Divided and vague as to their plans, the Liberals could hardly contribute to a debate on their own intentions.

The Unionist leaders were inhibited from making too much of Ministerial obscurity because of their own reluctance to countenance specific reform plans. They were however under considerable pressure to advance such plans. In the most circumlocutory sentence in his address Balfour acknowledged the need for reforms, but later in that address declared that reform schemes were not immediately relevant. On Christmas Day the *Spectator* told him that this was 'about the least appropriate thing that can be said of the reform of the House of Lords'. The journal warned the Unionists that if they declined to take up reform immediately they would gravely impair their chances of victory. Many Unionists agreed. In their election addresses half the Unionist candidates expressed dissatisfaction with the existing composition of the House.

Yet Balfour was reluctant to act, for his objections to reform in principle were now reinforced by tactical considerations. Writing on 23 December to Harcourt Kitchin, editor of the Unionist *Glasgow Herald*, who had pressed for a reform declaration, Balfour concentrated on the tactical aspect pointing out 'that our defence [of the Lords' action] would inevitably be weakened if we coupled it with the admission that the Second Chamber, which has carried out this (in our opinion, necessary) duty, was one which could not claim public confidence unless it were immediately reformed'.[66]

Yet whatever the logic of Balfour's position, Unionist unease rendered it increasingly difficult to maintain. Lansdowne, hard-pressed finally agreed to support limited reforms along the lines of the Rosebery Committee Report, which had urged curtailment of the hereditary element. With Balfour's reluctant concurrence, Lansdowne half-heartedly advised moderate reform at Liverpool on 5 January.[67] This modest avowal made little impact. Unionists who wanted an electorally palatable reform scheme showed little enthusiasm for the Rosebery Committee proposals, yet Lansdowne's speech gave notice that the Unionist leaders were not prepared to advance beyond them during the election. At the same time the circumspect response of the Liberal leaders inhibited debate. Thus the formulation of precise schemes was put aside by both parties until the election was over.

The New Year also saw the success of the Whole Hoggers. From the beginning the Liberal policy of concentrating on the Lords had encountered the contrary tactics of preaching 'the gospel of Tariff Reform at any and every opportunity.'[68] Joseph Chamberlain's election address, issued on Gladstone's centenary, contrasted with Balfour's in that it exemplified Whole Hogger tactics. It was devoted almost exclusively to Tariff Reform, claiming that now was the time to abandon an antiquated Cobdenism and introduce Colonial Preference, and warning that no further opportunity for fiscal change might occur if this one were 'thrown away'.[69] This address, not Balfour's, served as the model for most Unionist addresses; this address, not Balfour's seemed more closely geared to the main themes of Unionist propaganda.

The Unionist speakers kept the issue to the fore. Austen Chamberlain's campaign in the family stronghold was devoted almost exclusively to the family subject. As Bonar Law swept through Newcastle, Jarrow and Sunderland, areas of heavy unemployment, he hammered home the Tariff Reform case, presenting it primarily as a cure for unemployment.[70] The time allocation in the platform speeches of the City businessman Sir Joseph Lawrence, a member of the Tariff Reform caucus, was probably not untypical of Whole Hogger speeches: '2 minutes Budget, $\frac{1}{2}$ a minute H. of Lords, $57\frac{1}{2}$ minutes T.R. and Col'l Preference.'[71]

Milner was the favourite peer of the Whole Hogger wing, because he knew quite clearly what the election was, and was not, about. 'I am not going to let myself', he told his Huddersfield audience, 'be drawn into a discussion of the constitutional question to the neglect of what at this juncture is far more urgent and that is the trade question, the question of industry, of employment.'[72] Further peers were pressed into the cause. Curzon devoted as much attention in his New Year speeches to tariffs as to the Lords. Lansdowne too was recruited. On 28 December Sandars reported that Lansdowne 'is digging deep into all the controversial elements of the cotton question in connection with Tariff Reform. I have at last got him into communication with Hewins.'[73] The results of this tutoring were apparent in Lansdowne's Liverpool speech.

A joint pledge on Tariff Reform and the cost of living from Balfour and Joseph Chamberlain on the eve of the first polls set the seal on the victory within the party of the Highbury programme.[74] Despite its hyperbole, a eulogy of Joseph Chamberlain in the *National Review* for January 1910, captures the spirit and the tenor of the Unionist campaign: '[The Unionist Party] is more completely identified with

[Joseph Chamberlain] and intensely vitalised by him than at any previous moment of its existence. . . . Mr Balfour is the executor of the policy. Mr Chamberlain is the captain of the cause.'[75]

The strategy of the Whole Hoggers which had originally paralysed, now split the pathetic remnant of the Free Fooders. 'Divisions of opinion are so wide', Arthur Elliot noted in his diary for 2 November, 'the [Unionist Free Trade] Club cannot pronounce for a Budget Government or a Protectionist Opposition.' For some like the Cecils, Strachey and Cromer 'the need of getting rid of this Lloyd George and Winston-ridden Government' was paramount. For them 'predatory socialism plus demagoguery of the most reckless and unscrupulous description' plus Home Rule were worse than Tariff Reform.[76] But for other Free Fooders like James of Hereford, Balfour of Burleigh, Arthur Elliot, Professor Pollock, who placed Free Trade above other issues, 'the rejection of the Finance Bill of the year by the Lords, and the Conservative Leaders going to the country in favour of Protection form together too big a *bolus* . . . to swallow'.[77]

This division was apparent when the Unionist Free Trade Club met on 7 December to decide electoral policy. All it could do as a club was to refrain from any advice whatsoever for 'many speakers [were] determined to put Free Trade *first*; and to vote accordingly, [while] others [thought] we must defeat Socialism by voting for Balfour and the Tariff Reformers'.[78] Thus one effect of the insistence on Tariff Reform as the election issue was virtually to destroy the Unionist Free Trade Club, and to leak Free Food votes to the Liberals. But electoral defeat was necessary before the Unionist leaders concerned themselves overmuch with this leakage.

But not only was the Highbury policy *the* issue for Unionists, it also became in the New Year *the* issue of the campaign. Apart from Unionist insistence there appear to be four reasons for this. First, it was always likely that the fiscal issue might emerge as the most important, simply because Liberals were more willing to talk about Tariff Reform than were Unionists about the constitution. Many Liberals welcomed the Unionist effort to preach Tariff Reform, for they saw in this an opportunity to tar Tariff Reform with the unpopularity of the Lords. A poster cartoon, 'Tariff Reform Means Happier Dukes'[79], was widely used to suggest the inequity of the Highbury programme. Asquith delighted in his mastery of the subject; Churchill had established his Liberal reputation as a defender of Free Trade; both entered willingly into the fiscal debate.

Moreover, the improving economic climate encouraged Liberal rhetoric on the fiscal issue. Despite the onset of winter unemployment had continued to fall, and by the end of 1909 was at its lowest point since early 1908. Trade was again buoyant and it was apparent that the worst of the slump was over. The latest blue book statistics were widely used by Liberals to vindicate the Budget against charges that it was a depressant on economic activity, and to confound the economic pessimism of the Tariff Reformers. The Whole Hoggers had got their winter election but in economic conditions less favourable for their cause than they had anticipated.

Secondly, the critical role of Lancashire in the election emphasised the fiscal issue. Lancashire was considered the cockpit of the election. It was here that the Unionists had been overwhelmed in 1906, losing forty-one of the fifty seats they had held in Lancashire and Cheshire. If this result could be reversed, or the old balance even partially restored, then the foundation would have been laid for overthrowing the Liberal majority. But the possibility of Unionist recovery was shadowed by the fervid adherence of cotton to Free Trade.

It was to ensure this adherence that Churchill went north in early December. His campaign there had as a prominent text: 'Lancashire has everything to lose and nothing to gain from Tariff Reform.'[80] It was certainly a message his audiences wanted to hear. At his Manchester meeting it was observed that 'the name of Adam Smith was cheered as if it had been that of a contemporary politician who had just spoken at Limehouse'.[81] Lancashire brought out the fiscal side in everybody. Manchester revealed the Tariff Reformer in Curzon, and it was for a meeting in Liverpool that Lansdowne was tutored by Professor Hewins.

Thirdly, in the post-Christmas period, as if uncertain of the appeal of their constitutional arguments, the Liberals gave increasing attention to the bread and butter issues of politics, and thus to the fiscal question. Churchill's address to the Dundee electors, published nationally on 29 December, signalled the need to stress Liberal social reforms as positive antidotes to poverty and unemployment.

This shift of emphasis is even more apparent in the first post-Christmas speeches of Lloyd George. In London on New Year's Eve he devoted most of a speech to the problem of unemployment. Tariff Reform was not the answer, for in the United States 'this protectionist paradise . . . you find the serpents of hunger, want, unemployment, hissing in every glade'.[82] Rather the solution lay in the provisions of the Budget and in a thorough overhaul of the land system. The following afternoon at Reading social reform in a Free Trade system was his chief topic.

Finally and paradoxically, the return of that most reluctant of Tariff Reformers, Arthur Balfour, assured the primacy of the fiscal question in the New Year. While the Whole Hogger press watched him eagle-eyed for heresy, Asquith pursued him doggedly as he had once pursued Joseph Chamberlain. The platform duel that dominated this stage of the campaign was above all a duel about Tariff Reform. Asquith demanded details of tariff rates, the definition of raw materials, the explanation of how goods could be kept out yet revenue raised. If under Asquithian pressure Balfour was prone to grandiloquent general-isations, e.g. at Aberdeen Liberal fiscal policy was castigated as running counter to 'the experience of civilised mankind',[83] the debate was climaxed at York on 12 January by Balfour's specific pledge to impose 'import duties over a wide fiscal field', with a tax on foreign wheat, and with protective tariffs, so 'that our markets are not unduly trespassed upon by rival producers'.[84] While Balfour's York speech was the inevitable outcome of the autumn consensus in the Unionist Party, this debate between the party leaders in the days before the first polls finally established Tariff Reform as the paramount question on the hustings.

Of the four minor issues developed during the campaign, Old Age Pensions, the Osborne Judgement, Home Rule and the naval agitation, the Unionists succeeded in turning the naval agitation into a major scare with considerable benefit to their cause.

Old Age Pensions were an inevitable election issue. Nor only were they the outstanding Liberal achievement in social reform, but the measure's grudging acceptance by the Lords highlighted the disap-pointing record of the Unionists on this question. Liberals were not always scrupulous in their use of the issue, Liberal speakers hinting that the destruction of the Budget would mean the end of the pensions. Unionists retaliated by labelling any anti-Unionist remark on pensions as a lie. The *Daily Telegraph* fulminated against 'the deliberate attempt to saturate the constituencies with mendacity' on the subject, and urged that squire, clergy and Primrose dame should all work to repudiate the lies.[85] Balfour's public denials of various Liberal alle-gations were made into a leaflet by the Central Office, and sent out 'by the thousands to the Agents in districts where the lie still flourishes.'[86] Harassed Unionist M.P.s, pressed to explain their pensions voting record, and candidates bullied by hecklers about Joseph Chamberlain's failure to honour his pensions promises, all sought escape in charges of mendacity. All the Devonshire Unionist candidates issued a circular 'in order to remove doubts and anxiety caused by the lying statements of certain evil-minded persons'.[87] But the very vociferousness of the chorus suggests that the protestations were as much intended to cover Unionist vulnerability as to counter Liberal untruths.

The pensions issue was kept in the public eye by the first-anniversary celebrations on 1 January 1910, and was revitalised by an election-eve letter of Lansdowne's in which he unwisely, if tritely, intimated that the pensions provisions were not unalterable.[88] As Lansdowne confessed: '. . . my luckless letter . . . was harmless eno' . . . But I ought to have foreseen that my meaning would be distorted. . . .' It was. The Liberal press instanced the letter as revealing Tory intentions to substitute a contributory scheme. Nor could the letter have been more unfortunately timed, Lansdowne himself recognising that at a critical moment 'it helped to give wings to the pensions lie'. Lansdowne himself spent the next fortnight publicly assuring alarmed Unionist candidates that his letter had been grossly misinterpreted.[89]

A second issue favouring the anti-Unionist cause was injected into the campaign on 21 December when the Law Lords in the Osborne Judgement held that compulsory trade union levies for political purposes were illegal. The Osborne Judgement was soon lumped with the other crimes of the Lords by Radical and Labour men with a careless regard for constitutional niceties. The Unionist Party, condemned for its inaction on Taff Vale, was now treated as an accomplice in the Osborne Judgement.[90] Acland-Hood later claimed that the Judgement 'did us infinite harm' (in Lancashire and the North).[91] But this seems an exaggeration and the analogy with Taff Vale should not be pushed too far. As Snowden noted, the desire to challenge the Osborne Judgement lacked 'the unanimity and enthusiasm' of the agitation to reverse Taff Vale.[92] The Judgement did not stir the rank and file of the trade union movement, and a significant minority viewed with antipathy the efforts at reversal.

Home Rule was introduced into the election by Asquith's declaration at the Albert Hall. If it satisfied the Nationalists it brought little joy to the Liberals. At the Albert Hall itself 'it was remarkable that in a meeting boiling over with enthusiasm for so many far-reaching changes, the Prime Minister's inclusion of [Home Rule] produced a sensation of surprise and coldness. There was comparatively little cheering, and even that was without vigour.'⁹³ From the Albert Hall speech until the polls, there was virtually a conspiracy of silence on Home Rule among Liberal Ministers and candidates.⁹⁴ One reason for this was suggested by the Irish politician-historian Richard Barry O'Brien: 'All the Liberals I have met, with the exception of Scotchmen, are afraid of Home Rule, and would in fact have much preferred it if Asquith had never made his declaration . . .'⁹⁵ Nor did Ministers wish to encourage distractions from the central issue.

Yet despite Liberal anxieties Home Rule played little part in the election until the early returns indicated the Irish would hold the balance. The reasons for this neglect of Home Rule by the Unionists seem twofold. First, it was difficult to create feeling about an issue that had been dead for fifteen years. In late 1907 key men in the Unionist organisation were of the opinion that 'Home Rule is not the slightest use as a war cry in England'.⁹⁶ Even in December 1910, with the Irish question much more central to British politics, Walter Long discovered that 'in many parts of the country the view was accepted by our people that Home Rule had fallen into abeyance and that there existed no longer any need to expatiate upon its dangers'.⁹⁷ But the second reason for this neglect was more immediately significant. In the offices of the *Daily Mail* a greater scare was being prepared. The threat to the Union was soon to be submerged in the rising clamour over the threat to the nation.

The naval panic of March 1909 had been eclipsed by the debate on the Budget, and stilled by the decision in July 1909 to lay down the four contingent Dreadnoughts. But the scare had left the public fearful and suspicious of Germany. This feeling was reflected in, and encouraged by, best-selling spy stories and popular plays, and by exaggerated alarms in both the popular and the quality press.⁹⁸

Against this background the inflammable naval issue was introduced into the election by Admiral Lord Charles Beresford, Unionist candidate for Portsmouth, whose feud with Fisher had divided the navy since 1906. But Fisher's powerful Unionist allies were unhappy about Beresford's candidature, and were reluctant to support Beresford in what they looked upon as a personal vendetta.⁹⁹

Beresford, however, received support from the controversial H. H. Mulliner, ex-managing director of the Coventry Ordnance Works. Mulliner, disgruntled by the paucity of Admiralty orders to his firm and alarmed by naval construction in Germany, had passed on information about his dealings with the Admiralty to a number of Unionist politicians, and the Admiralty had retaliated by withholding all orders from the Coventry works until Mulliner resigned, which he did in July 1909.[100] The general election gave the indignant Mulliner new opportunities to attack the Admiralty and the Government. His correspondence to the press, always extensive, now became voluminous.[101]

But the efforts of Beresford and Mulliner would have been little but campaign footnotes had they not been joined by a third figure, Robert Blatchford, perhaps the strangest of the 'Trinity'.[102] Editor of the Socialist Clarion and author of the best-seller, 'Merrie England', Blatchford had assets the others lacked: a genius for mass propaganda, and a vehicle to utilise his talents – the Daily Mail, with its one million readers. Moreover, he had none of the personal rancour of Beresford or the suspect financial interests of Mulliner. Blatchford was seen as a patriot who, by doing his duty, was alienating himself from his Socialist comrades. Balfour wrote to a protesting Esher on 16 December 1909: '. . . it is something that an extreme Socialist should admit that he has a country worth making sacrifices to defend, so though doubtless he does talk nonsense, his nonsense is likely to be less injurious than usual.'[103] Whatever damage 'his nonsense' might do in the international sphere, it could only injure the governmental party in Great Britain.

Daily from 13 December until 24 December, the Daily Mail published a series of articles by Blatchford written, so the author claimed, because 'I believe that Germany is deliberately preparing to destroy the British Empire, and because I know that we are not able to ready to defend ourselves against a sudden and formidable attack'. Under sensational headlines such as 'Armageddon, the great Danger', 'Soldiery or Slavery', the articles were luridly alarmist and inflammatory, but they possessed a certain shrewdness, and undoubted vigour. Blatchford argued that Germany was bent on 'deliberate and ruthless conquest' and that the Cabinet realised 'our unreadiness, but lacked the moral courage to confess it'. His prescription included an expenditure of £50,000,000 on the navy, an army of 1,000,000 and two years' military service for all men. 'Unless the British people are ready to fight and pay and work . . . the Empire will assuredly go to pieces and leave us beggared and disgraced under the conquest of a braver, better trained and better organised nation.'[104]

The King and his courtiers might be dismayed, and the more delicate Unionists might stand aloof from the rantings of a Socialist demagogue,[105] but the impact of the articles was undeniable. 'Nothing that has appeared in the *Daily Mail* in recent years has attracted more attention, has aroused more discussion, or has been followed by our readers with closer interest', boasted the paper itself. Published as a pamphlet 1,600,000 copies were sold by the end of January, and nearly another 250,000 were given away.[106]

Many of the Unionist newspapers followed Blatchford, as did many Unionist speakers, often with the caveat that they were not themselves scaremongers. 'I am not an alarmist', Lord Curzon declared at Derby, 'but . . . I know there is a distinct and growing menace across the North Sea.' Cromer joined hands with Blatchford: 'We are both patriotic Englishmen', while Cawdor defended Mulliner and linked Home Rule and the naval scare by asking a Leeds audience, 'How, if they granted Home Rule, could they check a German fleet in Belfast?'[107] All over the land the Cassandra chorus was heard, and soon no Unionist speech was complete without some reference to the gravity of the naval situation.

The Liberal leaders, hoping that the issue would die of its own exaggerations or be calmed by the season of goodwill, left the question severely alone before Christmas. But the clamour mounted in the New Year with the publication of Mulliner's diary with its accusations of either 'culpable or criminal neglect' by the Government; with Beresford's sensational scenario of German tramps attacking the 'Mauretania'; and the circulation of a Navy League poster castigating as traitors all candidates and voters who did not accept the extravagant 'two keels to one' standard.[108] But it was the ex-Prime Minister who elevated the issue into one of the more formidable scares of a peace-time election.

For thirty-five minutes at Hanley on the evening of 4 January, Balfour lent his prestige to the naval scare and the related anti-German hubbub. Balfour was profuse in disclaiming that far from using the navy as a vote-catcher, the Unionists were 'driven by absolute necessity' – the Government's squandering of the naval supremacy bequeathed them by the Unionists – to raise the question. More sensationally he told his audience that the statesmen and diplomats of the lesser European powers were unanimously agreed that 'a struggle sooner or later between this country and Germany is inevitable and [that] . . . we are predestined to succumb'.[109]

Although the Liberal press might brand him 'war-monger', Asquith denounce his remarks as 'wanton', and Lloyd George accuse him of being a purveyor of 'a kind of society tittle tattle',[110] Balfour had given the agitation a new impetus. The imaginative flights of a Socialist journalist, or the vendettas of disgruntled admirals and company directors were one thing; the phrases of an ex-Prime Minister quite another.

Inflamed by Hanley the agitation distracted from other issues and brought returns to the Unionists. Its effects were obvious in the great naval dockyard towns of the South, always peculiarly sensitive to the jingo scare.[111] Thus the success of the Unionists in pushing the naval issue to the fore was a further factor in explaining their New Year recovery.

V

But interest was now rapidly shifting from the doings of the politicians to the decision of the voters. The appearance of the election writs on 10 January marked the disappearance of the peers, who in an effort to retain some semblance of constitutional nicety decided to refrain from active campaigning from that date on. Adherence to this decision was rigorously insisted on, Glasgow Unionists refusing to have Lord Cawdor on the 10th, for fear that Churchill, who was to speak later at Glasgow 'would make a great point of it'.[112]

Last-minute advice now showered on the voters from all quarters – from the Commoners still on the stump, from the press, and from poets, dramatists and novelists. Usually the alternatives presented were so stark that the advice could have been of little help to the genuinely undecided. In most general elections the voters are asked to condemn or commend a Government, to give a verdict on its performance. In January 1910 the electors were asked to give or withhold a mandate for a series of sweeping proposals with radical constitutional, economic, and political implications. Moreover the electors could not escape radical change. To deny the Liberals a mandate for their social and constitutional reforms was to opt for a radical transformation of the economic system.

Contemporaries were well aware of the significance of the election. It was not idle rhetoric when the *Morning Post* declared: 'Never have the two parties been separated by differences so vital and profound; never has there been so wide a gulf between their professed aims and between the policies for which they are appealing.'[113] Certainly not for decades had the parties been sundered by so many major issues of policy and principle. 'This is the one historical election that I have seen

since I was born, and perhaps the only one I shall see before I die.'[114]
There was general agreement with Chesterton that it was the most
momentous election for a generation, indeed the *Daily Mail* thought
since 1832, and the *Daily News*, characteristically, since the Civil War.[115]

Forecasts, Results and First Reactions

I

In the Parliament elected in 1906 the Liberals and their allies with a majority of 356 had enjoyed a superiority unequalled since the electoral landslide following the 1832 Reform Act. The Liberals alone had possessed a majority of 130 over all other parties. By the time of the dissolution in January 1910 the combined majority had been reduced to 334 and the absolute Liberal majority to 76.

TABLE 7.1 PARTY CHANGES 1906–JANUARY 1910 DISSOLUTION

	Unionist		Liberal		Labour		Nationalist		Others	
1906 Election	157		400		30		83		0	
	+	−	+	−	+	−	+	−	+	−
By-elections	12	0	0	15	2	0	0	0	1*	0
M.P.s changing allegiance	2	3	3	15†	13	0	0	0	0	0
Net Change	+11		−27		+15		0		+1	
1910 Jan. Dissolution	168		373		45		83		1	

Notes: *Victor Grayson (Colne Valley), independent Socialist.
　　　 † Includes thirteen Lib–Lab miners who severed their formal connections with the Liberal Party at the dissolution.

Assuming, as did most contemporaries, that the Nationalist and Labour totals would remain much the same, a Unionist net gain of thirty-nine seats would destroy the absolute Liberal majority, but the anti-Unionist majority would still remain formidable. For the Unionists to achieve an absolute majority they would have to double their representation, capturing 168 seats from their opponents. If the Unionists had a net gain of between forty and 168 then the Liberals would be to a lesser or greater extent dependent on Labour and the Irish Nationalists. What were the Unionist chances of achieving any of these objectives?

The campaign was throughout 'the most speculative Election which has occurred in our time'.[1] On the Sunday before the first polls the *Observer* published six forecasts from supposedly competent sources whose estimates ranged from a Unionist majority of ninety to an anti-Unionist majority of 200. The *Observer* considered this divergence 'evidence of probably the strongest conflict of anticipation that has yet been known in this country'.

The Radical crusaders were confident of a decisive victory, and the Liberal organisation was infected with their optimism. Although few agreed with the Baptist militant, Dr Clifford, that the Liberal majority would be unimpaired,[2] many shared Lloyd George's hunch that the Liberals 'would win by 90 excluding the Irish' i.e. a total anti-Unionist majority of about 170.[3] At Liberal headquarters prevailing opinion was said to expect a loss of some seventy seats, leaving an anti-Unionist majority of 200.[4] The Liberal press was chary about predictions, probably from fear of discouraging their supporters. But the *Review of Reviews* was as sanguine as any Radical could wish: Liberals 339; Labour 50; Nationalists 86; Unionists 189; – an anti-Unionist majority of 286, and an absolute Liberal majority of fourteen.[5] Thus the Radical rank and file, its chosen leader, and the party organisation all looked forward to an electoral triumph less overwhelming than 1906 but sufficient for the passage of the Budget and the attack on the Lords, and free from dependence on the Irish.

Equally confident were those Unionists whose spiritual home was Birmingham. Surrounded by evidence of the undoubted resurgence of Unionism in the Midlands, the family at Highbury was 'fully satis-fied that they [were] in for a great victory'. The master evidently expected a small but adequate Unionist majority.[6] The Whole Hogger *Globe*, one of the only two papers to produce a detailed forecast, held similar views, predicting a net gain of 175 seats and thus a narrow Unionist majority.[7] Expectations were high at Central Office. Despite occasionally disquieting reports from London and Lancashire the overall picture was promising. On 11 December 1909 Percival Hughes claimed most encouraging reports from all quarters.[8] With such reports continuing, the organisation's confidence grew in the New Year and on the eve of the polls Sandars was said to be sure of victory.[9] Garvin, who had access to Central Office figures, estimated on New Year's eve that 'making the results in Lancashire and the Cheshire fringe as bad as possible, the result ought to be one of the following: (a) Coalition 343; Unionist 327; (b) Unionist 357; Coalition 313'.[10]

But the Edwardian establishment – the moderate element in the Cabinet, the Balfourites, the Free Fooders, leading civil servants, The Times, and much of the press – expected that neither the Liberals nor the Unionists would secure an independent majority, and that once more the pivotal role would fall upon the Irish Nationalists. '. . . the most general opinion is that we shall be returned with a majority', wrote Lucy Masterman, 'but dependent on the Irish and Labour men.' Grey, Crewe and Haldane do not seem to have been very confident about the outcome, while Asquith had told the King in October that he expected the Irish to hold the balance.[11] Lansdowne and Curzon did not expect victory, probably sharing Milner's view that 'it would take two Parliaments to run [the anti-Unionist majority] out'.[12] The Free Fooders, who feared both victory and defeat, foresaw that the result would be to transfer the balance to the Home Rule party.[13] Independent observers confirmed the views of the centre politicians. Fitzroy, Clerk of the Privy Council, predicted an anti-Unionist majority between thirty and eighty. Esher agreed, believing the result would 'leave the Irish the controlling power'.[14]

In Fleet Street the Unionist press was far more apprehensive about the outcome than Highbury or St Stephen's Chambers. Garvin reported 'depression' at the Daily Telegraph and wild rumours of an increased Liberal majority at Printing House Square.[15] The most sophisticated forecast appeared in the Daily Mail on 13 January 1910, and supported the contention that neither side could gain a majority independent of the Irish. Using a swing calculation similar to that of the Nuffield electoral studies, the writer predicted an anti-Unionist majority of sixty-five in Great Britain, insufficient to render the Liberals, with Labour, independent of the Irish.

But the most substantial support for the establishment thesis came from The Times in fourteen exhaustive regional surveys and forecasts.[16] The series made miserable reading for Unionists, for although it held out some hope of reducing the Liberals to dependence on the Irish, it held out no hope whatever of a Unionist majority. Garvin was convinced that those who controlled The Times 'desire a Unionist disaster, in order to justify an attitude on the Budget to which they had not the courage to stick'.[17]

Not only can the sources of the conflicting estimates be identified but the geographical assumptions underlying them can be determined by an examination of the regional predictions of the two major forecasts, that of the Globe with its promise of Unionist victory, that of The

Times with its inescapable conclusion that the Unionists could not win.

Both papers predicted substantial Unionist gains in South-Eastern England, in the West Country, East Anglia, and the Midlands. Most Unionists shared these views; as did many Liberals, who were apprehensive about the 'rotten' southern counties; fearful of Unionist inroads in the West; and alarmed by the Unionist resurgence in Chamberlain's Duchy. As it was even the most exuberant forecast in the Unionist press underestimated the extent of the revulsion against the Liberals in the southern counties. Both forecasts, on the other hand, held out little hope for Unionist gains in Yorkshire and the North-East. Liberals were confident that their hold on these areas would not slacken, while it was widely conceded that there would be little change in Wales and Ireland.

But in three crucial areas – London, Lancashire and Scotland – there was a clear divergence in the predictions of the two papers. The Central Office seems to have shared with the *Globe* high expectations of London, although Hayes Fisher, in charge of the Unionist Metropolitan organisation, 'took the gloomish [*sic*] view of our prospects'.[18] Although worried, the Liberals hoped that Lloyd George would stem the reaction, limiting losses to a number of marginal middle-class seats.

Lancashire was the 'cockpit' and on the outcome there the papers differed sharply – the *Globe* predicting twenty-four Unionist gains, *The Times* about thirteen. In this they mirrored the division of opinion in Unionist ranks. Although Unionist organisers believed the situation there was improving,[19] Unionism was, as Garvin complained to Sandars, 'plagued into despondency by the stream of pessimism from Lancashire'. Garvin sought to nullify this pessimism by showing that 'the conditions there are peculiar and absolutely don't exist elsewhere; that the pendulum might fail to swing there without saving the Government from complete or sufficient disaster'.[20] Encouraged by the despondency of their opponents, heartened by Churchill's campaign and by good official reports, Liberals looked forward to the Lancashire results scotching all hope of a Unionist victory.

In Scotland the forecasts differed so markedly, and opinion was so solidly behind *The Times*, in its prediction, at best of, only eight Unionist gains,[21] that it is tempting to think that, as the Scottish article was the last in the *Globe* series, the eighteen gains predicted there were arbitrarily chosen so as to give the Unionists an absolute majority. But if isolated on this point, the *Globe* was not quite alone. Highbury too had high hopes of Scotland.[22]

The implication of *The Times*'s overall forecast is clear if unusual, and was stated in the introduction to the final article on 12 January:

There would seem to be a possibility of two distinct waves of popular feeling in the country, instead of one, as in 1906. Liberals in Lancashire believe that there is a storm rising in the North in their favour, a storm of indignation against the action of the Lords and in favour of Free Trade and the Budget. Shrewd observers in the Home Counties and the East and West foretell a storm in favour of the Unionists, directed by the winds of Tariff Reform and Unemployment.

If this were so, the North would offset the South and the Irish would hold the balance. But if the Liberals were justified in their confidence in industrial England and the Tories deluded about the rural and suburban South the Liberal Government would be returned entrenched and secure. If, on the other hand, the Unionists swept the Midlands and the South, and the North and Lancashire returned to a more traditional balance of forces, the Unionists would form the next Government.

II

On Saturday, 15 January, the voters of sixty-six English boroughs went to the polls in unprecedented numbers. At Lloyd's the Liberals were narrow favourites at 6:4 on, at the Stock Exchange the odds stood at evens.[23] The sixty-six constituencies polling were an excellent cross-section of the English boroughs. Once these results were to hand the general outcome in the remaining two hundred boroughs could be predicted with confidence.

Rain, intermittent in the afternoon in the South, but persistent throughout the day in Lancashire and the North, limited many of the customary polling-day tours of the constituency, and washed out final parades and demonstrations. But it did not deter the suffragettes from their efforts to compile a mammoth petition by collecting signatures at the polling booths. Nor did it prevent at the Hartlepools an 'intimidating' invasion of hired miners which was to cost the Liberal millionaire, Sir Christopher Furness, his seat.[24] And it did not prevent a hostile demonstration against Lloyd George at Grimsby, provoked by his breaking the custom that Cabinet Ministers should not speak in constituencies, other than their own, on polling day.[25] Above all, neither the rain, nor the Football Cup tie matches in London, deterred the voter. By the time the evening papers appeared, it was clear that the poll had been extraordinarily heavy. The average turnout for the day was in fact 88·9 per cent, dispelling fears that the long campaign may have induced apathy.

Excitement mounted as the hour for the first declarations approached. Great crowds gathered in the major cities from 8 p.m. onwards. In London, crowds poured into Trafalgar Square and packed the Strand and Fleet Street, bringing all traffic to a halt. At strategic points from Trafalgar Square to St Paul's huge screens had been erected on which the results could be flashed by lantern as soon as they came in.

The electoral efficiency of Manchester brought the first results through to London at 9.21: North Salford – Liberal, no change. At 9.27 came the first gain – a Liberal victory at North-West Manchester, the first of a number of by-election reversals. For a moment, many in the crowds must have sensed a second 1906. But not for long. In a three-cornered fight the Unionists won South-West Manchester, and soon afterwards came the swollen Unionist majorities at Birmingham, threatening Liberal losses throughout the Midlands. These came soon after at Wolverhampton and Wednesbury. Three hours later at 12.30 a.m. the final result – Bath reported a double Liberal loss. On the day's pollings the Unionists had captured eighteen seats and lost four, with an average swing in their favour of 4·4 per cent. These figures gave no hope of a Unionist majority, nor even the assurance that the Liberals would be reduced to dependence on the Nationalists.

The pattern of the results had soon been apparent. In Lancashire and Northern England the Liberal lines held; in the Midlands they were breached; in the South and West, outside London, they melted away. In the North the Liberals lost Stalybridge, and 'the meaningless folly of a split vote'[26] cost them two Lancashire seats, Burnley and South-West Manchester. But the Liberal Unionist Whip was turned out at Darlington by twenty-nine votes,[27] Sir George Doughty lost Grimsby by twenty-two votes, and the Liberals recovered North-West Manchester. The solidarity of the North cheered the anti-Unionists, and the only comfort the Unionists could find was the general decline in the Liberal majorities throughout Lancashire. Even this was denied them in Yorkshire, where Halifax, the only West Riding borough to poll, showed a swing against the Unionists.

But the bloated majorities in Birmingham symbolised the Unionist resurgence in the Midlands. 'The Radical attack on the great fortress of Tariff Reform has not merely been repulsed, but literally overwhelmed.'[28] Many Liberals attributed the disaster to 'Joe' rather than

to any political principle, and certainly his authority was being restored throughout the Black Country. Wednesbury, South Wolverhampton, West Wolverhampton were all recaptured on the first day,
although Amery failed for the third time at East Wolverhampton,
and the Liberals saved Dudley by a narrow margin.

In the South and the West the Unionist tide flowed even more
strongly. The cathedral towns of Salisbury and Gloucester were recaptured, and a heavy swing at Bath unseated both Liberals. In Cornwall
the Liberals lost the joint borough of Penryn and Falmouth, Liberal
since 1895, and in Kent, Rochester. At Reading, Rufus Isaacs scraped
home by 207 votes,[29] but the Liberals lost Cambridge. The loss of the
two seats at Devonport, and the near loss of the two at Plymouth,
were unwelcome news for Liberal candidates in naval towns still to
poll.

In London the situation was ambiguous. A mere three gains from
ten Liberal seats disappointed the Unionists. But the swing against
Liberalism in London on the first day was substantial, 6·3 per cent, and
luck seems as responsible as any other factor for limiting Liberal losses.
The four Islington constituencies were all held although the total
majority was only 1335, while Walworth was retained by 190 votes.

On 17, 18, 19 January the borough polls continued to dominate the
news, and nightly to attract crowds to the city centres. But the results
merely confirmed the pattern set on the first day. Turnout remained
exceptionally high, although it never again quite reached the heights
of the first day. The only new factor, the borough pollings in Scotland,
Ireland and Wales, merely endorsed the opinion of most commen-
tators that in these areas there would be little change.[30]

Massive pollings throughout Yorkshire on 17 January attested the
unbroken hold of Liberalism in the North. The political complexion
of every borough constituency in Yorkshire remained unaltered, the
Liberal and Labour parties retaining twenty seats to the Unionists'
five. The movement of opinion was slightly to the left, with small
swings to the Liberals and their allies in Bradford, Hull, Sheffield and
York. An unexpected double loss at Sunderland[31] and a further loss
arising from a triangular contest at Whitehaven, were the only Liberal
or Labour defeats in the far North, and these were offset by gains at
Stockton and Newcastle.

Apart from Liverpool, Sandars's 'green oasis in the desert of Lancashire',[32] where the Conservatives regained two seats, the constancy of
Lancashire delighted even the most optimistic Liberal. Wigan was

won by Labour, the Liberals gained a seat at Blackburn, and at Oldham the enormous Liberal majorities of 1906 were increased. The loss of two seats to the Conservatives at Preston, although disappointing, was not unexpected, and was attributed in part to the 'lamentable muddle of candidates which prevented a straight fight'.[33] North of a line running from Chester to Grimsby, the Liberal high-water mark of 1906 remained almost undiminished.

To the south the picture was wholly different. Birmingham continued to regain its influence, Walsall and West Bromwich falling to the Unionists on 17 January and Coventry, Kidderminster, and Warwick and Leamington on the following day. The contagion was limited to the West Midlands, for, with the notable exception of Nottingham where two seats were lost, the Liberal position remained practically unchanged in the cities of the East Midlands. In the South and West few Liberals survived the wreck. Liberal and Labour Members were ejected from the dockyard towns of Portsmouth and Chatham. In the West, Cheltenham and Exeter were lost; in the South-East, Bedford, Colchester, Christchurch and Brighton.

In London the Liberals continued to limit their losses to seats solidly Unionist before 1906,[34] managed to recover two by-election losses, and more surprisingly won Hoxton held by the Unionists in 1906. By the end of polling in London the Unionists had a net gain of eleven seats, below even the most modest of their expectations.

On 19 January the first of the counties went to the polls, and although a few boroughs had still to vote, interest rapidly shifted to the one great unanswered question – how would the English counties vote? On the answer to this question depended, not the return of the Liberal Government, for this had been virtually assured by the borough polls to date, but the independence of that Government. To have had any chance of a majority the Unionists would have had to capture about one in two of the Liberal borough seats; instead they had won only one in four. If the first Unionist objective was then unattainable, what of the second, the reduction of the Liberal Government to dependence on the Irish? In the first three days, with most of the borough polls completed, the Unionists had won forty-one seats from the Liberals. Could they secure from the English county pollings the further forty-four seats needed to deny the Liberals, with Labour, an absolute majority?

The Liberals thought not. For one thing they had fewer English county seats than boroughs to lose, so that even if the Unionists maintained a similar ratio of gains they would not get the necessary number of seats. Indeed, both the *Daily Chronicle* and the *Westminster Gazette* expected the Liberals to lose proportionately fewer seats in the counties than in the boroughs.[35] Despite warnings, the Liberal organisation remained confident that the counties would ensure their return with the desired, albeit reduced majority.[36]

'The results in the counties were often very different from the towns. . . . Such may be the case on this occasion.' This sibylline utterance of the *Morning Post* well-captured the uncertainty amongst Unionists on the morning of the first county polls. At the Central Office Hughes was confident, believing that the good borough results on Tuesday, 18 January, would 'have produced a favourable impression upon the Counties'. But Sandars was despondent: 'Gales, our county expert, attributes much more danger to the pensions lie than to the food question in the county districts and doubtless the use that is now being made of Lansdowne's unfortunate letter does not make our task easier in counteracting the lying accusations.'[37] On the other hand, the *Daily Telegraph* was optimistic since 'up to the present, Unionists have not lost a single urban constituency in an agricultural district . . . we have made gains all over the country in the old market towns, which are usually a sure guide to the state of feelings in the counties about them'. Whether they accepted this thesis or not, few would dispute the validity of the paper's claim that 'upon the verdict of the agricultural shires the whole character of the next Parliament will depend'.[38]

Forty-eight county constituencies polled on 19 January, but because of the scattered polling stations in most of them, the count did not take place until the 20th. On that day hopes of a Liberal and Labour majority independent of the Irish vanished. From all parts of the country came news of Liberal losses and enhanced Unionist majorities, but the reaction struck the Home Counties with greatest force. At Tonbridge a Liberal majority of 1283 became a Conservative majority of 3210, at Kingston a safe Conservative seat, the 1906 majority was increased by over 4000 votes, and the shift to Unionism occurred on a lesser but still impressive scale throughout rural England. Amid signs of panic the *Daily Chronicle* pressed Liberals to 're-double their efforts to arrest a Tory reaction in the rural districts'.[39]

But the reaction was not to be halted. On 19 January the Liberals lost thirteen out of thirty-two county seats; on 20 January eleven out of twenty-eight; on 21 January nineteen out of forty-five, although on that day they had their first county gains. 24 January was proportionately the worst day of the election for the Liberals, with nine out of seventeen seats lost. Only in Scotland, Wales and the industrial North was there resistance to the sweeping Unionist revival. The Liberal position was bleakest in the Home Counties, and outside London Liberal representation virtually disappeared from South-East England.[40] But the 'rot in the counties' was considerable elsewhere, substantial losses occurring in East Anglia, the Midlands and the West Country.

TABLE 7.2 RESULTS JAN 1910

	Unionist	Liberal	Labour	Nationalist	Others	
Seats at dissolution	168	373	45	83	1*	
						Losses
Won from Unionists		21	1			22
Won from Liberals	120		2			122
Won from Labour	6	2				8
Won from Nationalists	1					1
Won from Others		1				1
Gains	127	24	3			154
Net gain or loss	+105	−98	−5	−1	−1	
1910 Parliament	273	275†	40	82‡	0	

Notes: * Victor Grayson, independent Socialist (Colne Valley).
† Includes Cameron Corbett (Glasgow Tradeston) elected as an independent Liberal against official Liberal opposition.
‡ Includes 11 independent Nationalists, mostly followers of William O'Brien and T. M. Healy.

The Liberals were depressed. Carrington found it 'a sad and disastrous week' and apparently could not bring himself to go to church.[41] Chastened Liberals comforted themselves with the notion that the anti-Unionist majority was better than 1892, and with the hope that such a majority would prove united and irresistible. Unionist jubilation was unrestrained. 'All through the eastern, the southern, and the western counties they have been smitten hip and thigh, and the field is strewn with their stricken soldiery', with the result that Liberalism would once more 'stew in the Parnellite juice'.[42] The *Observer* on 23 January anticipated the propaganda themes of the next electoral contest.

The absolute majority is smashed, pulverised, annihilated . . . Mr. Asquith and his Government must exist in subjection to Mr. Redmond ['the Irish dictator'] or they cannot exist at all. Is the Second Chamber to be destroyed by the Irish

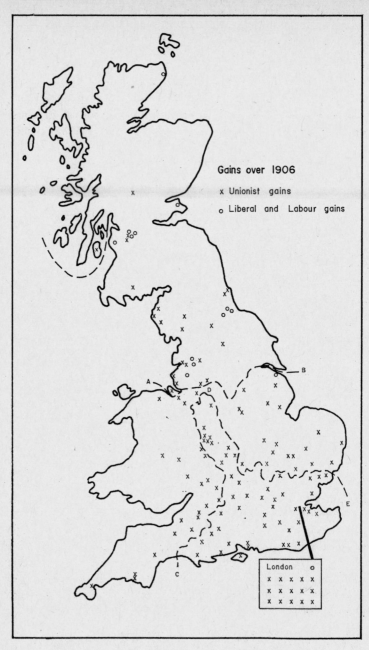

Gains over 1906

x Unionist gains

o Liberal and Labour gains

London

Map 7.1   DISTRIBUTION OF PARTY GAINS JAN 1910

Vote [and are] . . . free imports to be forced upon the neck of British Labour
by the money that has been raised in the Protectionist United States?

But for the Liberals the worst was now over, and interest in the
remaining polls subsided except for the question of which single party
would be the largest in the new House of Commons. This was resolved
in the Liberals' favour on 31 January with their capture of the Wick
Burghs, Unionist for nearly twenty years. The final polls gave both
sides a chance to sober up after the unsettling effects of the early county
polls. They enabled the Liberals to realise that, whatever their disappointment, they did possess a governmental majority of sorts, and
the Unionists to realise that whatever their success, they were still
His Majesty's Opposition. (See Map 7.1.)

III

'Our Victory – tho' substantial – is clearly Wagram not Austerlitz',
wrote a subdued Churchill, when the extent of the Liberal losses was
apparent.[43] But even this modest assessment seemed inappropriate, for
many Unionists seemed not to appreciate they had been beaten. Right
across the spectrum of opinion in the Unionist camp there was satisfaction with the results. Although saddened by the electoral failure
of their candidates, the Free Fooders welcomed the results as emasculating their enemies in both parties. 'The teeth and claws of the
Radical and Socialist tiger have been cut very effectually while at the
same time tariff reform cannot be carried in the present Parliament',
wrote Strachey.[44] The Whole Hoggers saw the victories of the party as
Tariff Reform victories. 'Where we won, we won on and by Tariff
Reform.'[45] All that was needed was one more push with 'a far more
definite and bolder policy of Tariff Reform' and the 'motley majority'
would crumble.[46] For the Balfourites the late-nineteenth-century
issues and the late-nineteenth-century situation had returned. Ireland
was the issue on which Balfour had established his political reputation;
he preferred arguing against Home Rule to arguing for fiscal change,
and the threat of Home Rule offered him an opportunity to reunite the
party.

Paradoxically while the defeated were undiscouraged, the victors
were depressed. Grey concluded that 'the moral of the election is that
neither party had succeeded in gaining the confidence of the country'.[47]
Many Liberals, unhappy about their losses, were frankly appalled by
the prospect before them. History gave them scant comfort. The

disaster of 1886 and the experiences of 1892-5 were hardly encouraging precedents for a Liberal Government dependent on Irish votes. Surrounded by Liberal gloom, Lloyd George was moved to protest. 'I don't know what possesses people to go about talking as if we were beaten. We've won this election. The other side are just frightening us into it.'[48] But even Lloyd George was all too aware of the limitations of this electoral Wagram.

These paradoxical reactions stemmed from the Government's loss of independence. Not that anyone worried much about the Government's relations with Labour, except in so far as they provided grist for Unionist propaganda. Labour's confidence in its own dynamism had been rudely shaken by the results, and what comfort it could draw from the retention of most of its seats in a strong swing to the right, was offset by its utter discomfiture in attack. Moreover its financial troubles made it virtually a sleeping-partner in the alliance. Although helping to stiffen the Radical wing of the Liberal Party, Labour was unlikely to pursue a strongly independent line.

The trouble was the Irish. First, their commanding position rendered dubious Liberal claims for a mandate on licensing, education and the Budget. None of these measures had been favoured with Irish support and their prospects in the new Parliament were uncertain. Moreover the more ingenious of the Whole Hoggers were even able to challenge the mandate for Free Trade by picturing the Irish as 'natural protectionists'.[49]

These were mostly debating-points, although they contributed to the confused post-electoral atmosphere. More seriously, the pivotal position of the Irish imperilled the Budget, and the situation was likely to be exacerbated once Redmond discovered that the Cabinet was weaker *vis-à-vis* the King than he suspected. There was no guarantee that the Budget could pass the new House of Commons let alone the House of Lords. Moreover Redmond's exposed flank in Ireland made manœuvres at Westminster difficult. Tactical errors over the Budget would be seized upon by O'Brien and Healy to serve their own domestic ends. Redmond had a great opportunity, but if he failed, the forces of disruption would be let loose in Ireland.

Most important of all, the Unionists argued that the composite majority, dependent on the anti-English 'Molly Maguires', gave the Liberals no authority to transform the constitution. On 23 January 1910 Garvin warned in the *Observer* against 'the grotesque iniquity of permanently devitalising the Second Chamber . . . by the aid of the

Irish votes given . . . without the least regard to the future interests of the United Kingdom as a whole'.

It is probable that the Unionist attempt to impugn the Liberal mandate could have been dismissed as merely the windy rhetoric of defeated politicians but for two crucial factors. First, the King's hand, revealed to Asquith six weeks before, had been immeasurably strengthened by those very features of the result stressed by the Unionists. Secondly, many moderate Liberals inclined to agree with the Unionist interpretation, seeing the electoral verdict as a brake on drastic changes.

The election results had been received with satisfaction by the Court. Writing to Balfour from Windsor, Esher reported: 'The recent elections have caused great relief here. . . . There can be no question, with this lowered majority, dependent upon the Irish, of Asquith trying to "bully" the King.'[50] This belief that the King could not now be 'bullied' into creating peers explained much of the Unionist confidence. As early as 23 January, Lansdowne was sure that the King 'will be in a position to snuff out peremptorily any demands for guarantees against the interference of the House of Lords. Even if we don't win another seat, enough has happened to justify our action.'[51] Without the consent of the King, the power of the House of Lords could not be broken, and at least one more election stood between the Unionists and the destruction of their entrenched constitutional position.

Strengthened by assurances from Balfour, conveyed through Esher, the King was 'quite clear that he will not assent to any request to make Peers'.[52] The King told Haldane on 3 February that he 'could not possibly consider the creation of peers without a much more definite expression of opinion from the country'.[53] Not that the King needed to worry. Despite the clamour of the Radical press, the Albert Hall policy was in ruins. It is possible that if the Liberals had retained an absolute majority, pressure on the King might have been renewed, but now there was no danger.

Indeed moderation not aggression was the keynote in influential Liberal circles. Spender feared that 'We shall go smash' unless the Radicals realised the difference between the old and the new majority.[54] Spender's paper, the *Westminster Gazette*, welcomed a proposal by *The Times* for a 'Round Table Conference between the leaders, and a policy of compromise upon some subjects, and abstention from others'.[55] In the Cabinet pressure for moderate Second Chamber reform rather than the suspensory veto gathered momentum.

It is not surprising that in this confused situation, with the Unionists defeated but convinced of the immediate frustration of their opponents, and the Liberals victorious but apparently unable to utilise their victory, the most common reaction of all to the election results was the expectation of a second election. Balfour spoke of 'the fight now going on . . . [as] but the first of a series of actions',[56] and the *Morning Post* of the struggle as 'only the first phase of a stern and prolonged contest . . . It seems to be . . . agreed that a second battle will take place before very long.'[57] Privately some Ministers concurred. 'Everything seems to point to an inevitable second Election this summer', Harcourt wrote Asquith when the worst of the county returns were in.[58] Opinions might vary as to when the election would occur, and as to its occasion – a rupture in the anti-Unionist alliance, a rejection of a further Liberal measure by the Lords, a clash with the King – but many believed it would come before the year was out. Only the Liberal rank and file did not share this conviction. But they were living in error, for they assumed that as the Government had retained office it possessed the guarantees from the King.

1910 was then not just a year in which two elections took place, but a year in which the possibility of the second election was omnipresent. In one sense the crowded politics of 1910 were simply the preparation of all parties for an inevitable second election.

The Months Between

I

In the early months of 1910 the demands of government and the electoral interests of the Liberal Party coincided. It was imperative that the Budget be passed into law as soon as possible. It was equally imperative that the Cabinet reach an agreed policy on the House of Lords. These were governmental necessities. They were also electoral necessities, for the Liberals could hardly face a second election with the Budget unpassed and policy on the House of Lords still undefined.

The Opposition were under no such immediate pressure to produce results. If the Government fell or split asunder as appeared possible, at least half the battle would be over. Furthermore they had a new propaganda asset in the 'Irish dictator' cry. Yet these advantages were to become excuses for inaction. The refurbishing of policy on the constitutional question, on the fiscal issue, on social reform, on Home Rule, all demanded by segments of the party, aroused antagonism in other quarters. Moreover, the split on most of these subjects tended to coincide, reviving the conflict between Balfourites and Whole Hoggers. It is understandable, therefore, that the Unionist leadership, hoping that events might render drastic changes unnecessary, hung back from policy revision.

The passage of the Budget depended on the attitude of the Irish in the Commons, and of the Tory majority in the Lords. For the Peers there was no alternative to accepting the Budget as their leaders had quickly realised. Whatever attitude Unionists might adopt in the Commons, and on this counsels were divided, it was clear that if the Budget passed the Commons the Lords could not possibly reject it a second time. 'As to the 1909 Budget,' Lansdowne informed Austen Chamberlain on the last day of January, 'if the new House of Commons sends that up to us, I would pass it even if it has been modified by the omission of the whisky tax.'[1]

Moreover the Unionists might well make a virtue of necessity. A declaration that the Lords would accept the verdict of the people on the Budget could be used to strengthen the Upper Chamber in the battle to preserve its prerogatives. Balfour had already taken action. Publicly he had interpreted the verdict as a decision on the Budget but not on Tariff Reform, Home Rule or the House of Lords.[2] Privately he authorised Sandars to develop his contacts with Sir Francis Hopwood, Permanent Under-Secretary at the Colonial Office, who appears to have acted as an intermediary between the right wing of the Cabinet and the Unionist leadership.[3] Sandars reported that Hopwood had told him that 'members of the Cabinet, with whom he was in contact, had grave doubts as to whether the Lords would, after such an encouraging answer as they had received from the constituencies', pass the Budget. Sandars, however, assured Hopwood that if the Budget survived the Commons the Lords would certainly pass it.[4] Whatever light this transaction throws on the state or morale among some of the Liberal Ministers, it is clear that by giving this assurance Balfour hoped to strengthen the moderate forces within the Cabinet, a group in which many of the Unionists placed high hopes.

But the acquiescence of the Lords would not solve the Liberals' problems in the Lower House. Although some Unionists favoured capitulation in the Commons, the leadership did not. In response to an enquiry from the King, Balfour made it clear that 'it would be vain to ask the Unionist Party on tactical grounds to vote black where they had before voted white'.[5] This left the fate of the Budget in the hands of the Irish.

The Nationalists wanted two things from the Budget: they desired particular concessions, especially on the whisky duty; and they wished to use the Budget as a bargaining-counter to compel the Government to adopt a strong anti-Lords policy. No doubt Redmond hoped to secure both, but there should never have been any doubt about his priorities.

It is possible that when Redmond threatened 'No Veto, No Budget' he was bluffing. Although at times he saw little to choose between the two major parties, and voiced hopes that the Unionists might yet barter the Union in exchange for Tariff Reform,[6] to overthrow the Liberal Government would have been a desperate resort. Yet the exigencies of the Irish situation – the unpopularity of the Budget and the revolt of the O'Brienites – compelled Redmond to take an intransigent line at Westminster.

If Redmond was not bluffing, concessions on the Budget but no strong veto policy would be of little use. At best they would only postpone the crisis. 'Don't make the mistake of thinking R's attitude is due to the Budget,' T. P. O'Connor warned Elibank, the new Liberal Chief Whip, in March. 'Redmond has to pick his steps very warily owing to the feverish excitement in Ireland – not on the Budget – but on what they consider the bold tactic R. has advised ... they cling to the idea that No Veto, no Budget, is the true, the courageous, the only policy.'[7] On the other hand, if Redmond could secure in exchange for Irish support on the Budget a limit on the veto of the House of Lords that would effectively pave the way for Home Rule, then the whisky question would be of little consequence.

One other consideration is relevant. When Redmond demanded Budget amendments he was the spokesman for a fairly limited sectional interest. When he opposed reform of the House of Lords, urged the settlement of the constitutional grievance before supply, and insisted on guarantees, he spoke at least for the whole left wing of the anti-Unionist front. As he admitted when a strong pledge on contingent guarantees was finally given in April: 'You fellows have done us. . . . If we vote you out now it is on whisky, where we shall get no sympathy from the priests or the British Radicals.'[8]

In the early weeks of the new Parliament the Cabinet glimpsed only intermittently and hazily Redmond's strength and weakness. 'Anti-Irish prejudice' and oversensitivity to any suggestion of surrender to the Irish 'obliterated all the bald necessities of the situation'.[9] Moreover while the Cabinet itself could not reach agreement on constitutional policy, it was impossible for it to respond to Redmond's demands. Instead, efforts were made by the more opportunist of the Ministers to seek a solution with Redmond through Budget bribes. These approaches were initiated sometimes with, sometimes without, Cabinet approval, but always the more fastidious of the Ministers baulked at their implementation. Anyhow, it is unlikely that such concessions would have satisfied Redmond. The various approaches merely exacerbated relations by encouraging Redmond to believe he could get Budget concessions as well as his veto policy.

Government equivocation ended with the reassertion of collective common sense at the Cabinet meeting of 13 April, when the Cabinet rejected any notion of amending the Budget on the grounds that 'to purchase the Irish vote by such a concession would be a discreditable transaction'.[10] Having preserved its integrity, the Cabinet proceeded to satisfy the Irish, the Labour Party, and most of its own supporters by adopting the guarantees policy outlined by Asquith in his momentous statement to the Commons on 14 April.[11] The Budget then passed the Commons with Irish support on 27 April, was accepted by the Lords on 28 April, and was given the royal assent the following day, exactly one year after its introduction.

Thus on one of the great issues of the first campaign the election was ultimately decisive. There were only echoes of the controversy in the second campaign. The Unionist organisation set itself firmly against attempts to commit the party to repeal the land taxes. '. . . in Lancashire and Yorkshire our friends recognise that the repeal policy . . . is very detrimental. It keeps alive the political prejudice against landowners and it saddles the party with the same burdens which they bore with such difficulty at the General Election last January.'[12] Moreover, as the Chief Whip warned Sandars, 'If we go in for repeal of the Land Taxes, we shall have the Licensing Trade clamouring for repeal of the Licensing Duties'.[13] In the second election Unionists contented themselves with temperate pleas for further relief for agricultural land and the building trade, and for allocating revenue from the urban land taxes to the municipalities.

But vacillations over the Budget left a more significant electoral legacy – the charge that Ministers had bought the Irish vote for the Budget by betraying the constitution. Governmental dithering in early 1910 gave weight to this charge. Having first allowed Redmond to usurp the leadership of the Radicals, the Cabinet had then moved gingerly towards him. Each step in this movement could easily be presented as a further cowardly surrender to the Irish, when each was rather a recognition of the demands of the Ministry's own supporters. As Spender noted, 'the appearance of bargaining with the Irish brought much discredit'.[14] In 1909 Liberal quarrels had helped to forge the greatest bogey of the first election – the naval scare. In early 1910 the Ministers gave substance to the chief weapon to be used against them in December – the cry that they were the puppets of the Irish.

But if the January election had ultimately been decisive on the Budget, it was decisive on little else. On the constitutional issue, the suspensory veto solution was jeopardised by renewed pressure for reform of the composition of the Lords. Those members of the Cabinet who had been but reluctant converts to the Campbell-Bannerman scheme, and whose scope for manœuvre had been restricted by the Budget crisis, now seized their opportunity. The nucleus of this group – Grey, Haldane, Crewe, and Runciman – believed that the ambiguous election result would compel the party to discard the veto policy, and adopt a scheme of Second Chamber reform.[15] Outside the Cabinet they received the powerful and vocal support of Spender, who believed that 'Liberal members having said (1) that a Second Chamber is necessary and (2) that the Hereditary principle is obsolete and absurd can scarcely propose the Peers in fetters as the final solution'.[16]

In a memorandum to Asquith which is the most persuasive of all the statements for the reform solution, Grey argued that 'it is the constitution of the House of Lords, and not its powers, which is an anomaly'.[17] But Grey was more interested in the immediate tactical situation than in restating his general policy position. Nothing illustrates better than this memorandum that the politics of 1910 were the politics of electoral preparation. Grey assumed the inevitability of any early election, and used it as his most telling argument for rejecting the suspensory veto scheme. 'I do not believe we can win with the so-called C.B. plan . . . It is open to the charge of being in effect a Single Chamber plan, and from a Single Chamber, I believe the country would recoil.' The electoral theme recurred throughout the memorandum: 'We should eventually appeal to the country upon [the policy of an elected Second Chamber] . . . the Opposition would have to fight as the defenders of privilege and hereditary right against the principle of election. We must in any case stake everything upon the next appeal to the country. . . .'

The reformists had in the past been in a minority in the Cabinet. Now they were strengthened by the erosion of the vetoists under the impact of the election results. Most notable among waverers in the veto wing were Churchill and Lloyd George. In addition Asquith's indecision contributed to the resurgence of reform.

Both on the eve of his departure for France early in February and on the Riviera, Churchill had discussed reform solutions. Soon after his return he told Masterman that 'We cannot defend intellectually our position on the Veto',[18] and he developed his ideas in a memorandum sent to Asquith. He did not abandon the suspensory veto completely, but coupled a version of it with drastic composition reform proposals, and it was this latter aspect that was uppermost in the memorandum. As with Grey electoral considerations were prominent.

> The C.B. Plan . . . is not sufficiently based on principle for a pitched battle on it alone. If we are to aim at winning another general election in July against the Lords, we must not deprive ourselves of the right to develop the full argument against the principle of hereditary legislators.[19]

Churchill and Grey were not alone in pressing such advice on Asquith. On 3 February Samuel, the newest recruit to the Cabinet and formerly a staunch supporter of the 'C.B. Plan', wrote to Asquith to urge a reform policy which, provided the Labour and Irish would agree, would put the Liberals 'in a much stronger position in an election than if we adhered to the C.B. plan'.[20]

The shift in the Cabinet was encouraged by the equivocation of Lloyd George. Lloyd George probably found reform attractive because it offered the possibility of a compromise between the major parties, and thus an escape from a protracted constitutional struggle. Six months later he was to try and circumvent such a struggle by promoting a coalition government. He returned from France in early February reportedly 'very bitten with the reform idea'. Yet no figure in the Cabinet was more tied, emotionally and politically, to the Radical wing of the party, and he was therefore acutely aware of its distrust of reform projects. In such cross-currents he seems temporarily to have lost all sense of direction. 'I have no vision . . . I cannot see what we are to do.' For once Lloyd George merely acquiesced in a policy of drift.[21]

The Prime Minister was the other key factor in the situation. Exhausted by the election and by personal worries[22] he set off for Cannes at the end of January and returned on 8 February still apparently with 'no ideas and no plan of any kind'.[23] Asquith might have stemmed the drift away from the veto plan, for he was later to prove both far-sighted and resolute, but for the moment he appears to have been at a complete loss. Confronted by the shift in the Cabinet, concerned over the general interpretation of the Albert Hall pledge, and with the composite majority palpably divided on the Budget, he seems to have lacked both grasp and nerve. As a result the Cabinet was allowed to drift towards that 'compromise between the Vetoists and the Reformists' embodied in the King's Speech, which was to outrage his followers and anger his allies.[24]

Within the Cabinet Harcourt alone was vocal in trying to prevent the drift. On 7 February he protested to Asquith: 'There is a deal of loose thinking *inside*, as well as outside, the Cabinet just now. We must stick tight to principles and not go a-whoring after false constitutions.'[25] But although Harcourt might speak for the party in the Commons and the country, within the Cabinet Ministers were actively pursuing the harlot. In early February the suspensory veto plan, ostensibly party policy on the House of Lords question, seemed in danger of being discarded in favour of some reform scheme, never sanctioned by the party, and actively advocated during the election by Grey alone.

But the great weakness of the reformist position, indeed of the Cabinet's position, was that while over-conscious of the electoral verdict as a vote for moderation, they overlooked or minimised the fact that the power structure in the Commons militated against any moderate compromise. Treating the Tory electoral recovery as an admonition against extreme courses, the reformists too easily neglected the fact that this very recovery rendered the Government dependent on groups determined, at the least, to limit the veto of the Lords. If pressed, many of the reformists might have preferred to remake the constitution with the Tories, rather than with their Radical wing and their Labour and Irish allies. That they might soon be faced with such a choice was apparent at the opening of the Parliament.

Asquith's icy disavowal of the near-universal interpretation of his Albert Hall pledge angered the Radicals, the Irish and Labour. They were alarmed by the suggestion of reform proposals in the King's Speech, and amazed by ministerial intentions to settle finance before taking up the constitutional question. On the floor of the House Redmond seized his chance to become the spokesman of the discontented, and in the lobbies his aide T. P. O'Connor stirred up the militants in all the anti-Unionist parties. For a few days 'the position was intolerable' and the Ministry seriously contemplated resignation.[26]

The clamour of this Radical–Labour–Irish alliance crystallised into three demands. On the procedural question, the alliance insisted that there be no settlement of outstanding financial business until the Commons had pronounced on a policy towards the House of Lords. By the old device of grievance before supply the rebels could insure themselves against their avowed enemies, the Tories, and against their suspected enemies, the Whiggish element in the Cabinet. On the substantive issue they wanted the Campbell-Bannerman plan and would have no truck with reform. Finally they wanted definite guarantees from the King to ensure that the veto legislation would become law.

After a week of utter depression the Ministry rallied. Contact with the Commons had ultimately a bracing effect. The threat of a serious revolt shocked some of the Ministers into their senses. Asquith began to recover his grip while some of his more opportunistic colleagues, who had clutched at reform as metaphorically the way out, now realised that it was literally the way out. The trend in the Cabinet towards a reform scheme was halted, then reversed.

The Ministry found it relatively easy to accede to the procedural demands of the rebels. On 28 February it was announced that a series of veto resolutions would be given priority over the Budget. The toughening fibre of the Cabinet was shown a fortnight later, when Lloyd George secured a vote on account for only five or six weeks instead of the customary five or six months. Grievance before supply was being practised with all the enthusiasm of the newly converted.

In the Cabinet, however, vetoists and reformists remained sharply divided. If the Ministry opted for reform the anti-Unionist front would disintegrate; if the Ministry opted for the suspensory veto the Cabinet seemed likely to split, and the front, if it survived, would be gravely weakened. In the circumstances Asquith opted for a masterly shuffle whereby the Cabinet was inched towards the adoption of the Campbell-Bannerman plan, without ever definitely abandoning reform – thereby preserving both the Cabinet and the anti-Unionist front.

His chief instrument in this manœuvre was his close friend, Haldane, himself a reformist, but also a master of ingenious compromises. He seems to have been the key figure in securing Cabinet agreement on establishing the priority of the suspensory veto, but primarily as the means whereby reform could subsequently be carried through.[27] His task was eased by the fact that, perhaps as a means of keeping everyone happy, Ministers were allowed to stress either veto or reform in their public speeches provided they paid lip service to the Haldane compromise.

By the middle of March three resolutions closely modelled on the Campbell-Bannerman plan had been approved by the Cabinet, although reform was apparently still vaguely endorsed as the ultimate objective. These resolutions provided that the Lords could neither reject nor amend a money bill; that the Lords could only delay other bills, which would become law without the Lords' assent if passed in three successive sessions by the Commons, provided that two years had elapsed between a bill's introduction and its final approval by the Commons; and finally that the maximum duration of a Parliament should be reduced from seven years to five. At this stage Grey and his allies baulked, realising that the vetoists were getting the substance, the reformists merely the shadow.[28] Once again a rupture was avoided by the resourceful Haldane, who devised a preamble for the Parliament Bill, which, with its promise of reform 'hereafter', apparently dispelled the qualms of the reformists.[29]

By this point – the beginning of April – pressure was growing for a decision on the other critical question, the contingent guarantees. Morley was the most vociferous opponent, behaving over a potential creation of peers as 'an orthodox Christian might if it were proposed to add a fourth person to the Trinity'.[30] Unfortunately the demand for contingent guarantees got mixed up with the current demand for Budget concessions to the Irish. Often both demands were pushed by the same Ministers, particularly Lloyd George and Churchill, and the distinctive opposition to each proposal tended to coalesce.

The crucial Cabinet of 13 April reached agreement by disentangling the two questions. First it refused to sanction any change whatever in the Budget. Having done this the Ministers seem to have found it relatively easy to agree to request contingent guarantees before a further election. Morley alone demurred but did not resign.[31] Asquith's tactics had paid off. The Cabinet and the anti-Unionist front had been preserved. The period of uncertainty was now over and the Cabinet began to prepare for a midsummer election.

One further subject demanded Cabinet attention before the dissolution – the attitude to be taken towards the Labour Party's insistent demand that the Osborne Judgement be reversed. Since the midsummer election was abandoned on the death of the King on 6 May, the subject was not seriously broached until the autumn. The Ministers then agreed that early steps should be taken to implement payment of Members and of official election expenses.

But beyond this some were unwilling to go. Robson, the Attorney-General, who reflected the attitude of the embattled North-Eastern Liberals, where the struggle with Labour was most acute, believed that 'the Liberal party will be driven to more open and direct battle with the Socialists in the constituencies'. He argued, therefore, for recognising 'the inevitable at once' rather than trying 'to stave it off for yet a little longer until the Socialist organisation, by our own assistance, have got command of this enormous war chest'. Nor would taking a strong stand against reversal injure the Liberals electorally, for when he had done so in January, he had 'received the united and enthusiastic support of the Trade Unionists of [South Shields] in that action'.[32]

The Cabinet, however, did not share Robson's assessment of the danger, and anyhow had no desire to provoke electoral troubles at this time. On the other hand they were not prepared to meet Labour's demand for an absolute and complete reversal of the Judgement. After considerable debate in Cabinet, a decision was belatedly arrived at on the eve of the second election, which, while restoring to the trade unionists their power to provide funds for political purposes, guaranteed the liberties of individual trade unionists by provisions for contracting out. This with the promise of payment of Members and of election expenses, was to be the substance of most Liberal declarations on the issue during the election. The Labour leadership was unhappy with the Government proposal but was unwilling to quarrel with the Liberals on the eve of the election.[33] The Liberals at least promised substantial revision. The Unionists were not only adamant against reversal, they also refused to commit themselves to payment of Members.

Thus after a hesitant beginning the Liberals had spent the year settling their major problems. This was much more than could be said for the Unionists, who, having failed to clarify their political stance on a number of key questions during the year, spent most of the election campaign trying to do so.

II

Untrammelled by office, the Unionists spent the months between the two elections in a rather casual attempt to refurbish their policies. Their first concern was what to do with the House of Lords. Those, noted Lansdowne, who treat the verdict as 'a vote of confidence' in the Lords 'urge us to sit tight'; those 'alarmed at the violence of the attack' urge us 'to set our house in order without an instant's delay'.[34] The old guard considered themselves vindicated, but moderates, Whole Hoggers, and the more far-sighted in the party desired reform either to assist an all-party compromise or to secure better ground on which to fight the next election. Writing to recommend an elective element in the Upper House, Curzon thought it necessary to construct a reform plan that 'will be an alternative when [the Liberals] go to the country on the Question of the Veto: or that would equally be the end at which we should aim in any Conference Committee or Royal Commission should such come about'.[35] Harcourt Kitchin, editor of the *Glasgow Herald*, who had urged a reform declaration during the election, 'made it quite plain to Lord Lansdowne that a General Election in Scotland and the north of England is perfectly useless . . . unless there is a really genuine project of reform before the country'.[36]

Electoral considerations were certainly uppermost in the minds of the Tariff Reformers. While their own schemes were currently under attack as electoral embarrassments, the Whole Hoggers were themselves convinced that their fiscal faith had been rejected not on its merits but because it had been shackled to unpopular causes. From a Scottish Unionist the Chamberlains learnt that 'there are more Tariff Reformers in Scotland today . . . but the trouble is that they voted on the Budget and on the House of Lords, and *not* on Tariff Reform'.[37] How to win the North was clearly the preoccupation of the writer of an article in the *Morning Post* urging drastic Second Chamber reform:

> No Unionist can contemplate with equanimity another election fought by the Unionists purely on the issue of upholding the power of the House of Lords as it at present exists. Defeat would be certain . . . great sections of the working class of Scotland and Northern England . . . simply get out of hand when you try to persuade them that the House of Lords is [a] strong, competent, disinterested and impartial body.[38]

To win these votes for fiscal change, the Whole Hoggers were prepared for major surgery on the House of Lords.

But Balfour and Lansdowne were most reluctant surgeons. Both Tory leaders were opposed in principle to the sweeping and varied reform schemes being pressed upon them from Highbury, Hatfield, Hackwood,[39] from less exalted residences, and from the editorial offices of the Tory press. They had neglected reform in the past, had put it aside during the election, and in the early months of 1910 their role was mostly obstructive.

They were, however, prepared for some concessions to strengthen the hands of the reformists in the Cabinet, with whom they were in touch through the ubiquitous Sir Francis Hopwood. Hopwood was particularly persistent in pressing for a reform declaration from the Unionists, and Sandars believed that he was the agent of those in the Cabinet 'who are most anxious to find some *modus* out of a difficulty which may be created by extravagant demands upon the King for assurances'.[40] But Lansdowne at least seems to have thought that a readiness to 'bless [reform] in principle' would be sufficient.[41] Both Balfour and Lansdowne were certainly adamant against the promulgation at this stage of a definitive reform scheme. 'I am terrified,' wrote Lansdowne to Balfour on 31 January, 'at the idea of reconstructing a part of the constitution during the next few days, and giving the result of our deliberations "forthwith" . . . to the public.'[42] They both recognised that they might 'in the end, have to harden our hearts and go a good deal further than you or I would probably like to go'.[43] In the meantime, they parried the desire for the publication of a reform scheme with a host of tactical objections. Such a course 'a little savours of panic'; would annoy many of 'our most steady-going friends'; and might well 'result in a violent cleavage of opinion within our own ranks'.[44]

If the Unionist leaders were at best lukewarm, some of the peers were frankly hostile. The aged yet formidable Lord Halsbury, thrice Lord Chancellor, was against any tinkering with the Lords whatsoever. 'It was impossible to make an institution more practically useful for its purpose than the present House.'[45] The distinguished Anglo-Catholic Lord Halifax, whose quaint reform proposals included inter alia the exclusion of all bishops holding sees created since the accession of Henry VIII, warned Sandars that 'the House of Lords is in more danger from its friends than its foes'.[46] The backwoodsmen, in general, could not be expected to view with favour schemes which, however diverse, usually had one feature in common: the expulsion of the backwoodsmen.

In these unpropitious circumstances leadership of the reform cause devolved on Rosebery. Consistent reformer though he had been, he was hardly the man to lead so forlorn a cause and he received little support from 'the medievals on the front Opposition bench'.[47] Moreover, the peers who did support Rosebery in principle displayed little agreement on specific reform proposals. Some wanted a purely elective, others a wholly nominated chamber. Others wanted a mixture of hereditary, elected, and nominated peers in varying proportions. Some wanted peers elected by their fellow peers, others by county councils; some wanted peers nominated by the King, others by the Prime Minister. Some favoured the inclusion of dominion representatives, some wished to see the Nonconformists represented, while Garvin was urging the presence of two or three Catholic Archbishops as 'the simplest and most certain way of getting a new and strong leverage upon the Irish situation . . . and [as] the only immediate way of queering the pitch of the Coalition in the Northern Boroughs'.[48]

A desultory meeting of the Unionist high command with Rosebery on 3 March revealed considerable disparity of views, a growing recognition by Balfour of the need for some reform 'in our democratic days', and the continued hesitation of Lansdowne.[49] Rosebery, however, went ahead and prepared the following five resolutions for debate in the Lords:

1. That a strong and efficient Second Chamber is not merely an integral part of the British Constitution, but is necessary to the well-being of the state, and to the balance of Parliament.

2. That such a Chamber can best be obtained by the reform and reconstitution of the House of Lords.
3. That a necessary preliminary of such reform and reconstitution is the acceptance of the principle that the possession of a peerage should no longer of itself give the right to sit and vote in the House of Lords.
4. That in future the House of Lords shall consist of Lords of Parliament
   (a) Chosen by the whole body of hereditary peers from among themselves and by nomination by the Crown;
   (b) Sitting by virtue of office, and of qualifications held by them;
   (c) Chosen from outside.
5. That the term of tenure for all Lords of Parliament shall be the same, except in the cause of those who sit *ex officio*, who would sit so long as they hold the office for which they sat.

The first three resolutions, rather vague statements of general principle, were regarded as relatively innocuous, but the last two, embodying more specific proposals, aroused considerable anxiety. Cautioned by Curzon, and by Lansdowne, who dreaded anything concrete,[50] Rosebery postponed tabling the last two resolutions until after the debate on the first three, which took place in mid-March.

The debate made it quite clear that the Unionist leaders had no agreed scheme, their followers an instinctive dislike for any specific suggestions. Sandars, present at the opening of the debate, reported that the reception of Rosebery's speech

> ... was not enthusiastic, more especially that part of it which related to his constructive proposals. Two or three persons whom I saw after the Debate dwelt upon the fact that when Rosebery came to his suggestions for introducing the elective element, and to the abolition of the hereditary principle, the sympathy if any was very cold.[51]

Despite the debate Rosebery was determined to plunge ahead with the more detailed resolutions. But his path now clearly diverged from that of Lansdowne, who, alarmed by the debate, wrote to warn Balfour at the end of March that '. . . the Rosebery resolutions . . . are, I fear, going to give trouble if he persists in dotting his i's too much'. Lansdowne himself was now tempted by the referendum, arguing for 'a policy based on H. of L. reform and the referendum' as against the Parliament Bill.[52] The influential Lord Selborne and the Cecils were 'hot for' the referendum,[53] for 'It exhibits trust in the people in its strongest and most undiluted form'.[54] Whether Lansdowne supported the referendum as a diversionary tactic, as a distraction from the vexed question of composition reform, or because he was convinced that it offered the most viable solution is not clear. Certainly Salisbury advanced the referendum partly because he opposed 'the absurdity of Rosebery's proposal' for an elected element in the reformed House.[55] What is clear is that by late March the discussion within the Unionist camp was diverted from composition reform to the referendum, to the relief of the majority of the peers. In addition, the injection of the referendum issue into the debate further delayed any final decision on Upper Chamber policy, a not unwelcome respite for Lansdowne, for all who subscribed to the virtues of delay and for those resistant to all change.

Nothing was done until November, the moratorium on politics that followed the death of the King enabling Lansdowne to prevent further discussion of the Rosebery resolutions. The results were wholly unfortunate. The Unionist leaders went into the Constitutional Conference[56] with no clear alternative to the veto plan, and although their own ideas on the constitutional question developed during the Conference, the election was upon them before they had any agreed plan before the public. The scramble to push through a reform policy in November – the notorious 'deathbed repentance' of the House of Lords – was the direct result of the abdication of Unionist leadership on this issue in the early months of the year.

But reform of the House of Lords was not the only issue raised by the January election. 'Protection is indeed not merely dead but damned,' trumpeted the Liberal *Morning Leader* on 18 January. Many Unionists were inclined to agree. Although it was not apparent at the time, the January election marked the zenith of Tariff Reform. The election completed the task the Confederates had begun. Free Food representation in the Unionist ranks was virtually eliminated. Nevertheless the Whole Hoggers were on the defensive. As always the Balfourites were the danger. Balfourite pragmatism challenged once again the fiscal ideology of Highbury. The landed classes who had hoped that Tariff Reform might save them from the burdens of the Budget were disenchanted; Unionists who had shared Birmingham's optimism concerning the popularity of Tariff Reform were disillusioned; while the party strategists saw that in the very areas where Tariff Reform was to have won seats, in the North and London, it had most singularly failed. Critics, silenced while Tariff Reform reigned unchallenged as the alternative to a detested Budget, reappeared. Dissent grew again in the Tory ranks.

What rendered the Whole Hoggers' position critical, and ultimately desperate, were the great problems now crowding upon the Unionist Party. The House of Lords and Home Rule were now at the heart of the political conflict. A long and rambling memorandum from the fourth Marquis of Salisbury was sent to Austen Chamberlain and Bonar Law on 1 February 1910.[57] This document, a familiar catalogue of Cecilian objections to the tariff programme, appealed far beyond the broken Free Fooders because it recognised the awful predicament in which the Unionist Party now stood.

> We are to be asked to risk everything upon the next throw . . . If we fail this time the power of the House of Lords must go, and with it the Union, the Church, the whole realm of religious interests to which we are attached, and the barrier against Socialism; and at the same time if it be true that the present government cannot be trusted in Imperial defence, perhaps the very existence of our Empire. Is it reasonable, is it possible, to ask us to enter into this struggle except upon the best ground we can find? If we can win without food taxation, but may very possibly be shattered with it, can we hesitate which choice to make?

In this lay the germs of the policy of retreat from the full Tariff Reform programme that was to characterise Unionist policy in the coming year. Salisbury admitted in his memorandum that 'the overwhelming mass of the Unionist Party believes in Tariff Reform'. But there was a great distinction between those who saw Tariff Reform as *the* policy of the party, and those who saw it as *a* policy of the party. The former might be, indeed some were, prepared to sacrifice both Union and House of Lords to secure their aims. The latter were prepared to abandon Tariff Reform if this would strengthen the resistance to threats against the traditional order. As Balfour had always been aware, once the danger to the Lords and to the Union was fully apparent he would be immensely strengthened in dealing with the tariff dogmatists. In the months ahead, as the threat to the constitution mounted, Salisbury's arguments came to possess a growing attraction for a desperate party.

Criticism was directed mainly at the food taxes, electorally the most vulnerable plank in the Tariff Reform programme. On the day after the first polls the *Sunday Times* declared: 'Even the trump card of a strong Navy and the appeal to the patriotism of the country lost their potency when coupled with proposals to tax the food of the people'; while on 29 January the *Spectator* argued that '. . . if the Tariff Reformers had distinctly abandoned all idea of taxing bread, meat and cheese, and confined their demands to the taxation of manufactured articles' the Unionists would have won. It was obvious that the critics hoped by these means to separate industrial protectionists from imperial preferentialists. Fabian Ware, militant editor of the Whole Hogger *Morning Post*, recognised that we are in a not very different position to that which followed the election of 1906. But now the enemy, instead of endeavouring to throw over the whole question of Tariff Reform, desires merely to jettison the Imperial side.'[58]

Economic developments during 1910 reinforced the movement against Tariff Reform. The sharp recession which had provided an admirable background for the propaganda of fiscal change was rapidly disappearing. The recovery noticeable in the second half of 1909 had been maintained, and if the boom conditions of 1906–7 were not yet restored, the indices of employment, production, and overseas trade were all rising. The only shadow on the otherwise resurgent Free Trade economy was the continued deterioration in real wages. But this very fact was bound to work against the Unionists, for, as Garvin observed, the people, 'only know that they are in the grip of high prices and they dread the possibility of an increase in a way that fills them in the closing days of an election . . . with a terror that makes great numbers of them vote against us in the end though sympathising with every other article of our creed'.[59] If a succession of bad winters had failed to bring victory to the proponents of fiscal change, could they hope to make much progress in a now rapidly reviving economy? Although the only formal change made to the Tariff Reform programme during 1910 was the decision in April to abandon the duty on colonial wheat, never a popular addition to Chamberlain's original scheme,[60] the tariff cause was extremely vulnerable on the eve of the second election. How vulnerable the campaign itself was to reveal.

The weakness of Tariff Reform was masked by the Whole Hoggers' aggressive response to the threats to their policy. In answer to Salisbury's memorandum of 1 February Bonar Law wrote:

> The Unionist Party is now committed to the whole policy of Preference, including food duties, and there is a large section of the Party . . . which regards Preference not as a political opinion but as something almost sacred. If [it were decided] to postpone this part of the proposal . . . there would, in my opinion, be a wholesale revolt among the rank and file which would cause a division in our Party more complete and more hopeless than has existed at any time since the fiscal controversy was raised.[61]

The threat was explicit. If the pragmatists excised key elements of the fiscal programme in their pursuit of electoral success, then the ideologues would wreck the party, giving it over once more to internecine strife.

Moreover the Whole Hogger interpretation of the electoral verdict ran directly counter to that of their critics. 'Tariff Reform was our trump card. Where we won, we won on and by Tariff Reform. Even where we lost, it was the only subject in our repertoire about which people really cared.'[62] Bonar Law stressed its success in the counties:

Tariff Reform . . . was popular in the purely agricultural parts of the Counties . . . the agricultural labourers cannot have been frightened by the food duties and the farmers . . . were attracted by them. To propose, therefore, to leave out the food duties would . . . be to run a serious risk of losing the advantage we have gained in the Counties, without any guarantee of securing an equivalent advantage in the towns.[63]

The corollary to the theory that Tariff Reform was 'our trump card' was that the Unionists had otherwise a bad hand, and the Whole Hogger objective throughout 1910 was to keep the trump suit and get rid of the rest. As has been seen, the Whole Hoggers were active in the effort to democratise the Lords. They were prominent too in an even more dangerous undertaking – the questioning of the *raison d'être* of the party, the Union with Ireland.

As the results came in in January it was perhaps inevitable that some Unionists would contemplate buying Irish support with a measure of Home Rule. Such a notion appealed to the Whole Hoggers, who saw the Irish as natural protectionists, and who were as a faction less wedded to the traditional view of the Union. Garvin, addressing Sandars on post-electoral strategy, was convinced that the Unionist position on Ireland needed rethinking, and that perhaps the Irish would accept 'the Quebec or Ontario model' of internal self-government.[64] Fabian Ware, the most militant propagandist of the tariff cause, apparently advised a bargain with the Irish.[65]

But Balfour was adamantly opposed to any bargain with the Irish. Whatever else the Unionist Party might stand for, it stood above all in his eyes for the unimpaired link with Ireland. He told Garvin plainly that trafficking with the Irish would be 'Eating Dirt'.[66] To Lansdowne he wrote in equally stringent terms on 29 January 1910.

I am already getting a certain number of letters urging an arrangement with the Irish on the basis of sacrificing the Union (more or less completely) in the interests of Tariff Reform. I do not, however, believe that this particular form of 'rot' has penetrated, or is likely to penetrate, into the Party organism.[67]

This attitude scotched the 'rot' in the early months of 1910.

But the Constitutional Conference, and particularly Lloyd George's proposals for a coalition, revived demands for a rethinking of Unionist policy on Ireland. A campaign for 'federal Home Rule' led by Garvin and a number of young Whole Hoggers, and treated not unsympathetically by Bonar Law and Austen Chamberlain, soon spread. '. . . some fundamental alteration of the Unionist attitude on the Irish question', Garvin told Maxse, 'is becoming indispensable if we are to have a fair chance of saving anything.'[68] Garvin's note of desperation was echoed in an opportunist party press. October found most of the Unionist newspapers, particularly the Whole Hogger papers, vying with each other to compromise the Union. The leading proponents of reappraisal were to a man Whole Hoggers, and the movement foundered on the opposition of Balfour, some of the Balfourites, the Free Fooders and the Orangemen.[69] Election necessities then forced a volte-face on all the advocates of compromise. October's charity to the Irish was replaced by November's unbending hostility.

One other development had been pushed, also without success, by the Whole Hoggers. Awed by the disasters in the North, they had called for a greater commitment to social reform. The *Morning Post* urged a programme of Poor Law reform, pensions, and national insurance, while Garvin took a similar line in the *Observer*, pressing the Lords themselves to take up the reform of the Poor Law.[70]

But these appeals generated no response within the party. The leaders were absorbed with other questions while, with its recent legislation and its much-advertised future plans, the Liberal Government had pre-empted the field. Anyhow, influential elements in the party looked askance on social reform as a threat to individual freedom and financial integrity. A weekend with the 'Hotel Cecil' in mid-February 1910 brought Beatrice Webb face to face with the negativism which was to frustrate the Whole Hoggers.

> To many of the more upright minds, failure at the polls would be the lesser evil compared with the downward course towards a collectivist organisation. They have a *blind* fear of any increase of social responsibilities; and, if they are to accept any measure of it, they would positively prefer to hide their heads in the sand and *refuse to see it*.[71]

If social reform made little progress in the party during 1910, the Osborne Judgement raised issues difficult for the Opposition to avoid. The Unionist organisation had been perturbed by the effects of the Judgement in the January election, and in October 1910 Bonar Law reported 'a great deal of fear of the effect of the Osborne Judge-

ment on the part of Unionist Members for the industrial centres'.[72]
But there was no likelihood of the Unionists favouring reversal.
Balfour was definite: 'I am quite clear that I individually could never
give my assent to a reversal of the Osborne Judgement.'[73] The Chief
Whip thought that none of 'our men' favoured reversal, but 'a great
many [of them] are in favour of payment of members as an alternative'.[74]

This raised a more controversial question, which divided the party
along all too familiar lines. Balfour was astride the fence, disliking
payment of Members but preferring it 'a hundred times' to any
reversal of the Osborne Judgement.[75] Bonar Law, leading the Whole
Hoggers and the younger men, argued for payment as the only 'real
alternative by which labour representation can be secured', and as a
means to 'kill the purely political influence of the Trade Unions'.[76]
He was strongly supported by F. E. Smith, Paddy Goulding and the
Whole Hogger press.[77]

The opposition was centred around the Balfourite old guard.
Lansdowne was opposed and Walter Long wrote to warn Balfour
that the adoption of payment of Members would 'frighten our friends'
and not win the workingmen.[78] Decisive, however, was the split in the
Whole Hogger ranks. Garvin 'hated' payment of Members,[79] and
the proposal was frowned upon by Highbury. 'We should shock many
people by supporting it', wrote Austen to Balfour, 'and we should
conciliate no one.'[80] Highbury's opposition ensured that the party
entered the election opposed both to reversal and to the payment of
Members.

Thus on the eve of the second election while the Liberals had passed
their Budget, defined their constitutional programme and adopted a
policy on the Osborne Judgement, the Unionists, apart from their
acquiescence over the Budget, had failed to modify or alter in any
significant way the programme on which they had been beaten ten
months before. The result was to be the most kaleidoscopic series of
policy changes ever to be carried out in Britain by a major party
during an election campaign.

III

The possibility of a second election was omnipresent during 1910.
In the first critical days of the new Parliament, an election often seemed
imminent although nobody wanted it. Then in late March, with the

Government bedevilled internally by the threat of the resignation of the reformist wing and externally by renewed Irish threats to vote against the Budget, the likelihood of an election loomed again. But the Prime Minister's guarantees pledge on 14 April ended the possibility of a spring election. All parties now prepared for a midsummer election. Both the major parties saw disadvantages in this: the Liberals, worried by the unpopularity of two elections in six months,[81] the Unionists fearing an August election, 'holiday time for the middle classes'.[82]

Their qualms were needless. The sudden death of King Edward on 6 May ended all talk of a midsummer election and gave an opportunity to all those who sought to avoid a second election. The forces seeking a compromise settlement, briefly visible in the confused aftermath of the first election, re-emerged, fortified now by somewhat surprising allies. Asquith, reluctant to ask for guarantees in the opening days of the new reign, was willing for a conference with the Opposition leaders. The reformists in the Cabinet welcomed such a conference as a further opportunity to canvass their schemes, while even the vetoists recognised that 'we should incur much public odium if we were thought to be unduly pressing the Crown at this moment'.[83]

On the Unionist side there was powerful press support for a conference. The *Observer*, for over a year the most aggressive of Unionist journals, now became the most ardent apostle of the spirit of compromise. *The Times*, with a far less heroic past, became a willing host to each and every proposal for a bipartisan solution. The Unionist leaders, although sympathetic to the King, approached the conference suggestion in their usual cautious and sceptical fashion, fearing perhaps that it was merely a device to enable the Liberals to postpone the election to some more propitious occasion. Sandars was initially hostile, fearing that 'to allow [sentiment] to weaken political action and decision . . . seems to me to be a folly we shall live to regret'.[84] Yet Balfour at least was astute enough to realise that such a conference offered the Unionists possibly their one real hope of retrieving their position.[85]

But the rank and file on both sides were unhappy. Two electoral defeats had merely encouraged the suicidal impulses of the unthinking, and even some of the thinking, sections of the Unionist Party. The events of the past few years had nourished, too, a pathological suspicion of all dealings with the enemy. Nor was the situation made any easier by the widespread distrust of the Unionist leaders among their own backbenchers. The Liberal Front Bench was likewise viewed with suspicion by its backbenchers, and by its Labour and Irish allies whose representation at the Conference seems never to have been suggested. The *post facto* judgement of the I.L.P. was that the 'only effect of the Veto Conference has been to accentuate suspicion of the Government's intentions'.[86] The early vacillations of the Liberal Ministry had not been forgotten and the Radical alliance feared that a Front Bench conclave might rob them of their triumph. Although they failed to prevent the Conference, these attitudes severely circumscribed the field for manœuvre. For five months the extreme wings of both parties were forced to watch in 'scarcely veiled hostility'[87] the secret and spasmodic attempts of the Constitutional Conference to find an agreed way out.

This unique event in British political history is of little concern here. The Constitutional Conference was called in the hope of averting, or at least delaying, the second election. When the Conference broke down on 10 November the situation was as before. True, the Conference compelled the Unionist leaders to formulate more precisely their reform plans for the Lords, but this did not become apparent until the campaign was under way. The Conference, too, had encouraged a surprising shift on Home Rule by one section of the Unionist Party, but this was abandoned as soon as the Conference failed. The Conference saw no advance on the situation existing in early May, no resolution of the issues then dividing the parties. All it did was to delay for five months the second election.

The election now came with startling suddenness. On 8 November, two days before the formal breakdown of the Conference, the Cabinet was informed that there was 'an apparently irreconcilable divergence of view' and that the end was imminent.[88] During the next two days there appears to have been a short, sharp verbal debate between those who wanted to postpone the election until January, and those who wanted it at once. A January election on the new register would, it was argued, favour the Liberals because it would minimise removals and allow the Government to pass the Parliament Bill through the Commons and thus redefine its programme. On the other hand there was a strong desire to get on with the election immediately, to strike before the Unionists could elaborate an alternative policy, and before Liberal enthusiasm was dampened, or the unity of the anti-Unionist forces impaired, by further delays. The disarray of the Unionists and the gloom of their press were added incentives for immediate action.[89]

Asquith appears to have favoured an immediate dissolution, considering it a waste of time to proceed further with the Parliament Bill.[90] But the decisive voice appears to have been that of Elibank, the Chief Whip, and the decisive event for him the by-election at Walthamstow on 1 November. Walthamstow was a constituency with a huge electorate on the periphery of London, and few constituencies had suffered more severely from removals. Yet the by-election revealed a slight swing to the Liberals. Apparently they need not worry overmuch about the effect of removals.[91] On 9 November Jesse Herbert, the Chief Whip's secretary, went carefully through all the English and Welsh constituencies and estimated a net gain of twenty-nine for the Liberals in an immediate election.[92] The popular tide was with them, their organisation was ready, and the enemy was divided and depressed. On 10 November, the Cabinet, which seems to have been thoroughly canvassed by Elibank, decided on a pre-Christmas election.[93]

There now remained the delicate negotiations with the new King over the contingent guarantees. On Friday, 11 November, Asquith travelled down to Norfolk for a preparatory discussion with the King at Sandringham on the post-Conference situation.[94] The discussion appears to have been characterised by excessive tact, and the King gained the mistaken impression that guarantees would not be requested before the election.

The King spent a pleasant weekend at Sandringham under this misconception while the Prime Minister, who returned to London on Saturday, prepared a memorandum to disillusion him.

There are four possible courses [wrote Asquith] which the King might be advised to take, in the event of the rejection by the House of Lords of the Commons Resolutions

(1) An immediate exercise or promised exercise of the prerogative of creation in the present Parliament without a dissolution.

(2) An immediate dissolution with an assurance by His Majesty that, in the event of the policy of the Government being endorsed by an adequate majority in the new House of Commons, he will be willing, if and when the occasion should arise, to make use of his prerogative, *and that the Government should be at liberty to announce that this is so.*

(3) The same as (2) without the concluding underlined words.

(4) An immediate dissolution without any such assurance or liberty of announcement, but with a clear understanding as between the King and his Ministers, that, if the electors give the Government an adequate majority, Ministers will find themselves unable to continue in office, unless they can, *thereupon*, be assured of the willingness on His Majesty's part to make use, in case of necessity, of the prerogative.[95]

All four courses involved either an immediate assurance from the King on the use of the Prerogative, or as in the case of (4) an assurance immediately upon the conclusion of the election, and even this latter course involved an understanding between the King and his Ministers prior to the election.

On Monday, 14 November, Lord Knollys, who had travelled up that day from Sandringham, was closeted with the Premier for two hours at Downing Street. There he was given either this memorandum, or an outline of the possible courses Ministers were likely to advise. Writing to the King that night, he expressed his surprise at the implications of the memorandum, and indicated the line of action the Ministry was likely to pursue. 'What [Asquith] *now* advocates is that you should give guarantees *at once* for the next Parliament.'

Next morning the Cabinet met at 11.30 to prepare a formal request to the King for contingent guarantees. During this meeting a telegram from the King at Sandringham was sent into the Cabinet room. 'The King has received from Lord Knollys the four possible courses which might be submitted to him by the Prime Minister. His Majesty regrets it would be impossible for him to *give contingent guarantees* and he reminds Mr Asquith of his promise not to seek for any *during this Parliament.*'[96] His reluctance to give guarantees compounded by his recent disappointment over Asquith's intentions had led the King to a blunt *non possumus*, which threatened an immediate breach with his Ministers. They for their part remained adamant. Despite the telegram, the minute formally requesting contingent guarantees was agreed to and despatched, softened only with the provision that the King's pledge should be kept secret unless and until the actual occasion for its implementation arose.

It was now up to the King and his advisers. For the next twenty-four hours Lord Knollys fought to persuade the King to accede to the ministerial request, which he considered the monarch could 'safely and constitutionally accept', and which he believed it would be folly to refuse. His chief opponent was the King's other private secretary, Sir Arthur Bigge, who feared that to give the guarantees would turn the monarch into 'a Partisan', and who criticised the secrecy provisions as 'not English' and 'childish'. Bigge was personally much closer to the King than Knollys, having been his private secretary for the previous ten years, whereas the King acquired Knollys only on his accession to the throne. Moreover, while the King remained at Sandringham Bigge was physically much closer. But by one o'clock on Wednesday, 16

November, Knollys had got the King back to Buckingham Palace and the battle was half won. In the next two hours he won completely, making full use of his greater political experience over Bigge, and particularly his role as confidant to Edward VII. His methods were not overly scrupulous. He seems to have deliberately concealed vital information concerning Balfour's attitude to assuming office, and possibly to have misrepresented Edward VII's views on guarantees. The dangers confronting the monarchy if George V had refused his Ministers' request must be Knollys's excuse. When Asquith and Crewe arrived at 3 p.m. for what Asquith described 'as the most important occasion of my life' the King reluctantly gave the required pledge. The way was now clear for the dissolution.[97]

Although these negotiations delayed the announcement they did not affect the timing of the election. The intrinsic interest of these events has often disguised the fact that only a little over twenty-four hours passed between the Cabinet's preparation of the minute requesting guarantees and the King's assent. There seems little evidence to sustain the King's claim to Lansdowne that 'it was owing to him that we had been allowed to have the Parliament Bill in the House of Lords at all',[98] nor the related assertion of one historian that the dissolution 'was deferred for ten days in order to permit the presentation in the House of Lords of the Government's Bill and Lord Lansdowne's alternative proposals . . .'.[99] It is true that in his interview with Asquith at Sandringham the King asked that the Parliament Bill be sent to the Lords before the dissolution, a request to which Asquith acceded.[100] Yet it seems most unlikely that the Government would have refused Lansdowne's request for the Bill, while in their minute to the King on 15 November, the Ministers made it quite clear that any discussion in the Upper House should not be permitted to postpone the date of the dissolution.[101]

On 18 November Asquith announced the dissolution for 28 November with first polls on 3 December. Few British elections have been so often anticipated, none have been characterised by so short an interval between formal notice of election and the first polls.

9

The Second Campaign

I

The December election, by contrast with January's, followed an autumn of relative political calm. The campaign itself was not only shorter, but also quieter than its predecessor. How far this was evidence of public apathy was much debated. Sidney Low described the election as 'the most apathetic within living memory',[1] but Sydney Brooks, another respected observer, noted that the 'uncanny decorum of the election did not imply disinterest'.[2] And in fact the turnout indicates that public interest remained high.[3] One other contrast with January is important. While the first election remained throughout a debate on all the great issues of the day, in the second election the constitutional question achieved the primacy denied it in January.

Initially, this appeared unlikely. The Unionists, gloomy about their prospects, were desperately searching for distractions. The Christmas election they denounced as wanton – because commercially ruinous – and, with more substance, as improper. By holding the election on the old register the Government denied the vote to at least a quarter of a million people, and this came ill from a party pledged to a broader franchise.[4]

A more significant distraction was the allegation that the dissolution was dictated by the dollar-financed Nationalist Party. The accusation of Irish dictation had been developed in the aftermath of the January election and drew substance from the Government's behaviour in the early months of the year. At the breakdown of the Constitutional Conference Redmond was at sea, returning from a successful fund-raising tour of the U.S.A. His boast on disembarking at Cork on the evening of 12 November that 'the sum we have received is the largest ever subscribed for Irish political purposes'[5] helped transform the 'Irish Dictator' into the 'Dollar Dictator'.

Abandoning the moderation of the autumn, the Unionists raged against Redmond, the 'uncrowned king of political mendicants' with 'his pockets bulging with American gold'.[6] The attack gained impetus from a belligerent speech of Redmond's in Dublin on Sunday, 13 November. 'I go', he declared, 'to the British Parliament with one purpose only – that is to endeavour out of the necessities of English parties to win freedom for Ireland . . .'[7] On the following day Unionist headlines warned that the House of Lords was to be destroyed in order to give Ireland a separate parliament. At the end of the week, when Asquith announced the dissolution, it was obvious to Unionists that 'the Dollar Dictator has forced his marionette ministry to stampede the House of Commons'.[8]

Throughout the week headlines, pictures and cartoons had elaborated the theme. Dollar signs decorated the front pages of the press as a constant reminder of Liberal infamy; the National Union issued a facsimile of a dollar note, with the legend: 'Will you be ruled by the dollar or the sovereign?'[9] The Dollar Dictator or Dollarver Cromwell, clutching his dollar bags, glared from many a hoarding. Redmond had replaced the German as the chief Unionist bogeyman.

Tariff Reform continued the first constructive plank in the Unionist platform, despite internal intrigues to get rid of it. The tariff cause was highlighted early in the election by Bonar Law's dramatic decision to give up his safe London seat, Dulwich, and to contest North-West Manchester, won by the Liberals in January. Lancashire, the greatest of Unionist disasters in 1906, the worst of Unionist disappointments in January 1910, was for Balfour 'the very key and centre of the next electoral battle'.[10] For the Whole Hoggers, Lancashire was even more important. Unless they could convert the industrial North, and particularly Lancashire with its traditional Conservative allegiance, not only would their programme be unrealised, but it might well be discarded by a thrice-defeated party. In October 1910 the Tariff Reform League had mounted an intensive campaign in Lancashire. In November the Whole Hoggers sent Bonar Law, by now their leading figure after the Chamberlains, to contest a marginal Lancashire seat. The result was to be ironical indeed.

All the Unionist war-cries were apparent in Balfour's speech at Nottingham on the evening of 17 November. Delivered before the announcement of the election, this speech was the first major platform event of the campaign. Balfour protested against a possible December election, spoke briefly on land reform, social reform and the navy, and promised relief to licence holders and to the payers of land taxes. As usual he defined Tariff Reform as 'the greatest constructive policy to which . . . the party stands committed',[11] but instead of hurrying on he stressed both its urgency and the marginal impact it would have on the cost of living. This part of the speech signalised the temporary defeat of those working to weaken the party's commitment to Tariff Reform.

Balfour then gave his support to Rosebery's resolutions on the reform of the composition of the House of Lords, and foreshadowed proposals to change the relations between the two Houses. Finally, he attacked the Labour Party and the Nationalists – the 'driving forces behind the revolution . . . log-rolling factions of men who care nothing for your Empire and your country'. Balfour had opened by promising that the Unionists would not be content with 'defensive warfare'. This speech summed up the wide offensive that characterised the opening days of the Unionist campaign.

Meanwhile the Liberal campaign hung fire, the Ministers pre-occupied, their press mainly on the defensive. The negotiations with the King were not finally completed until 16 November, ministerial policy on the Osborne Judgement not finally settled until 22 November, and certain items of parliamentary business awaited dispatch. In addition, the Government was bedevilled by the worst suffragette disorders to date, and by the riots of Tonypandy. The Unionists exploited both, accusing the Ministers, particularly Churchill, Home Secretary since February 1910, of disdaining the public interest for fear of losing votes.[12]

II

But upon this welter of distractions a single issue – the future of the House of Lords – was already asserting its dominance. Two roughly parallel series of events were responsible for this: the hurried commit-ment of the House of Lords to sweeping reforms, and the London opening of the Liberal campaign.

'Depend upon it, Sir, when a man is going to be hanged in a fort-night it concentrates his mind wonderfully.' Dr Johnson's adage, as Asquith observed, seemed peculiarly appropriate to the November activities of the Tory majority in the House of Lords.[13] If after the January election many Unionists had recognised that changes in the House of Lords were desirable, on the eve of the second election most Unionists considered them imperative. Balfour was now pressed from all sides to give a lead, the Unionist press clamoured for reform, and it was even suggested that the name of the Second Chamber be changed to convince people of the seriousness of Unionist intentions. Even Lansdowne no longer paralysed action by his doubts and hesitations.[14]

But speed was the essence of the situation. '. . . we must move', urged Austen Chamberlain on 13 November, 'quickly and dramatically . . . but above all quickly and decisively.'[15] They did. Liberal intransigence over the parliamentary timetable and over amendments preventing any worth-while debate on the Parliament Bill,[16] the Peers adjourned debate on that measure and turned instead to formulating their own alternative. In just over twelve hours of debate, the House of Lords passed a series of resolutions that would dramatically and decisively transform that venerable institution. Whether these reforms would eliminate the Tory bias remained controversial.

The first step was taken on 17 November when Lord Rosebery's fourth resolution outlining the composition of a reformed House of Lords, postponed from April, was passed without division after a debate of only three hours. The fifth resolution relating to terms of tenure was withdrawn on the grounds that 'it goes too far into details'. Rosebery confessed that the proposals were rather vague, but argued that they constituted the basis for an alternative that would avoid the 'incredible dangers and tyranny of Single Chamber Government'.[17] His Unionist allies did their best to fill in the gaps. The House would be smaller; it would be more distinguished; it would contain 'a democratic element replenished from time to time by contact, direct or indirect, with the people'.[18]

This, however, was but a beginning. The Rosebery resolutions challenged merely the preamble of the Parliament Bill, not its substance. On the relations between the two Houses Unionist views had matured during the Constitutional Conference. On Sunday, 20 November, the Unionist high command met at Curzon's Basingstoke home, Hackwood, to formulate their plans.[19] The result of their deliberations was made known in a series of resolutions presented to the House of Lords on the following day, and debated on November 23 and 24. Briefly, the so-called Lansdowne resolutions provided:

1. A joint sitting to settle disputes between the Houses arising on ordinary bills and persisting for over a year.

2 A referendum to settle a similar dispute when it arose on 'a matter of great gravity which had not been adequately submitted to the judgement of the people'.

3. A joint committee presided over by the Speaker to determine

whether a bill was a money bill or not. Provided such a committee
was established and provision was made against tacking, 'the Lords
are prepared to forego their constitutional right to reject or amend
Money Bills of a purely financial character'.

The Lansdowne resolutions raised as many questions as they answered. How were the joint sittings and the joint committee to be
composed? What was 'a matter of great gravity'? Who was to decide
whether or not a measure had been 'adequately submitted to the
judgement of the people'? Until these questions were answered, observed the *Westminster Gazette* on 21 November, 'whether the resulting
draught is to be a virulent poison, a bracing tonic, or a harmless potion
. . . cannot be ascertained'.

The short debate in the Lords did little to clarify the ambiguity of
the resolutions. Indeed, precision and detail were openly eschewed by
Lansdowne on the grounds of insufficient time, and by Rosebery as an
usurpation of the Government's prerogatives.[20] The Tory leaders were
striving to rally their followers and persuade the moderates. Clarity
would, in all likelihood, have either alienated the former or discouraged the latter.

Some writers have stressed the unreality of these debates, contrasting
them with the real fight, the developing struggle in the constituencies.[21]
Yet this is a false contrast, for the Lords were electioneering not
legislating, and were thus as much a part of the real struggle as the
constituency activists. '. . . we must try, before we are finally closured,'
wrote Lansdowne, 'to lay before the country a fairly complete account
of our policy as a whole.'[22] The candidates, the opinion leaders, the
enemy all hung upon the debate in the Lords. In every constituency
throughout the country the resolutions of the Upper House were to
be invoked and denounced, if often only hazily understood, while one
of the proposals, the referendum, was to determine the whole course
of the public debate.

How successful the resolutions were as electioneering is more
debatable. They certainly were not warmly received amongst the
Unionists. The *Morning Post* lamented 'the sacrifice of a great possession to the exigencies of party strife' while the *Sunday Times* was openly
hostile to the reforms.[23] The remainder of the Unionist press was barely
enthusiastic. Since most of them had clamoured for reform in January,
it is unlikely that they were upset by the schemes *per se*. It was the
timing that aroused disquiet. It was difficult to show enthusiasm for a
retreat which, even if skilled, verged on a rout. In addition, reform

resolutions at this stage suited Liberal tactics, for they helped to concentrate attention on the House of Lords.

Nor did the totality of the reforms get over to the electorate.
Garvin was 'amazed' to find that

> amid all the tumult the House of Lords debates were not read at all even by
> people of the shopkeeping class and that there exists no notion in the people's
> heads as to the measure of reform Lansdowne has offered or as to the kind of
> Upper House we propose to construct! We shall have to simplify somehow, so
> incredibly crude are the minds of the multitude . . .[24]

But it was not so much simplification that the reform schemes needed,
although this might have helped, but time. The very lateness of the
Unionist acceptance of these schemes left the press and the candidates
only a few days in which to explain them to the electorate. They came
too late for most candidates to include details in their addresses. Moreover, in many cases, Unionist candidates themselves were vague about
the reform proposals, and, like the Peers, had little idea about their
further elaboration.

It is not surprising then that the Unionist press and speakers seized
upon the simplest, most readily grasped and most attractive of the
proposals, the referendum, making it the core of their constitutional
case. After aggressive speeches in the West Country, in which he ran
through the whole gamut of Unionist electoral cries, Lord Selborne
reported to Balfour: 'I had magnificent meetings at Plymouth & at
Devonport. *Referendum tells immensely.*'[25] The *Morning Post*, not
enamoured of the reform schemes *in toto*, thought so highly of the
referendum that it was quite content to assign the rest of the reform
proposals to a preamble, leaving the referendum as 'the normal
solvent of deadlocks'.[26] If few Unionists went so far, most believed the
referendum their most attractive electoral asset.

It is at first sight strange that this instrument of direct democracy
should be embraced so fervently by the Unionist Party. But the device
commended itself both to the parliamentary strategists and to the
electoral tacticians and, although promulgated in haste, had been
carefully considered by the party leaders both prior to, and during, the
Constitutional Conference.

The referendum represented a realistic response to the predicament
of the Edwardian Unionist Party. From 1906 the Unionists were confronted with a dominant anti-Unionist front. Yet many of the measures
to which this front was committed were essentially sectional, and
although they might pass by *quid pro quo* agreements in the Commons,

it was doubtful whether they commanded majority support in the country. For a minority party which yet considered itself the guardian of the national interest, or perhaps the English interest, the referendum was most attractive. It would, as Lord Cromer pointed out to Moberly Bell, manager of *The Times*, prevent the 'very great danger that a coalition of discordant elements, e.g. Home Rulers, Socialists, Suffragists and I know not what besides, though differing entirely . . . on particular points, would yet manage to join together in order to defeat the wishes of what really is the majority of the nation'.[27]

Cromer belonged to that faction of the party which saw the referendum as a realistic solution to the party's internal difficulties as well. The Free Food *Spectator* had long canvassed the referendum, avowedly for the purpose of settling Tariff Reform. A referendum on that subject would permit Free Fooders to remain true to their fiscal faith without deserting the Unionist Party. But for the moment the Free Fooders did not surface, or were treated roughly when they did. There was, at this stage, little consideration of submitting Unionist – 'national' – measures to the referendum. While a modified but still Unionist Upper House was retained, it would be Liberal measures which would run the gauntlet of the referendum.

The electoral tacticians welcomed the referendum as an extension of the logic of November 1909. Then the Peers had defended their action by the demagogic plea that they had simply referred the Budget to the judgement of the people. Now all major issues other than finance, which deadlocked the two Houses would be referred to the people. In his letter to Moberly Bell Cromer noted: '. . . though I believe in truth [the referendum] will turn out to be a Conservative measure, [it] is distinctly hall-marked with the democratic stamp.'

While the Lords were adumbrating their plans for reform, the Liberals had launched their campaign with a series of ministerial speeches in London: Asquith to the National Liberal Club on Saturday, 19 November; Lloyd George at Mile End and St Pancras on 21 and 22 November; Churchill at Islington on 22 November. Both Churchill and Lloyd George dealt with the dollar agitation which the Liberal press had countered single-handed for the past week. Lloyd George initiated a spirited counter-attack.

> Since when have the British aristocracy started despising American dollars? (A Voice: Marlborough) I see you understand me. Many a noble house tottering to its fall has had its foundations underpinned, has had its walls buttressed by a pile of American dollars.[28]

It was soon a popular Radical response to the dollar cry.

But the essence of these speeches, indeed the sole matter of Asquith's, was the House of Lords. While Asquith confined himself to the strictly political misdeeds of the peers, and Churchill pointedly remarked that he was not attacking peers as individuals, Lloyd George had no such scruples, and his Mile End performance aroused a greater furore than any since his memorable defence of the Budget at Limehouse. He pilloried the peers as descended from 'French filibusters', church-plunderers and the ennobled 'indiscretions of Kings', and after giving them both a more ancient and a more dubious lineage than most could claim, he likened the aristocracy to cheese, 'the older it is the higher it becomes'.[29] The speech revealed both the strength and weakness of his style – the easy humour, the colloquial intimacy, the homely yet memorable imagery, the imprint of passion; but also the slipshod form, the disregard for facts, and the undisciplined vituperation lapsing often into sheer bad taste. The *Morning Post* was appalled: 'There is an indescribable note of the gutter about it, of women screaming at each other across a street, never yet heard in the whole long volume of English political oratory.'[30]

All three Ministers denied that the Parliament Bill would establish a Single Chamber government and they pounced on the Lords' still incomplete reform schemes. They needed to discredit such proposals, and the task afforded a welcome relief from more hackneyed themes. Asquith opened his campaign with a sustained satire on the 'death-bed repentance'.

> Ah, gentlemen, what a change eleven short months have wrought! This ancient and picturesque structure has been condemned by its own inmates as unsafe. The parricidal pick axes are already at work, and constitutional jerry-builders are hurrying from every quarter with new plans. . . . There must be something to put in its place . . . something that could be called a Second Chamber, with a coat, however thin, of democratic varnish.[31]

Outside London the Liberal campaign lost nothing of its single-mindedness. As the demands of the parliamentary session ceased, the Liberal leaders fanned out across Britain. Once more in the Celtic fringe, Lloyd George toured Midlothian on Saturday, 26 November, gave a major speech in Edinburgh that evening, and was in Cardiff on 29 November. In both capitals he sought to rouse the spirit of nationalism and anti-landlordism against the Peers.

Churchill visited Manchester and Bradford, then back to London and on to Colchester where on 28 November, in one of the few violent incidents of the election, he was pelted with mud and rotten fish. The Prime Minister had gone to Hull for the attenuated one-day annual meeting of the National Liberal Federation. There on the evening of 25 November, he subjected the Unionist reform schemes to the most ruthless scrutiny of the election. Four days later he was at Reading helping the sorely pressed Attorney-General, Rufus Isaacs.

With the single exception of Churchill's speech at Manchester, in which the fiscal question was paramount, all the speeches were devoted to the Lords. The other Ministers and the rank and file followed suit. The Liberal thesis was that the reform proposals involved a superficial modernisation which would in no way impair, and might very well strengthen, the Tory hegemony for as it was regularly pointed out, under the reform schemes deadlocks could no longer be broken by the King creating peers.

But like their opponents, the Liberals concentrated increasingly on the referendum. In a flurry of metaphor Churchill denounced it as another 'trick in order to gain time to load the dice again – a fair pretence to strike a fatal blow', while Lloyd George feared that the expense would make it 'a prohibitive tariff against Liberalism'.[32] Asquith's comprehensive attack on the referendum at Hull condemned it on party grounds as giving the Unionist peers 'the power . . . to compel . . . what would be to all intents and purposes a Dissolution and a General Election'; and on national grounds as 'strik[ing] a deadly blow at the very foundation of representative government in this country'.[33]

How far such arguments were effective answers to the Unionist plea that they would rather trust the People than the Commons is debatable. But the Liberals had a more simple and deadly counter: a challenge to Unionist sincerity. Introduced by Crewe in the Lords,[34] it was taken up by Lloyd George at St Pancras, repeated by Asquith at Hull, and soon figured in every Liberal meeting. This was the challenge to the Unionists to submit Tariff Reform to a referendum, since a device 'which does not refer all major questions is purely a one-sided party dodge'.[35] The cry became 'the strongest weapon in the armoury of the Radicals'[36] and its effectiveness was soon dramatically apparent. At the Albert Hall on 29 November, amid tumultuous acclaim, Balfour declared: 'I have not the least objection to submit the principles of Tariff Reform to Referendum.'

III[37]

This was one of the most fateful decisions ever taken by a British party leader under the stresses of an election campaign. In the short run, although it revolutionised the election debate, its impact on the electoral results was marginal. But in the internal history of the Unionist Party it was crucial. Its disruptive effects were already evident before the election was over, and the disintegration of the party in 1911 owed much to the pledge. In the history of Tariff Reform it was equally momentous. Since Chamberlain's declaration in May 1903, Tariff Reform had suffered two electoral rebuffs, and had lost its champion. None of these proved as effectually crippling as the retreat embodied in Balfour's pledge.

For the origins of the pledge we must turn back to the days immediately following the breakdown of the Constitutional Conference on 10 November. With the failure of the Conference the Unionists were faced with the situation foretold by Salisbury nine months before. The threat to the House of Lords was now imminent, that to the Union scarcely less so. Salisbury's challenge now confronted the party. 'Is it reasonable, is it possible, to ask us to enter into this struggle except upon the best ground we can find? If we can win without food taxation, but may very possibly be shattered with it, can we hesitate which choice to make?'[38] While the Peers moved to renovate the Upper House, other Unionists pressed their leaders to cast off the dead-weight of the food taxes. Three elements can be identified – the Free Fooders; leaders and organisers in the industrial areas, particularly the North and Scotland; and an opportunist party press.

The resilience of the economy had made most Free Fooders 'even more Free Trade' than at the previous election.[39] Cromer, their nominal leader, wrote to Austen Chamberlain begging the party leaders to 'ease down' on Tariff Reform.[40] The *Spectator* appealed to Joseph Chamberlain to save the Union a second time, by putting aside for this election Tariff Reform. Otherwise, wrote the editor to Selborne, 'I look upon the election with the gloomiest forebodings'.[41]

But the *Spectator* had long been a lone voice, and unless there was erosion in the ranks of the Whole Hoggers, the Balfourites would find it difficult to act. There was growing evidence of such erosion. The solidarity of the Whole Hoggers appeared to be crumbling, particularly in the industrial areas. 'Just now', wrote Austen Chamberlain on 16 November, 'we are all flooded with letters from "ardent" but wobbly

Tariff Reformers begging us to play hankypanky somehow with the Food Taxes, to run away from them today that we may live to fight for them again.'⁴² From the North-East, from Liverpool, even from the Duchy, Whole Hoggers wrote urging postponement of the food taxes.⁴³

Opportunism was rank among the party press. If Garvin ('Garvin – Garvin of all men') was the most notorious advocate of jettisoning the food taxes, he was far from alone. Buckle of *The Times* and Blumen-feld, editor of the strongly Tariff Reform *Daily Express*, both told Balfour that he could not win with the food taxes. The proprietors of the *Daily Telegraph* welcomed the idea of postponing the food taxes, while Northcliffe, the greatest newspaper proprietor of them all, was clearly willing to popularise such a policy, although reluctant to move without a lead from Balfour. Garvin was making no vain boast when he promised Balfour the backing of the entire Unionist press, except the *Morning Post* and the *Birmingham Daily Post*, if he pledged that the party would introduce no duty on food until after a further election.⁴⁴

If, having aired their views, most Unionist editors and proprietors were content to await a lead from the leader, Garvin was not. The *Observer* might maintain a discreet silence, but behind the scenes its editor was the most active Unionist proponent of a modified tariff line. Convinced that Lancashire was the key to the election, and that defeat throughout the North was certain unless the food taxes were put aside, Garvin put pressure on Sandars in order to influence Balfour.

> Since it is impossible that we can win upon this issue [food taxes] why should we be handicapped by it not only to no practical purpose whatever but in a way that endangers – the Second Chamber – the Constitution – the Union itself . . . and the next Imperial Conference and indirectly the whole future of the Empire as well as the whole future of the Unionist Party . . . the best chance for the whole policy of Imperial Preference itself is to go to the country now upon this cry, 'At *this* election your vote will tax the foreigner but will not tax your food.'⁴⁵

Garvin's suggestion amounted to postponing the imperial side of the programme while retaining industrial protection. The hard core of the Whole Hoggers rallied to defend what had always been the heart of Chamberlain's policy. '. . . hesitation now would be fatal to Preference *for ever*,' wrote Austen Chamberlain on 17 November.⁴⁶ Backed by Bonar Law, Austen strove to stiffen the wobblers, persuade or at least neutralise Northcliffe, and above all to harden Balfour against the temptations of expediency.⁴⁷

They had four assets. First, whatever the defections amongst the rank

and file, none of the Whole Hogger leaders, unless Garvin is so classified, deserted. Secondly, the widespread belief among Tories in
southern England, that to jettison the agricultural side of Tariff Reform
would be to invite party losses in the southern county seats, worked in
their favour; Austen pointed out to Balfour: '. . . if you give up all
agricultural protection and keep industrial duties, you may lose the
[agricultural] labourer. You will certainly lose the farmer, who will
cry out that agriculture is betrayed.'[48] Thirdly, in the period prior to
the Lords' commitment to sweeping reforms, the Whole Hoggers
could play upon the Unionist dread of doing battle on the constitutional
question alone.

> All our advisers – Liberal Unionist or Conservative – agree that in Scotland and
> the North of England the House of Lords is profoundly unpopular, and that to
> fight on that position is impossible. . . . It is Tariff Reform and Tariff Reform
> alone that holds our masses in the Midlands, or is winning the masses else-
> where.[49]

But above all, the tactical difficulties of opportunism provided the
real strength of the resistance. How could postponement be carried out?
The party, still less the country, had received little preparation for so
precipitate a step. Without public preparation it would all too easily
appear a hasty and ignominious retreat. 'Let us win or lose with credit',
pleaded Austen Chamberlain, who reserved his most cutting comments
for the renegade Garvin. 'Fancy going to the country on a policy which
is to keep the counties by persuading them that we *will*, and to win the
towns by persuading them we won't.'[50] Indefatigable in the struggle
to preserve his father's policy, his letters at this time capture something
of his father's tone.

> In the disasters of 1906 [he wrote to Lord Cromer] nothing was more fatal to us
> than the Babel of Unionist tongues. Nothing so shook the moral credit of the
> Party, or did more to court defeat. To give any excuse for the belief that as a
> Party we were wobbling again would, I believe, destroy us not merely now,
> but for a generation.[51]

And then there was Balfour. His own past record made it virtually
impossible for him to lead the renunciation. Balfour confessed to
Austen Chamberlain that 'He had come slowly to the Food Duties, but
having come to them, he didn't like to go back on them. The Party
had shed some members by adopting Tariff Reform, he wouldn't
split it by abandoning it.'[52] Whatever the sincerity of the first, the crux
lay in the second sentence. If Balfour postponed the food duties without

Highbury's approval, he would re-open the wounds of the party, would give it over once more to internecine strife. On this issue Balfour could not lead his party; only 'Joe could do it' and Joe would not.

On the evening of 16 November, the tired Austen Chamberlain knew he had won – 'Balfour stands firm and will nail the flag to the mast tomorrow, so all is well'.[53] Balfour's Nottingham speech on 17 November, with its declaration for food taxes, announced the defeat of the opportunists. Yet in the twelve days between Balfour's Nottingham speech and his Albert Hall declaration on 29 November the opportunists were to recover the initiative and the Whole Hoggers to be vanquished. This reversal arose from the weakening of all those elements of Whole Hogger strength noted above. The unity of the Whole Hogger leaders was broken, the rural objections became less relevant, Unionists became more confident about their constitutional policy, and above all, the tactical situation was transformed by the referendum issue.

While Balfour's Nottingham speech was an authoritative repudiation of the attempts to abandon the food taxes, it did not quell Unionist unease on the tariff issue. Four days later Sandars told Garvin: 'The Cries of candidates and constituencies are still about the Food Taxes, and they will increase.'[54] The limited attention paid to the fiscal issue in speeches and addresses hardly justified the description of Tariff Reform as 'the first constructive plank of the Unionist programme'.

In these uneasy conditions the referendum, introduced apropos of the constitutional question, fundamentally altered the whole debate on Tariff Reform. At first sight this seems surprising. The referendum was intended to resolve deadlocks between the two Houses, and it was inconceivable that Tariff Reform should deadlock the two Houses. But if no one envisaged Unionist measures being deadlocked, no Unionist wanted to make this obvious, and the Whole Hoggers probably feared that the Unionist Party might, if pressed, prove remarkably generous about the subjects submitted to the referendum. The Whole Hoggers had been wary of the referendum earlier in the year, and Garvin later claimed: 'I was not [then] in favour of the Referendum *just because it would mean submitting Tariff Reform*.'[55]

The Whole Hoggers appear to have protected themselves against this possibility. Both during the Constitutional Conference and at the vital Hackwood meeting on Sunday, 20 November, the Unionist leaders had 'specifically and deliberately excluded [finance]' from the

purview of the referendum.[56] Speaking to the resolutions, Lansdowne
left no doubt on this point. Budgets, however revolutionary, would no
longer be referred to the people, but left to the joint session.[57]

The debate on the resolutions was instructive. When the Free
Fooder St Aldwyn argued that the Lansdowne proposals 'would
enable the policy of Tariff Reform to be put to the people in the
simplest way that could be devised', Lord Ridley, President of the
T.R.L., rebuked him and denied this interpretation.[58] Although pressed
by Cromer to support St Aldwyn, Salisbury, personally sympathetic,
felt himself 'bound by what passed at Hackwood' and in winding up
the debate passed the matter by.[59]

But if the Whole Hoggers were still on top, the Free Fooders and
the wobbly Tariff Reformers grabbed at St Aldwyn's suggestion.
Whereas a week before they had pleaded for the dropping of the food
taxes, they now urged that Tariff Reform be submitted to a referendum.
On 26 November Sandars told Garvin: 'Correspondence pours in –
will Mr Balfour say that Tariff Reform will be referred by *Referendum*
to the people?'[60]

This proposal had all the advantages of the proposal to postpone
the food taxes and few of its drawbacks. It would rally the moderates,
particularly the Lancashire moderates. 'It is now absolutely clear . . .
that the Free Trade Conservatives do hold the balance in Lancashire
and that if the Referendum is to cut both ways, they will vote for us
to strengthen the Constitution', argued Garvin.[61] The two most
influential figures in Lancashire Unionism, Derby and Salvidge, the
'boss' of Liverpool, supported the proposal.[62] Cromer and Harold Cox,
ex-Liberal M.P. for Preston, believed that the proposal would win the
Unionists thirty seats in the North; Rosebery that it would win them
the election.[63]

At the same time, it could plausibly be argued that the referendum
stratagem was, as Garvin pointed out, 'utterly different from "dropping
the food-tax" ', and would not alienate the farmers by discriminating
amongst the tariff proposals. Indeed, its most enthusiastic advocate,
Garvin, considered it 'a pledge absolute to submit the food-tax to the
country'.[64] Apparently quite willing to jettison the Hackwood
commitment, Lansdowne asked: 'If the Tariff Reformers really believe
in their cause, and if they also believe in the Referendum, can they
reasonably object to test the one by the other?'[65]

Moreover, the tactical opportunity did not have to be created. As
Lansdowne later explained: 'We had been challenged, and a refusal

to pick up the glove would, I think, certainly have created a bad impression in the country.'[66] In such circumstances, Joe was discounted. 'Highbury', wrote Garvin, 'has doubtless a sort of special veto on Tariff Reform but surely not on what is *NOW* necessary for the maintenance of the Constitution.'[67]

These arguments triumphed quite suddenly. The catalyst was a meeting in Manchester some time on the morning of Saturday, 26 November, between Bonar Law and one Edward E. Marsden, the editor of an obscure trade journal. This meeting, in which Bonar Law revealed his sympathy with the proposal to submit Tariff Reform to a referendum, sparked off a series of events culminating in the Albert Hall pledge on 29 November. Marsden telegraphed to Garvin on Saturday morning: 'Lancashire can be won only if balfour announces that tariff on passing would be submitted for confirmation by referendum this is vital will you seek balfours approval and advocate it tomorrow mr bonar law suggests last proposal.' Dr Gollin has told of this telegram's dramatic impact. Already convinced of the necessity for such a pledge, Garvin seized upon the telegram as a belated but authoritative appeal from Lancashire, an appeal backed by a ranking member of the inner Tariff Reform caucus. The telegram did not reach him until late Saturday afternoon. There was no time for consultation, indeed it was already too late to alter the provincial editions of the *Observer*, but Garvin entirely rewrote the five-column leading article of the final London edition.[68]

The gist of the new editorial, 'Now to the Nation', was simple. 'Home Rule and Tariff Reform alike must be submitted separately to the people and judged on their merits or the Referendum cannot be honestly applied to either. There can be no cogging of the constitutional dice . . . That is the meaning of "trust the people".' Out to persuade the Unionists, he added an unfortunate aside: 'It is the principle, as we have the best reason to believe, that would sweep Lancashire.'[69]

The response of the Unionist daily press is indicative of their desperation. Despite an earlier understanding that Northcliffe would await Balfour's lead, the *Daily Mail* on Monday reproduced Garvin's appeal verbatim, and told its readers that the Unionists 'are not only willing but eager to submit Tariff Reform . . . to the people of England by referendum'. Its associate, the *Evening News*, expressed similar sentiments a few hours later. On the same day the *Daily Graphic* interpreted Garvin's statement as authoritative and assured Free Fooders that they need no longer fear that 'votes given to defend the constitution might be used against Free Trade'.

On Tuesday *The Times* and the *Standard* gave Garvin's proposal guarded editorial endorsement. The *Daily Express*, after a Monday of paralysed indecision and silence on the major news topic of the day, came down firmly for the proposal on Tuesday. Its readers were perhaps startled by its front-page slogan: 'Tariff Reform means the will of the people.' That evening the Whole Hogger *Globe* announced its support. Most of the press on Tuesday carried a letter from Lord Cromer stressing the necessity of including Tariff Reform among the 'matters of great gravity' for which the referendum was intended. Only the *Morning Post* remained faithful, castigating Garvin's 'extraordinary suggestion' as 'a dodge to sweep Lancashire'.[70] All this had taken place without public comment from any member of the Shadow Cabinet.

The developments in the press had rendered Balfour's Albert Hall speech critical since they aroused expectations which Balfour could not neglect on Tuesday night. The ferment in the press had also stimulated growing pressure within the party. It seemed to Balfour that the party was fast getting out of hand. 'So many [candidates] (poor dears!) are utterly floored by the question, "Are you going only 'To trust the people' when Radical legislation is in dispute?" – that I am convinced at least a large minority of our Party will find themselves pledged to the new project before we know where we are.'[71] The action of F. E. Smith was a portent. Although he had opposed the dropping of the food taxes on tactical grounds, he declared in Liverpool on 28 November that he personally favoured submitting Tariff Reform to the referendum.[72]

But the most significant message out of Lancashire was Bonar Law's letter to Balfour, written after the former's encounter with Marsden on 26 November, and which reached Balfour some time on Monday, 28 November. The Whole Hogger leader wrote as follows:

[The proposal to submit Tariff Reform to a referendum] would destroy the whole of the attack on the referendum as part of the proposals in regard to the relations between the two Houses which have been put forward by Lansdowne, and I cannot help thinking that it would make certain of securing the votes all over the country of people who still believe in Free Trade but are Unionist otherwise. From the point of view of Tariff Reform I cannot at the moment see that there is much objection to it, because we obviously could not carry a big change like this without a decent majority, and I doubt if we should want to carry it if we thought the country would given an adverse decision by means of the referendum.

He concluded in a characteristically ambivalent fashion:

> Of course, if it is to be done it must be done quickly, or it would be of no use,
> and I can hardly say that I feel that I have given enough thought to it even to
> recommend it; but I do think that it is worth your consideration.[73]

Lancashire had clearly left its mark on Bonar Law.

Inclined to moderation on Tariff Reform and conscious of the weight of Bonar Law's arguments, Balfour recognised in this letter the rift in the Whole Hogger caucus which might give him freedom to act. If Bonar Law favoured the referendum stratagem then Highbury's veto might well be circumvented. The importance Balfour attached to this letter is shown by the fact that he showed it to Lansdowne and forwarded it to Edinburgh in an effort to persuade Austen Chamberlain.

If Bonar Law's letter was influential so was the attitude of Balfour's closest colleague Lansdowne, with whom Balfour spent much of the critical Monday and Tuesday. Lansdowne displayed all the keenness of a late convert to the notion of submitting fiscal proposals to a referendum. Rarely had he been so exigent on any issue, and his unexpected fervour clearly impressed Balfour, who, in a subsequent justification, wrote: 'Lansdowne in particular is more emphatic in his expression of opinion than I have ever known him upon any subject whatever.'[74] Bonar Law, and to a lesser extent Garvin, gave Balfour his opportunity. Without Lansdowne's insistent and persistent pressure, Balfour might not have seized it.

By Monday afternoon Balfour appears to have made up his mind. The postscript to the letter he sent, with that of Bonar Law, to Austen Chamberlain read: 'On the whole I am disposed to think that I cannot be silent about the matter tomorrow – that I cannot wisely plead for delay and further consideration – that I had better therefore boldly accept the challenge thrown down to us, and say that we do *not* shrink from an appeal to a Referendum in the case of Tariff Reform.'[75]

Chamberlain received the letters in Edinburgh about midnight; his telegraphed repudiation, not unexpected, reached Carlton Gardens about 9 a.m. on Tuesday.

> I don't like proposal if of general application it is open to all the objections
> already expressed and is also a departure from plan just formally set forth in
> resolutions if confined to this particular occasion is weak and will be thought
> so and will not in either case as far as I can judge materially affect result further
> have its advocates considered practical difficulties they seem to me immense
> messenger brings letter suggesting alternative.[76]

The letter referred to did not arrive until 7 p.m., only about an hour before the Albert Hall meeting. It clearly revealed its midnight authorship, and elaborated the point of the telegram that a pledge to submit Tariff Reform to a referendum was neither desirable nor practicable. Chamberlain's one positive proposal was quite fantastic. The Unionists would offer a referendum on Tariff Reform if the Liberals accepted the Rosebery–Lansdowne resolutions and dropped their veto Bill.[77] The letter had little effect on Balfour and Lansdowne, whose intentions had already survived a much bigger shock.

At about midday a rather surprising telegram had arrived from Bonar Law. Apparently Balfour had aimed to get a more definite commitment from Bonar Law, for on Monday evening Sandars sent a telegram to Bonar Law which read: 'In confidence what do you think will be effect in manchester and district if chief in speech tomorrow declares for tr reference and especially if such a policy is endorsed by rosebery on wednesday?'[78] Bonar Law's reply indicated that Saturday's advocate had become Tuesday's cunctator.

> My experience too short to make my opinion of any value all wealthy unionists even strong tariff reformers would say such declaration would mean victory but I find all working class audiences only interested in tariff reform and declaration would do no good with them and might damp enthusiasm of best workers declaration would be excessively difficult to work in practice on the whole think we should gain by it at election but doubt whether subsequent difficulties are not too great to make it wise would there be any use in saying if government undertake in event of their obtaining majority not to pass home rule without referendum we would give same undertaking regarding tariff reform bonar law.[79]

This notion of a conditional pledge, apparently the tactic Bonar Law preferred, amounted to little more than a debating trick, for the Liberals would never have agreed.[80]

Balfour was unmoved. Bonar Law's letter of 26 November had been fundamental in triggering off a decision to which Balfour, and Lansdowne, were personally predisposed. As Balfour's latest biographer has written, the Albert Hall pledge 'represented no change in his essential middle-of-the-road attitude to tariffs, promulgated years before'.[81] By Monday evening Balfour had resolved to give the pledge and, backed by Lansdowne and Sandars, he was unshaken by Tuesday's missives.

This interpretation is strengthened by Balfour's failure to call a truncated Shadow Cabinet some time on the Tuesday afternoon, to discuss his momentous decision. He later claimed: 'I could do no more than I did to collect the views of the Party leaders.'[82] But what did he do? He sent a special messenger to Austen Chamberlain and a telegram to Bonar Law. He may also have seen Acland-Hood and Derby, who were in London that weekend. Yet it is unlikely that anyone but Lansdowne was informed of the situation as it stood at midday on Tuesday with the telegrams from Austen Chamberlain and Bonar Law to hand.

Two months later, a still indignant Walter Long rebuked his leader:

> You were good enough to tell us the other day 'that you regretted your inability to consult your Colleagues at the time: that we were in the flurry of an Election, were scattered to the four winds of heaven, and that consequently consultation was impossible'. . . . I ask you what must be the impression produced on our minds when we know that the use of the telephone for quarter of an hour by your Secretary would have brought . . . at least four or five [colleagues].[83]

Yet no effort seems to have been made to gather them together. Balfour later asserted: 'I suspect that if a Shadow Cabinet could have been called, the whole trend of its opinion would have been nearly unanimous in favour of the course which, on my own responsibility, I did actually adopt.'[84] But this is too facile an assumption. In the full Shadow Cabinet there would have been determined opposition. Would the truncated group that could have been called together faced with Bonar Law's hesitations, Chamberlain's repudiation, the Hackwood agreement, and the fact that polls were only four days away, have supported the referendum pledge? It is of course possible, considering the combined influence of Balfour and Lansdowne on such a council. But the more likely outcome would have been the acceptance of some compromise proposal such as the conditional formula suggested by Bonar Law. Intentionally or otherwise the issue was never put to the test.

IV

Small wonder that Balfour arrived at the Albert Hall looking 'a little tired'.[85] But he did not disappoint the eager crowd of nearly ten thousand awaiting him. The hostile *Morning Post* thought it perhaps the finest platform performance of his career.[86] He opened and closed with Ireland. The rest of the speech was devoted to the referendum.

Amid rising excitement he described the Radical demand for a referendum on Tariff Reform as

> ... simply an expedient for wriggling out of the proposal which gives the people their just claim to come in as arbiters in great cases of difference of opinion between the two chambers. . . . Nevertheless . . . Tariff Reform is a great change. . . . I have not the least objection to submit the principles of Tariff Reform to Referendum.

Someone shouted, 'That's won the election', and the whole audience 'rose to its feet in a tumult of cheering', waving handkerchiefs and programmes.[87] Although he challenged the Liberals to do so, Balfour did not make his pledge contingent on a reciprocal promise from them to submit Home Rule to a referendum.[88]

If Balfour's pledge was received with tumultuous acclaim in the Albert Hall, its reception by Unionists generally verged on the ecstatic. Balfour 'has breathed a new soul into the party', wrote a jubilant Garvin. He had responded to 'the higher logic', pontificated *The Times*, while for the Free Fooders, 'Mr Balfour has made a new heaven and a new earth in the region of politics.'[89] The impact on Lancashire was considered by most Unionists be to profound. Even the *Morning Post* was compelled to admit that the majority of the Unionist leaders and workers in Lancashire were in 'cordial agreement' with the pledge.[90] The full voting strength of Lancashire Unionism would now be polled for the first time since 1900.

The Whole Hoggers hid their chagrin under public declarations of loyalty. A discouraged and disappointed Austen Chamberlain brought himself publicly into line at West Bromwich on 30 November and he reiterated his support in speeches in the North-East on 1 and 2 December. At Darlington, however, he declared that if the referendum on Tariff Reform were unfavourable he would resign.[91] Bonar Law publicly adhered to the new policy in a press statement late in the evening of the Albert Hall speech, and in a speech on 30 November.[92] Ridley, who disliked the stratagem as much as Austen Chamberlain, nevertheless 'felt the only thing to do in the crisis was to back our leader'. So the central organisation of the T.R.L. came into line.[93]

But from Joseph Chamberlain at Highbury no word came, and his flow of letters to candidates suddenly ceased. His silence was indicative of the real feelings of the Whole Hoggers. Beneath the euphoric public surface swirled strong currents of antagonism.

Even in Lancashire support for the new line was not universal. The candidates for South Manchester, Gorton and Stretford expressed their disquiet in private, while one candidate, Austin Taylor (North-East Manchester) publicly repudiated the pledge.[94] Symptomatic of more violent feelings was the letter to Austen Chamberlain from Richard Jebb, a fanatical Tariff Reformer, long estranged from the party leaders. 'Henceforth', he wrote, 'Balfour is out of the question. Some Tariff Reformers may look to him to wriggle out of his pledge; but that would only make him impossible for others, and for the country which will never trust him again.'[95]

Unfortunately for the Unionists the discontent was not merely subterranean. Sullenly resigned on Wednesday, 30 November, the *Morning Post* rebelled the following day. Fabian Ware now counselled outright defiance: 'Let Tariff Reform candidates go straight ahead on their original course. . . . Let them boldly declare that, if elected, they will use their Parliamentary position in the ordinary way to get Tariff Reform at the earliest opportunity.' In the next few days the newspaper moderated its tone, but irreparable damage had been done.

Meanwhile, having deliberately wooed the moderate Free Trade vote at the Albert Hall, Balfour was himself seeking to placate the Whole Hoggers. Their immediate concern was with the widespread and not unnatural interpretation of the pledge as meaning that Tariff Reform was no longer an issue in the election, indeed had been postponed indefinitely. A worried Austen Chamberlain telegraphed Balfour on the morning of 30 November, urging him to stop this misinterpretation of his speech which was doing 'much mischief in doubtful seats'.[96] Whole Hogger apprehensions were increased by Rosebery's 'non-party' speech at Manchester on 30 November, in which he implied that the fiscal question had been removed from the election and would not be touched until the constitutional question had been settled.[97] The chief result of this was to turn Rosebery into a whipping boy on whom the Whole Hoggers could vent their anger without injuring the party.[98]

At Reading on 1 December Balfour carried out an intellectually impressive reassurance operation. He reasserted the pre-eminence of Tariff Reform in the Unionist programme, and claimed that its popularity was enhanced by the referendum proposal.[99] Austen seemed satisfied: '. . . given your decision in favour of the Referendum on Tariff Reform, it was exactly the right postscript to your Albert Hall speech.'[100] But others were not. On 5 December the influential City Whole Hogger, Sir Joseph Lawrence, sent an urgent appeal to Balfour. '. . . if we are to stop the "dry rot" that has set in, we must show that if we are returned, a Tariff Bill will be *at once introduced* in accordance with your promises that it is to be the *first constructive work of the Unionist Party*.'[101]

This raised the problem of what exactly was to be referred. 'There are certainly great difficulties to be faced when we get to close quarters with the idea of using the Referendum', observed Lansdowne, somewhat belatedly on 4 December.[102] Liberal speakers were making this only too plain. At the Albert Hall, Balfour had talked of referring tariff principles to the referendum, which was certainly the simplest procedure. But the Whole Hoggers, determined that the first task of a Unionist administration would be the framing of a Tariff Reform budget, declared that it would be this budget that would be referred. The point remained in doubt for nearly a fortnight, until at Dartford on 12 December Balfour yielded to the Whole Hoggers. By this date it was obvious that the stratagem had failed, and Balfour's need to placate the Whole Hoggers was correspondingly greater.

This question, and the persistent pressure of the Whole Hoggers, compelled Balfour to give considerable attention to Tariff Reform throughout the last phase of the campaign. While seeking Free Trade votes by relegating fiscal reform to the referendum, he had constantly to assure the Whole Hogger wing that its policy would be the first constructive act of a Unionist Government. Balfour accomplished this dialectical task with considerable skill, but it undoubtedly contributed to the electors' confusion as to where the Unionist Party stood. Asquith spoke for many, if not for himself, when he complained: 'It is difficult for a man of slow moving intelligence like myself to keep pace with such a bewildering series of twists, gyrations, and somersaults.'[103]

But the gyrations were not quite ended. The referendum had not quite run its wayward course. On 6 December Balfour telegraphed Waldorf Astor, Unionist candidate for Plymouth, that in the referendum 'Each voter would have the right to give one vote and no more', thereby in the view of one Unionist 'destroying our case against the Plural Voting Bill'.[104] Privately, Unionists were caustic. Fabian Ware, thoroughly disenchanted with Balfour wrote: 'I went to see Salome the other night – the dance of the Seven Veils made me think politics. If F.C.G. saw it he would certainly give us A.J.B. in the part throwing off the last veil (plural voting) before presenting himself denuded to the electors.'[105] The Unionists were rapidly becoming the victims of their own ingenuity.

What of the Liberal reaction to this response to their challenge? If

momentarily taken aback, they quickly recovered, and outside Lancashire the pledge does not seem to have caused them much alarm. As
the *Morning Post* had foretold, the scheme was mercilessly pilloried as
opportunist. Margot Asquith told Strachey: 'Your party have *doubled*
and shuffled and surrendered at every point and I shd. not be sur-
prised if their gross political dishonesty wd. lose as much as they
think it will gain.'[106] According to the old theory, argued the *Westminster Gazette*, 'the House of Lords was to stand between the country
and passing gusts of popular madness. According to the new theory
everything of importance is to be submitted to the popular madman
in the moment of his delirium.'[107] Much play was made over differences in the Unionist camp, and Liberals used the rifts to suggest that
the pledge was fraudulent. Asquith delighted in the technical difficulties.
What if the referendum were defeated? Austen might promise to resign
but what about the rest? 'Apparently the Government . . . are going to
sit on placidly at Westminster as though nothing had happened . . .
framing . . . new Budgets for fresh referenda year after year in a discredited House of Commons. . . .'[108]

But the prime purpose of Liberal speeches and editorials was to
present the Unionist decision as a retreat if not a rout. The theme was
treated most memorably by Churchill in a speech at Sheffield on
30 November.

> What a ridiculous and pitiful spectacle is the rout of a great political party.
> General Scuttle is in command, the white flag is hung out over the Tory clubs,
> over many a noble residence and many a public house. Army colours, baggage,
> ammunition – all are scattered behind along the line of flight. . . . In the very
> forefront of the retreat gleams the white feather of their leader. . . . We have got
> them on the run, and what you have to do is to keep them at it.[109]

But one aspect of the Albert Hall speech, the Home Rule challenge,
left Liberals uneasy. Many ignored it; others, like Asquith, argued
that it was absurd to ask Liberals to submit their measures to a form
of adjudication they opposed. As the early pollings revealed that again
the Irish would hold the balance, the air became thick with Unionist
taunts that the Liberals were afraid to trust the people on Home Rule.

In all his later speeches, Balfour repeated his challenge on Home
Rule and demanded details of the Liberals' Irish plans. What was meant
by the 'supremacy of the Imperial Parliament'; was devolution or
dominion status intended; what financial agreements would there be;
what of Irish representation at Westminster; what, above all, was the
future of Ulster?

Asquith replied with references to his earlier declarations, particularly his Albert Hall pledge on Home Rule in December 1909.[110] Asquith's biographers accept this as adequate response,[111] but Asquith's reply did not meet the gravamen of Balfour's charges. This was that in an election to elect a Parliament which would present a measure to enact Home Rule, Liberal Ministers had given no indication of the nature and scope of that measure. The reiteration of the earlier Albert Hall statement was no response to this criticism, for that promise was made primarily to keep the Irish in line, not to inform the British electorate.

The Liberals were not guilty, as was later charged, of deceiving the electorate, for most Ministers made it quite clear that once the constitutional issue was settled they would push through Home Rule. In this sense they could claim a mandate. But they failed lamentably to educate the electorate on the nature of one of the major items of their legislation. They had many excuses, but this failure gave their opponents a useful weapon in the tortuous controversies of 1912-14.

V

Balfour and Asquith dominated, as they had not in January, their parties' campaigns. Balfour indeed had no rivals and his platform campaign was more energetic and pugnacious than ever before. Sandars, no sycophant, told Balfour: '. . . you have never done so well, your speeches have never been more vigorous or more telling.'[112] They also of course had a flavour rare in election speeches, the quality of unexpectedness.

Asquith stood out equally, though, from a more able collection of platform colleagues. He achieved a rare blend of intellectual force and platform effectiveness. Churchill wrote to him when all was over:

> . . . everyone feels that your leadership was the main and conspicuous feature of the whole fight. It is not always that a leader's personal force can be felt amid all that turmoil. You seemed to be far more effectively master of the situation and in the argument than at the Jan election, and your speeches stood out in massive pre-eminence whether in relation to colleagues or opponents . . . I noticed that Liberal audiences responded to your name with increasing enthusiasm as the days wore on. The result was decidedly a victory, and decidedly your victory.[113]

It was a fair assessment.

Balfour was supported by Curzon, Lansdowne and Milner but the peers made less impact than in the previous election, perhaps because the novelty had worn off. Milner, however, had one of the few really rowdy meetings of the election at Bow on 28 November and there was an attempt by 'a large crowd of roughs' to storm his meeting at North Islington on 1 December.[114] F. E. Smith was the most active of the Unionist Commoners. Sandars regarded him as 'Next to [Balfour] . . . the leading figure on the platform during the recent Election. His speeches, though violent at times, have been brilliant, forcible and popular. In Liverpool he is what Joe used to be in Birmingham.'[115] Austen Chamberlain, apparently confident of the family fief, ventured further afield than before with major visits to Unionist black spots such as Scotland and the North-East. Bonar Law established a national reputation without moving from Manchester, where his constituency campaign received unequalled coverage.

After opening in London, Lloyd George devoted himself almost exclusively to the Celtic fringe. For sheer physical endurance Churchill's arduous campaign was unparalleled. His spectacular performance on the eve of the first polls on 3 December was characteristic. On Friday morning, 2 December, he visited Labour Exchanges and Liberal Party workers in Manchester, then travelled to address two afternoon meetings in the marginal constituency of Eddisbury in Cheshire. Midnight found him across England at Grimsby where before an audience in the skating rink, he replied to Balfour's speech delivered there four hours before. In the morning on to Lincoln, where an angry polling-day crowd refused him a hearing in the 'most exciting incident of the election'.[116] Tireless, he travelled west to speak at Chester that evening.

One pathetic incident fittingly closes this account of the second election – the electoral performance of that 'moderate man' Lord Rosebery. The ex-Liberal Prime Minister addressed two great 'non-party' meetings at Manchester and Edinburgh on 30 November and 3 December respectively. A decent pretence of non-partisanship was attempted at Manchester, but even this was abandoned at Edinburgh where the platform was mostly Unionist.

Although Rosebery was presented as the oracle of the moderate man, there was little in his speeches, apart from their undeniable polish, to distinguish them from the utterances of rabid Unionist partisans. He used the dollar cry, bewailed the Socialist menace, and claimed that the House of Lords 'has ceased to exist . . . It has surrendered its powers to the nation'.[117] He closed his Edinburgh speech with a description of 'Britannia, in her old age, casting away her helmet, and dancing a breakdown to the tipsy tune played to her by the Government, apparently prepared to revise at ten days' notice the Constitution of 800 years'.[118] Many must have thought his remarks more applicable to the Unionist Party than to Britannia and the Government.

His speeches were denounced by Liberals as 'unscrupulous and as cheap as the silliest mendacity in the repertoire of Tory demagogy'.[119] Lord Morley emerged to berate his one-time leader at Darwen and Asquith scoffed at his 'preposterous fears'.[120] Lloyd George was even more forthright. 'Lloyd George gave it to him at Glasgow . . . as he never got it before – called him a "chatterer", who had never done any good but only criticised others,' recorded the old Gladstonian Lord Armitstead, with ill-concealed relish.[121] Nor were Rosebery's new allies particularly appreciative. The Whole Hoggers abused him and the *Morning Post* rightly warned voters not to be seduced by his 'perfidious' suggestion that if the Government lost even five seats they could not proceed with their proposals.[122] With these two speeches Rosebery passed for ever from the public platform which he had so adorned, isolated and ineffectual, condemned by his one-time associates, used, abused, and ultimately discarded by his present friends.

Yet it was upon the Roseberys of the world, the moderate men, that the Unionists had gambled everything. To win their votes they had cast aside traditional principles; to secure their support they had jettisoned their own policies. Would the returns justify the sacrifices?

Winter 1910–11

I

The kaleidoscopic changes in Unionist policy during the election had stemmed above all from desperation. Sandars, critical of the failure of Balfour and the old guard to compromise, bluntly told his master on the eve of the Conference breakdown to prepare for 'our third consecutive defeat'.[1] A fortnight later Strachey wrote to Lansdowne: 'I hope I am not too pessimistic, but I confess to feeling very deep anxiety as to the course of the election. It seems to me almost impossible that we can obtain a majority or reduce the Government majority to a small figure. But nothing less than that can save the situation.'[2]

The 1910 by-elections had not been encouraging for the Unionists. Of the ten contested by-elections five had shown a swing to the Unionists, four against them and one, Mid-Glamorgan, a fight between Labour and Liberal, only confirmed the Liberals' ability to resist Labour expansion. At least until Balfour's pledge, prevailing opinion held that the result would range between a gain or loss of twenty-five seats for the Government.[3] Prior to the Albert Hall speech the odds at the Stock Exchange were 5/1 against a Unionist victory, and the market's estimate of the anti-Unionist majority stood at eighty, suggesting a Unionist net gain of some twenty seats.[4]

Unionist expectations certainly rose and the market's estimate of the Government's majority fell following Balfour's Albert Hall pledge. On the eve of the polls Strachey, immensely cheered by the developments of the past few days, wrote: 'Balfour and Chamberlain have both behaved splendidly and so has Lansdowne and I really feel we shall now win.'[5] The Stock Exchange did not endorse this extravagant optimism. If on the day following the pledge the estimate of the anti-Unionist majority tumbled to forty, second thoughts were more sober. On the morning of the first polls the estimate stood at sixty-three.[6]

However, if the Unionists had little hope of destroying the majority against them, they could hope to impair it sufficiently to thwart the

Government's constitutional designs. Unionists were ignorant, of course, of the guarantees, but even the guarantees were contingent not just on a majority, but on an 'adequate majority' (the phrase used in the Cabinet minute requesting guarantees).[7] Asquith had wisely hesitated to define an 'adequate majority', but when Knollys suggested fifty 'the King rather demurred to this number'. Knollys prayed that the issue would never arise. 'I am sure that as far as the King is concerned, it is very desirable the Government should maintain their majority, for then it appears to me that the course before him is pretty clear.'[8] If the Government's majority were seriously reduced then ministerial irresolution in dealing with the monarch might reappear, while Bigge and others who disliked the guarantees would be strengthened in their influence by heavy Liberal losses.

Unionist hopes and efforts were concentrated on those twenty-two seats lost against the national tide in January, and on another thirty to forty constituencies where Liberal majorities had been slim. Likewise Liberal hopes lay in regaining seats lost in triangular contests, recapturing surprise losses particularly of seats held both in 1900 and 1906, and in picking up seats amongst the thirty or so held with narrow Opposition majorities.

No one seems to have expected significant changes in Ireland, Scotland, Wales, or the North. Even in Lancashire itself *The Times* thought only one or two Unionist gains probable,[9] although there was an upward revision of Unionist expectations in Lancashire following the referendum pledge. Liberals had some prospects of recovery in the southern counties, but in the South-West they held a clutch of particularly vulnerable seats.

It was the concentration of marginal seats in London and its suburban fringe that provided the great question mark of the election. In his advance planning for the election the Liberal Chief Whip, Elibank, paid 'more particular attention to the 132 seats in London and the Home Counties'.[10] The Liberals had twenty marginal seats in this area. A slight swing to the Unionists in London coupled with gains in Lancashire could seriously damage the anti-Unionist majority. On the other hand the Unionists had over a dozen marginal seats in London. London therefore could well hold the key to an enhanced Government majority.

II

On Friday, 2 December, the first unopposed returns were announced; on Saturday, 3 December, sixty-four boroughs, returning sixty-nine Members, polled. In London that evening the results were eagerly awaited in the clubs and around the newspaper screens, although steady rain reduced the number of outdoor enthusiasts, turned Trafalgar Square into a sea of umbrellas, and dampened election-eve wit.

For Liberals, the first results, from Lancashire, were as depressing as the weather, suggesting as they did a strongly Unionist tide. Although Bonar Law failed in North-West Manchester, and the South-West division, lost in a triangular fight in January, was recovered by the Liberals, in all the other Manchester divisions the anti-Unionist majorities were alarmingly reduced. In adjoining Salford, the Southern division was lost and Liberal majorities cut back in the other two seats. In nearby Ashton-under-Lyne, in the most surprising result of the evening, the Liberal Member was toppled by an unknown young Canadian, Max Aitken, who had only been in the constituency five days.[11] To the north, in Wigan, the Labour Member was defeated; in the west, at Warrington, F. E. Smith's brother captured a further seat for the Conservatives. All over Lancashire, the anti-Unionist majorities fell.

It was with some trepidation that the Liberals awaited the London returns, for if the movement in Lancashire was reproduced the Government would be in trouble. But the London results changed 'the whole current of the fight'.[12] First came the news that the determined Unionist attack on the two vulnerable Shoreditch seats had been repulsed, then that the Liberal majorities had been increased in the two marginal Newington constituencies, and finally that the Unionist Member had been ousted at Peckham. Of the nine London constituencies polling, in only one did the Unionists increase their proportion of the vote. London had once again failed the Unionists and, as was soon plain, ended their chances of seriously reducing the majority against them.

In the industrial North, outside Lancashire, anti-Unionist majorities declined marginally, and Darlington was lost. In the Midlands and in the southern boroughs Unionist majorities fell slightly and the party lost Exeter[13] and Rochester. In the eastern counties however, the Unionists recaptured Grimsby and King's Lynn.[14] The one Scottish borough polling, Perth City, merely confirmed Liberal solidarity in the Celtic fringe.

On the day's polls, the Unionists had captured seven seats, the Liberals four. In thirty-six seats there was a swing to the Unionists, in twenty-five a movement to the anti-Unionists, in three no change. The slight shift in votes to the Unionists (under 1 per cent) was so marginal as to occasion little real danger for the Liberals.

Nor did the Unionists do better in the days that followed, despite the continued deterioration of the Liberal position in Lancashire. In Liverpool all the Unionist majorities were up: the one Liberal seat, Exchange, was lost and only 'the old, obdurate, impenetrable foxhole of Nationalism, the Scotland Ward',[15] prevented a clean Tory sweep. Across the Mersey, the electors of Birkenhead rejected one of the few remaining Lib-Labs, Henry Vivian. Labour lost to the Unionists at Newton and St Helens, although further Liberal losses at Darwen and Altrincham were partly offset by a gain at Burnley.

Throughout the rest of the North the substantial anti-Unionist majorities of January tended to fall, but this decline resulted in only one further Unionist gain, Eskdale. Indeed it was the anti-Unionists who were on balance successful. They recaptured the two seats at Sunderland,[16] won Wakefield for the first time since 1885, and regained Whitehaven and Cockermouth, lost on a minority vote in January. There was little change in the Midlands,[17] but Liberal gains in East Anglia and the southern counties offset several losses in Devon and Cornwall.[18]

Garvin's 'we have done rottenly in London'[19] summed up the Unionist reaction to the Metropolitan situation. Paradoxically, while after the first day the overall swing in London was to the Unionists, the anti-Unionists possessed an uncanny ability to get votes where they most mattered, winning, in addition to Peckham, Bow and Bromley, Stepney, Woolwich, and West Southwark, and losing only North Islington and West St Pancras.

In Scotland and Wales the position remained unchanged. The loss of Cardiff, considered by Unionists a distinct rebuff to Lloyd George,[20] was offset by the Liberal gain at Radnorshire. Similarly in Scotland the Unionists gained St Andrews, the Liberals Kirkcudbright. In Ireland, the Nationalists captured two Unionist seats, South Dublin and Mid-Tyrone, and effectively contained the O'Brienites.

The most striking feature of the results was the similarity of the verdict with that of ten months before. With the pendulum virtually

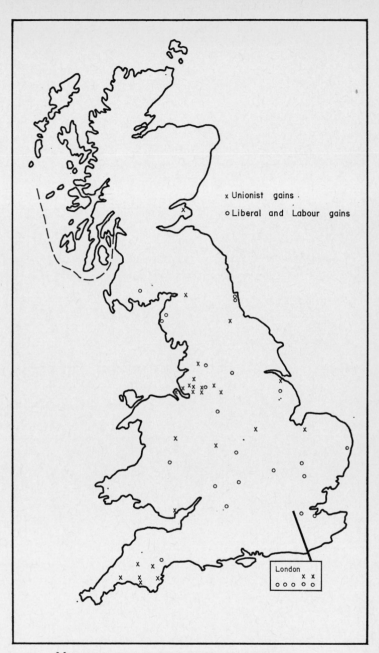

Map 10.1 DISTRIBUTION OF PARTY GAINS DEC 1910

stilled both sides picked up a number of their opponents' vulnerable seats. All but three of the Unionist, and five of the anti-Unionist, victories were in seats with majorities of less than 6·0 per cent in January.[21] '. . . if we put aside certain constituencies of habitual instability', concluded *The Times*, 'the identity of the verdict, though with the enfeeblement of the Liberal vote, with that of the last General Election, is remarkable.'[22] And this 'enfeeblement', the *Daily Mail* confessed, involved but 'a very slight and infinitesimal oscillation of the pendulum against the Government'.[23] It was certainly insufficient to save the House of Lords.

TABLE 10.1 RESULTS DECEMBER 1910

Seats at dissolution	Unionist 274★	Liberal 274★	Labour 40	Nationalist 82	
					Losses
Won from Unionists		23	4	2	29
Won from Liberals	24		1		25
Won from Labour	3				3
Won from Nationalists					0
Gains	27	23	5	2	57
Net gain or loss	−2	−2	+2	+2	
1911 Parliament	272†	272	42	84‡	

Notes: ★ The Liberal Member for Montgomery Boroughs, Sir John Rees, crossed the floor in the last week of the 1910 Parliament.

† Includes F. Bennett-Goldney (Canterbury), elected as an independent Conservative against official party opposition.

‡ Includes 10 independent Nationalists.

III

The coincidence of the figures, however, was the only parallel with January. For the results in December were decisive, and seen to be decisive, in a way that the identical results in January had not been. Unionists might comfort themselves that it was a 'dead heat' election, that the position was as before, but this was so only in a most formal sense. Even for most Unionists a further election was 'unthinkable'.[24] For Liberals the time for compromise was passed. Churchill spoke for the party and the Cabinet when writing to Asquith in the New Year:

We cannot parley with the Tories on any question until we can meet them on fair and equal terms. We cannot resume discussions where we argue and they decide, where we propose and they pronounce. . . . We ought to go straight ahead with the Parliament Bill and carry it to the Lords at the earliest date compatible with full discussion.[25]

The Ministry made certain immediately of the guarantees. On 17 December Lloyd George wrote to Asquith, stressing that it was 'vital' that the Prime Minister see the King at 'the earliest possible moment', for 'The Tory papers which he reads and whose opinions in the main he accepts and assimilates are busily engaged in persuading him that our majority is inadequate. . . . If he adopts the Tory view of the election now, and that aspect of it sinks into his brain your difficulties later on will be enormously increased and may well become insuperable.'[26]

Three days later Asquith had an audience with the King. The Prime Minister's confidence is conveyed clearly if crudely in Elibank's account of the meeting.

The P.M. has seen the King: the interview was cordial and satisfactory. Asquith pointed out that the majority was cohesive & formidable & had been 'returned' after what in effect had been a 'Referendum'. . . . The King trotted out the Bigge arguments re the Irish – which were at once demolished. The *British* majority being evidently a new idea to him![27]

Nor did the Ministry shrink from the idea of creating peers if the need should arise. Some even welcomed the prospect. Churchill, for one, argued that 'Such a creation would be in fact for the interest of the Liberal party and a disaster for the Conservatives' for it would facilitate the passage of Liberal legislation.[28] The occasion, however, would probably not arise, although if there were 'any dilatory vapourings in the Lords' it might be necessary to 'clink the coronets in their scabbards'.[29] The Ministry had emerged from the second election with an enhanced authority and a determination to use it.

Ministers derived assurance from the lamentable state of the Opposition. The Unionist Party 'are in a bad way, never worse', wrote the Prime Minister's secretary at the beginning of 1911. 'They have had to look on while their chief punctured their tyres and spilt their petrol and declare that such master strokes were never on this earth seen before.'[30] The fragile unity of the Unionist Party built up arduously from 1906 to 1909 and cemented in the anti-Budget campaign had been shattered.

The Albert Hall pledge was the cause of disunity. The advocates of the pledge assured their critics that it had saved the party from utter disaster. '. . . if I had taken a different line', wrote the author of the pledge, 'the Government anticipations would have been fulfilled, and we should have lost heavily.'[31] Lansdowne, on whom considerable responsibility for the pledge rested, agreed, being

> deeply persuaded that throughout the country Balfour's action gave immense satisfaction to our friends, and encouraged many who were comparatively luke-warm to give us their wholehearted support. . . . in many constituencies where we have won by narrow majorities we should have stopped short of winning but for the feeling which I have described.[32]

The most convincing evidence for this thesis was of course Lancashire. The reports from Manchester, and Salvidge's from Liverpool all supported Garvin's contention that 'the Referendum helped enormously in Lancashire and will help more yet'.[33] Elsewhere, however, success was limited.

Victory or substantial gains might have silenced the Whole Hoggers; defeat made them vocal. They had stood by and seen the Tariff Reform programme jeopardised, yet the party's electoral position was virtually unchanged. They did not, indeed could not, accept the argument that the pledge had saved the Unionist Party from catastrophe. For Highbury to accept the Balfour–Lansdowne thesis would be to admit that Tariff Reform was an electoral handicap.

Basing his case on a number of particular returns, Austen Chamberlain argued that 'the result has shown, that whilst wrong in itself, [the pledge] would not even serve the end in view and win seats'.[34] For the Whole Hoggers, the substantial body of Free Fooders, supposedly ensnared by the pledge, were a 'regiment without privates', 'non-existent outside the few counting houses and clubs where [the] conspiracies have been hatched'; 'not worth', in Austen Chamberlain's opinion, 'a hundred votes in any constituency'.[35]

Some of the Whole Hoggers went further. 'For every moderate Liberal or Unionist Free Fooder we have gained we have lost a thousand Tariff Reform votes amongst the working classes.'[36] The candidate for South-West Manchester claimed that the pledge 'did not help but it hurt me',[37] while the aggrieved Professor Hewins, defeated at Middleton, complained to Austen Chamberlain: 'I should have won but for the disastrous Albert Hall speech – this lost me hundreds of votes just in the districts where I stood to gain most by my uncompromising advocacy of Tariff Reform, and where it is impossible to win on the House of Lords issue.'[38]

Antipathy to Balfour grew, at first in secret. Leo Maxse of the *National Review* was particularly venomous. 'Balfour so palpably means continuous disaster. Up to now those who count in our Party have sacrificed the cause and their principles to this sinister individual, but I feel quite sure that this cannot last as the discontent is too profound and widespread.'[39] It could not remain bottled up until the election was over. Predictably, the banner of revolt was raised by the *Morning Post*. On 13 December Lawrence wrote to warn Chamberlain that 'Fabian Ware says Balfour has "led" us three times to destruction and he (Ware) is biding his time to explode . . .'.[40] The explosion came the following day, sparked off by Balfour's promise at Dartford on 12 December to submit a Tariff Reform budget rather than Tariff Reform principles to the referendum. With this promise, commented the *Morning Post*, 'the last vestige of practicability has vanished from the unfortunate proposal'. The *Morning Post* did not mince its words. 'It is no longer possible or desirable to ignore the gravity of the situation into which the Unionist Party has drifted in the past fortnight.' The Albert Hall pledge inspired by 'Mr Chamberlain's enemies within the Unionist camp' was 'a Radical departure from the time-honoured practice of the Constitution' and would shatter the basis of parliamentary government. Widening the indictment, it denounced the Rosebery–Lansdowne resolutions as 'an awkward load for Tariff Reform to carry' and pleaded for a return to the 'old Constitution'. It would be difficult to find during an election campaign so stark a disavowal of official policy as this.[41]

But apart from Ware and Maxse what other rebels were there? Discontent was widespread, mainly among the younger party members, the Jebbs and the Gouldings, and among politicians such as Milner, Wyndham and Ridley. None of these was a major figure in the party. Others of the Whole Hogger leaders had been compromised, for, as Austen Chamberlain noted: '. . . many men, and Tariff Reform leaders among them, did not wait to be consulted. They pressed this proposal on Balfour with unanimity and promised him victory if he would take their advice.' But in the next sentence of this letter, he indicated the one possible leader of the discontent. 'I was a voice crying in the wilderness I stood alone.' To Austen Chamberlain the rebels turned.[42]

Yet Austen was not the stuff from which rebels are made. His deep personal admiration for Balfour – 'he stands a head and shoulders above the rest of us' – immunised him against the bitter rancour felt by many Whole Hoggers for the party leader. Nor had he failed to appreciate the lessons of his father's career. 'We can only win by and through the Party ... *if we quarrel with it, we can indeed ruin it, but we can't carry Tariff Reform.*'[43] On the other hand the blow to his father's policy was 'a great discouragement'.[44]

He was to speak for the last time in the campaign at Buxton on 15 December, and was pressed to denounce the Albert Hall policy. His decision to do so resulted from mounting evidence that Balfour's pledge was to be a permanent feature of Unionist policy. The Free Fooders believed it should be so on grounds of principle; the Balfourites and their recently acquired allies from the Chamberlain faction worked to retain it because they saw it as indispensable for a future electoral victory – 'when the poorer constituencies understand that no votes for the Unionist Government ... can irrevocably commit them to the food tax the effect will be enormous',[45] or because the party could simply not afford to revoke it – 'we have to stand by his declaration for good or evil'.[46] The permanence of the pledge was implied in a letter from Balfour, received by Austen on the eve of the Buxton speech.[47] A further goad was the insinuation that Austen Chamberlain, like Bonar Law, had acquiesced in the pledge prior to its promulgation.[48]

While expressing his personal disagreement with the Albert Hall policy, Chamberlain's concern at Buxton was not with the past but with the future. He stressed that the pledge was 'for this election' and implied that it would not be repeated. The speech also seems to be the origin of the idea that Balfour only made a contingent pledge, a pledge dependent on the Liberals agreeing to refer Home Rule.[49]

This was going too far too early. Sandars, himself the recipient of 'violent remonstrances from more than one quarter' about the Buxton speech, was furious: 'What I care most about is the shocking example of disloyalty in high places: it is wholly indefensible. . . . And before the Election is over! The Radical papers are all screaming with delight . . . and I hear it is the staple joke at our expense at Election meetings during the last few days.'[50] From Lancashire Derby stormed: 'What the devil is the meaning of Austen's speech . . . Damn these Chamberlains – they are the curse of our party and of the country.' The real cause of Derby's anger was not the disloyalty but the fact that Austen was attempting to render temporary a policy which Derby and others wished to see permanent. 'I hold A.J.B.', wrote Derby, 'has bound his party to submit Tariff Reform to a Referendum – before it becomes law – that promise holds good for all time and not only as Austen says for *this* election.'[51]

While the *enragés* Tariff Reformers were committed to the revocation of the Albert Hall pledge, and in some cases to the overthrow of the party leader – Maxse's notorious 'Balfour Must Go' article appeared in the January 1911 issue of the *National Review* – other lines of cleavage were developing in the party. On future policy towards the House of Lords a divergence of opinion had appeared by the end of the election. This development was ominous, not simply because of the passions aroused, but because it cut across the factional lines on the fiscal question, not obliterating them but merely adding a new dimension to the disunity of the Unionist Party.

Garvin, who for the past two years had alternated between bouts of conciliation and compromise on the one hand, and stark extremism on the other, now demanded resistance to the bitter end on the Parliament Bill. On 18 December headlines in the *Observer* urged that 'The Puppet Peers be Made' so that the Government would perish in ridicule and ignominy. Privately, through Sandars, Garvin warned Balfour against surrender: 'You cannot conceive how hateful the remotest thought of surrender is to the broad masses of our party. Unionist leadership responsible for accepting the Veto policy without compelling the threatened guarantees (the obtained guarantees?) to be executed, never would be trusted or followed again.'[52] Balfour, however, shrank from such action and inclined to surrender 'hateful as it is'.[53] But not so for many among the angry activist element in the Tariff Reform wing, whose temperamental affinity for a last-ditch stand would merely be strengthened by knowledge that Balfour contemplated surrender. Nor were such emotions confined to the Whole Hoggers, for the frustrations engendered by the party's third successive defeat ensured a response to Garvin's call among Balfourites and Free Fooders too.

On the other hand it was the great vehicle of the Whole Hoggers, the *Morning Post*, that was most outspoken in condemnation of the Garvin policy. 'We are glad to see', Fabian Ware wrote on 21 December, 'that Unionists generally are inclined to deprecate the extraordinary suggestion that the House of Lords should in the last resort compel the Government to ask the Crown for 500 dummy Peers.' For once, Ware found an ally in Strachey and the *Spectator*. To a receptive Lansdowne Strachey stressed the existence among Unionists of 'a very strong desire not to run any risk of throwing the Monarchy after the House of Lords', and counselled, therefore, against 'violent or extra-constitutional action'.[54] In the *Spectator* editorial of 17 December he saw submission as inevitable: 'If [the Liberals] insist on taking their full pound of flesh, they cannot be prevented from doing so.' Thus did the rift between 'hedgers' and 'ditchers' begin to develop as the results came in.

Amongst many Unionists concern for the Lords was already over-shadowed by anxiety about the Union. The realisation that in the new Parliament 'to the Redmondite Canossa Mr Asquith must go'[55] might be humiliating for Liberals but it was alarming for Unionists. Some were already preparing to sacrifice the Lords in order to save the Union, as the year before they had given way on the Budget to save the Lords. Thus it was argued that the Liberals had a mandate for the Parliament Bill but not for Home Rule.[56] For Balfour the fatal flaw in Garvin's last ditch policy was that a mass creation of peers would facilitate the passage of Home Rule.[57] Better to hope that the cumbrous machinery of the Parliament Bill would, with the Liberals 'slaving for Mr Redmond' for three sessions, render the chances of Home Rule 'remote'.[58]

But so bleak was the prospect that an uglier note was heard. An Opposition whose effective constitutional veto was endangered hinted at a non-constitutional veto. Walter Long, the English Unionist most identified with Ireland, warned of civil war,[59] and the *Daily Express* observed that preparations for civil resistance in Ulster threw a 'grim shadow' over Christmas.[60] Would Asquith, challenged the *Morning Post*, be prepared 'to send British soldiers to rivet on the neck of the Protestant North the iron collar of the Redmondite domination?'[61] Even the usually sober *Times* played with the notion. 'Parnellite Home Rule will not be imposed upon Ireland except by physical force, which will be met by physical force. . . . The Government are rushing down a steep place into the sea, and unless the country cuts the connection in time, it, too, will share in the Gadarene catastrophe.'[62]

Thus the second election restored the authority, *élan* and purpose of the Liberal Government, while it left the Opposition factious, uncertain and desperate. The years immediately ahead were years of considerable achievement for the Liberals, but of frustration and internal dissension for the Unionists. Yet, ironically, the defeated were soon to dominate British politics for a generation, while the victors were never to win again.

PART THREE

The Parties and their Allies

The Parties and their Candidates

I

The total of 1313 candidates in January 1910 was greater than in any electoral contest since 1885.[1] Only the fact that the virtual single-party systems of Ireland had hardened in the generation since 1885 prevented the record total of that year from being surpassed. In Great Britain the total of 1171 candidates was the greatest ever. Never before had so few seats been uncontested, while a third party, Labour, placed its largest contingent in the field. Every seat was fought in Scotland and Wales; only eight were left unfought in England.[2] Even in Ireland, where the unopposed election had become the rule, the O'Brienite revolt resulted in the greatest number of contests – thirty-seven – since the intra-party troubles of the 1890s.

The Unionists, fighting on the widest front of any party – they had a broader flank than the Liberals in Ireland, and they fought Labour in every seat – put up 595 candidates; the Liberals 512. With the virtual exception of Southern Ireland, the major parties operated throughout the British Isles, but all the smaller parties were geographically confined. Labour's seventy-eight candidates were limited almost entirely to the major industrial conurbations and the coalfields, with a few appearing in smaller industrial centres and ports. With the exception of T. P. O'Connor at Liverpool Scotland, a colony of Irish immigrants, the eighty-four official Nationalist candidates were confined to Ireland. The nineteen independent Nationalists were even more circumscribed. Two-thirds were found in the province of Munster, for as they were mostly O'Brienites, 'Rebel Cork', O'Brien's stronghold, tended to be 'the Mecca of the Movement'.[3] The ten candidates of the Social Democratic Party were all put forward in industrial constituencies. In addition there was a mixed bag of fifteen Independents, including rejects from the major parties, a prohibitionist, and a women's suffrage candidate.

While the geographical patterns were if anything more marked in

December, the number of candidates declined. To reserve their efforts, their finances and their forces for the decisive contests, all parties reduced their candidatures in the strongholds of their opponents; but only four seats marginal in January were unfought in December.[4] In Great Britain ninety-five seats went uncontested. The decreased number of contests, a drastic pruning of Labour candidatures, and Liberal and Unionist withdrawals from some triangular contests, reduced the total of candidates in Great Britain to 1049, 122 below the January total. As if to illustrate the imperviousness of Irish politics to the ebb and flow of British politics, contested seats there in December rose by one to thirty-eight, although the number of candidates fell by five owing to the elimination of three-cornered contests and an increase in the number of multiple candidatures. This gave an overall

TABLE 11.1 PARTIES AND CANDIDATES 1910*

Standing	Unionist	Liberal	Labour	Nationalist	Ind. Nationalist	Other	Total
Both elections	431 (50)†	369	47	70	10	6	933‡
Only Jan	164 (37)	143	31	14	9	19	380
Only Dec	117 (4)	98	9	9	11	8	252
Total Jan	595 (87)	512	78	84	19	25	1313
Total Dec	548 (54)	467	56	79	21	14	1185
Total candidates	712 (91)	610	87	93	30	33	1565

Notes: * All Unionist and Liberal candidates recognised by the official local organisations have been classified as Unionist or Liberal even when they campaigned under qualified nomenclature, e.g. Samuel Storey (Sunderland), who stood as an independent Conservative, and G. R. Bethell (Holderness), who stood as an independent Free Trader, have been listed respectively as Unionist and Liberal because they received the official backing of the respective local associations. Independent Unionist or Liberal candidates who stood against the official candidate or were refused party endorsement have been classified under 'other'. Only candidates recognised by the N.E.C. have been classified as Labour. Nationalist classifications are based on the *Freeman's Journal*.

† Figures in brackets indicate number of Liberal Unionist candidates.

‡ 935 candidates stood at both elections but as two candidates stood under different party classifications in each election they have been listed separately in the 'only January' and 'only December' lines. The two candidates were A. Cameron Corbett (Glasgow Tradeston) Jan: ind. Liberal; Dec: Liberal. T. F. Richards (West Woverhampton) Jan: Labour; (East Northants.) Dec: ind. Labour.

total of 1185 candidates[5] of whom 548 were Unionists, 467 Liberals, 56 Labour, 79 Nationalists, 21 independent Nationalists, 3 Social Democrats and 11 Independents.

Of those who fought in December 79 per cent had contested the previous election. Although a number of these candidates tackled new constituencies, in only seventeen constituencies was there no candidate from January, while 142 contests were identical in personnel.

II

No party approached the elections of 1910 untroubled by internal problems. Nevertheless, all except the Nationalists presented a relatively united front during the elections, although the Unionist façade was cracking by the end of the second election. Table 11.2 suggests some of the ways whereby particular internal problems were solved prior to the first election.

TABLE 11.2 M.P.S AND THE JANUARY DISSOLUTION

	Unionist	Liberal	Labour	Nationalist
M.P.s changing allegiance (1906–10)	3	15	–	–
M.P.s at dissolution (10 Jan 1910)*	166	371	45	82
M.P.s retiring	17	70	1	5
M.P.s changing seats	6	10	–	1
M.P.s standing again for same seats	143†	291‡	44	76§

Notes: * These dissolution figures differ slightly from those given in Table 7.1 because owing to deaths two Liberal and two Unionist seats and one Nationalist seat were vacant at the dissolution. Nor is Victor Grayson, independent Socialist M.P. for Colne Valley, included in this table.

† Includes T. H. Sloan (South Belfast), standing as an independent Unionist against an official candidate.

‡ Includes Harold Cox (Preston) and Cameron Corbett (Tradeston), standing as independent Liberals against official candidates.

§ Includes nine M.P.s standing as independent Nationalists against official candidates.

The years 1906–10 saw the virtual elimination of the Free Fooders within the Unionist Party. All the floor-crossings, a majority of the retirements, and two of the seat-changes were related to the fiscal quarrel. In these cases the fiscal question was usually the crucial, if not always the exclusive consideration.

The three Unionists who crossed the floor, Austen Taylor (East

Toxteth), Cameron Corbett (Tradeston) and Alexander Cross (Camlachie) were part of that unrepentant core of Free Fooders who had survived the 1906 landslide. Taylor joined the Liberals in February 1906, following the publication of Balfour's Valentine letter on fiscal policy. Corbett crossed in the autumn of 1908, Cross at the beginning of 1909. Although the fiscal question was at the root of their desertion, all three shared other sympathies with the Liberals. Taylor voted throughout the Parliament with the Liberals. The actual occasion of Corbett's break with the Unionist Party was the Licensing Bill of 1908, and he claimed that from August 1909 – when he returned to the Commons after an illness – until the end of the session he had voted 323 times for the Government and only once against it.[6] Cross, too, supported the Liberals over licensing and education, and he was rejected by his constituency association for having shown a general lack of sympathy with the Unionist Party.[7] Taylor retired in January 1910 but Cross stood unsuccessfully as the official Liberal candidate at Camlachie, and Corbett successfully as the independent Liberal candidate for Tradeston.

The fiscal quarrel played a part in over half the relatively few Unionist retirements. Ten of those retiring had links with the Free Food faction, seven of them appearing on the proscription list issued by the *Morning Post* in January 1909.[8] Certainly age and ill health abetted the purge of the Free Fooders. Sir John Kennaway, the father of the House (Honiton), Sir John Batty Tuke (Edinburgh and St Andrews Universities), Sir Francis Powell (Wigan) and J. G. Talbot (Oxford University) were all septuagenarian Free Fooders and in poor health. There were signs too of decrepitude amongst the sixty-year-old Free Fooders. Sir William Hornby (Blackburn) decided to retire because he was getting quite deaf and felt 'depressed by the House'.[9]

How far some of the younger Free Fooders found the party uncongenial and voluntarily retired, and how far they were driven out, is not always easy to establish. W. F. D. Smith (Strand), the future Lord Hambledon, seems to have given up politics in disgust,[10] while at Aylesbury the Free Fooder Lionel Rothschild made way for a more pliant member of the same family. At Hertford Abel Smith was ejected by the Confederates. By mid-1909 there were rival Unionist associations in Hertford, one supporting the incumbent, the other organised by a resident Confederate, Henry Page Croft, running a Whole Hogger candidate, Mortimer. The rebel organisation, built up through the local T.R.L. branches, seemed the stronger of the two and claimed that it supported the whole policy of the party. A face-saving compromise for Abel Smith was devised in October 1909. It was well described by Page Croft: 'Mr Abel Smith decided to stand down on condition that our candidate, Mr Mortimer, stood down also, which he agreed to do, and we thereupon adopted an out-and-out tariff reformer. . . .'[11]

Of the six Unionist M.P.s who sought new seats, two, Walter Long and G. D. Faber, sought safer ones. Long gave up perilous South Dublin for the blue-ribbon Strand seat, and Faber gave up marginal York for the relative security of Clapham. The two Liberal M.P.s who had crossed to the Unionist side of the House, Commander Carlyon Bellairs and Major A. L. Renton, each sought more congenial surroundings than the seats they had won as Liberals in 1906. The remaining two Unionists seeking new seats were Lord Robert Cecil and Stewart Gibson Bowles – Free Fooders fleeing from troubles in their own constituencies.

Along with Abel Smith, Cecil (East Marylebone) and Bowles (Norwood) had been the chief victims of Confederate attention. Bowles was disowned in January 1909 by his local-association executive which had by August selected a new candidate and issued a manifesto against the sitting Member. The combative Bowles fought back by establishing a rival association, and a split Unionist vote seemed assured, Central Office attempts at compromise being thwarted by the irreconcilable spirit of the opposing factions in the constituency.[12]

A similar situation existed in East Marylebone. Here too a rival Whole Hogger organisation had been established. The rebels allied themselves with a local Conservative 'home-rule' movement, which desired to break away from the Marylebone Constitutional Union, the Conservative organisation which ran both parliamentary constituencies – East and West Marylebone – and was allegedly dominated by 'Westerners'. Once again the rebels showed a certain talent for organisation. While Cecil's agent struggled to get subscribers for the Marylebone Constitutional Union – only 25s. from two hundred letters – the new association quickly rounded up 1500 members, secured finance and won recognition from the Liberal Unionist Council.[13]

The prominence and connections of Lord Robert Cecil rendered the East Marylebone contretemps particularly disturbing to the Unionist leadership. Selborne, Cecil's brother-in-law, warned Balfour, Cecil's cousin, that if the East Marylebone 'rent' were not healed before the election 'we shall present this sorry spectacle to the world, half your old Cabinet including myself supporting Bob and half supporting a rival Unionist candidate and speaking on opposing platforms!'[14] A compromise proposed by Selborne in August was almost successful, but by this time the revolt in East Marylebone had acquired an independent momentum. When the rebel executive and the rebel candidate accepted the Selborne compromise they were thrown over by their followers.[15]

At this point Cecil and Bowles were persuaded to abandon their damaging fratricidal contests and to fight the two-member seat of Blackburn, a reputed Free Trade citadel. This solution had the approval of the Whips, 'the Bonar Law–Goulding lot', and had been actively canvassed by the Lancashire Free Fooders.[16] Blackburn had been represented in the 1906 Parliament by the Free Fooder Hornby and Labour's Philip Snowden. Until 1906 both seats had been solidly Conservative and, provided Hornby could pass on his strong personal vote, Blackburn seemed to offer a secure haven for at least one of the persecuted Free Fooders. Unfortunately this overlooked two further factors. If the local Labour and Liberal parties could achieve better relations than in 1906 then the anti-Unionist alliance might well capture both seats, particularly in the absence of the locally popular Hornby. Secondly, Blackburn was not only a stronghold of the Free Fooders, but also a bastion of the militant evangelicals, and Cecil and Bowles had been distinguished upholders of the high church position against the Protestant anti-ritualists. Both were to find that their transfer was a case of out of the Confederate frying-pan into the sectarian fire.

Liberal troubles were less dramatic and less easily defined, there being no dominant theme running through Liberal floor-crossings and retirements. Of the fifteen Liberal M.P.s changing their allegiance thirteen, the miners, went to the left, and two, Bellairs (King's Lynn) and Renton (Gainsborough) went to the right. The movement of Bellairs and Renton was more typical of the currents at work in the Liberal Party. Both had crossed the floor on the defence issue, Renton in November 1907, Bellairs in October 1909. Renton had voted with the Unionists on all major issues since 1907, while by the autumn of 1909 Bellairs was as much concerned about the 'socialistic' policies of Lloyd George and Churchill, as about the Government's external policies.[17] Both stood as Unionists in 1910.

But the most striking symptom of Liberal malaise was the large number of Liberal M.P.s retiring. In absolute terms Liberal retirements were four times as numerous as Unionist, and proportionately nearly double the rate amongst Unionists. Some withdrew in anticipation of preferment, for of the seventy retiring Liberals ten were created peers or took up judicial or administrative posts within the next twelve months. Some withdrew simply because they lacked vigour. Nearly half those retiring were over sixty and many advanced medical grounds for their departure. The seventy-year-old James Caldwell (Mid-Lanark) could not fight the election because after the arduous session it was 'imperatively necessary to take a lengthened sea voyage in order to avoid the winter climate and recuperate'.[18] Even a younger man like D. C. Erskine (West Perthshire) refused to stand again on the grounds that 'the strain of parliamentary duties was so severe'.[19]

But there were other factors explaining the wastage of Liberal M.P.s. Early in 1908, before the disastrous by-election sequence had sapped Liberal morale, Montagu had reported to Asquith: 'The Private Member seems to me unenthusiastic, listless, disappointed where he is not disaffected and disgusted.'[20] About one-third of the retiring Members could be classified with the 'disaffected or disgusted' as they had opposed one or more major items in the Government's programme. Some had disliked the Government's Scottish land policy; others such as Julius Bertram (Hitchin) and S. H. Whitbread (Huntingdon), both with links with the brewery trade, had voted regularly against the Government's licensing proposals. But the chief source of disaffection was the growing collectivist tendencies in Government policy. Sir Robert Perks, announcing his retirement at Louth, gave as his reasons dislike of the Budget and fear of further socialist legislation, as well as his own disappointment with the Government's handling of Nonconformist grievances.[21] The much-advertised lists of secessions from the constituency Liberal parties during 1909-10 suggest that Perks, in protesting against the un-Gladstonian currents in the Edwardian Liberal Party, spoke for a number of Liberals outside, as well as for some inside, Parliament.[22]

It is difficult to ascertain whether these M.P.s withdrew voluntarily, or were ousted by their constituency associations. The responsibility for discipline fell very much on the constituencies, as the Government's majority had allowed considerable tolerance at Westminster. Harold Cox, a root-and-branch critic of the Government's social reform policies, was thrown over by the Liberal association at Preston without central encouragement, indeed against headquarters' advice.[23] R. L.

Everett, an aged but persistent anti-Budget sniper, was rejected by his local association at Woodbridge, while H. C. Lea, who seems to have deliberately abstained on the third reading of the Budget, was refused renomination at East St Pancras.[24] Lord Dalmeny, Rosebery's heir, probably escaped a similar fate by disclaiming late in 1908 any intention to stand again for Midlothian. As he candidly confessed: 'It is being forced upon me more and more that my politics are not far enough advanced to meet the views of the Liberal Party as at present constituted. . . .'[25] A similar realisation, combined with a reluctance to perpetuate local differences, probably lay behind a number of other withdrawals. Certainly in Louth, Mid-Norfolk, Carlisle and Brighton there had been serious quarrels between Whiggish Members and their more advanced supporters, and in each case the Member retired. By contrast, Sir George Kekewich seems to have been rejected at Exeter for his advanced views, or perhaps because of his probity, Kekewich himself instancing his stand against bribery in a highly marginal borough as the chief cause of his failure to secure renomination.[26]

Nor had the stirring events of 1909 dispelled entirely the listlessness, lack of enthusiasm and disappointment amongst back-benchers noted by Montagu in 1908. For back-bench Members of the great majority, life in the Commons was too often tedious, frustrating and wearisome, and offered few opportunities for individual distinction. The novelist A. E. W. Mason, Liberal Member for Coventry 1906–10, excused his refusal to stand again on the grounds of the demands of literature: but, says his biographer, 'the reason went deeper than that. . . . The pettiness and the lack of individuality inevitable in party politics galled him bitterly.'[27] Some were easy victims of such disillusion for, in the words of a long-time Liberal M.P., 1906 'floated into the House (to their own great surprise in some cases) some men but ill equipped for it'.[28] Of one retiring Member, Lord Wodehouse (Mid-Norfolk), his father Lord Kimberley admitted to Asquith: '. . . my son does not care much for Political Life, in fact he was too young really when elected [in 1906] he being only 22 years and 1 month old when returned.'[29]

A realistic appraisal of their chances probably influenced some of the withdrawals. Many of the seats won in 1906 had never been Liberal before and were unlikely to be again. Contests were frequently expensive for candidates, and this may have acted as a deterrent in a number of the more hopeless constituencies. The *Sunday Times* considered that the heavy Liberal withdrawals indicated that 'the gentlemen who floated in on the crest of the wave in 1906 entertained no delusions as to the possibility of the wave rising so high again'.[30]

Of course the keen politician could seek a safer seat. Three Liberal M.P.s left obviously insecure seats for what appeared to be easier contests. The consequences were not always happy. Timothy Davies abandoned the hopeless struggle at Fulham, which the Liberals had never won prior to 1906, but failed to hold Louth, Liberal since 1892, probably because of dissension within the local Liberal party. The wealthy Austrian-born industrialist, Alfred Mond, fled the borough of Chester, which he had won by forty-seven votes in 1906, and sought sanctuary at Swansea Town. There he encountered an abusive independent Labour opponent in the dockers' leader, Ben Tillett; considerable anti-semitism fanned by the local Conservative paper; and a Conservative-instigated outburst of affronted Welsh nationalism, reflected in placards bearing the derisive slogan 'Vales for the Velsh'.[31] Only the translation of W. H. Cowan from Guildford, perhaps the most miraculous of the miracles of 1906, to the safe Liberal seat of East Aberdeenshire was an unqualified success.

Mixed motives lie behind the remaining seven Liberal seat changes. Elibank's move from Peebles and Selkirk to historic Midlothian was prompted by tactical considerations as Midlothian was considered 'the keystone of a number of the surrounding constituencies [and] it was wise that a man of experience should be put in the field'.[32] J. F. L. Brunner no doubt welcomed the offer of his father's seat at Northwich in which the family chemical works were situated, particularly as Labour intervention appeared likely in his own seat at Leigh. The growing tension in the South Wales coalfield probably contributed to the mine owner D. R. Thomas's decision to leave the safe mining borough of Merthyr Tydfil, which he had controlled for twenty years, in order to contest the prestigious but marginal seat of Cardiff. C. H. Lyell's departure from marginal East Dorset to challenge the sitting Unionist at West Edinburgh may have resulted from pressure by the locally powerful Wimborne clan, anxious to secure East Dorset for a scion of the family, or it may simply have reflected the desire of a Scotsman to fight a Scottish seat. The effort of the millionaire soap manufacturer, W. H. Lever, M.P. for Wirral 1906–10, 'to scale the castellated walls of Ormskirk',[33] the preserve of the Stanleys, seems to have been a heroic act of political self-destruction.

At Kidderminster and Wisbech the Liberal Members, E. B. Barnard and A. C. T. Beck had quarrelled with their local associations, Barnard over licensing, Beck over the Budget. Both left these marginal seats to contest constituencies with strong Unionist traditions. Barnard fought Hertford where he lived and where he hoped to profit from Unionist quarrels.[34] Beck became the Liberal candidate for Chippenham, with the help of the retiring Member, Dickson-Poynder, the leading Liberal opponent of the land taxes.

Liberal concern over the high wastage-rate amongst their sitting Members, and over seat-flitting, was heightened by the large number of Unionist candidates fighting seats in which they had been defeated in 1906. Altogether eighty-four Unionists defeated in 1906 fought the same constituencies in January 1910.[35] Approximately one-third of these had held the seats prior to 1906, often for a decade or more, but others persisted with well-nigh hopeless contests. Most had assiduously cultivated the constituencies in the years since 1906. Typical was S. Samuel, who had been soundly defeated by Herbert Gladstone at West Leeds in 1906. In March 1907 Joseph Henry, Gladstone's chairman, reported that 'Samuel is always about, he went to two bazaars a fortnight ago unexpected and left a few pounds for the poor. Not that it matters much what he does.' Eighteen months later the tale is the same. 'Samuel is still throwing his money about like rain.' But with the slump in Liberal electoral fortunes a note of alarm has crept in: '. . . many of our friends are uneasy about it'.[36] All over the country Unionists convinced that 1906 was an aberration worked the constituencies lost in that disastrous year.

Liberal concern over this activity was increased because of the neglect of their constituencies by a number of the Liberal Members. In the wake of the 1908 by-election defeats the Executive Committee of the N.L.F. condemned such slackness, instancing the failure of one Member to speak in his constituency despite the fact that his defeated opponent from 1906 had been working hard ever since, while in another seat nearly lost, even registration had not been carried out.[37] Moreover the fact that in three of the four years of the 1906 Parliament, the Session had been prolonged into December, rather than prorogued in August as was usual, contributed to the Members' neglect of their constituencies.

But Liberal retirements and the activities of defeated Unionists seem to have had little influence on the results. While all the figures in Table 11.3 incline in the expected direction, only that in column A suggests a significant Unionist advantage. However, this figure is probably biased since a consideration in many Liberal retirements was the fact that the M.P. held a traditionally Unionist seat, and it was in such seats that the swing to the Unionists in January was highest.

TABLE 11.3 EFFECTS OF RETIREMENTS AND PERSISTENT CANDIDATES
JAN 1910

Median swing (1906–J. 1910)	A Median swing in constituencies with Liberal M.P. retiring at dissolution.	B Median swing in constituencies with Unionist M.P. retiring at dissolution.	C Median swing in constituencies with defeated Unionist candidate 1906 fighting again.
+4·3	+5·2	+4·1	+4·4

No Labour M.P. left his seat to fight another. Of Labour's forty-five M.P.s all but one stood again. The difficulties at South-West Manchester, where the Labour Member G. D. Kelly retired, suggest the problems the young party might have faced had it lost other sitting Members.[38] As at South-West Manchester such retirements might well have tempted the Liberal Party to reassert its claim to the seats.

The removal of so many irritants from the body politic meant that in Great Britain there were very few constituencies with rival candidates from the same party. Only in Ireland was the party schism carried to the polls to a significant extent.

TABLE 11.4 INTRA–PARTY CONFLICTS JAN 1910

Unionist	Liberal	Labour	Nationalist
5	4	0	18

Dual candidatures in the Unionist Party were mostly related to the fiscal quarrel. Cecil's departure did not heal the rift in East Marylebone which saw the most acrimonious of the five Unionist intra-party conflicts. On Cecil's retirement the Marylebone Constitutional Union selected Lord Charles Beresford, and when he departed for Portsmouth, James Boynton, a moderate Tariff Reformer. But the rebel association, now bereft of most of its leaders, persisted with the candidature of Richard Jebb, a fanatical Whole Hogger whom Beresford considered 'a dangerous lunatic.'[39] Jebb was backed by the East Marylebone 'Home Rulers', by those who saw Boynton's candidature as a sign of continuing Cecilian influence, and by the *Morning Post*.[40] Boynton, on the other hand, was supported by Cecil's allies, by the central party organisation, and increasingly by Unionist moderates in

East Marylebone. This protracted and much-publicised quarrel did more to mar Unionist unity in the first election than any other single event, and left bitter feelings in its wake. 'It will take a long time', wrote Sandars, 'before I can forgive [Ware's] vain and disloyal action in East Marylebone, where in order to advertise his own contentions, he did his best to lose us one of the safest seats in London.'[41]

The other four intra-party Unionist conflicts occasioned much less publicity and much less concern. Two of them, at Aberdeen and Glasgow Universities and South Belfast, were straight fights between two Unionists. In the university seat Sir Frederick Pollock stood as a Unionist Free Trader but, as the nominee of the Liberal members of the university senates and as the leading jurist critical of the Lords' rejection of the Budget, he was treated frequently as the Liberal candidate. This contest further illustrated the disintegration of the Free Fooders, with Arthur Elliot endorsing Pollock and Lord Robert Cecil his opponent.[42] In South Belfast T. H. Sloan, the independent Orange M.P., was opposed by an official candidate. Sloan had allied himself with the Free Fooders in the 1906 Parliament, but he had also supported the Budget and the resolution condemning its rejection. C. H. Seely stood again as a Free Fooder at Lincoln where he had come second in a triangular contest in 1906, but he too received only limited support from leading Free Fooders. At Canterbury a personal feud between the sitting Member, Henniker Heaton, and the Mayor, Bennett-Goldney, led to two Unionist candidates there and exasperation at party headquarters. 'Canterbury is the devil', wrote Sandars to Balfour. '. . . You might delicately touch Heaton with the proverbial barge pole: but not Goldney.'[43]

Two of the four independent Liberal candidates – Harold Cox (Preston) and Pritchard-Morgan (Merthyr Tydfil) – ran in two-member seats where a single official Liberal was running in tacit understanding with a Labour candidate; these interventions will be discussed as an aspect of Liberal/Labour relations in the next chapter. At Tradeston where the Unionist M.P. Corbett had crossed to the Liberal side in 1908, things were complicated by the devious manœuvres of Corbett. He seems to have aimed at securing the Liberal nomination, while retaining the support of the Liberal Unionist association. He failed to do either but succeeded in disrupting the Liberal association and in keeping the support of the Liberal Unionist executive, described by one disgruntled Conservative as 'merely a standing committee in Mr Corbett's interest'.[44] This limited tactical achievement and his strong personal following were sufficient for electoral success. The most peculiar independent Liberal candidate was at Walton, where the official Liberal candidate in 1906, E. G. Jellicoe, insisted on running again although the local Liberals had selected another candidate. Jellicoe justified his intervention on the grounds that having spent £2,000 on the 1906 election the local 'junta of wirepullers' was not entitled to dismiss him. However, there is some evidence to sustain the theory that Jellicoe was induced to stand again by F. E. Smith, as a means of guaranteeing the latter's return for Walton.[45]

In Ireland the unity of the Nationalist Party was menaced by the most serious factional conflict since the struggles of the 1890s. In eighteen seats rival Nationalist candidates went to the polls, and in several other seats feuds threatened but did not materialise. Most of the independent Nationalists were followers of the rebel Irish leaders, William O'Brien and T. M. Healy, but general dissatisfaction with the Nationalist Party allowed other discontents to flourish and there were several non-O'Brienite independents. The one-party nature of much of Ireland reduced the electoral sanction against intra-party conflicts. In all but two of these eighteen contests, the only candidates were Nationalists.

III

However ambiguous the results of the January election nationally, these results, combined with the prior withdrawals and rejections, did much to clarify the internal problems of the parties, at least in Great Britain. Only one unofficial candidate, Cameron Corbett, was returned in Great Britain and he was quickly absorbed by the Liberal Party, whose leaders had stood aloof from the Tradeston imbroglio.[46] All other independent candidates and the S.D.P. candidates were defeated, in most cases soundly trounced. In Ireland, however, there were eleven independent Nationalist victories. There, loyalty to the sitting Member whether he was Redmondite or rebel provided the dominant pattern.[47]

Free Fooder representation in the Unionist ranks was virtually eliminated. Not only were Free Food rebel candidates defeated, but prominent Free Fooders with official recognition went down. Bowles and Cecil were defeated at Blackburn despite their becoming retaliationists. F. E. Lambton (South-East Durham), who had defied the Confederates to do their worst and who was the only Unionist candidate not to mention Tariff Reform in his election address, lost his seat. At Darwen John Rutherford, who tried to be all things to all men on the fiscal issue, also lost his seat. The *Morning Post* commented waspishly: 'The Unionist Free Traders and the faint-hearted Tariff Reformers have learnt from the bitter lessons of the polls that the country wants no half measures and no compromises.'[48]

The other Free Fooders proscribed in January 1909 and still in the field – R. Williams (West Dorset), G. W. Woolf (East Belfast), E. A. Brotherton (Wakefield), M. Hicks Beach (Tewkesbury), Sir Philip Magnus (London University) and F. Mildmay (Totnes) – seemed to have saved their seats by sacrificing their beliefs.[49] Lord Hugh Cecil, virtually smuggled into one of the Oxford University seats, was the Free Fooders' solitary consolation.

The disappearance of many of the personal sources of discontent, and the high premium placed on party solidarity because of the impending second election, helped ensure that the period between the two elections was characterised by few of the constituency under-currents that had marked 1909. The chief determinant of whether a candidate ran a second time in 1910 was his success or otherwise in the January election. Despite the similarity of the result in the two elections, a surprisingly large number of candidates enjoyed or suffered a reversal of fortunes in December.

TABLE 11.5 JANUARY RESULTS AND THE DECISION TO STAND AGAIN

	Won in Jan		Lost Marginally in Jan (Majority against under 10%)		Lost Heavily in Jan (Majority against over 10%)	
	Standing Dec	Not Standing Dec	Standing Dec	Not Standing Dec	Standing Dec	Not Standing Dec
Unionist	261 [237]	12	78 [26]	53	92 [3]	99
Liberal	247 [225]	27	74 [31]	37	48 [5]	79
Labour	39 [36]	1	6 [2]	4	3 [1]	25
Nationalist	66 [64]	5	2 [1]	3	2 [1]	6
Ind. Nationalist	8 [7]	2	1 [1]	2	1	5
Other	1 [1]	0	2 [1]	0	4	18
Total	622 [570]	47	163 [62]	99	150 [10]	232

Note: Figures in brackets indicate number successful in December. Candidates changing party classification between the two elections are listed under January classification. See Table 11.1, p.210.

Of the forty-seven successful candidates who did not stand again in December, six had died during the year, one was dying, and two, Sir Christopher Furness (Hartlepools) and E. O. Sullivan (East Kerry), had been unseated on petition. Liberal retirements still ran ahead of Unionist, the number of relatively young Liberals dropping out suggesting that the Liberal malaise had not quite run its course. But patronage seems the chief explanation of the difference, seven of the retiring Liberals receiving peerages or judicial appointments during 1910. The one Labour Member retiring, David Shackleton (Clitheroe), was also the beneficiary of governmental patronage, becoming Senior Labour Adviser at the Home Office.

Two Liberals, however, retired on well-publicised political grounds. At South Salford Hilaire Belloc's long-suffering committee broke at last with their heterodox M.P., whose obsession with the alleged evils of the party system – the political sham fight and the despotism of the related front bench oligarchies – increasingly coloured his political behaviour. Nor had he endeared himself to the local party activists by treating teetotalism as a fad.[50] The other was Sir John Rees (Montgomery Boroughs), who in the last week of the 'short Parliament' crossed to the Unionist side of the house. In a long letter to *The Times*, which read like a Tory manifesto complete with critical asides on Lloyd George and Churchill, Rees revealed his utter disagreement with practically every major item of Liberal policy.[51]

The rest of January's victors fought again, all but three fighting the same seat. Bonar Law's dramatic move from his safe London seat, Dulwich, to the marginal Liberal seat, North-West Manchester, the key commercial constituency in the heart of cotton Lancashire, seems to have had two objectives. First it sought to provide a much-needed fillip for the Lancashire Unionists: 'a great bomb in the enemy's camp' as the enthusiastic Goulding put it.[52] Secondly, it aimed at ensuring the loyalty of Lancashire Unionism to the Chamberlainite cause. Balfour's initial hesitancy was overcome by Derby's generous promise of his brother's seat at Ormskirk for Bonar Law should he fail at Manchester; Bonar Law's doubts were dispelled by the glittering prospect held out to him by the promoters of the scheme. 'It would make you', Garvin told him, 'conspicuously beyond all other men the standard bearer of our cause in the next battle. . . .'[53] Bonar Law's translation was significant for the course of the election and for his own future. It led to his referendum initiative and it made conceivable the leadership coup of the following November. Bonar Law was the only Unionist Front-

Bencher to emerge from the second election with a greatly enhanced reputation. The press attention given to North-West Manchester and his challenge to Churchill to fight the seat made Bonar Law something of a hero to the Tory rank and file. Moreover despite his tergiversation on the referendum and Tariff Reform, he had managed to avoid alienating influential sections of the party as had both Balfour and Austen Chamberlain.

On the Liberal side a Verney gave up the family seat of Buckingham to a younger Verney, and went off to fight Christchurch, while E. G. Hemmerde an able, ambitious young lawyer, gave up his seat to challenge Beresford at Portsmouth.

Of those who had failed in January, 117 found new constituencies, thirty-one of these being returned. The renomination of nearly all the victors, the successful search for better seats by a number of the defeated, and the minimal shift of opinion between the elections, left few opportunities for new candidates in December. Of the 250 new candidates in December, only twenty-seven were successful.

There was even less opportunity for rebel candidates. Bennett-Goldney, pursuing his feud with the official organisation in Canterbury, was this time successful, but the other persistent Unionist rebel, T. H. Sloan (South Belfast), did not do as well as in January. The Liberals had only one internal conflict, at South Hackney where the local Nonconformists, backed by the *Daily News*, ran the Rev. R. H. Roberts against the idiosyncratic Liberal and dubious financier, Horatio Bottomley.[54]

The national S.D.P. could only afford to run one candidate, Hyndman, at Burnley, but two local branches put up candidates.[55] All were unsuccessful. Grayson ran as an independent Socialist at Kennington where, as he admitted after the election, 'we have been handsomely pulverised'.[56] There were also unsuccessful independent Labour candidates at East Northants. and East Carmarthen.

The situation in Ireland was much changed from January. The events of 1910 had revived the confidence of the Nationalists. The breakdown of the Constitutional Conference, the abandonment of talk of devolution, and the dominant position of the Nationalists seemed to render Home Rule imminent. In these conditions it was easy to picture the O'Brienites as allies of those who 'hated' the Irish people 'their name, their faith and fatherland'.[57] Moreover, the presentation of Redmond as the dictator, if it damaged the Liberals in Great Britain, only enhanced his stature in Ireland. Their strengthened position enabled the official Nationalists to contain the O'Brienites and to display magnanimity towards Laurence Ginnell (North Westmeath) and John McKean (South Monaghan), returned as non-O'Brienite independents in January. Despite increased candidatures the O'Brienites merely held their own, losing South Mayo and North Louth and gaining seats at Cork City and South Cork. On Redmond's instructions Ginnell and McKean were returned unopposed and soon after readmitted to the party.[58]

IV

The patterns of the parliamentary and electoral experience of the candidates reflected above all the effects of 1906. That election had decapitated a generation of Unionist politicians and denied parliamentary opportunities to many younger Unionists. Thus it was with a relatively inexperienced team that the Unionists fought the January election. Only 36 per cent of the Unionist candidates had sat in the Commons, whereas 61 per cent of the Liberals and 56 per cent of the Labour candidates had done so, and this despite the heavy wastage among Liberal M.P.s. Persistence of defeated Unionist candidates from 1906 narrowed the gap in electoral expertise between the parties. In all 59 per cent of Unionist candidates had stood at least once before compared with 72 per cent of Liberal, and 69 per cent of Labour candidates.

If Unionist persistence and Liberal retirements moderated the effects of 1906 on the patterns of political experience in January 1910, the results of the January election served further to erase these effects in December. The proportion of Unionists with parliamentary experience still trailed their opponents, but Unionist successes in January had considerably bridged the gap. There was now little difference in the proportions of electorally experienced candidates put forward by the parties. Indeed, the outstanding feature in December is that the election was fought by experienced campaigners, only 18 per cent of all candidates being without electoral experience as compared with 34 per cent in January.

Most of these remarks are not applicable to the Irish parties for Ireland was unaffected by 1906. Of all the parties the Nationalists were pre-eminently the party of those with parliamentary experience, 80 per cent of the Nationalist candidates falling in this category. As Ireland was not subject to electoral shifts, indeed subject to very limited electoral competition, a candidate once nominated usually had a life tenure provided he could avoid factionalism in the constituency. This meant of course that electoral experience was limited, 41 per cent of the sitting Nationalist M.P.s in January 1910 having never previously faced a contested election.

An examination of career patterns reveals that only prior parliamentary experience was highly correlated with electoral success. In January 75 per cent of candidates with parliamentary experience were successful; in December, with little electoral movement, an even higher proportion, 86 per cent. There was little difference in party patterns, although the high ratio of Labour successes in defensive contests, and the static nature of politics in Ireland, gave the minor parties above average proportions in this respect in both elections, while in January, with the tide running strongly against them, only 69 per cent of Liberals with parliamentary experience were successful. And the impact of the electoral shift on the Liberal figure had been cushioned by the voluntary retirement of many Liberals sitting for vulnerable seats. Previous but unsuccessful electoral experience as a party nominee gave candidates a marginal advantage over those without such experience, 39 per cent of the former being successful in January as compared with 24 per cent of the latter. The comparative figures for December were 12 per cent and 9 per cent.

One-quarter of the Unionists and one-third of the Liberals had local government experience, but they did no better than candidates without it. Local government was a more important recruiting ground for the Labour and Nationalist parties,[59] slightly over half the candidates of both parties having had a period in local politics. Only, however, in the Labour Party did candidates with local government experience do distinctly better than those without.

Carpet-baggers were, as they had always been, familiar figures in British elections; the more prominent the politician the more likely he was to be a non-resident candidate.[60] Nearly half the candidates were carpet-baggers, and the practice seems to have caused some resentment in rural constituencies.[61] Unionist and Labour selection committees appear to have placed slightly greater emphasis on residence than the Liberals, while in Ireland the United Irish League deliberately encouraged 'adequate representation of the country constituencies by men familiar with their local problems'.[62] There appears to have been a certain advantage in being a local candidate, perhaps arising from the ability of the local man to secure a good local seat, and conversely the tendency to send carpet-baggers to the poorer seats. However, the fact that 53 per cent of Liberal carpet-baggers were successful, as compared with only 33 per cent of Unionist carpet-baggers suggests, as does other evidence, the greater willingness of the Liberal central authorities to seek out good seats for able candidates.[63]

When we turn to examine the social characteristics of the candidates the contrasts are not between the major parties, but between the major parties and the smaller parties. There are no sharp contrasts in the age, occupational, and educational profiles of the dominant Edwardian parties; but the Liberal and Unionist profiles differ markedly from the Labour and Nationalist patterns.

The oldest candidate, and he fought both elections, was the eighty-eight-year-old Nationalist, Samuel Young. The oldest candidate in Great Britain was the eighty-five-year-old Robert Cameron, Liberal Member for Houghton-le-Spring. In spite of some local Liberal dissatisfaction over Cameron's age, his irregular attendance at the House, and his neglect of the constituency, he fought and won both elections.[64] The youngest Unionist candidates were the twenty-two-year-old Marquis of Stafford, heir to the Duke of Sutherland, and three twenty-three year olds, Viscount Wolmer, Selborne's heir, the Hon. Jasper Ridley, son of Lord Ridley, and the Hon. Charles Mills, son of Lord Hillingdon. The youngest Liberal candidates were two twenty-four-year-olds, Francis McLaren, son of the millionaire Liberal M.P. Sir Charles McLaren, and the Hon. Peter Wodehouse, the Earl of Kimberley's second son. The youngest candidate in Ireland was John Redmond's twenty-four-year-old son, William. As always, a direct personal link with the political élite eased a young man's entry into politics.

The age profiles of the candidates of the two major parties are nearly identical, although the Unionists were somewhat younger, having a median age of forty-five to the Liberals forty-eight.[65] While the median age of the Labour candidates was also forty-eight, the distribution around the median was quite different. Labour was a party with a distinct middle-age spread. Two-thirds of its candidates were in their forties or fifties, by contrast with the Unionists and Liberals who had only half their candidates in these age groups. As a new party, Labour lacked elderly candidates, while the social situation of the classes from which it drew its candidates, and the attitude of the party leaders with their stress on proletarian service militated against the selection of younger men. This attitude was reflected in the clash with Grayson:

Keir Hardie's comment on the Colne Valley selection that 'men who had grown grey in the movement should not feel that they were put aside to make room for younger men'[66] typifying the generational conflict involved. In Ireland long years of service to the Nationalist cause were a usual prerequisite for nomination, and this, combined with political longevity, gives an elderly bias to the Nationalist profile. One-quarter of the Nationalists were over sixty, compared with 10 per cent and 15 per cent respectively for the Unionists and Liberals. But for the O'Brienite revolt and the consequent demand for new candidates, the proportion of older men in the Nationalist ranks would have been even higher.

The educational background of the candidates reveals the same broad similarities in the Liberal and Unionist patterns, which are markedly dissimilar from the patterns of the minor parties. A majority of the candidates of both the major parties (53 per cent of Unionists, 50 per cent of Liberals) had attended university or received some other form of higher education, while only 3 per cent of their candidates had left school at the elementary level. By contrast the overwhelming majority (82 per cent) of Labour candidates had left school at the elementary level; indeed it was a matter of pride in most Labour autobiographies to claim experience in the pit or at the factory bench at an early age. Only 6 per cent of Labour candidates had any form of higher education. The Nationalist pattern, with one-fifth of their candidates having only elementary schooling, and one-quarter with University education, lies roughly midway between those of the major parties and Labour.

The broadly identical patterns of the two major parties disguise some important differences. A larger proportion of Unionists than Liberals – 43 per cent to 22 per cent – had attended a major public school,[67] the difference arising mainly from the much greater number of Unionists going to the two leading schools Eton and Harrow – 153 Unionists to Eton, fifty-three to Harrow, compared with a total of fifty-nine Liberals to both schools. Nor did Harrow's latest recruit to the Liberal Cabinet bring it the Headmaster's vote. Dr Wood, although a Liberal, could not vote for the Government because of the land taxes and because he had 'no use for an old Harrow boy' in the Cabinet.[68]

In higher education, while Oxford and Cambridge dominated, they, and particularly Oxford, bulked larger in the education of Unionists, accounting for 67 per cent of Unionists with a higher education, but only for 51 per cent of Liberals. The newer universities, particularly

London, and the Scottish and Welsh universities made a more significant contribution to Liberal ranks (43 per cent of candidates with higher education) than to Unionist (20 per cent), while, as might be expected, the naval and military academies figured more prominently in the educational background of Unionists.

The major contrasts in the occupational background of candidates were again between the Unionists and the Liberals, on one hand, and Labour and the Nationalists on the other. Not that the latter had much in common. The preponderance of manual workers in the Labour ranks distinguished it from all other parties. The Nationalists were differentiated from the major parties first by the absence of financial and industrial entrepreneurs, reflecting Irish underdevelopment rather than any Nationalist prejudice; and secondly by a lower-middle-class bias in most of the major categories. Nationalists with a business background fell mainly into the category 'other business' which includes most of the small businessmen; in the landed group the Nationalists were predominantly farmers rather than landowners or country gentlemen; in the professions the lower status and the less lucrative careers figured more prominently in the Irish lists.

Both the Unionists and the Liberals drew the bulk of their candidates from the solid and upper-middle classes, but the occupational patterns are differentiated by an aristocratic bias in the Unionist, and a lower-middle-class element in the Liberal. Three times as many Unionists as Liberals were drawn from the landed interest, the country gentlemen and the military, naval and civil services, the interests and occupational preserves of the old governing élite. On the other hand, the greater lower-middle-class element amongst the Liberals was reflected in the greater number of Liberals in the 'other business' category and the occupational spread of Liberals in the professional group.

But if the partisans of the major parties were not sharply distinguished by age, occupation, or education, a religious cleavage was apparent. Unionist candidates were drawn overwhelmingly from the Anglican Church and the party itself was the traditional defender of the religious establishment. Less than 10 per cent of its candidates were drawn from Catholic, Nonconformist and Jewish congregations. By contrast the Liberal Party was the party of the Nonconformists. 'To talk of the Liberal Party without Nonconformists is precisely the same thing as to talk of the Unionist Party without Conservatives', declared the British Weekly.[69] Not quite. For one thing the Nonconformists were not a majority of the Liberal candidates. For another, as the

TABLE 11.6 OCCUPATIONS OF CANDIDATES 1910 ELECTIONS*

	Unionist No.	Liberal No.	Labour No.	Nationalist No.
A. *The Landed Interest*	110 (15%)	47 (8%)		18 (15%)
1. Landowners	46	15		2
2. Country gentlemen†	54	29		2
3. Farmers	10	3		14
B. *The Services‡*	121 (17%)	32 (5%)		1 (1%)
1. Military, Naval	104	17		1
2. Diplomatic, civil	17	15		
C. *Finance*	37 (5%)	23 (4%)		
1. Bankers	14	8		
2. Stockbrokers	10	7		
3. Insurance Directors	6	4		
4. Chartered Accountants	7	4		
D. *Industry*	101 (14%)	105 (17%)		2 (2%)
1. Ironmasters	18	17		
2. Textile manufacturers	21	31		
3. Transport industrialists	22	14		
4. Mineowners	10	11		
5. Brewers, Distillers	15	3		2
6. Other manufacturers	15	29		
E. *Other Business*	29 (4%)	72 (12%)	3 (3%)	23 (19%)
1. Publishers	2	15		
2. Wholesalers	18	37		9
3. Retailers	9	23	3	14
F. *The Professions*	251 (35%)	264 (43%)	4 (5%)	55 (45%)
1. Barristers	161	120		10
2. Solicitors	36	43		16
3. Doctors, dentists	6	11	1	3
4. Academics	14	22		2
5. Engineers	13	12	1	2
6. Architects, surveyors	8	6		
7. Clerics		8	1	
8. Teachers	5	6	1	5
9. Journalists, authors	8	36		17
G. *Manual Workers*	8 (1%)	14 (2%)	73 (84%)	3 (2%)
1. Miners	1	3	31	1
2. Textile workers	1		6	
3. Metal, eng. workers	3	3	8	
4. Building trade workers	1	2	9	
5. Other manual workers	2	6	19	2
H. *Miscellaneous*	7 (1%)	4 (1%)	4 (5%)	3 (2%)
I. *Details Unknown*	48 (7%)	46 (8%)	3 (3%)	18 (14%)

British Weekly itself observed, 'the prizes are captured for the most part by those who are not Nonconformists, or those who were once Nonconformists and have ceased to be so'.[70] Yet as Montagu warned Asquith: 'There is no getting away from the fact that ours is a Nonconformist Party, with Nonconformist susceptibilities and Nonconformist prejudices.'[71] The large body of Nonconformist candidates and members gave the Edwardian Liberal Party a distinctive ethos, tone and style, as well as committing it to particular causes. More than any other social factor, the different patterns of religious affiliation separated the two major parties. Thus the socio-political heritage of the nineteenth century still moulded the parties in the twentieth century, although the religious issue itself was of declining salience.

Labour too was closely linked to Nonconformity, containing an even higher proportion of Nonconformist candidates than the Liberal Party, although Unionist propaganda often painted the party as 'godless' and 'atheistic'. The mining communities particularly had been strongly influenced by Methodism, and in Northumberland–Durham and the Midlands the union hierarchies and the lay leadership of the Primitive Methodist Church were closely interrelated.[72] The remark, applied to the Lib-Lab John Wilson that he '. . . would never have been an M.P. if he had not been a P.M.',[73] was true of many Labour M.P.s who had prepared themselves for the platform by preaching from the pulpit. Here for once social cleavage coincided with political cleavage, the inherent dualism of the party system apparent at this point in the guise of the Nonconformist Left versus the Anglican Right.

Catholics were rather left out, being poorly represented at least in Great Britain. Catholics appear to have found it difficult to secure nomination in either of the major parties. Sandars considered that

---

Notes: Figures in brackets percentage of party's total candidates.

    * Where possible the formative occupation of the candidate has been selected, but for some candidates information on the current occupation only was available.

    † The term describes a way of life, rather than an occupation. It includes lesser landowners, and others with country estates who had not had an active business or professional career. In many cases their chief source of income was not land.

    ‡ As a period in the services was considered by many as part of a young man's education only those who served for ten years or longer have been listed under this head.

being a Catholic was electorally a 'grave disability'.[74] In some parts of
the country, e.g. Lancashire, it was practically impossible for a Catholic
to secure a Unionist nomination and Sandars, in the letter noted above,
dismissed as 'absurd' the suggestion that a Catholic candidate, 'however brilliant', could be nominated at Cambridge University. An
independent Unionist and Protestant candidate was threatened in
January at Deptford because the official nominee was a Catholic.[75]
It was probably equally difficult for a Catholic to secure Liberal nomination in strong Nonconformist areas.

TABLE II.7 RELIGIOUS AFFILIATIONS OF CANDIDATES
1910 ELECTIONS

	Unionist	Liberal	Labour	Nationalist
Anglicans +	639	344	46	7
Presbyterians –	21	18	1	2
Nonconformists	20	215	36	1
Catholics	14	10	4	113
Jews	18	23	–	–
	712	610	87	123

Notes: The religious press and the church year books provide authoritative and
       fairly exhaustive lists of Nonconformist, Catholic, and Jewish candidates.
       In a few instances these have been supplemented by the local press. All
       other candidates in Great Britain have been treated as Anglicans, unless
       identified as Presbyterians, as have Unionist, Liberal and Labour candidates
       in Ireland. As the Presbyterian lists are not complete this slightly inflates
       the number of Anglicans and deflates the Presbyterian figures. The Angli-
       can total will also contain some candidates without religious affiliation.
       Nationalist candidates have been treated as Catholics unless there was
       information to the contrary. The breakdown of Liberal Nonconformists
       was: Congregationalists 88; Wesleyan Methodists, 38; Baptists 22;
       Quakers 15; Unitarians 14; Calvinistic Methodists 12; Others 26.

The guardianship of Catholic interests on both sides of the Irish Sea
fell to the Nationalist Party. If its first task was to secure Home Rule
for Ireland, its second was to protect the Catholic Church in Great
Britain. About 90 per cent of its candidates were Catholics, the sprink-
ling of Protestant candidates being a gesture to broad-mindedness.[76]
Despite the small size of the Jewish vote – about 25,000, located
mainly in four cities, London, Manchester, Leeds and Glasgow[77] –
Jews appear to have found it easier to secure nomination from the

major parties than Catholics. Not that any specific religious appeal was countenanced by the leaders of the Jewish community. The *Jewish World* frowned upon party appeals to the Jews *qua* Jews, being alarmed by the argument 'boldly advanced that it is the duty of the Jewish voter to cast his vote in favour of a co-religionist rather than a Gentile'. To such a plea the journal was uncompromisingly hostile: '. . . the principle is wrong . . . the policy is pernicious . . . the consequences may be disastrous'.[78] It well recognised that such pleas could only fuel the fires of local anti-semitism, sometimes lit by the presence of a Jewish candidate.[79]

If there was much to distinguish the policies of the two major parties, there was little to distinguish their partisans. Only religion, the residuum of an earlier socio-economic and cultural division, provided any sharp contrast in the social background of the major parties' candidates. The challenge to the prevailing pattern of solid middle-class candidates in Great Britain came from the Labour Party, in terms of its candidates a more proletarian party than it was ever to be again.

The Containment of Labour

I

In 1906 it had been possible for working-class candidates to occupy an indefinite Lib-Lab position between the L.R.C. and the Liberal Party. By 1910 this was no longer a workable formal alternative to Liberalism or Labour. The alternative had ceased to be viable once its most powerful bulwark, the Miners' Federation, had surrendered to the Labour Party. There were only two new Lib-Lab candidates in 1910, A. J. Bailey in Central Sheffield at both elections and the Watermen's Secretary, Harry Gosling at North Lambeth in December. Of the sitting Lib-Labs, two – Richard Bell at Derby and J. Havelock Wilson at Middlesbrough – retired, nearly half were defeated, and the remainder were completely absorbed into the Liberal Party.

With formal Lib-Labism eclipsed, the lines between the Liberal and Labour parties were now more clearly drawn. The aim of the Liberal Party in 1910 was to prevent any further Labour infiltration across these lines. Their policy was one of electoral containment – to confine Labour to the seats won in 1906. This policy was made explicit in a long letter from Pease on 16 November 1909 to the Liberals of Bishop Auckland who were faced with the prospect of Labour intervention.

> . . . Liberals, so far as they can, should respect the seats which at the last general election returned L.R.C. candidates, and . . . the L.R.C. organisation should respect other Progressive candidates standing for seats held by other Labour representatives or Liberals in 1906. . . . If an aggressive attitude is persisted in by the Labour party, Labour cannot expect official Liberalism to stand to one side and allow their candidates to remain unnominated. . . . If [the Labour leaders] now press Labour Representation Committee candidates for seats which were won by Liberal or Labour members who have not signed the constitution, they must expect retaliatory attacks upon their own candidates standing for those seats which they now hold.[1]

Pease thus made it clear that most Labour efforts to expand would be treated as aggression. The thirty Labour M.P.s elected in 1906 would go unchallenged by the Liberals as would the miners' representatives who had since joined the Labour Party. Although the letter was obscure on the point, Labour was to be allowed a free hand in a further half-dozen constituencies, where it had been the main or only anti-Unionist contender in 1906. Any Labour deployment beyond these bounds would meet Liberal resistance and might incur Liberal retaliation. Liberal headquarters stuck to this policy, deviating from it only as a result of local pressure.

It was the obvious policy for the Liberals to pursue. Whatever the case in 1906, Labour expansion in 1910 was likely to be at Liberal expense. Thus the Liberal Party had little choice but resistance. At the same time the immediate circumstances rendered impossible a deliberate invasion of Labour-held seats. Not only were the Liberals unprepared for such a campaign in late 1909, they were also inhibited from attacking Labour seats. The argument that third-party intervention would endanger the progressive cause, so useful to the Liberals in the country as a whole, would recoil on the Liberals in the forty-five seats held by Labour. Moreover, there were working-class votes to be reaped by the Liberals throughout the country, in return for their toleration of Labour in these seats. Friendly relations with Labour would engender working-class support for the Liberals in urban and industrial constituencies generally, but such friendship would not be pursued at the expense of Liberal-held seats.

Labour's prospects of expansion were anyhow not good. The party's electoral record remained unencouraging. True, Labour had had an unexpected success at Attercliffe in May 1909 and had won the mining seat of Mid-Derbyshire in July. But Attercliffe had been a confused four-cornered fight, and Mid-Derbyshire a victory for the Lib-Labs in all but name, for J. G. Hancock, the Labour candidate, had in the words of one historian 'brought off a remarkable trick: he had been officially adopted by both the Liberal and Labour Parties'.[2] More typical of Labour's electoral performance were the dismal showing of the party in working-class Bermondsey in October, where with a good local candidate Labour captured only 15·9 per cent of the vote in a three-cornered contest, and the 'disappointingly slow' progress in the municipal elections in November.[3]

The electoral battleground itself could hardly have been less favourable to Labour, since the constitutional issue would undoubtedly overshadow the distinctive social and industrial objectives of the Labour Party. Keir Hardie might comfort himself and others with the notion that 'the battle against the Lords is peculiarly ours'.[4] But it was not. The S.D.P. candidate at Northampton, Harry Quelch, was nearer the mark in claiming that the 'House of Lords is as essential to the Liberals as the Devil to the Salvation Army'.[5] By virtue of long tradition the battle with the House of Lords was peculiarly a Liberal battle. In one sense the *Clarion* was right in warning Labour candidates that 'to confine their campaign to the great constitutional crisis would be madness. The great constitutional crisis is *not* the important thing for us.'[6] To give prominence to the Lords was to endanger the distinctive identity of the Labour Party.

Yet in so far as the constitutional crisis was the most important question for the nation, Labour could neglect the issue only at the risk of forfeiting the attention of the electorate. Of course, most Labour candidates neither could, nor would avoid the issue. 'When the very existence of [the House of Commons] as a potent instrument of reform is at stake,' wrote Philip Snowden, 'the Labour Party is bound to make that question, upon which all it hopes for in the way of reform depends, one of its battle cries.'[7]

The Budget posed a similar dilemma. Here the Liberals had appropriated Labour policies, stealing as the *Clarion* protested, 'our speeches, our statistics, and our arguments, everything in fact but our principles'.[8] It was not Labour's Budget, but the party could not disown it. It embodied, albeit inadequately, much of what the party had striven for, and the condemnation the measure earned from the rich only confirmed Labour support. Once more, on a key issue, Liberal and Labour positions merged, and Labour's identity was again threatened.

Under these conditions Labour was inevitably handicapped. Its distinctive features were obscured by issues not of its own making or choosing, yet issues on which it could not avoid taking a stand, even at the expense of its identity and independence. This rendered difficult any effort to expand against Liberal opposition, for such attempts would be open to the charge, peculiarly effective in these circumstances, of betraying the place to the enemy. Caution became not merely a virtue but a necessity.

The Labour leaders had already revealed their natural circumspection in their opposition since 1906 to contests where Labour had little chance. They also seemed to have doubted until the very end that the Lords would precipitate the election, and Ramsay MacDonald, their chief strategist, was in India when the crisis blew up. However, before departing in mid-September he had left with Masterman 'a little telegraphic code' so that he could be summoned back immediately. In addition he had assured Lloyd George that 'As the result of three or four days' steady negotiations, I think I have straightened out everything, and if an election should come, the anti-Budgetists will not get much comfort out of our relationships'.[9] MacDonald's assurance should not be construed as sacrificing Labour interests to a Liberal accommodation, but rather as an effort to earn Liberal goodwill from the harsh tactical realities of Labour's situation. Having not anticipated an election before late 1910, the party had a considerable contingent of candidates in the field, but many of these had not yet been officially approved by their union executives or by the National Administrative Council of the I.L.P., and even more had not been endorsed by the Labour Party Executive. In many cases little spadework had been done in the constituencies. Now, late in 1909, fearful that a series of ignominious defeats would impair the standing, morale and organisation of the party and aware that in the circumstances such defeats were likely, the Labour leaders strove to extricate the party from an overextended electoral position. It was a delicate operation. On the eve of the election they endeavoured to carry through a policy of electoral retrenchment, while at the same time maintaining the dynamic of the young movement.

Critics lurked on either wing, and each withdrawal served to multiply the foci for controversy within the Labour movement. Militants on the left saw each withdrawal as 'a dirty and treacherous bargain with the Liberal Capitalist Party',[10] a bargain motivated by 'the overweening anxiety of the politician Labour man to save his seat'.[11] Each retreat, each hint of compromise, each Liberal rallying-cry in a Labour mouth was but placing 'the Socialist movement in the Liberal pawnshop, in the dubious hope of some day recovering its moth-eaten remains'.[12] The militants' apocalyptic vision of the class struggle ignored the immediate realities of the electoral situation. Caution was merely cowardice: he who subordinated his Socialist principles to the immediate task of fighting the House of Lords was either 'a fool or a knave'.[13]

For the right wing, particularly the miners, there were not enough bargains. From this group came the demand for a declared entente with the Liberals. William Brace, one of the South Wales miners' leaders, urged an arrangement with the Liberals and the full cooperation in the constituencies of all the progressive forces.[14] Another miners' M.P., John Wadsworth, told the Hallamshire Liberal Association that the Labour Party constitution was too inflexible in its opposition to co-operation.[15] He, for one, seemed willing to ignore the constitution. The Yorkshire Miners' Association and the South Wales Miners' Federation, both with strong Lib-Lab traditions, were suspiciously eager to abandon projects for running additional Labour candidates.[16]

The Labour leadership avoided both the sterile extremism of the Left and the disruptive expediency of the Right. In the autumn of 1909 the Labour Party had contemplated about 110 contests at the next general election.[17] In a series of meetings in November and early December the National Executive working closely with the National Council of the I.L.P. and the Executive of the Miners' Federation pruned this number by some thirty candidatures. Ramsay MacDonald, who believed that three-cornered contests were 'foredoomed', favoured an even more drastic reduction but claimed that suspicion amongst the rank and file prevented further withdrawals.[18]

Thus the possibility of widespread conflict with the Liberals was considerably lessened. This does not, however, seem to have been the prime motive for Labour withdrawals. Many of the candidatures abandoned were in a purely preparatory stage. It was useless to continue with them, and they constituted the major proportion of the withdrawals. In a number of other cases plans were further advanced but the contests had not yet been endorsed by the central bodies. Nearly all these candidates were withdrawn. But only a handful of contests that had received central endorsement were abandoned.[19]

Throughout the Labour leaders appear to have made their decisions primarily on the basis of Labour's chances in the constituency. The condition of the local organisation, the unity of the local Labour bodies, indications of local electoral strength and the sufficiency of funds appear to have been the considerations on which Labour based a decision to run or not. The candidature at Keighley which had been in hand for eighteen months was withdrawn after a visit by the National Agent revealed local organisation to be inadequate. The National Administrative Council of the I.L.P. recommended that the contest at Midlothian be abandoned because the miners' officials in the constituency were opposed to a contest. The 'sole reason' for the withdrawal at Coventry was apparently finance.[20] Official Labour policy was stated by the *Labour Leader*: '. . . this is not the occasion for multiplying candidatures. It is an occasion for concentrating our efforts effectively on effective organised campaigns.'[21]

There is little evidence of bargaining between the parties over these withdrawals. True, the threatened Liberal interventions in South Wales and in Leeds were aimed at ensuring the maintenance of the existing balance of parliamentary representation in those areas and were not proceeded with once the point had been made.[22] Again the Labour Executive's refusal to sanction any new interventions in two-member constituencies held by two Liberals might be construed as a deliberate sacrifice in order to preserve the *status quo* in those two-member boroughs in which representation was already shared by the anti-Unionist parties.[23] But a simpler explanation seems likely. In single-member seats Labour intervention threatened to give one seat to the enemy, in two-member constituencies such intervention endangered both seats. The first was a heavy enough burden, the second was crippling. Moreover, in two of the two-member seats in which Labour contemplated intervening specific factors were decisive. At Oldham the locally powerful cotton operatives refused to support a Labour candidate;[24] in Southampton the candidature of Alderman Lewis had been promoted irregularly and had been resented from the outset by the central bodies.[25] In a third seat, Plymouth, the overpowering consideration behind withdrawal seems to have been the hopelessness of the contest.[26]

A detailed examination of the Labour withdrawals gives little hint of swaps and exchanges between the two parties. The fact was that in the first election Labour had no room to manœuvre, for the Liberals were unwilling to bargain. The Liberals were prepared to accept the decision of 1906 but they were not prepared to tolerate any further Labour advance. Labour might reap Liberal goodwill from the withdrawals, but they would not get reciprocity.

The Labour leaders were left with the difficult job of aligning Labour clearly with the anti-Unionist forces in order to gain Liberal support in straight fights, while at the same time stressing Labour's independence in order to justify a Labour vote in three-cornered contests. It was an impossible task. On the whole they succeeded in the first objective at the expense of the second. The highly publicised lists of Labour withdrawals emphasised progressive solidarity. The advice of the Labour leaders to Labour voters further strengthened the anti-Unionist alliance. Arthur Henderson, in speeches and letters, requested Labour voters in seats without Labour candidates 'to do everything in their power to secure the defeat of all candidates standing in defence of the Lords'.[27] The *Labour Leader* was more explicit, preferring a Liberal vote to the 'futility' of abstention in seats where there were no Labour candidates.[28] These tactics by blurring the differences between the anti-Unionist parties gained Liberal support for Labour in straight fights. But at the same time they further weakened Labour's already bleak chances in three-cornered contests.

The writ of the Labour Executive did not run through the whole Labour movement. At Colne Valley Victor Grayson pursued his independent course. Some desultory efforts were made late in 1909 to get Grayson to sign the Labour Party constitution, but there was little interest on either side.[29] Grayson was openly contemptuous of Labour's electoral tactics, deeming it 'more worthy to go down with a solid, clear-eyed three thousand Socialist voters, than to slink into Parliament at the coat-tails of a cynical and plutocratic Party'.[30] Between Grayson's idealistic, if arrogant and unrealistic, pursuit of socialist purity, and the Labour Executive's cautious, realistic and opportunistic pursuit of electoral success, there was an unbridgeable gap. Two others, the dockers' leader Ben Tillett at Swansea Town and Joseph Burgess at Montrose Burghs, defied the N.E.C. by persisting with contests without official endorsement. In addition, the ten S.D.P. candidates were also a challenge to the Labour Executive and an irritant in Liberal–Labour relations.

Yet the friction generated by these candidates was minimal, for official Labour's antipathy to them was strong and obvious. In a published letter to a Liberal journalist MacDonald wrote that if he had 'a vote in Swansea it would . . . not be given to Mr Tillett unless I were assured that his policy in Parliament was not to follow the lines of his criticism outside'.[31] In most of the constituencies with S.D.P. candidates the local L.R.C.s and the I.L.P.s vocally opposed them, and in some cases urged support for the Liberals.[32] At Sheffield Brightside the S.D.P. candidate was publicly repudiated both by MacDonald and by the Labour M.P. in adjoining Attercliffe.[33] These contests then tended to further rather than weaken the understanding between the Liberals and official Labour.

Moreover, Liberals were aware that S.D.P. opponents were not necessarily an electoral handicap, for such candidates might well split the anti-Government vote. The ex-Liberal Carlyon Bellairs, standing as the Unionist candidate for West Salford, considered that the presence of a Socialist candidate, A. A. Purcell, harmed him and benefited his Liberal opponent.

A Labour candidature may help [he wrote to Leo Maxse on 2 February 1910] but a socialist takes his socialists who will never vote for a Liberal and he also competes for the numerous *discontented* who want to vote against the government. The Socialist at Salford abused the Radicals & the government & told me himself that he got his extra support from men who would otherwise have voted for me.[34]

II

The Labour Party finally ran seventy-eight candidates in January 1910. Table 12.1 provides a breakdown of these candidatures in relation to the Liberal policy of containment. In the fifty-one seats which Labour or miners' candidates had won in the past or in which in 1906 a Labour candidate had been the only anti-Unionist candidate or had run second to the Unionist, Liberal intervention was sanctioned in only three. On the other hand in the twenty-seven seats which Labour had not fought before or in which in 1906 a Labour candidate had trailed the Liberal, Liberal intervention occurred in all but three.

TABLE 12.1 LABOUR AND THE LIBERALS JANUARY 1910

Contests Jan 1910 in:	Seats with no Liberal opposition Jan 1910	Seats with Liberal opposition Jan 1910	Labour victories Jan 1910
A. seats won by L.R.C. 1906			
(a) Two-member seats	11	0§	9
(b) Single-member seats	18	1	15
B. Seats won by miners 1906*	9	1	9
C. Seats won in by-elections†	4	1	4
D. Seats fought and lost by L.R.C. 1906‡			
(a) Labour only anti-Unionist candidate or ran second to Unionist	6	0	0
(b) Others	0	6	0
E. Seats not fought by L.R.C. 1906	3	18	3
	—	—	—
	51	27	40

Notes: *Does not include three seats where the miners' M.P.s refused to join the Labour Party, nor seats where miners stood as L.R.C. candidates in 1906.
  † Includes seats won by the miners in by-elections.
  ‡ Includes three seats fought by the Scottish Workers' Representation Committee in 1906.
  § There was unofficial Liberal opposition in two of these seats.

As in 1906 under the original compact, Liberal and Labour relations were at their best in those seats where a united front was most necessary, the eleven two-member boroughs in which the parties shared the representation. In Norwich the Liberal Two Hundred urged that the second Liberal vote be cast for the Labour man, an action commended by the *Nation* as 'the high water mark of politic good sense and local statesmanship'.[35] In Sunderland the Liberal candidate James Stuart hoped the electors would give their second vote to 'his old colleague Mr Summerbell' [the Labour Member].[36] Not all were quite so direct. In Halifax the Chairman of the Liberal association urged Liberals to vote so as to put the Liberal at the top of the poll and the single Conservative at the bottom.[37] In Newcastle the Labour Member, Hudson, asked his supporters not to plump for him but 'to give your first vote to me and the other to the man who will help me in Parliament'.[38] The Liberal *North Mail* shunned such circumlocution. 'It is the obvious and imperative duty of every true democrat, no matter what label he may choose to wear, to split fair between Mr Shortt [Liberal] and Mr Hudson.'[39]

Deeds accompanied words. In Blackburn, where there was Liberal resentment that Labour plumping had put Snowden into Parliament with a Unionist in 1906, Labour now went out of its way to co-operate with the Liberals. The allegedly reactionary record of the Tory candidates on social questions was cited as the excuse for Labour appeals urging the electors to vote for Snowden and the Liberal.[40] In Newcastle the Liberal association circulated polling cards supporting a vote for both progressive candidates.[41] In both Halifax and Sunderland the illness of the Liberal candidates left the brunt of the anti-Unionist campaign to the Labour Members, and this served further to cement the relationship between the two parties in these constituencies. In Sunderland on polling day Liberal blue and Labour white were worn intertwined by many voters.[42] This symbolised the relationship between the anti-Unionist parties not only in Sunderland but in most of the two-member boroughs.

In three of these eleven constituencies, Dundee, Merthyr Tydfil and Preston, this blessed state was endangered. In each case local Liberals were the source of disaffection and their activities were frowned upon by London. Dundee had not figured in the original Gladstone-MacDonald compact, and the Labour Member, Alexander Wilkie of the Shipwrights' Association, had wrested a seat from the Liberals in 1906. The bitterness resulting had been slowly erased by Wilkie's parliamentary performance, Dundee Liberals being satisfied with his voting record and finding his speeches unobjectionable. But the growing *détente* between Wilkie and the Dundee Liberals was shattered by the Dundee by-election of 1908. Despite the fact that the Labour Executive opposed second Labour candidates in two-member seats, and without consulting Wilkie or the Shipwrights' Association, a Labour candidate, G. H. Stuart, ran at the by-election. Although the seat was in no way imperilled and although Wilkie himself condemned the folly of Labour trying to capture both seats,[43] the anti-Wilkie forces within Dundee Liberalism were considerably strengthened.

This was apparent when on 6 November 1909, at a meeting of the Dundee Liberal Association, a majority favoured running a second Liberal candidate, although the final decision was left to the Executive Committee of the association, a body of some 400 members. When this body met five weeks later, both Churchill, the Liberal Member, and Asquith counselled delay until Labour's national attitude was clearer. The Executive Committee's decision to adjourn for a week was a tactical victory for those working for a Liberal–Labour arrangement, for the longer the decision was put off the less likelihood was there of a second Liberal candidate. Labour's publicised withdrawals and the restraining influence of the Liberal leaders ensured the ultimate success of the local supporters of the Liberal–Labour alliance. After a long debate on 20 December, the Executive Committee decided by a vote of two to one not to run a second candidate. From then on relations were cordial between the two parties in Dundee. Churchill's voting card warned against plumping – 'You can't give two votes to Churchill' – and his speeches indicated clearly to whom the other vote should be given.[44] The great majority of Liberal voters in Dundee seem to have followed his advice.

Merthyr Tydfil, like Dundee, had not been included in the original Gladstone–MacDonald compact, but Keir Hardie had retained his seat against two Liberals in 1906. In 1909 the Liberal association, after considerable debate, nominated only one candidate, the young Radical, Edgar Jones. But the hopes for amicable Liberal–Labour relations in the borough were frustrated by the intervention of an independent Liberal, the eccentric Pritchard-Morgan, Liberal M.P. for Merthyr from 1888 to 1900. Only one Unionist candidate was nominated.

A strange contest developed. While Jones debated with his Unionist opponent, and avoided linking his candidature with either Pritchard-Morgan or Keir Hardie, these latter two, continuing their 1900 vendetta, swapped abuse with each other. Stories spread that under the famed cloth cap Hardie was a man of wealth, with an estate in Scotland and £20,000 from the sale of the *Labour Leader*. The constituency was

swamped with anti-Socialist leaflets which warned Nonconformists
that socialism meant atheism, and Puritans that it meant free love.
Hardie retaliated, accusing Pritchard-Morgan of being the tool of the
Anti-Socialist Union, a body allegedly financed by dukes, millionaires
and sweaters of labour. Much was made of Pritchard-Morgan's
investments in Chinese coal mines. A wholly new version of the
Chinese Slavery agitation developed with Pritchard-Morgan, not
Milner, as the villain.

In this extraordinary situation Unionists were advised to plump;
Pritchard-Morgan urged a vote for the two Liberals; Keir Hardie
refused any advice as to the second vote; and Jones behaved with
exemplary caution. He was wary of flouting the conservative Liberals
supporting Pritchard-Morgan, but as it became increasingly clear that
Hardie not Pritchard-Morgan commanded the votes, Jones increasingly
revealed his sympathy for Keir Hardie. But his tentative overtures met
no response from Keir Hardie. Others, however, were at work to
align the votes behind Jones and Hardie. Redmond instructed the
Irish to split their votes between these two candidates. The Baptist
leader, Dr Clifford sent Nonconformists a telegram to the same effect.
As it was, although the rift probably diverted a number of votes from
Hardie, and left Jones at the top of the poll, it did not seriously endanger Hardie's seat.[45]

In Preston the situation bore a superficial resemblance to that in
Merthyr Tydfil. Here, too, the Liberals had nominated only one
candidate, the ex-Unionist, Sir John Gorst, and the disruptive factor
was the Liberal Member for Preston, Harold Cox, who had been
disowned by the local association. But in Preston the understanding
between Liberalism and Labour was much closer. Indeed, the independent Liberal candidate at Preston had the effect of strengthening
the progressive alliance. When local Unionists began distributing
false handbills urging Liberals to plump for Gorst, and Labour to
plump for Macpherson, the local Liberal paper declared: 'Sir John
Gorst and his Party are as anxious that every Liberal should split his
vote with Mr Macpherson as Mr Macpherson and his Party are
anxious that every Labour man should split his with Sir John Gorst.'[46]

There were three reasons for the differing impact of the independent
Liberal candidate in Preston as compared with Merthyr Tydfil.
Ideologically Cox was much closer to the Unionists than Pritchard-
Morgan. He was the last Liberal defender of undiluted *laissez-faire*, and
his vehement attacks on Old Age Pensions and the Budget had been

equalled by few Tories.⁴⁷ A visiting Liberal speaker was cheered when he said that he hoped everyone in Preston 'realised the importance of voting for two good democrats and not for one of the three Tory candidates'.⁴⁸ Secondly, Macpherson had better relations with the local Liberals than the dour and independent Keir Hardie. Finally, and perhaps most important, the Unionists were a very real threat in Preston, indeed they captured the seats. Thus it was more imperative in Preston than in Merthyr that no anti-Unionist vote be wasted. Despite the solidarity at the top the alliance did not work well at the level of the ordinary voter. Although no breakdown of the Preston voting is available there was a distinct leakage away from a split Liberal–Labour ticket.⁴⁹

Hence, in none of the eleven two-member seats in which representation was shared by the parties did the Liberal Associations sanction any effort to capture both seats, thus fully adhering to Pease's containment policy. The co-operation between the politicians and party workers produced co-operation among the voters. In the two-member seats, apart from Dundee, Merthyr Tydfil and Preston, there was little drift from a Liberal–Labour ticket. The greater drift amongst Liberal voters reflects a somewhat great willingness on their part to plump or, more likely, to split their votes with Unionists.

TABLE 12.2 LIBERAL–LABOUR VOTING IN TWO-MEMBER SEATS*

	% voting for the Liberal but not for the Labour candidate †	% voting for the Labour but not for the Liberal candidate †
	Figures in brackets – December 1910 percentages	
Newcastle	6 [6]	3 [5]
Stockport	6 [10]	7 [9]
Sunderland	7 [8]	3 [2]
Bolton	8 [10]	5 [8]
Halifax	9 [6]	5 [3]
Blackburn	11	6
Dundee	15 [8]	11 [10]
Merthyr Tydfil‡	20 [30]	14 [25]

Notes: * Detailed figures not available for Leicester, Norwich, and Preston.
    † It should be noted that these figures show the drift from the total vote of the candidate, a total made up of votes from Liberal *and* Labour supporters. It is impossible to discover what proportion of a candidate's votes came from Liberal voters, i.e. voters who would have voted Liberal if they had had only one vote, and what proportion from Labour voters, since the elector simply put two crosses on the ballot paper.
    ‡ Calculated from incomplete figures (plumpers only), January 1910.

In all but one of the nineteen single-member seats won by the L.R.C. in 1906 the Liberals did not intervene against the sitting Member. In these eighteen seats relations were friendly if perhaps not as close as in the two-member seats. In these seats Labour could not offer votes in return for Liberal support, but they did offer candidates whose policies were indistinguishable from the Radicals. In these constituencies the House of Lords was as regularly attacked, the Budget as regularly extolled, and Tariff Reform as regularly condemned, as in any constituency with a Liberal candidate. Henderson claimed that his victory at Barnard Castle was a Budget victory as he had kept the Budget to the fore throughout.[50] The Labour M.P. for Deptford horrified Socialists by proclaiming that it was inexcusable to introduce other issues besides the constitutional question.[51] At West Wolverhampton the Labour candidate, T. F. Richards, formally requested help from the Liberal association.[52] Over one-fifth of these members indicated in their addresses that the chief reason for a Labour vote was paradoxically the record of the Liberal Government, goaded to righteousness of course by the Labour representatives.

The Liberals responded by rallying their voters behind the Labour Members. The resolution of the Barrow-in-Furness Liberal Association typified the attitude of the Liberal Party in most of the single-member constituencies held by Labour.

Having regard to the serious issues involved in the forthcoming election, this Association considers it imperative that all party political feelings should be sunk in a strenuous desire to defeat the forces of reaction, and therefore requests all Liberal electors on this occasion to vote for the Labour candidate.[53]

In two seats containment was threatened and in one abandoned. In East Leeds a Liberal candidate was brought out against James O'Grady, the sitting Labour M.P. But the objective of this candidature seems to have been to deter rumoured Labour attacks on South and West Leeds. When these were definitely abandoned the Liberal withdrew at East Leeds, citing his retirement as an act of reciprocity. Pease may have been instrumental in securing this outcome; he certainly approved the Liberal withdrawal.[54]

The Chief Whip's influence was undoubtedly decisive at Chester-le-Street. Early in October 1909 the Liberal association decided to secure a candidate against the sitting Labour Member, J. W. Taylor, and appointed a subcommittee to consult the Chief Whip on the matter. Having consulted with Pease the subcommittee recommended that it would be 'imprudent' for the Liberals to fight the division, advice accepted by the local association.[55]

But at South-West Manchester the Liberals attacked a seat won by the L.R.C. in 1906. The excuse was provided by the retirement of the sitting Labour Member G. D. Kelly, the only Labour M.P. to retire. A further ostensible reason was that the socialism of the new Labour candidate, McLachlan, an I.L.P.er, was offensive to many Liberals who had supported the moderate ex-Liberal Kelly in 1906. Moreover, the N.E.C. itself was not that happy with McLachlan, and by the time that they had finally sanctioned his candidature, a Liberal, C. T. Needham, had been before the constituency for some months, and he and his supporters were determined to fight.[56]

But the situation in South-West Manchester cannot be understood without reference to the position in the adjoining constituency of East Manchester where an identical situation but with the roles reversed had developed. There the Liberal, T. G. Horridge, who had defeated Balfour in 1906, announced in 1908 his intention to retire at the dissolution. Labour was quick off the mark. The party had an excellent organisation in East Manchester, and a good candidate in J. E. Sutton, a miner's agent and a Manchester City Councillor.

The Liberals were prepared to give Labour a free hand in East Manchester, but the *quid pro quo* was McLachlan's withdrawal from the South-West. The Liberal preference for the South-West constituency was understandable. They had held that seat from 1886 to 1895, whereas East Manchester had never been won prior to 1906. South-West Manchester was a mixed-class constituency whereas East Manchester was almost entirely working-class. Moreover the miner Sutton was a more acceptable candidate to Manchester Liberals than the I.L.P.er McLachlan. The proposed deal would, while preserving the balance of representation, leave the Labour seat in the hands of a moderate.

When Labour refused to play ball the Liberals tried to scare Labour into an agreement by bringing forward in East Manchester L. W. Zimmerman, who was, in the opinion of an electoral expert on *The Times*, the strongest candidate the Liberals could have chosen, and who was regarded by many as one of the architects of the Manchester victories of 1906.[57] At a more trivial level, the Manchester Liberal Federation denied Labour the use of an empty club building until 'the settlement of an understanding between the Liberal and Labour forces'.[58]

But neither the advent of Zimmerman nor petty retaliation led

Labour to reassess its position in Manchester. The Manchester Liberal Federation next tried to do a deal with the national leaders of the Labour Party. Advised by Pease, the Executive Committee of the Federation resolved on 16 December, with only one dissentient, that 'the President and Chairman of the Executive be empowered to inform Mr Arthur Henderson that if Mr McLachlan were withdrawn from South-West, the Executive of the Manchester Liberal Federation would recommend to the General Committee of the Federation that the Liberal candidate should retire from East Manchester.'[59] But this too failed, for Henderson was apparently unwilling or unable to force McLachlan's withdrawal.

The Liberals were now growing desperate. Having failed either to frighten Labour into a swap or to strike a bargain with the Labour leaders, the Manchester Liberals now decided to shame Labour into retiring. On 20 December, with a small minority dissenting, the Executive Committee resolved that 'this Federation still considers it to be in the interests of Liberalism as a whole that the East Manchester Liberal Association should withdraw their candidature'. This time they had reckoned without the East Manchester Liberals. A deputation from East Manchester was in attendance and it unanimously decided to do no such thing. The Federation Executive now gave up, regretted the deputation's attitude and placed upon them full responsibility for the contest.[60] A policy initiated merely to secure an exchange of seats now threatened to give both seats to the Unionists.

The decision in East Manchester now passed to Zimmerman. Primarily an organisation man, he was privy to the suggestion of a bargain, and now that this had failed he recognised that his candidature was a liability to the Liberal cause. On Christmas Day he resolved the issue by withdrawing.

The situation immediately improved in East Manchester and deteriorated in the South-West. The *Manchester Guardian* acclaimed Zimmerman's retirement as 'a courageous and generous decision, conceived in a spirit of high disinterestedness' and asked the Liberals of East Manchester to give 'their hearty and unflinching support' to the Labour candidate. The Manchester Liberal Federation urged Liberals to support Sutton, 'the anti-Lords candidate', and Zimmerman himself campaigned for Sutton.[61] In the South-West Labour's failure to reciprocate only heightened the antagonism between the parties, while Zimmerman's abnegation made it easier for Liberals to present McLachlan as the traitor to progressive unity.[62]

The two campaigns moved to a predictable close. In East Manchester 'let every Liberal vote for [Sutton] as eagerly as if he were the Premier'; in South-West Manchester: 'It is simply because we know Mr Needham to have the greater chance of victory already that we urge every Labour man to vote for him . . .' Thus the *Manchester Guardian* on the eve of the poll.[63] In the East the advice appears to have been followed, the swing to the Unionists being less than in most of the Manchester seats. In the South-West Needham captured the bulk of Kelly's votes, but was still 108 votes short, the Unionist winning on a minority vote. To have abandoned one seat to Labour and lost the other to the Unionists was a most unsatisfactory result for the Manchester Liberals. Nevertheless, they had reasserted their right to be regarded as the major anti-Unionist party in South-West Manchester, a right they exploited ten months later.

In the thirteen seats won by the miners in 1906 necessity dictated Liberal policy. Once the Miners' Federation had joined the Labour Party, the Liberals could only save these seats if the sitting Members rebelled against joining the Labour Party.[64] Nearly all the constituencies were single-industry constituencies dominated by coal, and the Liberals would have encountered great difficulties in trying to oust the miners' representatives. There was, anyhow, little incentive for the Liberals to try. Nearly all the miners' M.P.s belonged to the older generation of union leaders, and were Lib-Lab in spirit and tradition. Typical was John Wadsworth, who assured his Liberal friends: 'I am really a Liberal–Labour candidate and during the election I will fight as Liberal–Labour candidate for Hallamshire.'[65] Wadsworth and his colleagues were unlikely to abandon the habits and attitudes of a lifetime. They would be a force for moderation and compromise in the Labour ranks, and could sustain the Liberal hope that the division in the progressive forces was not irrevocable.

In three of the thirteen constituencies, Morpeth, Wansbeck and Mid-Durham, the Liberals lost nothing, for the Members refused even formally to desert the Liberal Party. Thomas Burt, John Wilson, and Charles Fenwick had all sat in the Commons as Liberals for at least twenty years. They had fought a stubborn rearguard action to keep the Northumberland and Durham miners out of the Miners' Federation; they had fought a similar action to keep the Federation out of the Labour Party; now they were engaged in a personal struggle to keep themselves out of the Labour Party while yet retaining their parliamentary seats.

John Wilson, long a law unto himself in Mid-Durham, bluntly refused to sign the Labour constitution. He was not prepared to forgo his freedom to speak on Liberal platforms, or to oppose candidates who might be nominated by the Labour Party. The old individualist objected to giving a pledge of good conduct after forty years of public life. Wilson's position was unassailable. Mid-Durham was virtually his personal fief and it was hinted that if the Durham Miners' Association ran a candidate against him, Wilson would be backed by the Liberals, the local miners, and the Unionists.[66] He was left in undisputed possession of the constituency, one of the ten Members in Great Britain returned unopposed.

Burt and Fenwick had a tougher struggle. In early October 1909 Burt wrote to Bryce revealing his uneasiness with recent developments.

> Mr. Fenwick M.P. (a thoroughly good fellow) and I are being asked and pressed to sign the Constitution of the Labour Party. Both of us have refused to do so, and we shall not recede from that resolution. It may mean our leaving the H. of C. at the next general election. . . . The Fed. has affiliated itself with the Labour Party, and we are to be handed over body and soul to the Socialists. M.P.s and candidates are to be shackled by all sorts of bonds, such as cannot be for a moment tolerated by self-respecting liberty-loving men.[67]

But Burt and Fenwick had powerful allies. They could rely on considerable support both from the hierarchy of the Northumberland Miners' Association and from the rank and file. Burt particularly was widely liked and respected even by those who disagreed with him politically. The Northern Liberal Federation assured both Members privately that if they were jettisoned by the miners, the Federation would stand by them, while the *Newcastle Daily Chronicle* offered to pay their election expenses.[68] Moreover, their opponents were reluctant and divided. Those miners' officials, mainly the younger ones, who believed the candidates should join the Labour Party were reluctant to force the issue either from personal reasons or from fear of splitting the Northumberland Miners' Association. In addition, little love was lost between these officials and their potential allies, the local L.R.C.s dominated by the I.L.P., who wanted Socialist candidates in Morpeth and Wansbeck.

Above all, time was the ally of the incumbents. If a decision could be postponed, it might be too late for the cumbrous selection machinery of the Association to produce new candidates for the election. If new nominations could be avoided or delayed Burt and Fenwick might be left alone in the field, even if, in order to preserve its links with the

Miners' Federation, the Northumberland Miners' Association were forced to disown them. Recognising this, Burt and Fenwick fought a skilful delaying action. They were greatly assisted by the miners' reluctance to force a showdown. Despite sharp divisions of opinion, a majority of the Council of the Northumberland Miners' Association wished to retain Burt and Fenwick, but at the same time feared that this might lead to a breach with the Miners' Federation. Divided and hesitant over taking any irrevocable step, the Council tried to get a special dispensation for Burt and Fenwick, exempting them from having to sign the constitution. When this failed the Council appealed to the miners themselves, invoking protracted ballot procedures which were not completed until 13 December 1909. Although the ballot of the Northumberland miners revealed a small majority in favour of the two Members signing the Labour constitution, Burt and Fenwick disparaged the ballot and refused to desert their seats in view of the grave national crisis.[69] It was now too late for the miners to secure new candidates, and the Council of the Association accepted the proposal widely canvassed, not least by Burt and Fenwick, that the sitting M.P.s run independently and that the miners refrain from putting up candidates against them.

The decision pleased nearly everybody. Burt and Fenwick were satisfied: their seats were safe and the Labour constitution unsigned. The local Liberal associations were happy: they still had their two candidates. The leaders of the Northumberland miners were satisfied, for the seats were still held by two miners closely connected with the Association. A rupture within the Association had been avoided, yet relations with the Miners' Federation had been preserved, for the letter of the constitution had been observed. Only the local L.R.C.s were disgruntled, and they for the moment were powerless.

If these were the only three miners' Members who refused to desert the Liberal Party, most of the others deserted in name only. The leading authority on the miners in politics in this period, Dr Roy Gregory, writes: 'They had all signed the constitution, but for most of them their signatures made not a scrap of difference to the way in which they conducted their election campaigns.'[70] In the case of James Haslam (Chesterfield) hecklers during the election found it difficult to ascertain whether he had signed the constitution or not.[71] Some of the miners appeared before the local Liberal associations to secure their support. At Gower, the Liberal Association confidently expected that John Williams, who had reluctantly signed the Labour constitution,

would be 'a faithful and consistent follower of the Liberal Party'.[72]
Contrary to the Labour constitution, some miners' candidates allowed
Liberals to appear on the platform. The most notorious example of
this was Wadsworth in Hallamshire, who permitted the Liberal
H. J. Wilson, himself fighting a Labour candidate in near-by Holmfirth,
to speak from his platform.[73] In near-by Normanton the Liberal *Leeds
Mercury* reported that Fred Hall 'is a sound Liberal and although he
has accepted the L.R.C. ticket his principles have not changed', while
at Nuneaton William Johnson 'contrived to go right through both
campaigns without mentioning the Labour Party at all'.[74]

Liberals publicly distinguished between the miners and other
Labour Members. Speaking for Wadsworth in Hallamshire, Sir
William Clegg, leader of the conservative wing of the Sheffield
Liberals, distinguished between the 'Wadsworth type Labour man' and
'that other section' for whom he had a strong antipathy. Clegg went
on to urge support for Wadsworth and for Harvey and Haslam,
miners' M.P.s for the adjoining Derbyshire constituencies, but
deliberately ignored Pointer in neighbouring Sheffield Attercliffe,
whom he clearly regarded as one of 'that other section'.[75] Most
Liberals saw little need to contain the miners.

In these circumstances it is not surprising that Keir Hardie found it
necessary to plead with the delegates to the 1910 Labour Conference
that '. . . for this election they should not turn the searchlight too
fiercely on what was being done in certain mining constituencies',[76]
and this despite the fact that MacDonald's private remonstrances about
the electoral conduct of the miners had been blandly rebuffed by the
Miners' Federation.[77] But whatever anguish it caused to those wedded
to an independent Labour line, and whatever future problems it posed
for the Labour Party, the rampant Lib-Labism in these constituencies
ensured the full mustering of the anti-Unionist vote.

This ideal relationship was threatened in South Wales and shattered
at Gateshead. In South Wales the younger generation of miners, led by
Vernon Hartshorn, were not content that the miners should be
limited to four seats in South Wales – West Monmouthshire, South
Glamorgan, Gower and Rhondda. Hartshorn himself was nominated
against the Liberal Solicitor-General, Samuel Evans, in Mid-Glamorgan, and miners were nominated for East Carmarthenshire and East
Glamorgan. The Liberals retaliated by resuscitating their associations in
Gower and South Glamorgan and made ostentatious preparations to
select candidates.[78] In the face of these threats the Lib-Lab leaders of

the South Wales Miners' Federation, William Abraham (Mabon), Tom Richards and William Brace capitulated, abandoning their new candidatures. The rift between the generations in the Federation was obvious and public. A disappointed Hartshorn condemned the older leaders for not presenting a united front to the Liberals in Mid-Glamorgan, while his close associate, C. B. Stanton, rejected 'Mabon, Brace and the others' as his leaders.[79] But for the last time the old leaders prevailed. The Liberals reciprocated by waiving whatever plans they had for contesting Gower and South Glamorgan. Thus a tangled series of three-cornered contests was avoided in the mining districts of South Wales.

Gateshead, held by the miner John Johnson, was unique: the only seat in which a Labour or miners' M.P. elected in 1906 faced official Liberal opposition in January 1910. It was the most glaring breach of the containment policy, although Pease endeavoured to justify it on the odd ground that Johnson had changed his political faith since 1906.[80] But so formerly had most of the miners' M.P.s.

Johnson was partly to blame for this unique and unenviable distinction. While his colleagues in Northumberland and Durham sought to avoid signing the Labour pledge, Johnson trumpeted his commitment to the Labour Party. The *North Eastern Daily Gazette*, a not unsympathetic paper, thought that if he had been more tactful the difficulty would not have arisen.[81] This lack of tact was more surprising since Gateshead was a mixed industrial seat and not a mining stronghold. Nor was Johnson's hold on the seat secured by long tenure. But what made Johnson's actions fatal was the antipathy between Liberalism and Labour in the North-East. Perhaps only in Scotland was the rivalry between the two parties more intense. For in the North-East, alone in England, the Liberals genuinely feared they might soon be swamped by the rising Labour tide.[82] They were determined to prevent any further losses and to retrieve their position where possible. Gateshead offered them an excellent opportunity.

Liberal preparations to contest Gateshead began even before the Miners' Federation had formally affiliated with the Labour Party. The intention to seek a Liberal candidate was announced in January 1909 and a constituency reorganisation was under way by February.[83] It was later alleged that the Liberals had done everything possible to avoid a three-cornered contest.[84] It is true they wrote to the Miners' Federation asking whether Johnson could stand as a Liberal candidate but the answer to this was a foregone conclusion. Again, they suggested a postcard plebiscite to decide on the anti-Unionist candidate, but they would have been extraordinarily naïve if they believed a sitting Member would accept such a proposal. Rather, both these moves were designed to strengthen the case for Liberal intervention. In May 1909 the Northern Liberal Federation learnt that the Gateshead Liberals 'were determined to run a Liberal at the General Election'. Having secured in July a prominent Liberal in Harold Elverston as their candidate, they seem never to have wavered in this determination.[85]

Despite the fact that he was the sitting Member, Johnson, like so many Labour candidates in three-cornered contests, tended to be edged to the sidelines while a miniature national debate was conducted by Elverston and his Tory opponent. Johnson was forced more and more to explain his relevance to the contest, and as the campaign proceeded his language grew wilder with strong personal attacks on Elverston and the local Liberals, most of which the Liberals blandly ignored.[86] Johnson's chances were not improved by a postcard ballot, conducted by an amiable busybody, which showed him bottom of the poll.[87] He suffered a further blow on polling day when the constituency was invaded by ten thousand miners who, angered by Johnson's support for the locally unpopular Miners' Eight Hours Act, demonstrated against him bearing banners urging 'Down with Johnson. The Miners' Ruination. Vote for Elverston.'[88] As expected, Johnson was defeated, but Elverston's success in winning the seat against both opponents and his lead of more than 3000 votes over Johnson was the most effective testimony to the Liberals' recuperative power provided by the election.

Pease's letter had been uninformative concerning the five seats won at the by-elections. Were they to be regarded as Labour territory because they had Labour Members or, as post-1906 advances, would they be open to Liberal intervention? The three seats won by the miners presented no difficulties. North-East Derbyshire and North-West Staffordshire had been won before the Miners' Federation affiliated with the Labour Party, and no difficulties arose when the M.P.s concerned joined the Labour Party. Mid-Derbyshire was won after the affiliation with the Labour Party, but the candidate, J. G. Hancock, had fought the seat as a Lib-Lab with open Liberal support. There was no cause for dissension here.

At Attercliffe, won for Labour by Joseph Pointer in May 1909, the local Liberals accepted the by-election verdict and resolved not to run a candidate at the general election. But Sheffield Liberalism was deeply sundered by the attitude it should take to Pointer's contest. On the one side stood the aged but still active H. J. Wilson, an old-fashioned Radical and the dominant figure in local Liberalism for a generation. He favoured active co-operation with Labour, partly out of a genuine conviction that the future of both anti-Unionist parties depended on collaboration, partly in order to obviate the Labour threat to his own seat, the nearby working-class constituency of Holmfirth. He was abetted by his numerous relations located at key points in the Sheffield Liberal structure, particularly his cousin J. W. Wilson, who ran the Liberal machine in Attercliffe,[89] and by the local Liberal newspaper, the *Sheffield Daily Independent*. His support derived mainly from Liberals in the predominantly working-class divisions of Central Sheffield, Attercliffe and Brightside where the advantages of the alliance with Labour were most acutely recognised.

He was opposed by the conservative wing of Sheffield Liberalism led by Sir William Clegg and Sir Joseph Jonas, ex-Lord Mayors of Sheffield and respectively Chairman and Treasurer of the Sheffield Liberal Federation, who wished to prevent the Attercliffe Liberals from openly aligning with Pointer. Their support came principally from Hallam and Ecclesall, middle-class constituencies where the local party leaders were anxious to conciliate 'nervous Liberals'.[90] Clegg outlined his objections to any overt alliance with the 'revolutionary Socialist party' which 'has acted detrimentally and disastrously' towards the Liberal Party both 'imperially and locally', in a vehement memorandum circulated in mid-November 1909.[91] In it he condemned H. J. Wilson's support for Labour at the recent municipal elections as 'ill-advised and a tactical blunder' and warned Sheffield Liberalism that, 'if it does not disassociate itself publicly and by its actions from the "red tie brigade," it would alienate supporters, voters and financial resources'.

This broadside did not deter the Wilsons. On 13 December the Attercliffe executive, with representatives from the other Sheffield divisions present, decided to recommend to the Attercliffe Liberal Council that a manifesto be issued urging a vote for the 'Progressive candidate'. Three days later the Council approved the issue of the manifesto and, at the instigation of a Wilson client, went further adding the words 'Vote for Pointer' to the Liberal manifesto which was published next day in the *Sheffield Independent*. Despite the resignation of Jonas from the Attercliffe Association; despite the fulminations of Clegg against '*officially* assist[ing] the robber to continue to enjoy the fruits of his robbery'; and despite a delay in circulating the manifesto, occasioned by legal difficulties and a traditionalist counter-attack, the Liberal voters in Attercliffe appear to have rallied strongly behind Pointer. His vote in January was over a thousand greater than the combined Liberal and Labour poll in the previous May. Thus, in spite of the inauspicious circumstances created by the recent and bitter by-election, and the powerful local voices raised in opposition, Attercliffe proved a triumph for Wilson's ideal of positive co-operation with Labour.[92]

By contrast, in the other seat won by Labour at a by-election, Jarrow, the Liberals were determined to oust the Labour Member, Pete Curran. Like Gateshead it was a seat in the troubled North-East. Moreover, the 1907 by-election had been fought under peculiarly adverse conditions for the Liberals. From its creation in 1885 Jarrow had been a 'pocket borough' for the founder of Jarrow, the Liberal shipbuilder, Sir Charles Mark Palmer. The Unionists had never contested the seat; Labour had never troubled the incumbent. Thus by the time Sir Charles died in 1907 the Liberal organisation had decayed through lack of competition. Secondly, the by-election had seen the unusual candidature of an Irish Nationalist, whose intervention, in the opinion of many Liberals, cost them the seat.[93] Finally to replace a local magnate the Liberals had chosen as their candidate a carpet-bagger, the journalist Spencer Leigh Hughes.

All this was changed by 1910. The Jarrow organisation was over-hauled, and by February 1909 a full-time agent was at work in the constituency.[94] In 1910 the Irish vote was marshalled behind the Liberal candidate, who 'had pledged himself up to the hilt' on Home Rule, and who was safer on the Catholic schools than the secularist Curran.[95] Above all, the Liberal candidate was a Palmer, and thus a certain vote-getter in Jarrow.

The campaign was one of the quietest of all three-cornered contests, probably because both the Liberal and Labour candidates were ill for much of the time; indeed Curran died within a week of his defeat. There was little of the personal invective that characterised the contest in neighbouring Gateshead. Curran gave considerable attention to the Osborne Judgement, to local unemployment, and to distinguishing his position from that of the Liberals on the House of Lords. By contrast, Palmer relied mainly on his name. Despite their very great advantages over their by-election position, the Liberals just scraped home, Palmer leading Curran by a mere sixty-seven votes.

Finally, Labour was given a free hand in six seats in which it had done well in 1906. Liberal generosity was easy here for in most of these seats Liberal organisation was moribund. Five of the seats were in the Liberal black-spots of Birmingham, Liverpool and Belfast. Only in the sixth seat, Wakefield, where the Liberals had made a real sacrifice, were relations between the parties unsatisfactory. The local Liberal Association did nothing to help Stanton Coit, the Labour candidate, and left Liberals to vote as they pleased. It was rumoured that the older Liberals had not forgiven Coit for boasting in 1906 that 'he had killed the Liberal party in Wakefield'.[96] The results in 1910 do suggest Liberal alienation in January. Coit lost to the Unionist by 519 votes in January; a Liberal defeated the same Unionist by 166 votes in December. Coit's boast was not only unwise, it was also premature.

In the fifty-one seats examined above, the Liberal policy of containment was mostly a negative one, a policy of non-interference in seats in which the Liberals recognised Labour's claims. But in the remaining twenty-seven seats the policy of containment was mainly positive, resistance to Labour expansion. This was inevitable. Twenty of the seats were held by the Liberals, while six of the remaining seven had been won by the Unionists on a minority vote in 1906. Eight of the twenty-seven seats were in Scotland, where, as the *Clarion* later claimed, the Liberal Party had 'fought Labour virulently, bitterly and meanly every inch of the way'.[97] Another eight were in Lancashire–Cheshire–Yorkshire where Labour was already strongly entrenched and the Liberals hostile to further expansion. The acrimony resulting from these contests occasionally spilled over into neighbouring constituencies, left considerable local bitterness between the parties and threatened to damage the amicable relations between them at the national level.

In nearly all these contests, the Liberal candidate adopted the wise tactical course of ignoring Labour's campaign and arguments, and concentrating his fire on the Unionist, who was usually the more serious threat. The division in the nation was between Unionists and anti-Unionists. The Liberal tactic of ignoring Labour was an obvious method of deflating the chances of the anti-Unionist alternative to Liberalism. Few Liberals went so far as did their candidate at Huddersfield who openly declared that 'so far as this election was concerned he had seen no reason yet to discuss Mr Snell [Labour] or his candidature'.[98] Most Liberals, however, practised such tactics.

In one or two cases the Liberal did not, because he dared not, ignore the Labour challenge. Such a case was West Fife, a mainly mining constituency, where the sitting Liberal M.P. was faced with a powerful and able opponent in the local miners' leader, Will Adamson. No one believed the Unionist had much chance even in a triangular fight, and for once a vigorous cut-and-thrust developed between the progressive forces with the Unionist being neglected. But West Fife was an unusual contest both in form and result. For the most part it was the Labour man who stood disregarded on the sidelines.

No candidate can afford to be treated as an irrelevant outsider. Liberal tactics forced Labour candidates to feverish efforts in order to distinguish themselves from the Liberals and to secure attention. This task was made more difficult by the fact that in most of these industrial constituencies the Liberal Party candidate was a Radical, whose policies differed little from moderate Labour. At Cockermouth, Sir Wilfrid Lawson thought that 'Liberalism ought to include both Radicalism and Socialism',[99] while at Holmfirth H. J. Wilson built his campaign around his past activities on behalf of the working class.[100] Efforts to distinguish their candidatures forced Labour candidates into extremist stances in such constituencies. It was in the addresses of these candidates that greatest enthusiasm was found for nationalisation; it was among these candidates that criticism of the inadequacies of the Budget was strongest. In Holmfirth the Labour candidate, Pickles, fought on a single-chamber, single-tax, anti-Budget platform;[101] in Leigh the local Labour party issued a pamphlet on 'Liberal and Tory Crimes'.[102]

More scope was offered for Labour in those few seats where the Liberal candidate came from the conservative wing of the party. In such seats the Labour candidates proclaimed themselves the true followers of the Radical creed, presenting the choice as one between themselves and two Tories. In Spen Valley, the Labour candidate labelled the incumbent, Sir Thomas Whittaker, a Liberal critic of Lloyd George, as 'the greater Tory' of his two opponents.[103] At Leith in a fierce contest with the Scottish landowner, Munro-Ferguson, the Labour candidate, Sam Walker, declared himself the true Radical. 'I am out for Lloyd George, Munro-Ferguson is not, I am out for the whole Budget, Munro-Ferguson is not. . . . The Winston Churchill group would not touch [Munro-Ferguson] with a forty foot pole.'[104]

But if the Liberals generally ignored Labour, one aspect of the Labour candidates was universally stressed – that Labour intervention might well hand the seat to the Unionists. In Morley the Liberal placards warned: 'A split vote is the Tories' opportunity';[105] in Bow and Bromley Dr Clifford pressed Lansbury, the Labour candidate, that 'it would be serving the cause of the poor and the cause of liberty if you were to retire, and so make a clear course for a straight fight.'[106] In Cockermouth the rumour spread that the Unionist candidate, the ironmaster Sir John Randles, had paid the Labour candidate £150 to force a triangular contest.[107] Liberal publicity made full use of early polls which showed the damaging effects of Labour intervention. The early example of the disaster at Camlachie, where the Unionist won with 38·1 per cent of the vote, was instanced with fatal effects for Labour in Scotland.[108]

Thus Labour, the attacking party, was everywhere placed on the defensive. Labour candidates in the three-cornered contests found it necessary continually to justify their presence. Justifications based on working-class solidarity were common. 'Labour men', claimed Snell at Huddersfield, 'could better represent the workers than could nickel imitations of silver men.'[109] At Cockermouth the Labour cry was 'Workers representation from workers' ranks',[110] while Patrick Walls at Middlesbrough told an audience that unless they had a worker for a representative they would 'stop in the gutter or the mud'.[111]

Frequently Labour candidates claimed the seat belonged by right to Labour or had been promised to Labour. The Middlesbrough Liberal and Labour Association, unable to persuade its Lib-Lab M.P. Havelock Wilson to return from the U.S.A. in order to fight the election, and unable to secure a trade unionist, finally selected a young ironmaster, Penrys Williams, as its candidate. The local independent Labour forces selected a steel worker, Patrick Walls, and a dispute raged through the campaign as to which candidate was the true heir to the popular Havelock Wilson. Williams managed to get a letter from Wilson endorsing his candidature, but Walls made great fun of 'the Lib-Lab ironmaster'.[112] At Bishop Auckland and Mid-Lanark Labour claimed that the retiring Liberal Members had promised Labour the seats.[113] In West Fife, the miners claimed that it had long been understood that when the miners brought forward a candidate the Liberal M.P. would gracefully retire. Naturally the Member concerned denied this vehemently.[114] At Camlachie Labour claimed that the local Liberal Association's adoption of the ex-Unionist M.P., Alexander Cross, abrogated whatever claims the Liberals might have upon the seat.[115] The time and energy given to these often devious justifications is one measure of Labour's anxiety about the betrayal charge.

Containment was not insisted on in only three seats attacked by

Labour for the first time – East Manchester, Wigan and Derby. Each was a special case. The position at East Manchester, inextricably tied to the situation in the South-West constituency, has already been examined. Wigan was a seat in which an unofficial Labour candidate had come second to a Unionist in 1906, and was thus only formally a new contest. After some protests the reorganised Liberal Association at Wigan 'did good work for the Progressive cause'.[116] Derby, a two-member borough, had been represented in the 1906 Parliament by a Liberal and the Lib-Lab Richard Bell, General Secretary of the Railway Servants. Bell's relations with his union had seriously deteriorated during 1909 and he resigned his candidature at Derby in December. The 10,000 employees at the Midland Railway Company's works were the decisive element in the electorate, and their determination to have an official Labour candidate in J. H. Thomas, though opposed by Bell, was acquiesced in by the local Liberals.[117] Once again the electoral necessities of the two-member seat facilitated Liberal–Labour co-operation.

III

The election results in January proved a triumph for containment and a vindication of those Labour politicians, particularly MacDonald, who had preached retrenchment of Labour candidates. While Labour did well in the straight contests, it was uniformly unsuccessful in every three-cornered fight. In the three seats held by Labour but attacked by the Liberals, Labour lost Gateshead and Jarrow to the Liberals, South-West Manchester to the Unionists. Only in one of the three-cornered contests did the Labour candidate secure more votes than the Liberal. This was Lansbury at Bow and Bromley, 'the only good fight against adversity'.[118] In three other seats – West Fife, Jarrow and Huddersfield – Labour came second to the Liberals. In the remaining twenty-three three-cornered contests Labour finished at the bottom of the poll. Nor did Labour intervention seriously penalise the Liberals. Only four defeats – Bow and Bromley, Camlachie, Cockermouth and Whitehaven – could be attributed to Labour intervention.[119]

It was this 'shocking list of defeats in three-cornered contests'[120] rather than the Osborne Judgement or financial stringency that determined Labour policy for the second election. Labour could not afford another series of disastrous triangular contests consuming money, demoralising supporters, and lowering the prestige of the party.

Moreover, whatever the arguments for propaganda fights in January, the proximity of the two elections weakened such arguments in December. The January election was scarcely over before MacDonald enunciated electoral policy for December. '. . . we should contest only those seats which we hold with, in addition, those where local successes, financial preparedness, and the state of the organisation make a win practically assured.'[121] In his post-election memorandum to the N.E.C. he stressed the need to concentrate Labour's resources on one or two unconquered constituencies in Yorkshire and in Lancashire (he suggested South-West Manchester, Kirkdale and Huddersfield) rather than dissipate them widely over those two counties. Similarly in Scotland he recommended that the party should concentrate on Camlachie and West Fife.[122] At both the 1910 Labour Party and I.L.P. Conferences the party leadership prepared their supporters for drastic retrenchment in the number of candidates.

TABLE 12.3 LABOUR RESULTS JANUARY 1910

	Total	No. successful
A. Straight Fights		
(a) In two-member seats		
(in harness with Liberals)	12	10
(b) In single-member seats	39	30
B. Three-cornered Contests	27	0
	78	40

Labour eventually cut back its candidates in December to fifty-six.[123] In January Labour had fought most of the seats in which it had had a chance. Campaigning in new territory would have been foolhardy and only three seats not fought in January were tackled in December – South Leeds, Mid-Glamorgan and East Glamorgan – and of these only East Glamorgan was virgin territory. There was also a drastic pruning of contests in which Labour had done poorly in January. The party fought only seven of the twenty-six seats in which it had trailed the Liberals in January. In general the policy of concentration seems to have been adopted. In Lancashire only two seats not held by Labour – Kirkdale and Preston – were fought; in Yorkshire only two – Huddersfield and South Leeds; and in Scotland only three – Camlachie, Mid-Lanark and West Fife.

TABLE 12.4 LABOUR AND THE LIBERALS DECEMBER 1910

	Seats with no Liberal opposition Dec 1910	Seats with Liberal opposition Dec 1910	Labour victories Dec 1910
Contests Dec 1910 in:			
A. Seats won by Labour Jan 1910			
(a) Two-member seats	10	0	10
(b) Single-member seats	29*	1	27
B. Seats fought and lost by Labour Jan 1910			
(a) Two-member seats			
(in harness with Liberals)	2	0	1
(b) Labour only anti-Unionist candidate			
or ran second to Unionist	3	1	2
(c) Others	1	6	2
C. Seats not fought Jan 1910	0	3	0
	—	—	—
	45	11†	42

Notes: * In Chester-le-Street, West Monmouthshire and Normanton the Members were returned unopposed.

† In Gower, Mid-Glamorgan, and West Fife there was only Liberal opposition.

The Liberals persisted with their containment policy which had worked so successfully in January. Two elections in the one year plus the very success of the January operation did ensure a certain generosity. In Bow and Bromley, where Lansbury had run second to a Unionist in January, the Liberals desisted. Over local grumbling, Lloyd George and the local Liberal Association endorsed Lansbury,[124] who defeated the unlucky Amery. In Cumberland there was a swap. In January, Labour candidates came at the bottom of the poll in Cockermouth and Whitehaven, but in both cases their intervention lost the seat to the Unionists. In December, Labour did not bring forward a candidate in Cockermouth, while a Liberal and Labour conference in White-haven left the choice of candidate to the Labour Whip, subject to endorsement by the Liberal Whip. In both constituencies the anti-Unionist parties co-operated. Towards the close of the contest in Cockermouth Labour representatives appeared on the Liberal plat-forms; Labour issued placards denying friction between the progressive parties and urging a vote for the Liberals; and on polling day inter-twined blue and red ribbons were common, indicative of the local alliance. In Whitehaven the Liberal Association endorsed the Labour candidate and Liberals appeared on the Labour platform.[125] The anti-Unionists won both seats.

The Liberals could afford to be generous. Labour withdrawals enabled them not only to recover Cockermouth but also South-West Manchester. A Liberal took the place of Stanton Coit at Wakefield and won the seat where, despite the neutrality of official Labour, the miners and railwaymen rallied to the Liberal.[126] At Chatham where there had been a straight fight between Labour and Unionist in January, a Liberal intervened claiming that Labour had promised to abandon the seat after its January defeat.[127] Although failing to win the seat in December, the Liberal led the Labour man by over three thousand votes. And this was a seat won by Labour in 1906.

Relations between the two parties were generally good. They were excellent in the two-member seats, and so good in some of the mining seats that the Labour Executive considered disciplinary measures against three of the miners' M.P.s because of their Lib-Lab behaviour during the campaign.[128] While the Labour withdrawals annoyed the left wing, they served to further good Liberal–Labour relations in most constituencies. There was the threat of trouble from the local Liberals at Clitheroe where David Shackleton retired, the only Labour Member to do so at the second election. But Liberal headquarters persuaded the local Liberals to acquiesce in a new Labour candidate.[129] There were only three S.D.P. candidates and three independent Labour candidates and these did little to embarrass relations. Indeed John Burns welcomed the Socialist candidate at Battersea as 'a Lightning Conductor for votes that otherwise would go Tory but not to me'.[130]

There were scattered protests about the amity of relations. The S.D.P. which had advised Socialists to judge between candidates on their merits in January, now pressed a blanket vote against Liberals 'our worst enemies'.[131] The I.L.P. manifesto urged workers to make the Osborne Judgement 'the first of all election issues'[132] and a number of local Labour bodies urged abstention or a vote against the Liberal candidate because of his attitude to the Judgement. There was, too, a hangover from the bitter three-cornered contests in January, reflected in heavy abstentions in some of the seats contested by Labour in January but not in December. In Gateshead where the January contest had been marked by exceptional personal rancour the poll fell by 12·1 per cent. In Spen Valley where the Liberal victor at the January declaration of the poll claimed that the Labour campaign 'of personalities, of lies, and of slander . . . [had been] driven back to the gutter from which it came',[133] the poll fell by 10·2 per cent. At Middlesbrough it fell by 10·2 per cent; at Leith by 14·3 per cent. In many of these cases the local Labour parties advised voters to abstain, or adopted neutral positions with distinct anti-Liberal undertones, often with specific reference to the events of eleven months before.[134]

But these were scattered protests. Only in one region did Liberal–Labour relations notably deteriorate. The troubles on the South Wales coalfield had culminated in the riots at Tonypandy in early November. Liberal–Labour relations in the valleys were scarred by these events, and Keir Hardie's vehement denunciations of the Liberal coal-owners and the Government's actions exacerbated the situation.[135] Liberal annoyance with Keir Hardie was such that as late as 28 November the Merthyr Liberal Federation contemplated running a second candidate against him. Although a second Liberal did not appear, the discord in Merthyr was carried to the polls. 2595 Labour voters plumped for Keir Hardie, while 2172 Liberal voters plumped for Edgar Jones, and another 1484 split their votes between Jones and the conservative candidate.[136]

In the surrounding valleys the Young Turks in the South Wales Miners' Federation now successfully insisted on a broader assault on the Liberal position in Glamorgan. Vernon Hartshorn had already stood for Mid-Glamorgan in March 1910 on the retirement of the Liberal M.P., Sir Samuel Evans. Liberal headquarters had been willing to acquiesce in Hartshorn, 'but the local people were determined and got their man in by Tory votes'.[137] In December Hartshorn stood again for Mid-Glamorgan and C. B. Stanton, a leader in the Rhondda troubles, stood for East Glamorgan. Over London opposition the local Liberals retaliated, bringing out a strong anti-socialist against John Williams in Gower, the only case in the election of a sitting Labour M.P. being attacked by a Liberal.[138] At the polls however the *status quo* was maintained, all the sitting Members being returned. Although mounted under apparently favourable circumstances and in an overwhelmingly working-class environment, the Labour challenge failed to wrest the control of the Welsh industrial heartland from the Liberals.[139]

Labour's failure in South Wales was typical of its national failure to win new territory from the Liberals. Apart from holding Gower, Labour captured only one seat against Liberal opposition. This was West Fife, where the miner Adamson had run second to the Liberal

in January. In December the Labour attack benefited from the withdrawal of the Unionist, and the Liberal ran scared throughout, his
desperation revealed in his promises of the nationalisation of mines and
railways.[140] In other clashes with the Liberals Labour performed as
dismally as in January. Labour's only gains, apart from West Fife, came
in straight fights with the Unionists, though at Whitehaven and Bow
and Bromley such gains were the result of new Liberal abstentions.

TABLE 12.5 LABOUR RESULTS DECEMBER 1910

	Total	No. successful
A. Unopposed	3	3
B. Straight Fights		
(a) In two-member seats (in harness with Liberals)	12	11
(b) In single-member seats – against Unionists	30	26
(c) In single-member seats – against Liberals	3	2
C. Three-cornered Contests	8	0
	56	42

Labour had launched a cautious exploratory attack on Liberal
territory in January, which was almost totally repulsed. The result was
less than a dozen clashes with the Liberals in December, again mostly
disappointing. Liberal–Labour relations in the elections of 1910 had
been dominated by the Liberal tactic of containment. Few tactical
operations in electoral history can have been so completely successful.

Party Organisation

I

Party machines are often scapegoats for electoral defeat, and much of the abuse that was showered on the Conservative organisation in the aftermath of the 1910 defeats was both unfair and exaggerated. 'I have no doubt', wrote Balfour in January 1911, 'that the Central Office and all connected with it has been unjustly attacked. *But* I have also no doubt that the system which has been practically unchanged for 25 years requires overhauling.'[1] Others were markedly less restrained. Lord Malmesbury, who had considerable experience of the organisation in London and the Home Counties, attributed blame for defeat in December to 'an enormous extent' to 'the rottenness of our party organisation'.[2] The theme was elaborated in *Blackwood's Magazine*:

> Conservative organisation, bad at best, is reduced to chaos by a fight at short notice. . . . There is no supervision of local associations, no attempt to make backward localities efficient, no selection of the right men for the right seats. . . . It would be worth the Conservative Party's while to stay for ten years out of office, if thereby we could scrap the present party machinery and learn the rudiments of sane business.[3]

The organisational ills that plagued the Conservative Party in 1910 stemmed from age and decay in the party machine. According to Sandars: 'The C.O. has stood still for more than a generation. It lives the same cramped life; it employs the old methods; it works with the same class of man (in some respects they are not so good as in Middleton's day) and meanwhile the whole face of the political world and the party has changed.'[4] The rust, which had already begun in the last years of Captain Middleton's long tenure as Principal Agent, was in no way arrested by his incompetent and short-lived successors, Captain Wells (1903–5) and Colonel Haig (1905–6).[5] External pressure for reform at the Central Office after 1906 came to nothing because of the factional struggle. Nor was reconstruction likely to come from within. Acland-Hood was the last man to initiate reforms, while the new Principal Agent, Percival Hughes, lacked the experience and force of character to press for them.[6]

The woeful condition of the organisation was obvious to any who visited St Stephen's Chambers in Bridge Street where the Conservative Central Office was housed.

> The existing staff are badly accommodated and overcrowded and the arrange-ments for interviewing candidates, local deputations, etc., are so bad as to be a real menace to the harmony of the party. No man ... can spend half an hour or more (and more is the rule) in the poky little coal hole which serves partly as a waiting room and partly as a passage for clerks, without departing in a thor-oughly irritated and hostile frame of mind.[7]

Inside this warren administrative chaos reigned. Writing some twelve months after the second election, the newly appointed party manager, Arthur Steel-Maitland, indicted the running of the Central Office under Hughes.

> No attempt was made at departmentalising work. There was no control of ordinary office routine ... no proper system of reports from district agents; no control of their expenditure. What is more, there was no annual balance sheet. They could not tell you within £10,000 what the year's expenditure had been; probably not within £20,000. There was no proper classification of expenditure, no recovery of loans, no following up of lapsed subscriptions. No note was taken (except as regards General Election expenses) of interviews at which promises were made, pecuniary or otherwise. Vague verbal assurances were the rule, not satisfactory at the moment and productive of trouble later. Engagements were never practically kept. And in general work was done which could not be put off, but all problems and responsibilities were shelved if possible.[8]

Moreover the size of the administrative staff – fourteen, consisting of nine district agents and 'five responsible persons at headquarters' – was the same as in Middleton's day, and Acland-Hood had successfully resisted attempts to increase it.[9] The numbers were simply inadequate to cope with the demands of a general election. The indefatigable Sandars seems to have installed himself as chief executive officer at periods during both elections. If this reflects primarily on Hughes's capacity, it also reflects on the understaffing at party headquarters.

Recruitment policies compounded the weakness of the Central Office. The heads of departments were all promoted agents. Sandars summed up their qualities in a letter to Balfour on Christmas Day 1910. 'They are excellent men of their type, skilled in the technique of agents' election work, but they have no sympathy with new ideas, no imagination, no elasticity of method; in a word they are old fashioned.'[10]

Their limitations added to the work of the Principal Agent, for, as Sandars noted, it meant there was no one at Central Office, apart from Hughes, who could talk with the local chairmen 'on terms of social equality';[11] and Amery complained of 'the difficulty of getting hold of anybody at the Central Office who is in a position to deal directly and authoritatively with questions raised'.[12] Perhaps the most eloquent testimony to the competence of the Central Office staff was their fate under Steel-Maitland, who took charge in July 1911. Of the nine district agents five were to be pensioned off as soon as suitable replacements could be found. Of the five members of staff at headquarters one was labelled 'quite incompetent' and marked for dismissal, and a second 'absolutely valueless', except for 'his ability to make calculations'.[13]

Acland-Hood and Hughes seem to have cultivated the party agents, particularly the older men, so much so that Sandars considered that there was 'almost an Agents' ring, which is ultra-conservative in ideas, looks to, & gets support from, the C.C.O., & is very loyal to that institution because it recognises and protects its interests'.[14] After 1906 Acland-Hood refused to appoint any new young agents because owing to the 'general election slump' many dispossessed old agents had to be provided for first.[15] Steel-Maitland accused Hughes of 'gain[ing] great popularity with [the agents], partly by real sympathy, partly by lack of discipline, and by being ready, if a man is dismissed for gross incompetence, to recommend him elsewhere'.[16] It was charitable of the Central Office to act as a benevolent society, but this policy was not always conducive to efficiency. After the January election there was a demand for a complete revision of the agents' lists, and many agents were condemned as 'lazy' and 'incompetent'.[17]

The offices of the National Union of Conservative and Unionist Associations, which an article in *The Times* described as 'squalid, small and uncomfortable',[18] were also located in St Stephen's Chambers. But proximity did not lead to harmonious relations with Central Office. '. . . there is', confessed Henry Chaplin, Chairman of the National Union in 1910, '& always has been much jealousy of the Central Office.'[19] The fusion of the C.C.O. and the National Union, achieved through Middleton's joint occupation of the office of Principal Agent and Secretary of the National Union from 1885 to 1903, ended with his resignation. None of his three immediate successors as Principal Agent held executive position in the National Union. The key executive officer there in 1910 was the Secretary, Thomas Cox, a competent but unimaginative authoritarian. His administration was described as 'wooden and rigid' and apparently occasioned considerable friction with the constituencies. Steel-Maitland assessed him as 'an admirable foreman' but a 'bad head'.[20]

The factional struggle within the Conservative Party aggravated the inherent dualism at St Stephen's Chambers. In 1906 the Whole Hoggers had attempted to subvert the Central Office, the centre of organisational resistance to Chamberlain, but were repulsed by the Balfourites who saw the Whole Hogger move as an attempt 'to capture the Machine and the Party Chest, and to make the Chief Whip and the Central Office a subordinate department of the National Union'.[21] This victory left the Balfourites in control of the Central Office, as well as ending the prospects of any immediate reform of that institution.

The Whole Hoggers were more successful in their efforts to widen the powers of the National Union; they succeeded in extending its authority over constituency associations, and secured for it control over literature and speakers, These were Whole Hogger victories, for by 1908 at the latest the Whole Hoggers controlled the popular organisation. Yet these changes were ill-conceived, partly because factional were given more weight than organisational considerations. They emphasised the debilitating dualism of the party organisation, and impaired its electoral efficiency.[22]

As a result of these reforms the Central Office agreed to pay the National Union a fixed annual grant of £8500 to cover office establishment, publications and lectures, to be supplemented at by-elections by additional grants at the discretion of the Principal Agent and Chief Whip.[23] The latter provision led to irritation, for the 'National Union "stick" the Central Office – quite naturally – when they can', while generally Steel-Maitland considered that the National Union was poorly organised to use these funds with the result that much money was wasted.[24]

Although the agents reported regularly to the Central Office, the reaffirmation of National Union responsibility for constituency associations served to inhibit Central Office action, and to excuse inaction, in the field of local organisation. Nor was the National Union capable of carrying out effective local supervision. Information on the condition of constituencies was lacking for 'the National Union books, over-elaborate in other respects, are quite deficient in this'. In respect to stimulating 'backward constituencies' (if and when identified) 'the National Union, except in one or two counties, is absolutely useless for this purpose, though officially charged with it'.[25] The breakdown of an effective liaison between the National Union and the Central Office after 1903, and the reaffirmation of National Union responsibility for local organisation in 1906, contributed to headquarters' neglect of the constituency organisation.

The deleterious results of National Union control of literature and speakers was dramatically apparent in the January election. While in the years before the election the National Union had exercised full control over these activities, at the general election the work devolved willynilly on to the Central Office because so many members of the National Union committees concerned were themselves out of London. 'By some tacit understanding, at the General Election the duties were dumped . . . on the Central Office, which has been kept in ignorance of the previous course of the work, and which does not receive the reports made to the National Union.'[26] Chaplin was appalled:

> . . . something at all events *can* & *must* be done to put an end at the next [election] to the chaos & confusion which prevailed at the Last Election [January 1910], owing to the Dual Responsibility in many respects of the N.U. – & the Central Office. It can in my opinion be done only in one way. *For one thing after the election has begun & while it lasts* the responsibility for Sending Speakers . . . must be in the hands of *one* authority only & that authority it seems to me must be the Central Office. The Best men on the N.U. are all away fighting their own seats – & though I have the *Highest opinion* of Cox, he hasn't the same means of access to Front Bench men, and Prominent members of Parlmt. for which Constituencies are for ever asking, as the Central Office, even if his hands were free from a hundred other things & not weighted as they are.[27]

Some improvement in these relations was noticeable by December, but the Central Office and the National Union continued in the words of *The Times* to resemble 'two motor cars driven side by side along a narrow road, with the attendant risks of collision'.[28] It was primarily a result of the experience of this dualism in the elections of 1910 that led the Conservative Party in 1911 to reverse the reforms of 1906 and vest executive authority for local organisations, literature and speakers solely in the Central Office.

It was in its relations with constituencies and candidates that the defects of the central organisation were most apparent and most critical at election times. Inaccurate intelligence and assessment of local and regional situations were indicative of the poor liaison between headquarters and the constituencies. Above all, the parlous state of many local associations suggested things were seriously amiss. The long years of Unionist hegemony, the slow corrosion of the once superb Middleton machine, and the strained relations between the National Union and Central Office had sapped the vigour and vitality of the constituency associations. Even the traumatic shock of 1906 had failed to revitalise them.

In 1910 Central Office recognised that the machine in London 'was defective', that Manchester and Yorkshire were 'hopeless in the matter of organisation' while the Newcastle upon Tyne association was 'futile'.[29] At Newcastle in December 1910 'no less than 14,000 electors were never canvassed and 8000 removals never traced'.[30] In Manchester and the Yorkshire boroughs 'little or no work is done except at election times, and the result is there is no close touch between organisers and constituents'.[31] Even Acland-Hood saw that in Lancashire, Yorkshire and Scotland the 'methods, leaders and organisation are hopelessly out of date, and must be altered whether they like it or not'.[32] The *Daily Telegraph* recommended that in London, Lancashire, and Yorkshire, the Unionists should 'scrap the existing party machinery and . . . instal new plant'.[33] The Scottish machine was perhaps the classic case. Although nominally under the Principal Agent, the Scottish organisation was for all practical purposes quite divorced from the English authorities. It was decentralist in structure, and inherent centrifugal tendencies were fanned by the fact that there was no Scottish Whip, no fixed office or permanent staff for the Scottish Agent, and insufficient finance. Outside Clydeside and Midlothian constituency organisation was 'badly defective or non-existent' and local associations little more than 'social gatherings of lairds'.[34] According to *The Times* there was no adequate system for providing speakers, no requirement for registration reports, and the whole organisation desperately needed a businessman.[35]

Their failure to keep pace with developing democratic sentiment, and their related inability to mobilise the political resources available to them, were the most characteristic defects of the local organisations. It was frequently alleged that local associations were made up merely of paid agents and the nominees of the sitting Member, and that no attempt was made to give them a wider base.[36] A Unionist candidate, J. Foster Fraser, complained that policy 'is largely dependent upon what certain social big-wigs in the locality are in favour of'.[37] Too often in the urban constituencies of the North the local organisations were closed and complacent coteries of traditional notables. While running associations through local magnates might work in the countryside, it was often resented in the cities, and here also Unionist neglect of the working classes was widely noted. 'The working classes in this country', warned *The Times*, 'have been given electoral power, and the Unionist Party, if it is to rule, must rule with and through them.'[38]

Typical was the response of the Central Office to the imaginative lead of the *Standard*, which in late 1909 raised £6074 to run Unionist working-men candidates.[39] The Central Office ran four candidates with this fund, but in seats which had only gone Tory in moments of aberration. At least in three of the seats, Swansea District, Leicester and Clitheroe there was an industrial working-class vote to tap, but the decision to send the fourth candidate to Orkney and Shetland seems utterly inexplicable. All were defeated by overwhelming majorities.

Undaunted the *Standard* tried again in December. This time the newspaper received the active support of the Whole Hogger wing, and a motion from the National Union Conference stressed that the candidates should be given constituencies in which they would have 'a fair and reasonable chance of being returned'.[40] £7866 was raised and six hopeful working-men were run.[41] This time the Central Office treated their candidatures more sympathetically. No one was sent to Orkney, but only two stood in seats that could be considered winnable. Neither won.

The dominance of many associations by the 'social big-wigs' arose from their dependence on a few wealthy subscribers, or on the munificence of the local chairman or candidate, as well as from the deferential structure of English Conservatism. Special privileges naturally accrued to such paymasters, e.g. in most Unionist organisations subscriptions over a certain amount entitled the subscriber to a vice-presidency and a seat on the council of the local association. It was a frequent charge of the Tory democrats that 'by allowing wealth and social standing to preponderate over political ability, the Unionist Party had dulled the edge of its political organisation'.[42]

There was widespread disquiet about the calibre of candidates. An irate Sir Joseph Lawrence claimed: 'We lost Lancs and Yorks:– principally the former by rotten candidates. . . . Fancy that popinjay . . . Ian Malcolm with his perfume and his dilettantism . . . in a constituency where people walk in clogs and women wear shawls on their heads at meetings!'[43] The *Saturday Review* thought that at least twelve of the London candidates in December had no qualifications except 'social ambition, praiseworthy sentiments, and money'.[44] Money was the crucial requirement. 'It is not the fault of the Central Office so much', wrote Amery, 'nor the snobbery or greediness of constituencies as the system of looking directly to the candidate for the maintenance of the local organisation and for payment of the Agent which is responsible for the weakness of our candidates as a rule.'[45] When the East Dorset Unionist Association approached Lord Robert Cecil as a candidate for the December election, he was told that the candidate was expected to find £1000 a year plus his election expenses.[46] The millionaire Sir Edward Sassoon, M.P. for Hythe since 1899, spent £3000 a year on the borough, which was admittedly a 'demoralised' seat, i.e. one without effective organisation.[47] This 'cheque book system' of election, as one critic dubbed it,[48] was considered by many to be the chief explanation for the poor quality of Unionist candidates. Steel-Maitland recognised that 'the Central Office must reform its ways about candidates. . . . Wealthy candidates must be borne in mind . . . But it is no good running more Belilios and Profumos for Walworth or the High Peak division.'[49]

Dissatisfaction with candidates was linked to dissatisfaction with agents. The local agent was often the real arbiter in the selection of the candidate and tended to prefer 'a rich candidate who will pay expenses, however undesirable he may be in other directions'.[50] Above all, the agent looked for a candidate who could assure him of a satisfactory income. As his livelihood depended on what the constituency organisation was prepared to pay, and could vary from about £40 to £500 per annum,[51] he was most unlikely to underrate wealth as a qualification for association office or parliamentary candidature. Certainly agents wished to avoid the fate of the East Bristol Conservative agent who 'had to go round . . . collecting shillings and half crowns to make up his salary'.[52] Amery went so far as to allege that an agent's 'chief work therefore is not organisation, so much as finding, nursing and keeping a rich candidate'.[53]

The party headquarters proved incapable of dealing with this multitude of problems. Indeed it is doubtful whether the Central Office recognised many of them. Headquarters was poorly organised to do so. Unlike the Liberals, the Unionist Whips were not organised on a regional basis with regional responsibilities. The authority of the provincial divisions of the National Union was vitiated by the failure of the central organisations to support them in conflicts with refractory constituency associations. Little was done to stimulate local reorganisation, and even encouragement and help for the associations were lacking. Clinging to the tradition of non-interference in the selection of candidates, and ever considerate of the needs of the agents, Central Office seems to have been impervious to the rising disquiet about the quality of candidates. Sandars concluded that weaknesses in the constituencies were too often the result of weaknesses at the top.[54]

Even when defects were recognised action was dilatory. Much-needed reorganisation in London was frustrated by Acland-Hood and Hughes, who delayed approval of a decentralised system for the London constituencies until the eve of the first election.[55] Two months after the first election had revealed serious weaknesses in the Manchester area, Sandars was complaining to Balfour that nothing had been done and that 'Alick [Acland-Hood] now serenely says that the time before the next election is too short for organising the constituencies'.[56] In September 1910 Unionist unease was seen in widespread press criticism of 'the supineness of the officials, and the dilatory methods of the Central Office'.[57]

Much of the responsibility for the parlous state of the Conservative machine must rest on Sir Alexander Acland-Hood, Chief Whip since 1902, and to a lesser extent on J. Percival Hughes, Principal Agent since 1907. Acland-Hood was a blunt West Country squire, known familiarly as 'the Pink'Un' or 'Old Brickdust'. Trained as a Whip in the days of Akers-Douglas and Middleton, he was an unimaginative traditionalist averse, even hostile, to any tinkering with the Middleton machine. His knowledge of urban politics and organisation was minimal. Indeed, his predecessor Akers-Douglas alleged in 1910 that 'Alick is totally unacquainted with any details of provincial organisation outside the electoral division of West Somerset [his own constituency]'.[58] His characteristic bluntness was mingled with increasing irascibility as pressures mounted. The younger men, with whom he seems to have been completely out of sympathy, suffered most. Sandars learnt that during the second election 'Alick's behaviour towards the young men of the Party was most disheartening and . . . his brusquerie amounted to absolute rudeness'. Sandars's informant, Lord Lansdowne, 'as a rule the most pacific and moderate of men', felt so strongly on the subject that he 'hoped an early and honourable withdrawal' could be arranged for Acland-Hood.[59] Amery agreed, believing that nothing could be done to overhaul the party machine until the Chief Whip was either 'poisoned or pensioned'.[60] By the end of 1910 Acland-Hood possessed the unique and unenviable distinction of having presided over the party machine through three successive election defeats.

The Principal Agent, Percival Hughes, was something of a dilettante. By profession a barrister, he also had pretensions as a novelist and sculptor. When appointed Principal Agent in 1907 he had had only limited political experience, and none whatsoever of the Central Office, although this latter was not necessarily a handicap. Personable and loyal, he lacked drive, initiative and administrative ability. One of the junior Whips, Balcarres, thought him 'fit [only] for an old woman's tea party';[61] while Garvin found it 'grotesque' that he should take a Christmas holiday in the midst of the first election, leaving Sandars to keep the machine running.[62] By 1911 Hughes had 'completely broken down and was absolutely useless', and he resigned from the organisation early in 1912.[63]

Yet it would be unjust to attach all the blame for organisational failure to Acland-Hood and Hughes. Acland-Hood at least made no effort to cling to power, admitting after the first election that it would be best for the party if he retired.[64] However, although his inadequacies were widely recognised, he was kept in office, for the party leaders revealed no sense of urgency about the condition of the organisation.

Moreover, Acland-Hood was grossly overloaded. Balfour himself found it 'hard to believe that any single person can do the work demanded of a modern head Whip'.[65] Yet Balfour had been tardy in reaching this conclusion and even tardier in doing anything about it. Well before 1910 the task of combining the role of party disciplinarian, party treasurer, and chief organiser had become overwhelming, and the load had become unbearable as the result of the failure to find an adequate successor to Middleton at the Central Office. M.P.s complained that they could not contact Acland-Hood because he was always closeted with Hughes, or a party chairman, or a candidate, or a cartoonist; organisation men complained that it was hard to see the Chief Whip because of his parliamentary duties. To make matters worse the junior Whips were hardly equipped for their jobs because they never had a chance of conferring with Acland-Hood 'owing to the jostling of the multifarious claims upon his time'.[66] It is little wonder that Acland-Hood became increasingly irritable.

The factionalism that had riven the party since 1903 added to the Chief Whip's load. We have seen how it aggravated the dualism in the party organisation, complicating the tasks of the party officers. In more immediate ways it contributed to Acland-Hood's burdens. The correspondence of the leading Unionists reveals how much of his time in Parliament was consumed by disciplinary problems; and how much of his time outside the House was eaten up in trying to settle factional squabbles. On the eve of the first election Acland-Hood was exhausted and his never equable temper frayed. After a protracted quarrel with Lord Robert Cecil, he expressed to Sandars his regret that 'we are not living in 1809, in which case I would have called him out and shot him'.[67]

Finally, although the central authorities cannot escape a share of the responsibility for the lamentable state of many of the constituency organisations, they were faced with a herculean task. The dimensions of the problem were enormous, the weight of social conservatism, organisational inertia and entrenched administrative practices had all to be overcome. In addition the constituencies were often recalcitrant: '. . . it is,' complained Acland-Hood, 'precisely because these districts *will* run their own show, and will brook no interference from the Central Office that we did as badly there.'[68] In Manchester, the local chairman, Sir William Vaudrey, was 'a real obstruction'. Despite Central Office advice that 'no Chairman of a party ought to think of contesting a seat in his own area', Vaudrey stood for North-East Manchester in January to the detriment of the Manchester organisation.[69] The task of overhauling the local machinery of the party would have daunted abler and more determined men than Acland-Hood and Percival Hughes.

It was no doubt true, as *Reynolds News* observed, that even if Acland-Hood 'had been a Schnadhorst in organisation, a Chamberlain or a Lloyd George in demogoguery, a Gladstone in oratory, he could not have averted defeat in the last two elections'.[70] But his lack of Schnadhorst's qualities and the general ills of the Conservative organisation handicapped the party electorally. This handicap becomes more obvious when the Liberal organisation is contrasted with the Conservative. At Liberal headquarters Schnadhorst's successor had created a machine rivalling in quality the Middleton machine at the peak of its performance.

In Sir Robert Hudson, 'the Liberal Party's great wire puller' as Strachey wrote with reluctant admiration,[71] the Liberals had an organiser of genius. Schnadhorst's protégé, he was well fitted to succeed him. A man of quiet charm, courtesy and personal modesty, he was methodical, thorough, and perspicacious. He possessed also an excellent memory, considerable courage and tireless energy. As one close associate wrote: 'Hudson had in him . . . pluck and work for a dozen ordinary fellows.'[72] Inclined to be curt, even brusque in his business, he seems rarely to have provoked misunderstandings or personal animosities. In addition, he seems to have been an able suppliant for party funds. A measure of his ability is that during the sterile years from 1895 to 1903 there seems to have been no serious attempt to unseat him. By 1910 he had been the key figure in the Liberal machine for seventeen years but, aged only forty-six, he was now at the height of his powers.[73]

Hudson was the lynchpin of the Liberal organisation. He was secretary of the National Liberal Federation, the popular body, and of the Liberal Central Association, the headquarters organisation. He was treasurer of the Liberal Publication Department, of which his able brother-in-law Charles Geake, was secretary. He had had a long and intimate relationship with Jesse Herbert and R. H. Davies, the key officials in the Whips' Office. In addition he was a member of the executive and organising committees of the Free Trade Union. Acting as the liaison between the Chief Whip and the organisations of the party, and between the major party organisations themselves, Hudson gave the Liberal machine a unity that the Unionists conspicuously lacked.

The Liberal Party had not been quite so fortunate in its Chief Whips, having had three between 1906 and December 1910. The first of these, George Whiteley (1905–1908), was a blunt Yorkshire brewer who seems to have spent an excessive amount of time quarrelling with the Lord Chancellor over legal patronage. He did, however, restore the finances of the party.[74] He was succeeded by Joseph Pease, Chief Whip from April 1908 until February 1910. Pease had been a junior Whip for eleven years, and was regarded as a political lightweight. '... plenty of pluck, little knowledge of men, a devoted admiration of Winston, no political knowledge and a great liking for people who will feed and amuse him', was Montagu's assessment.[75] His term as Chief Whip proved that he had been much underrated. He pushed through a comprehensive scheme for grouping the local associations in regional federations and presided over the smooth functioning of the Liberal machine during the January election. Much to his joy he was rewarded with Cabinet office, and was followed as Chief Whip by the Master of Elibank, who had been Scottish Whip from 1906 to 1909.[76]

Alexander Murray, the Master of Elibank, Chief Whip of the Liberal Party during the critical months from February 1910 to August 1912, was probably the greatest Chief Whip of his generation. Characterised by 'chronic good humour'[77] and with the ample form of the jovial fat man, his outward *bonhomie* masked an iron determination, shrewd judgement, and great tactical boldness.

1910 was his year of achievement. He played a key role in ensuring the survival of the Government in the troubled early months of the year. If he did not 'lunch together every day, or sup together, or sleep together . . .' with the Irish and Labour Whips as he was advised,[78] he did establish excellent personal links with both Irish factions, and with the Labour leaders.[79] Outside Parliament he rehoused the over-crowded Liberal Central Association, and encouraged the organisation men by securing a knighthood for Jesse Herbert.[80] At the same time he kept the regional and local organisations attuned for an expected election, and pursued tirelessly the search for funds to fill the Liberal coffers. Amidst all this he found time to revive the moribund Liberal organisation in Ulster.[81]

Finally in December he was the architect of victory. He seems to have played a decisive role in determining the timing of the second contest.[82] During the election itself he was 'an inspiration to all who have come in contact with him, cool amid all the excitement, working almost night and day, and yet always quick to note the weak point and to repair its defect'.[83] One of his colleagues, R. H. Davies, wrote to him after the election: 'I have worked under quite a number of Chief Whips but, believe me, you leave them all far behind.'[84]

Not only were the Liberal Chief Whips abler, and better served, than Acland-Hood, but their burdens were eased by the organisational structure of the Liberal machine. Hudson's linking the Liberal Central Association and the National Liberal Federation avoided strains be-tween the two bodies by contrast with the bickering and dualism at St Stephen's Chambers. The L.C.A., composed of leading figures in Parliament and the country, while in no way infringing on the powers of the Chief Whip, did provide him with a source of intelligence and an informal means for raising and distributing funds. Again, the Whips' Office, ambiguously related to the L.C.A. and housed in 12 Downing Street, further eased the work load of the Chief Whip.[85] There was no parallel institution in the Unionist organisation.

Relations with the local constituencies reflected the vigour of the central leadership. In 1908 Pease initiated through the N.L.F. a group-ing of the local associations in England into eight regional federations. This reorganisation was completed by April 1909, and seems to have functioned well in both elections, Hudson reporting after the January election 'very gratifying testimony' to the usefulness of the regional federations.[86] The federations acted as intelligence outposts for the Chief Whip, as clearing houses for propaganda and speakers, as overseers of derelict constituencies, and as a funnel to the Whips' Office for local demands for candidates.

By contrast with the Unionists, the Liberal authorities were determined to make the regional federations effective. A junior Whip was attached to each federation as a liaison between the federation and the Chief Whip. Pease and Elibank seem to have developed close personal relations with the leading members of the federation executives. Financial assistance was forthcoming from the central bodies, although some of the federations seemed chary of accepting responsibility for allocating central funds to constituency associations, out of fear of local disputes over such allocation.[87] In the January election the N.L.F. supplied and financed fifty-seven speakers for the district federations, and organised through the federations some three to four hundred meetings a week.[88] The Chief Whip was generous with central funds, particularly for those federations with heavy responsibilities for derelict constituencies. The Midland Liberal Federation, faced with a considerable task in reactivating Liberal organisation, was promised £100 a year, plus further grants up to £500 per year on a pound for pound basis.[89] The efforts of the Lancashire and Cheshire Federation to revive Liberal organisation in constituencies held by Labour were underwritten from London.[90] In a healthy area such as Yorkshire, Pease promised the regional federation that financial assistance 'for extended operations' would be forthcoming if required.[91] Nor in extreme cases were the central authorities unprepared to use financial sanctions. In 1911 the National Liberal Federation withheld its annual £100 grant from the Western Counties Federation, within whose jurisdiction Liberal losses had been severe in December, and from the Eastern Counties Federation, until the two organisations showed signs of greater activity.[92]

The readiness of Liberal headquarters to exercise a firm if judicious authority towards the localities is apparent in other ways. The mobility of the leading Ministers has been noted. The same was true of the lesser fry. While *The Times* lamented that too many Unionists with safe seats 'seemed terrified to leave their constituencies for a moment',[93] Liberals in safe seats were encouraged by the central authorities to get out and work in the marginals. In the first election Pease circularised all the Welsh candidates, requesting them to place themselves at the disposal of the Welsh National Liberal Council as soon as their own contests were over. Similar requests seem to have been made of Liberal candidates in other regions. In Scotland in December, Elibank refused all help to Members with safe seats.[94]

Finance was frequently as crucial in the selection of Liberal as of Conservative candidates. One of the fiercest attacks on the role of the Member as a 'political relieving officer' came from a Liberal, Sir George Kekewich, M.P. for Exeter 1906–10. He argued, on the basis of his experience, that if a man 'is to have the honour of representing the people, he must first maintain them' and that 'if a member happens to become impecunious he is drummed out of the constituency and boycotted by the central caucus as well'.[95] Big donors were influential in Liberal caucuses and private means was a valuable asset for anyone wishing to be a candidate. The wealthy banker, H. H. Raphael, M.P. for South Derbyshire, spent nearly half his income in 1910 on 'politics and the attributes of politics'.[96]

Constituency associations looked to their candidates for financial aid, as in many cases did agents for their salaries. J. L. Walton, M.P. for South Leeds (1892–1908), paid his own agent. His successor, W. Middlebrook, paid the local association an annual subscription of £100 as did Herbert Gladstone the West Leeds Association. In addition the Leeds Liberal Members appear to have each contributed between £50 and £100 at municipal elections, earmarking the donations for work in their own constituencies.[97] Typical of constituency dependence on the candidate was an inquiry from the President of the Sheffield Attercliffe Liberal Association as to whether 'it would be desirable to ask Pease if he can make us a grant as we have no candidate to pay'.[98] When John Burns's ministerial salary was raised to £5000 in 1908 the Battersea Liberal and Radical Association refused to continue paying for registration and for an agent, for it was felt that 'a wealthy Liberal Member of Parliament in Battersea should act as wealthy Liberal Members do elsewhere and relieve the Association of all financial responsibility'.[99]

But the Liberal central authorities seemed to have shown a greater willingness to finance candidates of quality than did their opponents. Most of the Conservative critics of the cheque-book system of selection contrasted Liberal practice favourably with their own. Baumann alleged that the Liberal managers found seats for clever men irrespective of their bank accounts, Ellis Barker that the Liberals welcomed 'Every impecunious lawyer, writer, or working man . . . if he possessed political ability or debating power',[100] while the *Saturday Review* noted

that the Liberal organisations were better 'in excluding their well-to-
do noodles'.[101] These comments suggest that Liberal headquarters
were more concerned with investing in political talent than were their
rivals. Elibank's readiness to help is illustrated in the case of young
Joseph Davies, who wished to contest Hereford City in December but
who told Elibank that he could not afford to pay more than half the
election expenses. Elibank 'at once agreed to meet the other half from
the Central Fund'.[102] An obituary of Elibank in the *Westminster
Gazette* noted that 'many unknown men without a big bank balance
got their first chance in political life through Lord Murray'.[103]

This sharp contrast between the machines of the two parties needs
some qualification. Approximately one-eighth of the Unionist candidates were not the responsibility of the Central Office and the
National Union, but of the Liberal Unionist Council. If the separation
between the Unionist organisations had long since ceased to have
much justification, it had the unforeseen consequence of keeping the
Liberal Unionist organisation free from the muddle of Conservative
headquarters. With a much lighter load the Liberal Unionist Council
was generally regarded as a more efficient organ than the Central
Office. In December 1910 Lansdowne heard 'bitter complaints of our
lack of organisation – directed against the Conservative Office – but
not ours'.[104] Its list of election speakers was reputedly better than the
Central Office list, although the speakers themselves were often cold
shouldered by local Conservative bodies.[105] Some evidence of the
quality of Liberal Unionist personnel is seen in the fact that following
the amalgamation of the Unionist organisations in 1912 the first two
Principal Agents of the united party were Liberal Unionists – John
Boraston, in 1910 Organising Secretary of the Liberal Unionist Party,
and William Jenkins, in 1910 chief Liberal Unionist organiser in the
Midlands.

Nor was the local picture one of unrelieved Unionist gloom and
unalloyed Liberal brightness. The Unionist critics tended to concentrate their fire on the failure of the country squire, Acland-Hood, to
adapt the Conservative machine and the local organisation to a
predominantly urban setting. Little dissatisfaction was expressed with
the rural organisations of the party, for, even if old-fashioned, they
usually served the party well. Moreover under direction from Central
Office there had been considerable reorganisation in the Home Counties after 1906. By contrast Liberal organisations were often weak in
the rural areas, particularly in the South-East. In Kent the local associa-

tions had decayed; registration had not been completed; and the constituencies seem to have been neglected by both the Ministers and the central organisations.[106]

Some Conservative urban machines had also escaped the prevailing inertia of the Central Office. The Liverpool organisation, in the hands of an astute local party boss, Alderman Salvidge, had successfully incorporated working-men into a machine which was the envy of its opponents and the exemplar of all Conservatives striving for organisational reform.[107] A measure of the Liverpool organisation's efficiency was its success in December in tracing 21,000 out of a total 25,000 removals.[108] Birmingham was a second Unionist stronghold with well-developed local associations. The strength of the local organisations here was partly attributed to the fact that all the candidates' subscriptions were centrally pooled and allocated according to need.[109] It is perhaps significant that these two highly successful urban machines were divorced from the Central Office. At Liverpool, Salvidge 'had practically established Home Rule',[110] while the machine at Birmingham was Liberal Unionist and dominated by the family at Highbury.

The striking Unionist successes in January 1910 in two smaller urban centres, Portsmouth and Sunderland, were ascribed partly to organisation. At Portsmouth, where there was a phenomenal swing of 19·8 per cent to the Unionists, the local organisation had been thoroughly overhauled since 1906, strong ward associations established, and full attention paid to the 'social side' of organisation.[111] Sandars considered Sunderland, where there was a swing of 16·3 per cent, 'the best organised constituency in the North of England, and here you have the visible proof of technical management'.[112] There is a suggestion too that Unionist successes in the South-West in December could be partly attributed to improved organisation.[113]

The Unionist ancillary organisations, particularly the Primrose League, seem to have been more active than the less-developed ancillaries of the Liberal Party. The Primrose League knights and dames assumed responsibility for tracing and bringing removals and out-voters to the polls. Their work in December was praised by Elibank, who alleged that their efforts had frustrated his expectations in some thirteen or fourteen seats.[114]

II

The organisation of the Labour Party was at once more complex and more rudimentary than those of the major parties. The complexity arose from the lack of a clear-cut demarcation between organisational and parliamentary personnel, from the federal structure of the organisation, and from the great variety of constituency bodies. Yet this relatively complex organisation was at a most rudimentary stage of development.

Both characteristics are seen in the central organs of the party – the National Executive Committee and the Head Office. The former, the body responsible for the supervision of the organisation and for election strategy, consisted of representatives appointed by the constituent bodies of the Labour alliance – the trade unions, the I.L.P. and the Fabian Society. While the N.E.C. played a leading role in determining the number and the location of electoral contests, the constituent bodies were responsible for recognising candidates and for financing their election campaigns. The N.E.C. would sanction no contest unless the candidate concerned had been recognised as a parliamentary candidate by his trade union or the I.L.P. or the Fabian Society, and unless financial support had been guaranteed by the same body, or occasionally by a local trade council or L.R.C.

At the national level the uneasy alliance between the Socialist propagandists of the I.L.P., the intellectuals of the Fabian Society, and the non-doctrinal, often anti-Socialist leaders of many of the trade unions, worked reasonably well. Despite the disappointments since 1906, the accumulation of electoral expertise by the N.E.C. and the readiness of its I.L.P. members to discipline the factious wing of their own party to the needs of the alliance with trade union funds and organisation, assured the hegemony of the N.E.C. in electoral matters.

In contrast to the major parties, the leading Labour parliamentary figures played a leading role in the organisation. Hardie, Snowden, Henderson, and MacDonald were all members of the N.E.C. in 1909 and 1910. Two of these, MacDonald, the party Secretary, and Henderson, the party Treasurer, were the chief electoral tacticians of the party. These men combined with their parliamentary duties tasks shared in the major parties between the Chief Whips and their key organisational aides.[115]

This was a natural development in a small third party trying to break into the political system. To establish the party in the country was the primary objective, and to this task the leading Labour Parliamentarians gave most of their time and energy. Moreover, as the party's activities in Parliament were limited – in a real sense all the Labour M.P.s were back-benchers – parliamentary and organisational duties could be combined without undue strain. Finally, talent was scarce and a multitude of functions tended to be performed by the few able men. But this involvement did mean that during an election the party was virtually headless. As the chief figures in the N.E.C. scattered to their constituencies, the party almost ceased to function as a national organisation. Rather it succumbed to the atomistic tendency of a general election and became a diverse collection of constituency campaigns.

The situation was aggravated by the primitive state of Head Office, the administrative arm of the N.E.C. MacDonald as Secretary was in charge, but the day-to-day direction was in the hands of James Middleton, the Assistant Secretary. The parsimonious attitude of the trade unions and their ingrained suspicion of professional politicians had delayed the development of a permanent and adequate secretariat. In 1910 the Office was housed in two rooms in Victoria Street, and employed no more than seven persons.[116] Full-time travelling organisers were not appointed until 1914,[117] and thus the members of the N.E.C. were regularly itinerant. The position had been somewhat alleviated in 1908 when at the annual Conference the N.E.C. had secured, over the opposition of sentimentalists and cheeseparers, the appointment of a National Agent, Arthur Peters.[118] Between 1908 and 1910, Peters made several tours of the constituencies, and acted as election agent at most by-elections. But, starved of resources, Head Office was hardly adequate to the demands of a general election, and certainly, bereft of MacDonald and Henderson incapable of providing much day-to-day direction.

At the local level Labour organisations differed widely from constituency to constituency.[119] In many of the less-developed constituencies the I.L.P. provided the only local organisation. In most of the Midland and Yorkshire mining constituencies held by the party, the Members relied on their existing Liberal-staffed electoral machines. In Hallamshire in January it was reported that 'The campaign is being conducted just as in 1906', while at Nuneaton in both elections William Johnson's 'agent and election machinery were provided by the Nuneaton Liberals'.[120] Usually no alternative Labour organisation existed, but the miners' Members made little effort to establish one. Soon after the January election MacDonald urged that 'Labour Parties should be formed in their constituencies and the Agents they have appointed, or are about to appoint, should be clearly understood to be the Agents of these Parties'.[121] However, the recalcitrant Members were able to avoid any action along these lines, and on the eve of the second election the *Labour Leader* castigated Hall, Wadsworth, Harvey, Haslam, Johnson and Hancock 'for their refusal to create electoral machinery of their own along Labour lines'.[122] By contrast a few constituencies – Barnard Castle, Clitheroe, Woolwich – had fully developed local Labour parties with individual members.[123]

But the most common type of constituency organisation was the local trades council or local L.R.C. which, reflecting the federal pattern at the centre, consisted of delegates from the affiliated unions and Socialist societies, and occasionally from other working-class organisations. By 1910, 155 trade councils and L.R.C.s were formally linked with the Labour Party.[124] Sometimes these local federations were dominated by one or more of the Socialist societies. At Leicester, Ramsay MacDonald's constituency, which had the second largest I.L.P. branch in the country, 'the structure of the local party, although nominally indirect, may be seen in reality as a flourishing I.L.P. which was able at election time to merge itself in the Labour Party – a committee whose extra-I.L.P. function was to bring the power of the trade unions to help the promotion of Labour candidates'.[125] Others were firmly controlled by locally influential trade unions, while still others were characterised by an uneasy and often changing balance of forces.

These organisations functioned less smoothly than did their central counterpart, for often the particular local balance provided outlets for animosities frustrated at the national level. The local trade councils and L.R.C.s were often weakened by internal divisions, particularly between the trade unions and the Socialist societies. In December in Normanton, the local I.L.P. was unable to get in touch with the Labour Member, a miner, and was not invited to participate in the electoral organisation.[126] Often represented on the trade councils and antipathetic to the manner in which the Labour experiment was being conducted, members of the S.D.P. were, according to Peters, 'main causes of local friction and hostility'.[127] But even between the trade unions there were difficulties. The traditionally Lib-Lab miners were not particularly co-operative with fellow trade unionists, let alone with the I.L.P. and the S.D.P. At Holmfirth, W. Pickles, the candidate of the House and Ship Painters, complained that the locally powerful Yorkshire Miners' Association gave him no help in January, not even a resolution, and that its local officials were prominent on the platform of his Liberal opponent.[128]

As election machines, most Labour constituency organisations were primitive by comparison with those of their opponents. Keir Hardie observed after the first election: 'Save in comparatively few constituencies we have not yet either evolved the organisation or the esprit de corps which would enable us to cope successfully with out opponents.'[129] At Huddersfield, Snell, the Labour candidate, found the Labour organisation 'contemptible' by comparison with that of the Liberals.[130] Too often constituencies without the local organisation to sustain a campaign demanded candidates. In other cases, e.g. at St Helens, Newton and Wigan in December, the organisation appears to have collapsed during the election.[131] Registration was frequently neglected, there was 'a deplorable lack of canvassers' and some constituencies ordered no leaflets at all.[132] Agents were a constant source of worry. They were in short supply, only one-third of the more fully-worked constituencies having a full-time or part-time agent in 1908. Inevitably men were appointed 'who have no previous experience and who know practically nothing of their duties' and the National Agent thought that 'our success [in January] was considerably injured by incompetent men serving as agents'.[133]

Many of these weaknesses stemmed from the prevailing shortage of funds. The Sunderland organisation was 'crippled' through lack of finance resulting partly from heavy unemployment on the Wear.[134] In many constituencies funds were not adequate for election campaigns, let alone for the long-term construction of local organisation. Unless the constituency was nursed by the candidate of a wealthy trade union, or had been peculiarly fortunate in its organisers or in its location, campaign resources were likely to be rudimentary. The dedication of the party's rank and file, often the envy of the organisers of more wealthy parties,[135] and pressures towards working-class solidarity, frequently offset, if they did not always overcome these disadvantages.

III

In Ireland national solidarity greatly reduced the need for electoral organisation at all. Over much of Ireland the Nationalists were the only political party, and the mass party organisation, the United Irish League, scarcely had to worry about inter-party contests in these areas. It was concerned rather with confirming adherence to the Home Rule faith, preserving the unity of the Nationalist Party, and raising funds. Only in the areas of two-party competition, parts of Ulster and Dublin, was the U.I.L. a well-organised electoral machine.

The U.I.L. had helped to build up reserves of loyalty for the Nationalist Party and the Redmondite leadership, and had helped to give the official party a copyright on the Home Rule movement. But the mass organisation proved ill-adapted to the task of purging and restoring the party, particularly in the climate of discontent with official policies that prevailed in 1909. The National Directory of the League failed in nearly every case in its efforts to sack sitting M.P.s, failed in one or two cases to sustain a favoured Member, and saw many of its conventions for selecting candidates disrupted by the rebels.

One reason for this was that the very quiescence of Irish politics over the past decade had led to the atrophy of local organisations. Throughout most of Munster the U.I.L. had decayed, and had been replaced as the popular body by the Land and Labour Association, of which there were over a hundred branches in County Cork, mostly controlled by the partisans of O'Brien. In Cork City the U.I.L. organisation was not revived until October 1909, while in South-East Cork there appears to have been no U.I.L. organisation whatever.[136]

Moreover the U.I.L. had originally been designed by O'Brien to be 'the supreme arbiter of the national movement', superior to the political party.[137] Although this intention had been frustrated inasmuch as the central organs of the League – the National Directory and its Standing Committee – were dominated by the Parliamentarians, O'Brien's reform of the local organisations, particularly the conventions, rendered them relatively free from the central dictation of Parnell's heyday.[138] Thus while the central organs of the U.I.L. functioned as instruments of the party leadership, resistance was often encountered at the level of the local machine. In the disturbed climate of the first election the independence of the local divisions, or of influential factions within them, was often asserted, sometimes in a rowdy fashion.

The conventions were usually the focus of the disturbances. They were designed to be broadly representative of the interests in the constituency and were constituted to include the clergy, the divisional

U.I.L. executive, representatives of the local U.I.L. branches, representatives of local government bodies in the constituency and
representatives of the local branches of semi-political bodies such as the
Land and Labour Association, the Ancient Order of Hibernians, the
Irish National Foresters and the Town Tenants' Association.[139] In
County Cork in January it was difficult to establish representative
conventions because of the strength of O'Brienism. In a number of
cases in Cork hurriedly gathered caucuses seem simply to have sanctioned a Dublin nominee. In other parts of Ireland clericalism and
anti-clericalism, resistance to central direction, and personal quarrels
surfaced at the January conventions and frequently led to their disruption.[140] The cry that conventions were 'stuffed' or 'Tammany Hall'
jobs was frequent.

The convention system, designed to eliminate friction, exacerbated
it in January 1910 because of the general dissatisfaction with the party
to which the malcontents could appeal. In Dublin, where the National
Directory's writ ran most strongly and where the Tories were present
in some force, no conventions were held.[141] In December this practice
was generally adopted, and conventions were held only in those
constituencies which the official party did not hold.[142] The short
campaign provided the excuse, but it is likely that the real reason was
to avoid a repetition of January's strife. That the decision was accepted
with little dissent reflects the strengthened prestige of Redmond and
the recognition by the party generally of the threat posed by the
O'Brienite revolt.

14

Party Finance

The fog of secrecy which shrouds the party coffers makes an assessment of the financial resources of the parties difficult. We can begin by an examination of the returned costs for both elections which are set out in Table 14.1. Taking the most useful figure for comparison, the expenses per opposed candidate, three distinct levels of expenditure are apparent, first the major parties, then Labour, and then the Nationalists. If this provides a rough ranking of the parties according to their financial resources four qualifications need to be remembered. First, much expenditure by the central authorities is not recorded in these figures because it was not directly attributable to any candidate; secondly, there was probably some fudging of returns by candidates of the two large parties;[1] thirdly, the Labour average hides a rather unusual and significant distribution of costs per candidate; fourthly elections in Ireland were much cheaper than in Great Britain.[2]

Perhaps the most remarkable feature of the table is the similarity of Liberal and Unionist expenditure. In 1880 there had been a distinct difference between Conservative and Liberal expenditure, the Conservatives spending almost £200,000 more than the Liberals absolutely, and £400 more per candidate.[3] Since that date the flow of rich businessmen from the Liberals had meant that increasingly wealth was corralled in the Unionist camp.[4] This flow had probably quickened since 1906, while the exodus of Liberal entrepreneurs over the Budget may have caused acute financial difficulties in particular constituencies bereft of a leading subscriber on the eve of the election. It seems probable in 1910 that the potential financial resources of the Unionists were considerably greater than those of the Liberals.

Yet there is little evidence of this in the returned expenses. True, the surrender of a number of seats to Labour in 1906 and the considerable number of seats left uncontested in December 1910 reduced the absolute cost of the two elections for the Liberal Party. Yet the financial saving was only a secondary inducement in the original pact with

TABLE 14.1 RETURNED EXPENSES BY PARTY 1910
(£'s)

Party	JANUARY			DECEMBER		
	Total expenses	Expenses per candidate	Expenses per candidate in contested seats	Total expenses	Expenses per candidate	Expenses per candidate in contested seats
Conservative	558,822	1109	1137	454,635	918	1020
Liberal Unionist	92,593	1064	1101	48,120	891	1041
Liberal	550,234	1075	1077	411,845	882	940
Labour	67,836	881	881	41,241	736	774
Nationalist	9,954	120	304	11,692	144	330
Ind. Nationalist	5,561	293	293	6,862	298	357
Other	10,424	417	417	3,757	289	289
All candidates	1,295,424	992	1048	978,152	823	931

Source: *Parl. Papers* 1910, lxxiii 705–81 and *Parl. Papers* 1911, lxii 704–49.
Notes: 1. In January no return was provided by 4 Unionists, 2 Nationalists, 1 Labour, 1 independent Nationalist, and 1 independent Conservative. In December no return was provided by 2 independent Nationalists and 1 Independent.
2. The figures are approximations as each candidate's total expenses was taken to the nearest £ to simplify counting.

Labour, and the decision to curtail contests in December probably arose as much from Elibank's tactical realism as from financial exigencies. Some Liberal candidates, and no doubt some Unionists, found two elections in the one year tough going. Lansdowne in appealing for funds in November 1910 pointed out that 'Owing to the fact that there will have been two elections within the present year, our candidate will obviously experience more than usual difficulty in meeting their own expenses'.[8] E. H. Pickersgill (Liberal, South-West Bethnal Green), who 'was as poor as a church mouse, refused to take help from the Whips' Office, and used to start saving at the end of one election to pay the costs of the next. Two elections in the one year had hit him very hard, and in 1911 he was very hard up.'[6] But over all the Liberals do not appear to have wanted for money. Rather the contrary, as Amery observed: 'Considering the disproportion between the available wealth at the back of the Unionist Party, and that at the back of the Liberals, it is really absurd that they should, judging by all appearances and results, have at least as large, if not a larger, campaign fund than we have.'[7]

This discrepancy was probably not unrelated to the comparative efficiency of the two party machines. Acland-Hood does not seem to have fully utilised the financial resources available to him, Amery suspecting that the weakness stemmed from 'the absence of any really effective organised attempt to get the money'.[8] Steel-Maitland's later activities tended to confirm this suspicion by revealing the elasticity of Conservative supplies. Within a few months of taking over in 1911 he had increased the existing subscription list from £4000 to £34,000 per annum, and he hoped by the end of 1913 to have increased it by at least a further £70,000.[9] The Central Office under Acland-Hood does not appear to have suffered from a shortage of funds, but it seems to have failed to tap potential funds.

By contrast the Liberals, assisted by their control of patronage, seem to have exploited fully their more limited resources. Whiteley's great achievement as Chief Whip was to restore the finances of the Liberal Party. Herbert Gladstone had passed on £20,000 to Whiteley in 1906.[10] Two years later Whiteley handed on to Pease 'actual and collectable, all good money . . . £519,000 less under £5000 overdrawn at the bank.'[11] £400,000 of this was invested in Consols and not readily available, but even if Pease added little to the party chest, funds would have been quite sufficient for the January elections.

But the January election, the most expensive since 1880,[12] imposed a financial veto on a precipitate second election. 'Nobody wants a new election,' wrote Morley in February 1910, 'among other reasons because it is money that makes the electioneering mare to go, and all the war chests . . . are sadly depleted.'[13] The Liberal chest was at least as depleted as the others, although Hudson was confident that 'there are some very wealthy men who will fight Protection with their last farthing'.[14] One of Elibank's most pressing tasks on becoming Chief Whip was to collect these farthings.

Once more the Master revealed his talents. 'He soothed the rich Liberals who were uneasy about Limehouse, and got large cheques out of them to be used for their own despoiling.'[15] There are some suggestions that patronage was made to pay. The wealthy Liberal retailer, Sir Hudson Kearley, had earlier intimated that while he 'wasn't going to buy' a peerage; if he became a peer 'he would like to voluntarily help the party by £25,000 or so.'[16] Kearley became Lord Devonport in 1910. Lloyd George informed Elibank with respect to the 'general helpfulness' of 'our Cardiff friend' that 'his prospects are distinctly good when the next ennobling list appears'.[17] Elibank was still 'drumming for subscriptions' during the second election,[18] but the money seems to have been found. Geake told Herbert Gladstone after the election: 'Your successor, the Chief Whip, gives great satisfaction and apparently had plenty of money.'[19]

Although the evidence is inconclusive it does suggest that the Liberal managers, helped by the control of patronage, exploited their limited financial sources more fully than the Unionists their greater ones. A second explanation for the fact that, despite their disproportionate support from the wealthier segments of the community, the Conservatives apparently had little financial advantage over their rivals, is that possibly the Central Office was less willing to spend money than the Liberal Central Association. In his 1912 memorandum on Conservative organisation Steel-Maitland commended Acland-Hood as 'very good . . . as regards the getting of money'. But the evidence in his memorandum tends to refute this praise. What the memorandum does suggest is that Acland-Hood was very good at hoarding money. '. . . he started without any invested funds, and left a nest egg of over £300,000.'[20] A traditionalist view of Central Office functions plus an inclination to thrift may explain for example the frequent unfavourable contrasts drawn between the Central Office and the Liberal Central Association as regards the financing of impecunious but able candidates.

The similarity in the candidates' expenses by the major parties has been noted. Election expenditure by the central authorities seems also to have been similar. In his memorandum Steel-Maitland stated: 'An Election costs from £80,000 to £120,000.' As Steel-Maitland was writing soom after the two 1910 elections, the first of which was long and expensive, the second short and relatively cheap, it is a likely conjecture that these figures are based on Central Office expenditure in the 1910 elections.

Expenditure by the Liberal central authorities was probably similar. In 1906 the Liberal Chief Whip spent £100,000 on the general election[21] and, given the improved state of Liberal finances and the increase reflected in the returned expenses, it is unlikely that Pease spent less than £100,000. The returned expenses of the January 1910 election show an 11 per cent increase over those for the 1906 election. If the expenditure from Liberal central funds increased in the same proportion then the cost of the January election to the Liberal authorities would have been approximately £111,000. This is probably a minimum figure. Doubtless less was spent in December, but it seems unlikely that expenditure would have fallen much below the £80,000, the minimum suggested for the Central Office.

While the evidence remains tentative it seems likely that electoral expenditure from central party funds in no way reflected the preponderance of the Conservatives amongst the wealthy element of the community. Finally it is possible that the wasteful and muddled procedures of the Central Office may have devalued Conservative expenditure. As one disgruntled Unionist complained: 'A shilling given to a Liberal organisation goes almost as far as a sovereign given to a Unionist organisation.'[22]

In one sphere, the provision of motor cars, Unionist wealth told. Motor cars had first been used extensively in the election of 1906, but their use had been 'trivial in comparison with the universality of their employment last month [January 1910]'.[23] Not only were they valuable in getting the voter, particularly the out-voter, to the polls, but they facilitated intensive campaigning in the county seats and provided perambulating rostrums in the towns. *The Motor* claimed that a candidate who did not have thirty cars working for him considered himself poorly off, while the more fortunate had armadas of one hundred or more. In Coventry and the surrounding constituencies the Rover, Swift and Daimler companies generously supplied cars to the Unionist candidates. It was estimated that, with an average of one hundred and twenty cars per constituency, thus eighty thousand cars altogether, each carrying fifty voters, some four million were transported to the polls by car in January.[24]

The Unionists seem to have been much better supplied with motor vehicles. The N.L.F. reported an 'overwhelming disparity' between the parties in the supply of motors.[25] The Liberal press frequently bemoaned the Liberal lack of cars, instancing detailed cases of Liberal hardship and pressing for legislation to limit the Tory advantage. Even in Scotland, where wealthy Liberals were numerous, the Scottish Liberal Association complained of the shortage of vehicles throughout the country.[26] In England the differences between the parties in the boroughs do not seem to have been great, although on polling day in Bermondsey, where the narrow streets were so glutted with cars that voters 'had difficulty in getting to the polling booth through the besetting herds of motors', the Unionist candidate had fifty cars by 8 a.m. while his Liberal opponent still had only two traps at 10 a.m.[27] In the country constituencies the Unionists were usually much better off than their rivals.

Yet the effect of this disadvantage should not be exaggerated. The preponderance of beribboned and placarded Tory motors testified to Unionist backing amongst the wealthier classes. But though a few voters may have been seduced from their allegiance by the novelty of a car ride, Liberals tempted by a Tory offer could heed the advice of the Daily News. 'Never mind who takes you to the polls. Vote Liberal. The ballot is as secret as the grave.'[28] Thus in many cases the gaily decked chariots were Trojan horses, hurrying the Greeks to the polls.

'Ride to the poll in Tory and Liberal motor cars, but vote for Whitehead' read a Labour polling-day placard in Cockermouth.[29] It was the only way most Labour voters could secure a ride, for Labour candidates had few if any cars at their disposal. Even in a well-organised constituency such as Henderson's at Barnard Castle, the Unionist had fifty cars to Henderson's one.[30] Drawing its support from the poorer sections of the community, Labour encountered unique financial handicaps.

In the sphere of electoral finance, there was a fairly clear demarcation of responsibility.[31] The N.E.C. administered the Labour Party's Parliamentary Fund, raised by an annual per capita levy of 2d. on all members of affiliated trade unions and societies. However, the bulk of this fund was for the payment of M.P.s' salaries, and the only specific responsibility for election finance accepted by the N.E.C. was the

payment out of this fund of one-quarter of the returning officers'
expenses. This payment amounted to £4,227 in January, and £2,965
in December, and represented about one-fifteenth of total Labour
election expenses.[32] The party's General Fund financed the cost of
producing literature, election travelling expenses, and extra office
assistance over the election period. The total cost of these operations
amounted to £1450 in the January election, but this was considerably
offset by income from the sale of leaflets and posters, Ramsay Mac-
Donald estimating that the total cost to the General Fund of the first
election was only about £250 in all.[33]

This left the bulk of election financing with the trade unions and the
Socialist societies, for the remaining expenses had to be found by the
union or society sponsoring the candidate and by local subscriptions
in the constituency. Of the £67,836 spent by Labour candidates in
January, £4227 came from the Parliamentary Fund, £3108 from the
central funds of the I.L.P., and about £1000 from the Fabian Society.
This left about £59,000 to be found by the trade unions or through
local subscriptions. Of the £41,241 spent in December, £2965 came
from the Parliamentary Fund, £1036 from the central funds of the
I.L.P., and about £800 from the Fabian Society, leaving about £36,400
to be found by the trade unions and local appeals.[34]

This pattern of financial responsibility meant that money was as
influential in the selection of candidates in the Labour Party as in the
major parties. At the 1909 Labour Conference MacDonald criticised
'constituencies that had dilly-dallied and hung over for the last moment
until they could get a candidate with £1000 in his pocket – and not to
risk local money'.[35] But as there was usually little local money to
risk and little in the way of finance from central party funds, impover-
ished local organisations naturally preferred a nominee from one of the
great trade unions – the miners, the cotton operatives, the railway
servants or the engineers, all with ample parliamentary funds – rather
than from the chronically poor I.L.P.

Of the fifteen candidates sponsored, or part-sponsored, by the I.L.P.
in January, none received more than £400 from I.L.P. central funds.[36]
Only in two cases, in poverty stricken Sunderland and in the critical
three-cornered fight at Camlachie, did the National Council advance
more than half the total expenses. This was not due to parsimony on
the part of the national I.L.P. but simply to the fact that the I.L.P.
had no more money. The I.L.P. raised its election funds by levies
on its members in election years. For the first 1910 election it raised

£3043 11s. 10½d. and spent all of it. For the second election it was able to raise only £1035 12s. 1d., and was compelled to prune severely its grants to a reduced number of candidates. Even then it was forced to turn to the central funds of the Labour Party for special assistance. This meant that local financial resources were particularly important in constituencies with I.L.P. candidates. By contrast the Miners' Federation had an election fund of £25,661 for the first election, alleviating local financial worries in constituencies with miners' candidates.[37]

A trade union candidate, with substantial funds behind him, was therefore much more likely to secure adoption than an I.L.P. man, irrespective of the merits of the two candidates. In 1910 over three-quarters of the Labour candidates were sponsored by the trade unions, and nearly half came from five large trade unions. It might be argued that this still left a generous proportion of candidatures to the Socialist societies, for they provided less than 2 per cent of the membership of the Labour Party. But such a comparison ignores the fact that while the bulk of the trade union membership was a purely formal membership, the great majority of the Fabians and I.L.P.ers were party activists.[38] Moreover, the candidates of the Socialist societies and the lesser unions tended to get the more difficult contests, the seats in which Labour's chances of success were least.

TABLE 14.2 LABOUR CANDIDATES FINANCE AND SUCCESS 1910

	Miners	Cotton Operatives, Rly Servants, Engineers, Carpenters and Joiners	Other Unions	Socialist Societies
No. of candidatures	49	23	31	31
Expenses per candidate in contested seats	£1255	£731	£666	£467
Expenses expressed as % of Unionist expenses in same seats	100	76	70	57
% of seats won	67	70	58	48

This predominant position of the unions within the Labour movement, and the whole financial structure of the Labour Party, had been endangered by the decision of the Law Lords in the Osborne case. Some historians have attributed Labour's disappointing electoral record in 1910 in part to the effects of this decision, and there have been specific claims that the considerable pruning of Labour candidates in the second election arose partly from difficulties caused by the Judgement.[39] Yet this seems unlikely. The threat of the Judgement was primarily long-run, its short-term effects being virtually nil in the first election, and marginal in the second.[40]

The authors of *A History of British Trade Unions since 1889* note: 'The Osborne judgement had virtually no effect on the finances of the party in the first election because the only injunction in force was that against the Railway Servants.'[41] Most Labour contests had been fixed before the Law Lords' decision, and there seem to have been no withdrawals in consequence. The three candidates of the Railway Servants, W. Hudson (Newcastle), J. H. Thomas (Derby), and G. J. Wardle (Stockport) were each provided with substantial emergency loans from the Labour Party Parliamentary Fund.[42] Indeed the N.E.C. appeared so confident of coping with any difficulties arising that, contrary to practice, it endorsed Thomas's candidature without prior reference to his union.[43]

While the Judgement had no effect on Labour in the first election, it does not seem to have significantly affected the number of candidates in the second. Labour's withdrawals in December were nearly all made on tactical grounds, which meant abandoning seats where Labour had done badly only ten months before. This is not to argue that financial considerations did not enter into some of the withdrawals. As with the other parties, two elections in the one year imposed a heavy strain on Labour's resources. Neither the N.E.C. nor the prudent union executives were likely to throw money away on contests in which, judging from January, the chances of success were non-existent. The I.L.P. was in financial difficulties, and required special assistance from the N.E.C. Financial considerations led it to abandon the contest in Jarrow to a nominee of the Carpenters and Joiners, incidentally one of the unions with an injunction against it.[44] Many of the constituency organisations were in a bad way financially. In these circumstances, finance was an added inducement to abandon hopeless contests. But this is very different from arguing that the Labour Party was compelled to abandon seats it would otherwise have contested because of the Osborne Judgement.

The N.E.C. was able to face the December election, if not the future, with equanimity because owing to the affiliation of the Miners' Federation in 1909 the Parliamentary Fund had never been healthier. Despite heavy demands on it the balance in the Fund at the beginning of 1911 was only £1300 below the January 1909 figure. The healthy condition of the Parliamentary Fund, plus a special appeal fund which contained £1738 just before the December election, enabled the N.E.C. to tide over with loans and special grants most of the financial difficulties of union candidates.[45]

The boast of the N.E.C. after the election that 'we have seen that every one of the candidates who were duly selected for the recent election were not stinted for want of funds'[46] seems to have been justified. Loans totalling £750 were again provided for the three candidates of the Railway Servants; while G. H. Roberts (Norwich), the candidate of the Typographical Association, was lent £500, and C. W. Bowerman (Deptford) of the London Compositors £200.[47] There was a loan of £122 to the Carpenters' and Joiners' candidate at Jarrow.[48] A £260 grant from the special appeal fund was made to J. Pointer (Attercliffe) of the Patternmakers Association.[49] The only case discovered of a union refusing to accept financial responsibility for a candidate owing to the Osborne Judgement was that of the Boot and Shoe Operatives' refusal to sanction the candidature of T. F. Richards at East Northamptonshire.[50] Richards anyhow went ahead and contested the seat as an independent Labour candidate. Labour's abandonment of Wakefield and West Wolverhampton may have stemmed partly from difficulties produced by the Judgement.[51]

Apart from meeting the difficulties arising from the Osborne Judgement, central funds provided aid for the I.L.P. at Kirkdale, Chatham, Whitehaven and for the abortive contest at West Wolverhampton. In addition, grants of £5 in cash, and £5 in posters were offered to all candidates.[52] These further departures from N.E.C. financial practices reflect local needs, but they also reveal the willingness and the ability of the N.E.C. to take a wider share of financial responsibility in the second election. Nor is it certain that all the expenditure discussed here covers the total contribution of the central funds.[53] Given all these factors it seems unlikely that the number of candidates or the financial resources available to them were much affected by the Osborne Judgement.

The Irish Nationalist candidates were mostly personally better off than their Labour counterparts, though the U.I.L. did not command financial resources comparable with the trade unions. Nevertheless, probably a greater proportion of electoral expenses was covered from central funds by the Nationalists than by any other party. This was possible because of the usually small number of contests fought by the Nationalists and because of the generosity of the overseas Irish. When in 1910 the number of contested seats rose significantly, the Irish turned to their overseas brethren for help.

Despite the healthy condition of Irish funds after 1900,[54] the two elections of 1910, each involving more contests than in any election for over a decade, imposed an unprecedented demand on Nationalist finances. That the party survived both elections without severe financial difficulties was due to help from across the Atlantic. T. P. O'Connor's winter tour of Canada in 1909 yielded £10,000, sufficient for the immediate electoral needs of the party.[55] But the rumour in London, when the new Parliament assembled in February 1910, was that the most disruptive element among the anti-Unionist forces was also the most impecunious. According to Ilbert 'the Irish political chest is absolutely empty and some of the members are said to be heavily in debt'.[56] The writer of a detailed and well-informed memorandum for Elibank on the Irish situation reported in March 'unmistakable signs of a shortness of cash at the Nationalist Treasury'.[57]

But things were not as bad as the Liberals imagined or perhaps hoped. Certainly the Nationalists were prepared to fight a midsummer election, preferring that to the Constitutional Conference which they viewed with intense mistrust.[58] Nevertheless whatever their dislike of the Conference the opportunity it provided to recoup the party's finances prior to a further election was not unwelcome to the Nationalist leaders. They were insistent against an autumn election because of their September commitments in the U.S.A. 'To cancel these engagements', Redmond told Elibank, 'would be for us an *exceedingly serious* thing.'[59] The 1910 autumn tour of Redmond, Boyle and Devlin to the United States and T. P. O'Connor to Canada was the most successful the Nationalists had undertaken in thirty years. All told the tour yielded 100,000 dollars (£20,000) and ended the financial worries of the Nationalists.[60]

The independent Nationalists were primarily dependent on personal contributions from Ireland and Great Britain. O'Brien had considerable financial resources of his own, and local caucuses of anti-Redmondite Nationalists subscribed to the costs of the independent candidates. They also seem to have received financial assistance from moderate Unionist landlords, such as Dunraven and Castletown, sympathetic to O'Brien since the Land Conference of 1903,[61] and moderate Liberals with Irish interests such as Lord Brassey.[62] A more extraordinary source was Garvin, who went 'cadging' money for O'Brien in November 1910 with considerable success, for he appears to have raised at least £10,000 for the O'Brienites.[63] O'Brien seems to have spurned pure Tory money, and had doubts about accepting devolutionist money.[64] In the event the O'Brienites do not seem to have suffered from a shortage of funds in the second election, but rather from a shortage of candidates.

Two elections in the one year, and one of them the most expensive for thirty years, posed serious financial problems for all the party organisations. To their credit all seemed to have overcome these difficulties, for no party was unduly or unusually handicapped in December.

Publicising the Issues

I

The coverage of the elections in the press was both massive in scope and highly partisan in treatment. The Unionists had a distinct preponderance, both in the number of papers and in circulation, in the London daily press. In addition no London quality morning newspaper supported the Liberals. This was partly offset by Liberal backing

TABLE 15.1 LONDON DAILIES: CIRCULATION AND POLITICAL ALLEGIANCE 1910

UNIONIST		LIBERAL	
Morning		*Morning*	
★3*d. The Times*	45,000	½*d. Daily Chronicle*	400,000
★1*d. Daily Telegraph*	230,000	½*d. Daily News*	320,000
★1*d. Morning Post*	60,000	½*d. Morning Leader*	250,000
★1*d. Standard*	80,000		
½*d. Daily Express*	425,000		
1*d. Daily Graphic*	50,000		
½*d. Daily Mail*	900,000		
Evening		*Evening*	
★1*d. Globe*	Under 20,000	½*d. Star*	330,000
★1*d. Pall Mall Gazette*	10,000	★1*d. Westminster Gazette*	20,000
1*d. Evening Standard*	160,000		
½*d. Evening News*	300,000		
	About 2,280,000		About 1,320,000
INDEPENDENT			
½*d. Daily Mirror*	630,000		

Notes: ★ Quality papers.
Sources: *Advertising*; T. B. Browne's *Advertiser's A.B.C. 1910*; A. P. Wadsworth, 'Newspaper Circulations 1800–1954', *Transactions, Manchester Statistical Society 1954–5*; and various newspaper histories and editors' biographies,

from the prestigious *Westminster Gazette*, widely regarded as the most influential evening paper, and by the growing national reputation of

the *Manchester Guardian*. Furthermore, while the Unionists controlled
the two serious Sunday journals, the *Observer* and the *Sunday Times*,
the figures, although incomplete, suggest that the circulation advantage
in the London Sunday press lay with the Liberals. They got support
from *Reynolds News* and *Lloyds Weekly News*, which, with the independent *News of the World*, commanded the biggest readerships in the
Sunday press. Outside London the two parties were evenly matched
as regards major daily newspapers, although amongst the English
weekly and twice weekly press, particularly in the smaller towns, the
Unionists had a distinct superiority.

By 1910 there had been considerable penetration of the provincial
press by the London newspaper magnates, Northcliffe of the *Daily Mail*
and Pearson of the *Standard* each having a stable of provincial newspapers. In addition more overt penetration had brought the London
newspapers themselves to the provinces by 1910. Nor only had better
transport accelerated distribution, but some of the London papers were
now printing local editions in the major provincial centres. The *Daily
News* and the *Daily Mail* both published Birmingham and Manchester
editions, while the *Daily Chronicle* also had a Midland edition. During
the first election, at least, Northcliffe also published special issues of the
Daily Mail for East Anglia and the North-East.[1]

TABLE 15.2 POLITICAL ALLEGIANCE OF MAJOR PROVINCIAL DAILIES
(Newspapers published in towns with population of 50,000 or more)

	Unionist	Liberal	Nationalist	Independent
England	33	36	–	23
Scotland	8	6	–	2
Wales	3	4	–	–
Ireland	8	–	6	2
	52	46	6	27

Sources: *Willing's Press Guide 1910*; *Mitchell's Newspaper Press Directory 1910*;
Constitutional Year Book 1911.

Not that Harmsworth expansion was always in the Unionist interest.
In July 1910 Elibank was able to report that Harold Harmsworth,
Northcliffe's younger brother, 'is doing splendidly with his paper
[*Glasgow Daily Record*]. He is sending reporters and special editions to
constituencies where we are not strong, and is generally doing his ut-
most to carry out his obligations.'[2]

The advantages which may have accrued from the Unionist preponderance in the national daily press were considerably dissipated by
poor relations between the party organisation and the press, and by a
lack of solidarity amongst the Unionist press itself. In the first weeks
of the first election the Unionists were troubled by an inadequate
liaison between the Central Office and the press. In mid-December
1909, considerable Unionist concern about their newspapers' coverage
of Liberal speeches was reflected in the correspondence columns of the
press. Even in January, after some improvement had occurred, Lord
Ampthill was still complaining to Maxse that 'Something is very
wrong with the Unionist Press', and its failure to use its opportunities
'is more than disappointing; it is a grave scandal'.[3] On some days even
in Unionist newspapers there was a distinct imbalance in speech
reports in favour of the Liberals. As Ampthill pointed out: 'When
Winston Churchill was speaking in Lancashire he got a whole page of
the "Times" (six columns) every day and every "obiter dictum" of
his was reported "verbatim". At the same period Austin [sic] Chamberlain, the former Chancellor of the Exchequer, was only getting half a
column in the "Times".'[4] Sandars indeed was led to protest to Northcliffe about 'the great prominence he had given to Winston's Lancashire efforts. . . .'. Northcliffe responded by complaining about the
paucity and quality of Unionist speakers.[5] But this was only part of
the answer. The imbalance arose as well from the contrasting relations
established between the press and the rival party organisations in the
early days of the election.

Relations between Liberal headquarters and the press were in the
hands of a propagandist of great ability, Sir Henry Norman, Secretary
of the Budget League and M.P. for South Wolverhampton. An ex-
journalist himself – he had served on the editorial staffs of the *Pall Mall
Gazette* and the *Daily Chronicle* – he had during 1909 assiduously wooed
the press and the news agencies, and had presided over the imaginative
and successful propaganda campaign that popularised the Budget. His
suggestions were not always felicitous. His melodramatic request that
the Liberal press should appear black-edged on the morrow of the
Budget's rejection was turned down by the Liberal editors on the
sensible grounds that rejection was a matter for rejoicing not mourn-
ing.[6]

By the time of the first election Norman had established a relationship with the press which was the envy of the Unionists. 'Our opponents,' wrote Sandars, 'through that ex-journalist Sir Henry Norman,

have gained so much by cultivating their own press.'[7] And not only with their own press. Fabian Ware was astounded to find that while the Press Association was not even reporting Austen Chamberlain's Midland speeches, it was urging him to take its verbatim reports of Churchill's Lancashire tour.[8] Sandars was of the opinion that the Press Association had been 'pampered by the Radicals who have practically captured it. Result – long reports of Radical meetings & speeches – ours often relegated to a few lines.'[9] Norman was helped by Lloyd George and Churchill, adept and unwearying in their cultivation of the press. Churchill's own newspaper experience had made him fully conversant with press needs. Apparently during his Lancashire tour he deposited all his speeches with the Press Association before delivery 'applause and everything else inserted by the author'.[10]

Conservative headquarters had no form of press bureau nor any officer carrying out functions similar to those of Norman. Once again those two indefatigable workers in the Unionist cause, Sandars and Garvin, sought to remedy the weakness. Garvin approached S. J. Pryor, Northcliffe's man at *The Times*, to stress the need for a greater coverage of Unionist speeches, in the belief that 'if *The Times* did it, the rest would follow very quickly'. At the same time, he discreetly encouraged Unionist speakers such as Austen Chamberlain to be a little more active in self-advertisement, instancing Churchill.[11] Sandars and Pryor drafted a circular on the inadequate coverage, Hughes signed it and it was then sent out to all sympathetic editors. Sandars encouraged Hughes to follow this up with personal interviews and no doubt prompted Hughes' request to leading Unionists to forward summaries of their speeches in advance, so that leader writers could prepare their comments. By the fourth week in December, Sandars could feel that 'now we are on a level with our opponents'.[12]

A more serious dissipation of the Unionist press advantage arose from a lack of solidarity amongst Unionist newspapers. The intimate relations between politicians, proprietors and editors meant inevitably that the press reflected the factionalism within the parties. This mattered little for the Liberals who were relatively united. The three London morning dailies, the evening *Star*, the Liberal Sunday newspapers and the weekly *Nation* were yoked to the Radical wing of the party. The *Westminster Gazette* spoke for the moderate elements in the party, but disagreed little with the Radical press in the emphasis placed on electoral issues.

But the Unionist press reflected the much deeper divisions within the Unionist Party. From the beginning the Whole Hoggers had realised the importance of the press. The Pearson press – the *Standard*, *Evening Standard*, *Daily Express* and several provincial papers – had rallied early to Chamberlain.[13] With the advent of Fabian Ware to the editorial chair of the *Morning Post* in 1905 and J. L. Garvin's appointment as editor of the *Observer* in 1908 the Whole Hoggers had gained respectively their most militant and their most influential press advocate. From 1908 to 1911 the *Globe* ardently supported the tariff crusade, losing Hildebrand Harmsworth £80,000 in the process.[14] The Unionist Sunday journal the *People* appears to have conceived its chief political task as the conversion of the working classes to Tariff Reform.

Outside London the internecine war within the Unionist Party had been paralleled by plots and counter-plots as the factions strove for control of the provincial journals. Success lay mostly with the Whole Hoggers. In 1904 they captured the *Birmingham Daily Post* and ousted the Free Trade editor.[15] In 1908 the Free Trade editor of the *Yorkshire Post* was 'faced with the alternative of turning to my "vomit" or retiring from the Y.P.'.[16] He apparently took to his 'vomit'. In 1909 the Whole Hoggers gained control of the *Glasgow Herald*.[17]

The Balfourites commanded the unswerving loyalty of the *Daily Telegraph*, while *The Times* throughout remained Balfourian in tone, Buckle, the editor, being 'a thorough and life-long Balfour man'.[18] Northcliffe's other papers, with the notable exception of the *Observer*, had pursued an erratic but generally middle course on the fiscal question. Northcliffe himself at all times displayed a keen awareness of the electoral difficulties of 'the stomach tax'. The *Pall Mall Gazette* prided itself on being a loyalist paper, while the pictorial *Daily Graphic*, with a Free Trade editor and Tariff Reform directors, hewed close to the middle way.[19]

The Free Fooders had neglected the press and were seriously handicapped. Their only regular supporter was the weekly *Spectator* under the dedicated Strachey. However, the *Sunday Times*, the most reactionary of the Unionist newspapers, revealed a growing sympathy for the Free Food cause in 1910.

During the first election the Unionist press remained relatively united, but as the party cracked under the impact of the referendum pledge in December, so did the press. Even in the first election, however, the factional alignments of the press are apparent in the emphasis placed upon different issues in the various Unionist newspapers.

The *Morning Post*, the *Globe* and the *People* all stressed Tariff Reform as the key to electoral victory with a single-mindedness not found elsewhere. Even the development of the naval scare was not permitted to distract from the central theme. Their heroes were Austen Chamberlain, Milner and Bonar Law, who 'force Tariff Reform to the front on every possible occasion'.[20]

None of the other Unionist papers displayed this concentration. Some, indeed, revealed their antipathy for Tariff Reform. The *Spectator* advised Free Fooders to 'choose the lesser evil and therefore vote for the Tariff Reformer rather than the Liberal'.[21] But it made no effort to hide its conviction that Free Fooders had only a choice of evils. The opposition of the *Sunday Times* was more covert. Editorially it virtually ignored Tariff Reform, devoting its election leaders mainly to a bravura defence of the House of Lords. But its contempt for much of Whole Hogger propaganda was revealed in an aside in a foreign policy leader on 26 December 1909: '. . . we have been treated to columns of blither about "Sober Sunday" here and "Golden Sunday in Berlin" – apparently for the sole object of exciting the cupidity of the uninformed in this country and alluring them to Protection.'

In the remainder of the press Tariff Reform was prominent although not pre-eminent. *The Times* revealed a greater interest in the fate of the House of Lords than in the fate of Tariff Reform, as did the *Daily Graphic*. The *Daily Telegraph* displayed a venomous negativism, concerning itself far more with the destructive policies of the Liberals than with the constructive policy of the Unionists. But, always close behind Balfour, the *Telegraph* stepped up attention on the fiscal issue, following the added emphasis given in Balfour's speeches in January 1910.

In the press directly controlled by Northcliffe Tariff Reform was not neglected, but it was certainly demoted as the naval scare and the related Germanophobia convulsed the newspapers issuing from Carmelite House. Although the timing was opportunistic, the Blatchford articles were in accord with the long-term anti-Germanism of the *Daily Mail* and its proprietor. They were also attuned to the inflammatory alarmism that had characterised the *Mail* in recent months. But the publication of the articles was also prompted by Northcliffe's unhappiness about the strategy of concentrating on Tariff Reform. He well recognised the demagogic potential of the Budget and the House of Lords issues for the Liberals, and the German naval scare was his answer. It would serve both the immediate tactical needs of the hard-pressed Unionists and the long-term Northcliffe policy of bring-

ing home to Englishmen the nature and extent of the German
menace.

If the naval agitation dominated the *Daily Mail, Evening News,* and
Sunday Dispatch, its influence on the press was felt well beyond Carmelite House. Garvin, who had begun by stressing social and tariff
reform, felt by mid-December that what was needed was a 'cannon-
ball . . . something over and above tariff and social reform'.[22] He, too,
found it in the naval agitation and this subject increasingly shared
prominence with Tariff Reform in the most influential of the Unionist
Sunday journals.

Its impact on the Pearson press was equally dramatic. Throughout
December 1909 the Pearson press stuck, as might have been expected,
to a Tariff Reform line, the *Standard* and *Evening Standard* somewhat
stodgily, the *Daily Express* in more sprightly vein. The latter published
daily on its front page a list of dumped goods, and every day in large
letters in a special box the favourite tariff slogan of its editor, Blumen-
feld, 'Tariff Reform means Work for All'. But the *Daily Express* had
been founded as a 'patriotic' paper, and it had ever been a willing
competitor in jingoism with the Northcliffe press. Accordingly during
January 1910 the naval menace increasingly overshadowed Tariff
Reform in the columns of the *Daily Express.* A similar development
took place in the *Standard.*

Press support for Tariff Reform ebbed away during 1910. Opportunistic by occupation and untrammelled by the cares of party responsibility, many Unionist editors, faced with the second election,
believed that only drastic remedies could bring success. The Unionist
press was riddled with men convinced that one such remedy was
nothing less than a piece of major surgery, the excision of Tariff
Reform, or at least the food taxes, from the party programme. Right
across the ideological spectrum this course was actively canvassed – in
the columns of the Free Food *Spectator,* in the offices of the great
Balfourite organs, *The Times* and the *Daily Telegraph,* and in the editorial sanctums of the Whole Hogger *Daily Express* and *Observer.*[23]

The extent of the decay was apparent when Garvin launched his
public appeal for a referendum on Tariff Reform. Within forty-eight
hours and before any front bench Unionist had spoken, the bulk of the
Unionist press had declared its sympathy for the proposal.[24] But if the
referendum pledge revealed publicly the collapse of Tariff Reform's
hold on the Unionist press, it also revealed the disunity of that press.
The *Morning Post*'s refusal to acquiesce in these 'manifestations of

Unionist opportunism'[25] was an irreparable blow to the whole operation, casting doubt on the authority of the pledge and providing the Liberals with splendid ammunition. In the dog days of the second election Fabian Ware inflamed the rebels against the party establishment to such an extent that before the elections were over 'society folk talk[ed] of "boycotting" the *M. Post* for its "persistent attacks on A.J.B." '.[26] The Unionist advantage in numbers and circulation in the press had for some years been jeopardised by factional rifts; in the second election it was much dissipated by this public rupture.

The one party severely handicapped through lack of press support was the Labour Party. The I.L.P. weekly, the *Labour Leader*, gave the party solid support through the elections, but two other Socialist weeklies, *Clarion* and *Justice*, were more often hostile than friendly. In straight contests between Labour and Unionists the Liberal press backed Labour, and occasionally in three-cornered contests the Radical press was sympathetic. But the difficulties of an electoral fight against a hostile Liberal, as well as Unionist, press had been apparent at the Bermondsey by-election in October 1909, which a Unionist won on a minority vote. This contest on the eve of the Budget debate in the Lords was fought in the full glare of press publicity. The *Morning Leader*, arguing that a vote for Labour was a wasted vote, was distributed free to every house in the constituency. Salter, the Labour candidate, attributed his defeat chiefly to the lack of a daily Socialist paper, and the *Labour Leader* saw the by-election as an ominous foretaste of the impending general election with 'all the capitalist organs surpass[ing] Ananias and Baron Munchausen in the concoction of the wildest and weirdest falsehoods, and in circulating the most leprous lies'.[27]

Spurred on by Bermondsey, the National Labour Press proposed to publish for the duration of the general election a daily evening paper modelled on the popular *Manchester Evening News*. It would consist of four pages and would be supplied to all constituencies with Labour candidates. However, for the scheme to be practicable the representatives of the National Labour Press insisted that the Labour Party would have to agree to take at least 140,000 copies a day, at a cost of £1 6s per thousand copies. The minimum cost for a four-week campaign would therefore have been over £4000. The cost, plus the short time left to organise production and determine control, prevented the experiment. Thus in the 1910 elections, the presentation of the Labour case went largely by default, particularly in the national press.[28]

II

This quantitative analysis of press alignments neglects the quality of press partisanship. In London with the exception of the *Daily Mirror* and the *News of the World* all the press was unashamedly partisan. 'The daily newspapers have ceased to be retailers of news – they are merely mammoth political pamphlets of the most violent partisan type.'[29] There were, however, considerable variations in the intensity and temper of this partisanship. Generally the penny dailies were more moderate in tone than their halfpenny rivals. Certainly the *Westminster Gazette* – 'the last word in authoritative journalism on the Liberal side'[30] – possessed little of the shrill self-righteousness too often charac-teristic of the halfpenny Liberal morning dailies. Nor did the 'sea green incorruptible' sink to the crudities typified in the *Morning Leader*'s presentation of the issues as a contest between the 'citizens' and 'a herd of inferior rich men, led by a handful of prigs'.[31]

On the other hand no Unionist papers equalled the savagery of the penny *Daily Telegraph*, most virulent of all the Unionist press in its assault on the Ministry and the Ministers. It was the only quality Unionist paper actively to abet the raking up of Lloyd George's activities during the Boer War; indeed its invective against him made most of the Unionist press look squeamish by comparison.[32] Its contempt for the 'Yellow Parliament . . . born in the mendacity of the Pigtail elections; . . . exist[ing] upon folly and fanaticism; . . . perish[ing] under the burden of a policy of social bribes and Imperial betrayal' was unbounded.[33]

By contrast *The Times*, opposed to the rejection of the Budget, grasping at every compromise and plagued by internal difficulties, was almost genteel in its partisanship.[34] One strong partisan, Garvin, complained that *The Times* reminded him 'of the impartiality of the Irish historian, who was so impartial that he was quite unfair to his friends'. In a less-guarded moment he denounced the paper as 'a national curse'.[35]

While the press was characterised by strong partisanship, accom-panied by factional undertones, it was also characterised by an extra-ordinary preoccupation with things electoral. For eight weeks from 3 December 1909, and for a month following 19 November 1910 the press was literally dominated by the elections. For these twelve weeks the elections provided the chief source of news. Throughout these two periods an election item was almost invariably the main news item of the day. Only the death of Leopold of the Belgians on 17 December 1909 and the great Paris floods of late January 1910 displaced the first election as the major news topic of the day. In the second election concentration was uninterrupted until the third week of December when, with the result clear and interest waning, the popular press began to turn to more exciting topics – the *Mauretania*'s challenge for the blue riband, the Houndsditch murders and a dramatic spy trial in Germany.

TABLE 15.3 NATIONAL MORNING DAILIES: SPACE GIVEN TO
ELECTION MATERIAL

(Period 3 Dec 1909–31 Jan 1910)

Newspaper	Column Inches (To nearest 100)	% Total Editorial Space
Manchester Guardian	36,900	40
Standard	26,000	29
Daily Telegraph	25,700	23
Daily Chronicle	24,200	39
Daily News	23,500*	40
The Times	23,200*	25
Morning Post	20,400*	28
Morning Leader	14,200	28
Daily Express	12,600	32
Daily Mail	11,500	24
Daily Graphic	10,100	31
Daily Mirror	7,400	25

Note: * As the columns of these newspapers were wider than the average a measurement in column inches somewhat underestimates the total space given to election news in these papers, relative to the other papers.

In the eight-week period of the first election no London morning newspaper gave less than one-fifth of its total editorial space to election material. In the shorter and more concentrated second election the minimal figure was about one-quarter.[36] In the provinces the quality journals allotted even more space, for, with their unrivalled local sources, an election offered them an opportunity to compete with the expanding national press.

The total amount of space given to the election in any newspaper was chiefly a function of its size, the large penny dailies giving many more columns than their smaller halfpenny rivals. In the national press, two halfpenny dailies, the *Daily News* and the *Daily Chronicle* were exceptions to this rule. One explanation for this was that A. G. Gardiner of the *Daily News* and Robert Donald of the *Daily Chronicle* were probably more politically involved than other editors of the halfpenny press, while the proprietors concerned regarded their papers as party instruments in a fairly narrow sense. But it is also probable that the Liberal press was more politicised than the Unionist. An examination of the proportions of editorial space given to election material shows that the Liberal newspapers, with the exception of the *Morning Leader*, a paper given more to sport than politics,[37] allotted a greater proportion of space to election material than the Unionist newspapers. A general Radical tendency to political engagement, the Liberals' idealistic belief in the efficacy of reasoned argument, and perhaps a desire to offset their numerical inferiority, as well as particular personal factors, seem possible explanations for this.

It is impossible to determine the impact of this flood of words on the voter. The bias of most of the press was such that it is difficult to imagine that it provided much help to the genuinely undecided. Rather than change votes, it is more likely that it confirmed existing prejudices and provided rationalisations for established loyalties.

If we can only speculate about the impact of the press, we can be a little more definite about its role. First, the press, particularly the popular papers, provided the cues and tokens of party loyalty and partisan reactions: slogans like 'The Peers Against the People', symbols such as dollar signs and Union Jacks, images, e.g. the buffoon peers and the foreign dumper. Secondly, the press played a key role in structuring the national debate, witness the part played by the Unionist press in the first election in shifting the debate from the constitutional issue to fiscal and naval questions.

But on three occasions the press did more than simply structure the argument; it altered profoundly the course of the debate. The first and most individual of these initiatives was the publication of the Blatchford articles by the *Daily Mail*. The second was the *volte face* in the Unionist press in November 1910. Here the Irishman, treated kindly in the autumn, became once more a creature of sin and treason. The portrait of Redmond, puppet master of the Ministry and underwrit with foreign gold, was primarily a press achievement. The third and greatest of the press initiatives was the role of the Unionist newspapers in securing the referendum pledge on Tariff Reform. Garvin's appeal and the press response compelled a decision, when the time for decision had almost gone. It is perhaps as much a comment on party leadership as on the press that these three major initiatives were taken by the Unionist press.

III

The second major source of publicity was the parties themselves. In the eight-week first election the country was flooded with political leaflets, posters and other propaganda material to an extent unequalled in previous elections. 'The [January] election', noted *The Times*, 'was characterised by a greater output of campaign publications of all kinds, posters, pamphlets and leaflets than any which has occurred since the passing of the Reform Bill of 1832.'[38] The Liberal Publication Department had not expected to exceed the record output of 1906, yet by the time the election was over the 1906 figures had been surpassed by over 50 per cent. In all, the L.P.D. issued 41,135,000 separate items during the election.[39] The National Union produced over 50,000,000 leaflets, pamphlets, books, postcards and posters,[40] and even the Labour Party's modest 5,000,000 leaflets, 50,000 picture posters, and 800,000 copies of the party manifesto was a substantial increase over 1906.[41]

The January election saw the use of the pictorial poster on an unparalleled scale. Never before had the advertisement hoardings been made to serve so completely the purpose of the political platform, and for the first time the picture poster was widely used in the villages and the countryside. The *Daily Mail* estimated that by early January 1910 the posters originating from London alone would cover some two million square feet of wall space.[42]

Pride of place in the Liberal gallery went to the peers. Coroneted, ermined, gartered and robed, the peer capered across the hoardings of the country. The coronet was usually tilted to suggest irresponsibility, the visage frequently beery, the paunch bloated; and many a peer clutched his bags of unearned increment.[43] The Unionists produced no single rival, prominence in their cartoons being given to the pathetic figure of the unemployed workman and to Garvin's 'bogey . . . the freely importing foreigner',[44] often Herr Dumper, decked out in the trappings of the *nouveau riche*. 'England expects that every foreigner will pay his duty' was one of the most widely used of Unionist slogans.

In the second election the volume of material naturally declined – the total output being approximately half that of the previous contest – as did its quality.[45] Much of the material used was second-hand, and the inventive powers of poster designers and pamphleteers appeared exhausted. Nevertheless, the amount of material that issued from the party headquarters was still voluminous, for the output of the four-week December campaign roughly equalled that of the seven-week 1906 election.

While the spread of the poster was the most noticeable development in January, December saw the beginning of what is now a regular feature of electoral propaganda, the large page or half-page party advertisement in the press. Although a writer in *Blackwood's Magazine* thought it 'the most idiotic form of waste that can be conceived', the parties bought some £30,000 worth of newspaper space.[46] Most of the Liberal newspapers accepted the advertisements of both major parties, justifying this lucrative policy by claims to fair play. Most Unionist papers however refused Liberal advertisements, on the grounds that acceptance would involve a prostitution of their principles.

The most professional propaganda machine was that of the Liberal Publication Department under the capable direction of Charles Geake, Hudson's brother-in-law. A self-effacing man, who 'positively revelled' in the work,[47] he had been secretary of the L.P.D. since 1892. The smooth running of the administrative side of the Department reflected this experience; the contemporary format and immediacy of Liberal propaganda revealed an imaginative and up-to-date outlook. Unionists admired the 'red hot, brief, pungent style' of Liberal literature, contrasting if favourably with their own.[48]

There were certain unsatisfactory features. The Department's publicity shared with Liberal policy a distinctive urban emphasis, and there were complaints that it was unsuited to rural campaigning.[49] Again, Geake's belief that 'you must scatter your shot to bring down your bird'[50] led to large numbers of small posters each on a different issue which could be massed on a single hoarding. These were perhaps less effective than the single large posters favoured by the Unionists. Nevertheless, the national publicity of the L.P.D. provided a most satisfactory complement to the national campaign of the party leaders. 'In no election,' asserted the *Westminster Gazette* in January, 'has the Liberal literature been prepared with such care and thoroughness.'[51]

The same could not be said for the publicity of the National Union. On the eve of the first election Garvin attacked the campaign literature of his party as 'largely dead stuff. It is nearly all too abstract, academic and verbose.' Pictorially too much of it was inept. '. . . the British workman must appear in all our pictures as a fine fellow, not the debased, and uncouth and grotesque person that he seems in some of our pictures.' Garvin concluded that 'the inferiority of our party literature for its campaign purposes is a most serious disadvantage and indeed a very real danger'.[52]

Attempts were made to rectify this weakness. But much remained to cause disquiet. During the election the society weekly the *World* found that some Unionist posters were 'almost irritatingly feeble'.[53] The *Morning Post* criticised one Unionist poster on the grounds that an octopus representing Socialism had an 'absurdly benevolent appearance'.[54] The unfortunate portrayal of the British workman continued. 'The debauched looking ruffian', complained the *World*, 'who glares from the picture called "A Victim of Free Trade" might have been more suitably labelled "A Victim of Free Drink".'[55] Moreover distribution was often poor, *The Times* reporting that 'at present in many cases little or no discrimination is shown as to the kind of literature distributed, and appeals which might influence artisans are made to agricultural labourers and vice versa'.[56]

This inadequacy in Unionist publicity stemmed from the general weakness in Unionist organisation, particularly from that fitful effort at democratic reorganisation attempted in 1906. Previously control of publicity had been shared by the National Union and the Central Office; in 1906, however, the National Union was given complete control. This was exercised by an unwieldy National Union committee of twenty-five members, most of whom were M.P.s, candidates, or local organisers. During the campaign most of the committee members left London for their constituencies and responsibility for publicity had to be taken by the Central Office which in the preceding years had had little or no contact with the selection and distribution of party literature. Confusion inevitably resulted. In addition the Literary Department of the National Union was poorly staffed. In Chaplin's opinion it contained no one who could be considered an expert on publicity.[57]

Nevertheless an average of one million items a day left the National Union dispatch office during the January election, while the Unionist poster output was almost double that of the L.P.D. The *Westminster Gazette* admitted that in London the Tories made the biggest display on the hoardings.[58] The most widely reproduced poster in either election, T. B. Kennington's melodramatic portrayal of poverty and unemployment under Free Trade, was a National Union product.[59] Moreover the gigantic output of the T.R.L., which far surpassed any other pressure group or party ancillary, reinforced in quantity and quality the Unionist argument on the hoardings, the shop fronts and in the letter boxes.

Labour's propaganda was the responsibility of an *ad hoc* committee set up on 6 October 1909. There was little delegation and the sub-committee consisted of members of that already overburdened core of party leaders and officials. All but one were candidates in both elections. Limited financial resources resulted in a maximum payment of only five guineas for any poster design.[60] The result was a collection of competent but pedestrian posters and pamphlets, lacking in visual impact and too often overloaded with detail.

IV

The most individual item of publicity was the candidate's address, in which he stated his personal views on the issues before the electorate.[61] The election address is one of the more immutable features of British electoral practice. The addresses of fifty years ago differed little in format from those of today.[62] Over 75 per cent of them consisted of a single folded sheet, averaging about 1000 words. A number of the bigger productions, sometimes with stiff covers, amounted to twenty or thirty pages. In the sample available length ranged from the laconic 125-word address of Sir Charles Dilke (Liberal, Forest of Dean) to the elaborate twenty-eight-page address of E. Hoffgaard (Unionist, South-West Bethnal Green).[63]

Less than half the addresses carried a photograph of the candidate, and only a few that of his wife. Occasionally an ancestral home was used instead of a personal portrait. Both the Union Jack and the Royal Standard appeared, while the photographs of several candidates were garlanded with acorns and oak leaves, primroses and thistles. Neither the use of national and royal emblems, nor that of county and traditional insignia, was restricted to any one party. One of the most heraldic of covers was that of the Labour M.P. for Preston, J. T. Macpherson, which carried the Royal Standard, the Union Jack and the red rose of Lancashire.

One difference between the parties was in their use of candidates' photographs. 77 per cent of the Labour, but only 42 per cent of the Unionist, and 45 per cent of the Liberal addresses carried them. Perhaps Labour felt a greater need to reassure the electors about the respectability of its candidates, a feature which the photographs did much to stress. Most Labour addresses were in black and white, but many Liberal and Unionist addresses were printed in the colours of the local party – e.g. Unionist red in South London, blue in most of the rest of London; Liberal red in Lancashire, but blue in Liverpool – thus reflecting that patchwork of local party colours, one of the survivals from the localisation of nineteenth-century politics.

It is difficult to glean much biographical information from the addresses. Only a few gave adequate short biographies, while over 50 per cent gave no biographical information at all. Such material as there was related mainly to a candidate's parliamentary services. The Unionist member for Grimsby, Sir George Doughty, devoted half his address to supporting the assertion that 'no member of the House of Commons can claim to have been more zealously watchful of the interest of his constituency than myself'. Some attempted a quantitative assessment of their services. Sir William Collins, Liberal M.P. for West St Pancras claimed that he had recorded 1300 votes in the division lobbies, and he instanced his speeches to show that he was no 'silent voting machine'. But his record was surpassed by the eccentric Arnold Lupton (Liberal, Sleaford) who claimed 1379 votes and 226 columns of *Hansard*.

The parochial aspect is seen in residential and ancestral references and in the emphasis by candidates on particular local issues. In London there was wide support for the equalisation of rates; in the East End Unionists urged stricter administration of the Aliens Act; in the coastal constituencies of Scotland there were demands for stiffer action against foreign trawlers in Scottish waters; and in the Glasgow area the controversial letting system was attacked by the candidates of all parties.

But the real interest of the election address lay in the candidate's personal statement on the national issues before the country. The addresses cannot tell us what issues, if any, were decisive in determining the voters' choice of party. They can tell us more conveniently than anything else what issues the politicians thought would determine that choice, and therefore what questions figured most prominently in the constituency campaigns, and how such questions were tackled.

In the first election few addresses were written before Christmas, and most not until the New Year. With some weeks of electioneering behind them the candidates had a volume of speeches and a wealth of comment on which to draw. For many Liberals Asquith's Albert Hall speech was the distinctive signpost, and his formulas on the constitutional issue and Home Rule were echoed in many addresses.

Balfour's manifesto was a less popular guide, inspiration for Unionists coming more often from Birmingham. The candidates had undoubtedly had opportunities to sense the opinions of the electorate, to gauge what issues aroused it, to estimate what subjects should be avoided or played down, to learn the best ways of tackling questions – all this before writing their addresses. In general, the January addresses blend the views of the party leaders both with the candidates' personal convictions and the politicians' awareness of local responses. In the

TABLE 15.4 ISSUES IN CANDIDATES' ADDRESSES JAN 1910*

Issue	% of total addresses mentioning issue	% of Unionist addresses mentioning issue	% of Liberal addresses mentioning issue	% of Labour addresses mentioning issue
(Figures in brackets % of candidates ranking issue first.)†				
House of Lords	96 (47)	94 (15)	99 (82)	99 (58)
Tariff Reform – Free Trade	93 (38)	100 (74)	88 (3)	82 (4)
Budget	85 (5)	84 (6)	88 (5)	80 (1)
Government record‡	43 (6)	25	63 (10)	46 (19)
Old Age Pensions	76	76	75	82
Defence	73 (2)	96 (4)	57	18
Home Rule	62	82 (1)	39	70
Education	56	71	44	27
Disestablishment§	19	33	8	1
Licensing	35	29	38	61
Electoral reform	36	16	51	84
Agriculture	45	68 (1)	27	1
Social reform	53 (1)	40	64	80 (6)
Right to work	5 (1)	–	–	62 (11)
Nationalisation	3	–	–	39 (1)
Payment of Members	4	5	3	31
Osborne Judgement	1	–	–	13

Notes: * Based on analysis of 1124 addresses (522 Unionist, 498 Liberal, 74 Labour). Includes all available addresses for Great Britain of official party candidates except two Liberal addresses in Welsh and the idiosyncratic address of Horatio Bottomley (Liberal, South Hackney).

† Ranking based on candidate's declaration, or on space given to issue in address.

‡ References to all Government measures 1906–9 except those rejected by the Lords, plus Old Age Pensions, and measures relating to defence.

§ Mainly references to Welsh Disestablishment.

flurry of the December election the position was more confused. About 70 per cent of all the addresses appear to have been written after the passage of the Rosebery resolutions, but before the introduction of the Lansdowne resolutions. It seems likely that during the weekend 19–20 November, while the Unionist leaders formulated their final proposals for Second Chamber reform, most candidates were hastily scribbling their addresses. As a result, only about 20 per cent of the addresses dealt with the referendum and joint session proposals, and a mere handful with Balfour's pledge on Tariff Reform. Thus, while the January election addresses give an adequate picture of what the election was about, or at least what the politicians thought it was about, the more fluid situation in December is less perfectly mirrored in the election addresses.

In January the candidates recognised the importance of the three major and interrelated questions – the House of Lords, the Budget and Tariff Reform. Although the Budget was the logical crux of these issues, it was superseded in all parties by the controversies it had stimulated. But there were variations in party emphasis. The Unionists

TABLE 15.5 LABOUR ADDRESSES JAN 1910

Issue	Straight Fights (47 addresses) % treating issue	Triangular Fights (27 addresses) % treating issue
House of Lords	100 (64)	93 (48)
Tariff Reform – Free Trade	85 (4)	82 (4)
Budget	92	63
Government record	60 (23)	33 (7)
Old Age Pensions	85	78
Defence	13	11
Home Rule	66	78
Education	34	15
Disestablishment	2	–
Licensing	62	63
Electoral reform	79	89
Agriculture	2	–
Social reform	77 (4)	89 (18)
Right to work	53 (4)	74 (22)
Nationalisation	30	56
Payment of Members	30	37
Osborne Judgement	10	22

Note: Figures in brackets % of candidates ranking issue first.

advocated Tariff Reform as never before; the Liberals concentrated
on the constitutional issue; Labour men, while accepting Liberal
priorities, paid more attention than the other parties to social reforms.
Lansbury (Bow and Bromley) summed up the Labour position: 'We
are fighting Peers and Plutocrats, Pauperism and Poverty.' While for
some Unionists the constitutional question was 'an electioneering
dodge',[64] for seven Liberal candidates including one Cabinet Minister,
Harcourt, it was the only issue worth mentioning. Conversely, while
for many Unionists Tariff Reform was the panacea for the ills of the
nation, Liberals variously dismissed it as 'undiluted quackery', 'a silly
myth' and 'a hoary old fraud'.[65]

Labour's treatment of the issues, and the attention accorded them,
depended considerably on the type of contest involved. In straight
fights with Unionists Labour addresses closely followed those of the
Radicals; but in triangular contests Labour candidates tended to concentrate on distinctive Labour themes in order to distinguish themselves
from the Liberals.

An address is usually a simple document in which complex issues are
reduced to stark essentials or even to slogans. On the constitutional
question abstruse arguments, and the subtleties which fascinated
constitutional lawyers and filled the correspondence columns of *The
Times*, were shunned by both sides. Most Unionists were content simply
to claim that the House of Lords had both a right and a duty to refer
the Budget to the people. While rebutting this claim, 'a colossal piece
of impudence and hypocrisy',[66] Liberals contended that the rejection
was an assault on, and a threat to, representative government. Most
Liberal addresses treated the validity of the charge as self-evident.
'Every vote given to the Unionists in this election is a nail in the coffin
of democracy.'[67]

The aggressive stance of the Liberals was reinforced by reference
to the history of rejected and mutilated Liberal measures. 51 per cent of
Liberal candidates referred to the destruction of Liberal bills, though
few enjoyed the metaphorical flourish of the Member for Orkney and
Shetland, with his description of Liberal measures 'condemned by the
lynch law of the Wild Western Backwoodsmen'. Over one-third of
the Liberal candidates devoted a paragraph of abuse to the Lords, and
on this subject Liberal eloquence was unrestrained. Perhaps the most
comprehensive denunciation came at North Manchester, where
Manchester's leading Liberal, Sir Charles Swann, attacked the Lords
as 'land grabbers and stealers of commons . . . the fleecers of farmers,

miners and cities; the Shylocks of the slums; the friends and obsequious servants of the brewers'.

Rhetorical flashes were less in evidence in the more defensive posture of Unionists. The distinctively Balfourian line, the dread of a single uncontrolled chamber, appeared in almost 70 per cent of the addresses. Despite lack of encouragement from their leaders 50 per cent of the Unionists declared for reform of the House of Lords. 'I entirely refuse to be identified with an unreformed House of Lords' protested the candidate for Luton, while the Unionist in the Stirling Burghs assured the electors that the reform of the Lords would be the 'first task of a Unionist administration'. Most reformers urged that somehow the Lords should be made 'more representative'. One candidate even went so far as to advocate the expulsion of 'unworthy peers'.[68]

Lack of Cabinet unanimity on the constitutional problem was mirrored in a similar lack of unanimity in the addresses. 20 per cent of the Liberal addresses advanced no constructive solution at all. Of the remainder, just over half urged the restriction of the legislative veto. The rest divided evenly between a distinguished group including two Cabinet Ministers, Grey and Haldane, which found the solution in a reform of the composition of the Lords with at most the abolition of the financial veto, and another which coupled restriction of the legislative veto with composition reform. Only a handful supported the abolition of the House of Lords and then mostly in the spirit of the Member for Holmfirth: 'I have desired to see it abolished, but am told the difficulty is too great. If that be so, it must at least be deprived of its power for evil.'

Labour Party candidates were mostly for abolition. Of those suggesting a solution, fifty-two favoured abolition as against eleven for veto restriction, and one, Albert Stanley (North-Western Staffordshire) for the so-called Grey plan. There was much suspicion of the Liberal veto plans. The Labour candidate at Huddersfield promised that while 'the Liberal Party proposes to put the House of Lords in a cage, I propose to put it in a coffin'. The danger of a rift in the anti-Unionist forces on this point was minimised by many Labour candidates, particularly the M.P.s, who indicated their willingness to accept adequate veto restriction as a short-term solution.

The division between the parties on the fiscal issue was stark. Unionists presented Tariff Reform as the basic requisite for the social and economic well-being of the state, while Liberals saw it as class-biased solution bringing in its wake a host of attendant evils. Unionists supported their case with considerable facts and figures, and a wealth of economic argument. By contrast the Liberal attack on Tariff Reform seemed more a matter of faith than economics. Over one-third of the Liberals accompanied their attack on Tariff Reform with a genuflection towards the altar of Free Trade, 'the application in international relations of the principles of the gospel'.[69]

TABLE 15.6 BENEFITS FROM TARIFF REFORM JAN 1910

Benefit	% Unionist candidates mentioning benefit
Increase wages or employment	90
Provide revenue by taxing foreigner	55
Combat foreign dumping	40
Increase economic negotiating power	34
Help agriculture	13

Liberals denied that tariffs would increase employment and wages – rather the reverse – and argued that commerce and trade would be injured, the consumers' tax burden increased, and trusts and cartels would proliferate. One-third of the Liberal addresses claimed that a tariff system would benefit the rich at the expense of the poor, for 'tariffs are trumps for the Shylocks of industry and the Sharks of landed property, filling their bank balances to bursting, but for the people they are robbery and spoliation'.[70] Above all, as it had been the kernel of the Free Trade case against tariffs for a hundred years, Liberals argued that the fiscal theories of Birmingham would increase the price of food. This charge was levelled in three-quarters of the Liberal addresses, and Unionists were sensitive to it. 60 per cent endeavoured to counteract it by pledging that there would be no increase in the cost of living under Tariff Reform, and at least one-third of these promised adjustment of the existing food duties to ensure this.

The Labour addresses bore out the Lib-Lab miner Thomas Burt's assessment that 'the socialist is nearly always an earnest free trader, and the ordinary trade unionist is . . . almost without exception, a convinced and determined free trader'.[71] The attention paid by Labour to the fiscal question and the arguments used were virtually identical with the Liberal position.

While Unionists regarded the blessings of the tariff as inestimable, the form of the tariff remained obscure. On the protection of manufactures, 2 per cent of Unionists, including Free Fooders such as Lord

Robert Cecil, Stewart Gibson Bowles, Derby's brother Arthur Stanley and Sir Arthur Bignold, committed themselves merely to retaliatory measures against foreign dumping. Another 40 per cent were vaguely protectionist, although what they would protect was by no means clear. The candidate for Tottenham wrote: 'In fact I am a Tariff Reformer because I am at heart a Free Trader.' Another 15 per cent supported duties on competitive manufactures. Many of these were hardly distinguishable from retaliationists. Finally 45 per cent supported a general tariff on all manufactured goods.[72]

On colonial preference the position was even more ambiguous. Cecil and Bowles declared themselves unequivocally opposed to any duty on meat, corn or dairy products for the purposes of colonial preference.[73] No other Unionist displayed this sort of courage, although Lambton at South-East Durham showed his distaste for Birmingham economics by being the only Unionist candidate not to mention Tariff Reform in his address. In 15 per cent of the Unionist addresses there was no suggestion that Tariff Reform had anything to do with the Empire. In another 15 per cent there was a vague imperial reference, but the candidates baulked at the phrase 'imperial preference'. A majority of the candidates – 51 per cent – claimed they stood for imperial preference, but dropped no hint that this involved tariffs on foodstuffs. Only 17 per cent declared that their schemes involved the taxation of food, and only 2 per cent, including the most ancient and ardent protectionist of them all, Henry Chaplin, suggested that the fully-fledged Tariff Reform programme involved a tax on colonial, as well as on foreign, foodstuffs. 'There was', observed the Conservative *Saturday Review* in a classic understatement, 'something shamefaced about the way many Unionists tackled the [food tax] issue.'[74]

Too much should not be read into these figures. Because of shortage of space and tactical considerations many who fell into the doubtful categories were, in fact, ardent Tariff Reformers. However, many others fell into these categories because they themselves were dubious or muddled about features of the Tariff Reform programme. There was certainly much hesitation about its form, although little about its benefits. The men of the Balfourite middle way had accepted the slogans of the Whole Hoggers as the Budget crisis engulfed the party, but the extent of their commitment was obscure and far from whole-hearted.

The Unionists' fiscal arguments were directed at the working classes: the Liberal defence of the Budget at the same groups. As the Liberals had argued that Tariff Reform would lay its burdens unfairly on the poor, so they now argued that the Budget's taxes fell most heavily on the shoulders most able to bear them. This was the most common defence of the Budget occurring in 60 per cent of the addresses. It was buttressed by another appeal to the working classes: that the Budget would lay the foundation for social reform (50 per cent of Liberal addresses). The land taxes were acclaimed by urban Liberals, although worried Liberals in the rural constituencies found it necessary to stress that the taxes did not affect agricultural land.

Labour support for the Budget was almost as enthusiastic as Liberal. T. F. Richards at West Wolverhampton thought it 'the greatest measure for the poor ever introduced to Parliament'; Keir Hardie (Merthyr Tydfil) praised it for having its roots in socialism; and Robert Smillie (Mid-Lanark) eulogised its land taxes which 'follow reverently in the steps of the old Hebrew prophets' by treating the soil as the natural inheritance of the people. Again Labour was virtually at one with the Liberals.

Unionists too directed their anti-Budget arguments at the proletariat, charging that the Budget would be 'a workhouse Budget',[75] detrimental to the economy and thus to the employment and wages of the workers (60 per cent of Unionist addresses). Some 20 per cent of Unionist candidates protested against the 'beer and baccy taxes' pointing out that while the Budget 'might sheer the rich [it] would assuredly skin the poor'.[76] The Unionists' popular case against the Budget was summed up in the jingle:

> Dearer Baccy, dearer Bread
> Dearer Living, dearer Dead
> Dearer Whisky, Beer and Gin
> Is what you get when Rads are in.[77]

But this type of appeal was uneasily harnessed with a conservative defence of the wealthier classes against predatory and vindictive taxation. The addresses did not hide the anger of the classes against a Budget designed to woo the masses, 40 per cent of the addresses alleging the taxes were vindictive or unfair, or, as in the words of one Unionist, 'revolutionary, Socialist, un-English'.[78] The charge of socialism was levelled against the Budget in one-third of the addresses.

Of all the matters dealt with in the addresses, these three topics took up approximately two-thirds of the space. The only other issue referred to in at least three-quarters of the addresses was Old Age

Pensions. The most popular measure of the social reform programme of the Government, it was a bandwagon on which all tried to climb. The Liberals claimed credit for providing pensions, the Labour men that their insistence had secured them, and some Unionists that their party had fathered them.

Two further issues secured attention in more than 60 per cent of the addresses – defence and Home Rule. Both were prominent in Unionist addresses and played down or neglected by Liberals. Particularly did the Unionists seize upon the naval scare. References to the navy appeared more often in Unionist addresses than any other subject except Tariff Reform. Twenty-two Unionists made the same decision as the candidate for Gainsborough: 'Recent disclosures as to the strength and condition of the navy are of so serious a nature that I feel bound to place this question in the forefront of my address.'

This scare overshadowed fear of Home Rule, about which the Liberals were even more reticent. While 57 per cent of the Liberal addresses had defence references, only 39 per cent of the Liberals referred to Home Rule despite Asquith's pledge. Moreover, one-quarter of these referred to the question only to oppose it, or to support some measure of devolution unlikely to be acceptable to the Irish, or to promise complicated and distant plans for Home Rule all round.

The Labour Party did not share this reluctance, 70 per cent of its candidates declaring for Home Rule. This enthusiasm was not solely the result of principle. It arose partly because the majority of Labour candidates stood in constituencies with a significant Irish vote. It is easy to understand the bitterness of the Labour Party when this strong Home Rule stand met little response from the Irish leaders, who marshalled the Irish vote behind the Liberals in most triangular contests.[79]

Education, disestablishment and licensing were dying controversies in the country as a whole. Only in Wales did education and disestablishment receive a reference in a majority of Liberal addresses, while the attention paid by Liberals to licensing in Scotland and Wales was much greater than that paid in England. These issues were increasingly the causes of minority interests within the Liberal Party, which met by contrast much general resistance from Unionists. Except on licensing, where many Unionists seemed unprepared to give overt support to the brewers' cause, and where Labour Party feeling was strong, the establishment secured much wider support among Unionists than did its enemies among the Liberals and Labour men.

Just under half the candidates discussed rural land policy, but the lead given by Balfour in his address, plus on the whole the better quality of Unionist candidates in rural England, appears to have given the Unionists an advantage in this sphere. Certainly twice as many Unionists discussed agricultural questions in their addresses, which were usually more informed on rural issues and reflected more clearly the rural disquiet over local taxation.

In an election concerned mostly with what the Liberals or Unionists were going to do, less attention than usual was paid to the Government's record. Almost two-thirds of the Liberals thought aspects of the record worthy of mention, but only 10 per cent considered it the chief justification for a Liberal vote. A smaller proportion of Labour candidates praised the Government's record, but those who did so showed considerable enthusiasm, 19 per cent of Labour candidates making it the leading feature of their addresses. Indeed, some of these addresses read as though a Labour Government had been in power for the previous four years. Criticism from Unionists was muted, though there were grumbles about governmental profligacy with money and over the expanding bureaucracy.

The only other subjects to receive widespread attention in the addresses were social and electoral reforms. While a natural conservatism restrained the Unionists from too vigorous a competition, in the field of social reforms the Liberals were challenged by the left. The *Labour Leader* urged Labour candidates to emphasise the party's originality and initiative in this sphere and to stress that the Liberal programme of social reform 'past, present and future, is a badly bowdlerised edition of the Labour Party programme'.[80] There was agreement among all parties that the two chief measures of social policy required were poor law reform and a system of national insurance, to which the Labour Party added provision of a minimum wage, shorter working hours, and a right to work measure.

Apart from those committed to female suffrage and redistribution, Unionists were little interested in electoral reform. Interest was much greater in the Liberal Party, and close to universal in the Labour Party. Liberal and Labour candidates were usually concerned with a much wider range of electoral reforms than the Unionists, including extension of male suffrage, abolition of plural voting, registration reform, one-day elections, and changes in the voting system. The attention paid to these subjects was some measure of the grievances of the working classes against the system of 1884–5.

In January three questions – the House of Lords, the Budget and Tariff Reform – were each mentioned in 85 per cent or more of the addresses; in December only one issue – the House of Lords – appeared in 85 per cent or more of the addresses. In January, while Liberal and Labour addresses emphasised the House of Lords, Tory addresses gave first place to Tariff Reform; in December all parties agreed on the primacy of the constitutional controversy. In January there had been a profusion of issues, eight issues being mentioned by more than half the candidates; in December only four issues aroused the interest of over half the candidates.

TABLE 15.7 ISSUES IN CANDIDATES ADDRESSES DEC 1910*†

Issue‡	% of total addresses mentioning issue	% of Unionist addresses mentioning issue	% of Liberal addresses mentioning issue	% of Labour addresses mentioning issue
(Figures in brackets % of candidates ranking issue first)				
House of Lords	†99 (86)	†99 (74)	†100 (98)	†100 (79)
Tariff Reform – Free Trade	83 (9)	96 (17)	71 (1)	66
Budget 1909	44	45	43	43
Government record	4	–	10	–
Old Age Pensions	27	18	36	40
Defence	62 (1)	89 (2)	37	†25
Home Rule	†66 (1)	†88 (5)	†41	68
Education	28	35	22	15
Disestablishment	9	14	3	†8
Licensing	16	10	21	30
Electoral reform	27	16	34	62
Agriculture	40	63	†18	†4
Social reform	48 (1)	†49	44	66 (8)
Right to work	3 (1)	–	–	43 (6)
Nationalisation	1	–	–	25
Payment of Members	†17	†15	†16	†34
Osborne Judgement	†27 (1)	†22	†25	†81 (6)
Timing of election	34 (1)	62 (2)	29	13

Notes: * Based on analysis of 981 addresses (496 Unionist, 432 Liberal, 53 Labour). Includes all available addresses in Great Britain except two Liberal addresses not susceptible to such an analysis.
† Indicates increased attention over January.
‡ See notes Table 15.4.

The December addresses reveal the acceptance by both sides of the pre-eminence of the constitutional question. Every address except two mentioned the question. Fifty-one addresses considered no other topic. 86 per cent of the addresses gave the issue pride of place. This entailed only a slight hardening of Liberal and Labour concentration, but for the Unionists it marked a complete reversal of emphasis. Only 17 per cent of Unionists gave Tariff Reform first place in December compared with 74 per cent in January, and this dramatic relegation took place before Balfour's referendum pledge.

This concentration was accompanied by a decline in the attention paid to most other issues. Reference fell most dramatically to subjects already accomplished – the Budget, Old Age Pensions, and the other legislative achievements of the Government. Outside Scotland and Wales attrition of interest in traditional Radical objectives proceeded apace. References to disestablishment, education and licensing fell by half in December.

The heart had gone out of the Budget controversy, few Unionists in December bothering to query Liberal claims that the economic recovery was partly the result of the Budget. While a few Unionists (7 per cent) demanded abolition of the land taxes, a larger number (25 per cent) promised merely amendment. What tariff would follow a Unionist victory was an even murkier question than in January. Most addresses had been written before Balfour's referendum pledge, but thirty-two late addresses included the pledge. No Unionist candidate in his address repudiated his leader's promise.

Three issues apart from the constitutional question received more attention from candidates in December than January. The references to Home Rule increased slightly in number and considerably in vehemence. In January with the Home Rule scare overshadowed by the navy bogy, most Unionists had simply used pejoratives such as 'cataclysmic', 'catastrophic', 'disastrous' to evoke the desired response. Now, with Home Rule imminent, all the old arguments were trundled out. Home Rule would destroy the integrity of the Empire (67 per cent); would be thrust upon the country by alien dollars (36 per cent); would endanger the Protestant loyalist minority (25 per cent); had been decisively rejected in the past (15 per cent); was urged not in the national interest but in the interest of the opportunistic Liberal Party (9 per cent); would threaten national security (8 per cent); and anyhow the Irish were unfit to govern themselves (8 per cent). For the first time in many years, Unionist candidates evoked the spectre of civil war (8 per cent). Despite, or perhaps because of, this vigorous denunciation, a majority of Liberals continued to ignore the issue.

Events during the year had also compelled candidates, particularly those in industrial areas, to take up positions on the Osborne Judgement and payment of Members. While the Labour candidates who dealt with the subject were for outright reversal and adequate payment for all M.P.s, Liberals mostly accepted payment, but equivocated on the Judgement while most Unionists opposed both payment and reversal.

One new question intruded. Two-thirds of the Unionists voiced their indignation at the sudden November dissolution. First, because it was unseasonal; secondly, because it was another *diktat* pressed on the craven Liberals by their Irish master – 'Redmond's Yuletide election';[81] thirdly, because it took place on the stale register. Other reasons advanced were that somehow the dissolution was unconstitutional and that there had not been enough time to discuss the issues.

But only one issue really mattered. The Liberal plan embodied in the Parliament Bill was endorsed enthusiastically by nearly every Liberal candidate,[82] one indeed printing the whole of the Parliament Bill in his address.[83] 15 per cent desired composition reform, not as an alternative, but as an addition, to veto restriction. The Labour Party followed in the Liberal wake. With the Parliament Bill before them, most Labour candidates favoured it at least as the immediate solution. There remained, however, a distrust of Liberal intentions, reflected in Snell's warning to the Huddersfield electors that increased Labour representation was needed to 'prevent the Whigs from once more betraying the people'.

Although there was inevitable confusion, the spirit of reform was sweeping the Unionist Party. 95 per cent of the Unionists pledged themselves to reform of the composition of the Lords, a remarkable conversion. One-third, writing their addresses after the reform session of the Lords or vouchsafed previous inspiration, urged the use of the referendum to solve deadlocks. Criticism and derision greeted this conversion in roughly half the Liberal addresses.

Unlike the Liberals, whose case against the Lords was much as in January, the Unionists developed two new lines of defence. First that the Parliament Bill was the result of a 'log-rolling Radical coalition, which has degraded our public life';[84] and secondly that Home Rule would be the inevitable consequence of the Parliament Bill. Each charge occurred in just over half the Unionist addresses. On these points the addresses were rather wild. 'George V is my king. John Redmond is the Radical Party's. It is for you to choose who will be yours,' wrote the candidate for Poplar. At Eskdale the candidate warned that soon that choice would be non-existent: 'The Irish would abolish the Lords, The Socialists would abolish the king.' Reading the Unionist addresses on this subject, it is difficult to avoid the conclusion that, faced at last with Armageddon, many Unionists verged on the hysterical.

The Interests, the Suffragettes, and the Churches

I

No Ministry since the first great Government of Gladstone had challenged the *status quo* at so many points as had those of Campbell-Bannerman and Asquith. The result was the enmity of many of the most powerful interests in the land. Assessing the position in early 1908 Montagu wrote: 'The Liberal Party is once more in its old and almost traditional position: it has tickled up the sore points in pretty nearly every interest in the country – Land is against it, Property is against it, Beer is against it.'[1] To his list Montagu might well have added the Anglican and Catholic Churches, the Tariff Reformers, the Irish and the suffragettes. Nor had the Government satisfied many of the groups that had helped sweep it to power. The Education and Licensing Acts remained unamended, while Welsh Disestablishment had been fobbed off with the appointment of a royal commission.[2]

The Budget revived enthusiasm for the Government among many of the groups supporting it, particularly the land reformers and the temperance people. At the same time it heightened the hostility of many already antagonised. Against the Budget the brewers organised an expensive but more subtle campaign than that against the 1908 Licensing Bill, linking their own protest against the licensing duties with the broader indictment of the measure.[3] The organisations of the landed interest, which feared the Budget as 'an incubus on agriculture . . . all the more mischievous . . . because in many ways its effects are indirect',[4] were well to the fore. So were the Liberty and Property Defence League, the Property Protection Society, and the various anti-Socialist leagues. Above all the Tariff Reform League girded itself for what it conceived as a life or death struggle for fiscal sanity.[5]

Against this background it is not surprising that the January election saw the incursion of a probably unprecedented range of pressure groups and a vast expenditure on pressure group activities and propaganda. At West Southwark the Paymaster-General R. K. Causton was overwhelmed. 'I never had to meet such an united combination of forces against me. Hops, Beer, Church, Roman Catholics (my opponent is a Catholic), Tariff Reformers amongst the poorest . . . together . . . they were too much for me.'[6] In the field of the secular pressure groups the Unionists had a clear advantage. Not only were the majority of the organisations ranked on their side, but in the T.R.L. they had the most electorally active of all the pressure groups. In the religious field the balance was more even for, if the Anglican and Catholic organisations had greater potential numbers, the spiritual leaders of these churches were less willing to commit their churches than were their Nonconformist counterparts.

In the second election the pressure groups played a less notable part. The salience of the House of Lords issue led the pressure groups, both religious and secular, to stand aside. Moreover a disenchantment with Unionist policies weakened the links between the Unionist Party and some of its allied interests. Both the brewers and the Land Union were unhappy over the party's readiness to accept, with only minor modifications, the duties and taxes of 1909. The brewers were noticeably less active in the second election.

The electoral prominence of the issues with which they were concerned, the breadth of their interests and the strength of their organisations determined the electoral importance of the various secular pressure groups. Because the issue with which they were concerned was central to the electoral debate, because they encompassed a broad spectrum of particular interests, and because they commanded powerful organisations, two secular pressure groups stood out. These were the great rival fiscal organisations, the Tariff Reform League and the Free Trade Union, whose 'battle of the pamphlets . . . reached its peak of intensity with the two elections of 1910'.[7]

Each was intimately connected with the political party which favoured its fiscal creed. In many constituencies the Unionist candidate was the formal nominee of both the local Unionist association and the local T.R.L. committee; indeed in some constituencies the T.R.L. committee seems to have possessed a virtual veto over Unionist nominations. T.R.L. workers operated from Unionist committee rooms, and according to one member of the T.R.L. executive, 'we save money and increase efficiency of all Unionist parties by avoiding duplication of Lecturers, Literature, and helpfully interchanging services and concerting all efforts'.[8] Not that the relationship was always harmonious. Sandars feared that the T.R.L. drained the Unionist coffers of money, and the Unionist organisations of men. Certainly in many constituencies the T.R.L. committees were often better financed, better organised and more aggressively led than the local party organisations.[9]

Less ambitious, the Free Trade Union functioned as an auxiliary rather than as a partner of the Liberal Party. Strachey considered that G. Wallace Carter, Secretary of the F.T.U., was 'a regular Party politician and only working for the Liberal administration under the cloak of abstract Free Trade'.[10] This estimate seems merited. Carter and the F.T.U. worked closely with the Liberal organisations, liaison being provided by Hudson. Activities were closely concerted, a subcommittee of the National Liberal Federation in April 1908 recommending that the F.T.U. be entrusted with combating the T.R.L. in the constituencies, while the more strictly organisational duties be left to the Chief Whip and the L.C.A.[11] During the election its propaganda was distributed through the Liberal organisation.

The T.R.L. was undoubtedly the more formidable of the two organisations. Its means were ample. 'Apparently there is no limit to the number of their agents or the extent of their financial resources,' wrote the envious Carter.[12] Its propaganda output rivalled that of the major parties. In the period January 1909–January 1910 the T.R.L. issued 53,169,716 leaflets, pamphlets and posters, five-sixths of which were distributed during the general election.[13]

By contrast the F.T.U. was a relatively puny organisation. While defeat in 1906 had stimulated the T.R.L., victory had rendered the F.T.U. complacent. Between 1906 and early 1908 F.T.U. educational work 'stopped'.[14] After an organisational overhaul, the F.T.U. began to stir itself during the recession of 1908, but found itself lagging badly behind the T.R.L. In London and the Home Counties during the first election the F.T.U. had only one agent for every twenty-seven constituencies, while the T.R.L. had one for every three or four constituencies.[15] Its leaflet output was only about one-third of the T.R.L.'s.[16] Yet by contrast with most pressure groups, the F.T.U.'s electoral contribution was impressive. At the end of 1909 it opened fifty offices throughout England, each run by a representative controlling a panel of speakers. Altogether the F.T.U. had about a thousand speakers at its disposal.[17]

The various defenders of 'the Trade', the Brewery Debenture Holders, the National Trade Defence Association, the Licensed Victuallers' Defence League, the Brewers' Society and the various distillers' groups, did not have an organisation comparable with the T.R.L. or the F.T.U. But they had two assets. First, a great willingness to spend money in defence of their interests, and secondly a network of established propaganda points. They appear to have spent more money buying space in newspapers during the elections than all the other pressure groups put together. The nature of 'the Trade' was also exploited for political ends. The rejection of the Budget led to an immediate reduction in the price of beer and whisky. The pubs themselves frequently became local rallying-points for the Unionist campaign. 'Every public house has become a Tariff Reform agency', wrote the Clerk of the House of Commons with pardonable exaggeration,[18] while the Liberal candidate at St Augustine's complained: 'Every little beershop was covered by my opponent's bills, until you might have mistaken them for Tory committee rooms. Every inn was a recruiting ground for Toryism, with the publican as agent.'[19] At Burton, an important brewing centre, the local Liberals decided that 'nothing could be done at present on ordinary Liberal lines until the Licensing Clauses of the Budget were out of the way'. Despite pressure from London, they refused to bring forward a Liberal candidate in January, and in the second election accepted only with reluctance a candidate sent down by Liberal headquarters.[20]

One further secular pressure group secured considerable attention although the issue it raised was considered by most politicians as peripheral or even irrelevant to the electoral debate. This was the movement for women's suffrage which, although weakened by internal schisms, commanded substantial financial resources, and a network of committed and dedicated workers.[21] By 1910 the movement was broken into three rival and often quarrelling organisations: the moderate National Union of Women's Suffrage Societies, the militant Women's Freedom League, under Mrs Despard, and the highly militant Women's Social and Political Union commanded by the formidable Pankhurst clan. The movement succeeded in securing public attention primarily because the militant groups were prepared to flout the conventional rules governing pressure-group behaviour. The 'Vixens in Velvet'[22] who flooded Parliament Square in the dying days of the short Parliament of 1910, and the ubiquitous female heckler, often present only as the result of heroic feats of endurance or acrobatics, ensured that female suffrage was not forgotten.

Common to nearly all the secular pressure groups was the issue of a manifesto to the press, in which the interest tried to relate its specific concern to broad national considerations and thus legitimise its electoral intervention. For instance, the National Union of Women's Suffrage Societies' manifesto argued that 'the crisis of the hour is ... of such a character that it cannot be discussed without raising the fundamental principles of representative government, and therefore the injustice and impolicy of excluding the whole female sex from representation'.[23] In different vein but with a similar intention the Brewery Debenture Holders' manifesto pointed out that the predatory taxation of 'the Trade' was a foretaste of the treatment of other interests.[24] Centralising the temperance issue, the United Kingdom Alliance pictured the Lords as 'driven to revolution by the crack of the brewers' whip'.[25]

At the local level most pressure groups catechised the candidates. Sometimes the queries met with exceedingly blunt responses from the more courageous or foolhardy candidates. Hilaire Belloc (South Salford) replied to a women's suffrage circular thus: 'Dear Madam ... In my opinion the agitation to which you refer is grossly immoral, and I will have nothing to do with it.'[26] H. C. F. Luttrell (Liberal, Tavistock) got himself into trouble by disclosing that he had put the National Farmers' Union questionnaire into the waste-paper basket.[27]

Yet nearly all the pressure groups interrogated candidates either by letter or deputation, and nearly all candidates submitted to such interrogation, their answers evasive when not affirmative. Even the Licensed Victuallers' Defence League instructed its member associations to 'interview every candidate irrespective of party'.[28] Some of its affiliates, however, revolted. The Yorkshire Licensed Trade meeting at Leeds, 14 December 1909, decided: '... in view of the unvaried and universal hostility meted out to this trade during the last two years by all Yorkshire members of Parliament other than those belonging to the Unionist Party this meeting is of the opinion no useful purpose can be served by putting test questions during the coming election.'[29] The Licensed Trade in Birmingham followed the Yorkshire example.[30] Other organisations, e.g. the National Farmers' Union, used the candidates' responses as the basis for voting directives to their members.[31] Others simply published the responses.

Most pressure groups contented themselves with the issue of a manifesto and the catechism of the candidates. Only a few conducted extensive publicity campaigns during the elections. Both the T.R.L. and the F.T.U. issued pamphlets, leaflets and posters, and made great use of lantern slides and gramophones. An original contribution to propaganda were the T.R.L. dump shops, exhibiting foreign-made goods which competed with local products. The liquor interests sought extensive publicity through newspaper advertisements. These presented the attack on the brewers not just as an attack on the British way of life, but on 'the very foundations upon which civilised society has for generations been held together and upon which the greatness of our vast Empire has been maintained'.[32] The Anti-Socialist Union used part of the proceeds of its million shilling fund for extensive anti-Labour publicity. The women's suffrage societies also provided a wide range of pamphlets and posters, those of the W.S.P.U. defending militancy and condemning alleged atrocities against imprisoned suffragettes.

Most of the very active pressure groups were also highly articulate, providing their own speakers and meetings. The F.T.U. planned 5000 meetings for the first election,[33] and elaborate T.R.L. rallies were features of both campaigns. The Anti-Socialist Union organised a campaign in every constituency in which a Labour or Socialist candidate was standing, sending lady orators to the 'most politically depraved' areas.[34] Local publicans were urged 'to use every effort' to secure the return of favourable candidates and appear to have done so.[35]

Active campaigns were mounted by the three major female suffrage organisations. The campaign of the W.S.P.U. was frankly anti-Liberal. 'We urge every Liberal, whether man or woman to help us in stamping out the false and spurious Liberalism affected by Mr Asquith and the Government.' An equally negative but less anti-Liberal campaign was undertaken by the W.F.L., its guiding principle being 'opposition to foes, not the support of possible friends'. The W.F.L. concentrated its attack on Cabinet Ministers for 'failing to use their opportunity', and on inveterate anti-suffragists, irrespective of party. The National Union of Women's Suffrage Societies pursued a more positive campaign supporting all candidates who promised women's suffrage in their addresses, and organised a petition in most constituencies on polling day. It strove to utilise its resources to the best advantage by sending its workers to support candidates of the same political complexion as themselves. In the second election the W.F.L. worked with the constitutionalists, leaving the W.S.P.U. to pursue alone a militantly negative course.[36]

Venturing beyond the usual province of pressure group activities, the suffrage societies supported three female suffrage candidates. All polled pitifully: 639 votes at Rossendale, where a Labour appeal was coupled with the suffrage agitation in January, and thirty-five votes and twenty-two votes respectively at Camlachie and East St Pancras in December. This was a salutary lesson to the pressure groups on the dangers of openly competing with the parties.

But it was not their association with single-issue candidates but the campaign tactics of the militant wing, that most distinguished the women's suffrage movement from other Edwardian pressure groups. The suffragettes were uninhibited by many of the usual restraints on pressure-group activities, and broke as well some of the customary rules of British electoral warfare. At Leith the suffragettes attempted to storm Grey's meeting and provoked a riot; at Southport Churchill's meeting was disrupted by three suffragettes lashed to the window frames in the roof; outside the Queen's Hall Lloyd George was roughly handled by a suffragette who leapt into his car; at Liverpool Asquith narrowly escaped being hit by a stone ginger-beer bottle thrown by a suffragette disguised as an orange-seller; at Battersea Burns's pamphlets and cards were damaged by an acid-throwing female. On the evening before Asquith's speech, the suffragettes had held a rally in the Albert Hall. Inevitably a number of suffragettes secreted themselves around the hall and the police spent much of the next day flushing them out, an organ-tuner finding one 'dusty woman among the tubes in the heart of the instrument, with a cushion under her head, and food and a megaphone by her side'.[37]

Although it has been claimed that the Pankhursts called off militancy for the first election,[38] there was little evidence of a truce before the New Year, while even in January there were sporadic acts of militancy. The second campaign opened with suffragette bands attempting to rush the Houses of Parliament. On 18, 22 and 23 November Parliament Square was disfigured by sharp clashes between suffragettes and police. During these days ministerial houses were stoned, an assault on Downing Street foiled, and a trail of shattered glass left along Whitehall. Several Ministers were assaulted, the unfortunate Birrell being incapacitated for the election campaign. However, after this the suffragettes, exhausted, or perhaps conciliated by ministerial statements, waged a relatively subdued campaign.

Fearful of personal assault and even possibly of assassination – rumours were circulating in late 1909 that some suffragettes were having pistol practice[39] – and apprehensive about the disruption of electoral meetings, the Ministry took strong security precautions during both elections. Churchill apparently favoured locking up all dangerous suffragettes for the duration of the first election,[40] but the Ministry finally contented itself with the exclusion of all women from most major meetings, the erection of protective barriers around the entrance to the halls, increased numbers of stewards, and strong police guards for Ministers. The politicians' rhetoric was full of revolution, and the barricades, the long lines of police and the closely guarded Ministers lent substance to their words. Yet ironically the only revolutionaries were but a handful of courageous female fanatics.

In numbers, resources and industry the pressure groups linked with the Unionist cause outweighed those linked with the other parties. Many had been actively working against the Government for months, or even years, before the elections. It is likely that this persistent activity by many powerful interests did more to sap Liberal support than the Unionist campaigns themselves. Yet at the same time the very weight of the interests ranged against the Ministry lent strength to the Liberal contention that they stood for the people against wealth and privilege. The Liberal press almost daily linked the peers personally and collectively with the various pressure groups arrayed behind the Unionist Party, and fulminated against the perversion of the electoral process by moneyed interests.[41] Thus the manifest superiority and abundant resources of the complex of pressure groups around the Unionist Party may have produced a reaction in the Liberal favour amongst many voters.

The impact of the suffragettes requires separate consideration. Sweeping claims have been made for their influence. The Pankhursts believed that 'the disappearance of the Government's majority was largely, if not simply, due to the woman suffrage issue',[42] while more cautiously Pethick-Lawrence claimed that the suffragettes cost the Liberals thirty to forty seats.[43] The activities of the militants were anti-Liberal, but it is difficult to substantiate such sweeping claims. Whatever their impact at by-elections, and despite their flair for publicity, the suffragettes were weakened by the dispersal of their limited forces in, and the submergence of their single-issue obsession by, the general election. In the seats in which they conducted their most sustained campaigns, those held by Cabinet Ministers, there is little evidence for their claims. In January 1910 in five of these seats the Ministers did better than Liberals in adjacent constituencies, in six they did worse. The three Ministers who faced the most intensive barrage, Asquith, Burns and Harcourt, were amongst the five who did better than neighbouring Liberals.

Yet the impact of the female suffragist agitation cannot be dismissed quite so simply. The direct effect of the electoral activities of the suffragettes may have been of little moment, but the issue itself was inimical to the Liberal cause. No Unionist supporter of women's suffrage need have any pangs about voting against the Government, yet Liberal supporters of the suffragists were torn. The issue had provided a challenge to Liberalism which a Liberal Government had lamentably failed to meet. Female suffrage was a liberal cause, and the majority of Liberal Members favoured the principle, even if they did not always agree on the political wisdom of various enfranchising proposals. The failure of the Liberal Government to grasp this difficult nettle disappointed many ardent Liberals, while the Government's unimaginative and insensitive handling of the militants outraged them.

The last months of 1909 were a peculiarly inopportune time to begin the unwise policy of forcibly feeding hunger-striking suffragettes. Two able Liberal journalists, H. W. Nevinson and H. N. Brailsford, resigned from the *Daily News* in October 1909 in protest against that paper's wavering stand on women's suffrage, the forcible-feeding question being the occasion for their going.[44] An angry Liberal vicar wrote to the Home Secretary, Herbert Gladstone:

> It was from your honoured father that many like myself learned how Liberal and Progressive thought is seen to be consistent with loyalty to old Church principles. With what grief and amazement do we see you, his son, driven to sanction brutal outrages upon defenceless women whose offence is primarily political. Is this a time, when the Government will need every assistance to carry through its fiscal policy, to arouse the righteous indignation of those who have never yet given a vote to the political opponents of the Government, but who must now withhold sympathy and support from what is seen to be tyranny masquerading as Liberalism?[45]

The vicar was exaggerating. Yet the Government's 'do-nothing' policy and its harsh administrative practices not only exacerbated the problem, but compromised the very spirit of Liberalism. At the very moment the Government was seeking to rally all its supporters, it was antagonising some of its most ardent partisans. Such men, despite their threats, probably voted for the Liberals in 1910: but they probably also refrained from active work in the Liberal cause. Brailsford for one devoted his talents to ousting the Liberal Belloc, a vocal anti-suffragist.[46] The harm to Liberal fortunes came not from the aggressive electoral campaigns of the suffragettes but rather from the disillusion of good Liberals with the Liberalism of their own Government.

II

While the secular pressure groups were primarily or even solely organised for political ends, the churches were not. They were communities of varying coherence bound together by purposes distinctly non-political. Within or related to these communities, there were organisations closely comparable to the secular pressure groups, e.g. the National Society, the Catholic Association, and the Liberation Society. But the activities and influence of these organisations were greatly limited by the prevailing attitudes within the particular church, and their authority circumscribed by the spiritual leaders of the various churches. Probably the key role in setting the political tone of a church was played by its spiritual leaders. But the extent of their influence also depended on how far their views related to prevailing attitudes amongst the lesser clergy and laity.

Much has been written of the forces that in the last years of the nineteenth century were undermining denominational religion and eroding the religious habits of the nation.[47] By 1910 these had made themselves felt in declining church attendance, in declining church building and, particularly in the Anglican Church, in the falling off in recruits for the ministry. The boom in church membership characteristic of the second half of the nineteenth century had ended, although the long-term trend had been masked by the Welsh revival of 1904-5 and the apparent vitality of the Nonconformist churches. But by 1910 even the sluggish growth of the Nonconformists has ceased. Nevertheless it seems probable that a substantial minority of voters still had more than a merely nominal connection with a church.[48] And, as we have seen, although the partisans of the major parties were not sharply distinguished by age, occupation or education, a partisan religious cleavage was apparent.

Furthermore, recent events tended to involve the churches in politics and hence encourage partisan attitudes among church members. The controversy aroused by Balfour's Education Bill of 1902 had produced sectarian conflicts to a degree unknown for a generation, and the controversy was far from exhausted in 1910. Indeed, the events of the 1906 Parliament had served to exacerbate feelings, at least among the militants on both sides. The conduct of the House of Lords on this issue, as well as its treatment of the Licensing Bill and its known attitude to Welsh Disestablishment, drew the churches into the constitutional conflict central to the two elections.

Although the educational controversy revived the traditional alliance
between the Anglican Church and the Tory Party, and although since
1906 the Church had depended on the House of Lords to preserve its
educational position, the leaders of the Anglican Church strove to
maintain a position of non-alignment. Led by the astute Randall
Davidson, Archbishop of Canterbury, who possessed the facility
amounting to genius of appearing moderate on any issue, doctrinal or
political, the bishops as a whole resisted identifying themselves too
closely with the Unionist Party. The majority of the spiritual peers
displayed a genuine sympathy for Liberal social legislation, in marked
contrast to the expedient acceptance of such measures by the Unionist
peers. Most of the bishops showed sympathy for Liberal licensing
legislation.

On the education question the majority of the bishops were markedly
more moderate than the Tory peers, indeed one of their number,
Percival, Bishop of Hereford, supported the Liberal measures. While
the fiery Knox, Bishop of Manchester, fulminated against the 1906 bill,
the Archbishop of Canterbury was 'so strongly in favour of [a com-
promise] that he is no longer consulted by the Tory Chiefs'.[49] When
the attempt at conciliation was renewed in 1908, a clear majority of the
bishops favoured the compromise proposals of the Runciman Bill, but
were foiled by a revolt of the clergy and laity.[50]

The non-alignment of the Anglican hierarchy was furthered by the
Budget controversy. In private Randall Davidson advised strongly
against rejection, despite Sandars's lurid picture of the use of a money
bill to disestablish the Church. In public he advised the bishops to
abstain from what would be a strictly party division, reiterating his
growing belief that 'the Bishops act wisely in . . . sitting loose to party
ties'.[51] Most of the spiritual peers followed the advice of the Primate,
while the exceptions to this self-denying ordinance tended to strengthen
the non-party image of the church. Five of the spiritual peers, including
the Archbishop of York, Cosmo Gordon Lang, who made a telling
maiden speech against rejection, voted with the Liberals. Only one, the
aged Bishop of Lincoln, voted with the Opposition.

In their diocesan letters on the elections, the Archbishop of Canterbury and the majority of the bishops warned against the profound
spiritual damage done in using the pulpit for political ends, and avoided
all mention of controversial topics. Canterbury himself deprecated
churchmen forcing politico-religious questions such as Welsh Disestablishment and education during the elections. 'I honestly believe

that we best serve the interests both of Church and Nation by abstaining from identifying ourselves vociferously with one side or the other in an acute political conflict wherein Church questions occupy really a subordinate place.'[52]

Some of the bishops disagreed with this policy on the grounds expressed by Liverpool in his annual diocesan letter that it would be impossible for him to vote for anyone who 'intended to oppose definite religious education in our elementary schools' or 'was prepared to support the disestablishment of the Church'.[53] Some were partisan on more broadly political grounds. In embattled Wales, the Bishop of St David's urged an anti-Liberal vote not only because of Disestablishment, but also because it was necessary to preserve the veto of the House of Lords as 'a guarantee for national stability'.[54] Like all Irishmen, the Anglican Primate, the Archbishop of Armagh, saw politics in terms of a single issue, Home Rule. 'Morally, it is the great betrayal; logically it is the great fallacy; religiously it is the great break-up; imperially it is the great breakdown.'[55] Knox, the Bishop of Manchester, actively campaigned, appearing on Unionist platforms, arguing publicly for the Unionist cause, and writing letters commending particular Unionist candidates to their constituents.[56] On the other hand, the Liberal Percival of Hereford wrote to all his clergy stating that 'the plain duty of everyone of us is to support the Government and the House of Commons as the representatives of the people in their conflict with the Lords'.[57]

Nevertheless these were exceptions: non-alignment remained throughout the prevailing philosophy of the episcopal bench. Not so for the Church as a whole, which not surprisingly disliked neutrality. The Liberal attack on the voluntary schools had aroused the fighting spirit of the lesser clergy and the laity, and in the ultra-Tory Cecils and Halifax, and in Sir Alfred Cripps, Vicar-General of Canterbury and York, the laity had its leaders. Leading lay activists had distrusted the moderation of the bishops on the education question; now Cripps condemned the 'harmful inaction' of Canterbury as beneficial to the Liberals.[58]

Throughout the country the various organisations set up to defend the Anglican schools were active, and many of the clergy were vocal in their service. The Bishop of Hereford accused Lord Robert Cecil of degrading the National Society by turning it into 'the electioneering office of one particular party'.[59] Lord Salisbury appealed to his coreligionists to consider the 'preservation of the endowments of the

Church and the maintenance of religious teaching in the schools as taking precedence of all political issues'.[60] His advice was widely echoed. 'It is simply painful', wrote one of George Lansbury's clerical sympathisers, 'to see the way in which church folk are being given the tip to vote Tory under cover of Church Defence in Wales (i.e. of money bags) & of opposing Liberal Education policies.'[61] A *Te Deum*, arranged at Plumstead by the local vicar to celebrate the defeat of the Labour M.P., Will Crooks, was cancelled on the orders of the Bishop of Southwark.[62]

It was in Lancashire that the Anglican–Unionist alliance was most evident. A vigorous Tory bishop in Manchester, a strong evangelical tradition, and a large resident Catholic-Irish population, produced a spirit of militant co-operation between the Church and the party. 'In Liverpool', claimed the *Manchester Guardian*, 'the divisions are religious rather than political. . . . The German Emperor gives place to the Pope as the real bogy, and the Protestant workman . . . will show to you beyond doubt that the real objection to Home Rule is that under an Irish Government Ireland would be simply a jumping-off ground for the Papal Bodyguard.'[63] One of the junior Whips, Balcarres, who sat for a Lancashire constituency, wanted from the party leaders 'some reference to Education in order to show Lancashire that our interest has not abated in the question.'[64] Lancashire's certainly had not, and many Liberal candidates in the county hedged their commitment to the party's education and disestablishment policies. The *Lancashire Daily Post* considered that the Conservative victors at Preston 'owe their overwhelming victory . . . mainly to the religious question'.[65]

But Anglican fervour did not always benefit the Unionists. Lancashire's Anglicanism was strongly evangelical, protestant and anti-ritualistic. It was ominous that at a Liverpool demonstration of the Church Association, at which most local Unionist candidates were present, the theme of the meeting was 'neither Home Rule in Ireland nor Rome Rule in England'. One speaker even attacked Balfour for helping 'to Romanise the Bench of Bishops'.[66] All the Unionist candidates in Liverpool gave their allegiance to the strongly protestant policy of the powerful Laymen's League.[67] Ironically, the High Churchman Lord Robert Cecil, who had worked harder than most to arouse the Anglican laity in the Conservative interest, was the most prominent victim of Lancashire's anti-ritualism. Throughout his campaign at Blackburn he was attacked for his opposition to the anti-ritualist Ecclesiastical Disorders Bill and on polling day sandwichmen paraded with boards proclaiming, 'Every vote given to Cecil is a vote against

Protestantism'.[68] A more congenial campaign to the militant Low Churchmen was probably that at West Ham led by John Kensit, the most notorious anti-ritualist of the day, against the Liberal High Churchman and junior Minister, Charles Masterman, who was suspected of 'Popish tendencies'. Kensit's charges, however, were offset by the staunch support given to Masterman by that impeccable anti-papist the Baptist leader, Dr Clifford.[69]

It could be argued that all this Anglican activity made little difference because for social and economic reasons the Anglican voter leant naturally towards Unionism. In such circumstances, even the Canterbury policy of non-alignment favoured the Unionist interest. Yet Anglican apathy appears to have damaged the Unionists in 1906,[70] and the need to activate the Anglican vote in the Unionist cause should not be under-estimated, particularly in Lancashire, where Anglicanism and affluence did not always go hand in hand.

While the activation of the Anglican vote in the Unionist interest was probably only marginally significant, the aligning of the Nonconformist vote with the Liberals was more crucial. Unlike the Anglican, the Nonconformist voter was much more likely to be subject to cross pressures, his economic and class interests pulling him towards Unionism, his traditional and religious ties towards the Liberals. In 1906 these conflicting forces had been resolved in the Liberal favour, for the forces of dissent had been 'united in wrath' against the Government of Arthur Balfour;[71] in 1910 ominous cracks appeared. One ran horizontally, separating clergy from congregations; another vertically, separating the denominations.

By contrast with the Anglicans the militant keynote was struck by the leading Nonconformist divines. John Clifford of the Baptists, Silvester Horne of the Congregationalists, Scott Lidgett of the Wesleyan Methodists, were in the electoral vanguard of Nonconformity, and Free Church clergymen throughout the country gave them solid backing. Even 'the quiet men' of the ministry 'rally at the present time as they have never done before'.[72]

For most of the leading Nonconformist clerics religious issues were the immediate cause of their involvement. For Clifford, of passive-resistance fame, education was the first consideration. 'Sectarianism must be cast out of the state schools. Its presence is an intolerable wrong to the child, to the teaching profession, to the ratepayers, and to the nation.'[73] The election manifestos of the National Free Church Council gave education first place. Licensing too stirred clerical passions. Scott

Lidgett confessed that 'the contemptuous rejection of the Licensing Bill ... is the determining motive of my own action',[74] as did many Methodists who considered that licensing was 'our question before the party politicians made it a party question'.[75]

But few of the clerics were concerned only with religious questions. It may be, as a Nonconformist critic of political Nonconformity argued, that the educational struggle had encouraged Nonconformists 'to a greatly intensified activity in the general fields of politics, with which, as Nonconformists, they had no concern at all'.[76] Yet it could be argued that wider political questions were of concern to Nonconformists as Nonconformists. The recent acts of the House of Lords were challenges to Nonconformity. '... the Upper House is the champion and bulwark of sectarianism in the schools ... and of the Drink Trade. Unless that power of Veto is destroyed no reforms in these directions are possible.'[77] Moreover traditionally the House of Commons had widened political and social opportunity for Dissenters. 'Our history, our principles, and our needs,' wrote Scott Lidgett, 'make us extremely tenacious of the privileges of the House of Commons.'[78] Equally, the House of Lords had fought a stubborn rearguard action against such changes. Finally, it was the Civil War come again. For the Reverend John Shakespeare Lords Milner and Curzon were 'simply Strafford Redivivus'.[79] Thus from a mixture of immediate interest, sentiment and tradition the Nonconformist leaders were active partisans in the political struggle.

But a wide social concern also bound many of the Nonconformist clerics to the Liberal cause. Partly in reaction to the excessive individualism of Victorian Nonconformity, partly in an effort to reconcile the working classes to the chapels and partly from a real sympathy for the plight of the Edwardian poor, a number of Nonconformist leaders had laid great stress on the social gospel, on the role of the churches as agents for social reform.[80] The social gospel had much in common with, indeed was often the inspiration of, the 'new Liberalism' which sought, in the words of one writer 'a via media between Collectivism, Conservative or Socialist, and the decaying individualism of the Benthamite and Cobdenite epoch...'.[81] These ideas provided a further link between the Liberals and the Nonconformist élite, and the rejection of the Budget was seen not just as a refutation of the new Liberalism, but as a denial of the social gospel. John Clifford echoed Lloyd George in seeing the election as a 'contest ... between the idea that human life is ... a brotherhood of man with man, and the idea that it is the subjection of one class to the service and to the pleasure of another'.[82]

For many of the Nonconformist divines these motives merged to give the electoral struggle the character of a crusade. In the *Baptist Times* Clifford wrote: 'Intrinsically it is a fight for truth, for justice, for humanity ... it is also a war between Christian and anti-Christian ideals of individual and national living.'[83] Writing privately to a friend he prophesied: '... at last it seems possible to have a hand-to-hand fight with all the tyrannies and despotisms at once ... 1910 will open with Armageddon.'[84]

The National Free Church Council might protest that it had been forced reluctantly into the political fray, but there were few signs of reluctance in its preparations for battle. The 1910 Report of the Council noted: 'Free Church demonstrations were arranged everywhere, and all possible steps were taken to influence the opinion of Free Churchmen in the crisis.'[85] These demonstrations were organised in major centres at both elections, and were usually addressed by clergymen, although the most spectacular of them all, at the Queen's Hall on 16 December 1909, had Lloyd George himself. During the first election the Council distributed 1,500,000 leaflets.[86] As the indignant Nonconformist layman, Sir Robert Perks protested: '... manifestoes are being showered upon their people as though they were revelations from heaven.' He decried the fact that 'the fiery cross is to be carried throughout the land by preachers who have convinced themselves that they are called by God to smite "the hereditary foes of Nonconformity" hip and thigh'.[87] Clifford himself appealed to all Free Churchmen to give up their week-night meetings and canvass for Liberal and Labour men.[88] By his prodigious activity he set a notable example. Up and down the country the dissenting clerics were on the platform. 'If you can submit to the tyrannical yoke of landlordism then you are worse than wriggling worms,' cried one during the second election.[89] 'In no election in our memory', commented *Blackwood's Magazine* on the January campaign, 'was there so much ill-omened activity among the dissenting clergy.'[90]

In such an atmosphere the chapels themselves did not remain inviolate, often functioning as *de facto* committee rooms and serving as meeting places for the Liberals. It was alleged that in Wales a chapel was completely covered with Liberal posters,[91] while in Colne Valley, according to Grayson, the Liberals organised chapel parties 'to lubricate the Nonconformist conscience with gratuitous coffee'.[92] In the words of the *Blackwood's Magazine* article quoted above, 'Every Pleasant Sunday Afternoon sent forth a horde of canvassers, convinced by much

turgid oratory that the cause of Liberalism was the cause of God'. The
Pleasant Sunday Afternoon programme at the Congregational Church
in Walsall during the first election was typical – discussions on 'The
Tyrant Lords'.[93]

Even divine service could not escape the political fervour. The Welsh
chapel garbed outside in posters had its pulpit decked with Liberal
placards. While the prayer

> Take my vote and let it be
> Consecrated Lord to thee.
> Guide my hand that I may trace
> Crosses in the proper place.[94]

heard in a Sheffield pulpit was innocuous, some sermons sought to
indicate 'the proper place'. The *Standard* complained of 'ferocious
partisan harangues ... delivered on the Sabbath to a congregation
supposed to be assembled for religious worship'.[95] One Shropshire
Unionist M.P. heard on 'good authority' that 'in Wales many of the
Nonconformist Ministers tell their congregations from the pulpit that
anybody voting Tory will be drafted straight to Hades'.[96] In a sermon
at Plymouth a Methodist minister refused to accept that 'at a time when
braggart privilege and vested interest sit enthroned in our land, the
pulpit of Jesus Christ is to be silent'. He then proceeded to castigate the
enemy with a vehemence that would have earned plaudits from Lloyd
George.[97] At Grimsby a service was brought to a premature close when
one of the congregation protested against a political sermon.[98]

The *Standard* concluded, in an article on the Nonconformist campaign, that 'Nonconformity remains the backbone of the Liberal Party,
which would fare very badly indeed without the assistance of the
pastors and the votes of their flocks'.[99] If this contemporary conclusion
is too sweeping we can at least agree with the more moderate statement
of a recent student of the Edwardian Liberal Party that 'the party's
association with the Free Churches undoubtedly enabled it to win
support among what would otherwise have been Conservative social
groups: merchants, professional men, manufacturers'.[100]

Yet many Nonconformists in these social groups were faltering in
their allegiance to the Liberal Party. The historian of the Congregational Union, one of the more political of the sects, has noted that 1906
'was probably the last occasion on which the denomination as represented by the Union stood solidly behind the Liberal ... party'.[101] Even
Clifford, a born enthusiast, confessed in December 1910 that in the

January contest 'Free Churchmen fought . . . with less unity, energy and organisation than before'.[102] The monolithic nature of Nonconformist support for Liberalism, weakening in the late nineteenth century but restored by the agitation over Balfour's Education Bill, was breaking, this time irretrievably, on the social and economic policies of the Liberal Government.[103]

A correspondent to *The Times* summed up one of the splits developing: 'It may be that a majority of Free Church Ministers support the present Government, but a very large proportion of the laity do not follow them.'[104] The electoral revolt of the laity was personified by Sir Robert Perks, Liberal M.P. for Louth, 1892–1910. His Nonconformist credentials were impeccable – a founder of the National Free Church Council, chairman of the House of Commons Nonconformist committee, and the leading layman of the Wesleyan Methodist Church. He was also a wealthy financier and engineering contractor, and as has been seen a Roseberyite who disliked many of the tendencies of modern Liberalism and had broken openly with the party over the Budget.

A few days after Lloyd George's Queen's Hall meeting, Sir Robert wrote a letter to *The Times* which revealed the disquiet of a significant segment of the Nonconformist laity. In this letter Perks challenged the authority of the Free Church Council to represent the Free Churches, particularly the Wesleyan Methodist Church, condemned the political clergymen, denied that the Liberal Government had done or was likely to do much for Nonconformity and claimed that Nonconformists bitterly rued the day that they had chosen to follow Gladstone and Home Rule.[105]

The critics dismissed Perks as representing 'only a small knot of comparatively wealthy Methodists'.[106] He certainly did this. Many of the prominent organisers and supporters of the Nonconformist Anti-Socialist Union, founded in April 1909 with the apparently contradictory aims of resisting socialism and ousting politics from the churches, seem to have been wealthy Methodists.[107] But Nonconformist discontent with the Liberals spread beyond this narrow body. Many middle- and lower-middle-class Nonconformists feared socialism more than they disliked the Education Act or the Welsh establishment. This fear led to suspicion of the social gospel. Perks referred to the only two Wesleyan clerics on Lloyd George's platform as 'avowed socialists of a somewhat nebulous type'.[108] Another prominent Methodist layman, Henry Fowler, Viscount Wolverhampton, formerly Perks's law partner and now equally disillusioned with most aspects of Liberalism except office, was much disturbed by the 'socialistic teaching given in many ... [Methodist] pulpits'.[109] The secretary of the Nonconformist Anti-Socialist Union, admittedly biased, alleged that 50 per cent of Non-conformist ministers had socialist ideas.[110]

Nonconformist dissatisfaction was reinforced by the feeling among many of the militants that the Liberal Government had not been noticeably diligent to remedy Nonconformist grievances, and that in education matters it had been all too willing to give concessions to Catholics at the expense of Nonconformist principles.[111] On the other hand, less rabid Nonconformists were realising that in practice the Balfour Education Act was not so damaging to their interests as had been feared: '... while politicians are trying unsuccessfully to settle it, the education question is quietly settling itself.'[112]

Nor should spiritual disquiet be ignored as a further factor under-mining the Liberal–Nonconformist alliance. There were those in the Nonconformist congregation who feared that the soul was neglected in the social gospel, that 'Nonconformity cannot ... afford to leave unregarded the possibility that, in the winning of some meaner world, it has lost, or is losing, its own soul'.[113] A renewed emphasis on the spirit was not uncongenial to the growing social conservatism of the Nonconformist laity.

Not only was there this split between elements of the laity and the clerical élite, there were also distinctions between the Free Churches themselves. Amongst the Calvinistic Methodists with their strong Welsh base, and amongst the Primitive Methodists, most proletarian of the Nonconformist denominations, there were few of the cross-pressures affecting affluent and English Nonconformists. The Congrega-tionalists and the Baptists maintained with somewhat diminished vigour the militant radicalism that had long set them apart. On the other hand the Wesleyan Methodist Church, the aristocrat of the Nonconformist denominations with probably the wealthiest congrega-tion, was the centre of disquiet. Many of the strongest critics of political Nonconformity and most of the Unionist Nonconformist candidates came from this sect.[114] The President of the Wesleyan Methodist Conference seems to have been the only leading Nonconformist clergy-man to declare publicly for a policy of political neutrality.[115] The *Methodist Recorder*, widely distributed among the Wesleyans, also followed a course unique in the Nonconformist press. It was quite untainted with the prevailing enthusiasm for Liberalism, demanding that church life be kept 'free from the intrusion of alien matters', and lamenting the approach of the second election as harmful to the churches if not to the country.[116] There were, of course, many Wesleyan Methodist ministers active in the Liberal cause, but resistance to the Nonconformist–Liberal alliance does seem to have been peculiarly strong among the Wesleyans.

Nonconformist support for the Liberals was undoubtedly still substantial, but the elections revealed a breach between the clerical élite and significant elements of the laity, as well as between the sects. The distinctive middle-class drift from the Liberals, apparent in the results, was almost certainly in part a Nonconformist drift. The solidarity of the Nonconformist vote for the Liberals in 1906 had been a temporary phenomenon, not a lasting renewal of the traditional allegiance of Dissent. As the sectarian passions unleashed by Balfour's Education Bill died down and as Liberal policies alienated middle-class opinion, so the old alliance was eroded.

The Church of Scotland played no active political role, although the Liberalism of the agricultural Scottish lowlands was explained partly in terms of the separation between the Anglicised and Episcopalian gentry and the Presbyterian middle and labouring classes.[117] In Ireland the Presbyterian Church was firmly aligned with the Protestant establishment in defence of the Union. This church and some of the Irish Nonconformist churches exported their Ulster clergymen to Great Britain to preach against Home Rule to their fellow Protestants. These itinerant clerics were common during the elections, in Nonconformist Devon and Cornwall, sectarian Lancashire, and the Hibernian Clyde Valley.

Clifford, frank as ever, declared during the first election that 'the mass of the English Romanists will be against us',[118] The adjective is important for the problems facing the Catholic Church during the elections were ethnic as well as religious. In Great Britain the Church was composed of two disparate elements: the relatively well-to-do English Catholics, and the mainly working-class Irish Catholics. Here was the source of political tension within the Catholic community.

The Catholic Church was as committed as the Anglican to maintaining its entrenched educational position under the Balfour Act, 'the Magna Carta of our liberties',[119] and was hostile to Liberal attempts to amend the Act. On the other hand, the Catholic Church in Ireland was the ally of the Nationalists, and thus of a Ministry pledged to Home Rule. Thus there were difficulties in linking the Catholic Church in Great Britain with the hereditary enemies of Ireland in defence of the

Church schools. The difficulties were aggravated in the second election when, with the Irish question to the fore, the equation of Home Rule with Rome rule bred anti-Catholic prejudice throughout Great Britain.

In the January election the Catholic hierarchy in England seemed more concerned with its schools than with Ireland. Under the lead of Francis Bourne, Archbishop of Westminster, the Catholic bishops issued a pastoral letter stressing education, and containing a question to be addressed to all candidates.[120] In a few cases Liberal answers were denounced from the pulpit, and in most cases the responses secured by the local branches of the Catholic Federation were placed on the church notice boards.[121] In Lancashire at least, the Catholic Federation classified all responses as satisfactory or otherwise, and forwarded their classified list to parish priests and the press. This action was approved by the *Tablet*, which condemned 'all sorts of equivocations and cryptic replies' and commended the officers of the Catholic Federation for foiling 'these shuffling tactics'.[122] Rowland Hunt, Unionist M.P. for Ludlow, found that 'The Catholic priests in my division, & I believe in the whole of Shropshire, worked very hard for the Unionists. I think that most if not nearly all the non-Irish priests did the same.'[123]

But Hunt spoke of, and the London *Tablet* for, conservative English Catholicism. Very different was the attitude of the *Catholic Times* of Liverpool. It disapproved of the emphasis on education, and was far more lenient with candidates' replies than the *Tablet*.[124] Although it had little love for the fanatical Nonconformists, it had even less love for the Orange candidates in Liverpool. Thus it urged Liberals to respond affirmatively to the bishops' questions, noting of that ambiguous catechism that it was 'one that candidates of any political party should find no difficulty in answering satisfactorily'.[125] A considerable number of anti-Unionist candidates complied, particularly in Lancashire where, of course, they were also subject to strong Anglican pressure on the education question.

The Irish Nationalists, in pursuit of a Home Rule majority, also actively encouraged a Liberal vote amongst Catholics in Great Britain. Leading Irish Members crossed to England to get out the Irish Catholic vote for the Liberals. They appealed to their co-religionists to support the party pledged to Home Rule, while promising them that the Catholic Nationalist Party would protect their schools. The local branches of the United Irish League came to life, issued manifestos, and following directions from above instructed the local Irish to vote for the anti-Unionist candidates.

The Irish vote was concentrated in several key areas – Clydeside, Lancashire, Tyneside and Durham – and seems to have been fairly effectively marshalled behind the anti-Unionists. Unionists estimated that this vote gave their opponents an extra twenty seats in England,[126] while the *Scotsman* estimated that, if the Irish had abstained, the Unionists would have won eight more seats and, if they had voted with the Unionists, the party would have won altogether an extra nineteen seats in Scotland.[127]

TABLE 16.1 SEATS WON BY LIBERALS IN JAN 1910 IN SCOTLAND IN WHICH LIBERAL MAJORITY LESS THAN ESTIMATED IRISH CATHOLIC VOTE

Seat	Irish Catholic Vote	Liberal	Labour	Unionist	Majority
Dumbartonshire	2200	8640		7607	1033
West Fife	1900	6159	4736	1994	1423
North-West Lanark	2000	8422	1718	7528	894
Mid-Lanark	2000	5792	3864	5401	391
North-East Lanark	2400	9105	2160	7012	2093
North Ayrshire	250	6189	1801	5951	238
College	1300	6535		5823	712
Partick	700	10093		9522	571

Source: Irish Catholic figures, *Scotsman*, 18 Nov 1909.

The Unionists were not the only victims of the Irish vote. The Labour Party suffered too. In the very areas where the Irish vote was concentrated, the Labour Party was trying to break into the political system. Irish working-class support or the lack of it was frequently crucial for the Labour candidate.

In January 1910 the U.I.L.'s instructions to Irish voters were unequivocal. In all straight fights they were to vote for the anti-Unionist candidate whether he be Liberal or Labour. In three-cornered contests Redmond outlined U.I.L. policy at Leigh, one of the seats concerned:

> Their policy as between Liberal and Labour was to choose the one who was going to win, and advise the Irish electors to vote for him. They were perfectly impartial, but there was one type of Labour candidate which they always refused to adopt, and that was the hopeless and the wrecking one.[128]

In practice the U.I.L. tended to treat every Labour candidate in a triangular contest as a 'hopeless and wrecking one'. In every triangular contest in Scotland the Irish vote was ordered behind the Liberal.[129] In England the Irish vote was instructed for Labour in only two triangular contests – at Gateshead, one of the two seats in which a sitting Labour M.P. was being attacked by the Liberals,[130] and at Middlesbrough where the Labour candidate, Patrick Walls, was himself a Catholic, and a strong defender of the Catholic schools. Even at Middlesbrough, where Irish Catholics constituted some 15 per cent of the electorate, strong local pressure was necessary before the U.I.L. leaders declared for Walls.[131]

The Labour leaders were naturally angered by these directives. In his address from the chair at the 1910 Labour Party Conference Keir Hardie condemned this anti-Labour marshalling of the Irish vote 'without regard being taken to the actual facts or circumstances of the local situation', and warned that the rallying of the working class to the Home Rule cause would not be 'hastened by the heads of the Irish organisation . . . using their power to bludgeon down Labour candidates in every case in which the Liberals think fit to oppose them'.[132] Hardie's bitterness is understandable and his charges justified. There seems to have been little effort to assess the local situation; instead the vote seems to have been allocated automatically to the Liberals. For example at Camlachie the Labour candidate, O'Connor Kessack, took a much stronger line on Home Rule than the ex-Unionist M.P. and now Liberal candidate, Alexander Cross, yet the Irish vote was instructed for Cross.[133]

The Irish position however is understandable. The *petit bourgeois* Nationalist Party had little in common with the Labour Party, and certainly no desire to share a possibly pivotal position in the new Parliament. Moreover Redmond was giving Asquith his *quid pro quo* for the Home Rule pledge. He had no wish to devalue the significance of the Irish vote in Great Britain by permitting its dissipation. The course seems too to have been tactically sound. Any division of the Irish vote between the two anti-Unionist candidates would have cost the anti-Unionists seats, while in many cases even if the Irish vote had been given solidly to the Labour man, he would still not have won the seat. If in Table 16.1 we assume that the Labour candidate had no Irish votes and the Liberal candidate all the Irish votes, an even division of that vote would have cost the anti-Unionists two of the five three-cornered contests. Using the same assumptions, if the whole of the Irish vote had been transferred from the Liberal candidate to the Labour candidate, the Labour Party would have won two seats, and the other three would have been lost to the Unionists.

Thus considerable Liberal compliance with Catholic educational demands and the work of the U.I.L. gave the Liberal Party substantial Catholic support in January 1910. In the second election the strains on the Catholic vote were considerably reduced. With their schools firmly secured by the dominating parliamentary position of the Nationalists, and with the emphasis on Home Rule stirring ugly anti-Catholic sentiment,[134] the Catholic bishops contracted out, counselling that the election involved no strictly religious principle.[135] While the strains on Catholic consciences were thereby reduced, the strains on Irish working-class voters were also eased by the minimal number of triangular contests in the second election. It seems likely that the Irish Catholic vote in Great Britain was in December 1910 more solidly behind the Liberals than for many years. This was certainly the opinion of T. P. O'Connor, who had been fighting English elections since 1885. '... the Irish masses', he wrote during the second election, 'are voting with an enthusiasm and a unanimity ... unparalleled in any previous contest ... at least for the last twenty years.'[136]

PART FOUR

The Results Examined

The Electoral System

I

'Our present system of representation was an accumulated patchwork, composed partly of a little conviction, partly of a little concession, and partly of a little cowardice.' So spoke Lewis Harcourt of the electoral system under which the 1910 elections were fought.[1] That 'patchwork' was composed of five major acts passed a generation before – the Ballot Act (1872), the Corrupt and Illegal Practices Act (1883), the Franchise Act (1884), the Redistribution Act (1885) and the Registration Act (1885) – plus a host of lesser measures passed over several centuries. Much of the electoral system, particularly the franchise and registration elements, had evolved haphazardly through a long process of cumulative legislation. As Lowell observed in 1908: 'The present condition of the franchise is, indeed, historical rather than rational.'[2]

It was also excessively complicated. This complexity flowed not only from a lack of logic in the system's evolution, and an accompanying failure to codify the law, but also from the circumstances of the reforming acts of the 1880s. Each of the measures was the product of a Whig Liberal Cabinet palsied by the decay of the old coalition and presided over by a Prime Minister who considered it his 'singular fate to love the antiquities of our constitution much more even than the average Tory of the present day'.[3] If all the measures originated from a Cabinet compromise, some were passed with the co-operation of the Conservative Opposition. The Corrupt Practices Act was passed with the active support of the Opposition Front Bench;[4] the details of the Redistribution Bill were framed by an incongruous cabal composed of Gladstone, Dilke, Hartington, Salisbury and Northcote.[5] One result was the preservation of anomalies that a more coherent Cabinet or a more united and confident party would have swept away; a second was the tainting of Liberal principles with Whig and Conservative practices.

The generous principles of the Franchise Act were undermined by the failure to overhaul the antiquated registration machinery. The

Redistribution Act of 1885, although the most sweeping of the century, embodied 'at best only a vague approximation to equal electoral districts'.[6] The support engendered on both sides of the House for the Corrupt Practices Act resulted from the fact that while the measure embodied Radical principles it also served a conservative objective. The measure aimed not so much at broadening the ruling class, as at securing it from the assault of the plutocracy.[7]

No interpretation of the results of the 1910 elections can be worth while unless based on an understanding of this hodge-podge of conviction, concession and compromise. The biases and imperfections of the electoral system influenced the pattern of representation. With no public opinion polls and no detailed breakdown of constituency figures, a study of the elections of 1910 can provide only tentative conclusions as to why people voted as they did in January and December of that year, but it can provide some estimate of the contribution of the electoral order to the particular results which ensued. The reduction of the working-class electorate by the registration process, the distinctive bias in favour of the Celtic fringe in the distribution of seats, the inflation of the solid middle- and upper-class vote through plural voting all condition any interpretation of the results.

Moreover in the elections of 1910 the election system itself was at issue in the campaign, references to electoral matters occurring in 36 per cent of the candidates' addresses in January and in 27 per cent in December.[8] The peremptory rejection of the Plural Voting Bill of 1906 and the London Elections Bill of 1909 appeared among the lesser crimes in the Liberal indictment against the House of Lords. Plural voting, remaining franchise limitations, and the registration procedures were condemned by Liberal and Labour candidates; gross discrepancies in the distribution of seats by Unionists. Lastly, the ubiquitous suffragettes were a constant reminder of the most comprehensive disfranchisement of all.

II[9]

The state of the franchise in 1910 was a maze in which few felt competent to tread. It is possible to distinguish seven distinct franchises: the property, freemen, university, occupation, household, service and lodger franchises. Of these, the household franchise was by far the most important. With the occupation franchise, a relatively minor franchise with which it was coupled in the register, it accounted for 85·2 per cent of the electorate in the United Kingdom in 1910. Apart from the sex disqualification the franchise provisions appear both liberal and comprehensive. The household franchise would seem to establish a head of household suffrage; the service franchise was generous although erratic and open to manipulation, and while the £10 value level for lodgings had been deliberately exclusive when introduced in 1867,[10] by 1910 it was less so. Yet in 1910 there were only 7,695,602 voters on the register of the United Kingdom out of an estimated adult male population of 11,911,618. Even this proportion, approximately 65 per cent, exaggerates, for the register contains at least half a million plural voters so that in fact only about 60 per cent of all adult males were entitled to vote in 1910. Why?

Lunatics, criminals, aliens, paupers, peers and certain officials concerned with the conduct of elections were explicitly debarred. These accounted for about 800,000 of the nearly five million adult males not on the register. A larger but more indefinite number, including bachelors living with their parents, domestic servants resident with their employers, soldiers living in barracks and most seamen were indirectly excluded because their accommodation failed to conform to any of the franchise requirements. Not counting bachelors living with their parents, for whom it is impossible to give a figure, those indirectly excluded numbered about one million.[11]

There thus remained about three million adult males whose nonappearance on the register was unexplained by specific disfranchisements or by the various gaps in the franchise system. The explanation for their absence seems to lie in the registration system. Strict successive occupation clauses meant an annual disqualification of about one million voters. To qualify, all but owners had to have continuously occupied the qualifying premises for twelve months preceding 15 July, except that any changes of residence within the same franchise and the same borough, or within the same county division, did not count as a break in continuity.

Apathy undoubtedly swelled the ranks of the unregistered but apathy itself was fostered by a registration system 'so replete with technicalities, complications and anomalies that every obstacle is put in the way of getting on, and every facility exists for getting struck off, the register'.[12] For example many problems arose out of the disputed definitions of separate dwelling and separate occupation. '... the law of household suffrage is in such a condition of confusion, muddle and scholastic refinement that it is in many cases absolutely impossible to decide whether a person is a householder or a lodger.'[13] Yet the distinction was often crucial. The latchkey decisions in Devonport, which according to the Liberals cost them the two Devonport seats in 1910, turned on the definition of separate lodgings.[14]

The registration courts were full of hazards. The party agents battling for advantage used technicalities and even clerical errors to eliminate claimants. The whims of the revising barristers added a further unpredictable element, particularly in relation to the much contested lodger and service franchises. 'Some are most niggardly in allowing claims. Others again seem to think it their duty to dispense votes with a hand as profuse as the most liberal interpretation of the law will allow.'[15]

The lodger was probably worst off. He was often disqualified because in practice an above average weekly rent was necessary in order to meet the annual value qualification,[16] and he suffered peculiarly from the vagaries of the registration system. He alone had to apply personally to be put on the register each year, and his mobility was limited to a change of rooms in the one house. Greater mobility disfranchised him.

The patchwork of lodger votes across the nation tended to be a blueprint of party needs rather than a map of the location of the lodger population. Unless prodded, cajoled, and managed by energetic party agents, few lodgers would make the effort of pushing their claims. Under such pressure the lodger vote in 1910 proved extraordinarily elastic. With expectations of a second election, the party organisations pursued the lodger with such diligence that the number of lodgers on the new register rose by nearly one-third, and in the marginal seats the increases were usually very much greater.[17] Unfortunately only in Scotland was this effort of any avail, for elsewhere the second election was fought on the old register.

This raises another unsatisfactory feature of the registration system. The register was always outdated by the time it came into effect on 1 January because the original claims and entries had been compiled six months before. The position was better in Scotland where a more efficient registration process had the new register ready by 1 November. The effective register then, even when fresh, contained the names of some who had died or changed residence since 15 July. In the event of an election the removals could only vote by returning to the constituency in which they were registered. As the year wore on the register became increasingly stale and by the end of the year, i.e. eighteen months after the preparation of the register, removals in urban areas could amount to one-third of the electorate.

The state of the register was an important tactical consideration in the timing of both elections, and the decision to dissolve on the old

TABLE 17.1 REMOVALS IN URBAN CONSTITUENCIES BETWEEN
JULY 1909 AND DECEMBER 1910

Constituency	Removals	Removals as % of Electorate
London		
Croydon	7000	26
Fulham	5000	24
Haggerston	2000	25
Hoxton	2500	29
Hornsey	5000	21
Kennington	3000	30
Newington West	3000	31
Peckham	4000	32
St Pancras West	3000	35
Tottenham	8000	27
West Ham North	4–5000	26–32
Watford	4000	22
Other Urban Areas		
Birmingham Central	2000	20
Birmingham East	6000	39
Birmingham South	5000	33
Blackburn	8000	35
Bolton	7000	33
Dudley	4000	23
Leeds North	7000	30
Manchester (6 constituencies)	20–30000	29–44
Middlesbrough	7000	32
Oldham	10000	28
Tyneside	10000	39
Wolverhampton West	4000	30
Liverpool (9 constituencies)	26000	31

Sources: Based on figures culled from the national and provincial press.

register in December 1910 was considered a blunder by some Liberals who argued that if the Government had shown a little patience it would have won twenty or thirty more seats.[18] It was widely assumed that a majority of removals were Liberals, and that as well the Unionists were more successful in tracing their missing.[19] Undoubtedly the stale register imposed an enormous extra burden on the party machines in the second election, for in London and the major provincial centres the removals appear to have averaged between 30–40 per cent of the electorate. By contrast the fresh register in Scotland kept removals there to a minimum.

Most of these direct and indirect limitations on adult male suffrage affected adversely the poorer classes, and thus the anti-Unionist parties. In a memorandum prepared for the Liberal Chief Whip in November 1911 J. R. Seager, head of the Liberal Registration Department, reported:

> It is universally agreed by Liberal Agents that the present Registration Laws are prejudicial to the Liberal Party. Whether it be the non-resident owner, or the Plural Voter, the £10 occupier, or the Lodger Franchises, they give large opportunities of enfranchising one class, while by the rules made by legislation or by Revising Barristers, every obstacle is placed in the way of the poorer potential Elector.[20]

Wealthy families escaped the disfranchisement of sons living at home by providing facilities for a lodger franchise, well-to-do farmers by giving their sons £10 occupation rights. It was claimed that the lodger vote was 'a serious injury to the Liberal Party', for lodgers were 'more easily obtained by Tories than Liberals'. Some evidence for this claim is provided by a breakdown of the Glasgow and Edinburgh lodger-voters on the 1910 register. Again it seems likely that the migratory habits of many workingmen coupled with the successive occupation provisions severely cut back working-class numbers on the register.

TABLE 17.2 LODGER VOTERS GLASGOW EDINBURGH

	Liberal	Unionist
Edinburgh lodgers	2885 (45%)	3539 (55%)
Glasgow lodgers	3230 (28%)	8170 (72%)

Source: Scottish Liberal Association, minutes, Eastern Organising Committee, 14 Oct 1909 and Western Committee, 2 Nov 1910.

The impact of these provisions was not entirely one-sided. Mobile professional groups such as clergymen, teachers, and government officials were also handicapped by successive occupation, while Liberal disinterest in the exclusion of soldiers arose probably from the widespread belief that 'Soldiers usually vote Tory'. But overall these limitations told against the anti-Unionist parties: and Labour probably suffered even more than the Liberals. Liberal agents recognised that whatever benefits might accrue to the Liberals generally from a shorter qualifying period and a simpler low-rental lodger franchise, in areas where the Labour Party was growing 'young men with no votes at present would give the Labour Party an enormous addition of strength'.

A further aspect of the franchise which worked in the Unionist favour was the plural vote. In 1910 there were about 550,000 plural votes in the United Kingdom, and the motor car facilitated the turnout of plural voters in both elections. '. . . the plural voter has suddenly developed new power with the aid of the motor car', wrote the Liberal editor J. A. Spender. 'Every man of them polled, & motors were racing up and down the country taking them from point to point.'[21] The significance of the plural vote was enhanced by the fact that it tended to be concentrated in six types of constituency – in Metropolitan seats; in the commercial constituencies of the major cities; in the suburban county seats to which the borough freeholders were allocated; in rural county constituencies within whose boundaries lay one or more parliamentary boroughs; in the few city seats with a significant freeman vote; and in the six university constituencies.

The Unionists' public defence of plural voting and their private correspondence shows they were well aware of their advantage but the extent of its impact has probably been exaggerated. Liberals believed it had cost them between thirty and fifty seats in each election in 1910 on the assumption that the plural vote divided 4:1 in the Unionist favour.[22] But an examination of election results in seats with a high plural vote suggests that this exaggerates the bias of the plural vote and that a more likely split in 1910 would lie somewhere between 6:4 and 7:3. It is unlikely therefore that the plural vote cost the Liberals more than seventeen seats in January and twenty-one in December.[23]

Over-all the franchise provisions combined with the registration machinery prevented the middle classes from being swamped by working-class voters. A sense of political efficacy and a high level of education – both of which seem to correlate positively with electoral participation, and which are likely to be more widespread in middle-class communities – probably further diminished the gap between the proportion of middle-class and working-class voters on the register. No precise figures can be given but using Routh's occupational breakdown of the 1911 census,[24] an estimate can be made. If we classify professionals, employers, administrators, managers and clerical workers (Routh's categories 1, 2, 3) as middle class, then in 1910 there were 2·38 million adult males in this class, i.e. 20 per cent of the adult male population. If all 0·55 million plural votes are allocated to this class, then the potential middle-class vote was 2·93 million. If all were registered this class would account for 38 per cent of the votes on the 1910 register, i.e. proportionately they would be almost twice as well represented on the electoral register as they were in the adult male population as a whole. No doubt there were failures to register amongst the middle class, but it seems clear that the electoral system cushioned the impact of democracy in Edwardian England.

III

The most radical achievements of the Reform Acts of 1884–5 were in the field of redistribution, with the substitution in principle of the representation of numbers for that of localities, and the establishment as typical of the single-member division. The first represented a triumph for the Radicals, the second has been described as 'one of the cardinal features of the British Constitution'.[25] Yet they resulted from a compromise imposed on a reluctant Commons by the leadership of the two parties and, as with all compromises, principles were but vaguely endorsed and loosely applied.

The Redistribution Act embodied an approach to, rather than the realisation of, equal electoral districts. The Whig leaders never sanctioned the principle of numerical equality and denied that they aimed at mathematical accuracy of representation. Throughout, Gladstone disavowed strict adherence to the numerical principle as disruptive of tradition, and backed qualifications to that principle on the grounds that sparsely populated areas needed greater representation than densely populated areas, and that regions remote from London deserved especial consideration.[26] Thus the ratio of one seat to every 52,000 inhabitants taken as the average was considerably modified by the wide tolerance shown to existing boroughs, and by the generous representation given to the distant rural areas. The geographical distribution of the small boroughs preserved meant a continued overweighting of the South-West as against the Midlands and the North-East.[27] The Gladstonian regard for the sparsely populated and remote constituencies served to inflate the representation of the rural areas, particularly the rural Celtic fringe. Ireland was particularly favoured since in addition legal, historical, and sociological arguments of considerable sophistry were used in support of unchanged Irish representation. The result of these modifications was that in 1885 the approximate ratio between the largest and smallest electorate was 8:1.[28]

The years following the 1885 Redistribution Act witnessed the aggravation of these anomalies as the result of continued population decline in the small boroughs and the Celtic fringe contrasting with large population increases in the major conurbations. Population in most of the small boroughs, saved from Conservative and Radical hatchets in 1885, continued to decline or at least remain stationary in a period of increasing population. There was steady population decline too in rural Wales and Scotland.

But Ireland was the classic case of over-representation as a result of depopulation. In 1885 Ireland retained 103 seats, when on a strict population basis she would have been allotted only ninety-two. The often bitter debates in 1884–5 were concerned not so much with this marginal over-representation, as with the future implications of unchanged Irish representation. As Goschen with admirable prescience warned, 'the injustice to England will be an injustice increasing from year to year, because the population is increasing continually while the population of Ireland is stationary, if not diminishing'.[29] He was right. Between 1881 and 1911 the population of Great Britain increased by over 11,000,000. In the same period the population of Ireland declined by nearly 800,000. Ireland's marginal over-representation of 1885 had by 1910 become a gross inflation. By 1910 any scheme of redistribution accurately mirroring population would involve a loss of some forty Irish seats.[30]

By contrast, the thirty years prior to 1910 saw an enormous growth in suburbia and the creation particularly in the north of England of vast urban sprawls as the suburban fringes of one industrial community merged with those of another.[31] Large electorates were created in the residential seats of the large cities, and gigantic ones in the adjoining county divisions. In 1885 no seat in the new dispensation had a population greater than 100,000. By 1891 there were eleven such seats, by 1901 fifty and by 1911 one hundred.[32]

These contrasting population developments soon rendered obsolete the redistribution of 1885, and emphasised the surviving anomalies. Thus by 1910 the ratio between the largest and smallest electorates was 30:1, the extreme cases being Romford (58,984) and Kilkenny (1742). Nor were these discrepancies confined to a few extreme cases: nearly one-third of the electorates diverged from the average by 50 per cent or more. The geographical patterns and contrasts resulting from these antithetic developments are shown in Map 17.1.

How far did the pattern of seats stemming from the decisions of 1885 and the subsequent population movements benefit one or other of the parties? The Unionists clearly believed it operated against them.

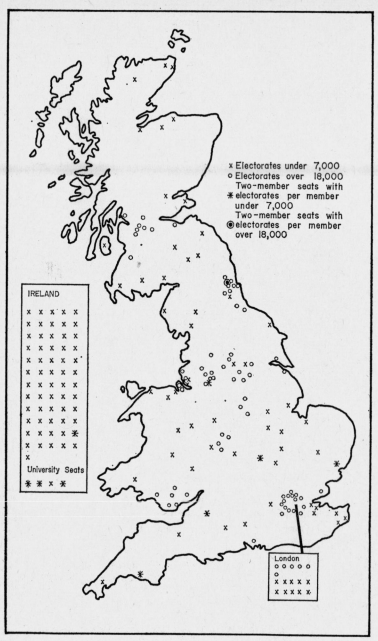

Map 17.1 DISTRIBUTION OF VERY SMALL AND VERY LARGE ELECTORATES 1910

'Liberalism flourishes', wrote a Unionist pamphleteer, 'on the over-representation of the most backward parts of the country and on the ignorance, envy and hostility to the Union of its inhabitants.' The gist was clear: '. . . illiterate, priest-ridden Ireland' had an unfair number of seats.[33] Ever since 1885 Conservatives had frustrated Liberal electoral reform plans by demanding redistribution, and had themselves in the badly managed redistribution proposals of 1905, the so-called 'gerry-Balfour', planned to prune Irish seats. When the 1910 elections revealed the pivotal position of the Irish the complaints were renewed:

> . . . the Government majority will be very largely dependent on the gross electoral anomaly and injustice, the over-representation of Ireland . . . It cannot be doubted that if electoral justice were done as between England and Ireland, the majority for the Government if it did not disappear altogether, would be reduced to insignificant proportions.[34]

But it is all a matter of what is meant by 'electoral justice'. Despite the over-representation of Ireland, the distribution of seats in the period 1885–1910 worked quite clearly in the Unionist favour. Table 17.3 shows the actual majorities, the majorities that would have ensued if seats had been distributed in proportion to votes, and the theoretical

TABLE 17.3 ELECTORAL MAJORITIES 1885–1910

Election	Actual Majority	Proportional Majority	Theoretical* Majority
1885	L 158†	L 92	L 276
1886	U 104	L 18	L 52
1892	L 44	L 40	L 120
1895	U 150	U 2	U 4
1900	U 134	U 2	U 4
1906	L 356	L 114	L 340
1910 J	L 124	L 54	L 160
1910 D	L 126	L 46	L 136

Notes: * The theoretical majority is calculated using the cube law. This states that, given a two-party system and fair and equal constituencies, if votes are divided between the parties in the ratio A:B then seats will be divided in the ratio $A^3:B^3$. For a full discussion see Butler, *Electoral System*, pp. 195–202.

† 'L' in the table stands for all the anti-Unionist parties.

Sources: Actual and proportional majority calculations, except for December 1910, from the Royal Commission on Electoral Systems, *Parl. Papers*, 1910, xxvi 308. The allowance made in these calculations for uncontested seats is fairly crude, but more sophisticated calculations, while they might alter particular entries, would be unlikely to affect the general implications of the table.

majorities to be anticipated given the relation between votes and seats in a single member first-past-the-post electoral system. In every election from 1885 to December 1910, with the exception of 1906, the distribution of seats served to exaggerate Unionist victories beyond the level to be expected under such a voting system, and to moderate Unionist defeats.

Table 17.4 shows how the Unionist disadvantage arising from Irish over-representation was offset in 1910. While under the electoral system the Labour Party was handicapped by the fact that most of its votes were polled in large seats, and the Nationalists favoured by their successes in small seats, over-all neither the anti-Unionists as a whole nor the Unionists were harmed by inequalities in the size of seats. This was primarily due to the fact that Unionist successes in small seats in Great Britain offset the Unionist disadvantage arising from the over-representation of Ireland. But if, in this respect, the system was unbiased as between the contending forces, Table 17.5 reveals the great wastage of anti-Unionist, particularly Labour and Nationalist votes in the safe seats. This meant that the Unionist vote was more effectively distributed for winning seats. Thus, while the apparent unfairness to the Unionists resulting from the over-representation of Ireland was offset by counter-vailing influences, a more neglected and more ineradicable bias in the distribution, in the form of the geographic concentrations of the anti-Unionist forces, prevented the anti-Unionists from capitalising to the full on their popular majority in 1910. As Spender complained, 'taking *Great Britain alone* the majority in votes which gives us a majority of 64 seats is practically the same as gave Salisbury a majority of 213 in 1895'.[35] Certainly it was harder for the anti-Unionists to win.

To the second great achievement of the 1885 Redistribution Act – the establishment as the norm of the single member geographically contiguous seat – there were three exceptions, the six university constituencies, the twenty-four two-member boroughs, and the twenty-two grouped boroughs.

The six university seats were havens of the plural voters and, with a total electorate of 48,154 in 1910, elected nine Members to the House of Commons. They were blue-ribbon Conservative seats, and the three old university constituencies, Oxford, Cambridge and Dublin, functioned almost as nomination boroughs. There were no contests in these three seats in 1910, indeed there had been only one contest, an intra-party quarrel in Cambridge, in these three seats since 1885. Country clergymen tended to dominate the Oxford–Cambridge electorate,[36] doctors the Scottish university electorates.[37]

TABLE 17.4 PARTY VICTORIES IN DIFFERENT-SIZE ELECTORATES JAN 1910

Size of electorate ('000)	GREAT BRITAIN						IRELAND						UNITED KINGDOM			
	Unionist		Liberal		Labour		Unionist		Liberal		Nationalist		Unionist		Anti-Unionist	
	No.	%	No.	%	No.	%	No.	%	No.	%	No.	%	No.	%	No.	%
Under 5	22	9	16	6	0	0	3	14	1	100	21	26	25	9	37	9
5–10	74	29	72	26	7	18	14	67			60	73	88	32	140	35
10–15	106	42	108	40	15	38	3	14			1	1	109	40	124	31
15–20	31	12	57	21	13	33	1	5					32	12	70	18
20–25	11	4	15	5	4	10							11	4	19	5
25–30	6	2	4	1	1	3							6	2	5	1
Over 30	2	1	2	1	0	0							2	1	2	1
	252	99	274	100	40	102	21	100	1	100	82	100	273	100	397	100

Notes: 1. Two-member seats divided and treated as two single seats.
2. Rounding explains why some percentages do not add up to 100.
3. The one Nationalist seat won in Great Britain included with Nationalist totals in Ireland.

TABLE 17.5 PARTIES AND SAFE SEATS JAN 1910

	GREAT BRITAIN			IRELAND		UNITED KINGDOM	
	Unionist	Liberal	Labour	Unionist	Nationalist	Unionist	Anti-Unionist
Seats with majority:							
20–40%	50	55	16	4	2	54	73
Over 40%	18	20	5	9	74	27	99
	—	—	—	—	—	—	—
Total safe seats	68	75	21	13	76	81	172
Safe seats as % of total seats won	27%	27%	53%	62%	93%	30%	43%

Notes: 1. Majorities in uncontested seats estimated from previous contested elections.
2. In Ireland constituencies with two Nationalist candidates treated as safe seats unless previous elections indicated otherwise.

The two-member seats, saved by Gladstonian insistence in 1885, were the most distinctive Whig feature of the Redistribution Act. Although few in numbers in 1910 these seats contained 6·7 per cent of the entire electorate; and because of the double vote used in these constituencies, approximately 13 per cent of the total vote came from these twenty-four seats. Ironically these elements of an earlier electoral dispensation played a key role in the rise of the Labour Party. Originally the scene of Whig–Radical alliances, in the early twentieth century they became one of the bases of the Liberal–Labour pact. In each of the elections of the first decade at least one-quarter of the parliamentary strength of the Labour Party derived from the two-member boroughs.[38]

The district boroughs were limited to Scotland and Wales. Usually these boroughs were groupings of neighbouring rural towns, but there were exceptions, e.g. the combination of industrial Cardiff with the agricultural towns of the Vale of Glamorgan, or the 220 miles by land and sea from Dingwall in Cromarty to Kirkwall in Orkney, both parts of the Wick Burghs, or the many miles between lowland Ayr and highland Oban, both units of the Ayr Burghs. Surprisingly these distances did not prevent effective organisation and campaigning, in so far as this can be measured in turnout figures, e.g. in January 1910 the turnout in the Wick Burghs was 92·7 per cent, that in Ayr Burghs 89·5 per cent, both well above the national average. In Wales the system of grouped boroughs tended to favour the Unionists, giving them urban victories by majorities which would have been swamped if the boroughs had been included in the Radical country electorates. In the elections of 1910 four of the five Unionist victories in Wales were won in the district boroughs, in three cases by majorities of less than sixty votes.

IV

Most other aspects of the conduct of the elections were governed by the comprehensive Corrupt and Illegal Practices Act of 1883, 'by far the most stringent [act] ever passed in Britain against electoral malpractices'.[39] Corrupt practices – bribery, treating, intimidation, personation, false statement concerning expenses – were punishable by one year's imprisonment and a fine of £200, as well as by loss of the offender's political rights. Illegal practices, mainly spending in excess of the legal maxima, payment for conveyance for voters, provision of party favours, were liable to fines and to a limited loss of political rights. If agency was established, that is if the responsibility for the corrupt or illegal practice was traced to the candidate or his agent, the seat was forfeit. The second and more popular part of the Act defined maximum expenses by laying down a scale of maximum expenditure based on the type of constituency and the number of voters in it. The scale ranged from £200 in Irish boroughs with under 500 voters to £710 plus £60 for every additional thousand voters in British county constituencies with 2000 votes and over.[40]

The Act was accepted by politicians doubtful of the value of old practices in a rapidly expanding electorate; stressed by parties concerned with their image; paradoxically supported by an aristocracy afraid of the encroachments of the plutocracy and by lower-middle- and working-class groups reaching out for political power. Respect for the Act was fostered by a moral climate increasingly critical of once tolerated electoral malpractices.[41] The number of election petitions was drastically reduced despite the greater number of contested seats and the broader scope for petitions. Similarly election costs were severely cut from the 18s. 9d. per vote of 1880 to the 3s. 11d. per vote of January and the 3s. 8d. per vote of December 1910.[42]

Some evils still occasionally flourished in defiance of the Act, particularly in the smaller constituencies.[43] Bribery was so rampant at Exeter during the January election that the Chief Constable was authorised by the City Council to take steps to prevent a reoccurrence at the second election.[44] In Coventry a Citizens' Vigilante Society was established to prevent corruption but the defeated Liberal candidate, the author Silas Hocking, still complained that he was beaten through votes bought with liquor. On polling day 'from 6–8 p.m. [the drunks] were carted away in batches from the public houses, happy and no doubt grateful for an abundant supply of cheap beer . . .'.[45] Personation seems to have been rife where one might most have expected it, in England's 'Tammany City' Liverpool. James Sexton, Labour candidate for West Toxteth alleged that 'a great many men came from the cemetery to vote against him', while the Labour agent at Kirkdale claimed that the small Tory majority there could be 'attributed to one cause, the skill in which absent voters were personated from 6 p.m. to 8 p.m.'.[46]

More significant were activities permitted, or not clearly prohibited, by what was on the whole a relatively comprehensive law. The Act did not guard against dubious practices between elections and many acts involved in the assiduous nursing of the constituency would have invoked the most serious penalties had they been committed within the imprecise but limited period in which the law applied. Holcombe Ingleby, the Conservative victor at King's Lynn in December had, as Mayor of that borough during 1910, dispensed the most lavish hospitality; entertainments for fishermen, dock labourers, police, and artisans; gifts of rabbits, ducks, pheasants and partridges for those not present at the festivities. Ingleby's plea that his hospitality was in accord with his mayoral pledges, and that it took place before he became the candidate, was accepted.[47] Similarly, in East Nottingham, where during 1910 the sitting Conservative had distributed charity with a generous hand, but had ceased to do so as soon as the second election appeared imminent, the judges decided that his conduct was 'honest charity' not bribery.[48] By contrast at Central Hull the open-handed manner in which the sitting Conservative, Sir Seymour King, celebrated in November 1910 his silver jubilee as Member cost him his seat. The timing was all-important for as the judge commented when declaring the election void, 'This charity in Central Hull, unlike that at King's Lynn and East Nottingham, went on while the election was in actual progress'.[49]

Again the salting of the constituency over long period of time did not come within the purview of the Act. E. A. Brotherton, Unionist Member for Wakefield, was thought quite secure against both the attacks of Tariff Reform fanatics and the local Liberal and Labour alliance because of his munificence: '... practically every society and institution benefits both by [his] subscriptions and other evidence of [his] goodwill.' He had provided every child in the city with a savings bank book credited with one shilling, and had put aside £10,000 to provide old-age pensions.[50] It is perhaps worth noting that the only independent candidate successful in January in Great Britain, Cameron Corbett, had a reputation for 'princely liberality'.[51]

The difficulty of proving agency permitted numerous questionable activities by the party associations, and, even more important, by the great pressure groups.[52] As one Unionist organiser wrote later: 'Availing themselves immoderately of this loophole political strategists enlarged it into a gaping breach of the law.'[53] The pressure groups were often closely linked with a party, but since their intervention was not aimed at the return of a specific candidate, it was difficult, and with the agency problem almost impossible, to bring it within the framework of the Act. The enormous expenditure on pamphlets, posters, dumping shops, slides, cartoons and speakers by organisations such as the Tariff Reform League, the Free Trade Union, the Anti-Socialist Union, and the Licensed Victuallers' associations never appeared in returns of

official expenses. But the problem was not just one of financial account-
ability for here was an opening for corruption, which could not be
attributed to any candidate or agent and therefore could not void an
election.

Again the high costs, the difficulty of proving agency, the fact that
verdicts were often based rather on trivial and technical grounds than
on the gravamen of the petition, and the local unpopularity incurred
all militated against the bringing of election petitions. The National
Liberal Federation argued that the fact that no cases were brought
against Unionists in the counties proved little about the extent of rural
corruption for 'nothing is so difficult as to make out a legal case of
intimidation, even when the facts are clear'.[54] The local Conservatives
seem to have persevered with the petition against the powerful Whig
Guests of Canford Manor in East Dorset chiefly because the party headquarters pressed the petition believing that 'unless a determined effort
is made to break [the Guest influence] down, that seat will become a
pocket borough of Canford'.[55]

Finally, because of the agency problem and the legislative difficulties
of curbing basic freedoms, there was a host of practices contrary to the
spirit of the Corrupt Practices Act but either outside or difficult to
bring within its scope. It was not possible to void an election because
of, and difficult to substantiate charges against, an employer who used
his position to support the Tariff Reform or the Free Trade case.
Innumerable examples can be found of subtle and not so subtle threats
of unemployment and warnings of reduced wages if the Budget were
passed, Tariff Reform rejected, or Free Trade abandoned. At Denbigh
the Unionist candidate, Ormsby-Gore 'saw Radical employers standing
at the door of the polling booths catching hold of their workmen &
saying "Remember which side your bread is buttered"'.[56] In the West
Midlands, in particular, Tariff Reform slogans were prominent on
factory gates, and local industrialists were active tariff evangelists.

Even more widespread was the pressure of the landed interest in the
counties. The National Liberal Federation thought that in January 'in
the county districts the feudal influence was worked against Liberalism
as perhaps it has never been worked before, with the result that intimidation and undue influence was rife to an unparalleled degree'.[57] The
Daily Chronicle alleged 'a state of terrorism' unlike anything since the
passing of the Corrupt Practices Act.[58] The Asquiths were inundated
with 'masses of letters all telling the same tale of funk and pressure',[59]
while F. W. Hirst, editor of the Economist and Liberal candidate for

Sudbury, alleged he was 'destroyed [by] . . . Beer & Feudalism & sheer brutality'.[60] Spender was of the opinion that 'while the threats of the Dukes to dismiss labourers, stop pensions, lower wages etc. have exposed them to derision in the towns, they have caused genuine fear in the villages.'[61] Support for Liberal complaints came from a well informed article on the January election, appearing in the *North American Review* which argued that 'unquestionably there has been a great deal of social intimidation in the rural districts . . . the village labourer . . . was either converted to Tariff Reform or else cowed and dragooned by the local magnates into voting the Unionist ticket'.[62] What seems certain is that landlords, squires, parsons and publicans used the weight of their social, economic and moral power to influence the verdict in 1910 to an extent not attempted for many years.

The Unionists had great advantages in the countryside. 'Every taproom is the centre of a Tory propaganda, every employer has a rostrum of his own in his farmyard . . . while the identification of the Church with the party invests opposition with the character of irreligious discontent.'[63] Margot Asquith reported that the upper classes in Somerset had 'moved their accounts from small shops unblushing';[64] a Liberal parson in Honiton wrote to Herbert Gladstone that 'A Liberal tradesman in Ottery St Mary who took an *active* part on the Liberal side wd. assuredly lose custom'. The same writer pointed out how pressure was brought to bear through the canvass, through the presence of prominent Tories at Liberal meetings, and through the farmers taking their labourers to the polls.[65] That both elections took place near Christmas enabled charity to be combined with influence. Moreover in the rural districts there was widespread and not entirely unjustified suspicion about the secrecy of the ballot. 'It is so hard to persuade the rustic voter', wrote Gladstone's clerical correspondent, 'that the ballot is really secret. And it is so hard for *him* to keep secret from "Those in authority over him", and from his companions what he has done or is going to do.'[66] Social intimidation, aspersions on the secrecy of the ballot, and the pervasive authority of the rural social structure all worked against the Liberals in 1910.

It is difficult to determine the point at which such pressures should be regarded as illegitimate. It is 'not perhaps exactly "intimidation" ', wrote the Devonshire parson referred to above, 'but it is strong *pressure*, "pressure" so strong as practically to be next door to intimidation if not actually intimidation itself.'[67] This perhaps does not give sufficient weight to the highly deferential structure of rural society, which facilitated the task of persuasion. Moreover it was extremely difficult to bring most of these activities within the ambit of penal legislation.

Ironically, the one English county petition to come before the courts in 1910 or 1911 was East Dorset, where the Liberal Guests were charged with the very offences – bribery, treating, intimidation – allegedly widely practised by the Unionists in the rural areas. It is doubtful how far generalisations about the behaviour of county families can be made from the East Dorset case. Certainly the Guests were typical of the politically active county families except for their party label, and even this was recent, the result of a switch in 1904. It is therefore possible that the pressure they exercised, if perhaps unique in its blatancy,[68] was not untypical of county family political activity. On the other hand, as Hanham has pointed out, when discussing this and other cases, 'the dangers of coercion were greatest when a landlord changed his politics'.[69] Thus their change of party in 1904 may have compelled the Guests to use pressures not needed by their less fickle contemporaries.

East Dorset, however, does lend substance to the N.L.F. complaint that intimidation was very difficult to prove. Despite considerable evidence suggesting intimidation, the election was not voided on this ground but because of excessive and unentered election expenses.[70] East Dorset also suggests that county family influence when exercised was not ineffective. The only county constituency in all of south-eastern England to show a swing to the Liberals in January 1910 was East Dorset.

This was the complex formal framework within which the election took place. Registration and the exclusion of women compromised the universality of the franchise; concessions marred the attempt at an equitable distribution of seats and time aggravated these blemishes; ancient customs influenced the conduct of the elections; corruption was dying but not dead. In 1910 for the last time the general elections were conditioned by an electoral system which was in form and actuality a product of the nineteenth century.

The Results

I

In Great Britain in January 1910 the electoral commitment of the political parties, as reflected in the number of candidates, was unprecedented, while the intensity of pressure group activity had rarely been paralleled. The response of the electorate was equally unprecedented. Never before had so many voters gone to the polls, while the proportion of registered electors voting, 87·0 per cent in Great Britain, and 86·7 per cent in the United Kingdom, has never been surpassed in any modern British election.

TABLE 18.1 ELECTION TURNOUT 1910 UNITED KINGDOM
(% of electors voting in contested constituencies)★

	England	Wales	Scotland	Great Britain	Ireland	United Kingdom
1906	83·4	81·1	80·7	83·0	82·1	82·8
	(+4·0)	(+2·6)	(+3·5)	(+3·9)	(+1·9)	(+3·9)
Jan 1910	87·5	84·8	84·5	87·0	80·1	86·7
	(−5·8)	(−6·7)	(−3·4)	(−5·6)	(−2·3)	(−5·6)
Dec 1910	82·0	77·7	81·6	81·7	74·7	81·4

Notes: Figures in brackets indicate the increase in turnout between 1906 and January 1910 and the fall in turnout between January and December 1910 *in seats contested in both of the elections being compared.* This is of significance in 1910 when the crude turnout figures mask the drop in turnout between the two elections, because of the large number of safe seats with a tendency to low turnout contested in January and not in December.

★ All votes in two-member seats treated as half votes, except in cases where there was only one Unionist or one anti-Unionist candidate in which case that candidate's votes treated as whole votes.

† University seats included only in United Kingdom totals.

The increase in turnout over 1906 seems to have been the result mainly of increased participation by Unionist supporters. Liberal losses resulted not so much from any significant falling off in the Liberal vote, as from a greatly augmented Unionist vote. In its first comment on the election results the *Westminster Gazette* observed: 'Conservatives who abstained in 1906 have voted strongly at this election.' Detailed examination gives weight to this supposition. While the turnout in Great Britain rose by 4·0 per cent, or by 3·9 per cent in seats contested in both elections, the average swing to the Unionists between the two elections was 4·3 per cent. The relation between turnout and swing in individual seats suggests that the similarity in these national averages was more than fortuitous.

TABLE 18.2 TURNOUT AND SWING 1906–JAN 1910 GREAT BRITAIN

Seats with:	No. Seats*	Median swing to Unionists
Turnout decrease	39	1·9%
Turnout increase of:		
0–1·9%	112	2·0%
2–3·9%	157	4·7%
4–5·9%	94	4·2%
6–7·9%	63	6·2%
Over 8%	57	7·5%

Notes: * Two-member seats treated as two single seats.

Thus one major explanation for the Unionist achievement in January 1910 was renewed support for the party from Unionists who had abstained in 1906. Indeed, the relationship between turnout and swing in January 1910 lends support to the thesis that significant Unionist abstention in 1906 was masked by the general rise in turnout in that year.[1] But the relation between turnout increase and Unionist recovery, in association with the very high poll, suggests that in January 1910 the Unionists also secured support from numbers of habitual abstainers. Ramsay MacDonald, in examining the Chatham figures, noted: 'In some way or other the Conservatives have tapped a reserve of voters which has hitherto been untouched by both Parties.'[2] Nor was the phenomenon limited to Chatham. The turnout figures do suggest that there was a residue of potential Tory voters, particularly in traditionally Conservative regions, untapped in the past but brought to the polls by the intensity of the partisan struggle in 1910. This may explain why the election of January 1910 does not fit the thesis advanced by Cornford that Unionist success was related inversely to the size of the poll, i.e. the larger the poll the poorer the Unionist result.[3] In January 1910, on a significantly larger poll than 1906, the Unionists did very much better than in 1906.

The reduction in the number of contests in December led to a fall in the total votes cast; and in the seats that were contested there was a decline in the proportion voting. But by confusing these two points, and by ignoring the state of the register, historians have concocted a myth of the bored electorate of December 1910. Halévy writes that 'half a million voters who had taken the trouble to poll in January *decided* to stay at home in December', while Jenkins notes that 'over one in six, indeed, of those who had previously voted *declined* to do so, and the total poll fell by more than a million votes'.[4]

The fall in the numbers voting was in fact 1,349,254; but the chief reason for this decline does not lie in any voluntary decision by the voters. Rather the parties, by curtailing the electoral struggle, denied the opportunity of a vote to approximately one million electors who had voted in January. Whereas in the United Kingdom in January there were contests in 571 seats with an electorate of 7,201,890, in December there were contests in only 485 seats with an electorate of 6,011,934. In these 485 seats the turnout dropped by 5·6 per cent over turnout in the same seats in January. This means that in these constituencies approximately 350,000 electors who had voted in January did not do so in December. But even this figure exaggerates the voluntary decline for in England, Wales and Ireland the second election was fought on a stale register. In Scotland, where the election was held on the new register, the turnout decline in seats contested in both elections was 3·4 per cent, compared with 5·8 per cent in England, 6·7 per cent in Wales, and 2·3 per cent in Ireland.[5] Approximately 80,000 of the 350,000 who did not vote in December in the contested constituencies were dead, although their names still stood on the registers in England, Wales and Ireland. In addition, the party organisations experienced considerable difficulty in tracing and bringing removals to the polls. It seems likely that if the new register had been in operation in England and Wales the turnout decline would have been no greater than in Scotland.

Indeed, it is possible that the decline would have been less than in Scotland. The major factor influencing voluntary abstention in December was the safety or otherwise of the seat. The closer the result in January the smaller was the fall in turnout in December. As the proportion of marginal seats (i.e. seats won with a majority of less than 10 per cent of the total vote) to total seats in England and Wales was

54 per cent while in Scotland it was only 38 per cent, it seems probable that the minimising effects of such seats on turnout decline would have been more noticeable in England and Wales. While a precise calculation is impossible it seems probable that if there had been an up-to-date register throughout the country the overall drop in turnout in the contested constituencies would have been about 2 per cent or 100,000 votes.

When these considerations are taken into account, and when it is noted that December 1910 was one of the wettest Decembers on record, the fall in turnout was surprisingly low.[6] *The Times* on 15 November 1910 had anticipated a turnout of about 75 per cent. Instead, on the stalest register of any election in the period 1885–1910, the turnout of 81·4 per cent was the third highest of the eight elections in this period. As the *Westminster Gazette* rightly observed on 16 December 1910, in the midst of much comment to the contrary, 'There have been no signs of apathy. Due allowance being made for the old register, there has been an enormous poll'. In its efforts to belittle the result, Unionist propaganda stressed the apparently heavy abstentions. Too often such arguments have been accepted uncritically and even extended. One modern historian has written: 'The two general elections of 1910, and particularly the second, produced more excitement among the candidates and less among the electors than perhaps any others of modern times.'[7] It is difficult to determine criteria for electoral excitement. What is clear, however, about both elections in 1910 is the remarkable interest of the electorate, as measured by the only meaningful criterion that can be used – the proportion of the electorate which could and did cast its vote.

II

By the end of polling in the second week of February 1910, the Liberal and Labour candidates had polled 3·13 million votes, 52·0 per cent of the poll, in Great Britain, compared with the Unionists 2·85 million votes, 47·4 per cent of the poll. This clear majority of the poll gave the anti-Unionists a majority of seventy seats in Great Britain. The results in Ireland increased the size but added to the heterogeneity of the anti-Unionist majority.

The feature of the results which aroused speculation and occasioned disquiet was the unusual geopolitical division of the country.

What is remarkable [wrote Beatrice Webb] is the dividing of England into two distinct halves each having its own large majority for its own cause – the south country, the suburban, agricultural, residential England going Tory and tariff reform, and the north country and dense industrial populations (excluding Birmingham area) going Radical–Socialist . . .[8]

J. A. Spender found the cleavage between the Liberal North, Scotland and Wales and the Unionist South both 'striking' and 'disagreeable' while the *Westminster Gazette* feared the breakdown of the political consensus in this stark alignment of the two nations.[9]

TABLE 18.3 RESULTS JANUARY 1910

	GREAT BRITAIN			UNITED KINGDOM†		
	Total Votes*	% Total Votes	Seats	Total Votes*	% Total Votes	Seats
Unionist	2,848,461	47·4	245	2,930,153	46·9	273
Liberal	2,694,521	44·8	273	2,719,481	43·5	274
Labour	431,815	7·2	40	435,766	7·0	40
Nationalist	2,943	–	1	76,990	1·2	71
Ind. Nationalist				40,138	0·7	11
Other	34,940	0·6	1	41,904	0·7	1
	6,012,680	100·0	560	6,244,432	100·0	670

Notes: * All votes in two-member seats treated as half votes, except in cases where there was only one Unionist or one anti-Unionist candidate in which case that candidate's votes treated as whole votes.
† University seats included only in United Kingdom figures.

This sharp and in one respect novel division along geographical lines is the most significant feature of the 1910 results. North of a line drawn from the Humber to the Dee (A–B on the maps)[10] the anti-Unionists held 169 seats and in Wales a further thirty-two. This total of 201 seats accounted for 64 per cent of the total anti-Unionist seats in Great Britain. South of the Humber–Dee line the Unionists held 192 seats or 78 per cent of their total seats. In one sense this cleavage marked merely a historic division, for the Unionists had long been strong in the South, while the North and the Celtic fringe contained the traditional citadels of Liberalism. Moreover, in 1906 the Liberals and their allies had won even more seats in the North, Scotland and Wales, and in other elections since 1885 the Unionists had done even better in the South. What was new was that never before had the anti-Unionists done so well in the North, Scotland and Wales while doing so badly in the South; never before had the Unionists done so well in the South, while doing so badly elsewhere.

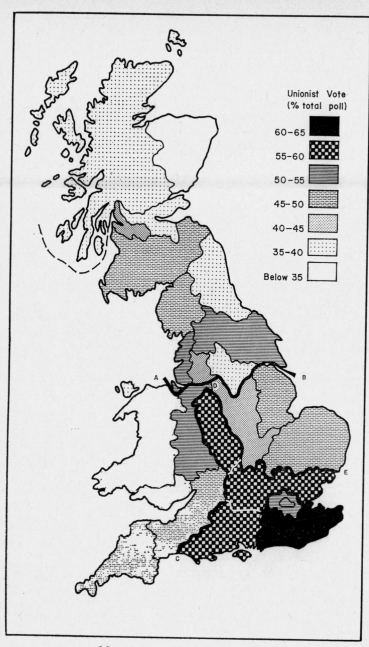

Map 18.1 RESULTS JANUARY 1910

TABLE 18.4 BROAD REGIONAL CONTRASTS 1885–DEC 1910
GREAT BRITAIN

	1885	1886	1892	1895	1900	1906	Jan 1910	Dec 1910
Liberal and Labour								
% of Northern, Scottish Welsh seats won	69	53	66	48	46	84	79	77
% of Southern seats won	52	19	36	18	23	70	37	39
Unionist								
% of Northern, Scottish Welsh seats won	31	47	34	52	54	16	21	23
% of Southern seats won	48	81	64	82	77	30	63	61
% difference between Northern, Scottish, Welsh seats won and Southern seats won	17	34	30	30	23	14	42	38

This broad geographical analysis requires certain refinements. In two of the thirteen regions into which the North, Scotland and Wales have been divided for this study the Unionists had a majority of the votes. In the North and East Ridings of Yorkshire a Liberal majority in the boroughs was more than offset by the Unionist majority in the agricultural county seats. In Western Lancastria (the mixed rural, seaside residential and industrial region of coastal Cheshire and Lancashire) the Unionists won 52·7 per cent of the vote against a mixed bag of opponents. In a third region, Cumbria, where the Unionists polled only 48·1 per cent of the vote, they yet held seven out of ten seats. Unionist minority vote victories at Cockermouth and Whitehaven, and an unopposed Unionist return at Penrith explained this discrepancy. In the remaining regions of the North of England – the West Riding, the North-East, and Eastern (or cotton) Lancastria – the anti-Unionists swept all before them, although not without occasional friction between themselves. Their superiority throughout Wales and Scotland was even more impressive.

In the South the picture was more complex. The Tory heartland was a roughly triangular area based on Dorset in the west and Kent in the east, and with its apex in the Western Midlands – 'a solid and broadening reef of Toryism and Protection stretching from Birmingham and the Western Midlands to the Southern Counties broken by industrial London'[11] (C–D–E on the maps).[12] In every region of this triangle save London and Outer London the Unionist vote averaged over 55 per cent. In Kent, Surrey and Sussex it was over 60 per cent; in Birmingham the Unionist proportion was 74·3 per cent, a Unionist poll unapproached in any other of the great urban centres of Britain.

To the east and west of this heartland Unionist predominance faded and in many cases disappeared. The Eastern Midlands was now a southward extension of the central spine of Liberalism, giving a clear majority of votes and seats to the anti-Unionist parties. Farther east, Lincolnshire and East Anglia were highly marginal areas with votes and seats shared almost equally between the two parties. In the Western Marches Unionist recovery was less than in most rural regions and, although the party possessed a clear majority of votes and seats, the party's poll was proportionately lower than in any election during the hegemonic period. To the south-west along the Severn, Unionist predominance fell away and in the South-West Peninsula the Liberals possessed a majority of seats and votes. The London conurbation was a divided enclave almost in the centre of the Tory heartland. The business and residential West End was staunchly Unionist, where with 65 per cent of the vote they captured all fifteen seats. In the East End the anti-Unionists won 54·9 per cent of the vote and eight out of eleven seats. The remaining parts of London were more evenly divided. Outer London tended to reflect in exaggerated form the politics of the contiguous metropolitan areas.

Results in individual constituencies highlight the main features of this geographical division. Of the fifty-eight seats in which the Unionists gained more than 60 per cent of the vote, all but one, Everton, were in the South, and all but three of these fell within the Tory heartland, inclusive of London. Of the seventy-four seats in which the Liberals gained over 60 per cent of the vote, only eight were in the South. Of the remaining sixty-six, forty-five were in Scotland and Wales. The Labour pattern was similar though not so dominated by the Celtic fringe. Of the twenty seats in which Labour secured more than 60 per cent of the vote three were in the South, one in Scotland, five in Wales and eleven in the North.

The clarity of this geographic dualism resulted primarily from the unusual movement of opinion in the January election. The swing in January was marked by a lack of uniformity and by elements of polarity unequalled since 1886. In the North, in Scotland and in Wales the pendulum hardly wavered, but the South swung sharply back to the Unionists, sweeping away the absolute Liberal majority in the process. Never before had one half of the nation moved so violently in one direction, while the other half had remained almost stationary. In the North, Scotland and Wales the Liberal position of 1906 was slightly eroded; in the South it was washed away in the tide of Unionist reaction.

The average swing to the Unionists in Great Britain between 1906 and January 1910 was 4·3 per cent. In Birmingham, the symbolic capital of Unionism in January 1910, the swing was 6·0 per cent. To the north of Birmingham the movement against the Government and its allies ebbed away. In England north of the Humber–Dee line in only one region out of six did the swing to the Unionists average above 3 per cent. Indeed in three sub-regions, North-East Lancashire, Tees-side, and the boroughs of the North and East Ridings, there was a swing against the Unionists. In Scotland the pro-Unionist swing was only 1·8 per cent. Similarly to the west of Birmingham the Unionist momentum petered out, the swing to the Unionists in Wales averaging only 1·9 per cent. Eastwards, however, through the rural parts of the Eastern Midlands and into East Anglia the Birmingham level was maintained. And to the south the tide of Unionist resurgence mounted, and in the South-East it virtually obliterated all anti-Unionist representation outside Greater London. Throughout the Home Counties the average swing to the Unionists was over 8 per cent and in two sub-regions, Surrey–Sussex and the Hampshire Ports, it was over 10 per cent. Only in London and the West Country was the Unionist tide partially stemmed. [See Map 18.2.]

This movement of opinion in the South in January destroyed the absolute parliamentary majority of the Liberals and greatly reduced the anti-Unionist majority in Great Britain. Unionist gains were heavily concentrated south of the Humber–Dee line. Over 80 per cent of their gains were in the South, and over 50 per cent within the Tory heartland, inclusive of London. [See Map 7.1, p. 140.]

A comparison of the geography of the Unionist hegemony and that of January 1910 indicates the critical and lasting features of the election of 1906. [See Maps 1.1, p. 18, and 18.1, p. 382.] The Unionist heartland in 1910 was an attenuated version of the great triangle of Unionist strength characteristic of the days of their hegemony. The great triangle had been shorn of its northern and western lands by the attrition of Unionist support in Western Lancastria, the Western Marches and

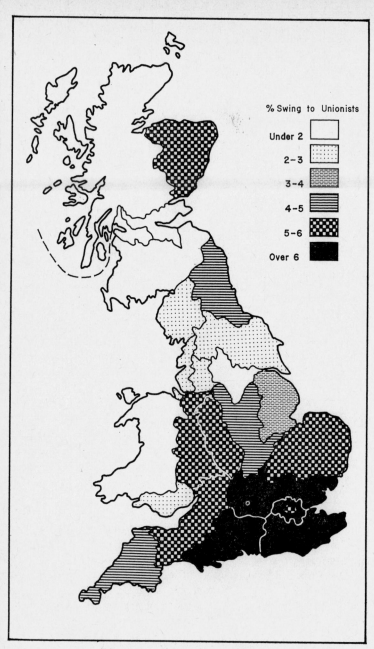

Map 18.2 SWING 1906 – JAN 1910

TABLE 18.5 RESULTS DECEMBER 1910

| | GREAT BRITAIN | | | UNITED KINGDOM | | |
	Total Votes	% Total Votes	Seats	Total Votes	% Total Votes	Seats
Unionist	2,230,521	47·5 (47·4)	245	2,289,508	46·8 (46·9)	271
Liberal	2,136,464	45·5 (44·8)	271	2,157,324	44·1 (43·5)	272
Labour	309,930	6·6 (7·2)	42	309,930	6·3 (7·0)	42
Nationalist	2,458	0·1	1	90,417	1·9 (1·2)	74
Independent Nationalist				31,234	0·6 (0·7)	10
Other	13,840	0·3 (0·6)	1	16,765	0·3 (0·7)	1
	4,693,213	100·0	560	4,895,178	100·0	670

Notes: Figures in brackets % of total votes January.

in the Severn Valley and weakened at its centre by the decline of Unionism in the London conurbation. On the other hand by comparison with the 1886–1900 situation, the Liberals had restored their 1885 dominion over Scotland, and to the Liberal bedrock areas of North-East England and the West Riding the anti-Unionists had added two further bastions, Eastern Lancastria and the Eastern Midlands, marginal regions during the years of the Unionist hegemony. In addition most of the other marginal regions of the hegemonic period now leant to the anti-Unionists.

The second election merely confirmed the new order. The December result was unique, for never before or since has an electoral decision so endorsed the previous verdict. 'The pendulum does not swing, it merely oscillates about the fixed point of last January.'[13] There was a slight Unionist bias in this oscillation. Table 18.5 fails to show this movement towards the Unionists, for it does not allow for uncontested seats. In the seats that were contested in both elections there was a swing of 0·8 per cent to the Unionists. In 256 seats there was a swing to the Unionists, in 171 a swing to their opponents, and in fourteen no swing.

The variations in swing were much less marked than in January. Only in one region, Eastern Lancastria, with a swing to the Unionists of 3·3 per cent, was there a deviation of more than 2·0 per cent from the national average. There was a tendency for seats and regions that had an above-average swing to the Unionists in January to have a below-average swing in December, and vice versa. Of the eleven regions with an above-average swing in January, ten had a below-average swing in December. Of the thirteen regions with a below-average swing in January, nine had an above-average swing in December. Thus the geographical contrast of January was marginally modified in December.

This minimal movement of opinion produced a virtual repetition of January in terms of seats. Although fifty-five seats changed hands in Great Britain between the two elections the Unionists had a net gain of only one.[14] [See Map 10.1, p. 199, for distribution of party gains.] The anti-Unionists did better than might have been expected given the slight swing against them, because they picked up five seats lost to the Unionists on a minority vote in January, and possibly because of better Liberal organisation.

The electoral fluctuations in Great Britain in 1910 found no parallel in Ireland, for there the political division, based on a coincidence of social, ethnic and religious cleavages, was too deep to be subject to much electoral oscillation. Three features of the Irish results in 1910

deserve note. First, there was a marginal erosion of Unionist strength
vis-à-vis the Nationalists. Joseph Devlin strengthened his grip on West
Belfast won in 1906 after fourteen years in Unionist hands, while in
December the Nationalists recovered South Dublin, 'the Alsace-
Lorraine of Ireland', which the Unionists had held for the better part of
the previous twenty-five years. Secondly, there was the eclipse of the
Liberals, who lost to the Unionists the two seats captured in 1906.
Finally there was the establishment and geographical confinement of a
rebel Nationalist party. The prevailing pattern in the factional contests
was the victory of the sitting Member. Thus the O'Brienite revolt, in
origin a parliamentary revolt based mainly on Cork M.P.s, had few
successes in January outside County Cork. The events of 1910 by
restoring the utility of the Liberal alliance, enhanced the authority of
Redmond and the official party, and enabled the Nationalists to confine
the revolt almost entirely to its Cork base in December.

III

Before proceeding to an interpretation of the election results, it is
worthwhile examining the performance of the Labour Party, a distinct
element in the anti-Unionist forces. In January 1910, seventy-seven
Labour candidates were put forward in Great Britain.[15] This represented an increase of twenty-two over official Labour candidates in
1906, and Labour's share of the total vote rose from 5·4 per cent in 1906
to 7·2 per cent in January 1910. Labour which had won thirty seats in
1906 held forty seats after the first 1910 election. Yet these indices of
expansion are misleading for by 1910 Labour's fortunes were on the
wane. Labour's additional strength came almost entirely from the
adherence of the miners' Members, not from any continuing popular
movement in Labour's favour. Labour's incursions into new territory
in January 1910 were almost uniformly disastrous. Nor did Labour
escape the general reaction to Unionism. In the forty-three seats with
official Labour candidates in both 1906 and January 1910 there was a
median swing to the Unionists of 3·6 per cent.[16] Thus while the party
broadened its attack, the average vote per Labour candidate fell from
45·1 per cent in 1906 to 44·5 per cent in January 1910, and this fall
would certainly have been greater except for the cushioning effects of
the miners' seats with their impressive Labour majorities. The party had
forty-five seats at the dissolution. It returned chastened from the polls
with forty, having lost eight and won three.

TABLE 18.6 LABOUR PARTY RESULTS

Regions*	1906§				JAN 1910				DEC 1910			
	Candidates	M.P.s	% Total Vote	Average % Vote	Candidates	M.P.s	% Total Vote	Average % Vote	Candidates	M.P.s	% Total Vote	Average % Vote
Lancashire–Cheshire	16	13	12·8	57·6	21	13	13·5	45·8	15	10	12·4	52·1
Yorkshire	8	3	6·5	41·7	12 (2)	6 (2)	10·3	44·8	8†	6	8·8	51·7
Northumberland–Durham	7	4	17·1	48·7	7 (1)	3	15·3	43·9	6†	4	13·7	46·1
Midlands	4	2	2·9	49·5	11 (6)	8 (6)	9·0	52·8	8	8	8·7	58·7
London (including Outer London)	4	3	3·8	49·1	4	2	3·3	49·5	4	4	4·1	56·0
England–Remainder	5	2	1·5	38·3	7	1	1·3	26·0	3	2	0·6	39·5
England	44	27	5·6	49·6	62 (9)	33 (8)	6·9	44·6	44	34	6·4	52·1
Scotland	9	2	4·9	28·4	10	2	5·1	29·5	5	3	3·5	42·7
Wales	2	1	3·5	40·2	5 (4)	5 (4)	14·9	72·9	7†	5	17·7	53·3
Great Britain	55	30	5·4	45·1	77 (13)	40 (12)	7·2	44·5	56‡	42	6·6	51·3

Notes: * The regions are mostly self-expanatory. The Midlands includes the following counties: Derby, Hereford, Leicester, Northampton, Nottingham, Shropshire, Stafford, Warwick, Worcester. London and Outer London: regions A and B in Appendix I.
† Includes one unopposed candidate.
‡ Includes three unopposed candidates.
§ Includes the five candidates of the Scottish Workers Representation Committee and J. W. Taylor (Chester-le-Street).
The average percentage vote is calculated by averaging the percentage vote of opposed candidates.
The figures in brackets in the Jan 1910 columns indicate the number of miners' M.P.s who joined the Labour Party at the dissolution.

Even the fact that their losses had been relatively lighter than those of the Liberals was small compensation, for Labour strength was mainly in the North, Scotland and Wales, where the pro-Unionist tide ran much less strongly. Whatever comfort could be drawn from Mac-Donald's assertion that 'the Labour Party has shown itself capable of holding what it has got',[17] it was impossible to hide disappointment at Labour's utter failure to make any inroads on the Liberal position.

It was a considerably subdued party that embarked upon a policy of electoral retrenchment after January. In December the party put forward only fifty-six candidates – three of whom were unopposed.[18] If by abandoning a number of hopeless three-cornered contests the Labour share of the total vote was reduced to 6·6 per cent, conversely the average vote per candidate rose to 51·3 per cent. This greater concentration, plus limited Liberal acquiescence, enabled the Labour Party to improve its parliamentary representation by two. Although the pro-Unionist wave in Lancastria cost Labour three seats, these were offset by five scattered gains.

The pattern of Labour polls is quite distinct from that of the major parties. [See Figure 18.1, p. 392.] This abnormal distribution of Labour results is a reflection of the Labour Party's unique position in the electoral system. In January the Labour Party fought three types of contest: paired with a single Liberal against two Unionists in double-member constituencies, against a single Unionist, and against both Unionist and Liberal opposition. In December were added three straight fights against Liberals. Labour's individual achievement was closely related to the type of contest concerned, in other words to the degree of

TABLE 18.7 LABOUR RESULTS ACCORDING TO TYPE OF CONTEST
1910 GREAT BRITAIN

Type of Contest	No.	No. of Wins	Median Labour Poll (%)
Labour + Liberal v. Unionist (two-member seats)	24	21 ⎫	
Labour v. Unionist	68	56 ⎭	56·2
Labour v. Unionist v. Liberal	35	0 ⎫	
Labour v. Liberal	3	2 ⎭	22·4
Labour unopposed	3	3	
	133	82	

infiltration into the political system permitted by the Liberal Party. Of the ninety-two contests in which Labour faced no official Liberal opposition, they won seventy-seven; of the thirty-eight contests in which the party faced Liberal rivals they won only two, and these only where there was no danger of letting a Unionist in. The median figures

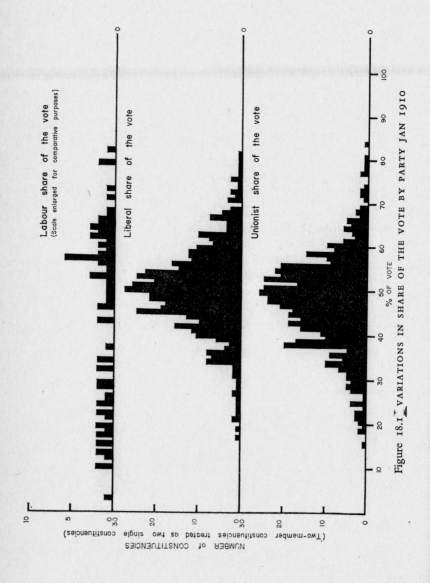

Figure 18.1 VARIATIONS IN SHARE OF THE VOTE BY PARTY JAN 1910

merely underline the contrast between results in the two types of contest.

The remarkably high ratio of Labour successes in seats without Liberal intervention was due to the fact that most of the seats lay in the industrial regions where the Unionist reaction was weakest in 1910. Many of these seats had been Liberal strongholds in the past. Others, where the pre-1906 record might have given rise to anxiety, were transformed into relatively secure seats by the Unionist Party's failure to recover support in previously Tory working-class areas. This was particularly true of Lancashire, a Tory fastness in the past and the scene of major Labour infiltration in 1906. Moreover nearly all the straight fights were defensive, fought in seats already held by Labour, and mostly by the sitting Labour Member. In nearly all these seats Liberal abstention was a guarantee of Labour success.

There were of course a few straight fights which were offensive rather than defensive, and where there was little chance of success. These were mainly in constituencies where the Liberal organisation was lamentably weak or the Liberal cause hopeless, e.g. in Birmingham and Liverpool. But these were exceptions to the general rule that Labour's straight fights were defensive and in constituencies safe or relatively secure.

Labour's uniformly disastrous results in three-cornered contests were the most striking manifestation of its failure to expand. While the party had consolidated its 1906 gains, mainly secured through the compact with Herbert Gladstone and the acquiescence of local Liberal organisations, the 1910 election revealed its inability to break through the bonds of the electoral system. The compact had enabled the Labour Party to escape the full rigours of an electoral system favouring the established parties. But the Liberals would tolerate no further subversion of the existing dualism in Great Britain, particularly as the Labour attack was now mainly directed against the Liberals. This acted as a virtual prohibition on Labour's advance.

Of the thirty-five three-cornered contests fought by Labour three were in defence of Labour-held seats and a further eight in seats held by Unionists. The remaining twenty-four contests were in seats held by Liberals. Perhaps the January contests at Bow and Bromley and Whitehaven could be placed on the credit side as they led in December to Liberal withdrawal and Labour success. Perhaps to have deprived the Liberals of victory at Cockermouth in January and at Camlachie on both occasions might be listed as some form of achievement. But the debit side was daunting. In twenty-nine of the thirty-five contests, the Labour Party came bottom of the poll, in the other six second, and only once did the Labour man finish in front of the Liberal.

More detailed examination reinforces the impression of Labour impotence in attack. In nine of the three-cornered contests in January 1910 there had also been three-cornered struggles in 1906. In all nine seats the Labour proportion of the poll declined, while in only four cases did the Liberal proportion fall.[19] This was particularly noticeable in the Clyde Valley, where four losses had occurred as the result of Labour intervention in 1906. Liberal recovery and Labour decline enabled the Liberals to recapture three of these seats – North Ayrshire, Govan and North-West Lanark – in 1910. Camlachie and Huddersfield enjoyed the dubious distinction of having triangular contests in 1906 and both 1910 elections. Both constituencies reveal a steady deterioration in the Labour vote. The evidence suggests that, if Labour failed on the first occasion, a process of attrition set in, a process accentuated if Labour intervention cost the anti-Unionists the seat. Liberal or Unionist withdrawals as at Bow and Bromley, Whitehaven and West Fife produced exceptions to this general rule.

TABLE 18.8 LABOUR DECLINE IN TWO THREE-CORNERED CONTESTS

		1906	1906 by-election	Jan 1910	Dec 1910
Huddersfield	Liberal	38·2	36·0	39·8	37·5
	Labour	35·2	33·8	31·6	29·0
Camlachie	Liberal	33·6		33·0	40·6
	Labour	30·0		28·9	18·1

Nor should the success of the limited Liberal counter attack be underrated. The Liberals recovered Jarrow, Gateshead and South-West Manchester from Labour. The Liberal victory at Wakefield in December, after Labour's failure in January, instanced the electoral advantages to the party that held the middle ground. And a Liberal defeat was perhaps the most impressive example of Liberal resilience. The Chatham figures tell their own story:

	1906	Jan 1910	Dec 1910
Lab.	6,692	6,130	1,103
U.	4,020	7,411	6,989
Lib.	–	–	4,302

These admittedly few indications tend to confirm Cole's contention that 'any serious clash with the Liberal Government might have endangered every Labour seat, except perhaps a very few which were "pocket boroughs" of the Miners' Federation'.[20] These were but straws in the wind, but it was an ill wind for Labour. The party's efforts to expand broke on the rocks of Liberal opposition and the bias of the electoral system.[21]

IV

In the absence of reliable survey material the electoral historian must rely on two sources for the interpretation of electoral behaviour. First, the voting returns which in 1910 provide particularly valuable clues because of the distinctive regional trends; and secondly, the views of contemporary participants and observers, often intelligent and perceptive but inevitably impressionistic, and frequently distorted by political commitment. However, by marrying these comments with the statistical evidence it is possible to reach some tentative conclusions on voting behaviour.

In Great Britain the results of both elections were governed by the swing in January 1910. Implicit in the geographic contrast which resulted from this movement of opinion was a significant political division. The contrast between the North with the Celtic fringe and the South was in part a contrast between Liberal and Unionist Britain. At the regional level the swing in January 1910 correlated closely with the political tradition of the region. Generally. the stronger the Unionism of a region in the past, the bigger the swing to Unionism in January 1910. And at the constituency level the movement against the Government was greatest in seats with Conservative antecedents, least in seats with a Liberal tradition. The result was that the two political Britains were more clearly juxtaposed than at any election since 1885. In the Unionist heartland, outside the London conurbation, the Unionists were as strong as in the heyday of their long hegemony. At the same time the strength of the anti-Unionists in their traditional northern strongholds and in the Celtic fringe was close to the levels reached in the peak Liberal year of 1906. Underlying the obvious geographic contrast was an evident political polarisation.

This suggests that in 1910 traditional partisan loyalties overrode all other considerations to an extent rare in British elections. While party identification is the prime determinant of voting behaviour, in any particular election immediate events and personalities are superimposed upon this basic orientation. These lead to temporary deviations in voting

behaviour which favour the party benefiting from the short-term
factors. But in 1910 contemporary events and personalities either made
little impression or, more likely, served to reinforce the traditional
partisan division in the nation. Fears for the political consensus were
perhaps not unwarranted.

TABLE 18.9 SWING AND THE POLITICAL TRADITION OF REGIONS
JAN 1910 GREAT BRITAIN

Unionist ranking	Region	% of total seats won by Unionists 1886–1900	Swing 1906–Jan 1910
1	South-East England	98	9·6
2	Outer London	97	8·3
3	Wessex	91	8·5
4	Western Lancastria	90	2·7
5	Thames Valley – Essex	90	8·1
6	Western Marches	88	5·2
7	London	79	5·7
8	Western Midlands	77	5·3
9	Severn	75	5·8
10	North and East Ridings	72	2·1
11	Eastern Lancastria	70	2·2
12	Lincolnshire	67	3·1
13	Cumbria	65	2·3
14	East Anglia	63	5·4
15	Southern Scotland	62	1·1
16	Clyde Valley	57	1·3
17	South-West Peninsula	53	4·3
18	Scottish Highlands	46	0·6
19	Eastern Midlands	42	4·0
20	West Riding	29	1·4
21	North-East England	26	4·2
22	Forth Valley	25	1·2
23	Industrial Wales	21	2·6
24	Rural Wales	19	1·5
25	North-East Scotland	8	5·6

In 1910 factors that might have blurred a sharp political division
along traditional party lines were mostly absent. Neither major party
was fragmenting as in 1886, nor splitting into openly contending
factions as in 1904–5. The disruptive Irish issue was not, in January at
least, as salient as in 1886, 1892 and 1895. No major party was damaged
by its patent inability to govern, as the Liberals had been in 1895 and
the Unionists in 1906. Nor was the country swept by jingo fervour as in

1900, or by a tidal revulsion against a party too long in power as in 1906. Thus forces which in the past had led voters to deviate from their party identification into non-voting or cross-voting were not present in 1910.

TABLE 18.10 SWING AND THE POLITICAL TRADITION OF
CONSTITUENCIES JAN 1910 GREAT BRITAIN

Seats won by Unionists 1885–1906	No. Seats	Median swing to Unionists
6 times	87	5·4
5 times	112	6·2
4 times	86	4·9
3 times	52	3·1
Twice	54	3·7
Once	45	2·8
Not at all	86	3·2

Party loyalties were confirmed because so many of the issues in dispute were old controversies, and all issues were involved in one long-standing dispute, that over the powers of the House of Lords. The transitional nature of Edwardian politics ensured there was a mixture of old and new questions in 1910. The taxation proposals of the Budget, Tariff Reform and the collectivist policies of the Liberals aroused the kinds of controversy that were to dominate the political debate in the decades ahead. But the elections also involved a host of disputes which were hangovers from the nineteenth century. The President of the National Liberal Federation, Sir William Angus, told the annual Council of the Federation on the eve of the second election: 'Many of the good causes for which generations of Liberals have patiently laboured have suddenly matured. Harvest is upon us.'[22] The institutional role of the House of Lords, the constitutional position of Ireland, the role of the Anglican Church in Wales and in education, the land question, franchise extension, and policy towards the liquor trade had been dominant issues in politics for at least a generation. Moreover Tariff Reform although recent in origin revived old controversies. Above all, the dispute over the powers of the House of Lords involved all other questions. All the anti-Unionist parties were prepared to subordinate their particular causes to the struggle against the Lords, while for Unionists the preservation of the traditional order seemed dependent upon the survival of a strong Upper Chamber.

Furthermore it was on the controversies of the past thirty years that the elections were most likely to be decisive. Taxation proposals could always be moderated, a point which too many Unionists neglected until the first election was upon them; fiscal change would take time to accomplish; while the passage of social legislation would be a gradual and was probably anyhow an inevitable process. But the emasculation of the House of Lords, the disestablishment of the Church in Wales and the granting of Home Rule appeared likely to follow speedily on a Liberal victory, and once accomplished were probably irreversible. Whatever distaste 'Whiggish' Liberals might feel for some of the more modern features of Liberal policy, most seemed prepared to stick with the Government because of the prospect of the immediate settlement of traditional grievances. Likewise, moderate Unionists who deplored the rejection of the Budget, or Unionist Free Fooders who disliked official fiscal policy, were yet drawn to support their party from fear of the immediate and irretrievable consequences of a Liberal victory. The choice for Free Fooders, as Lord Hugh Cecil reminded his ally Cromer, 'is not . . . between the devil and the deep sea, but between the devil who is very close, and a sea which is shallow and remote'.[23] St Aldwyn typified these attitudes in that, although a Free Fooder and opposed to rejection of the Budget, he nevertheless publicly urged all Unionists to support their party because of the momentous consequences of a Liberal victory.[24]

Finally most of the modern issues strengthened traditional allegiance. The Liberals' tentative steps towards a distribution of income through social reform and taxation confirmed the loyalty of the working classes, the basis of Liberal strength, outside the Celtic fringe, for a generation, while antagonising the middle classes, the basis of Unionist urban support in the same period. While Tariff Reform may have confused partisan loyalties among sections of the middle class, it strengthened the allegiance of the working classes to the Liberals and of rural England to the Unionists.

A wry post-election comment in the Conservative *Blackwood's Magazine* recognised something of the Liberal appeal to all the forces associated with the party.

> The Government went to the country [in January] with a magnificent electioneering battery. The liberties of England, the food of the people, the pensions of the old, the job of the workman, the future of the trade unions, the continuance of Nonconformity, the authority of the Ten Commandments – all were in imminent peril from the Conservative party.[25]

In the circumstances the appeal of the Liberal Party to all identified with it was immensely strong. Conversely the Liberal J. A. Hobson noted: 'The [January] election presents more plainly than ever before the instinctive rally of the classes and interests, whose possessions, prestige, privileges and superiority of opportunity are menaced . . .'[26] All the causes and interests which the Unionists had defended during their long hegemony were subsumed in the constitutional question and threatened by a Liberal victory. It behoved all true Unionists to put away the apathy and defection that had characterised their behaviour in 1906.

But if this interpretation, with its emphasis on the role of traditional partisan loyalties, is correct why did the country fail to return to the customary balance of political forces, why in fact was the Unionist hegemony not restored? One explanation is that the hegemony had been essentially negative, maintained not by majority identification with the Unionist Party, but by the fact that the forces distorting partisan loyalties from 1886 to 1900 were mostly anti-Liberal. A second is that in certain critical regions a realignment of voter loyalties appears to have taken place to the advantage of the anti-Unionists.

In the elections between 1886 and 1900 Gladstone's obsession with Ireland, the internal feuds of the Liberal Party, and the Unionist posture as the guardians of empire, worked at different times to prevent the Liberals from establishing a hold on electors who might otherwise have supported them. Thus it has been argued that the hegemony was negatively sustained by Liberal deviation, particularly into abstention, rather than positively by a clear majority identification with the Unionist Party.[27] In 1910, without such anti-Liberal currents running, the full strength of the traditional Liberal vote could be realised. Although jingo and Home Rule appeals were not absent from the 1910 elections, they seem to have been less detrimental to the Liberals than in the past. The naval scare probably harmed the Liberals in the dockyard towns, but outside these it does not appear to have had a significant impact. On Home Rule Sandars warned Balfour before the second election that 'we shall hug a delusion if we imagine that Home Rule will alarm the average voter of 1911 as it did in 1886 & 1895'.[28] And if any party suffered electorally from feuding in 1910 it was the Unionists not the Liberals. Thus the Liberals stood to benefit from the absence of forces that had handicapped them in the last fifteen years of the nineteenth century.

But it was not simply Liberal freedom from the ills that had plagued the party in the past that explains the Liberal victory. But for the fact that some of the elements of change in 1906 proved permanent, the anti-Unionists would have scored less impressive victories. Without a degree of realignment resulting from durable changes in party identification, it is unlikely that the anti-Unionists would have secured a majority of seventy seats in Great Britain in 1910. In Scotland the realignment took the form of a restoration of the Liberal pre-1886 supremacy. The two regions Southern Scotland and the Clyde Valley, which had been marginally Unionist during the hegemonic period, now remained strongly Liberal. The swing to the Unionists in these regions in January 1910 was minimal, and much lower than in other regions with a similar Unionist tradition [see table 18.9]. Here at least the 1906 reversal of traditional voting patterns seems to have been maintained.

In England the realignment appears to have been related to socio-economic factors. This involves consideration of a further dimension implicit in the geographic divide. For in England, in a crude sense which will require later qualification, the division was between two nations, between urban, industrial working-class England and rural, suburban, and middle-class England. Again the movement of opinion in January clarified the distinction. In terms of class and community the variance of the swing in January 1910 was reminiscent of the changes in the critical realigning election of 1886. The swing in the predominantly middle-class, rural, and urban–rural constituencies was distinctly above average; in the mixed-class constituencies average; and in the predominantly working-class and mining constituencies distinctly below average.

TABLE 18.11 TYPE OF CONSTITUENCY AND SWING
ENGLAND JAN 1910

Type of constituency	No.	Swing (%)
A. *Urban*		
1. Predominantly middle-class	55	6·2
2. Mixed-class	95	4·9
3. Predominantly working-class	118	3·8
B. *Mixed Urban/Rural*	49	6·0
C. *Rural*	96	6·0
D. *Mining*	21	0·5
	434★	Average swing England 4·9

Notes: ★ Does not include university constituencies. Two-member constituencies treated as two single constituencies. Swing not calculable in twenty-two constituencies.

This social division was in part a facet of the traditional political contrast. Between 1886 and 1906 the Unionist strength had lain mainly in the rural counties, the market, county and cathedral towns, in suburbia, spas and seaside resorts, and in the middle-class and commercial constituencies in the great cities. Liberal strength in England lay above all in the industrial regions, particularly the two great urban concentrations of the West Riding and the North-East. But in sharpening the division between industrial England on one hand, and rural and suburban England on the other, the swing weakened, at least relatively, both major parties in regions where they had been traditionally strong but where their support had been socially atypical. Thus Unionist recovery was mostly disappointing in those key industrial areas with a Tory tradition – Lancastria and working-class London, regions in which they had possessed majorities between 1886 and 1906. Similarly, although of less electoral significance because of the number of seats involved, the swing against the Liberals in rural regions which in the past had leant towards them, was greater than might have been anticipated from the traditional pattern. The Liberals could usually command a narrow majority in the poor agricultural regions west of the River Exe and they had done reasonably well amongst the Nonconformist small-holders and rural workers of East Anglia. The shift away from the Liberals in these regions in January was greater than in most of the industrial regions, and notably greater than in most regions with a comparable level of Liberal support in the past. It was particularly strong in East Anglia – a 5·4 per cent swing – whereas the real slump in Liberal fortunes in the South-West Peninsula did not come until the December election, which gave the Unionists a majority in the Peninsula for the first time since 1886.

But the contrast between the swing in industrial England and rural and suburban England highlighted not merely the growing socio-economic cleavage, but the durability of critical features of the 1906 election, which were closely related to this socio-economic polarisation. In a number of predominantly working-class regions there was no return to the Unionist ascendancy that prevailed prior to 1906. It was the almost total failure of the Unionists to recover their traditional position in cotton Lancastria and London, and their only limited success in Western Lancastria, that robbed them of all chance of a majority in Great Britain.[29]

The Celtic fringe appears the classic case of a strong traditional partisan response. 'Scotland at present', wrote the Scottish landowner and

Unionist candidate Seton-Karr in February 1910, 'appears hopelessly Radical. It is, in fact, worse (from our Unionist view) that at any time during the past twenty years.'[30] In Scotland the anti-Unionist total of seats was better than in any year since 1885, in Wales better than in any year except 1906. Unlike England, the cities and the counties of the Celtic fringe were united in repudiation of the Unionists.

The ascendancy of the Liberal Party in Wales and Scotland had resulted from the traditional identification of local nationalism with Liberalism.[31] The struggle for particular national goals – social, religious, economic – had for long been carried on in a political climate different from that in England, and the Liberal Party had been for a generation the champion of these national reforms. Such traditional issues were once more to the fore: in Wales pressure for Welsh Disestablishment and frustration over education legislation; in both parts of the Celtic fringe an enthusiasm for licensing legislation unmatched by the Liberals in England.[32] Land, another traditional issue, was also prominent. There were voters in 1910 who had had personal experience of the Scottish Crofters War of the mid-1880s, and the Welsh Tithe riots of 1887–92. And for those who did not, Lloyd George was merely the most prominent of the speakers to recall the past oppression of the landlords.[33] Thus in the words of *Blackwood's Magazine*:

> . . . the election, being largely fought on old issues, resurrected much of the old Liberalism of the eighties. Scottish Liberalism is one of the most stubborn and feudal forms of Conservatism that we know. It is loyalty partly to a tradition, and partly to a man, for the spirit of Mr. Gladstone still walks on Scottish soil, and the echoes of Midlothian have not died away.[34]

With so formidable a ghost on the other side it is little wonder that Austen Chamberlain concluded his analysis of the Scottish returns in January with the assertion: 'Our only chance of winning Scotland is to change the issue on which Scotsmen vote. As long as it is the land, the landlords, and the rest of the Radical programme we shall be beaten.'[35]

Yet it had been the House of Lords which, by flouting national sentiment, had ensured that regional nationalism was fully mobilised behind the party of Gladstone in 1910. The Lords' rejection of Liberal palliatives for the Scottish land problem had been widely denounced in Scotland. The defeat of the Licensing and Education Bills brought a storm of protest from Wales, while the frustration of Welsh national objectives by the House of Lords was the major theme of Lloyd George's campaigns in Wales. The climax came with the rejection of a budget popular in Wales and Scotland if for no other reason than its obvious unpopularity with the landlords. 'In Scotland', Balfour confided to his cousin Salisbury, 'I have no doubt whatever that there is a genuine and strong feeling against what they call "the hereditary principle" . . . it is the sort of *doctrinaire* point which appeals to the less educated among my countrymen.'[36] But Balfour's condescension could not erase the political impact of the 'doctrinaire point'. As the *Scotsman* bluntly told Unionists: '. . . the feeling in the Highlands is now so strong against the House of Lords that it seems hopeless to think of even contesting a Highland seat until . . . the question of the House of Lords is settled.'[37] Thus the Lords cemented, and Lloyd George exploited, the traditional alliance between Liberalism and regional nationalism. In Scotland and Wales the Lords were neither presented nor seen simply as the enemies of the Liberals, of the Nonconformists, of the tenant farmers and the labourers, but as the hereditary foes of the Welsh and Scottish peoples.

It is likely that this explanation is most relevant to the rural parts of Wales and Scotland, where in January 1910 the swing was not typical of most rural regions, and where anyhow a regional culture was most likely to have greatest vitality. In the industrial regions of the Clyde and South Wales, with a mixed population and social structures similar to that of the English industrial concentrations, regional nationalism was less strong. Here the success of the anti-Unionists probably derived from influences similar to those which ensured the supremacy of the anti-Unionists in most of the English industrial regions. The realignment on the Clyde for instance has close parallels with that in Lancastria. Nevertheless even on the Clyde and in South Wales Liberal strength *vis-à-vis* the Unionists was probably aided by national sentiment, while it seems likely that the alignment of Liberalism with nationalism enabled the Liberals to face with confidence the challenge from the left.

The Unionist recovery in the Tory heartland stemmed also from a strong traditional response, although here antipathetic to the Government. The fertile agricultural areas of South England had long been the foundation of the electoral strength of a party which saw itself as the guardian of the traditional order. Here the threat to that order aroused unparalleled opposition. 'I verily believe', wrote Salisbury, 'that we only prevailed amongst the agricultural constituencies because the leaders of opinion in the upper & middle classes . . . *strove as they have never striven before* to gain the support of the electors.'[38] This activity of the rural hierarchy took place in an environment characterised by a tradition of more harmonious rural class relations than in Scotland and Wales. As the Liberals themselves confessed, abuse of the landlords did not pay off here because 'the peasant class do not dislike their landlords personally'.[39]

To traditional partisan feelings the rural hierarchy added more immediate grievances. They disliked Liberal land policies and feared that the valuation of agricultural land was the prelude to land taxation. J. A. Pease, himself a victim of the rural landslide, admitted that the rural districts 'failed to understand the Budget';[40] Tories, of course, claimed that they understood its implications all too well. Nor was support for the Unionists based simply on traditional or negative grounds. One Unionist Free Fooder considered that 'the large majority of [farmers] were out and out Protectionists', and thus active supporters of the positive side of the Opposition programme.[41] Sandars concluded in a letter to his master in January 1910 that 'All our evidence goes to show that the County elector is really more keen on Tariff Reform than his urban brother.' He attributed this partly to 'the fact that the dear food cry is more easily dealt with in the country districts than in the towns'.[42]

The result was that in the rural heartland, as Spender lamented to Bryce, 'the landlords & farmers have taken the labourers with them to the polls on the grounds that the Govt. is "taxing land" and hitting the countryside, whereas the other party proposes to help agriculture and restore rural prosperity by keeping out the foreign foodstuffs'.[43] The political traditions of rural Southern England, the community of interest in rural society, the intense activity of the local leaders of opinion on behalf of the Conservative Party, the acceptance of Tariff Reform as a panacea for rural ills, and no doubt a certain amount of pressure revived the fortunes of Unionism in the countryside. While the reaction was most pronounced in the South, it was felt throughout rural England, and in the market and county towns which served the agricultural areas.

While rural England swung back to the Unionists, the political polarisation in terms of class became sharper in urban England. Table 18.11 (p. 400) confirms the first impression of the *Daily Telegraph* on 17 January 1910 that the Unionist gains were mostly in those constituencies 'where a middle-class residential element is strong'. London provides a microcosm of the national picture, with the swing to the Unionists tending to be larger the greater the proportion of the middle class in the constituency.[44] In the commuter belt around London, the major suburban agglomeration in the kingdom, the swing to the Unionists was greater than anywhere but in the rural Home Counties.

It appears, therefore, that the movement of the middle classes to Unionism, halted or even reversed in 1906, was now running apace again as both the tensions within Nonconformity and the discontent on the Whiggish wing of the Liberal Party had presaged. With the sins of Balfour's Government receding into the past, it was probably Liberal social and financial policies accompanied by 'Lloyd Georgism' that renewed the trend of the middle classes to the right.[45] Bonar Law ascribed this swing 'to the wholesale revolt of the middle classes against the Radical Party'.[46] The Budget no doubt sped and spread the process, for, as Fitzroy recognised, the 'Government in their efforts to tax the rich, never seem to have realised the risk they ran by exciting the fears of small property owners . . . [who] are far more sensitive to the cry of confiscation than those who enjoy a wider margin'.[47]

TABLE 18.12 SWING AND CLASS JAN 1910 LONDON

Middle class % of electorate	No. constituencies	Average % Swing
Less than 10	15	4·5
10–20	12	4·7
20–40	12	6·1
Over 40	18	7·2

Source of classification: Thompson, *Socialists, Liberals and Labour*, pp. 301–2. City of London not included.

This strong middle-class reaction against the Government seems to have occurred in suburban seats, resorts and residential constituencies in the South, but it appears to have been muted in the North. While it is possible that the low swing in Northern England hid a significant middle class move to the right, offset by Liberal gains over 1906 amongst the working classes, this seems unlikely for there is little evidence of a distinctive middle-class swing in constituencies in which such a movement might be detected. For instance in the thirty-seven predominantly middle-class and mixed class urban constituencies in the North, the average swing to the Unionists in January was only 3·0 per cent, only 0·6 per cent above the average swing in the North. Again, the ability of the Liberals to hold such commercial and residential constituencies as North Leeds, Central Leeds and North-West Manchester never held prior to 1906, and the fact that the Liberal share of the poll in the residential and commercial parts of Sheffield had never been better, tend to support the contention that the middle-class shift to the Unionists in the North was at most a marginal one.[48]

Radical sentiment and militant Nonconformist habits probably limited Liberal losses amongst the middle classes in the North. Unlike the South, the Liberal tradition was much stronger amongst the middle classes of the North particularly in the West Riding and the North-East. Wealthy Liberals might grumble about the Budget, but the opportunity to settle old scores with the hereditary enemy provided a countervailing force in middle-class communities with a Liberal tradition.

Equally important was the opposition of the middle classes in the North to Tariff Reform. Thomas Burt, the Northumberland miners' leader, with not unjustified pretensions to amateur sociology, told Bryce that though 'some large capitalists and great employers of Labour . . . have been captured by Tariff Reform . . . [it] has scarcely touched the middle class' in the North-East.[49] This was an even more significant consideration in the textile manufacturing areas, above all in Lancashire where the Liberal hold on middle-class voters was not abetted by a radical tradition. The threat of Tariff Reform to the competitive position of Britain's textile exports outweighed for many the fears of Socialistic legislation. 'It is agreed by the electioneers of both parties', wrote Spender, 'that . . . in Lancashire the business and middle classes are voting with us against Tariff Reform of any kind.'[50] Some support for this distinction between middle-class behaviour in the North as compared with the South comes also from an election survey conducted by the *Daily Mail* amongst one middle-class group, the retailers. The survey discovered that while only 25 per cent of London retailers supported Free Trade, 40 per cent of retailers in Lancashire did so. And the Unionist newspaper admitted that the Lancashire figure was an underestimate as many Free Traders refused to co-operate.[51]

While the middle classes at least in the South swung away from the Government, the working classes particularly in the North appear to have remained remarkably loyal. This behaviour was crucial to the electoral outcome. The working classes of the North-East and the West Riding had long furnished the sinews of Liberal strength. The anti-Unionists as a result of the realignment of 1906 now found comparable support amongst the workers of the Eastern Midlands, cotton Lancastria, the Clyde Valley and working-class London.

Once again traditional factors played a role. The Liberal election slogans of 1910 were well designed to appeal to the radical element in the working classes. Austen Chamberlain echoed a widely held opinion in his belief that the West Riding 'voted against the Lords, above all, against the landlords',[52] favoured targets of Radical wrath. A Liberal candidate in a northern industrial city reported that it was 'simply useless to attempt a defence of the Lords in the open air'.[53] The Irish working-class garrisons were also rallied to the Liberal side in pursuit of another long-standing objective.

The working classes shared with many northern entrepreneurs an antipathy to Tariff Reform. Often it was linked in a vague demonology with the Lords and the Tories. As a Conservative correspondent to the *Daily Telegraph* observed, 'Many working men . . . have hazily gathered . . . that Tariff Reform is the name of a plot between the Tories and the peers, involving dear bread, black bread, or the likelihood of no bread for the people'.[54] Although there may have been something in Burt's belief that 'some of the unemployed, and the very poor, who naturally are ready to credit any quack promise of amelioration, take more or less readily to tariff reform',[55] the great majority of workers seem to have rejected the Tory nostrum. The political and trade union leaders of the working classes were almost to a man strong Free Traders, and this constituted a formidable obstacle to the conversion of the workingman to Tariff Reform.[56] Above all, 'the ordinary workman has got fixedly in his head . . . that whatever tariff reform may mean, or may not mean, it will inevitably increase the price of food. That stands and will ever stand, as a barrier in the way of protection.'[57] It was a fixation fatal to Tariff Reform.

There was too a more positive appeal. The Liberals, particularly Lloyd George and Churchill, had set out in 1908 to restore the fortunes of their party by restoring morale and by rallying working-class support. They sought to achieve this latter objective by pre-empting aspects of Labour's social programme, and by presenting the Budget, Lloyd George's morale booster, as a method of benefiting the 'have-nots' openly or implicitly at the expense of the 'haves'. The elections of 1910 yielded dividends on this policy.

> . . . the working class constituencies of Lancashire, Yorkshire and Cheshire . . . were lost [wrote Lt. Col. Bromley-Davenport, Conservative candidate for Macclesfield] because masses of the extremely poor have been attracted by the Lloyd Georgian programme of vague suggestions that something is to be given to them which at present belongs to somebody else. They do not know what it is, but want to take their chance of getting it whatever it may be. . . .[58]

The economic climate was particularly propitious for the Lloyd

Georgian operation. In an age of ostentatious consumption the level of real wages was at best stationary, and the working classes were particularly attuned to the Liberal campaign with its strong class motif.[59] Lord Wolmer, Unionist candidate for Newton, ascribed 'our defeat in Lancashire to class feeling', arguing that 'the other side relied wholly on class feeling'.[60] *Blackwood's* was of the same opinion. 'Lancashire and Yorkshire on the whole have given a class vote. . . . The workman is begining to stick by his class in politics as for some years he has stuck by it in industrial disputes. The Tory working man, who used to be common in Lancashire, is fast disappearing.'[61] This response to the Liberals in working-class areas was in part the measure of the success of the Liberal effort to rally the working classes to the party, while the losses in suburbia were in part the cost of the operation.

The economic conditions which helped this campaign might well have been expected to benefit Labour, but the critical nature of the election, the tradition-orientated response of the electorate, and the tactical difficulties of a small third party in a predominantly two-party system all helped the Liberals to contain Labour. In addition the personalities and policies of Lloyd George and Churchill limited Labour's opportunities. 'The big thing', wrote Beatrice Webb at the end of 1910, 'that has happened in the last two years is that Lloyd George and Winston Churchill have practically taken the *limelight*, not merely from their own colleagues, but from the Labour Party.'[62] In so far as Labour co-operated with the Liberals they were successful. When the party challenged the Liberals they were almost uniformly unsuccessful.

But the Labour Party's contribution to the anti-Unionist victory was not just the forty or forty-two seats it won. This was recognised on all sides. Austen Chamberlain wrote:

> The combination of the Liberal and Labour Parties is much stronger than the Liberal Party would be if there were no third party in existence. Many men who would in that case have voted with us voted on this occasion as the Labour Party told them, i.e. for the Liberals. The Labour Party . . . is much stronger than at first appears from the electoral returns, for on this occasion it has chiefly served as a cat's-paw to pull Liberal chestnuts out of the fire.[63]

A similar complaint came from the left. The S.D.P. journal, *Justice*, noting that Liberal successes had been most striking where Socialists had been most active, blamed the Labour leaders for this deflection of votes, imputing it to 'their unqualified adulation of the Asquith administration' and 'their unbounded praise of the Budget'.[64] Liberals were simply thankful. With pardonable exaggeration from one who was the chief

Liberal architect of the alliance, Herbert Gladstone wrote: 'In England itself but for a fairly solid alliance with Labour Liberals would have been done.'[65]

Undoubtedly the strong Labour endorsement of the ostentatious Liberal efforts to benefit the working classes by redressing the balance of income distribution in their favour through legislation, and the friendly relations that existed between Liberals and Labour men in many constituencies helped rally the working classes behind the Liberals. Professor Hewins attributed his party's poor showing in Yorkshire to the solidarity of the Liberal–Labour alliance, a solidarity in his view deriving from a common social policy.[66] But perhaps Labour's major contribution to augmenting the Liberal vote amongst the working classes was simply the strong anti-Unionist stand it took on all the major issues in dispute. Labour's role continued critical in maintaining the breaches into the erstwhile Tory working-class areas, above all Lancastria, achieved in 1906. As in 1906 this was very much a combined effort by the anti-Unionist parties, and its success was perhaps the most crucial feature of the post 1906 realignment.

TABLE 18.13 BREAKTHROUGH IN LANCASTRIA

Results 1885–1900 Won by Unionists	1906	Jan 1910	Dec 1910
5 times but won by Labour	8	9	6
„ „ Liberal	10	6	2
4 times but won by Labour	1	1	1
„ „ Liberal	9	9	7
Total Labour	9	10	7
Total Liberal	19	15	9

Thus sustained by traditional Radicalism, antipathy to Tariff Reform, a strong current of class feeling and a mutually beneficial relationship with the Labour Party, the Government retained its grip on most of industrial working-class England, and therefore on the Treasury benches. Only in the Western Midlands, where the small-scale paternalistic structure of much of local industry muted class antagonisms, where foreign competition made industrial protection particularly attractive, and where the Chamberlain mystique was powerful, was there an above average swing in a predominantly industrial region.[67] Even here the Unionist reaction was less than might have been expected given the electoral tradition of the region.

In addition the Unionists were spectacularly successful with one scattered group of workers, those in the naval ports and always fickle dockyard towns. These saw some of the biggest shifts against the Government in the January election e.g. swings of 19·8 per cent at Portsmouth, 17·2 per cent at Chatham and 8·2 per cent at Devonport. Here, at least, the naval agitation seems to have paid dividends. Moreover retrenchment and unemployment had been severe in these centres, and the naval scare was usually coupled with fears for employment. Typical was the appeal issued by the *Western Morning News* on 15 January, polling day in the Devon Ports:

> [The prosperity of Devonport and Plymouth] must decline unless there is in power a strong Government, determined to maintain our Navy at sufficient strength to repel aggression and to keep Britain mistress of the seas ... The possibility of fresh discharges from the Dockyards immediately after the election of the Radicals, as was the case in 1906, is not pleasing to contemplate.

The twin appeal to patriotism and self-interest seems to have worked well in the dockyard towns. It probably also lay behind Will Crooks's defeat at Woolwich, variously ascribed to the 'Jingo scare' and unemployment at the Arsenal.[68]

We have been concerned mainly with opinion changes in January, for these determined the outcome of both elections. Not unexpectedly, few voters appear to have changed their minds between the two elections. They had little reason to do so. Despite the clarification of the Liberal constitutional position and some important changes of Unionist emphasis, December was very much in the nature of an uncluttered rerun. The spelling out of the Liberal position on the House of Lords was unlikely to affect the vote, while the Unionists' tactical changes probably came too late to leave much mark. Except perhaps in the euphoric aftermath of Balfour's pledge on Tariff Reform, few on either side expected much change.

Only in Lancastria was the movement of opinion sufficient to warrant more detailed attention. How far was this shift in Lancastria due to the pledge of a referendum on Tariff Reform? The Whole Hoggers belittled the general effect of the pledge by instancing a number of marginal seats, e.g. Lincoln, Cheltenham, Wakefield (supposedly abodes of the Free Fooders in which the referendum failed to help the Unionists), and other seats e.g. Ashton-under-Lyne, South Salford, Wigan, Warrington and North Manchester where Whole Hoggers either repudiated or ignored the pledge and did better than their more faint-hearted colleagues.[69] But against these particular cases could be set the over-all shift to Unionism in Free Trade Lancashire. Most contemporaries agreed with the *Economist* that Unionist successes in Lancashire 'were undoubtedly due to a belief that Mr Balfour had shelved tariff reform'.[70] Most historians have concurred in this view.[71]

It receives support from the fact that there was an above average swing to the Unionists in Scotland and the South-West Peninsula, two other regions where the Free Fooders were strong. In Scotland a post-election survey of Unionist candidates revealed 'an overwhelming body of belief that the referendum promise was of service', although there was also general agreement that 'the promise came too late for its full advantage [to be] reaped'.[72] Yet this coincidence raises a doubt. Lancastria, Scotland and the South-West all had in common a sensitivity to another issue – Home Rule. And if Tariff Reform was apparently shelved in the second election, Home Rule appeared a more immediate menace than in January. The Unionist *Western Morning News* attributed Unionist gains in Devon and Cornwall to Home Rule, as did the Liberal *Westminster Gazette*.[73] Others advanced the alarm of the Irish Tories and the revival of anti-Irish sentiment as at least partial explanations for the pro-Unionist movement in Lancastria and Scotland.[74]

In addition the slight anti-Unionist decline in nearly all the English industrial and urban regions suggests that they might have been marginally handicapped by the stale register in those regions where removals were greatest.[75] Thus any explanation of the Lancastrian shift must take into consideration not only the referendum pledge, but the increased prominence of Home Rule and the possible weakening of the anti-Unionist vote owing to involuntary abstention. It appears likely therefore that even in Lancastria the referendum pledge had at the most but a marginal effect.

The unusual movement of opinion in January 1910 defined the contours of the new electoral order emergent in 1906, but hidden in that election beneath the massive repudiation of Unionism. The swing in 1910 represented a sorting out of the stable and unstable elements in the shift of 1906. In retrospect the landslide of 1906 resulted from two forces: a short-term deviation into Liberalism or abstention by many Unionist identifiers, and a more fundamental and durable commitment to the anti-Unionist parties by erstwhile Unionists and frequent abstainers.

In 1910 the temporary deviants returned to the Unionist fold. It was this movement in the Tory rural heartland and in the Conservative

suburban strongholds by contrast with Liberal solidarity in the industrial central spine and the Celtic fringe, that accounts for the strong
traditional element in the geopolitical contours of 1910. Here old
causes, old issues, old allegiances lie at the heart of electoral change or
lack of change, with the Liberals marginally benefiting from the
absence of the negative forces that helped sustain the Tory hegemony.

But the second element in the landslide of 1906 was not a temporary
but a long-run desertion from Unionism, and its impact is therefore
still apparent in 1910. Here the sharpening socio-political cleavage,
encouraged by Liberal policies and by the Liberal–Labour alliance and
reinforced, as well as occasionally blurred to the Liberal advantage,
by Unionist fiscal policy, seems critical both to electoral change and
to the failure to restore the Unionist hegemony.

Thus the elections of 1910 were characterised by a partial reaction
to the upheaval of 1906, a reaction which clarifies the new electoral
order, ushered in by 1906 but obscured in that election by the unstable
and short-term charges inherent in any critical election.

The elections of 1910 produced the last but not the least of Liberal
victories. Electorally less overwhelming than 1906, their legislative
yield was greater. On the issue formally referred on each occasion to
the electors, the results were decisive: Lloyd George's Budget was
passed in April 1910; the Parliament Act in August 1911. Legislative
dividends were paid to the Government's supporters: for the working
classes a further instalment of the Liberal social programme in the
National Insurance Act; for its Labour allies payment of Members and
a partial revision of the Osborne Judgement; for the Celtic fringe a
start, under the cumbersome procedures of the Parliament Act, with
measures to disestablish the Church in Wales and to grant Home Rule
to Ireland.

On the other hand for those involved in rejecting the Budget
nemesis followed quickly. Balfour, who had presided over rejection,
lost his leadership, and Lansdowne, who had moved rejection, his
authority, as a result of the ruination of the House of Lords. The
leaders of the party organisation, Acland-Hood and Percival Hughes,
who had encouraged rejection, lost their posts. The Whole Hoggers,
the vanguard of the movement for rejection, saw the imperial side of
their programme jettisoned in the wake of defeat.

The thrice-defeated Unionist Party relapsed into an intransigence
marked by a growing alienation from a political system that seemed to

favour its opponents. Obsessed with the fear of a permanent minority status while the Irish Members remained in the Commons, the Unionists were yet unprepared to support a generous constitutional settlement for Ireland. Many preferred to die in 'the last ditch' for the Lords, and to risk civil war to preserve the Union. In so doing they contributed to the undercurrent of violence that marked British politics and society in the years preceding the outbreak of war in 1914. If the struggle to preserve the Union helped restore the morale of the Unionist Party, the risks were great. But for the war the Unionists might well have yielded to temptations which could have wrecked both the party and the political system. The threatened breakdown of the political consensus in 1914 had been foreshadowed in the political polarisation of January 1910, and in the desperate response of many Unionists to their third successive defeat in December. Both had boded ill for the politics of pragmatism and compromise.

The dynamism of Edwardian Liberalism resulted from the yoking together of the Radical drive to reform the structures of political power with the social reformer's desire to redress the economic imbalance. In the elections of 1910 these aims were obviously harnessed, and the calibre and orientation of the Liberal Party leadership promised their joint pursuit in the future. In addition the changes in partisan identification, which appeared to underline the realignment of 1906–10, suggested that the Liberals would not want for opportunities to put their policies on the statute book. Yet their electoral position was vulnerable because of its critical dependence on the traditionalism of the Celtic fringe and on the symbiotic relationship with the Labour Party. Liberal strength deriving from the first might well be eroded after the satisfaction of traditional objectives; Liberal strength from the second as a result of the pretensions and ambitions of Labour.

The settlement of outstanding political and national grievances might undermine Liberal support in the party's Celtic strongholds. The alliance with the Irish Nationalists might not survive the dissolution of the Union. The removal of the barrier of the Lords left the way clear for action on Welsh and Scottish questions. If the Liberals were successful they might well hasten the growth in Wales and Scotland of the politics of class, a development likely to be detrimental to their position in both kingdoms. On the other hand if the Lords turned out to have been an excuse for, rather than the cause of, Liberal inaction, disillusion could equally well weaken the alliance between nationalism and Liberalism.

With Liberal strength in England increasingly dependent on the working classes, the relationship with Labour would become increasingly significant. The Labour Party was unlikely to continue to accept the constraints on its development implicit in the existing relations with the Liberals. The party had been effectively contained in 1910, but its problem of identity was likely to be less acute in the future. Although the party would continue to encounter Liberal resistance within an electoral system biased against third parties, it was unlikely again to be as tactically handicapped as in the elections of 1910. Traditional Radical issues with their appeal to existing loyalties were unlikely to be as prominent in the future, while the party's opportunity to differentiate its platform from that of the Liberals would probably be greater. In 1910 the Labour Party did not, because it could not, disassociate itself from immediate Liberal objectives. But with these attained and with welfare questions coming to the fore, Labour's opportunities to outbid the Liberals would be increased. It seemed likely that at the next general election the Labour Party would endeavour to capitalise on its specifically working-class appeal by mounting a broad offensive against the Liberals in working-class areas. While such an offensive would invite Liberal retaliation and endanger the seats already held by Labour, the conflict engendered could well reverse the general trend of the working classes to the Liberals, a phenomenon in part attributable to Liberal–Labour relations in the Edwardian decade.

But Labour's future was as dependent on Liberal adaptability as on its own initiative. Could the Liberal Party, given the sources of its finance and the social composition of its parliamentary and local elites, compete successfully for working-class votes in an environment less sympathetic to Liberalism? There were signs of strain in the Liberal Party in 1910. But they arose from the successful advance of the Radical wing not from any effective holding operation by the conservative elements in the party. If the elections of 1910 revealed the increasing dependence of the Liberals on working-class votes, they also revealed the readiness of leading Liberals to accept the policy consequences of this dependence, even if it meant shedding followers on the right. The Liberal Party might well sacrifice, as in the past, its 'Whiggish' element in order to shore up its electoral base. Pre-emption of Labour programmes promised to be the future policy, the continued containment of Labour the future strategy, of the Liberal Party. And if containment proved a partial failure, a renovation of the electoral system in order to ensure the survival of both anti-Conservative parties, as in much of continental Europe, was perhaps the most likely outcome.

But the Great War intervened, postponing the election of 1915, disrupting the party system and leaving the historian to speculate on what might have been. The repercussions of war shattered the Liberals, destroyed the Nationalists, and gave a new purpose to Labour. The split in the Liberal Party gave Labour an opportunity which it ruthlessly exploited to establish itself as the second party in the system. But the destruction of a great political party, even one so obviously spent as the post-war Liberal Party, is usually a messy and protracted operation – and a costly one. In Britain it hobbled the Left for a generation.

Yet what succumbed to Labour in the post-war decade was but a shadow of the Edwardian Liberal Party. Labour may have finished off the Liberal Party in this period, but the crippling blow had already been dealt. The split of 1916 doomed the Liberal Party, robbing it of its dynamism, much of its leadership and of its entrenched position in the electoral system. The split resulted not from the challenge of Labour, nor from revolt in the Celtic fringe, nor because the party was somehow unfitted for the realities of the twentieth century. It resulted from the inability of the Liberal Government to win, lose or abandon the war, and from the personal rivalries unleashed thereby. The Liberal Party might, of course, have survived this blow if its enemies had been less numerous, less organised and less determined, and if its own electoral position had been less vulnerable. As it was, to cripple the party was to make its demise inevitable.

Thus victory in 1910 was ultimately fatal to the Liberal Party. It may well be that power tends to corrupt; between 1914 and 1918 it tended rather to destroy its possessors. Many of the institutions of old Europe were brought to the grave by their inability to cope with the cataclysm. The Liberal Party of Great Britain was not the least of these victims. Given power in 1910, it was destroyed in 1916 by the ambivalence of that gift.

Notes

CHAPTER 1   THE UNIONIST HEGEMONY 1886–1902

1. For this development see Paul Smith, *Disraelian Conservatism and Social Reform* (London, 1967); E. J. Feuchtwanger, *Disraeli, Democracy and the Tory Party* (Oxford, 1968), particularly ch. iv; James Cornford, 'The Transformation of Conservatism in the Late Nineteenth Century', *Victorian Studies*, vii (1963) 35–66; and J. P. D. Dunbabin, 'Parliamentary Elections in Great Britain, 1869–1900: A Psephological Note,' *English Historical Review*, lxxxi (1966) 82–92.
2. *Parl. Deb.*, 3rd ser., ccxxxv, 564–5 (29 June 1877).
3. Donald Southgate, *The Passing of the Whigs 1832–1886* (London, 1962) p. 408.
4. Quoted ibid., p. 376. It is relevant to note that Southgate entitles his chapter on the Whigs and the second Gladstone Administration 'The Defence of "Liberty and Property" '.
5. Smith, *Disraelian Conservatism*, p. 192.
6. W. H. G. Armytage, *A. J. Mundella, 1825–1897. The Liberal Background to the Labour Movement* (London, 1951) p. 136, Mundella to Robert Leader, 5 Oct 1873.
7. See Smith, *Disraelian Conservatism*, p. 314 n. 5; Feuchtwanger, *Disraeli, Democracy and the Tory Party*, pp. 80–3; and Dunbabin, *EHR*, lxxxi (1966) 88–9.
8. Trevor Lloyd, *The General Election of 1880* (Oxford, 1968) p. 150.
9. Armytage, *Mundella*, p. 228, 19 June 1885.
10. C. H. D. Howard, 'Joseph Chamberlain and the "Unauthorised Programme" ', *English Historical Review*, lxv (1950) 488, 30 Oct 1885.
11. For the results in the London conurbation see Henry Pelling's pioneering and invaluable guide to politics at the grass roots, *Social Geography of British Elections 1885–1910* (London, 1967) chs ii and iii.
12. J. L. Hammond, *Gladstone and the Irish Nation* (London, 1938) p. 398, Gladstone to Grosvenor, 27 Nov 1885.
13. This distinction between short-term switches and long-run partisan change is critical to the classificatory scheme developed for American presidential elections in Angus Campbell, Philip E. Converse, Warren E. Miller and Donald E. Stokes, *Elections and the Political Order* (New York, 1966) chs ii–viii, a work which has influenced my approach in this book. See also the seminal article by V. O. Key, Jr, 'A Theory of Critical Elections', *Journal of*

Politics, xvii (1955) 3–18, and the use of the classification with historical data in Gerald Pomper, 'Classification of Presidential Elections', ibid., xxix (1967) 535–66.

14. The effect of both questions on the Irish vote in Great Britain is examined in C. D. H. Howard, 'The Parnell Manifesto of 21 November, 1885 and the Schools Question', *English Historical Review*, lxii (1947) 42–51.

15. J. L. Garvin and Julian Amery, *The Life of Joseph Chamberlain* (London, 1935–69) ii 121; Bernard Holland, *The Life of Spencer Compton, Eighth Duke of Devonshire* (London, 1911) ii 76.

16. Quotations in this paragraph from S. Gwynn and G. M. Tuckwell, *The Life of the Rt. Hon. Sir Charles Dilke* (London, 1917) ii 182–3; A. R. D. Elliot, *Life of George Joachim Goschen, First Viscount Goschen, 1831–1907* (London, 1911) i 308; and *Annual Register 1885*, p. 174.

17. Derek W. Urwin, 'Development of Conservative Party Organisation in Scotland until 1912', *Scottish Historical Review*, xliv (1965) 90–6.

18. For this realignment see C. C. O'Brien, *Parnell and His Party 1880–1890* (Oxford, 1957); and H. J. Hanham, *Elections and Party Management, Politics in the Time of Disraeli and Gladstone* (London, 1959) pp. 179–87.

19. Kenneth O. Morgan, *Wales in British Politics 1868–1922* (Cardiff, 1963) pp. 22, 65; and Lloyd, *General Election of 1880*, p. 150.

20. Garvin and Amery, *Chamberlain*, ii 141.

21. A. G. Gardiner, *Life of Sir William Harcourt, 1827–1904* (London, 1923) i 594, 11 July 1886.

22. For method of calculation see Appendix III.

23. Two Liberal Unionists stood for Dundee, a two-member seat. In addition there were seven Liberal Unionist candidates in Ireland, mostly in Ulster. See D. C. Savage, 'The Origins of the Ulster Unionist Party, 1885–6', *Irish Historical Studies*, xii (1961) 185–208.

24. G. E. Buckle (ed.), *The Letters of Queen Victoria*, third series (London, 1930) i 143, journal entry, 8 June 1886. For a detailed account of this crucial period in Scotland see D. C. Savage, 'Scottish Politics, 1885–6', *Scottish Historical Review*, xl (1961) 118–35. Savage gives weight to disquiet over proposals for disestablishment and disendowment of the Church of Scotland as a further reason for the Liberal decline.

25. Peter Fraser, *Joseph Chamberlain. Radicalism and Empire, 1868–1914* (London, 1966) pp. 166–7, 27 Jan 1895. Chamberlain's stress on the discrete character of Liberal Unionism, or rather Radical Unionism, is a key theme in Michael Hurst, *Joseph Chamberlain and Liberal Reunion. The Round Table Conference 1887* (London, 1967).

26. *Aylesbury*

1885 Lib. (Rothschild)	5,476	1866 L.U. (Rothschild)	4,723
Cons.	2,624	Lib.	1,680
Radical	296		

West Derbyshire

| 1885 Lib. (Cavendish) | 5,020 | 1886 L.U. (Cavendish) unopposed. |
| Cons. | 4,138 | |

For the character of change in the Western Marches see Pelling, *Social Geography*, pp. 197–201.

27. Jesse Collings and Sir John L. Green, *Life of the Rt. Hon. Jesse Collings* (London, 1920) pp. 191–2.

28. John P. Mackintosh, *The British Cabinet* (London, 1962) 197–2–3, 484–9. For a valuable critique of this thesis see G. N. Sanderson, 'The "Swing of the Pendulum" in British General Elections, 1832–1966', *Political Studies*, xiv (1966) 349–60.

29. R. C. K. Ensor, *England 1870–1914* (Oxford, 1936) p. 284.

30. P. Corder, *The Life of Sir Robert Spence Watson* (London, 1914) p. 269, Harcourt to Watson, President, National Liberal Federation, 23 July 1895.

31. J. G. Kellas, 'The Liberal Party and the Scottish Church Disestablishment Crisis', *English Historical Review*, lxxix (1964) 31–46; and Pelling, *Social Geography*, pp. 373–5, 381–6.

32. Beatrice Webb, *Our Partnership* (London, 1948) p. 201. Henry Pelling, *Popular Politics and Society in Late Victorian Britain* (London, 1968) pp. 92–5, argues against interpreting the swing in working-class seats in 1900 as a positive proletarian response to the Boer War, attributing it rather to working-class antipathy to alien immigration in London's East End and to a pro-Unionist shift in the Irish Catholic vote. This is hardly an adequate explanation of the general phenomenon, nor does it explain the swing in working-class constituencies without significant Irish or alien immigrants e.g. in the mining constituencies. Furthermore, Pelling's argument for a pro-Unionist movement amongst Irish Catholics in 1900 fails to take account of the hostility of the reunited Nationalist Party, the most 'pro-Boer' of all the political parties, towards the Unionists on the chief issue of the election, the British intervention in South Africa. Nor were the pro-Unionist shifts he identifies in two Glasgow constituencies typical of the swing in Scottish constituencies with a significant Irish Catholic vote.

33. For these difficulties in London see Paul Thompson, *Socialists, Liberals and Labour. The Struggle for London 1885–1914* (London, 1967) ch. v.

34. Barry McGill, 'Francis Schnadhorst and Liberal Party Organisation', *Journal of Modern History*, xxxiv (1962) 27–8.

35. A. L. Thorold, *The Life of Henry Labouchere* (London, 1913) p. 299.

36. Hurst, *Chamberlain and Liberal Reunion*, pp. 377–8, Labouchere to Herbert Gladstone, 9 July 1886.

37. *Annual Register 1886*, p. 224.

38. *EHR*, lxxxi (1966) 94.

39. *Victorian Studies*, vii (1963) 54–5. This relationship had been noted much earlier by the Conservative M.P. Lord George Hamilton, *Parliamentary Reminiscences and Reflections, 1868–1885* (London, 1916) p. 65. See below, pp. 36–7, for criticism of the thesis in relation to the election of 1906.

40. *Annual Register, 1900*, p. 204.

41. *EHR*, lxxxi (1966) 96.

CHAPTER 2   THE END OF THE HEGEMONY 1902-6

1. xxvi (Aug 1902) 115.
2. Rosebery Papers, 83, Hugh Cecil to Rosebery, 7 Feb 1910.
3. *Annual Register 1902*, p. 143.
4. xxvi (Sept 1902) 228.
5. Garvin and Amery, *Chamberlain*, iv 494.
6. p. 71.
7. *Review of Reviews*, xxx (Aug 1904) 121.
8. Asa Briggs, 'The Political Scene', in Simon Nowell-Smith (ed.), *Edwardian England, 1901-14* (London, 1964) p. 56.
9. Élie Halévy, *A History of the English People in the Nineteenth Century*, v. *Imperialism and the Rise of Labour*, 2nd ed. (London, 1951) 209. Pelling, *Social Geography*, p. 293, notes 'a Nonconformist explosion' in North Leeds in 1902.
10. Garvin and Amery, *Chamberlain*, iv 495.
11. See Pelling, *Social Geography*, pp. 61-2, 75.
12. Holland, *Devonshire*, ii 283-4, Sir Henry James to Devonshire, 6 Aug 1902.
13. Ibid., 284, 22 Sept 1902.
14. Fraser, *Chamberlain*, p. 234, 21 Sept 1902.
15. For Bury see *Annual Register 1902*, p. 143; and for Woolwich see Frank Bealey and Henry Pelling, *Labour and Politics 1900-1906. A History of the Labour Representation Committee* (London, 1958) p. 144.
16. Garvin and Amery, *Chamberlain*, iv 495, Chamberlain to Balfour, 4 Aug 1902.
17. Detail in this paragraph from Bealey and Pelling, *Labour and Politics*, particularly chs. v, vi.
18. *National Review*, xlvi (Feb 1906) 950-1.
19. Dunbabin, *EHR*, lxxxi (1966) 98-9.
20. See Alfred Gollin, *Balfour's Burden; Arthur Balfour and Imperial Preference* (London, 1965) chs. i, ii.
21. Quoted in Briggs in Nowell-Smith, *Edwardian England*, p. 50.
22. Holland, *Devonshire*, ii 356. The letter as printed has 'Greenwich' not 'Woolwich'. The reference, however, was obviously to the Woolwich by-election.
23. Austen Chamberlain, *Politics From Inside* (London, 1936) p. 28, Balfour to Austen Chamberlain, 10 Sept 1904.
24. Holland, *Devonshire*, ii 308, Balfour to Devonshire, 4 June 1903.
25. *1903*, pp. 231, 191.
26. Gollin, *Balfour's Burden*, p. 246, Balfour to Chamberlain, 18 Feb 1905.
27. The economic arguments for and against Tariff Reform and the economic interests involved are surveyed in Halévy, v, *Imperialism and Labour*, 285-356; and in Bernard Semmel, *Imperialism and Social Reform. English Social-Imperial Thought 1895-1914* (London, 1960) chs. iv, v.
28. Michael Craton and H. W. McCready, *The Great Liberal Revival 1903-6* (London, 1966) pp. 4, 22.
29. There is a massively documented account of the feud within the Unionist Party in Garvin and Amery, *Chamberlain*, vols. v, vi. The two major commentaries on the feud are Gollin, *Balfour's Burden*, as the title indicates, Balfourian in sympathy; and Fraser, *Chamberlain*, chs. x, xi, a more balanced account, sympathetic to Chamberlain. The following paragraphs also draw

heavily on the opening section of my article, 'Free Fooders, Balfourites, Whole Hoggers. Factionalism within the Unionist Party, 1906-10', *Historical Journal*, xi (1968) 95-124.

30. Gollin, *Balfour's Burden*, p. 206.
31. Pelling, *Social Geography*, p. 232.
32. See the stimulating essay by J. R. Jones in Hans Rogger and Eugen Weber (eds.), *The European Right* (London, 1965) pp. 29-70, which concentrates on the radical Right in Britain in the years before 1914, and which is notable, amongst other things, for a convincing rehabilitation of Lord Willoughby de Broke.
33. Balfour Papers, Add. MS. 49759, ff. 185-98, Lord Hugh Cecil to Balfour, 4 May 1907.
34. James Cornford, 'The Parliamentary Foundations of the Hotel Cecil', in Robert Robson (ed.), *Ideas and Institutions of Victorian Britain* (London, 1967) pp. 282-3.
35. Kenneth Young, *Arthur James Balfour* (London, 1963) pp. 213-14, Balfour in the Commons, 10 June 1903.
36. Blanche E. C. Dugdale, *Arthur James Balfour, First Earl of Balfour* (London, 1936) ii 84-5.
37. The history of the Free Fooders is traced in H. W. McCready, 'The Revolt of the Unionist Free Traders, 1903-6', *Parliamentary Affairs*, xvi (1963) 188-206; and R. A. Rempel, 'The Abortive Negotiations for a Free-Trade Coalition to Defeat Tariff Reform: October 1903 to February 1904', *Proceedings of the South Carolina Historical Association*, 1966, pp. 5-17. It is clear from Randolph Churchill, *Winston S. Churchill*, ii, *Young Statesman 1901-14* (London, 1967), that Tariff Reform was the excuse rather than the cause of Churchill's departure from the Unionist Party. See chs. i, ii, and particularly the revealing letter to Hugh Cecil on pp. 70-2. The pre-1906 desertion or retirement of the Liberal element amongst the Free Fooders reduced the Free Fooders after 1906 to a small rump of Cecilian Conservatives and Whiggish Liberal Unionists, whose general ideological outlook was the most conservative of the factions within the Unionist Party.
38. *The Times*, 23 Jan 1911.
39. A. K. Russell, 'The General Election of 1906' (D.Phil. thesis, Oxford, 1962) p. 142.
40. Ibid., p. 519.
41. See Fraser, *Chamberlain*, pp. 271-3; and Gollin, *Balfour's Burden*, pp. 274-6.
42. Includes J. W. Taylor (Chester-le-Street), who was returned as an independent Labour candidate and joined the Labour Party in February 1906.
43. See Cornford, *V.S.*, vii (1963), 56, for argument and statistical evidence on this point.
44. Russell, 'Election of 1906', p. 505.
45. Pelling, *Social Geography*, p. 432 n. 3, draws attention to Cornford's failure to allow for the stale register and the natural increase in the electorate.
46. Gollin, *Balfour's Burden*, pp. 252-3.
47. Harcourt Papers, reports of London Liberal agents to W. M. Crook, Secretary, London Liberal Federation, May 1906. In several constituencies less than 50 per cent of the London outvoters went to the polls in 1906.

48. See below, pp. 377–9.
49. Includes the fifty L.R.C. candidates plus J. W. Taylor (see p. 421, n. 42) and the five Scottish Workers Representation Committee candidates. There is a seat-by-seat analysis of Labour successes and failures in Bealey and Pelling, *Labour and Politics*, pp. 266–74.
50. See Appendix IV.
51. p. 541.
52. See Campbell *et al.*, *Elections and the Political Order*, pp. 75–6; and Pomper, *J. Polit.*, xxix (1967) 535–66.
53. Ibid., 561.

CHAPTER 3   WINTER 1908–9

1. Bryce Papers, MS. 13, ff. 132–5, Sir Courtenay Ilbert, Clerk of the House of Commons, to Bryce, 30 Jan 1908. All references are to the English manuscripts unless otherwise noted.
2. Cecil Papers (Papers of Lord Robert Cecil, later Viscount Cecil of Chelwood), Add. MS. 51158, W. F. D. Smith (Conservative M.P., Strand, 1891–1910) to Robert Cecil, 18 Jan 1908; Bryce Papers, MS. 13, ff. 132–5, Ilbert to Bryce, 30 Jan 1908; *Liberal Magazine*, xvi (1908) 24–7; and Burns Papers Add. MS. 46326, diary, 18 Jan 1908. Buxton was a cadet of one of the great Liberal families of the period. The family derived its wealth from brewery interests, and was noted both for its Anglicanism and its Radicalism.
3. Roger Fulford, *Votes for Women* (London, 1947) p. 161.
4. Burns Papers, Add. MS. 46326, diary, 18 Jan 1908.
5. Ibid., Add. MS. 46330. Burns kept two diaries and appeared to use them indiscriminately. There are frequently entries for the same day in both diaries.
6. Spender Papers, Add. MS. 46389, ff. 167–70, Fitzmaurice to Spender, 10 Dec 1908. Fitzmaurice was the younger brother of the Marquess of Lansdowne, the Unionist leader in the House of Lords.
7. I am indebted to Dr. A. S. King for allowing me to use his transcript of the Carrington Diary.
8. Lucy Masterman, *C. F. G. Masterman* (London, 1939) pp. 110–12. Charles Masterman was a junior minister at the time, and a confidant of Lloyd George.
9. Burns Papers, Add. MS. 46326, diary, 11 Dec 1908.
10. Roy Jenkins, *Mr. Balfour's Poodle* (London, 1954) pp. 33–4.
11. See, e.g., Spender Papers, Add. MS. 46391, ff. 246–7, Bryce to Spender, 29 May 1908; and Carrington Diary, 25 Mar 1908.
12. Burns Papers, Add. MS. 46326, diary.
13. See Arthur J. Taylor, 'The Edwardian Economy' in Nowell-Smith, *Edwardian England*, pp. 111–12.
14. See A. H. H. Matthews, *Fifty Years of Agricultural Politics: being the History of the Central Chamber of Agriculture* (London, 1915) 137–43. The antipathy of the rural interests to the existing political set-up is also reflected in the movement for an agricultural party independent of both the major parties. Ibid. pp. 341–8, 408–15.

15. The historian of the Temperance movement claimed that Asquith's Licensing Bill 'brought the whole Trade out in the most violent political campaign of its history'. G. B. Wilson, *Alcohol and the Nation* (London, 1940) p. 185. See also Lord Newton, *Lord Lansdowne: A Biography* (London, 1929) pp. 367–8.

16. Bryce Papers, MS. 13, ff. 126–39, Ilbert to Bryce, 12 Mar 1908. Asquith's parliamentary private secretary, Edwin Montagu, warned his master to the same effect a few days later. '. . . in the constituencies . . . not only Members, but organisations are very, very frightened.' S. D. Waley, *Edwin Montagu: A Memoir and an Account of his Visits to India* (Bombay, 1964) p. 27, Montagu to Asquith, 17 Mar 1908.

17. For details see *Liberal Magazine*, xvi (1908) 172; and National Liberal Federation, *Report, Thirtieth Annual Meeting* (1908) p. 78.

18. The best short account of the Edwardian economy is the chapter by A. J. Taylor in Nowell-Smith, *Edwardian England*, pp. 103–38. There is also a useful discussion with particular reference to the 1907 recession in W. W. Rostow, *The British Economy of the Nineteenth Century* (Oxford, 1948) pp. 26–37.

19. Harcourt Papers, Cabinet memorandum, Report on Unemployment in the United Kingdom in September 1908, 10 Oct 1908.

20. The most comprehensive account of this controversy is to be found in A. J. Marder, *From the Dreadnought to Scapa Flow*, i, *The Road to War 1904–14* (London, 1961) ch. vii. For a fascinating and complementary account, particularly on the roles of Fisher and Garvin and the publicity surrounding the panic, see A. M. Gollin, *The Observer and J. L. Garvin 1908–14* (London, 1960) ch. iii.

21. Asquith Papers, 21, ff. 61–7, marked 'secret'.

22. Balfour Papers, Add. MS. 49797, ff. 89–90, Gwynne to Sandars, 30 Mar 1909.

23. Masterman, *Masterman*, p. 110.

24. 12 Dec 1908.

25. 20 Feb 1909.

26. *H.C. Deb.*, 5th ser., i, 13 (16 Feb 1909).

27. See Sir Almeric Fitzroy, *Memoirs* (London, 1925) i 372; and Scottish Liberal Association, Report of meeting between Scottish organisers and Scottish Whip, 4 Jan 1909.

28. Bryce Papers, MS. 13, ff. 160–3, and ff. 164–5, Ilbert to Bryce, 4, 9 July 1909. In a Cabinet memorandum of 30 Jan 1909 Lloyd George made the same point. '. . . we have been driven to consider the possibility of circumnavigating the House of Lords by incorporating a scheme for the valuation and taxation of land in a Budget.' Asquith Papers, 99, ff. 26–8.

29. See Jenkins, *Balfour's Poodle*, pp. 40–1.

30. Roy Jenkins, *Asquith* (London, 1964) p. 193.

31. Ibid. p. 196.

32. See, e.g., the contrasting views of Gollin, *Garvin*, pp. 95–7; Élie Halévy, *A History of the English People in the Nineteenth Century*, vi, *The Rule of Democracy* 2nd ed. (London, 1952) i 286; and Peter Rowland, *The Last Liberal Governments*, i, *The Promised Land 1905–1910* (London, 1968) p. 213.

33. 16, 23 Jan 1909.

34. *Labour Leader*, 2 Apr 1909. The Labour figures for South Leeds and Croydon were:

	1906	1908–9
South Leeds	4,030 (32·6%)	2,451 (19·4%)
Croydon	4,007 (20·2%)	886 (4·2%)

35. There is as yet no work on the Labour Party post-1906 to compare with the detailed studies of the pre-1906 period by Poirier and Bealey and Pelling. The fullest account is J. H. Stewart Reid, *The Origins of the British Labour Party* (Minneapolis, 1955) chs. ix–xiii, but this concentrates on Westminster and neglects the party in the country. Chapter ii of Henry Pelling, *A Short History of the Labour Party* (London, 1961), entitled 'A Pressure Group under Pressure (1906–14)' is the best short survey of this period of Labour history.

36. Elibank Papers, MS. 8801, f. 92, Churchill to Elibank, 23 Sept 1906.

37. I.L.P., *Report, Eighteenth Annual Conference (1910)* p. 35. The speaker was F. W. Jowett, Labour M.P. for West Bradford.

38. Labour Party, *Report, Ninth Annual Conference (1909)* p. 62.

39. Ibid., pp. 4, 61–2; Labour Party Documents, ii, ff. 92–3, minutes, N.E.C., 10 Sept 1908; Laurence Thompson, *Robert Blatchford, Portrait of an Englishman* (London, 1957) pp. 193–4; and I.L.P., *Report, Seventeenth Annual Conference (1909)* pp. 65–6.

40. See the comments of J. B. Glasier, editor of the *Labour Leader*, in the *Labour Leader*, 2 Apr 1909; and also of Keir Hardie, I.L.P., *Report, Seventeeth Annual Conference (1909)* p. 66.

41. See Margaret Cole, *Makers of the Labour Movement* (London, 1948) p. 220; and Pelling, *Popular Politics and Society*, pp. 136–46.

42. Pelling, *Short History of the Labour Party*, p. 21, Hardie to Glasier, 27 Dec 1908.

43. Denis Gwynn, *The Life of John Redmond* (London, 1932) pp. 113–17; F. S. L. Lyons, *The Irish Parliamentary Party, 1890–1910* (London, 1951) pp. 111–14; H. W. McCready, 'Home Rule and the Liberal Party, 1899–1906', *Irish Historical Studies*, xiii (1963) 316–48; F. S. L. Lyons, *John Dillon* (London, 1968) pp. 273–82; and Russell, 'Election of 1906', ch. vii, *passim* and pp. 192–5.

44. Elibank Papers, MS. 8801, ff. 213–14, T. P. O'Connor to Elibank, 14 Apr 1909.

45. Lyons, *Irish Parliamentary Party*, pp. 172–22. Surprisingly Gwynn's biography of Redmond has nothing on Redmond's relations with O'Brien and Healy in the period 1906–9. Lyons, in his recent study of Dillon, adds little to his earlier account, arguing that the 'importance – except to O'Brien – [of] these tiresome squabbles … should not be overrated'. *Dillon*, p. 304. The two fullest accounts, both O'Brienite, are William O'Brien, *An Olive Branch in Ireland and its Failure* (London, 1910) pp. 345–460, and T. M. Healy, *Letters and Leaders of My Day* (London, 1928) ii 475–89.

46. See Lyons, *Irish Parliamentary Party*, 124–5; O'Brien, *Olive Branch*, pp. 433–51.

47. 16 Dec 1908. For similar comments on the Trades Disputes Bill by the Duke of Devonshire and on the Old Age Pensions measure by Professor Dicey see Lord Askwith, *Lord James of Hereford* (London, 1930) p. 294, and Strachey Papers, Dicey to Strachey, 8 July 1908.

48. Strachey Papers, Strachey to Margot Asquith, 15 Dec 1908 [copy].

49. Balfour Papers, Add. MS. 49696, ff. 167–70, St Aldwyn to Balfour, [?] Aug 1908; and Milner Papers, Milner to Earl Grey, 29 Nov 1908.

50. Balfour Papers, Add. MS. 49730, ff. 52–5, notes on House of Lords reform by Lansdowne, 31 Jan 1910.

51. Jenkins, *Balfour's Poodle*, p. 92.

52. Chamberlain, *Politics From Inside*, pp. 145, 151. Reports at the Liberal Unionist headquarters indicated a Liberal majority of twenty, but the party Organiser, John Boraston, thought the reports too pessimistic. Ibid.

53. For the renewal of the conflict in the immediate aftermath of the election see Peter Fraser, 'Unionism and Tariff Reform: The Crisis of 1906', *Historical Journal*, v (1962) 149–66; and Garvin and Amery, *Chamberlain*, vi, ch. cxvi. The remaining section of this chapter is developed in greater detail in Blewett, *Hist. J.*, xi (1968) 95–124.

54. See ibid. 96–7, for a discussion of the evidence on, and the controversies over, the size of these factions.

55. Balfour Papers, Add. MS. 49771 ff. 166–7, Acland-Hood to Wilfred Short, Balfour's personal secretary, 14 Jan 1907.

56. Cromer Papers, F.O. 633/18, pp. 129–32, comments on Cromer memorandum from Balfour of Burleigh, 9 Jan 1909.

57. Charles Petrie, *The Life and Letters of the Rt. Hon. Sir Austen Chamberlain* (London, 1939) i 205, Balfour to Austen Chamberlain, 9 Feb 1907.

58. See Dugdale, *Balfour*, ii, 41–6.

59. Sir Charles Petrie, *Walter Long and His Times* (London, 1936) pp. 109–10.

60. Bonar Law Papers, 18/3/28, Maxse to Law, 2 Jan 1907.

61. Fraser, *Chamberlain*, 287–8; and Chamberlain Papers, AC 17/3/64, Arthur Lee to Austen Chamberlain, 28 Oct 1907.

62. Bonar Law Papers, 18/4/66.

63. R. B. Jones, 'Balfour's Reform of Party Organisation', *Bulletin of the Institute of Historical Research*, xxxviii (1965) 94–101.

64. See Balfour Papers, Add. MS. 49765, ff. 10–16, and ff. 34–8, Sandars to Balfour, 22 Jan 1907, and 2 Apr 1907.

65. Cecil Papers, Add. MS. 51159, typed memorandum, 1 Jan 1909, by G[eorge] H[amilton].

66. Balfour Papers, Add. MS. 49771, ff. 170–3, Acland-Hood to Sandars, 11 Jan [1908].

67. *The Times*, 20 Jan 1909.

68. Balfour Papers, Add. MS. 49376, ff. 12–15, 9 Feb 1907 [copy].

69. Ibid., Add. MS. 49708, ff. 106–30, Balfour to Selborne, 6 Mar 1908.

70. Ibid., Add. MS. 49771, ff. 170–3, Acland-Hood to Sandars, 11 Jan [1908].

71. The pertinent description of Goulding is from Gollin, *Garvin*, p. 103, and of Winterton from the Balfour Papers, Add. MS. 49737, ff. 84–5, Robert Cecil to Balfour, 13 Jan 1908. I am grateful to Mr W. D. Rubinstein of Johns Hopkins University for comments on the composition and nature of the Confederacy.

72. For evidence of Central Office complicity see Bonar Law Papers, 18/5/87, Goulding to Law, 25 Jan 1909; and Chamberlain, *Politics From Inside*, p. 142.

73. 10 Feb 1909.

74. Arthur Elliot Papers, E. G. Brunker (Secretary, Unionist Free Trade Club) to Elliot, 5 Feb 1909. See also ibid., memorandum by Robert Cecil, Feb 1909.

I am indebted to Dr R. Rempel for allowing me to use his transcript of the Arthur Elliot Papers.

75. See Asquith Papers, 12, ff. 3–10, for correspondence marked 'secret' between Asquith and Robert Cecil. See also Cecil Papers, Add. MS. 51159, for Cecil's correspondence with C. E. Mallet of the Liberal-dominated Free Trade Union.

76. Elliot Papers, Brunker to Arthur Elliot, 5 Feb 1909.

77. Cecil Papers, Add. MS. 51072, Cromer to Robert Cecil, 25 Dec 1908. See also Cromer Papers, F.O. 633/18, pp. 99–113, 'Memorandum on Position of Unionist Free Traders', Dec 1908.

CHAPTER 4   THE BUDGET OF LLOYD GEORGE

1. For details see Bernard Mallet, *British Budgets 1887–8 to 1912–13* (London, 1913) pp 298–313.

2. William George, *My Brother and I* (London, 1958) p. 220.

3. Generally, although not universally, regarded as an oratorical flop. John Burns who found the speech 'nervous, overweighted, tedious and pitiably diffuse . . . sighed for an hour of Gladstone and 20 minutes of Asquith'. Burns Papers, Add. MS. 46327, diary, 29 Apr 1909.

4. Rowland, *Last Liberal Governments*, i 220, Masterman to Gladstone, [?] Feb 1910, discussing his work with Lloyd George on the Budget. Ilbert told Bryce on 11 August that 'The Treasury people tell me that Lloyd George, who began with knowing nothing about the Bill, now knows it better than anyone else'. Bryce Papers, MS. 13, ff. 176–9.

5. See the letters to Asquith on 7 April 1909 from Sir George Murray, Permanent Secretary to the Treasury, and Walter Runciman, who had himself spent a year at the Treasury, Asquith Papers, 22, ff. 127–30, 132–5. See also the *Economist*, 1 May 1909 and the *Liberal Magazine*, xviii (1910), 217–18.

6. The words are those of the Permanent Secretary to the Treasury. Asquith Papers, 22, ff. 127–30, Murray to Asquith, 7 Apr 1909.

7. Quoted in Stephen McKenna, *Reginald McKenna* (London, 1948) p. 67.

8. Asquith Papers, 99, ff. 127–8, Cabinet memorandum on the Taxation of Land Values, 13 Mar 1909, from Lloyd George. See also Riddell, *More Pages From My Diary 1908–14* (London, 1934) p. 65.

9. See Mallett, *British Budgets*, 433–6, 449–64; L. G. Chiozza Money, *Riches and Poverty*, 10th ed. (London, 1911), ch. iii; A. L. Bowley, *The Change in the Distribution of the National Income 1880–1913* (London, 1920) 10–22.

10. This calculation is based on an allocation of tax loads suggested in Mallett, *British Budgets*, pp. 449–50. Moreover it should be remembered that the tax load was highly concentrated on the upper segment of the income-tax payers.

11. Taylor in Nowell-Smith, *Edwardian England*, p. 130.

12. Strachey Papers, Dicey to Strachey, 25 Sept 1909. What disturbed Dicey even more was his fear that 'the bribe has been, or probably will be, accepted'.

13. See Asquith Papers, 22, f. 123, Murray to Asquith, 7 April 1909, for Murray's mystification over the allocation of the revenue from the motor and petrol

taxes; and Churchill, *Churchill*, companion volume ii 885, for Churchill's warning to Lloyd George that 'You must not seem to be looking about for excuses to spend public money'.

14. Churchill was very close to Lloyd George at the time, and was as well busily canvassing the Ministry and the country with plans for social reform. See particularly Churchill, *Churchill*, ii ch. ix; and Winston Spencer Churchill, *Liberalism and the Social Problem* (London, 1909).

15. Churchill, *Churchill*, companion volume ii 887.

16. George, *My Brother and I*, p. 220, Lloyd George to William George, 6 May 1908.

17. Fitzroy, *Memoirs*, i 379; Sir Walter Runciman, *Before the Mast – and After* (London, 1924) pp. 281–2; and Robert Rhodes James, *Rosebery, A Biography of Archibald Philip, Fifth Earl of Rosebery* (London, 1963) pp. 465–6.

18. See Rosebery Papers, 42, for Perks's correspondence with Rosebery, mid-1909. There is a savage portrait of Perks – 'a combination of Gradgrind, Pecksniff and Jabez Balfour' – in Webb, *Our Partnership*, pp. 231–2.

19. Robert Speaight, *The Life of Hilaire Belloc* (London, 1957) p. 233.

20. *Nation*, 1 May 1909.

21. Spender Papers, Add. MS. 46386, ff. 198–200, 24 May 1909. Some allowance no doubt should be made for the natural enthusiasm of the measure's creator.

22. 14 May 1909.

23. See the *Labour Leader*, 7 May 1909 and Philip, Viscount Snowden, *An Autobiography* (London, 1934) i 196–9. Snowden's 1909 ILP pamphlet, *A Few Hints to Lloyd George* had foreshadowed many of the new taxes.

24. Burns Papers, Add. MS. 46327, diary, 23 July 1909. The swing to the Unionists in the three by-elections was Mid-Derby (where a Labour candidate stood with Liberal backing) 6·5 per cent; Dumfries Burghs 5·0 per cent; High Peak 2·3 per cent.

25. Bryce Papers, MS. 13, ff. 176–9, Ilbert to Bryce, 11 Aug 1909.

26. Balfour did not speak on a public platform between 21 May and 27 July, and Lansdowne not between 3 May and 16 July.

27. Speech in the City, 28 June, *The Times*, 29 June 1909.

28. Maxse Papers, 460, f. 365, Viscount Ridley, President T.R.L., to Maxse, 15 Aug 1909; and Gollin, *Garvin*, p. 102.

29. 31 July 1909.

30. 22 Aug 1909.

31. Joynson-Hicks quoted in Emily Allyn, *Lords versus Commons* (New York, 1931) p. 180.

32. National Union, minutes, Council, 14 May 1909.

33. Maxse Papers, 460, ff. 373–6, Winterton to Maxse, 18 Aug 1909. Winterton's source, the M.P. in question, is not identified, but evidence in the letter suggests it was F. E. Smith. Winterton, unlike his Confederate friends, also doubted the wisdom of rejection.

34. Gollin, *Garvin*, pp. 105–11, 119–22.

35. Gollin has argued convincingly for placing Balfour's decision in early August. Ibid. pp. 113–16.

36. 15 May 1909.

37. Bryce Papers, MS. 13, ff. 170–5, Ilbert to Bryce, 3 Aug 1909.

38. Ibid.

39. Based mainly on information in *Who's Who 1910*. As peers for whom information concerning landholdings was not available have been treated as owning less than 5,000 acres, this probably underestimates the number of substantial landholders voting against the Budget. *The Daily News*, 28 Dec 1909, in an article entitled 'The Lords who killed the Budget', estimated that the peers voting against the Budget owned in all 10,376,995 acres.

40. Balfour Papers, Add. MS. 49766, ff. 1–3, Sandars to Balfour, 15 Sept 1909.

41. Cromer Papers, F.O. 633/18, pp. 250–2, Strachey to Cromer, 3 Sept 1909.

42. *The Times*, 24 June 1909.

43. Ibid.

44. Cromer Papers, F.O. 633/18, pp. 285–6, Salisbury to Cromer, 21 Nov 1909.

45. Bonar Law Papers, 18/5/100, Maxse to Bonar Law, 29 July 1909.

46. Lady Victoria Hicks Beach, *Sir Michael Hicks Beach, Earl St Aldwyn* (London, 1932) ii 258.

47. Quoted in Arthur Redford, *Manchester Merchants and Foreign Trade* (Manchester, 1934–6) ii 105.

48. Joseph Chamberlain's Birmingham home.

49. Strachey Papers, Northumberland to Strachey, 7, 13, and 21 Sept 1909.

50. Newton, *Lansdowne*, pp. 378–9, Lansdowne to Balfour of Burleigh, 2 Oct 1909.

51. Strachey Papers, Dicey to Strachey, 25 Sept 1909.

52. Ibid., Strachey to Dicey, 2 July 1909 [Copy]. Strachey was passing on information received from Cromer.

53. Newton, *Lansdowne*, p. 379, Lansdowne to Balfour of Burleigh, 2 Oct 1909.

54. Balfour Papers, Add. MS. 49719, ff. 106–9, Esher to Sandars, 11 Oct 1909. See also Hicks Beach, *Hicks Beach* ii 259–61 St Aldwyn to Balfour, 20 Sept 1909.

55. Newton, *Lansdowne*, p. 379.

56. National Union, minutes, Executive Committee, 25 Aug 1909.

57. Chamberlain, *Politics From Inside*, p. 181.

58. Cromer Papers, F.O. 633/18, 253–5, Balfour of Burleigh to Cromer, 8 Sept 1909, confidential. Burleigh was 'satisfied that if the Lords reject the Budget there will be a complete débâcle of the Conservative Party in Scotland'. Ibid. pp. 274–5, Burleigh to Cromer, 25 Oct 1909.

59. M. V. Brett and Oliver, Viscount Esher (eds.), *Journals and Letter of Reginald, Viscount Esher* (London, 1934–8) ii 407. See also Goulding's similar estimate in Gollin, *Garvin*, p. 118.

60. Strachey Papers, Lichfield to Strachey, 29 Sept 1909.

61. Balfour Papers, Add. MS. 49766, ff. 15–16, Sandars to Balfour, 11 Oct 1909.

62. Newton, *Lansdowne*, pp. 378–9, Lansdowne to Balfour of Burleigh, 2 Oct 1909.

63. Balfour Papers, Add. MS. 49860, ff. 133–4b, John P. Croal, editor of the *Scotsman*, to Balfour, 19 Aug 1909.

64. Gollin, *Garvin*, p. 118, Sandars to Garvin, 26 Aug 1909.

65. Balfour Papers, Add. MS. 49860, f. 167, Balfour to Colonel Denny, 13 Nov 1909 [copy].

66. Gollin, *Garvin*, p. 110.

67. George, *My Brother and I*, p. 230. Masterman, *Masterman*, p. 140, notes that in August Lloyd George began to hope for rejection.
68. Lloyd George's letters to his brother provide evidence for all these assertions. See George, *My Brother and I*, pp. 230–2.
69. James, *Rosebery*, p. 465.
70. Gollin, *Garvin*, pp. 122–3; Chamberlain, *Politics From Inside*, 181–2. Lloyd George, recognising Rosebery's failure to give a lead on rejection, correctly interpreted the speech as 'a soft-nosed torpedo'. *Nation*, 18 Sept 1909.
71. Jenkins, *Balfour's Poodle*, p. 58.
72. Quotations from *The Times*, 23 Sept 1909. See also Chamberlain, *Politics From Inside*, pp. 182–3.
73. Ibid.
74. Haldane Papers, MS. 5981, ff. 121–2.
75. Harcourt Papers, Harcourt to Marks.

CHAPTER 5   THE COMING OF THE FIRST ELECTION

1. George, *My Brother and I*, p. 232, Lloyd George to William George, 22 Oct 1909.
2. This Cabinet was held a fortnight before Balfour's Bingley Hall speech and most Ministers probably still believed that rejection was unlikely. Burns noted in his diary after the Cabinet: 'Serious discussion on what will not occur.' Burns Papers, Add. MS. 46331, diary, 8 Sept 1909.
3. A typed undated copy of this memorandum is in the Asquith Papers, 22, ff. 214–23, while a printed copy dated July 1909 is in the Harcourt Papers.
4. Asquith Papers, 5, ff. 150–1, Asquith to the King, 8 Sept 1909 [copy].
5. Harcourt Papers, Cabinet memorandum, 'Action Consequent on Rejection', from Churchill, 1 Oct 1909.
6. Material and quotations in this paragraph from Asquith Papers, 5, ff. 150–1, Asquith to the King, 8 Sept 1909 [copy]; Harcourt Papers, Cabinet memorandum from John Burns, 4 Oct 1909; and ibid., Churchill memorandum, 1 Oct 1909.
7. Ibid.
8. The reason for this coincidence is examined below, p. 97.
9. CAB. 41/32/42, Asquith to the King, 24 Nov 1909. For the course and outcome of the debate see pp. 99–100 below.
10. CAB. 41/32/41, Asquith to the King, 17 Nov 1909; and ibid. 41/32/44, Crewe to the King, 16 Dec 1909.
11. National Liberal Federation, minutes, Executive Committee, 15 Dec 1909.
12. On the morning of 16 December, Archibald Gordon, younger son of Lord Aberdeen, and a close friend of Asquith's eldest daughter, Violet, had died as a result of injuries in a car accident. In the ensuing weeks Asquith, deeply attached to his family, was much concerned about his daughter's health. Much that remains inexplicable in his conduct in these weeks probably stems from this personal worry added to his heavy political burdens.
13. CAB. 41/32/44, Crewe to the King, 16 Dec 1909.

14. Fitzroy, *Memoirs* i 391.

15. Asquith Papers, 23, ff. 200–6, telegrams, George Haw (with Lloyd George in Wales) to Vaughan Nash, Asquith's private secretary, 22 Dec 1909, and Asquith to Nash, 23 Dec 1909.

16. Ibid. 1, ff. 245–6, Knollys to Nash, 25 Dec 1909.

17. Balfour Papers, Add. MS. 49766, ff. 48–9, Sandars to Short, 25 Dec 1909.

18. Asquith Papers, 22, ff. 229–30, Cabinet memorandum, 'Effect of the Rejection of the Finance Bill by the House of Lords', from Sir George Murray, 7 Sept 1909.

19. Ibid., ff. 236–7, Cabinet memorandum, 'The Finance Bill and the Lords' from 'the pen of a high constitutional authority', 9 Sept 1909. For the identification of Ilbert as the author of this memorandum see Bryce Papers, MS. 13, ff. 186–188, Ilbert to Bryce, 4 Nov 1909.

20. CAB. 41/32/40, Asquith to the King, 3 Nov 1909.

21. See Asquith Papers, 22, ff. 259–61, for a copy of this measure, dated 5 Nov 1909.

22. Bryce Papers, MS. 13, ff. 186–9, Ilbert to Bryce, 4 Nov 1909.

23. This paragraph is based on Ilbert's account of a meeting between himself, Lloyd George, Churchill and Chalmers at Churchill's office at the Board of Trade on 12 November 1909. Ibid. ff. 190–1, Ilbert to Bryce, 13 Nov 1909. It is worth noting that three days before this meeting Sandars had written to Maxse complaining that the Civil Service and particularly Sir Robert Chalmers 'is disgustingly partisan'. Maxse Papers, 460, f. 450.

24. Asquith Papers, 22, ff. 274–9, Cabinet memorandum, 'The Finance Bill and the Lords', from Sir Courtenay Ilbert, 16 Nov 1909. Part of this memorandum is quoted in Jenkins, *Asquith*, p. 201.

25. CAB. 41/32/41. This letter also reveals that the revenue officials had now drastically reduced the estimate for the temporary deficit from £50,000,000 to £20,000,000, and put the 'irrecoverable loss of revenue' at less than £1,000,000.

26. Ibid., 41/32/42, Asquith to the King, 24 Nov 1909.

27. The whole of this long letter is published, Gwynn, *Redmond*, pp. 166–7. A copy of the letter was forwarded by Morley to Asquith, Asquith Papers, 46, ff. 1–3.

28. Gwynn, *Redmond*, pp. 168–9.

29. See J. A. Spender, *The Life of the Right Hon. Sir Henry Campbell-Bannerman, G.C.B.* (London, 1924) ii 348–57; and a series of Cabinet memoranda circulated in October, November 1909 by Asquith, Crewe, Churchill and Loreburn, Asquith Papers, 102, ff. 152–4, 159–60, 183–7.

30. Harcourt Papers, Montagu to Asquith, undated, draft copy enclosed in Montagu to Harcourt, 9 Nov 1909. Montagu noted in his letter to Harcourt that the original had been altered substantially in detail but not in principle. The original letter does not appear to be in the Asquith Papers. Part of this letter has been published in Waley, *Montagu*, p. 34.

31. Asquith Papers, 12, ff. 64–5, Churchill to Asquith, 10 Nov 1909.

32. For the memorandum see H. H. Asquith, *Fifty Years of Parliament* (London, 1926) i 79; for the Albert Hall speech see below pp. 108–9; and for Asquith's address see the *Liberal Magazine*, xviii (1910) 48–9.

33. *H.L.Deb.*, 5th ser., iv, 1342 (30 Nov 1909); Lloyd George's speech, National Liberal Club, *The Times*, 4 Dec 1909; Churchill's speech at Manchester, *Manchester Guardian*, 7 Dec 1909; and J. A. Spender and Cyril Asquith, *Life of Lord Oxford and Asquith* (London, 1932) i 268.

34. At the Albert Hall Asquith stuck closely to his notes, a point Burns noticed critically in his diary. See Burns Papers, Add. MS. 46331, diary, 10 Dec 1909. This suggestion that the key passages of the speech were prepared in the Cabinet may explain the mystification of both Ilbert and Nash at the vague language of the Premier, usually 'a master of precise language'. Bryce Papers, MS. 14, ff. 1–4, Ilbert to Bryce, 17 Feb 1910.

35. Brett and Esher, *Esher*, ii 423–5, Esher to Knollys, 1 Dec 1909. Esher's informant was Haldane.

36. See his speech at the opening of the new Parliament, *H.C.Deb.*, 5th ser., xiv, 52–61 (21 Feb 1910). The trouble is that at no time did Asquith explain exactly what he meant by his pledge. Nicolson endeavours to explain the discrepancies in Asquith's utterances by claiming that 'Mr. Asquith's consistent purpose was to keep the name of the King out of party polemics'. (Harold Nicolson, *King George V, His Life and Reign* (London, 1952) pp. 128–9.) If such was Asquith's intention it is difficult to understand why the words at the Albert Hall were used at all.

37. It was not a question of 'assuming office'. The Liberal Government was 'in office', and therefore could not 'assume office'; it could only 'continue in office' or 'resign from office'. In context the correct 'resign' would have sounded rather petulant, so the incorrect 'not assume' was apparently preferred.

38. Bryce Papers, Uncatalogued, Lord MacDonnell to Bryce, 25 Feb 1910.

39. Asquith Papers, 12, ff. 77–9a. Ten days later, however, Harcourt thought the Cabinet should request contingent guarantees. Ibid., ff. 114–15, Harcourt to Asquith, 7 Feb 1910.

40. Brett and Esher, *Esher*, ii 450–1. See also Masterman, *Masterman*, p. 156.

41. Spender and Asquith, *Asquith*, i 261.

42. See Bryce Papers, Uncatalogued, Lord MacDonnell to Bryce, 25 Feb 1910.

43. Cromer Papers, F.O. 633/18, 243–5a, Arthur Elliot to Cromer, 25 Aug 1909. This letter is an excellent summary of the Free Fooder case against rejection.

44. Newton, *Lansdowne*, pp. 378–9, Lansdowne to Balfour of Burleigh, 2 Oct 1909.

45. Strachey Papers, Dicey to Strachey, 22 July 1909.

46. Ibid., Pollock to Strachey, 13 July 1909.

47. See Anson's letter to *The Times*, 22 Oct 1909.

48. Strachey Papers, Dicey to Strachey, 16 Sept 1909.

49. Ibid., Balfour to Strachey, 13 July 1909. For a full version of the Strachey thesis see the long leading article in the *Spectator*, 10 July 1909.

50 Strachey Papers, Strachey to Dicey, 5 Aug 1909 [copy].
    Balfour Papers, Add. MS. 49796, ff. 180–2, Balfour to Iwan-Muller, 7 July 1909 [copy].

52. Ibid., Add. MS. 49765, ff. 245–9, Sandars to Balfour, 26 Aug 1909.

53. Newton, *Lansdowne*, pp. 378–9, Lansdowne to Balfour of Burleigh, 2 Oct 1909.

54. Haldane Papers, MS. 5908, f. 189, Asquith to Haldane, 9 Oct 1909. This suggests that Asquith at least wished to scare the Lords away from rejection.

55. Balfour Papers, Add. MS. 49730, ff. 11–20, Milner to Lansdowne, 2 Nov 1909. See also Milner Papers, Lansdowne to Milner, 30 Oct 1909.

56. Balfour Papers, Add. MS. 49730, ff. 21–6, Sandars to Lansdowne, 6 Nov 1909 [rough copy]. The information had come from Lloyd George via Esher, who had had a tête-à-tête luncheon at the Carlton Restaurant with the Chancellor. It is possible that Lloyd George leaked this information to encourage rejection.

57. For the points and quotations in this paragraph see Chamberlain, *Politics From Inside*, p. 184.

58. See Jenkins, *Balfour's Poodle*, p. 58.

59. Balfour Papers, Add. MS. 49730, ff. 11–20.

60. Strachey Papers, Finlay to Strachey, 11 July 1909; ibid., Dicey to Strachey, 12 July 1909; Hicks Beach, *Hicks Beach*, ii 259; Anson's letter to *The Times*, 22 Oct 1909.

61. Strachey Papers, Dicey to Strachey, 2 July 1909.

62. Ibid., Finlay to Strachey, 11 July 1909.

63. Balfour Papers, Add. MS. 49730, ff. 21–6, Sandars to Lansdowne, 6 Nov 1909. There is an unconscious irony in Sandars' apologia: 'I daresay this sounds rather like claptrap, but really it is election business proper. It may read like the plea of the wirepuller rather than the reasoning of a Dicey or an Anson. But it is practical politics.'

64. Ibid., ff. 27–8, Lansdowne to Balfour, 10 Nov 1909; and ibid., f. 29, Balfour to Lansdowne, telegram, 11 Nov 1909 [copy].

65. Ibid., Add. MS. 49795, ff. 10–11, 1 Dec 1909.

66. Ibid., Add. MS. 49766, ff. 23–4, Sandars to Balfour, 29 Nov 1909.

67. *H.L.Deb.*, 5th ser., iv 954 (24 Nov 1909).

68. Hicks Beach, *Hicks Beach*, ii 262, 1 Dec 1909.

69. *H.L.Deb.*, 5th ser., iv, 1030, 1080 (25 Nov 1909), 1257 (30 Nov 1909).

70. Balfour Papers, Add. MS. 49795, ff. 1–2, Garvin to Sandars, 29 Nov 1909. Part of this letter is reproduced in Gollin, *Garvin*, p. 125.

71. Based on accounts in the London press, 1 Dec 1909.

72. The Home Rule Bill of 1893 was defeated on second reading in the House of Lords by 419 to 41.

73. Haldane Papers, MS. 5982, ff. 213–14, Haldane to his mother, 1 Dec 1909.

74. Asquith Papers, 1, ff. 233–4, Knollys to Nash, 1 Dec 1909.

75. All quotations from *H.C.Deb.*, 5th ser., xiii, 546–58 (2 Dec 1909).

76. The Clerk of the House of Commons, a perhaps not unprejudiced witness, thought his speech 'thin and poor, but which one must hope was found satisfactory by his friends'. Bryce Papers, MS. 13, ff. 192–4, Ilbert to Bryce, 3 Dec 1909.

77. All quotations from *H.C.Deb.*, 5th ser., xiii 558–74 (2 Dec 1909).

78. Burns Papers, Add. MS. 46331, diary, 3 Dec 1909.

CHAPTER 6   THE FIRST CAMPAIGN

1. *Annual Register 1910*, pp. 1–2.
2. For these occurrences see *The Times*, 7, 10 Jan 1910; *Morning Post*, 10 Jan 1910; and Cromer Papers, F.O. 633/19, pp. 8–9, Lambton to Cromer, 29 Jan 1910.
3. Chamberlain, *Politics From Inside*, p. 196.
4. *The Times*, 6 Dec 1909.
5. *Daily News*, 1 Dec 1909.
6. In both the *Daily Chronicle* and the *Morning Leader*, 1 Dec 1909.
7. Burns Papers, Add. MS. 46331, diary, 30 Nov 1909.
8. *The Times*, 6 Dec 1909.
9. Ibid. 4 Dec 1909. All later quotations from this speech are from this report.
10. Annabella Rainy, *Life of Adam Rolland Rainy* (Glasgow, 1914) p. 335. Rainy was Liberal M.P. for Kilmarnock Burghs.
11. *Sunday Times*, 5 Dec 1909.
12. Maxse Papers, 460, f. 408, Garvin to Maxse, 28 Sept 1909.
13. All quotations from the press of 1 Dec 1910.
14. 2 Dec 1909.
15. Balfour Papers, Add. MS. 49795, ff. 1–2, Garvin to Sandars, 29 Nov 1909.
16. The phrase was Garvin's. Ibid.
17. *Spectator*, 11 Dec 1909. The *Spectator*'s admiration stemmed no doubt from Churchill's defence of Free Trade.
18. *National Review*, liv (Jan 1910) 753.
19. *The Times*, 4 Dec 1909.
20. Maxse Papers, 460, f. 495, Garvin to Maxse, 22 Dec 1909.
21. See below, pp. 303–4.
22. His biographers claim that this speech 'laid down the lines for the controversies that were to occupy Parliament up to the outbreak of war'. Spender and Asquith, *Asquith*, i 268.
23. 11 Dec 1909. All quotations from the Albert Hall speech are from this report.
24. Ibid.
25. Strachey Papers, Margot Asquith to Strachey, 23 Jan [1910].
26. Jenkins, *Asquith*, p. 205, n. 1.
27. F. E. Hamer (ed.), *Personal Papers of Lord Rendel* (London, 1931) pp. 235–6. Rendel excused Lloyd George as 'a Welsh peasant, simply outside social veneration . . .'.
28. Bryce Papers, Uncatalogued, Spender to Bryce, 3 Feb 1910. See below, pp. 380–5, 400–10.
29. Strachey Papers, Margot Asquith to Strachey, 23 Jan [1910].
30. Violet Bonham Carter, *Winston Churchill As I Knew Him* (London, 1965) p. 186.
31. Montagu used the phrase with reference to the Budget campaign, Waley, *Montagu*, p. 35.
32. *The Times*, 22 Dec 1909.
33. Burns Papers, Add. MS. 46332, diary, 17 Jan 1910.
34. Rosebery Papers, 42, Perks, quoting Burns, to Rosebery, 15 Sept 1909. See also William Kent, *John Burns: Labour's Lost Leader* (London, 1950) pp. 202–3.

35. *The Times*, 4, 10 Dec 1909; and the *Morning Post*, 22 Dec 1909.

36. See *The Times*, 4 Dec 1909, and *Morning Leader*, 18 Dec 1909, for references to Rothschild and Revelstoke in his N.L.C. and Walworth speeches.

37. All quotations from the report in *The Times*, 17 Dec 1909. The spirit of this meeting was apparent from the outset. An attempt to sing 'For he's a Jolly Good Fellow' was silenced, the meeting opening with the apposite hymn 'Downward from his place defeated, shall the enemy be hurled'.

38. G. K. A. Bell, *Randall Davidson, Archbishop of Canterbury* (London, 1952) i 600, Davidson to the Methodist Scott Lidgett, who attended the meeting.

39. At Southport and Manchester, 4, 6 December, *Manchester Guardian*, 6, 7 Dec 1909.

40. At Liverpool, 21 December, *The Times*, 22 Dec 1909.

41. At Walworth, 17 December, *Morning Leader*, 18 Dec 1909.

42. At Cardiff, 21 December, *Morning Post*, 22 Dec 1909.

43. Maxse Papers, 460, f. 496, Oliver to Maxse, 23 Dec 1909.

44. E. T. Raymond, *Uncensored Celebrities* (London, 1918) p. 179.

45. *Daily Mirror*, 15 Dec 1909.

46. For the address, see *The Times*, 11 Dec 1909.

47. Report of the Committee of Privileges, *Parl. Papers*, 1909, viii 349–55. Anson, writing in 1897, pointed out that as such a sessional order could not affect the legal rights of non-members of the House of Commons and, moreover, would be inoperative during a prorogation or a dissolution of Parliament, 'the abstention of the peers from political activity [at elections] must be regarded as an act of courtesy extended by one House to the other'. Sir William R. Anson, *The Law and Custom of the Constitution*, part i, *Parliament*, 3rd ed. (Oxford, 1897) p. 119, n. 2.

48. Balfour Papers, Add. MS. 49730, ff. 21–6, Sandars to Lansdowne, 6 Nov 1906.

49. Thirty-nine peers were organised from the Central Office by Lord Hindlip and the campaigns were related to the overall needs of the party. These thirty-nine peers addressed a total of 257 meetings. (See the *Daily Mail*, 10 Jan 1910 and Milner Papers, diary, 8 Dec 1909.) In addition another dozen peers including Salisbury, Londonderry, and Dunraven pursued campaigns independent of the Central Office. These figures do not include peers who were active only in the constituency in which they lived.

50. Amongst the fifty-one were two Viceroys of India, two Viceroys of Ireland, several Indian provincial governors, and Cromer and Milner. The epithet 'prancing proconsuls' was frequently applied to the leading figures.

51. Maxse Papers, 462, f. 795, Nan Lyttelton (sister, Unionist candidate for Droitwich) to Maxse, undated but mid-December 1909.

52. Ibid., 461, ff. 548–51, Ampthill to Maxse, 10 Jan 1910.

53. Ibid.

54. Balfour Papers, Add. MS. 49766, ff. 28–30, Sandars to Balfour, 18 Dec 1909. [This letter has been incorrectly dated 16 Dec 1909.]

55. Ibid., 16 Dec 1909.

56. Ibid.

57. Ibid., 17 Dec 1909.

58. At Burnley, 21 December, ibid. 22 Dec 1909.

59. At Burnley, 17 December, *Manchester Guardian*, 18 Dec 1909.

60. Jenkins, *Asquith*, p. 203; and G. P. Gooch, *Under Six Reigns* (London, 1958) p. 157.

61. *The Times*, 6, 8 Jan 1910; *Daily Telegraph*, 29 Dec 1909; and *Daily Express*, 31 Dec 1909.

62. 12 January, *Daily Chronicle*, 13 Jan 1910.

63. In a speech at Plymouth, 8 January, *Daily Chronicle*, 10 Jan 1910. See also his speech at Wolverhampton, 12 January, ibid. 13 Jan 1910.

64. 'Blackbread and Blatchford', *Fortnightly Review*, lxxxvii (Mar 1910) 435–446; articles in *Daily Telegraph*, 8, 10 Jan 1910; and *Morning Post*, 11 Jan 1910.

65. See his speech at Alnwick, 10 December, *Morning Post*, 11 Dec 1909. Haldane took a similar line in his election address, but owing to illness he played little part in the campaign.

66. Balfour Papers, Add. MS. 49860, ff. 185–7. See also ibid., ff. 183–4, Kitchin to Balfour, 22 Dec 1909; and *Glasgow Herald*, 23 Dec 1909.

67. Newton, *Lansdowne*, pp. 385–6; and *The Times*, 6 Jan 1910.

68. *Morning Post*, 6 Dec 1909.

69. *The Times*, 30 Dec 1909.

70. *Newcastle Daily Chronicle*, 22, 23, 24 Dec 1909.

71. Maxse Papers, 461, ff. 567–8, Lawrence to Maxse, 2 Feb 1910.

72. 17 December, *The Times*, 18 Dec 1909.

73. Balfour Papers, Add. MS. 49766, ff. 50–5, Sandars to Short, 28 Dec 1909. Professor W. A. S. Hewins was secretary of the Tariff Commission and one of the leading academic proponents of Tariff Reform.

74. *The Times*, 14 Jan 1910.

75. liv 752, 760.

76. Strachey Papers, Strachey to Hugh Cecil, 30 Oct 1909, confidential [copy]. See also Rosebery Papers, 83, Cromer to Rosebery, 14 Dec 1909.

77. Strachey Papers, Elliot to Cromer, 29 Sept 1909.

78. Arthur Elliot Papers, diary, 7 Dec 1909.

79. *Pamphlets and Leaflets* 1909, pamphlet 2262.

80. At Manchester, 4 December, *Manchester Guardian*, 7 Dec 1909.

81. *The Times*, 7 Dec 1909.

82. Ibid., 1 Jan 1910.

83. Ibid., 11 Jan 1910.

84. Ibid., 13 Jan 1910.

85. 21 Dec 1909.

86. Balfour Papers, Add. MS. 49766, ff. 44–7, Sandars to Balfour, 22 Dec 1909.

87. *Western Morning News*, 10 Jan 1910.

88. The letter was published first in the *Westminster Gazette*, 13 Jan 1910. It appeared in most other papers the next day.

89. Paragraph based on, and quotations from, Balfour Papers, Add. MS. 49730, ff. 45–9, Lansdowne to Sandars, 23 Jan 1910.

90. See above, pp. 28–9, for the role of Taff Vale in the Unionist decline in the years after 1900.

91. Chamberlain, *Politics From Inside*, p. 200.

92. Snowden, *Autobiography*, i 223.

93. *The Times*, 11 Dec 1909.
94. Balfour later claimed that he had had 149 election speeches of Cabinet Ministers examined and in only one was there any voluntary reference to Home Rule. See *H.C.Deb.*, 5th ser., xiv 46 (21 Feb 1910).
95. Bryce Papers, Uncatalogued, O'Brien to Bryce, 30 Dec 1909.
96. Balfour Papers, Add. MS. 49859, ff. 173–6, Lord Rutland to Balfour, 18 Oct 1907.
97. Stanley Salvidge, *Salvidge of Liverpool* (London, 1934) p. 103, Long to Sir Archibald Salvidge, 29 Dec 1910.
98. For details see Sir Frederick Maurice, *Haldane, The Life of Viscount Haldane of Cloan* (London, 1937–9) i 254–6; and Marder, *From the Dreadnought to Scapa Flow*, i 179–82.
99. Balfour Papers, Add. MS. 49795, ff. 10–11, Garvin to Sandars, 1 Dec 1909.
100. Marder, *From the Dreadnought to Scapa Flow*, i 156–9, has a curiously incomplete account of the Mulliner affair. For details of Admiralty pressure omitted by Marder see Sir Reginald Bacon, *From 1900 Onward* (London, 1940) pp. 177–80. There is an exhaustive account of the public aspects of the Mulliner affair in Philip Noel-Baker, *The Private Manufacture of Armaments* (London, 1936) pp. 449–505. Fisher considered Mulliner 'pitch'. Gollin, *Garvin*, p. 67.
101. Letters or diary extracts from Mulliner were published in *The Times* on 14, 17 Dec 1909; 1, 3, 6, 7, 8, 12, 15, 18 Jan 1910.
102. '. . . what a trio to engineer a scare! A discredited Socialist, a shady company promoter, and a blatant Admiral. What a Trinity!' Arthur J. Marder, *Fear God and Dread Nought*, ii, *Years of Power* (London, 1956) p. 288, Admiral Fisher to Arnold White, 11 Jan 1910.
103. Balfour Papers, Add. MS. 49719, f. 119. As usual Balfour had not read the newspaper articles in question.
104. Paragraph based on, and quotations from, the eleven articles in the *Daily Mail*. Somewhat contradictory accounts of Blatchford's relations with the *Daily Mail* and of the origin of his articles are given in Laurence Thompson, *Blatchford*, pp. 212–16; Hamilton Fyfe, *Sixty Years in Fleet Street* (London, 1949) pp. 143–4; and Kennedy Jones, *Fleet Street and Downing Street* (London, 1920) pp. 249–53. See also Robert Blatchford, *My Eighty Years* (London, 1931) pp. 221–3.
105. See Brett and Esher, *Esher*, ii 442 and 426, and the critical comment in the *Sunday Times*, 19 Dec 1909. *The Times* was editorially silent on the Blatchford articles.
106. *Daily Mail*, 23 Dec. 1909, 22 Jan 1910.
107. Quotations from speeches on 17, 18 December, *The Times*, 18, 20, Dec 1910.
108. Mulliner's diary, *The Times*, 1, 3 Jan 1910; Beresford's speech at Grimsby, 31 December, *Daily Telegraph*, 1 Jan 1910; and reproduction of Navy League poster, *Morning Leader*, 28 Dec 1909.
109. *The Times*, 5 Jan 1910. *The Times* thought Balfour 'less felicitous than usual' in some of his statements. Balfour's biographers have handled the incident with exemplary discretion. See Dugdale, *Balfour*, ii 53–4, and Young, *Balfour*, p. 273.

110. Headline in *Daily Chronicle*, 6 Jan 1910; Asquith speech, Bath, 6 January, *The Times*, 7 Jan 1910; and Lloyd George speech, Peckham, 6 January, *Daily Chronicle*, 7 Jan 1910.
111. See below, p. 410.
112. Balfour Papers, Add. MS. 49766, ff. 50-5 and 56-7, Sandars to Short, 28, 29 Dec 1909.
113. 3 Jan 1910.
114. G. K. Chesterton in *Daily News*, 15 Jan 1910.
115. See respective editorials, 15 Jan 1910.

CHAPTER 7 FORECASTS, RESULTS AND FIRST REACTIONS

1. Bryce Papers, Uncatalogued, R. Barry O'Brien to Bryce, 30 Dec 1909.
2. *Daily Chronicle*, 14 Jan 1910.
3. Balfour Papers, Add. MS. 49791, ff. 169-70, Sir Joseph Lawrence to Sandars, 20 Nov. 1910, reporting a wager with Lloyd George. See also Masterman, *Masterman*, p. 150. But for a conflicting estimate from Lloyd George see Riddell, *Diary 1908-14*, p. 18. For Harcourt's expectation of a majority independent of the Irish, see Asquith Papers, 12, ff. 77-9a, Harcourt to Asquith, 26 Jan 1910.
4. *Review of Reviews*, xli (Jan 1910) 4.
5. Ibid.
6. Webb, *Our Partnership*, p. 437; and Margot Asquith, *Autobiography* (London, 1922) ii 133. For a less optimistic report out of Highbury see Fraser, *Chamberlain*, p. 293.
7. The forecast was based on a series of articles appearing on 19, 30 Oct; 9, 20, 25 Nov; 3, 10, 16, 23, 28 Dec 1909; 13 Jan 1910.
8. Fitzroy, *Memoirs*, i 390.
9. Marder, *Fear God and Dread Nought*, ii 289, Fisher to McKenna, 13 Jan 1910. See also Balfour Papers, Add. MS. 49766, ff. 30-5, Sandars to Short, 28 Dec 1909.
10. Balfour Papers, Add. MS. 49795, ff. 40-3, Garvin to Sanders, 31 Dec 1909.
11. Masterman, *Masterman*, p. 149; Margot Asquith, *Autobiography*, ii 124; Fitzroy, *Memoirs*, i 390; Webb, *Our Partnership*, p. 444; and Haldane Papers, MS. 5908, ff. 180-3, précis of conversation between Asquith and the King, 6 Oct 1909.
12. John Evelyn Wrench, *Geoffrey Dawson and Our Times* (London, 1955) p. 70, Milner to Dawson, received 19 Dec 1909. For Lansdowne see Newton, *Lansdowne*, pp. 378-9; and for Curzon see Milner Papers, Curzon to Milner 27 Jan 1910.
13. James of Hereford's forecast – Progressives 322, Unionists 254, Nationalists 84 – was both accurate and typical of Free Fooder opinion, *Daily Chronicle*, 14 Jan 1910.
14. Fitzroy, *Memoirs*, i 392; and Brett and Esher, *Esher*, ii 437.

15. Balfour Papers, Add. MS. 49795, ff. 12–13, 17, Garvin to Sandars, 14, 22 Dec 1909.

16. The articles were published on 13, 15, 16, 22 Nov; 10, 21, 23, 28, 30 Dec 1909; 4, 8, 10, 11, 12 Jan 1910.

17. Balfour Papers, Add. MS. 49795, ff. 40–3, Garvin to Sandars, 31 Dec 1909. Garvin had discovered that the author of the articles was A. M. Drysdale of 'Manchester Guardian antecedents, and whom I knew of old to be as innate a Radical as could be'. Ibid., ff. 12–13, Garvin to Sandars, 14 Dec 1909.

18. Ibid., Add. MS. 49772, ff. 43–4, Sandars to Akers-Douglas, n.d. but probably late Jan 1910. For the 'brightish' view of London prospects see the Observer, 2 Jan 1910, forecasting twenty-five to thirty gains.

19. Chamberlain, Politics From Inside, pp. 197–8; and Balfour Papers, Add. MS. 49766, ff. 50–5, Sandars to Short 25 Dec 1909.

20. Ibid. Add. MS. 49795, ff. 40–3, Garvin to Sandars, 31 Dec 1909.

21. See, e.g., Westminster Gazette, 15 Jan 1910; Morning Post 23 Dec 1910; and Lord James' forecast, Daily Chronicle, 14 Jan 1910.

22. Chamberlain, Politics From Inside, pp. 196–7. The Birmingham Daily Post, 4 Jan 1910 shared these hopes, predicting up to twenty Unionist gains in Scotland.

23. Observer, 16 Jan 1910.

24. Cornelius O'Leary, The Elimination of Corrupt Practices in British Elections 1868–1911 (Oxford, 1962) p. 223.

25. The Times, 17 Jan 1910. Grimsby provided one of the four Liberal gains on the first day.

26. Morning Leader, 17 Jan 1910.

27. The Darlington electorate had increased by over one thousand since 1906, mainly as the result of an influx of railway and metal workers. Newcastle Daily Chronicle, 11 Jan 1910.

28. Daily Telegraph, 17 Jan 1910.

29. Isaacs attributed the reduction in his majority 'to the effect produced by Lloyd George's [Reading] speech'. Rosebery Papers, 42, Perks to Rosebery, 29 Jan 1910.

30. The Unionists captured one Welsh borough, and captured one and lost two Scottish burghs. The borough representation in Ireland remained unchanged.

31. Sunderland was contested in the Unionist interest by James Knott, shipbuilder and shipowner, whose company launched a ship on the Wear during the election, and by Samuel Storey, who stood as an independent Tariff Reformer. Storey who had previously been Chairman of the Durham County Council, President of the Northern Liberal Federation, and Liberal M.P. for Sunderland 1881–95, was an exceptionally strong candidate. These personal factors, excellent organisation, the control of the local evening newspaper, and heavy unemployment in the town, explain the most remarkable turnover of votes in the North of England.

32. Salvidge, Salvidge, pp. 93–4, F. E. Smith to Salvidge, 4 Feb 1910.

33. Manchester Guardian, 18 Jan. 1910. There was an independent Liberal candidate, see below, pp. 224–5.

34. Of the fourteen seats lost by the Liberals in London, eight had never returned

a Liberal prior to 1906, and another four had only returned a Liberal once before that date.

35. *Daily Chronicle*, 19 Jan 1910; and *Westminster Gazette*, 20 Jan 1910.

36. Sir Almeric Fitzroy suggested to Lord Pentland that the Government was likely to lose heavily in the Home Counties, but was informed that this was not what the Liberal election agents expected. Fitzroy, *Memoirs*, i 392–3. See also the warnings of D. C. Peddar, 'The Corruption of the Cotter,' *Contemporary Review*, xcvi (Dec 1909) 690.

37. Balfour Papers, Add. MS. 49766, ff. 71–4, Sandars to Balfour, 19 Jan 1910.

38. 20 Jan 1910.

39. 21 Jan 1910.

40. In the counties of Kent, Surrey, Sussex, Hampshire, Essex, Hertfordshire, Oxfordshire and Berkshire, the Liberals held only seven seats – three London overspill constituencies, three borough seats, and one solitary rural county division, Buckingham.

41. Carrington Diary, 23 Jan 1910.

42. *Sunday Times*, 23 Jan 1910.

43. Haldane Papers, MS. 5909, f. 1, Churchill to Haldane, 24 Jan 1910.

44. Strachey Papers, Strachey to Hugh Cecil, 24 Jan 1910 [copy].

45. Chamberlain, *Politics From Inside*, pp. 196–7.

46. Pro Patria (J. L. Garvin), 'The General Election and the Next', *National Review*, liv (Feb. 1910) 933.

47. Asquith Papers, 23, ff. 63–6, typed memorandum by Grey, 31 Jan 1910, forwarded to Asquith, 7 Feb 1910.

48. Masterman, *Masterman*, p. 152.

49. *Observer*, 23 Jan 1910.

50. Brett and Esher, *Esher*, ii 440, Esher to Balfour, 24 Jan 1910.

51. Balfour Papers, Add. MS. 49730, ff. 45–9, Lansdowne to Sandars, 23 Jan 1910. See also Milner Papers, Curzon to Milner, 27 Jan 1910, making the same point.

52. The details of these extraordinary activities are contained in Brett and Esher, *Esher*, ii 435–42.

53. Maurice, *Haldane*, i 260.

54. Bryce Papers, Uncatalogued, Spender to Bryce, 3 Feb 1910.

55. *The Times*, 25 Jan 1910. *The Times* on the previous day had suggested a provisional Government under a neutral head. Although this proposal was quickly dropped it is revealing of the Unionist attitude to the electoral verdict. The *Westminster Gazette* took up the conference proposals on 25 Jan 1910.

56. In his last election speech, Haddington, *The Times*, 25 Jan 1910.

57. 28 Jan 1910.

58. Asquith Papers, 12, ff. 77–9a, Harcourt to Asquith, 26 Jan 1910.

CHAPTER 8   THE MONTHS BETWEEN

1. Chamberlain Papers, AC 8/5/4.

2. See his speech at Haddington, 24 January, *The Times*, 25 Jan 1910.

3. Balfour suspected that Hopwood, who was the senior Civil Servant in Crewe's ministry, was acting for Crewe. Balfour Papers, Add. MS. 49766, ff. 114–16, Balfour to Lansdowne, 29 Jan 1910 [copy].

4. Ibid. ff. 90–3, Sandars to Balfour, 26 Jan 1910.

5. Young, *Balfour*, p. 292, Balfour to the King, 15 Feb 1910.

6. See Wilfred Scawen Blunt's account of his conversation with Redmond on 13 Feb 1910, Wilfred Scawen Blunt, *My Diaries. Being a Personal Narrative of Events 1884–1914* (London, 1932) pp. 702–3.

7. Elibank Papers, MS. 8802, ff. 19–20, O'Connor to Elibank, 22 Mar 1910.

8. Masterman, *Masterman*, p. 162.

9. Ibid. pp. 159–60.

10. Jenkins, *Asquith*, p. 209, Asquith to the King, 13 Apr 1910.

11. Spender and Asquith, *Asquith*, i 278–9.

12. Balfour Papers, Add. MS. 49767, ff. 13–17, Sandars to Short, 24 Oct 1910. Sandars was reporting a conversation with Hughes, the Principal Agent.

13. Ibid., ff. 21–2, [?] Oct 1910. Acland-Hood noted in this letter that Unionists in the rural districts generally favoured repeal of the land taxes, but not so Unionists in the urban areas.

14. Bryce Papers, Miscellaneous Correspondence, Spender to Bryce, 20 Apr 1910.

15. The most fully documented account of the travails of the Liberal Cabinet on the constitutional question is A. S. King, 'Some Aspects of the Liberal Party 1906–14' (D.Phil. thesis, Oxford, 1962) ch. iv, 'The Fall of the House of Lords', to which this section is much indebted. King lists McKenna, Samuel and Churchill in addition to the above four as reformists in February 1910.

16. Bryce Papers, Uncatalogued, Spender to Bryce, 3 Feb 1910.

17. Asquith Papers, 23, ff. 63–6. This typewritten memorandum, dated 31 Jan 1910, was forwarded to Asquith on 7 February with a covering note from Grey. The major part of this memorandum has been published in G. M. Trevelyan, *Grey of Fallodon* (London, 1937) pp. 194–5.

18. Masterman, *Masterman*, pp. 158–9.

19. Asquith Papers, 23, ff. 70–6, Churchill memorandum, 14 Feb 1910. Parts of this memorandum are quoted in Churchill, *Churchill*, ii 335–6, and Jenkins, *Asquith*, pp. 206–7.

20. Asquith Papers, 12, ff. 105–5, Samuel to Asquith, 3 Feb 1910.

21. Quotations in this paragraph from Masterman, *Masterman*, p. 158.

22. Despite his biographers' assertions (Spender and Asquith, *Asquith*, i 270) the Premier does seem to have been 'knocked out' at the end of the election. See Brett and Esher, *Esher*, ii 444, and Masterman, *Masterman*, p. 154. Anxiety for his daughter's health, the motive for his hurried visit to France, probably contributed as much to his exhaustion as the wearying election campaign. See Hamer, *Rendel*, 175–6; and Bryce Papers, MS. 14, ff. 1–4, Ilbert to Bryce, 17 Feb 1910.

23. Masterman, *Masterman*, p. 158.

24. Arthur C. Murray, *Master and Brother* (London, 1945) pp. 38–9; and A. G. Gardiner, *Pillars of Society* (London, 1915) pp. 119–20.

25. Asquith Papers, 12, ff. 114–15.

26. Murray, *Master and Brother*, p. 41; and Spender and Asquith, *Asquith*, i 273–274.
27. Carrington Diary, 26 Feb 1910; and King, 'Liberal Party 1906–14', p. 134.
28. Asquith Papers, 23, ff. 82–2a, Grey to Asquith, 25 Mar 1910.
29. Jenkins, *Asquith*, pp. 208–9.
30. Harold Spender's description, see Masterman, *Masterman*, p. 195. For Morley's 'obduracy' see Haldane Papers, MS. 5909, ff. 18–19, Morley to Haldane, 10 Apr 1910.
31. Jenkins, *Asquith*, pp. 206, 209–10.
32. Asquith Papers, 104, ff. 134–7, Cabinet memorandum on the Osborne Judgment, 10 Oct 1910.
33. *The Times*, 23 Nov 1910; and the *Labour Leader*, 2 Dec 1910.
34. Balfour Papers, Add. MS. 49730, ff. 52–5, Lansdowne's notes, 31 Jan 1910, on Salisbury's memorandum on House of Lords reform.
35. Ibid., Add. MS. 49733, ff. 122–6, Curzon to Balfour, 1 Feb 1910, confidential.
36. Rosebery Papers, 83, Kitchin to Rosebery, 9 Mar 1910.
37. Cromer Papers, F.O. 633/19, pp. 91–6, Austen Chamberlain to Cromer, 17 Nov 1910, reporting views of a member of a Scottish deputation to Balfour after the January election.
38. 26 Jan 1910.
39. The homes of Joseph Chamberlain, Salisbury and Curzon respectively.
40. Balfour Papers, Add. MS. 49766, ff. 104–6, Sandars to Balfour, 28 Jan 1910. The Unionist leaders' response to this persistence is dealt with in Newton, *Lansdowne*, pp. 386–8. Newton's comment on this response is that both leaders 'were apparently labouring under the double fallacy that some measure of support might be expected from their opponents, and that the approaching conflict could be fought, not upon the powers but upon the constitution of the House of Lords'. Neither assumption was fallacious at the time, with compromise in the air, and the Cabinet inclining to composition reform.
41. Ibid., pp. 387–8, Lansdowne to Balfour, 1 Feb 1910.
42. Balfour Papers, Add. MS. 49730, ff. 50–1.
43. Newton, *Lansdowne*, pp. 387–8, Lansdowne to Balfour, 1 Feb 1910.
44. Ibid., p. 386, Balfour to Lansdowne, 29 Jan 1910; and Balfour Papers, Add. MS. 49730, ff. 52–5, Lansdowne's notes, 31 Jan 1910, on Salisbury's memorandum on House of Lords reform.
45. Jenkins, *Balfour's Poodle*, p. 96, quoting Halsbury, House of Lords, 16 Mar 1910.
46. Balfour Papers, Add. MS. 49860, ff. 219–25, Halifax to Sandars, 2 Mar 1910 [letter and memorandum].
47. Cromer Papers, F.O. 633/19, pp. 40–1, Rosebery to Cromer, 16 Apr 1910.
48. Balfour Papers, Add. MS. 49795, ff. 69–77, Garvin to Sandars, 14 Feb 1910. Parts of this letter are quoted in Gollin, *Garvin*, p. 177.
49. Chamberlain, *Politics From Inside*, pp. 219–22.
50. Rosebery Papers, 82, Curzon to Rosebery, 8 Mar [1910]. This letter suggests there were originally six resolutions. If so the sixth was never tabled.
51. Balfour Papers, Add. MS. 49766, ff. 178–85, Sandars to Balfour, 15 Mar 1910. See also Chamberlain, *Politics From Inside*, p. 233.

52. Balfour Papers, Add. MS. 49730, ff. 68–70, Lansdowne to Balfour 27 Mar 1910. See also ibid., f. 67, Lansdowne to Sandars, 23 Mar 1910; and Chamberlain, *Politics From Inside*, pp. 249–50, 263–4.

53. Ibid. p. 264. See also Balfour Papers, Add. MS. 49708, ff. 184–5, memorandum from Selborne, 23 Feb 1910.

54. Ibid., Add. MS. 49758, ff. 243–4, memorandum from Salisbury, undated.

55. Ibid. ff. 239–42, Salisbury to Balfour, 10 Apr 1910.

56. See below, pp. 164–5.

57. Chamberlain Papers, AC 8/5/5, confidential [typed carbon copy].

58. Ibid., AC 8/3/12, Ware to Austen Chamberlain, 25 Jan 1910, confidential.

59. Balfour Papers, Add. MS. 49795, ff. 145–8, Garvin to Sandars, 14 Nov 1910.

60. Ibid., Add. MS. 49766, ff. 186–95, Sandars to Balfour, 18 Mar. 1910, confidential; Chamberlain, *Politics From Inside*, 227–8; and Balfour's letter to *The Times*, 16 Apr 1910.

61. Bonar Law Papers, 20/34, note on position of T.R., 4 Feb 1910 [copy].

62. Chamberlain, *Politics From Inside*, pp. 196–7.

63. Bonar Law Papers, 20/34, note on position of T.R., 4 Feb 1910 [copy].

64. Gollin, *Garvin*, p. 172, Garvin to Sandars, 27 Jan 1910.

65. In an undiscovered letter, which Sandars described as 'a characteristic letter, and very typical of *Morning Post* policy . . . It seems to me that it is taking us back to the famous Carnarvon interview of 1885, and that kind of Randolphian scheming which did us as a Party so much damage.' Balfour Papers, Add. MS. 49766, ff. 94–6, Sandars to Balfour, 26 Jan 1910.

66. Gollin, *Garvin*, p. 184.

67. Balfour Papers, Add. MS. 49766, ff. 114–16, Balfour to Lansdowne, 29 Jan 1910 [copy]. This is the final paragraph of the letter, parts of which are quoted in Newton, *Lansdowne*, p. 386.

68. Maxse Papers, 462, ff. 727–30, Garvin to Maxse, 6 Oct 1910.

69. There are two excellent and complementary accounts of these developments in Gollin, *Garvin*, pp. 208–34, and Ronan Fanning, 'The Unionist party and Ireland 1906–10', *Irish Historical Studies*, xv (1966) 162–71.

70. *Morning Post*, 26 Jan 1910; *Observer*, 23 Jan 1910.

71. Webb, *Our Partnership*, p. 444.

72. Bonar Law Papers, 18/8/12, Bonar Law to Austen Chamberlain, 1 Oct 1910 [copy].

73. Chamberlain Papers, AC 8/6/12, Balfour to Austen Chamberlain, 21 Sept 1910.

74. Ibid., AC 8/6/15, Acland-Hood to Austen Chamberlain, 23 Sept [1910]. The letter is misdated 1911.

75. Ibid., AC 8/6/12, Balfour to Austen Chamberlain, 21 Sept 1910.

76. Bonar Law Papers, 18/8/12, Bonar Law to Austen Chamberlain, 1 Oct 1910 [copy].

77. For Smith and Goulding see *The Times*, 27 Sept 1910; for the Whole Hogger press, see *Morning Post*, 9 Sept 1910; *Globe*, 27 Sept 1910; *Standard*, 12 Sept 1910.

78. Balfour Papers, Add. MS. 49730, ff. 121–3, Lansdowne to Balfour, 24 Sept 1910; and ibid., Add. MS. 49777, ff. 68–71, Long to Balfour, 3 Oct 1910.

79. Maxse Papers, 462, ff. 727–30, Garvin to Maxse, 6 Oct 1910.

80. Balfour Papers, Add. MS. 49736, ff. 91–6, 23 Sept 1910. See also Bonar Law Papers, 18/6/125, Austen Chamberlain to Bonar Law, 29 Sept 1910.

81. Asquith Papers, 103, ff. 60–1, Cabinet memorandum, 'In Regard to an Early Election', 30 Mar 1910. This memorandum from Pease, the ex-Chief Whip, suggested all elections on the one day in order to minimise the unpopularity.

82. Chamberlain, *Politics From Inside*, p. 264.

83. Asquith Papers, 12, ff. 136–8, Harcourt to Asquith, 9 May 1910.

84. Maxse Papers, 461, ff. 647–8, Sandars to Maxse, 24 May 1910. Persuaded by Garvin his attitude changed and in November he was a critic of Balfour's decision to abandon the Conference.

85. See Gollin, *Garvin*, pp. 185–96, for the developments on the Unionist side as well as some interesting sidelights on ministerial attitudes.

86. I.L.P. manifesto, *The Times*, 25 Nov 1910.

87. Fitzroy, *Memoirs*, ii 418.

88. Spender and Asquith, *Asquith*, i 291. The quoted phrase is from Asquith's letter to the King, 8 Nov 1910, but he had outlined the situation to his Cabinet that afternoon in similar terms. See Carrington Diary, 8 Nov 1910; and CAB 41/32/70, Asquith to King, 9 Dec. 1910.

89. Carrington Diary, 11 Nov 1910.

90. Spender and Asquith, *Asquith*, i 296.

91. See Elibank's speech at Reading, 5 November, *The Times*, 7 Nov 1910. There were 12,000 removals, almost one-third of the electorate. Ibid., 1 Nov 1910.

92. Elibank Papers, MS. 8802, ff. 129–30, Jesse Herbert to Elibank, 9 Nov 1910, confidential.

93. For Elibank's role see Murray, *Master and Brother*, p. 59, and Masterman, *Masterman*, pp. 175–6. Jenkins, *Balfour's Poodle*, p. 118, n. 1, has disputed Elibank's role but his argument rests on the rather unrealistic assumption that anticipatory discussions on election timing had not taken place during the final days of the Conference.

94. Unless otherwise indicated the sources for this account of the negotiations with the King are Nicolson, *George V*, pp. 133–9, and Spender and Asquith, *Asquith*, i 296–8.

95. Asquith Papers, 23, ff. 160–1, memorandum on the Royal Prerogative, 14 Nov 1910, secret, from Asquith.

96. Asquith Papers, 23, ff. 124–5, telegram Sir Arthur Bigge to Nash, 15 Nov 1910. The second sentence of this telegram is quoted in Nicolson, *George V*, p. 134.

97. The chief commentaries on these negotiations are Jenkins, *Balfour's Poodle*, pp. 118–25, sympathetic to the Government and exculpatory towards the actions of Lord Knollys, and Young, *Balfour*, pp. 300–5, critical of the Government and continuing Balfour's feud with Lord Knollys, which resulted from these events.

98. Newton, *Lansdowne*, p. 410.

99. Allyn, *Lords Versus Commons*, p. 196.

100. Nicolson, *George V*, p. 133.
101. Ibid., p. 136.

CHAPTER 9   THE SECOND CAMPAIGN

1. 'The End of the Old Constitution', *Fortnightly Review*, Jan 1911, quoted in Jenkins, *Balfour's Poodle*, p. 128.
2. *Daily Express*, 8 Dec 1910.
3. See below, pp. 379–80.
4. The new register for England, Wales and Ireland, operative from 1 January 1911, showed an increase of 183,623 over the old. Moreover the old register contained the names of many who had died since it had been compiled eighteen months before, so that the actual increase in new voters was about 250,000. In addition the old register included many who had shifted and could not be traced and brought back to the polls. See below, pp. 360–1.
5. *The Times*, 14 Nov 1910.
6. F. E. Smith, 12 Nov, *Observer*, 13 Nov 1910.
7. *The Times*, 14 Nov 1910.
8. *Observer*, 20 Nov 1910.
9. Conservative Research Office, Leaflets 1910.
10. Balfour Papers, Add. MS. 49743, ff. 17–18, Balfour to Derby 6 Oct 1910, private [copy]. This letter seems to be the same as that published in part in Randolph Churchill, *Lord Derby, King of Lancashire* (London, 1960) p. 121, but there dated 10 October.
11. All quotations from the Nottingham speech from *The Times*, 18 Nov 1910.
12. See, e.g., the following editorials, 'The Vote Market' and 'The Vacillating Autocrat', *Daily Mail*, 24, 25 Nov 1910; and 'Tony Pandering', *Daily Express*, 25 Nov 1910.
13. Spender and Asquith, *Asquith*, i 300.
14. Balfour Papers, Add. MS. 49708, f. 212, Selborne to Balfour, 12 Nov 1910; Add. MS. 49861, ff. 66–9, Camperdown to Balfour, 12 Nov 1910; Newton, *Lansdowne*, pp. 399–400.
15. Chamberlain, *Politics From Inside*, p. 301.
16. *H.L.Deb.*, 5th ser., vi, 698, 702, 705 (17 Nov 1910).
17. Ibid. 757. For the text of the resolutions see above, pp. 156–7.
18. Curzon, ibid. 726. Lansdowne desired 'to see a certain proportion of the reformed House chosen from outside, and by this I mean elected in some way or other outside this House'. Ibid. 748.
19. It has not been possible to determine exactly who was present at this vital meeting. Fitzroy, *Memoirs*, ii 423, notes that according to Lady Lansdowne 'Arthur and the whole gang' were there. Balfour, Lansdowne, Curzon, and Salisbury were certainly present. Walter Long was not. It is possible that Balfour met with the leading Unionist peers and not the whole Shadow Cabinet. This would suggest in addition Cawdor, Middleton, and Selborne, who had met with Lansdowne, Curzon and Salisbury earlier in the week to discuss reform. See *Daily Express*, 18 Nov 1910. The importance of the

Hackwood meeting is attested by Balfour Papers, Add. MS. 49758, ff. 247–8, Salisbury to Balfour, 29 Nov 1910.

20. *H.L. Deb.*, 5th ser., vi 839 (23 Nov 1910); and ibid. 1000 (24 Nov 1910).

21. See, for example, Newton, *Lansdowne*, p. 405; and Halévy, vi, *The Rule of Democracy*, i 341.

22. Strachey Papers, Lansdowne to Strachey, 19 Nov 1910.

23. *Morning Post*, 18 Nov 1910; and *Sunday Times*, 20, 27 Nov 1910.

24. Balfour Papers, Add. MS. 49795, ff. 166–9, Garvin to Sandars, 12 Dec 1910.

25. Ibid., Add. MS. 49708, ff. 215–16, Selborne to Balfour, 26 Nov 1910 [my italics].

26. 23 Nov 1910.

27. Cromer Papers, F.O. 633/19, pp. 267–72, 3 Dec 1910.

28. At Mile End, *The Times*, 22 Nov 1910. Both the eighth and ninth Dukes of Marlborough had married wealthy Americans.

29. *The Times*, 22 Nov 1910.

30. 23 Nov 1910.

31. Quoted in Spender and Asquith, *Asquith*, i 299–300, where it is, however, mistakenly referred to as a passage from Asquith's Hull speech, 25 November. Most writers have followed Asquith's biographers in stating that Asquith opened the campaign at Hull on 25 November 1910, when in fact he opened the campaign six days before, with this speech at the N.L.C.

32. Churchill, Bradford, 26 November, *Daily Chronicle*, 28 Nov 1910; and Lloyd George, Edinburgh, 26 November, *The Times*, 28 Nov 1910.

33. Ibid., 26 Nov 1910.

34. See *H.L.Deb.*, 5th ser., vi 855 (23 Nov 1910).

35. Lloyd George at St Pancras, 23 November, *The Times*, 24 Nov 1910.

36. Balfour Papers, Add. MS. 49730, ff. 134–5, Cromer to Lansdowne, 28 Nov 1910.

37. This section owes much to the detailed account of the referendum pledge in Gollin, *Garvin*, ch. viii, 'Dollar Dictator and Referendum'. Gollin's account inevitably tends, because of its biographical nature, to enhance the role of Garvin, and to underrate the influence of other figures, particularly Lansdowne; nor does he give sufficient weight to the genesis of the Albert Hall pledge as a response to the electoral debate.

38. See above, p. 159.

39. Chamberlain Papers, AC 8/7/9, Cromer to Austen Chamberlain, 15 Nov 1910.

40. Ibid.

41. *Spectator*, 12 Nov 1910; and Strachey Papers, Strachey to Selborne, 16 Nov 1910 [copy].

42. Chamberlain, *Politics From Inside*, p. 300.

43. Ibid., p. 298; Balfour Papers, Add. MS. 49861, ff. 70–1, Sir Thomas Wrightson to Balfour, 15 Nov 1910; and Gollin, *Garvin*, p. 240.

44. Details and quotations in this paragraph from ibid., pp. 240, 245; and Chamberlain, *Politics From Inside*, pp. 298–300.

45. Balfour Papers, Add. MS. 49795, ff. 145–8, Garvin to Sandars, 14 Nov 1910.

46. Gollin, *Garvin*, p. 248, Austen Chamberlain to Garvin. Chamberlain warned Balfour that 'if he now took Preference off his flag, he could never put it back again'. Chamberlain, *Politics From Inside*, p. 298.

47. Ibid., p. 300.
48. Ibid., p. 299.
49. Cromer Papers, F.O. 633/19, pp. 91–6, Austen Chamberlain to Cromer, 17 Nov 1910.
50. Fraser, *Chamberlain*, p. 299, Austen Chamberlain to Balfour, 15 Nov 1910.
51. Cromer Papers, F.O., 633/19, pp. 91–6, 17 Nov 1910.
52. Chamberlain, *Politics From Inside*, p. 298.
53. Ibid., p. 300.
54. Gollin, *Garvin*, p. 255, Sandars to Garvin, 21 Nov 1910.
55. Balfour Papers, Add. MS. 49795, f. 163, Garvin to Sandars, 27 Nov 1910, private [my italics]. Gollin, *Garvin*, p. 260, prints nearly all this letter, but strangely omits the words in italics.
56. Chamberlain, *Politics From Inside*, pp. 310–12, Austen Chamberlain's letters to Balfour and Lansdowne; Balfour Papers, Add. MS. 49758, ff. 247–8, Salisbury to Balfour 29 Nov 1910; ibid., Add. MS. 49736, ff. 113–16, Austen Chamberlain to Balfour, 28 Nov 1910; and Petrie, *Chamberlain*, i 268–72, Austen Chamberlain to Richard Jebb, 7 Dec 1910.
57. *H.L.Deb.*, 5th ser., vi 847 (23 Nov 1910).
58. Ibid. 862, 886.
59. Balfour Papers, Add. MS. 49758, ff. 247–8. Salisbury to Balfour, 29 Nov 1910. This letter makes it clear that the Unionist leaders agreed at Hackwood to exempt all financial measures from the referendum.
60. Gollin, *Garvin*, p. 257.
61. Balfour Papers, Add. MS. 49795, f. 164, Garvin to Sandars, 28 Nov 1910, private. This letter is quoted in part in Gollin, *Garvin*, p. 262–3.
62. For Salvidge, see Salvidge, *Salvidge*, p. 102; for Derby see Churchill, *Derby*, pp. 159–61.
63. Gollin, *Garvin*, pp. 260–1.
64. Ibid., pp. 262–3, Garvin to Sandars, 28 Nov 1910.
65. Balfour Papers, Add. MS. 49730, ff. 132–3, Lansdowne to Balfour, 28 Nov 1910.
66. Chamberlain Papers, AC 8/7/19, Lansdowne to Austen Chamberlain, 14 Dec 1910.
67. Gollin, *Garvin*, p. 262, Garvin to Sandars, 28 Nov 1910.
68. This paragraph is based on ibid. pp. 258–9.
69. *Observer*, 27 Nov 1910.
70. *Morning Post*, 28 Nov 1910.
71. Chamberlain, *Politics From Inside*, pp. 303–4, Balfour to Austen Chamberlain, 28 Nov 1910.
72. *The Times*, 29 Nov 1910.
73. Bonar Law Papers, 18/8/14 [copy]. The original of this letter seems to have disappeared. It is not in the Balfour or Austen Chamberlain Papers.
74. Chamberlain, *Politics From Inside*, pp. 305–6, Balfour to Austen Chamberlain, 30 Nov 1910.
75. Ibid., p. 304. This postscript reveals a distinct hardening of opinion and significantly was written after a visit from Lansdowne, and perhaps less significantly after Balfour had learnt that the *Daily Mail* had taken up the referendum pledge on Tariff Reform.

76. Balfour Papers, Add. MS. 49736, ff. 122–4.
77. Ibid., Add. MS. 49736, ff. 113–16.
78. Bonar Law Papers, 18/6/137. This supports the contention that Balfour made up his mind on Monday. It also reveals that Balfour knew well his Bonar Law.
79. Balfour Papers, Add. MS. 49693, ff. 6–9.
80. Bonar Law Papers, 18/8/16, Bonar Law to Derby, 19 Dec 1910 [copy].
81. Young, *Balfour*, p. 300.
82. Chamberlain, *Politics From Inside*, pp. 306–7, Balfour to Austen Chamberlain, 13 Dec 1910.
83. Balfour Papers, Add. MS. 49777, ff. 79–81, Long to Balfour, 20 Jan 1911. This letter is quoted at length in Peter Fraser, 'The Unionist Débâcle of 1911 and Balfour's Retirement', *Journal of Modern History*, xxxv (1963) 356.
84. Chamberlain, *Politics From Inside*, pp. 306–7, Balfour to Austen Chamberlain, 13 Dec 1910.
85. *The Times*, 30 Nov 1910.
86. *Morning Post*, 30 Nov 1910.
87. *The Times*, 30 Nov 1910.
88. This point is relevant to later controversies and is contrary to the statement of some historians. Robert Blake, *The Unknown Prime Minister. The Life and Times of Andrew Bonar Law, 1858–1923* (London, 1955) p. 107, states: 'He made the offer in carefully guarded words as a *quid pro quo*, if the Liberals would promise a referendum on Home Rule'. Churchill, *Derby*, p. 161, similarly claims that Balfour 'had made it contingent on a reciprocal pledge' from the Liberals on Home Rule. It is impossible to construe the speech as making a conditional pledge in the sense suggested by these writers.
89. Balfour Papers, Add. MS. 49795, f. 165, Garvin to Sandars, 29 Nov 1910. (an excited Garvin misdated this letter which appears to have been written on the 30th); *The Times*, 30 Nov 1910; and the *Spectator*, 3 Dec 1910.
90. 30 Nov 1910.
91. Balfour Papers, Add. MS. 49736, ff. 129–31. Austen Chamberlain to Balfour, 2 Dec 1910; and *The Times*, 2, 3 Dec 1910. The *Daily Telegraph*, 30 Nov 1910, had already dealt airily with this problem: '. . . if the national ballot did not succeed the first time, a Unionist Government would simply stay in office and submit the question again'.
92. *The Times*, 30 Nov, 1 Dec 1910.
93. Chamberlain Papers, AC 8/7/25, Ridley to Austen Chamberlain, 12 Dec 1910. See also Bonar Law Papers, 18/6/150, Ridley to Bonar Law, 27 Dec 1910; and Ridley's telegram to the *Pall Mall Gazette*, 30 Nov 1910.
94. Balfour Papers, Add. MS. 49791, ff. 271–2, Sir Joseph Lawrence to Balfour, 5 Dec 1910, urgent. Taylor's public repudiation was widely reported in the press.
95. Chamberlain Papers, AC 8/7/17, Jebb to Austen Chamberlain, 6 Dec 1910.
96. Chamberlain, *Politics From Inside*, p. 302.
97. *The Times*, 1 Dec 1910.
98. See, for example, Goulding's speech at Worcester, 1 December, *The Times*, 2 Dec 1910; and the *Morning Post*, 1 Dec 1910.

99. *The Times*, 2 Dec 1910.
100. Balfour Papers, Add. MS. 49736, ff. 129–31, Austen Chamberlain to Balfour, 2 Dec 1910.
101. Ibid. Add. MS. 49791, ff. 271–2.
102. Strachey Papers, Lansdowne to Strachey, 4 Dec 1910.
103. At Newcastle, 3 December, *The Times*, 5 Dec 1910.
104. Chamberlain Papers, AC 8/7/21, Sir Joseph Lawrence to Austen Chamberlain, 9 Dec 1910.
105. Ibid., AC 8/7/27, Ware to Austen Chamberlain, 12 Dec 1910. 'F.C.G.' was Sir Francis Carruthers Gould, the brilliant cartoonist of the *Westminster Gazette*.
106. Strachey Papers, Margot Asquith to Strachey, 3 Dec 1910.
107. 3 Dec 1910.
108. At Wolverhampton, 1 December, *The Times*, 2 Dec 1910.
109. *Daily News*, 1 Dec 1910.
110. See his speeches at Bury St Edmunds and Bacup, 12, 15 Dec, *The Times*, 13, 16 Dec 1910.
111. Spender and Asquith, *Asquith*, i 301.
112. Balfour Papers, Add. MS. 49767, ff. 34–7, Sandars to Balfour, 14 Dec 1910, private.
113. Churchill, *Churchill*, ii 347–50, 3 Jan 1911.
114. *The Times*, 29 Nov, 2 Dec 1910; and Milner Papers, diary, 28 Nov, 1 Dec 1910.
115. Balfour Papers, Add. MS. 49767, ff. 74–5, Sandars to Balfour, [?] Dec. 1910 [incomplete].
116. *The Times*, 5 Dec 1910. Unionist comment on this event was unrestrained. The Unionist Sunday newspaper, the *People*, 4 Dec 1910, headlined its report 'A Rat on the Run'. Such comments were not limited to the press. Sandars wrote: 'I see the little animal invaded Lincoln today and that there has been a free fight in consequence.' Balfour Papers, Add. MS. 49767, ff. 27–30, Sandars to Balfour, 3 Dec 1910.
117. At Manchester, *The Times*, 1 Dec 1910.
118. Ibid., 5 Dec 1910.
119. *Daily News*, 5 Dec 1910.
120. *The Times*, 2, 6 Dec 1910.
121. Gladstone Papers, Add. MS. 46031, ff. 167–71, Armitstead to Gladstone, 7 Dec 1910.
122. 7 Dec 1910.

CHAPTER 10 WINTER 1910–11

1. Balfour Papers, Add. MS. 49767, ff. 23–4, 9 Nov 1910.
2. Strachey Papers, 22 Nov 1910.
3. See the judicious and detailed surveys in *The Times*, which appeared daily from 21 Nov to 3 Dec 1910. Moberly Bell told Cromer on 2 Dec that 'my late Election Meteorologist who was fairly right last time ... tells me he

expects 4 Liberal gains as the net result – 28 Liberal gains and 24 Unionist'. Cromer Papers, F.O. 633/19, pp. 126–7. This forecaster's uncanny accuracy in 1910 would be the envy of any modern psephologist. See also *Morning Post*, 29 Nov 1910; *Review of Reviews*, xlii (Dec 1910) 524; Carrington Diary, 17, 28 Nov 1910; and Masterman, *Masterman*, p. 176.

4. *The Times*, 3, 6 Dec 1910.

5. Strachey Papers, Strachey to Lord Onslow, 2 Dec 1910 [copy]. See also the similar view of Austen Chamberlain, although he considered 'the set was all in our favour' before the Albert Hall pledge. Balfour Papers, Add. MS. 49736, ff. 129–31, Austen Chamberlain to Balfour, 2 Dec 1910.

6. *The Times*, 6 Dec 1910.

7. For the importance one Minister, Crewe, attached to this stipulation, see Jenkins, *Balfour's Poodle*, p. 119, n. 1.

8. Asquith Papers, 2, ff. 77–8 and 81–2, Knollys to Nash, 28 Nov, and 8 Dec 1910.

9. 23 Nov 1910.

10. Harcourt Papers, Elibank to Harcourt, 21 Apr 1910.

11. No newspaper appears to have forecast Aitken's victory. A detailed account of this contest, planned like 'some great business enterprise', can be found in F. A. Mackenzie, *Beaverbrook* (London, 1931) pp. 46–57.

12. *Daily News*, 5 Dec 1910.

13. There were several recounts at Exeter, where the result, a Liberal victory by four votes, was not announced until 1.53 a.m. See the *Western Morning News*, 5 Dec 1910. This decision was later reversed as the result of a petition for recount.

14. Grimsby, a surprise Unionist loss in January, was won back by Sir George Doughty, despite the alleged efforts of Radical shipowners to keep the pro-Doughty fishermen at sea during the poll. See *Sheffield Daily Telegraph*, 3 Dec 1910.

15. *Liverpool Courier*, 6 Dec 1910.

16. The Unionists were handicapped by the retirement of the sitting Members, particularly that of Storey, widely credited with the responsibility for the January victories. See above, p. 438, n. 31.

17. In the Midlands the Liberals won Coventry and Leek, and lost Dudley, Melton and High Peak.

18. The Liberals won Louth in Lincolnshire; Bedford, Newmarket, Lowestoft and Saffron Walden in East Anglia; and Cheltenham, Banbury, Dartford and Cricklade in the South. In the West they lost the two Plymouth seats plus Ashburton, Bodmin, Tavistock and Torquay.

19. Balfour Papers, Add. MS. 49795, ff. 166–9, Garvin to Sandars, 12 Dec 1910.

20. Liberals attributed it to the Bute influence – the Marquess of Bute's brother was the Unionist candidate – and to a poorly organised Liberal campaign.

21. The exceptions were: *Unionist victories*: King's Lynn, St Helens, Cardiff. *Anti-Unionist victories*: Whitehaven, Cockermouth, Bow and Bromley, Mid-Tyrone (all with a split anti-Unionist vote in January), Wakefield.

22. 9 Dec 1910.

23. 21 Dec 1910.

24. Strachey Papers, Lansdowne to Strachey, 9 Jan 1911, strictly private.

25. Churchill, *Churchill*, ii 347–50, Churchill to Asquith, 3 Jan 1911.
26. Elibank Papers, MS. 8802, ff. 159–60 [copy].
27. Ibid., ff. 161–2, Elibank to Lloyd George, 21 Dec 1910 [copy]. The reference to the '*British* majority' refers to the fact that in Great Britain the anti-Unionists had a majority.
28. Churchill, *Churchill*, ii 347–50.
29. Ibid. My reading of the letter in the Asquith Papers, 13, ff. 1–4, leads me to prefer 'clink' to 'chink'.
30. Gladstone Papers, Add. MS. 46070, ff. 160–1, Nash to Gladstone, 9 Jan 1911.
31. Chamberlain, *Politics From Inside*, p. 307, Balfour to Austen Chamberlain, 13 Dec 1910.
32. Chamberlain Papers, AC 8/7/19, Lansdowne to Austen Chamberlain, 14 Dec 1910. See also Balfour Papers, Add. MS. 49730, ff. 149–50, Lansdowne to Sandars, 17 Dec 1910.
33. Balfour Papers, Add. MS. 49795, ff. 166–9, Garvin to Sandars, 12 Dec 1910, private. For Lancashire reports see Gollin, *Garvin*, p. 272 and Salvidge, *Salvidge*, p. 102.
34. Petrie, *Chamberlain*, i 268–72, Austen Chamberlain to Richard Jebb, 7 Dec 1910. The most detailed statement of Austen Chamberlain's arguments from particular constituencies is in Chamberlain, *Politics From Inside*, pp. 307–11. The validity of these arguments is examined below, pp. 410–11.
35. *Morning Post*, 5, 7 Dec 1910; and Petrie, *Chamberlain*, i 269.
36. Chamberlain Papers, AC 8/7/21, Sir Joseph Lawrence to Austen Chamberlain, 9 Dec 1910.
37. Ibid., AC 8/7/8, Arthur Colefax to Austen Chamberlain, 14 Dec 1910.
38. Ibid., AC 8/7/14, Hewins to Austen Chamberlain, 15 Dec 1910. Sandars noted that Hewins was 'sore all over' and attributed his complaints to the fact that 'he has not been provided with a safe seat by the Party managers'. Balfour Papers, Add. MS. 49767, ff. 34–7, Sandars to Balfour, 14 Dec 1910.
39. Bonar Law Papers, 18/6/145, Maxse to Bonar Law, 14 Dec 1910.
40. Chamberlain Papers, AC 8/7/22.
41. *Morning Post*, 14 Dec 1910. It was paradoxical that Balfour's Dartford promise should have provoked the *Morning Post*, for as has been seen this constituted a surrender to those Whole Hoggers who demanded a referendum, not on Tariff Reform principles, but on a Tariff Reform budget. But the *Morning Post* was quite consistent for it had opposed a referendum on any sort of financial measure, and the budget promise was therefore for the *Post* the ultimate absurdity.
42. Petrie, *Chamberlain*, i 268–72, Austen Chamberlain to Jebb, 7 Dec 1910.
43. Ibid.
44. Balfour Papers, Add. MS. 49736, f. 128, Austen Chamberlain to Balfour, 1 Dec 1910.
45. Ibid. Add. MS. 49795, ff. 166–9, Garvin to Sandars, 12 Dec 1910.
46. Ibid. Add. MS. 49861, ff. 99–102, R. Blumenfeld (editor, *Daily Express*) to Sandars, 17 Dec 1910.
47. Chamberlain, *Politics From Inside*, pp. 306–7.
48. Chamberlain Papers, AC 8/7/27, Ware to Chamberlain, 12 Dec 1910.

49. *The Times*, 15 Dec 1910.
50. Balfour Papers, Add. MS. 49767, ff. 38–41, Sandars to Short, 15 Dec 1910.
51. Churchill, *Derby*, p. 160, Derby to Sandars, 15 Dec 1910.
52. Gollin, *Garvin*, p. 314, Garvin to Sandars, 21 Dec 1910.
53. Ibid. pp. 309–11; and Newton, *Lansdowne*, pp. 407–8.
54. Strachey Papers, Strachey to Lansdowne, 15 Dec 1910 [copy]. For Lansdowne's sympathetic if ambiguous reply see ibid., Lansdowne to Strachey, 19 Dec 1910.
55. *Morning Post*, 8 Dec 1910.
56. Ibid. 17 Dec 1910.
57. Gollin, *Garvin*, pp. 319–21.
58. *Morning Post*, 12 Dec 1910.
59. Speech at Whitechapel, 6 December, *The Times*, 7 Dec 1910.
60. 21 Dec 1910.
61. 8 Dec 1910.
62. 6 Dec 1910.

CHAPTER 11   THE PARTIES AND THEIR CANDIDATES

1. There were 1315 candidatures because two Irish candidates each contested two seats.
2. This compared with seventeen seats uncontested in Great Britain in 1885 and thirty-one in 1906, the two most broadly based of earlier general elections. Nine Unionists were returned unopposed in the following seats: Oxford University (2); Cambridge University (2); Penrith (the Speaker); West Birmingham (Joseph Chamberlain); Durham City; Bury St Edmunds and Burton. One Liberal, John Wilson (Mid-Durham), was returned unopposed.
3. Elibank Papers, MS. 8802, ff. 39–45, unsigned memorandum on the Irish situation, 31 Mar 1910, quite confidential.
4. The four seats were York, Bootle, North and South Mayo. York, a two-member borough, had returned one Liberal and one Unionist in January after a close-fought election. The *status quo* was maintained in December by a mutual arrangement between the local associations whereby each nominated only one candidate. Bootle was one of the most populous constituencies in the kingdom and although the percentage margin between the parties had been small (5·8 per cent), the vote margin (1085) was daunting. In Mayo the independent Nationalists failed unexpectedly to nominate.
5. Because of multiple candidatures in Ireland there was a total of 1191 candidatures.
6. Harcourt Papers, Corbett to Harcourt, 8 Jan 1910.
7. *The Times*, 26 Jan 1909.
8. See above, p. 66.
9. Cecil Papers, Add. MS. 51159, Hornby to Robert Cecil, 7 Feb 1909.
10. See his letter informing Robert Cecil of his intention to end his Central Office subscription. Ibid. 21 Jan 1909.
11. Lord Croft, *My Life of Strife* (London, 1949) pp. 41–2; and Balfour Papers, Add. MS. 49860, ff. 136–7, Central Office memorandum on East Hertfordshire, 17 Aug 1909.

12. Cecil Papers, Add. MS. 51072, Bowles to Robert Cecil, 24 Aug 1909; ibid. Add. MS. 51071, Sandars to Robert Cecil, 23 Sept 1909; Balfour Papers, Add. MS. 49771, ff. 179–80, Acland-Hood to Sandars, 1 Oct [1909]; and *The Times* 20 Jan 1909.

13. Balfour Papers, Add. MS. 49860, ff. 146–9, Central Office memorandum on East Marylebone, 23 Aug 1909; Cecil Papers, Add. MS. 51158, J. S. Underhill (Cecil's agent) to Robert Cecil, 8 Jan 1909; and *Morning Post*, 10 Dec 1909, circular from a ward chairman of the rebel association.

14. Balfour Papers, Add. MS. 49708, ff. 173–5, Selborne to Balfour, 28 Aug 1909.

15. Cecil Papers, Add. MS. 51157, Selborne to Robert Cecil, 25 Aug 1909; Cromer Papers, F.O. 633/18, pp. 252–3, Robert Cecil to Cromer, 6 Sept 1909; and *The Times*, 21 Sept, 9, 23 Oct 1909.

16. Balfour Papers, Add. MS. 49737, f. 111, Robert Cecil to Balfour, 8 Oct 1909.

17. *The Times*, 25 Sept 1909.

18. Ibid., 7 Oct 1909.

19. Ibid. 4 Oct 1909.

20. Waley, *Montagu*, p. 26, Montagu to Asquith, 11 Feb 1908.

21. *British Weekly*, 18 Nov 1909.

22. See the Unionist press generally in the first fortnight of Jan 1910, for lists of seceders, often accompanied with reasons for particular secessions. Some of the secessions were rather bogus, e.g. Unionist Free Fooders returning to the Unionist fold after having voted Liberal in 1906, but the lists do suggest a dribble of local notables away from the Liberal Party.

23. *The Times*, 21 Sept 1909, letter, Pease to Cox, 16 Sept 1909. See also Pease's support for another Liberal 'troglodyte', Agar-Robartes, at St Austell, *Western Daily Mercury*, 9 Nov 1909.

24. *The Times*, 12, 14 Jan 1910.

25. Ibid., 1 Feb. 1909, Dalmeny to chairman, Midlothian Liberal Association, 26 Dec 1908.

26. Sir G. W. Kekewich, *The Education Department and After* (London, 1920) pp. 252–3.

27. R. L. Green, *A. E. W. Mason* (London, 1952) p. 110.

28. Harcourt Papers, J. E. Ellis to Harcourt, 9 Feb 1910.

29. Asquith Papers, 11, ff. 127–36, Kimberley to Asquith, 23 May 1908, strictly private. See also Pelling, *Social Geography*, p. 99.

30. 5 Dec 1909.

31. Henry Bolitho, *Alfred Mond, 1st Lord Melchett* (London, 1933) pp. 152–3; *South Wales Daily Post*, 6, 7 Dec 1909; and Morgan, *Wales in British Politics*, p. 150.

32. Scottish Liberal Association, minutes, Eastern Organising Committee, 20 May 1909.

33. Lever's words, *Manchester Guardian*, 21 Dec 1909.

34. In Dec 1910 Barnard returned to Kidderminster on condition that he was unpledged on the licensing question. See *Birmingham Daily Post*, 22 Nov 1910.

35. Six of these had already recaptured the seat at a by-election.

36. Gladstone Papers, Add. MS. 46037, ff. 31–2, 93–4, Henry to Gladstone, 25 Mar 1907, 14 Sept 1908.

37. National Liberal Federation, *Report, Thirtieth Annual Conference (1908)* pp. 42-3.

38. See below, pp. 247-9.

39. Balfour Papers, Add. MS. 49713, ff. 216-17, Beresford to Balfour, 6 Nov 1909.

40. See Fabian Ware's publicised clash with Acland-Hood over East Marylebone, *Morning Post*, 6 Jan 1910.

41. Balfour Papers, Add. MS. 49766, ff. 94-6, Sandars to Balfour, 26 Jan 1910.

42. *Glasgow Herald*, 14, 26, 27 Jan 1910.

43. Balfour Papers, Add. MS. 49766, ff. 31-41, Sandars to Balfour, 18 Dec 1909.

44. *Glasgow Herald*, 15 Dec 1909. There were reports, letters and articles on Tradeston in the *Glasgow Herald* almost daily from mid-November until the poll.

45. See Salvidge, *Salvidge*, pp. 88-9; and *Liverpool Courier*, 11, 15 Dec 1909, 4 Jan 1910.

46. Both Tradeston Liberal candidates were on Churchill's platform when he spoke in Glasgow. See *Glasgow Herald*, 13 Jan 1910. Lewis Harcourt beat a hasty retreat after rashly endorsing Corbett's Liberal opponent. See Harcourt Papers, Corbett to Harcourt, 8 Jan 1910; and *Glasgow Herald*, 12 Jan 1910.

47. Only four sitting Nationalist M.P.s were defeated. Two were independent Nationalists, two were official Nationalists.

48. 26 Jan 1910.

49. An examination of their election addresses indicates that they all took a vague Tariff Reform position.

50. Speaight, *Belloc*, pp. 237-8, 293-4. See also Belloc's last speech in the Commons, *H.C.Deb.*, 5th ser., xx 98-104 (18 Nov 1910); and Hilaire Belloc and Cecil Chesterton, *The Party System* (London, 1911).

51. 17 Nov 1910.

52. Bonar Law Papers, 21/3/10, Goulding to Bonar Law, 4 Aug 1910.

53. Blake, *Bonar Law*, pp. 66-7; Churchill, *Derby*, pp. 121-2; Bonar Law Papers, 21/3/14, Derby to Goulding, 10 Oct 1910; and ibid. 21/3/12, Garvin to Bonar Law, 10 Aug 1910. In the event Derby's brother did not prove amenable and another seat had to be found for Bonar Law.

54. *Daily News*, 19, 20 Nov 1910.

55. *Justice*, 3 Dec 1910. Four local candidates were named, but only two of them were finally nominated.

56. *Clarion*, 9 Dec 1910.

57. William Redmond at Cork City, *Freeman's Journal*, 20 Nov 1910.

58. Ibid. 3, 5, 7, 8 Dec 1910.

59. For the remainder of this chapter the term Nationalist includes official and independent Nationalist candidates.

60. Of Liberal Cabinet Ministers Asquith, Birrell, Buxton, Churchill, Haldane, Harcourt, McKenna, Pease, Runciman and Samuel were all carpet-baggers.

61. See Matthews, *Fifty Years of Agricultural Politics*, p. 347. But see Graham Wallas, *Human Nature in Politics* (London, 1908) pp. 39-40, who argued that the agents favoured a non-resident candidate, but preferably one who could claim an *ad hoc* local character by 'hiring . . . a large house each year in which he lives a life of carefully dramatised hospitality'. Information on residence was not available for 8 per cent of the candidates.

62. Lyons, *Irish Parliamentary Party*, p. 178.

63. See below, pp. 280–1.
64. *Newcastle Daily Chronicle*, 21 Dec 1909.
65. These figures probably overstate the median age as figures are not available for 18 per cent of Unionist candidates and 16 per cent of Liberal candidates. These were mostly defeated candidates without parliamentary experience, and probably consisted of a high proportion of younger men. Figures were also unavailable for 14 per cent of Labour candidates and for 16 per cent of the Nationalists.
66. I.L.P., *Report, Sixteenth Annual Conference (1908)* p. 51.
67. Those used in W. L. Guttsman, *The British Political Elite* (London, 1963), viz. Charterhouse, Cheltenham, Clifton, Eton, Fettes, Haileybury, Harrow, Loretto, Malvern, Marlborough, Oundle, Radley, Repton, Rossall, Rugby, Sedbergh, Sherborne, Shrewsbury, Uppingham, Winchester.
68. Sir Percy Harris, *Forty Years In And Out of Parliament* (London, 1947) pp. 45–6. Crewe was also an old Harrovian but presumably the reference was to Churchill.
69. Quoted in 'A Nonconformist Minister', *Nonconformity and Politics* (London, 1909) pp. 111–12.
70. Ibid.
71. Waley, *Montagu*, p. 30. Montagu was reporting some disquiet among M.P.s over the presence of a dancer, Miss Allen, at an Asquith garden party. He noted, however, that 'it is equally characteristic of our Party that so many Members who object to meeting the lady were able apparently to recognise her'.
72. See R. F. Wearmouth, *The Social and Political Influences of Methodism in the Twentieth Century* (London, 1957) pp. 80–161.
73. Ibid., p. 118.
74. Balfour Papers, Add. MS. 49767, ff. 84–5, Sandars to Short, 8 Jan 1911.
75. *Daily Telegraph*, 6 Dec 1909, 4, 8 Jan 1910.
76. See Lyons, *Irish Parliamentary Party*, p. 166, n. 2.
77. *Jewish World*, 10 Dec 1909, estimated that over half the Jewish vote was concentrated in these four cities.
78. Ibid. 9 Dec 1910.
79. See above, p. 217, for reference to the strong current of anti-semitism unleashed by Alfred Mond's candidature at Swansea Town.

CHAPTER 12   THE CONTAINMENT OF LABOUR

1. *Manchester Guardian*, 17 Nov 1909.
2. Roy Gregory, *The Miners and British Politics 1906–14* (Oxford, 1968) p. 149. For detailed accounts of the by-election see ibid. pp. 147–50; and J. E. Williams, *The Derbyshire Miners* (London, 1962) pp. 498–500.
3. For Bermondsey see Fenner Brockway, *Bermondsey Story, The Life of Alfred Salter* (London, 1949) pp. 36–9; and Thompson, *Socialists, Liberals and Labour*, p. 173. For the municipal elections see *Labour Leader*, 19 Nov 1909; and the *Economist*, 6 Nov 1909.

4. Labour Party, *Report, Tenth Annual Conference (1910)* p. 56.
5. Quoted by Ben Tillett in *Justice*, 11 Dec 1909.
6. 10 Dec 1909.
7. *Daily Mail*, 28 Dec 1909, article by Snowden, 'The Labour Party's Dilemma'. Even the S.D.P. journal *Justice* tended to treat the House of Lords as the supreme issue. See *Justice*, 4, 11 Dec 1909.
8. 28 Jan 1910.
9. Lloyd George Papers, C/5/11/1, MacDonald to Lloyd George, 17 Sept 1909.
10. *Clarion*, 26 Nov 1909, article by Grayson.
11. *The Times*, 28 Dec 1909, letter from Ben Tillett.
12. *Clarion*, 26 Nov 1909, article by Grayson.
13. Ibid. 10 Dec 1909.
14. Speech at Bridgend, 19 November, *Liverpool Daily Post*, 25 Nov 1909.
15. *Labour Leader*, 10 Dec 1909.
16. For the jettisoning of such candidates in the interests of 'Progressive unity' see Gregory, *The Miners*, pp. 112, 128–30.
17. This calculation is based on the number of seats the party actually contested plus those from which candidates were withdrawn. This is a minimal figure as all withdrawals may not have been traced.
18. *Labour Leader*, 4 Feb 1910. MacDonald would have cut a further ten to fifteen Labour candidatures.
19. The candidatures at Coventry, Keighley, Montrose Burghs and Plymouth seem to have been the only instances of fully endorsed candidatures being abandoned.
20. Labour Party Documents, ii, ff. 124–6, minutes, N.E.C. sub-committee on I.L.P. candidates, 3, 10 Nov 1909; *Yorkshire Observer*, 8 Dec 1909; *Glasgow Herald*, 22 Nov 1909; and *Birmingham Daily Post*, 6 Dec 1909.
21. 19 Nov 1909.
22. See below, pp. 246, 252–3.
23. Labour did persist, without success, in its efforts to capture one of the Portsmouth seats, and ran a replacement for Richard Bell at Derby, but these could not be considered new interventions.
24. *Manchester Courier*, 7 Dec 1909. Internal differences at Oldham apparently arose out of 'religious troubles' and from a clash between the local I.L.P. and the textile unions. See Labour Party, minutes, N.E.C., 13 Apr 1910, special memorandum on elections from Ramsay MacDonald. This memorandum consists of MacDonald's commentary on detailed constituency reports by the National Agent, Arthur Peters. Many of these reports are quoted verbatim in the memorandum. I am indebted to Mr Ross McKibbon for this reference.
25. Labour Party Documents, ii, ff. 109–10 and 118–23, minutes, N.E.C., 16 Feb 1909 and 8 Oct 1909.
26. *Western Daily Mercury*, 29 Nov 1909, speech by the Labour candidate, J. Belcher.
27. *The Times*, 30 Dec 1909.
28. 3 Dec 1909.
29. *Leeds Mercury*, 6, 20 Dec. 1909.
30. *Clarion*, 28 Jan 1910.

31. *South Wales Daily News*, 14 Jan 1910.

32. For the opposition of local Labour bodies to the Socialist candidates see *Carlisle Express and Examiner*, 11 Dec 1909 for Carlisle; *Glasgow Herald*, 29 Nov 1909 for North Aberdeen; and *Manchester Guardian*, 23 Dec 1909 for Rochdale.

33. *Justice*, 29 Jan 1910.

34. Maxse Papers, 461, f. 569.

35. 15 Dec 1909.

36. *Newcastle Daily Chronicle*, 8 Jan 1910.

37. *Yorkshire Post*, 13 Dec 1909.

38. *Newcastle Daily Chronicle*, 14 Jan 1910.

39. 14 Jan 1910.

40. *Labour Leader*, 21 Jan 1910.

41. *North Mail*, 14 Jan 1910.

42. *Newcastle Daily Journal*, 18 Jan 1910.

43. Labour Party, *Report, Ninth Annual Conference (1909)* pp. 61–3.

44. *Scotsman*, 7 Nov; 14, 21 Dec 1909; and 17, 19 Jan 1910.

45. This account of the Merthyr contest is based on W. Stewart, *J. Keir Hardie, A Biography* (London, 1925) p. 305; and *South Wales Daily News*, Jan 1910, *passim*.

46. *Lancashire Daily Post*, 15 Jan 1910.

47. Indeed his behaviour has deceived at least two historians. Reid, *Origins of the British Labour Party*, treats Cox throughout as a Tory Member. (See particularly references pp. 134 and 157.) Asa Briggs in Nowell-Smith, *Edwardian England*, p. 94, presents him as a leader of 'a section of backbencher Unionists'.

48. *Manchester Guardian*, 6 Jan 1910.

49. The results were: Unionist 9526   Labour   7539
                         Unionist 9160   Liberal   6281
                                          Ind. Liberal 2704

    Gorst attributed the leakage as due to 'Roman Catholic splits' between Macpherson and Cox. Churchill, *Churchill*, companion volume ii 964.

50. *Newcastle Daily Chronicle*, 21 Jan 1910.

51. See National Liberal Club, Election Addresses, Jan 1910, ii 10.

52. I.L.P., *Report, Eighteenth Annual Conference (1910)* p. 71.

53. *North Western Daily Mail*, 12 Jan 1910.

54. *Leeds Mercury*, 14 Dec 1909.

55. *Newcastle Daily Chronicle*, 20 Dec 1909.

56. *Manchester Guardian*, 4 Jan 1910.

57. *The Times*, 23 Dec 1909.

58. Manchester Liberal Federation, minutes, Executive Committee, 2 Dec 1909.

59. Ibid. 16 Dec. 1909. The single dissentient was Harold Elverston, who was himself involved in a three-cornered contest at Gateshead. See below, pp. 253–4.

60. Ibid. 20 Dec 1909.

61. *Manchester Guardian*, 27 Dec 1909; 6, 13 Jan 1910.

62. Ibid. 4 Jan 1910; and *Labour Leader*, 21 Jan 1910, article by McLachlan.

63. 14 Jan 1910.

64. The authoritative account of the affiliation of the Miners' Federation with the Labour Party is Gregory, *The Miners*, ch. iii.

65. *Sheffield Daily Telegraph*, 1 Dec 1909.

66. *North Eastern Daily Gazette*, 16 Dec 1909, interview with Wilson; and *Newcastle Daily Chronicle*, 30 Dec 1909.

67. Bryce Papers, Miscellaneous Correspondence, Burt to Bryce, 13 Oct 1909.

68. Gregory, *The Miners*, p. 75; and *Newcastle Daily Chronicle*, 19 Oct 1909.

69. Gregory, *The Miners*, pp. 74–6; and *Newcastle Daily Chronicle*, 6, 11, 25, 27, 28 Oct; 17, 19 Nov; and 15, 17 Dec 1909.

70. Gregory, *The Miners*, p. 42.

71. Ibid. p. 150.

72. *South Wales Daily Post*, 20 Dec 1909.

73. Labour Party, *Report, Tenth Annual Conference (1910)* p. 58.

74. Gregory, *The Miners*, pp. 113, 170.

75. *Sheffield Daily Telegraph*, 1 Dec 1909. In a memorandum dated 15 Nov 1909 Clegg made a similar distinction between 'genuine Labour' i.e. the 'Liberal-Labour' party and 'the Keir Hardie type of socialism'. H. J. Wilson Papers.

76. Labour Party, *Report, Tenth Annual Conference (1910)* p. 64.

77. Gregory, *The Miners*, pp. 42–4.

78. Gregory, *The Miners*, p. 128; *Liverpool Daily Post*, 25 Nov 1909; and *South Wales Daily Post*, 1 Nov 1909.

79. See Gregory, *The Miners*, p. 129, for this capitulation; and *South Wales Daily Post*, 7, 9 Dec 1909, for Hartshorn's and Stanton's reactions.

80. See Pease's letter, *Manchester Guardian*, 17 Nov 1909.

81. 20 Nov 1909.

82. At the dissolution the seats in Northumberland–Durham were distributed as follows: Liberal 14 (including seats of Burt, Fenwick and Wilson which the party would probably only retain while the incumbents lived), Labour 6, Unionist 4.

83. *The Times*, 6 Jan 1909; and Northern Liberal Federation, minutes, Executive Committee, 8 May 1909.

84. See the speech of the President, Gateshead Liberal Association, 14 December, *Newcastle Daily Chronicle*, 15 Dec 1909.

85. Northern Liberal Federation, minutes, Executive Committee, 8 May 1909. Elverston was Treasurer of the Manchester Liberal Federation and a member of the Executive Committee of the National Liberal Federation. His record in Manchester (see above, p. 456, n. 59.) suggests he was opposed to any compromise with the Labour Party.

86. *Newcastle Daily Chronicle*, 7 Dec 1909, 5, 17 Jan 1910.

87. Ibid. 21, 22, 24 Dec 1909.

88. Ibid. 18 Jan 1910.

89. A nephew J. H. Wilson was Secretary of the Sheffield Liberal Federation, and a son, O. C. Wilson, Secretary, Brightside Liberal Association.

90. H. J. Wilson Papers, J. W. Wilson, 9 Dec 1909.

91. Ibid. Clegg memorandum, 15 Nov. 1909.

92. Paragraph based on *Yorkshire Post* and *Sheffield Independent*, Dec 1909–Jan 1910, and on the following material in the H. J. Wilson Papers: History of Attercliffe Liberal Association manifesto *re* general election Jan 1910, 16 Feb

1910; J. W. Wilson to H. J. Wilson, 15 Dec 1909; Clegg to J. W. Wilson, 17 and 21 Dec 1909.

93. Bryce Papers, Miscellaneous Correspondence, Lord Pentland to Bryce, 14 July 1907. See also the account of this by-election in Pelling, *Popular Politics and Society*, pp. 133–6.

94. Northern Liberal Federation, minutes, Executive Committee, 20 Feb 1909.

95. *Newcastle Daily Chronicle*, 10, 21, 26 Jan 1910; and *Labour Leader*, 4 Feb 1910.

96. *Yorkshire Post*, 1, 11 Jan 1910.

97. 23 Dec 1910. The temper of Scottish Liberalism is seen in the close eleven to seven vote whereby in November 1909 the Western Committee decided that it was advisable to co-operate with headquarters in any efforts to reach an accommodation with Labour. Scottish Liberal Association, minutes, Western Committee, 24 Nov 1909.

98. *Yorkshire Observer*, 4 Jan 1910.

99. *West Cumberland Times*, 8 Jan 1910. The Liberal fighting Grayson at Colne Valley described himself as 'an evolutionary socialist'. *Yorkshire Post*, 19 Jan 1910.

100. *Yorkshire Observer*, 8 Jan 1910.

101. Ibid.

102. See *Manchester Guardian*, 26 Jan 1910.

103. *Yorkshire Observer*, 11 Jan 1910.

104. *Scotsman*, 7 Jan 1910.

105. *Yorkshire Observer*, 13 Jan 1910.

106. *Daily Chronicle*, 18 Jan 1910. R. C. K. Ensor working for Lansbury thought that the publication of this letter and one from Lloyd George to the Liberal candidate cost Lansbury 'hundreds of Liberal votes'. Lansbury Papers, iv, ff. 18–19, Ensor to Lansbury, 20 Jan 1910. See also George Lansbury, *My Life* (London, 1928) p. 113.

107. *Labour Leader*, 18 Feb 1910.

108. Ibid. 11 Feb 1910.

109. *Yorkshire Observer*, 3 Jan 1910.

110. *Carlisle Express and Examiner*, 11 Dec 1909.

111. *North Eastern Daily Gazette*, 17 Dec 1909.

112. Ibid. 9, 21 Dec. 1909.

113. For Bishop Auckland see Gregory, *The Miners*, pp. 77–8; and for Mid-Lanark see *Glasgow Herald*, 27 Jan 1910.

114. Ibid. 12 Jan 1910.

115. Ibid. 30 Nov 1909.

116. Lancashire and Cheshire Liberal Federation, minutes, annual meeting, 8 Apr 1910.

117. Gregory Blaxland, *J. H. Thomas, A Life for Unity* (London, 1964) pp. 53–7. There is a more melodramatic account in *J. H. Thomas, My Story* (London, 1937) pp. 24–6.

118. Lansbury Papers, iv, f. 23, E. R. Pease, Secretary, Fabian Society to Miss Lansbury, 21 Jan 1910.

119. Burnley was also lost as a result of the intervention of Hyndman of the S.D.P.

120. *Labour Leader*, 28 Jan 1910.

121. Ibid. 4 Feb 1910.

122. Labour Party, minutes, N.E.C., 13 Apr 1910, special memorandum on elections from Ramsay MacDonald.

123. The party had intended to contest at least fifty-seven seats but after three candidates and considerable confusion West Wolverhampton was abandoned. See *Birmingham Daily Post*, Nov 1910, *passim*; and *Labour Leader*, 2 Dec 1910.

124. *The Times*, 22 Nov, 7 Dec 1910.

125. *North Western Daily Mail*, 26 Nov 1910; and *West Cumberland Times*, 30 Nov, 7 Dec 1910.

126. *Yorkshire Observer*, 2 Dec 1910.

127. *Labour Leader*, 9 Dec 1910. The Labour candidature at Chatham was hopelessly mismanaged. The candidate was selected late, he was destitute of national Labour literature, and possessed not a single conveyance. And this occurred in a constituency recognised by the National Agent as one in which 'it is advisable to keep the Liberals out, otherwise they may again assert themselves, the only result being to "spoil the pitch" for Labour altogether.' Labour Party, minutes, N.E.C., 13 Apr 1910, special memorandum on elections from Ramsay MacDonald.

128. Labour Party Documents, ii f. 168, minutes, N.E.C., 20 Dec 1910. See also Gregory, *The Miners*, pp. 44–6, 151–3. Haslam, Harvey and Hancock were the three accused.

129. *Lancashire Daily Post*, 19, 28 Nov 1910.

130. Burns Papers, Add. MS. 46, 332, diary, 3 Dec 1910. As the swing against the Unionists at Battersea was the greatest in South London, Burns may well have been right.

131. *Justice*, 8 Jan, 24 Dec 1910.

132. *The Times*, 25 Nov 1910.

133. *Yorkshire Observer*, 24 Jan 1910.

134. See, for example, the local Labour attitude in Spen Valley, *Yorkshire Observer*. 6 Dec 1910; in Middlesbrough, *Yorkshire Post*, 2 Dec 1910; and in Leigh, *Liverpool Courier*, 12 Dec 1910.

135. See Morgan, *Wales in British Politics*, pp. 247–55, and for speeches of Keir Hardie see *South Wales Daily News*, 1, 10 Dec 1910. On the other hand 'Mabon' defended the Government's actions. Ibid. 9 Dec 1910.

136. Ibid. 29 Nov, 10 Dec 1910.

137. Carrington Diary, 31 Mar 1910. There is an account of this by-election in Gregory, *The Miners*, pp. 130–2.

138. *South Wales Daily News*, 28, 29 Nov, 1, 2 Dec 1910. The Liberal campaign in Gower was financed by Cory Yeo, one of the coal owners attacked by Hardie.

139. For a detailed study of the conflict in each constituency see Gregory, *The Miners*, pp. 132–3.

140. *Glasgow Herald*, 1 Dec 1910.

CHAPTER 13   PARTY ORGANISATION

1. Eric Alexander, Viscount Chilston, *Chief Whip. The Political Life and Times of Aretas Akers-Douglas, First Viscount Chilston* (London, 1961) p. 347, Balfour to Akers-Douglas, 17 Jan 1911.
2. Maxse Papers, 462, ff. 789–80, Malmesbury to Maxse, 28 Dec 1910.
3. clxxxix (Jan 1911) 153.
4. R. B. Jones, 'Balfour's Reform of Party Organisations', *Bulletin of the Institute of Historical Research*, xxxviii, no. 97 (May 1965) 99, Sandars to Short, 3 Oct 1910.
5. R. T. McKenzie, *British Political Parties* (London, 1955) pp. 178, 267.
6. See below, pp. 274–6.
7. Balfour Papers, Add. MS. 49775, ff. 149–60, memorandum on Unionist organisation, 31 Jan 1911, from Leopold Amery.
8. Bonar Law Papers, 41/1/2, memorandum on party organisation from Steel-Maitland, strictly private, n.d. but written early 1912. Parts of this memorandum have been quoted in Blake, *Bonar Law*, p. 100. Steel-Maitland was a Chamberlain protégé and his memorandum was no doubt influenced by Whole Hogger dissatisfaction with the Central Office, but his criticisms are amply documented and substantially confirmed by other sources.
9. Bonar Law Papers, 41/1/2, Steel-Maitland memorandum; and Jones, *Bull. of the Inst. of Hist. Res.*, xxxviii, no. 97 (May 1965) 99.
10. Balfour Papers, Add. MS. 49767, ff. 58–61, confidential.
11. Ibid. A. L. Lowell, *The Government of England* (London, 1908) i 482, notes that agents 'are not of the class from which members of Parliament are taken'.
12. Balfour Papers, Add. MS. 49755, ff. 149–60, Amery memorandum.
13. Bonar Law Papers, 41/1/2, Steel-Maitland memorandum.
14. Balfour Papers, Add. MS. 49767, ff. 58–61, Sandars to Balfour, 2 5Dec 1910, confidential.
15. Acland-Hood Papers, p. 52, newspaper cutting.
16. Bonar Law Papers, 41/1/2, Steel-Maitland memorandum.
17. See articles in *Daily Telegraph*, 4, 5 Feb 1910.
18. 30 Jan 1911. This is the last of three articles on Unionist organisation, the others appearing in *The Times*, 16, 23 Jan 1911. They were extensively used in McKenzie, *British Political Parties*, chs. iv, v.
19. Bonar Law Papers, 18/6/118, Chaplin to Bonar Law, 13 Mar 1910.
20. Ibid. 41/1/2, Steel-Maitland memorandum.
21. Acland-Hood Papers, p. 50, note in Acland-Hood's hand.
22. *The Times*, 16, 23, 30 Jan 1911; National Union, minutes, special Conference, 27 July 1906; and Jones, *Bull. of the Inst. of Hist. Res.*, xxxviii, no. 97 (May 1965), 99.
23. National Union, minutes, Executive Committee, 3 June 1907.
24. Bonar Law Papers, 41/1/2, Steel-Maitland memorandum.
25. Ibid.
26. *The Times*, 23 Jan 1911.
27. Bonar Law Papers, 18/6/118, Chaplin to Bonar Law, 13 Mar 1910.
28. 30 Jan 1911.

29. Balfour Papers, Add. MS. 49766, ff. 75-80, Sandars to Balfour, 21 Jan 1910.
30. Bonar Law Papers, 26/1/76, memorandum, n.d., from Walter Long.
31. Balfour Papers, Add. MS. 49766, ff. 75-80, Sandars to Balfour, 21 Jan 1910, private.
32. Ibid., Add. MS. 49771, ff. 189-90, Acland-Hood to Sandars, 5 Feb 1910.
33. 2 Feb 1910.
34. *Scottish Hist. R.*, xliv (1965) 109.
35. 16 Jan 1910.
36. *National Review*, lii (Jan 1909) 744.
37. Acland-Hood Papers, p. 67, newspaper cutting.
38. 16 Jan 1911.
39. *Standard*, 14 Dec 1909.
40. National Union, minutes, Annual Conference, 17-18 Nov 1910.
41. *Standard*, 21 Nov, 14 Dec 1910. Candidates were run at Attercliffe, Hyde, Macclesfield, Norwich, Radcliffe-cum-Farnworth and Stockport.
42. J. Ellis Barker, 'How the Unionists Might Win', *Fortnightly Review*, lxxxvi (Nov 1909) 804. Lowell, *Government of England*, i 489-90, considered these special privileges one of the most obvious contrasts between Liberal and Conservative local associations.
43. Maxse Papers, 461, ff. 567-8, Lawrence to Maxse, 2 Feb 1910.
44. 10 Dec 1910.
45. Balfour Papers, Add. MS. 49775, ff. 149-60, Amery memorandum. Amery himself had trouble in finding a seat in late 1910. He hoped for Croydon, a safe seat, but noted that 'one or two richer men are in the field'. Milner Papers, Amery to Milner, 9 Nov 1910. One of the richer men got the seat and Amery had to content himself with marginal Bow and Bromley.
46. Robert Cecil Papers, Add. MS. 51160, Earl of Shaftesbury to Robert Cecil, 3 Oct 1910.
47. It was also the last of the pocket boroughs, having 'nearly always been held by the Rothschilds or a relation, & they have a very long standing connection with the place. They are the most generous of all our supporters and that without asking for any return. They give us £12,000 a year and large sums at Elections and subscribe very largely to the L.U.'s also.' Bonar Law Papers, 26/3/39, Steel-Maitland to Bonar Law, 26 May 1912.
48. Arthur A. Baumann, 'Money and Brains in Politics', *Fortnightly Review*, lxxxvi (Oct 1909) 598-604. Baumann had had considerable experience as an unsuccessful Conservative candidate.
49. Bonar Law Papers, 41/1/2, Steel-Maitland memorandum. Belilios and Profumo aroused antipathy among the xenophobic Whole Hoggers as much because of their foreign ancestry as for alleged failings as candidates.
50. *The Times*, 30 Jan 1911.
51. This is the range for Liberal agents, and although Conservative agents averaged slightly higher salaries the range was probably much the same. See Lowell, *Government of England*, i 482-3, 489.
52. Bonar Law Papers, 16/1/76, memorandum, n.d., from Walter Long. East Bristol was a 'backward' constituency with no organisation 'worth speaking about'.
53. Balfour Papers, Add. MS. 49755, ff. 149-60, Amery memorandum.

54. Ibid., Add. MS. 49767, ff. 44–9, Sandars to Balfour, 19 Dec 1910.

55. Ibid., Add. MS. 49772, ff. 43–4, Sandars to Akers-Douglas, n.d. but probably Jan 1910.

56. Ibid., Add. MS. 49766, ff. 186–95, Sandars to Balfour, 18 Mar 1910, confidential.

57. *Globe*, 19 Sept 1910.

58. Balfour Papers, Add. MS. 49766, ff. 186–95, Sandars to Balfour, 18 Mar 1910, confidential.

59. Ibid., Add. MS. 49767, ff. 52–7, Sandars to Balfour, 24 Dec 1910, confidential.

60. Bonar Law Papers, 18/6/146, Amery to Bonar Law, 16 Dec 1910. Acland-Hood was 'pensioned' with a peerage in June 1911.

61. Chamberlain Papers, AC 8/7/22, Joseph Lawrence to Austen Chamberlain, 13 Dec 1910.

62. Balfour Papers, Add. MS. 49795, ff. 19–20, Garvin to Sandars, 28 Dec 1909.

63. Bonar Law Papers, 41/1/2, Steel-Maitland memorandum.

64. Balfour Papers, Add. MS. 49771, ff. 185–8, Acland-Hood to Balfour, 29 Jan 1910.

65. Chilston, *Chief Whip*, p. 348, Balfour to Akers-Douglas, 17 Jan 1911.

66. Balfour Papers, Add. MS. 49767, ff. 44–9, Sandars to Balfour, 19 Dec 1910.

67. Ibid., Add. MS. 49771, ff. 179–80, Acland-Hood to Sandars, 1 Oct [1909].

68. Balfour Papers, Add. MS. 49771, ff. 189–90, Acland-Hood to Sandars, 5 Feb 1910.

69. Ibid., Add. MS. 49766, ff. 75–80, Sandars to Balfour, 21 Jan 1910.

70. Acland-Hood Papers, p. 70, newspaper cutting.

71. Strachey Papers, Strachey to Rosebery, 23 July 1908, confidential [copy].

72. Corder, *Life of Robert Spence Watson*, p. 265. Spence Watson was President, National Liberal Federation 1890–1902.

73. Material in this paragraph based mainly on J. A. Spender, *Sir Robert Hudson, A Memoir* (London, 1930).

74. See below, p. 291.

75. Waley, *Montagu*, p. 31.

76. Elibank was not Pease's first choice as a successor, Pease fearing he 'is a bit too scheming, & needs a steady hand over him.' Asquith Papers 12, ff. 107–10 Pease to Asquith, 4 Feb 1910, secret.

77. J. A. Spender, *Life, Journalism and Politics* (London, 1927) i 235.

78. Elibank Papers, MS. 8802, f. 13, W. T. Stead to Elibank, 15 Feb 1910.

79. Murray, *Master and Brother*, pp. 47–8; and Gollin, *Garvin*, p. 181.

80. Elibank Papers, MS. 8802, ff. 3–4, R. H. Davies to Elibank, 2 Jan. 1911 [misdated 1910] with praise for the rehousing; and ibid., MS. 8803, ff. 84–5, Herbert to Elibank, 8 Aug. 1912, for Jesse Herbert's fulsome thanks.

81. *The Times*, 18, 19 Oct 1910.

82. See above, p. 166.

83. Comments in the *Westminster Gazette*, 20 Dec 1910, quoted in Murray, *Master and Brother*, p. 67.

84. Elibank Papers, MS. 8802, ff. 3–4, Davies to Elibank, 2 Jan 1911 [misdated 1910].

85. On the Liberal organisational structure in this period see Spender, *Hudson*, ch. iii; King, 'Liberal Party 1906–14', ch. i; and Viscount Gladstone, 'The Chief Whip in the British Parliament', *American Political Science Review*, xxi, no. 3 (Aug 1927) 519–28.

86. N.L.F., minutes, Executive Committee, 16 Feb 1910.

87. See, e.g., Northern Liberal Federation, minutes, Finance and General Purposes Committee, 23 July 1908.

88. N.L.F., minutes, Executive Committee, 16 Feb 1910.

89. Midlands Liberal Federation, minutes, Executive Committee, 22 Apr 1909.

90. During 1910 the Chief Whip seems to have paid nearly £300 to cover registration and propaganda activities in the derelict constituencies of Lancashire and Cheshire. Based on the accounts of the Lancashire and Cheshire Federation for 1910.

91. Yorkshire Liberal Federation, minutes, Executive Committee, 25 Nov 1908. I am indebted to Dr A. S. King for this reference.

92. N.L.F., minutes, Executive Committee, 25 Jan, 22 Feb 1911.

93. 16 Jan 1911.

94. N.L.F. minutes, Executive Committee, copy of letter, Pease to W. H. Hughes, organising secretary, Welsh National Liberal Council, 25 Nov 1909; ibid. N.L.F. circular, 29 Nov 1909; and *The Times* 16 Jan 1911. *The Times* attributed the December fall in Liberal majorities in safe seats as due to Elibank's decision.

95. Kekewich, *Education Department and After*, pp. 342–4.

96. Elibank Papers, MS. 8802, ff. 173–4, Raphael to Elibank, 14 Jan 1911.

97. Gladstone Papers, Add. MS. 46037, ff. 91–2, 95–6, Joseph Henry to Gladstone, 6 Aug, 13 Oct 1908.

98. H. J. Wilson Papers, J. W. Wilson to H. J. Wilson, 17 Dec 1909.

99. Kent, *Burns*, pp. 211–12.

100. *Fortnightly Review*, lxxxvi (Oct–Nov 1909) 598–604, 803.

101. 10 Dec 1910.

102. Sir J. Davies, *The Prime Minister's Secretariat* (Newport, 1951) p. 33.

103. Elibank Papers, MS. 8804, ff. 299–300, typed copy.

104. Chamberlain Papers, AC 8/7/19, Lansdowne to Austen Chamberlain, 14 Dec 1910. See also Balfour Papers, Add. MS. 49755, ff. 149–60, Amery memorandum.

105. *Daily Telegraph*, 4 Feb 1910.

106. *Daily Chronicle*, 28 Jan 1910.

107. For details see *The Times*, 16 Jan 1911. See also B. D. White, *History of the Corporation of Liverpool, 1835–1914* (Liverpool, 1951) pp. 192–201.

108. *Liverpool Courier*, 9 Dec 1910.

109. Balfour Papers, Add. MS. 49755, ff. 149–60, Amery memorandum.

110. Ibid., Add. MS. 49767, ff. 58–61, Sandars to Balfour, 25 Dec 1910, confidential.

111. *Daily Telegraph*, 4 Feb 1910.

112. Balfour Papers, Add. MS. 49766, ff. 71–4, Sandars to Balfour, 19 Jan 1910.

113. See Pelling, *Social Geography*, p. 173, n. 2.

114. Acland-Hood Papers, p. 67, newspaper cutting.

115. McKenzie, *British Political Parties*, pp. 343–4 and 561–2; and Snowden, *Autobiography*, i 220–2.

116. There were only seven employees at Head Office in 1914 and the numbers were probably less in 1910. See McKenzie, *British Political Parties*, p. 562.
117. W.B. Gwyn, *Democracy and the Cost of Politics in Britain* (London, 1962) p. 170.
118. Ibid. p. 168; and M. A. Hamilton, *Arthur Henderson* (London, 1953) p. 75. Opinions differed about Peters' abilities. See contrasting judgements ibid., p. 76; and McKenzie, *British Political Parties*, p. 563, quoting Beatrice Webb.
119. Bealey and Pelling, *Labour and Politics*, p. 236, describe the local organisations as incorporating 'the rich and intricate social and institutional pattern of British life'. For other descriptions of the local Labour organisations at this time see McKenzie, *British Political Parties*, pp. 476–9; G. D. H. Cole, *British Working Class Politics 1832–1914* (London, 1941) ch. xviii. There is a well-documented analysis of London constituency organisations in Thompson, *Socialists, Liberals and Labour*, ch. xi.
120. Gregory, *The Miners*, pp. 113, 170.
121. Labour Party, minutes, N.E.C. 13 Apr 1910, special memorandum on elections from Ramsay MacDonald.
122. 18 Nov 1910. See also Gregory, *The Miners*, pp. 42, 112–13, 150–1, 170–1.
123. For the Labour Party at Woolwich, soon to become the exemplar for Labour constituency organisation, see Thompson, *Socialists, Liberals, and Labour*, pp. 250–64.
124. Labour Party, *Report Tenth Annual Conference* (1910) p. 6.
125. David Cox, 'The Labour Party in Leicester: A Study in Branch Development', *International Review of Social History*, vi (1961) 210.
126. Labour Party, *Report, Eleventh Annual Conference* (1911) p. 70.
127. Labour Party Documents, ii, ff. 87–91, National Agent's report, 27 July 1908.
128. Labour Party, *Report, Tenth Annual Conference* (1910) p. 58.
129. Ibid. p. 55.
130. Lord Snell, *Men, Movements and Myself* (London, 1936) p. 187.
131. Labour Party, *Report, Eleventh Annual Conference* (1911) p. 3.
132. *Labour Leader*, 4 Feb 1910, article by National Agent; and Labour Party Documents, ii, ff. 87–91, National Agent's report, 27 July 1908.
133. Ibid. and Labour Party, minutes, N.E.C., 13 Apr 1910, special memorandum on elections from Ramsay MacDonald.
134. Labour Party Documents, ii, ff. 87–91, National Agent's report, 27 July 1908.
135. See, e.g., Elibank Papers, MS. 8801, ff. 145–51, memorandum on Socialist and Labour Movement in Scotland, forwarded to P.M., Feb 1908, in which admiration and envy are quite unconcealed.
136. *Freeman's Journal*, 3 Feb, 17 Nov 1910; and *Irish Independent*, 16, 22 Dec 1909.
137. Lyons, *Irish Parliamentary Party*, p. 198.
138. Ibid. pp. 195–200.
139. For the detailed constitution of the conventions as laid down by the National Directory in 1909 see *Irish Independent*, 14 Dec 1909.
140. For the conventions at South Monaghan and East Limerick which degenerated into brawling, and the one at Mid-Tyrone which split into two separate conventions see ibid. 16, 30 Dec 1909; and *Freeman's Journal*, 29 Dec 1909, 4 Jan 1910.
141. Ibid. 13 Jan 1910.
142. Ibid. 30 Nov 1910.

CHAPTER 14   PARTY FINANCE

1. One successful candidate in January F. E. Guest (Liberal, East Dorset) was unseated for exceeding the maximum expenditure permitted, an excess not shown in his return. John Derry, defeated Liberal candidate for Sheffield Ecclesall, did not reveal in his return that he had exceeded the maximum by over £300. J. H. Wilson, secretary, Sheffield Liberal Federation, explained to Elibank that this excess was due to 'six weeks of strenuous electioneering' (H. J. Wilson Papers, 28 Apr 1910 [copy]), an excuse available to many in January.

2. The expenses per opposed Conservative candidate in Ireland in January 1910 averaged £578 as compared with the United Kingdom Conservative average of £1137.

3. Gwyn, *Democracy and Cost of Politics*, p. 94.

4. Ibid. pp. 93–5. See also Lowell, *Government of England*, ii 124–5.

5. Cromer Papers, F.O. 633/19, pp. 112–13, Lansdowne to Cromer, 28 Nov 1910.

6. Harris, *Forty Years*, p. 47.

7. Balfour Papers, Add. MS. 49775, ff. 149–60, Amery memorandum.

8. Ibid.

9. Bonar Law Papers, 41/1/2, Steel-Maitland memorandum.

10. Gladstone Papers, Add. MS. 46021, ff. 152–9, memorandum prepared for Honours Enquiry, 1922, from Herbert Gladstone [draft].

11. Asquith Papers, 11, ff. 139–40. Whiteley to Asquith, 29 May 1908. See also Riddell, *Diary 1908–14*, p. 60.

12. Gwyn, *Democracy and Cost of Politics*, p. 55.

13. Dunlop Smith Papers, Morley to Minto, 10 Feb 1910. I am grateful to Mr Martin Gilbert for this reference.

14. Bryce Papers, MS. 14, f. 14, Ilbert to Bryce, 17 Feb 1910.

15. Spender, *Life, Journalism and Politics*, i 235.

16. Elibank Papers, MS. 8802, ff. 146–7, Pease to Elibank, 18 Nov 1910. Pease added that he felt sure that 'if you now approached him he would like to respond in the direction indicated by him . . . & I know full well how much a whip needs all he can get for a general election!'

17. Ibid. ff. 157–8, Lloyd George to Elibank, 17 Dec 1910, very secret. The 'Cardiff friend' was not identified.

18. Gladstone Papers, Add. MS. 46031, ff. 161–6, Armitstead to Gladstone, 25 Nov 1910.

19. Ibid., Add. MS. 46042, ff. 198–201, Geake to Gladstone, 11 Jan 1911.

20. Bonar Law Papers, 41/1/2.

21. Gladstone Papers, Add. MS. 46021, ff. 152–9, memorandum prepared for Honours Enquiry, 1922, Herbert Gladstone [draft].

22. Ellis Barker, *Fortnightly Review*, lxxxvi (Nov 1909) 804.

23. *The Motor*, 15 Feb 1910.

24. Details from ibid.; and *Birmingham Daily Post*, 22 Jan 1910.

25. N.L.F., minutes, Executive Committee, 16 Feb 1910.

26. Scottish Liberal Association, minutes, Eastern Organising Committee, 5 May 1910.

27. *Morning Post*, 22 Jan 1910; and *The Motor*, 25 Jan 1910.

28. This slogan and variants on it appeared daily in the *Daily News* during the last fortnight of January 1910.

29. *West Cumberland Times*, 22 Jan 1910.

30. *Newcastle Daily Chronicle*, 21 Jan 1910.

31. The best account of Labour Party finance in this period is in Gwyn, *Democracy and Cost of Politics*, pp. 159–77.

32. Labour Party, *Report, Eleventh Annual Conference (1911)* p. 34.

33. Labour Party, minutes, N.E.C., 13 Apr 1910, special memorandum on elections from Ramsay MacDonald.

34. Sources for calculations: Table 14.1 (above, p. 290); I.L.P., *Report Eighteenth Annual Conference* (1910), p. 9; ibid., *Nineteenth Annual Conference (1911)* p. 34; *Labour Leader*, 25 Mar, 23 Dec 1910; Passfield Papers, ix I (i), ff. 90–1, Fabian Society circular appealing for funds 18 Nov 1909; ibid., ff. 93–5, Fabian Society Memorandum on 'The Forthcoming General Election: the Fabian Society's Candidates', 21 Nov 1910. These calculations ignore certain relief grants and loans paid from the Parliamentary Fund by the N.E.C. See below, pp. 297–8.

35. Quoted by Gwyn, *Democracy and Cost of Politics*, p. 171.

36. Sources for information on I.L.P. finance in this paragraph are I.L.P., *Report, Eighteenth Annual Conference (1910)*; I.L.P., *Report, Nineteenth Annual Conference (1911)*; and *Labour Leader*, 25 Mar 1910, 23 Dec 1910, articles by T. D. Benson, I.L.P. Treasurer.

37. R. Page Arnot, *The Miners, A History of the Miners Federation of Great Britain, 1889–1910* (London, 1949) p. 368.

38. Some members of the I.L.P. were, of course, nominated by their unions, as was one member of the S.D.P., Will Thorne (South West Ham).

39. For one or both of these contentions see Cole, *British Working Class Politics 1832–1914*, pp. 202–3; and Pelling, *Short History of the Labour Party*, p. 24.

40. There is an excellent account of the impact of the Osborne Judgement on the Labour Party in Gwyn, *Democracy and Cost of Politics*, ch. vii.

41. H. A. Clegg, Alan Fox and A. F. Thompson, *A History of British Trade Unions since 1889*, i, 1889–1910 (Oxford, 1964) 419.

42. Hudson and Wardle received loans totalling £850. See Gwyn, *Democracy and Cost of Politics*, p. 196. Thomas also received a loan of about £400. See Labour Party Documents, ii, ff. 148–54, minutes, N.E.C., 29 Sept 1910.

43. Labour Party, *Report, Tenth Annual Conference (1910)* p. 63.

44. I.L.P. *Report, Nineteenth Annual Conference (1911)* pp. 47–8. The National Council of the I.L.P. apparently told Jarrow it could not endorse an I.L.P. candidate for the constituency unless the local organisation could find £600.

45. Gregory, *The Miners*, p. 36; Clegg, Fox, Thompson, *History of British Trade Unions*, i 419; and Gwyn, *Democracy and Cost of Politics*, pp. 194–6.

46. Labour Party, *Report, Eleventh Annual Conference (1911)* p. 10.

47. Gwyn, *Democracy and Cost of Politics*, p. 196.

48. Labour Party, *Report, Eleventh Annual Conference (1911)* p. 34.

49. Gwyn, *Democracy and Cost of Politics*, p. 196. The H. J. Wilson Papers reveal that the Wilson clan gave financial assistance to Pointer at both elections.

50. Labour Party Documents, ii, ff. 155–6, minutes, N.E.C. 30 Sept 1910.

51. *Yorkshire Observer*, 25 Nov 1910; and *Birmingham Daily Post*, 24 Nov 1910.
52. Gwyn, *Democracy and Cost of Politics*, p. 196; I.L.P. *Report, Nineteenth Annual Conference (1911)* p. 48; Labour Party Documents, ii, f. 179, minutes, N.E.C. 31 Jan 1911; and ibid. f. 160, minutes, emergency committee, N.E.C., 21 Nov 1910.
53. See Gwyn, *Democracy and Cost of Politics*, pp. 196-7, for some of the mysteries remaining.
54. See Lyons, *Irish Parliamentary Party*, pp. 215-17.
55. *The Times*, 28 Dec 1909.
56. Bryce Papers, MS. 14, ff. 1-4, Ilbert to Bryce, 17 Feb 1910.
57. Elibank Papers, MS. 8802, ff. 39-45, unsigned memorandum on Irish situation, 31 Mar 1910.
58. Ibid., ff. 67-8, Redmond to Elibank, 1 June 1910; and ff. 78-9, Dillon to O'Connor, 9 June 1910 [copy].
59. Ibid., ff. 67-8, Redmond to Elibank, 1 June 1910.
60. Gwyn, *Democracy and Cost of Politics*, p. 184.
61. Carrington Diary, 11 Feb 1910. See also Gollin, *Garvin*, p. 249.
62. Brassey, who had landholdings in Ulster, gave £500 to the O'Brienites in late 1910. See *Irish Independent*, 30 Nov 1910.
63. Gollin, *Garvin*, pp. 249-50.
64. Ibid.

CHAPTER 15   PUBLICISING THE ISSUES

1. Balfour Papers, Add. MS. 49766, ff. 44-7, Sandars to Balfour, 22 Dec 1909.
2. Asquith Papers, 12, ff. 70-6, Elibank to Asquith, 13 Jan 1910. Northcliffe claimed that he never read Harold's 'beastly paper'. Reginald Pound and Geoffrey Harmsworth, *Northcliffe* (London, 1959) p. 400.
3. Maxse Papers, 461, ff. 548-51, Ampthill to Maxse, 10 Jan 1910.
4. Ibid.
5. Balfour Papers, Add. MS. 49766, ff. 28-30, Sandars to Balfour, [18] Dec 1909. [This letter is misdated 16 Dec in the British Museum file.]
6. See *The Times*, 1 Dec 1909, for Norman's circular; and ibid. 2 Dec 1909, Norman's letter to the editor.
7. Balfour Papers, Add. MS. 49766, ff. 44-7, Sandars to Balfour, 22 Dec 1909.
8. Chamberlain Papers, AC 8/3/6, Fabian Ware to Austen Chamberlain, 21 Dec 1909.
9. Balfour Papers, Add. MS. 49766, ff. 31-41, Sandars to Balfour, [18] Dec 1909.
10. Chamberlain Papers, AC 8/3/6, Fabian Ware to Austen Chamberlain, 21 Dec 1909. Ware noted one of the difficulties of such a procedure: 'I hear that the newspaper account of the Oldham speech is unrecognisable, as far as applause is concerned, by those who were present.'
11. Chamberlain Papers, AC 8/3/3, Garvin to Austen Chamberlain, 15 Dec 1909. Pryor was Northcliffe's first appointment to the editorial staff of *The Times*.
12. Balfour Papers, Add. MS. 49766, ff. 31-41, Sandars to Balfour [18 Dec] 1909; ibid. ff. 44-7, Sandars to Balfour, 22 Dec 1909; and Bonar Law Papers, 18/5/108, Hughes to Bonar Law, 21 Dec 1909.

13. See Bernard Semmel, *Imperialism and Social Reform*, pp. 110–12.

14. Pound and Harmsworth, *Northcliffe*, p. 293.

15. H. R. G. Whates, *The Birmingham Post 1857–1957* (Birmingham, 1957) p. 199.

16. Cecil Papers, Add. MS. 51158, J. S. R. Phillips to Cecil, 28 Feb 1908, confidential.

17. Bonar Law Papers, 18/5/94, James Kennedy to Bonar Law, 4 Apr 1909.

18. *History of the Times*, iv, *The 150th Anniversary and Beyond* (London, 1952) part i 13.

19. See Cromer Papers, F.O. 633/19, pp. 9–10, Harold Cox to Cromer, 31 Jan 1910.

20. *Morning Post*, 28 Dec 1909.

21. This advice was offered at the beginning and end of the election. See the *Spectator*, 27 Nov 1909 and 15 Jan 1910.

22. Balfour Papers, Add. MS. 49795, ff. 14–16, Garvin to Sandars, 20 Dec 1909. Part of this letter is quoted in Gollin, *Garvin*, pp. 129–30. Neither the evidence provided by Gollin, nor anything seen by the writer, seems to justify Gollin's claim that it was Garvin who 'revived the question of the naval rivalry with Germany'.

23. See above, p. 179.

24. See above, pp. 183–4.

25. *Morning Post*, 28 Nov 1910.

26. Chamberlain Papers, AC 8/7/22, Lawrence to Chamberlain, 13 Dec 1910.

27. *Labour Leader*, 5 Nov 1909. See also Thompson, *Socialists, Liberals, and Labour*, p. 173.

28. The material in this paragraph is based on Labour Party Documents, ii, f. 125, minutes, N.E.C. sub-committee on the press, 10 Nov 1909.

29. *Reynolds News*, 2 Jan 1910. *Reynolds News* contributed its fair share of violent partisanship each election Sabbath.

30. J. D. Symon, *The Press and Its Story* (London, 1914) p. 151.

31. *Morning Leader*, 4 Dec 1909.

32. See editorials, *Daily Telegraph*, 28 Dec 1909 and 1 Jan 1910.

33. Ibid. 11 Jan 1910.

34. The editorial staff of *The Times* at this period was politically mixed. See *The History of the Times*, iv part i 51–2.

35. Chamberlain Papers, AC 8/3/3, Garvin to Austen Chamberlain, 15 Dec 1909; and Balfour Papers, Add. MS. 49795, ff. 40–3, Garvin to Sandars, 31 Dec 1909.

36. Calculations have been made for only six newspapers in the second election. All show some increase in the proportion of space given to election material in the four week period of the second election. Percentage of editorial space given to election material, 19 Nov–21 Dec 1910: *Standard* 32 per cent; *Daily News* 41 per cent; *Morning Post* 30 per cent; *Daily Express* 36 per cent; *Daily Mail* 25 per cent; *Daily Graphic* 36 per cent.

37. See Fyfe, *Fleet Street*, p. 76. Not that in the *Morning Leader* politics was entirely excluded from the sporting pages. On 15 Jan 1910 the main sporting story was headlined: 'Today's English Cup Ties. You Must Vote Before Going to See Your Favourite Team Win.'

38. 30 Nov 1910.

39. This included 34,553,000 leaflets, 2,697,000 booklets, 900,000 Liberal Month-lies, 989,000 copies of Liberal songs and 662,000 posters. N.L.F., minutes, Executive Committee, 16 Feb 1910; and N.L.F., *Report, Thirty-Second Annual Conference (1910)* p. 17. Figures for publicity in 1906 are given in Russell 'Election of 1906', p. 172.

40. The main items were 46,000,000 leaflets, 1,147,000 posters, 2,844,590 post-cards and 460,000 copies of the special number of *The Conservative and Unionist*. National Union, annual report of Publication Department, 1910.

41. Labour Party, *Report Tenth Annual Conference (1910)*, p. 6.

42. 4 Jan 1910.

43. Some of these posters had annoyed Churchill, who thought the poster peer bore too close a likeness to his cousin, the Duke of Marlborough. Changes were made to satisfy the Minister. See Spender, *The Prime Minister*, p. 169.

44. Balfour Papers, Add. MS. 49795, ff. 3–9, Garvin memorandum on campaign literature, n.d. [Filed with November 1909 letters.]

45. Figures are available only for Liberal publicity which fell by just over 40 per cent. See N.L.F., minutes, Executive Committee, 25 Jan 1911; and N.L.F., *Report, Thirty-Third Annual Conference (1911)* pp. 21–2. It is likely that the amount of publicity put out by the other parties fell off in much the same proportion.

46. 'The Elections and After', *Blackwood's Magazine*, clxxxix (Jan 1911) 153; and *Newspaper Owner*, 3 Dec 1910.

47. Spender, *Hudson*, p. 189.

48. Balfour Papers, Add. MS. 49795, ff. 3–9, Garvin memorandum on campaign literature, n.d.

49. See complaints of Liberal agents on this point, Yorkshire Liberal Federation, minutes, Executive Committee, 13 Oct 1909. I owe this reference to Dr A. S. King.

50. *Westminster Gazette*, 8 Dec 1909, interview with Geake.

51. 7 Jan 1910.

52. Balfour Papers, Add. MS. 49795, ff. 3–9, Garvin memorandum on campaign literature, n.d.

53. Quoted in *Westminster Gazette*, 7 Jan 1910.

54. 14 Dec 1909.

55. Quoted in *Westminster Gazette*, 7 Jan 1910. Similar criticisms were voiced in the *Daily Mail*, 10 Jan 1910, and within the National Union, minutes, Executive Committee, 11 Mar 1910.

56. 30 Jan 1911.

57. Bonar Law Papers, 18/6/118, Chaplin to Bonar Law, 13 Mar 1910.

58. 7 Jan 1910.

59. Over 11,000 large and expensive coloured reproductions of this poster were issued during the first election, and most newspapers published a copy. See *Daily Mail*, 4 Jan 1910.

60. Labour Party Documents, ii, ff. 113–16, minutes, N.E.C., 6 Oct 1909. The committee consisted of Keir Hardie, Snowden, Henderson, G. H. Stuart and E. R. Pease.

61. It was customary to issue the addresses through the post and also to publish them in the local press. Most candidates would probably have agreed with the

Newspaper Owner, 26 Nov 1910, that 'election addresses printed in newspapers are a practically effete form of newspaper publicity,' but they were often virtually blackmailed into publishing their addresses for fear that if they did not, the local newspaper would boycott their campaigns. Owing to the diligence of the secretaries of the National Liberal Club, 98 per cent of the addresses issued in Great Britain in 1910 have been preserved either in their original format or as they appeared in the local press. The addresses are bound in four volumes, two for each election. Volume i in each set contains the addresses for London, Wales, Scotland and Ireland; volume ii contains the addresses for English provincial boroughs and English counties. As the addresses are filed alphabetically by constituency within each of these divisions it has not been thought necessary to give volume and page references. Forty per cent of the addresses are as issued to the electors, while the remainder are newspaper reproductions of the addresses.

62. All quantitative statements concerning format are based on the 455 January addresses filed in their original form in the N.L.C. volumes. There seems no reason to suspect that this is not a representative sample.

63. This latter address was attacked by the *Daily Chronicle*, 15 Jan 1910, as 'the most inconsistent, lying and rubbishy election address in the country'.

64. Unionist address, Tavistock.

65. Liberal addresses, Hoxton, Coventry, and South-West Bethnal Green respectively.

66. Liberal address, Caithness.

67. Liberal address, Aston Manor.

68. Unionist address, Leicester.

69. Liberal address, Horncastle.

70. Liberal address, Brentford.

71. Bryce Papers, Miscellaneous Correspondence, Burt to Bryce, 13 Oct 1909.

72. Vagueness about the general pattern of the tariff did not prevent generous promises of protection to local industries. In South-West Bethnal Green tariffs would protect artificial flowers, tin ware, door mats; in Fulham tramway rails; in Kent hops; in East Anglia market gardening; in Cornwall granite; in the Potteries pottery; in Nottingham glassware; in the Midlands iron and steel; in Caithness fishing and flagstones.

73. Unionist address, Blackburn.

74. 19 Feb 1910.

75. Unionist address, Chester.

76. Unionist address, Mile End.

77. National Union Leaflet, in Conservative Research Office, Pictorial Volume, 1910 elections.

78. Unionist address, Middlesbrough.

79. See below, pp. 351–2.

80. 10 Dec 1909.

81. Unionist address, Whitechapel.

82. T. Gibson Bowles, ex-Unionist M.P. and Liberal Member for King's Lynn was the only Liberal openly critical. He feared that the principles of the Bill were 'in some respects manifestly imperfect, in some respects incompatible with the Parliamentary system of the country'.

83. Liberal address, South-West Bethnal Green.
84. Unionist address, Clapham.

CHAPTER 16   THE INTERESTS, THE SUFFRAGETTES, AND THE CHURCHES

1. Waley, *Montagu*, p. 27.
2. The best account of the politics of Welsh Disestablishment in this period is Morgan, *Wales in British Politics*, pp. 231–40.
3. Wilson, *Alcohol and the Nation*, p. 185.
4. Matthews, *Fifty Years of Agricultural Politics*, p. 151.
5. The Budget League and the Budget Protest League are not treated here as they were discrete arms of the party organisation rather than pressure groups, and were merged with the parties once the election began.
6. Gladstone Papers, Add. MS. 46068, ff. 228–9, Causton to Gladstone, 24 Jan 1910. See also Pelling, *Social Geography*, pp. 50–1.
7. Semmel, *Imperialism and Social Reform*, p. 113.
8. Balfour Papers, Add. MS. 49791, ff. 226–9, Lawrence to Balfour, 6 Nov 1907.
9. Ibid. Add. MS. 49765, ff. 10–16, Sandars to Balfour, 22 Jan 1907.
10. Cecil Papers, Add. MS. 51158, Strachey to Robert Cecil, 26 Mar 1908, confidential.
11. Minutes, Executive Committee, 8 Apr 1908.
12. Cecil Papers, Add. MS. 51158, Carter to Robert Cecil, 5 Mar 1908.
13. See annual report of T.R.L. 1910, quoted in T. J. Macnamara, *Tariff Reform and the Working Man* (London, 1910) p. 19. See above, pp. 311–12, for comparable output of major parties.
14. Cecil Papers, Add. MS. 51158, Carter to Cecil, 5 Mar 1908.
15. *Daily Chronicle*, 28 Jan 1910.
16. *Daily News*, 23 Dec 1909, interview with Carter.
17. Ibid.
18. Bryce Papers, MS. 13, ff. 192–4, Ilbert to Bryce, 3 Dec 1909.
19. *Westminster Gazette*, 28 Jan 1910.
20. Midlands Liberal Federation, minutes, Executive Committee, 18 Oct 1909, 10 Feb 1910; and *Birmingham Daily Post*, 5 Jan, 26 Nov 1910.
21. There is a lively, if facetious, account of the women's suffrage agitation in Roger Fulford, *Votes for Women*. A more analytic as well as a more sympathetic account is Constance Rover, *Women's Suffrage and Party Politics in Britain 1866–1914* (London, 1967).
22. John Burns's phrase. See Burns Papers, Add. MS. 46332, diary, 22 Nov 1910.
23. *The Times*, 18 Dec 1909.
24. Ibid., 22 Dec 1909.
25. Ibid., 16 Dec 1909.
26. Fulford, *Votes for Women*, p. 219.
27. *Western Morning News*, 15 Jan 1910.
28. *The Times*, 9 Dec 1909.
29. *Yorkshire Post*, 15 Dec 1909.
30. *Birmingham Daily Post*, 23 Dec 1909.

31. See Yorkshire N.F.U. executive recommendations, *Yorkshire Observer*, 7 Jan 1910; and *Western Morning News*, 18 Dec 1909 and 1 Jan 1910.

32. *The Times*, 10 Jan 1910. For other examples of political advertisements by 'the Trade' see the *Standard*, 28 Dec 1909; *Daily Mail*, 24 Dec 1909; and *Weekly Dispatch*, 4 Dec 1910.

33. *Daily News*, 23 Dec 1909.

34. *The Times*, 16, 25 Dec 1909.

35. This appeal was issued by the Licensed Victuallers' Defence League in the week before the January poll. See ibid. 11 Jan 1910.

36. Material and quotations in this paragraph from *The Times*, 8, 9 Dec 1909 and 30 Nov 1910; and Fulford, *Votes for Women*, p. 233. The general policies and strategy of the various female suffrage societies are discussed in Rover, *Women's Suffrage*, chs. vi, vii.

37. For these incidents see *The Times*, 11, 17, 22 Dec 1909, 3 Jan 1910; *Daily Mail*, 6 Dec 1909; and *News of the World*, 12 Dec 1909.

38. See Fulford, *Votes for Women*, p. 222. But see also Christabel Pankhurst, *Unshackled* (London, 1959) p. 148, which suggests there was no truce until after the election campaign.

39. Asquith Papers, 22, ff. 224-8, memorandum from Permanent Under-Secretary, Home Office to the Home Secretary, 27 Sept 1909.

40. Rowland, *Last Liberal Governments*, i 356, Gladstone to Churchill, 18 Mar 1910.

41. See, e.g., *Daily News*, 13 Dec 1909, editorial, 'Money versus the People'.

42. Pankhurst, *Unshackled*, p. 148.

43. Fulford, *Votes for Women*, p. 219.

44. H. W. Nevinson, *More Changes, More Chances* (London, 1925) pp. 324-5. The whole chapter, pp. 304-39, is an excellent and sympathetic treatment of the suffragette movement by an avowed but eminently rational supporter.

45. Gladstone Papers, Add. MS. 46067, ff. 219-20, Sussex vicar (signature indecipherable) to Gladstone, 5 Oct 1909.

46. See *Manchester Guardian*, 28 Nov 1910.

47. See Ensor, *England 1870-1914*, pp. 305-9, 527-31; E. R. Wickham, *Church and People in an Industrial City* (London, 1957) pp. 166-205; and G. S. Spinks, *Religion in Britain Since 1900* (London, 1952) pp. 11, 14-16, 38-9, 45-8.

48. *Church numbers United Kingdom 1910.*
    Anglicans: 2,485,000 (Easter communicants)
    Nonconformists: 2,113,000 (mostly members but in some cases communicants)
    Presbyterians: 1,603,000 (Communicants)
    Catholics: 6,034,000 (Total population)
    Sources: Whitaker's Almanack and the year-books, directories and handbooks of the churches. For difficulties of comparing denominational statistics see Michael Argyle, *Religious Behaviour* (London, 1958) pp. 4-5.

49. Brett and Esher, *Esher*, ii 208. See also Bell, *Davidson*, i 513-30.

50. Ibid. i 530-40.

51. Ibid. i 595-6, 597.

52. Ibid. i 603–4.
53. *The Times*, 1 Jan 1910.
54. Ibid. 18 Dec 1909.
55. *Irish Times*, 10 Jan 1910.
56. See *Manchester Courier*, 8 Jan 1910; and *Manchester Guardian*, 1, 6, 20 Jan 1910.
57. *The Times*, 10 Jan 1910.
58. Bell, *Davidson*, i 602–3.
59. *The Times*, 21 Dec 1909.
60. Ibid. 12 Jan 1910.
61. Lansbury Papers, 3, ff. 142–3, Rev. G. R. Bruggenkate to Lansbury, 12 Jan [1910] [the letter is misdated 1909].
62. *Daily Chronicle*, 21 Jan 1910.
63. 12 Jan 1910.
64. Balfour Papers, Add. MS. 49766, ff. 50–6, Sandars to Short, 28 Dec 1909. The 'Education people' were 'much distressed' at Balfour's neglect of education in his election manifesto. Ibid. 49758, ff. 213–16, Salisbury to Balfour, 16 Dec 1909.
65. 18 Jan 1910.
66. *Liverpool Courier*, 14 Dec 1909.
67. See *The Times*, 18 Jan 1910.
68. *Lancashire Daily Post*, 17 Jan 1910. See also *Manchester Guardian*, 11 Nov 1909, for the early development of the protestant opposition.
69. *Daily Telegraph*, 14 Jan 1910; and *Westminster Gazette*, 14 Jan 1910.
70. See Russell, 'Election of 1906', pp. 388–91.
71. Ibid. pp. 381–2.
72. Bell, *Davidson*, i 601, Scott Lidgett to the Archbishop of Canterbury, 19 Dec 1909.
73. *The Times*, 9 Dec 1909.
74. Bell, *Davidson*, i 601 Scott Lidgett to Canterbury, 19 Dec 1909.
75. *The Times*, 25 Dec 1909.
76. 'A Nonconformist minister', *Nonconformity and Politics*, pp. 66–8. This work is a polemic against the political involvement of Nonconformity with the Liberal Party.
77. *Baptist Times*, 10 Dec 1909.
78. Bell, *Davidson*, i 601.
79. *British Weekly*, 6 Jan 1910.
80. See John W. Grant, *Free Churchmanship in England 1879–1940* (London, 1955) pp. 169–80; and King, 'Liberal Party 1906–14', pp. 61–5.
81. William G. Addison, *Religious Equality in Modern England 1714–1914* (London, 1944) p. 166.
82. *Baptist Times*, 3 Dec 1909.
83. 3 Dec 1909.
84. Sir James Marchant, *Dr John Clifford, His Life, Letters and Reminiscences* (London, 1924) pp. 131–2.
85. *Free Church Year Book, 1910*, p. 213.
86. Ibid. p. 214.
87. *The Times*, 21 Dec 1909.
88. Ibid., 8 Jan 1910.

89. *Western Morning News*, 12 Dec 1910.
90. 'The Elections and their Moral,' *Blackwood's Magazine*, clxxxvii (Mar 1910) 431.
91. *Daily Express*, 28 Jan 1910.
92. *Clarion*, 28 Jan 1910.
93. *Birmingham Daily Post*, 15 Jan 1910.
94. *Observer*, 16 Jan 1910.
95. 18 Jan 1910.
96. Maxse Papers, 461, f. 571, Rowland Hunt to Maxse, 4 Feb 1910.
97. *Western Daily Mercury*, 13 Dec 1909.
98. *Yorkshire Observer*, 5 Dec 1910.
99. 18 Jan 1910.
100. King, 'Liberal Party 1906–14', p. 66.
101. A. Peel, *These Hundred Years. A History of the Congregational Union of England and Wales, 1831–1931* (London, 1931) p. 366.
102. *Baptist Times*, 2 Dec 1910.
103. For a general discussion see John F. Glaser, 'English Nonconformity and the Decline of Liberalism,' *American Historical Review*, lxxiii (1957–8) 353–63. Glaser appears to underrate the signifiance of the recrudescence of the politico-religious controversy in Edwardian England, dismissing the resistance to Balfour's Education Bill as 'an artificial resurgence'.
104. *The Times*, 27 Dec 1909.
105. Ibid. 21 Dec 1909. This letter provoked an interesting and lengthy correspondence in *The Times*.
106. Ibid. 23 Dec 1909.
107. See the statement of aims, and the list of supporters of the Nonconformist Anti-Socialist Union, ibid. 10 Dec 1909.
108. Ibid. 21 Dec 1909.
109. Edith Henrietta Fowler, *The Life of Henry Hartley Fowler, First Viscount Wolverhampton* (London, 1912) p. 587.
110. *The Times*, 4 Jan 1910.
111. See Glaser, *Amer. Hist. Rev.*, lxxiii (1957–8) pp. 361–2; and also Perks's letter to *The Times*, 21 Dec 1909.
112. King, 'Liberal Party 1906–14', p. 55, quoting anonymous writer to the *British Weekly*, 10 Dec 1908.
113. 'A Nonconformist minister', *Nonconformity and Politics*, p. 8.
114. It is not always easy to identify Nonconformist Unionist candidates because the chief source of such details, the *Christian World* deliberately did not include Unionists in its lists of Nonconformist candidates since 'the experience of the last ten years had demonstrated the unwisdom of expecting anything . . . from Conservative Free Churchmen in Parliament'. *Christian World*, 8 Dec 1910.
115. *The Times*, 30 Dec 1909.
116. 13 Jan, 17 Nov 1910.
117. See the *Saturday Review*, 10 Dec 1910, which alleged that a common Sunday spectacle in the Lowlands was 'the lairds and their families driving to the Episcopalian church, often many miles distant, and passing on the roads their tenants and agricultural labourers going to the parish kirk near at hand'.

118. *Baptist Times*, 17 Dec 1909.
119. *Tablet*, 1 Jan 1910.
120. *The Times*, 27 Dec 1909.
121. *Tablet*, 29 Jan 1910.
122. Ibid. 15 Jan 1910.
123. Maxse Papers, 461, f. 571, Hunt to Maxse, 4 Feb 1910.
124. *Tablet*, 8, 15 Jan 1910; and *Catholic Times*, 14 Jan 1910.
125. *Catholic Times*, 31 Dec 1909.
126. *Daily Telegraph*, 20 Jan 1910.
127. 2 Feb 1910.
128. *Manchester Guardian*, 24 Jan 1910.
129. *Scotsman*, 13 Jan 1910.
130. *Newcastle Daily Chronicle*, 6 Jan 1910.
131. *North Eastern Daily Gazette*, 20 Dec 1909. Some of his Socialist supporters thought that Walls spent too much time wooing the Irish Catholic vote, apparently without much benefit for 'the Catholics have done what they liked in spite of their instructions to vote for him'. Lansbury Papers, iv, ff. 6–7, Marion Hansen to George Lansbury, 19 Jan 1910.
132. Labour Party, *Report, Tenth Annual Conference (1910)* p. 55.
133. See *Glasgow Herald*, 14, 17 Dec 1909; and *Scotsman*, 20 Jan 1910.
134. See *Catholic Times*, 25 Nov 1910, 'Anti-Catholic Bigots and Home Rule.
135. Ibid. 16 Dec 1910.
136. *Reynolds News*, 4 Dec 1910.

CHAPTER 17 THE ELECTORAL SYSTEM

1. *Parl. Deb.*, 4th ser., clxvi, 624 (3 Dec 1906).
2. Lowell, *Government of England*, i 213.
3. Agatha Ramm, *The Political Correspondence of Mr Gladstone and Lord Granville, 1876–86* (Oxford, 1962) ii 228.
4. O'Leary, *Elimination of Corrupt Practices*, ch. vi.
5. Cecil, *Salisbury*, iii 118–24; Gwynn and Tuckwell, *Dilke*, ii ch. xxxvi.
6. H. L. Morris, *Parliamentary Franchise Reform in England and Wales 1885–1918* (New York, 1921) p. 11.
7. See O'Leary, *Elimination of Corrupt Practices*, p. 172; and Gwyn, *Democracy and Cost of Politics*, pp. 51–2.
8. See above, pp. 318, 326.
9. This section of the chapter draws heavily on my article, 'The Franchise in the United Kingdom 1885–1918', *Past and Present*, No. 32 (Dec 1965) 27–56.
10. See F. B. Smith, *The Making of the Second Reform Bill* (Melbourne, 1966) pp. 193–5.
11. For these estimates see S. Rosenbaum, 'The General Election of January 1910, and the Bearing of the Results on Some Problems of Representation', *Journal of the Royal Statistical Society*, lxxiii (1910) 473–7.
12. S. Buxton, *A Handbook to Political Questions of the Day*, 9th edn. (London, 1892) pp. 114–15.

13. P. A. Chance (Nationalist, South Kilkenny), *Parl. Deb.*, 4th ser., iv 1825 (25 May 1892).

14. *Western Daily Mercury*, 30 Dec 1909; *Western Morning News*, 17 Jan, 25 Nov, 5 Dec 1910.

15. M. MacDonagh, 'The Making of Parliament', *Nineteenth Century and After*, lix (Jan 1906) 31.

16. A rent of about 5s. a week was necessary to qualify and, in cities outside London and particularly in the rural areas, this was a high rent for lodgings. Even in London the average middle zone weekly rent for two rooms in 1912 was only 5s. 6d., while for similar accommodation in the major provincial cities the average was only 3s. 1½d. See points made by Dilke in discussion of Rosenbaum's paper, *J. R. Statis. Soc.*, lxxiii (1910) 519–22, and *The Year Book of Social Progress for 1913–14* (London, 1914) pp. 371–4.

17. For details see Blewett, *Past and Present*, no. 32 (Dec 1965) 42–3.

18. See Gladstone Papers, Add. MS. ff. 34–7, Joseph Henry to Gladstone, 29 Dec 1910.

19. See *The Times*, 3 Dec 1910.

20. Harcourt Papers, Cabinet memorandum 16 Nov 1911. This memorandum consists of Seager's report to Elibank, 8 Nov 1911, on a number of issues relevant to the Franchise Bill being prepared by the Cabinet, and a detailed summary, with verbatim quotes, of the replies to a set of questions circulated by Seager in September to the secretaries of the regional federations. Details and quotations in this and the following paragraph from this document unless otherwise noted.

21. Bryce Papers, Uncatalogued, Spender to Bryce, 3 Feb 1910. A four-page article in *The Car*, 26 Jan 1910, recounts how a septuagenarian plural voter was sped by a racing motorist to six widely separated constituencies in the one day. See also Grace A. Jones, 'Further Thoughts on the Franchise 1885–1918', *Past and Present*, no. 34 (July, 1966) 137, for the high turnout of plural voters in 1910.

22. N.L.F., minutes, Executive Committee, 16 Feb 1910; Bryce papers, Uncatalogued, J. A. Spender to Bryce, 3 Feb 1910; Gladstone Papers, Add. MS. 46042, ff. 198–201, Geake to Gladstone, 11 Jan 1911; *Liberal Magazine*, xviii (1910) 150–2, 665–8.

23. See Blewett, *Past and Present*, no. 32 (Dec. 1965) 48–50, where the problem is examined in greater detail. I accept the point made by Grace Jones, *Past and Present*, no. 34 (July 1966) 136, that this claim about the partisanship of the plural voter 'needs further systematic testing at the constituency level'. It seems likely that there were regional differences in the division of the plural vote, arising from differing patterns of socio-political cleavage in various parts of the country. Some pointers to the pattern: at Lewes it was estimated that as many as 90 per cent of the plural voters were Conservatives, and at Leigh 66 per cent (ibid. 136–7): at Elland the plural vote split 61/39 in the Unionist favour in January 1910 (*Yorkshire Post*, 6 Dec 1910); at Stretford Liberals expected that the out-voters would be shared evenly between the parties (*Manchester Guardian*, 12 Jan 1910).

24. Guy Routh, *Occupation and Pay in Great Britain 1906–60* (Cambridge, 1965). As Routh's figures relate to all males gainfully employed, exclude Ireland and

are for 1911, they have been crudely adjusted to include Ireland, exclude males under twenty-one, and allow for population change between 1910 and 1911.

25. Sir Ivor Jennings, *Party Politics*, i, *Appeal to the People* (Cambridge, 1960) p. 28.

26. Charles Seymour, *Electoral Reform in England and Wales* (New Haven, 1915) pp. 506-7.

27. Ibid. p. 515.

28. See D. E. Butler, *The Electoral System in Britain since 1918*, 2nd ed. (Oxford, 1963) p. 213.

29. *Parl. Deb.*, 3rd ser., cclxxxv, 426 (3 Mar 1884). Gladstone, ever an optimist where Ireland was concerned, was not willing to accept the inevitability of continuing population decline in Ireland. Ibid., cclxxxvi, 1836 (7 Apr 1884).

30. Rosenbaum, *J. R. Statist. Soc.*, lxxiii (1910) 482-4.

31. It should be noted that the exodus to the suburbs produced declining electorates in the heart of some of the great cities, most notably London and Liverpool.

32. Figures for England and Wales are given in *Parl. Papers*, 1912-13, cxii 6, and to these have been added the Scottish and Irish figures. Double member constituencies included when population exceeds 200,000.

33. Ellis Barker, *Fortnightly Review*, lxxxvi (Nov 1909) 802-3.

34. *Spectator*, 22 Jan 1910.

35. Bryce Papers, Uncatalogued, J. A. Spender to Bryce, 3 Feb 1910. Spender's comparison is, of course, weakened by his failure to allow for the large number of uncontested seats in 1895.

36. Seymour, *Electoral Reform*, p. 475; and Lowell, *Government of England*, ii 110.

37. It was claimed that Sir Frederick Pollock, the independent Unionist candidate for Glasgow and Aberdeen Universities in January 1910, was defeated by the vote of the English country doctors. '. . . all country doctors in England voted for Craik [the official Unionist]. They say a country doctor in England has to be Conservative.' Bryce Papers, Miscellaneous Correspondence, Professor G. A. Smith (Returning Officer for Aberdeen University) to Bryce, 23 Apr 1910.

38. In 1900 two Labour Members came from these seats, in 1906 eleven, in Jan 1910 ten, and in Dec 1910 eleven.

39. O'Leary, *Elimination of Corrupt Practices*, p. 175.

40. Ibid.

41. For an elaboration of these themes see ibid. pp. 178, 229-33; and Gwyn, *Democracy and Cost of Politics*, pp. 90-2.

42. O'Leary, *Elimination of Corrupt Practices*, pp. 206, 238.

43. See Pelling, *Social Geography*, pp. 429-30.

44. *Western Morning News*, 25 Nov 1910. See also Kekewich, *Education Department and After*, p. 345. There is an exhausting account of the 1910 December election petition at Exeter in L. M. Helmore, *Corrupt and Illegal Practices, A General Survey and a Case Study of an Election Petition* (London, 1967).

45. *Birmingham Daily Post*, 22 Jan 1910, interview with Hocking. In view of its composition and bias the Vigilante Committee was dubbed 'The Society for Threatening the Prosecution of Tories'. Ibid. 13 Jan 1910.

46. Labour Party, *Report Tenth Annual Conference (1910)* p. 75; Labour Party,

minutes, N.E.C. 13 Apr 1910, special memorandum on elections from MacDonald.

47. See Conservative Research Office, *Election Petitions 1911*, King's Lynn and *Liberal Magazine*, xix (1911) 183–5.

48. Ibid. 433–4 and Conservative Research Office, *Election Petitions 1911*, East Nottingham. Approximately 1300 East Nottingham residents each received a postal order for ten shillings from their Member.

49. *Liberal Magazine*, xix (1911) 436. King distributed over a thousand bags of coal to the poor, and eight thousand boxes of chocolates, bearing his name and the Conservative Party colours, to the children of Central Hull.

50. Cecil Papers, Add. MS. 51072, M. Warren (Wakefield) to E. G. Brunker, 17 Mar 1909. [Confidential copy, forwarded to Cecil]; and *Yorkshire Post*, 1 Jan 1910.

51. *Glasgow Herald*, 29 Nov 1909. Churchill in 1906 considered Corbett 'absolutely unassailable having given parks, mountains and other things to his beloved native town'. Churchill, *Churchill*, companion volume ii 416.

52. See Mosei Ostrogorski, *Democracy and the Organisation of Political Parties*, trans. F. Clarke (London, 1902) i 472–81; Wallas, *Human Nature in Politics*, p. 213; and Lowell, *Government of England*, i 223–5.

53. P. Cambray, *The Game of Politics* (London, 1932) p. 155.

54. *Report, Thirty-Second Annual Conference (1910)* pp. 20–1.

55. Balfour Papers, Add. MS. 49766, ff. 135–8, Sandars to Balfour, 3 Feb 1910.

56. Maxse Papers, 462, f. 782, Ormsby-Gore to Maxse, 11 Dec 1910.

57. *Report, Thirty-Second Annual Conference (1910)* pp. 20–1.

58. 28 Jan 1910.

59. Strachey Papers, Margot Asquith to Strachey, 31 Jan 1910.

60. Gilbert Murray Papers, Hirst to Murray, 21 Jan 1910. I owe this reference to Dr Keith Robbins.

61. Bryce Papers, Uncatalogued, Spender to Bryce, 3 Feb 1910.

62. Sydney Brooks, 'The British Elections', *North American Review*, cxci (1910) 410–19.

63. D. C. Pedder, 'Intensive Electioneering', *Contemporary Review*, xcvii (Mar 1910) 277.

64. Strachey Papers, Margot Asquith to Strachey, 31 Jan 1910.

65. Gladstone Papers, Add. MS. 46068, ff. 308–15, Rev. G. Reade to Gladstone, 17 Feb 1910.

66. Ibid., ff. 292–7, Reade to Gladstone, 14 Feb 1910. See discussion of this·question in Pelling, *Social Geography*, pp. 12–13. See also N.L.F., minutes, Executive Committee, 16 Feb 1910.

67. Gladstone Papers, Add. MS. 46068, ff. 308–15.

68. Sandars told Balfour: 'The exercise of the Wimborne influence, and the direct pressure of her Ladyship upon the voters at this election exceeds anything outside Ireland that I have ever heard . . .' Balfour Papers, Add. MS. 49766, ff. 135–8, Sandars to Balfour, 3 Feb 1910.

69. Hanham, *Elections and Party Management*, p. 12.

70. O'Leary, *Elimination of Corrupt Practices*, p. 223, notes that during the campaign 'some sinister things happened', e.g. allotment holders were given notice, a workman sacked, and a Guest estate agent with notebook recorded

attendance outside a polling booth. O'Leary's account is, however, rather garbled. He has the Guests mixed up, the candidate being F. E. Guest not Ivor Guest; the Member who made way for Guest was a Liberal not a Conservative; O'Leary's scheduled maximum for expenses is £1000 below the actual maximum; and his account implies the petition was dismissed. For details see *Parl. Papers*, 1910, lxxiii 454–67.

CHAPTER 18   THE RESULTS

1. See above, p. 37.
2. Labour Party, minutes, N.E.C., 13 Apr 1910, special memorandum on elections from Ramsay MacDonald.
3. See above, p. 22.
4. Halévy, vi, *The Rule of Democracy*, i 342; and Jenkins, *Balfour's Poodle*, p. 128 [my italics].
5. The small Irish decline is explained by the fact that the low January turnout in Irish seats contested for the first time in many years, offered opportunities and, if the factional fight had been close, provided the incentive to increase the turnout in December even on a stale register.
6. With the exception of December 1896 more rain fell in the first fifteen days of December 1910 than in any whole December month for the previous thirty years. See *Daily News*, 16 Dec 1910.
7. A. J. P. Taylor, *Lloyd George, Rise and Fall* (The Leslie Stephen Lecture, Cambridge, 1961) p. 19.
8. Webb, *Our Partnership*, pp. 443–4.
9. Bryce Papers, Uncatalogued, Spender to Bryce, 3 Feb 1910; and *Westminster Gazette*, 22, 24 Jan 1910.
10. See Maps 7.1 (p. 140) and 18.1 (p. 382).
11. *Nation*, 22 Jan 1910.
12. See Maps 7.1 (p. 140) and 18.1 (p. 382).
13. *Westminster Gazette*, 9 Dec 1910. The two other elections in the modern period in which the results closely paralleled the previous election were 1900 and 1951. In 1900 the Liberals had a net gain of nine over their 1895 position while in 1951 the Conservatives had a net gain of twenty-three over 1950.
14. These figures include Montgomery Boroughs, whose Liberal Member crossed to the Unionists in the last week of the 1910 Parliament.
15. As in 1906 there was also a Labour candidate in North Belfast.
16. This swing was lower than the national average of 4·3 per cent because Labour's seats were mostly located in regions where the general swing to Unionism was low.
17. *Labour Leader*, 4 Feb 1910.
18. At West Monmouth, Normanton, and Chester-le-Street.
19. The seats were North Ayrshire, Camlachie, Eccles, Govan, Huddersfield, North-East Lanark, North-West Lanark, Portsmouth, South-West Manchester. Moreover, while the total Labour vote fell in every case, only at Camlachie was the Liberal poll less than in 1906.

20. G. D. H. Cole, *The History o, the Labour Party from 1914* (London, 1948) p. 4.
21. A more favourable account of Labour's performance in the 1910 elections has recently been given in Pelling, *Popular Politics and Society*, 114–15.
22. *The Times*, 26 Nov 1910.
23. Cromer Papers, F.O. 633/18, pp. 278–81, Hugh Cecil to Cromer 27 Oct 1909.
24. See *The Times*, 21 Dec 1909.
25. 'The Elections and Their Moral', *Blackwood's Magazine*, clxxxvii (Mar 1910) 431.
26. 'The General Election: A Sociological Interpretation', *Sociological Review*, iii (Apr 1910) 116.
27. See above, pp. 20–3.
28. Balfour Papers, Add. MS. 49767, ff. 7–10, Sandars to Balfour, 18 Oct 1910.
29 This leaves three regions in Table 18.9 (p. 396) with an idiosyncratic swing not accounted for in the above paragraphs. Both the North and East Ridings and Lincolnshire had relatively low swings to the anti-Unionists in 1906 (see Table 2.1, p. 38) and this may have moderated the level of the pro-Unionist move-ment in 1910. The above average swing to the Unionists in North-East Scotland probably arose from an unusual combination of electoral factors all adversely affecting the anti-Unionist vote viz., three ministerial retirements, and an increase in the number of Independent and independent Labour candidates.
30. Balfour Papers Add. MS. 49860, ff. 213–17, memorandum on Scottish elec-tions from H. Seton-Karr, 5 Feb 1910. See also the article by E. N. Mozley, 'The Political Heptarchy. An Analysis of Seven General Elections', *Contem-porary Review*, xcvii (Apr 1910) 400–12, which stresses the hardening of opinion in Scotland and Wales.
31. The most useful studies dealing with this relationship are Sir Reginald Coup-land, *Welsh and Scottish Nationalism* (London, 1954); and Morgan, *Wales in British Politics*.
32. See above, p. 324, for evidence on these points.
33. See above, p. 112. See also K. O. Morgan, *David Lloyd George: Welsh Radical and World Statesman* (Cardiff, 1963) pp. 16, 44, for the prominence of refer-ences to the Tithe riots in Lloyd George's oratory at this time. Seton-Karr told Balfour: 'The amount of poisonous nonsense that has been uttered by the Lord-Advocate [Alexander Ure] and others . . . from Scotch political platforms, on the land question particularly, is . . . a lasting disgrace to our methods of political controversy, and a danger to our national life'. Seton-Karr memoran-dum, 5 Feb 1910.
34. 'The Elections and Their Moral', clxxxvii (Mar 1910) 435.
35. Chamberlain, *Politics From Inside*, p. 198.
36. Balfour Papers, Add. MS. 49758, ff. 231–2, Balfour to Salisbury, 4 Feb 1910.
37. 3 Feb 1910.
38. Chamberlain Papers, AC 8/5/5, memorandum from Salisbury, 1 Feb 1910 [copy] [my italics]
39. *Westminster Gazette*, 28 Jan 1910, letter from Liberal rural organiser.
40. Rosebery Papers, 42, Perks to Rosebery, 29 Jan 1910, reporting conversation with Pease. See also above, pp. 76–7.

41. Balfour Papers, Add. MS. 49859, ff. 183–5, A. E. Fellowes to Balfour, 24 Oct 1907.
42. Ibid., Add. MS. 49766, ff. 75–80, Sandars to Balfour, 21 Jan 1910.
43. Bryce Papers, Uncatalogued, 3 Feb 1910.
44. Dr Paul Thompson, *Socialists, Liberal and Labour*, p. 167, has endeavoured to disparage this contrast arguing that in January 1910 'the majority of lost Liberal voters must have been working class, for while the percentage of [the total electorate] voting Liberal fell in working class constituencies it rose in middle class constituencies'. This contention is based on table 8, ibid. p. 303 which however contains an arithmetic error fatal to Thompson's argument. I have recalculated the relevant rows in that table using Thompson's procedures with the following results. Where my figure differs significantly for the argument from Thompson's his figure is given in brackets.

Group	A Over 90% w.c.	B 80–90% w.c.	C 60–80% w.c.	D less than 60% w.c.
1906	47·5	44·6	41·4	35·0 [30·5]
1910 J.	45·8	43·3	40·5	32·9

Thus the percentage of the total electorate voting Liberal fell more steeply in middle-class constituencies, and this despite the generally much greater increases in turnout in the middle-class constituencies.
45. For Liberal opinions on Lloyd George's impact on middle-class voters see above, pp. 110–11.
46. Bonar Law Papers, 20/34, note by Bonar Law on position of T.R., 4 Feb 1910 [copy].
47. Fitzroy, *Memoirs*, i 393. A Liberal candidate in the Home Counties echoed Fitzroy: '. . . there was a real terror of what was called "Socialistic legislation" – a nightmare that seems particularly to possess the man who is beginning to gather a little property.' *Westminster Gazette*, 26 Jan 1910.
48. Population shifts may have favoured the Liberals in some of these constituencies.
49. Bryce Papers, Miscellaneous Correspondence, Burt to Bryce, 13 Oct 1909.
50. Ibid., Uncatalogued, Spender to Bryce, 3 Feb 1910.
51. *Daily Mail*, 4, 5 Jan 1910.
52. Chamberlain, *Politics From Inside*, p. 197.
53. *Westminster Gazette*, 28 Jan 1910.
54. 7 Feb 1910.
55. Bryce Papers, Miscellaneous Correspondence, Burt to Bryce, 13 Oct 1909.
56. T. J. Macnamara, *Tariff Reform and the Working Man* (London, 1910) 14, 17, laid stress on the importance of this opposition. See also Semmel, *Imperialism and Social Reform*, pp. 106–21.
57. Bryce Papers, Miscellaneous Correspondence, Burt to Bryce, 13 Oct 1909.
58. Maxse Papers, 461, f. 574, Bromley-Davenport to Maxse, 8 Feb 1910.
59. For class consciousness fostered by awareness of income mal-distribution see Taylor in Nowell-Smith, *Edwardian England*, pp. 126–35. See also above, pp. 70–1.
60. Chamberlain Papers, AC 9/3/64, Wolmer to Austen Chamberlain, 1 Feb 1910.

61. clxxxvii (Mar 1910) 436.
62. Webb, *Our Partnership*, p. 465.
63. Chamberlain, *Politics From Inside*, p. 198.
64. 29 Jan 1910.
65. Samuel Papers, Gladstone to Samuel, 30 Dec 1910. I am indebted for this quotation to Dr A. S. King.
66. *Morning Post*, 19 Jan 1910.
67. See Pelling, *Social Geography*, ch. ix; and Cornford, *V.S.*, vii (1963) 62–3.
68. *Labour Leader*, 21 Jan 1910; Pelling, *Social Geography*, p. 40.
69. See Chamberlain, *Politics From Inside*, pp. 307–9.
70. 10 Dec 1910.
71. Seen Ensor, *England 1870–1914*, p. 426; and Halévy, vi, *The Rule of Democracy*, i 341. Jenkins, *Balfour's Poodle*, p. 131, enters a caveat noting that five of the eight Unionist gains were away from the 'predominantly cotton areas'. Nevertheless, the swing was greater in Eastern or cotton Lancastria than in Western Lancastria.
72. *Scotsman*, 5 Jan 1911.
73. *Western Morning News*, 16 Dec 1910; *Westminster Gazette*, 20 Dec 1910.
74. See *Review of Reviews*, xliii (Jan 1911) 8.
75. On the other hand it should be noted that in Scotland, on a new register, there was a slight swing against the Liberals in every region.

APPENDIX I

Classification by Regions

NOTES

1. An effort has been made to group constituencies in regions based on common social geography and where possible on common political traditions. Some examples illustrate the approach adopted:

(a) The constituencies Honiton, Tiverton and Exeter in the good agricultural lands of east Devon, a strongly Unionist area, have been placed in the Severn region with which agriculturally and politically they have much in common, while the poorer agricultural and more Liberal areas of west Devon are included with Liberal Cornwall in the South-West Peninsula region.

(b) Lancastria (i.e. Lancashire and the adjacent north Cheshire fringe) has been divided into two regions – the mixed industrial, seaside residential and rural area of Western Lancastria, and Eastern Lancastria centred on the cotton industry. Both tended to be Unionist between 1886 and 1906 but Western Lancastria much more strongly so.

(c) The industrial and mostly Liberal constituencies of Middlesbrough and Cleveland have been taken out of the mainly rural and Unionist North and East Ridings and grouped with urban, industrial and mainly Liberal Tees-side.

2. *Definition of regions and sub-regions.*
(Reference to a county includes all county and borough constituencies therein unless otherwise specified.)

A. LONDON
   1. *South of the Thames.*
   2. *Business and residential:* Chelsea, City, Fulham, Hammersmith, Hampstead, Kensington, Marylebone, Paddington, St George's Hanover Sq., Strand, Westminster.
   3. *East End:* Bethnal Green, Shoreditch, Tower Hamlets.
   4. *Remainder:* Finsbury, Hackney, Islington, St Pancras.

B. OUTER LONDON
  1. *Middlesex – Essex:* Middlesex plus Romford, Walthamstow, West Ham.
  2. *Kent – Surrey:* Dartford, Sevenoaks, Kingston, Wimbledon, Croydon.

C. SOUTH-EAST ENGLAND
  1. *Kent:* minus Dartford, Sevenoaks.
  2. *Surrey – Sussex:* minus Kingston, Wimbledon, Croydon.

D. THAMES VALLEY – ESSEX
  1. *Oxon. – Berks. – Bucks.*
  2. *Herts. – Essex:* minus Romford, Saffron Walden, Walthamstow, West Ham.

E. WESSEX
  1. *Hampshire Ports:* Portsmouth, Southampton.
  2. *Rural Wessex:* Hampshire, plus Dorset plus Devizes, Wilton, Salisbury.

F. EAST ANGLIA
  1. *Norfolk.*
  2. *Suffolk:* plus Saffron Walden.
  3. *Bedford – Cambs. – Hunts.*

G. SOUTH-WEST PENINSULA
  1. *Cornwall.*
  2. *Devonshire:* minus Honiton, Tiverton, Exeter.
  3. *Devon Ports:* Devonport, Plymouth.

H. SEVERN
  1. *Somerset – Devon:* Somerset plus Honiton, Tiverton, Exeter.
  2. *Glos. – Wilts:* minus Devizes, Wilton, Salisbury.

I. WESTERN MIDLANDS
  1. *Birmingham:* plus Aston Manor.
  2. *The Black Country:* Handsworth, Kingswinford, Walsall, Wednesbury, West Bromwich, Wolverhampton, Nuneaton, Tamworth, Coventry, East Worcestershire, North Worcestershire, Dudley.
  3. *Potteries – South Cheshire:* North-West Staffordshire, Hanley, Newcastle-under-Lyme, Stoke-on-Trent, Crewe, Macclesfield.
  4. *Staffs. – Warwick:* Burton, Leek, Lichfield, West Staffordshire, Stafford, Rugby, Stratford-on-Avon, Warwick and Leamington.

J. **WESTERN MARCHES**
1. *Hereford – Worcs.:* Herefordshire plus Bewdley, Droitwich, Evesham, Kidderminster, Worcester.
2. *Cheshire – Salop:* Shropshire plus Eddisbury, Knutsford, Northwich, Chester.

K. **EASTERN MIDLANDS**
1. *Derbyshire – Notts.:* minus Chesterfield, North-East Derbyshire.
2. *Leicester – Northants.*
3. *Major Cities:* Derby, Leicester, Northampton, Nottingham.

L. **LINCOLNSHIRE:** plus Rutland.

M. **WESTERN LANCASTRIA**
1. *Merseyside:* Bootle, Widnes, Liverpool, Wirral, Birkenhead.
2. *West Lancashire:* Blackpool, Chorley, Newton, Lancaster, Ormskirk, Southport, Preston, St Helens, Warrington.

N. **EASTERN LANCASTRIA**
1. *Manchester Conurbation:* Gorton, Stretford, Manchester, Salford, Altrincham, Stockport.
2. *South-East Lancastria:* Eccles, Heywood, Leigh, Ince, Middleton, Prestwich, Radcliffe-cum-Farnworth, Westhoughton, Ashton-under-Lyne, Bolton, Bury, Oldham, Rochdale, Wigan, Hyde, Stalybridge.
3. *North-East Lancashire:* Accrington, Clitheroe, Darwen, Rossendale, Blackburn, Burnley.

O. **WEST RIDING**
1. *West Yorkshire conurbation:* Colne Valley, Elland, Keighley, Morley, Otley, Pudsey, Shipley, Sowerby, Spen Valley, Bradford, Dewsbury, Halifax, Huddersfield, Leeds.
2. *South Yorkshire:* Remainder West Riding minus Barkston, Ash, Ripon, Skipton plus Chesterfield, North-East Derbyshire.

P. **NORTH AND EAST RIDINGS**
1. *Counties:* plus Barkston Ash, Ripon, Skipton, minus Cleveland.
2. *Boroughs:* minus Middlesbrough.

Q. **CUMBRIA:** Cumberland, Westmorland plus North Lonsdale, Barrow-in-Furness.

R. NORTH-EAST ENGLAND
1. *Tyneside:* Chester-le-Street, Houghton-le-Spring, Jarrow, Gateshead, South Shields, Sunderland, Tyneside, Newcastle upon Tyne, Tynemouth.
2. *Tees-side:* South-East Durham, Darlington, Hartlepools, Stockton, Cleveland, Middlesbrough.
3. *Remainder:* remaining constituencies in Durham and Northumberland.

S. INDUSTRIAL WALES
1. *Glamorgan.*
2. *Monmouth.*

T. RURAL WALES
1. *Counties.*
2. *Boroughs.*

U. SCOTTISH HIGHLANDS: Argyll, Bute, Caithness, Inverness, Orkney and Shetland, Perthshire, Ross and Cromarty, Sutherland.

V. NORTH-EAST SCOTLAND
1. *Aberdeen – Dundee:* cities of Aberdeen and Dundee.
2. *Remainder:* Aberdeenshire, Banff, Elgin and Nairn, Forfar, Kincardine.

W. FORTH VALLEY
1. *Edinburgh:* plus Leith Burghs.
2. *Remainder:* Clackmannan and Kinross, Midlothian, Fife, Linlithgow, Stirlingshire.

X. CLYDE VALLEY
1. *Glasgow Conurbation:* Glasgow plus East Renfrew, Govan, Partick.
2. *Clydeside:* Dumbarton, Mid-Lanark, North-East Lanark, North-West Lanark, West Renfrew, Greenock, Kilmarnock, Paisley.

Y. SOUTHERN SCOTLAND: Ayrshire, Berwick, Dumfriesshire, Haddington, Kirkcudbright, South Lanark, Peebles and Selkirk, Roxburgh, Wigtown.

Z. IRELAND
1. *Belfast.*
2. *Ulster.*

3. *Dublin*: city and county.
4. *Connaught, Leinster and Munster.*

3. *Sources in preparing this classification were:*
Philips's *Handy Atlas and Gazeteer of the British Isles. A series of detailed county maps showing local government and parliamentary divisions* (London, n.d.).

Pelling, *Social Geography.*
C. B. Fawcett, *Provinces of England* (London, 1919).
T. W. Freeman, *The Conurbations of Great Britain* (Manchester, 1959).
Edward Krehbiel, 'Geographic Influences in British Elections', *The Geographical Review*, ii (Dec 1916) 419–32.

Constituency Classification

A. All constituencies in England were classified into one of four categories.

  1. *Mining:* all constituencies with a mining vote in 1910 of 30 per cent or more. (Source: Gregory, *The Miners*, pp. 12–13.)

  All remaining constituencies:

  2. *Urban:* borough constituencies.
     : county constituencies with less than 30 per cent of population in rural districts.

  3. *Mixed Urban/Rural:* county constituencies with 30–60 per cent of population in rural districts.

  4. *Rural:* county constituencies with over 60 per cent of population in rural districts.

B. The urban constituencies were further divided using an index developed by Henry Pelling, *Social Geography*, to measure the social status of constituencies.

  1. *Predominantly middle-class:* constituencies with over 250 female domestic servants per 1000 households.

  2. *Mixed-Class:* constituencies with between 100 and 250 female domestic servants per 1000 households.

  3. *Predominantly working-class:* constituencies with less than 100 female domestic servants per 1000 households.

C. The 1911 Census was the source for population and occupation figures used in this classification. Estimates of plural voters were considered in determining both the urban-rural distinction, and the social status classification in a number of cases. Paul Thompson, *Socialists, Liberals and Labour*, was used, although not always followed, in the classification of the London constituencies.

D. The following limitations should be noted.

1. The use of rural districts is not completely satisfactory for at least two reasons:
   (a) administrative definition tended to lag behind urban development.
   (b) a degree of guesswork is involved in apportioning rural districts between various county constituencies, for administrative and parliamentary boundaries rarely coincided.

2. It is not possible from the 1911 Census to obtain female domestic servant ratios for constituencies within a divided borough. For such constituencies the chief source for the social status classification has been Pelling, *Social Geography*, supplemented with newspaper analyses of the social composition of the relevant constituencies.

3. With urbanised county seats, and with a number of borough seats in which the parliamentary boundaries differ significantly from the administrative boundaries, an element of guesswork is involved in making use of the female domestic servant ratios.

E. Classification (arranged in alphabetical order by counties).

Key: A. Urban – predominantly middle-class.
     B. Urban – mixed-class.
     C. Urban – predominantly working-class.
     D. Mixed Urban/Rural.
     E. Rural.
     F. Mining.
     * Two-member seats.

BEDFORDSHIRE
Biggleswade (E)
Luton (C)
Bedford (A)

BERKSHIRE
Abingdon (E)
Newbury (E)
Wokingham (E)
Reading (B)
Windsor (A)

BUCKINGHAMSHIRE
Aylesbury (E)
Buckingham (E)
Wycombe (D)

CAMBRIDGESHIRE
Chesterton (E)
Newmarket (E)
Wisbech (D)
Cambridge (A)

CHESHIRE
Altrincham (D)
Crewe (C)
Eddisbury (E)
Hyde (C)
Knutsford (E)
Macclesfield (C)
Northwich (B)
Wirral (B)
Birkenhead (B)
Chester (B)

CHESHIRE—*cont.*
Stalybridge (C)
*Stockport (C)

CORNWALL
Bodmin (E)
Camborne (D)
Launceston (E)
St Austell (E)
St Ives (D)
Truro (E)
Penryn and
   Falmouth (B)

CUMBERLAND
Cockermouth (D)
Egremont (D)
Eskdale (E)
Penrith (E)
Carlisle (C)
Whitehaven (F)

DERBYSHIRE
–Mid (F)
–North-East (F)
–South (E)
–West (E)
Chesterfield (F)
High Peak (D)
Ilkeston (F)
*Derby (C)

DEVONSHIRE
Ashburton (D)
Barnstaple (D)
Honiton (E)
South Molton (E)
Tavistock (E)
Tiverton (E)
Torquay (A)

Totnes (E)
*Devonport (C)
Exeter (B)
*Plymouth (B)

DORSET
–East (D)
–North (E)
–South (B)
–West (E)

DURHAM
–Mid (F)
–North-West (F)
–South-East (F)
Barnard Castle (F)
Bishop Auckland (F)
Chester-le-Street (F)
Houghton-le-Spring
   (F)
Jarrow (C)
Darlington (B)
Durham (B)
Gateshead (C)
Hartlepools (B)
South Shields (B)
Stockton (B)
*Sunderland (B)

ESSEX
–South-East (D)
Chelmsford (E)
Epping (E)
Harwich (E)
Maldon (E)
Romford (B)
Saffron Walden (E)
Walthamstow (C)
Colchester (B)

West Ham
–North (C)
–South (C)

GLOUCESTERSHIRE
Cirencester (E)
Forest of Dean (D)
Stroud (E)
Tewkesbury (E)
Thornbury (E)
Bristol
–East (C)
–North (B)
–South (B)
–West (A)
Cheltenham (A)
Gloucester (B)

HAMPSHIRE
Andover (E)
Basingstoke (D)
Fareham (D)
Isle of Wight (D)
New Forest (E)
Petersfield (E)
Christchurch (A)
*Portsmouth (B)
*Southampton (B)
Winchester (A)

HEREFORDSHIRE
Leominster (E)
Ross (E)
Hereford (B)

HERTFORDSHIRE
Hertford (D)
Hitchin (E)
St Albans (D)
Watford (B)

HUNTINGDONSHIRE
Huntingdon (E)
Ramsey (E)

KENT
Ashford (E)
Dartford (B)
Faversham (D)
Isle of Thanet (B)
Medway (E)
St Augustine's (D)
Sevenoaks (A)
Tonbridge (D)
Canterbury (B)
Chatham (C)
Dover (B)
Gravesend (B)
Hythe (A)
Maidstone (B)
Rochester (B)

LANCASHIRE
Accrington (C)
Blackpool (D)
Bootle (B)
Chorley (D)
Clitheroe (C)
Darwen (C)
Eccles (C)
Gorton (C)
Heywood (C)
Ince (C)
Lancaster (D)
Leigh (F)
Middleton (C)
Newton (F)
North Lonsdale (D)
Ormskirk (D)
Prestwich (C)

Radcliffe-cum-
   Farnworth (C)
Rossendale (C)
Southport (A)
Stretford (B)
Westhoughton (C)
Widnes (B)
Ashton-u-Lyne (C)
Barrow-in-Furness
   (C)
*Blackburn (C)
*Bolton (C)
Burnley (C)
Bury (C)
Liverpool
   –Abercromby (B)
   –East Toxteth (B)
   –Everton (C)
   –Exchange (B)
   –Kirkdale (C)
   –Scotland (C)
   –Walton (B)
   –West Derby (B)
   –West Toxteth (C)
Manchester
   –East (C)
   –North (C)
   –North-East (C)
   –North-West (A)
   –South (B)
   –South-West (C)
*Oldham (C)
*Preston (C)
Rochdale (C)
St Helens (C)
Salford
   –North (B)
   –South (C)
   –West (B)
Warrington (C)

Wigan (F)

LEICESTERSHIRE
Bosworth (F)
Harborough (D)
Loughborough (D)
Melton (D)
*Leicester (C)

LINCOLNSHIRE
Brigg (E)
Gainsborough (E)
Horncastle (E)
Louth (E)
Sleaford (E)
Spalding (E)
Stamford (E)
Boston (B)
Grantham (B)
Grimsby (B)
Lincoln (B)

LONDON
Battersea (C)
Clapham (B)
Bethnal Green
   –North-East (C)
   –South-West (C)
Camberwell
   –North (C)
   –Dulwich (A)
   –Peckham (C)
Chelsea (A)
Deptford (B)
Finsbury
   –Central (C)
   –East (C)
   –Holborn (A)

LONDON—*cont.*
Fulham (B)
Greenwich (B)
Hackney
—Central (C)
—North (A)
—South (C)
Hammersmith (B)
Hampstead (A)
Islington
—East (B)
—North (B)
—South (C)
—West (C)
Kensington
—North (B)
—South (A)
Lambeth
—North (C)
—Brixton (A)
—Kennington (C)
—Norwood (A)
Lewisham (A)
*City (A)
Marylebone
—East (A)
—West (A)
Newington
—West (C)
—Walworth (C)
Paddington
—North (B)
—South (A)
St George's, Han. Sq.
    (A)
St Pancras
—East (C)
—North (B)
—South (B)
—West (B)

Shoreditch
—Haggerston (C)
—Hoxton (C)
Southwark
—West (C)
—Bermondsey (C)
—Rotherhithe (C)
Strand (A)
Tower Hamlets
—Bow & Bromley
    (C)
—Limehouse (C)
—Mile End (C)
—Poplar (C)
—St George's (C)
—Stepney (C)
—Whitechapel (C)
Wandsworth (A)
Westminster (A)
Woolwich (C)

MIDDLESEX
Brentford (B)
Ealing (A)
Enfield (B)
Harrow (B)
Hornsey (A)
Tottenham (C)
Uxbridge (A)

NORFOLK
—East (E)
—Mid (E)
—North (E)
—North-West (E)
—South (E)
—South-West (E)
Great Yarmouth (B)
King's Lynn (B)
*Norwich (B)

NORTHAMPTON-
    SHIRE
—East (C)
—Mid (E)
—North (E)
—South (E)
*Northampton (C)
Peterborough (B)

NORTHUMBERLAND
Berwick-on-Tweed
    (D)
Hexham (E)
Tyneside (B)
Wansbeck (F)
Morpeth (F)
*Newcastle (B)
Tynemouth (B)

NOTTINGHAMSHIRE
Bassetlaw (D)
Mansfield (F)
Newark (E)
Rushcliffe (D)
Nottingham
—East (C)
—South (B)
—West (C)

OXFORDSHIRE
Banbury (E)
Henley (E)
Woodstock (E)
Oxford (A)

RUTLAND
Rutland (E)

SHROPSHIRE
Ludlow (E)

Newport (E)
Oswestry (E)
Wellington (B)
Shrewsbury (B)

SOMERSET
  –East (E)
  –North (E)
  –South (E)
Bridgwater (E)
Frome (E)
Wellington (E)
Wells (D)
*Bath (A)
Taunton (B)

STAFFORDSHIRE
  –North-West (F)
  –West (F)
Burton (B)
Handsworth (B)
Kingswinford (D)
Leek (E)
Lichfield (B)
Hanley (C)
Newcastle-u-Lyme
  (B)
Stafford (B)
Stoke-on-Trent (C)
Walsall (C)
Wednesbury (C)
West Bromwich (B)
Wolverhampton
  –East (C)
  –South (C)
  –West (B)

SUFFOLK
Eye (E)
Lowestoft (D)

Stowmarket (E)
Sudbury (E)
Woodbridge (E)
Bury St Edmunds (B)
*Ipswich (B)

SURREY
Chertsey (A)
Epsom (D)
Guildford (D)
Kingston (A)
Reigate (D)
Wimbledon (A)
Croydon (B)

SUSSEX
Chichester (D)
Eastbourne (A)
East Grinstead (E)
Horsham (E)
Lewes (D)
Rye (E)
*Brighton (A)
Hastings (A)

WARWICKSHIRE
Nuneaton (D)
Rugby (D)
Stratford-on-Avon
  (E)
Tamworth (D)
Aston Manor (C)
Birmingham
  –Central (B)
  –East (C)
  –North (C)
  –South (C)
  –West (C)
  –Bordesley (C)
  –Edgbaston (A)

Coventry (C)
Warwick & Lea-
  mington (A)

WESTMORLAND
Appleby (E)
Kendal (D)

WILTSHIRE
Chippenham (E)
Cricklade (D)
Devizes (E)
Westbury (D)
Wilton (E)
Salisbury (A)

WORCESTERSHIRE
  –East (B)
  –North (D)
Bewdley (E)
Droitwich (E)
Evesham (E)
Dudley (B)
Kidderminster (C)
Worcester (B)

YORKSHIRE
EAST RIDING
Buckrose (E)
Holderness (E)
Howdenshire (E)
Hull
  –Central (B)
  –East (C)
  –West (B)
*York (B)

NORTH RIDING
Cleveland (D)
Richmond (E)

NORTH RIDING
—*cont.*
Thirsk & Malton (E)
Whitby (E)
Middlesbrough (B)
Scarborough (B)

WEST RIDING
Barkston Ash (E)
Barnsley (F)
Colne Valley (C)
Doncaster (F)
Elland (C)
Hallamshire (F)
Holmfirth (D)
Keighley (C)

Morley (F)
Normanton (F)
Osgoldcross (F)
Otley (B)
Pudsey (B)
Ripon (D)
Rotherham (F)
Shipley (C)
Skipton (D)
Sowerby (C)
Spen Valley (C)
Bradford
   –Central (C)
   –East (C)
   –West (B)
Dewsbury (C)

*Halifax (C)
Huddersfield (C)
Leeds
   –Central (B)
   – East (C)
   –North (B)
   –South (C)
   –West (C)
Pontefract (B)
Sheffield
   –Central (B)
   –Attercliffe (C)
   –Brightside (C)
   –Ecclesall (A)
   –Hallam (A)
Wakefield (B)

APPENDIX III

Results 1885–Dec 1910

(Unionist percentage of total poll)

A. *By Regions*

Region	Seats	1885	1886	1892	1895	1900	1906	Jan 1910	Dec 1910
London	59	52·5	59·2	53·1	59·7	63·1	48·2	53·9	54·3
Outer London	16	55·5	68·4	60·0	64·7	66·5	45·4	53·7	52·9
S.E. England	26	57·6	64·4	59·9	61·8	60·7	52·3	61·9	61·4
Thames Valley – Essex	22	52·6	61·5	55·6	59·4	58·7	48·8	56·9	56·7
Wessex	19	51·3	57·2	53·6	54·4	56·3	47·6	56·1	55·8
East Anglia	28	46·7	51·8	49·3	52·5	52·0	43·6	49·0	48·1
S.W. Peninsula	17	43·8	59·2	49·9	49·9	49·9	42·7	47·0	48·1
Severn	27	48·3	55·0	51·7	54·5	53·1	44·0	49·8	50·0
Western Midlands	36	43·4	50·8	55·7	60·5	60·6	49·8	55·1	54·6
Western Marches	17	49·8	58·3	57·4	61·9	59·0	49·5	54·7	54·9
Eastern Midlands	27	43·4	47·3	47·4	50·9	49·5	40·4	44·4	45·1
Lincolnshire	12	48·7	56·6	50·7	54·3	52·9	45·8	48·9	49·8
Western Lancastria	23	58·2	57·9	56·7	61·7	63·6	50·0	52·7	55·2
Eastern Lancastria	39	50·3	52·0	50·0	52·7	53·5	40·0	42·2	45·5
West Riding	37	41·2	43·8	44·6	48·5	48·8	36·0	37·4	38·8
North and East Ridings	15	50·5	53·5	51·2	53·5	55·5	48·4	50·5	51·0
Cumbria	10	49·0	51·8	49·3	53·8	53·4	45·8	48·1	49·7
N.E. England	26	38·4	42·6	44·0	45·4	48·2	35·1	39·3	39·9
ENGLAND	456	48·7	54·5	52·0	55·6	56·1	44·5	49·4	50·0
Industrial Wales	14	30·4	31·6	32·0	39·7	37·2	28·5	31·1	33·6
Rural Wales	20	42·2	44·6	41·0	44·3	42·8	32·6	34·1	34·9
WALES	34	37·3	39·2	37·3	42·4	40·5	30·4	32·3	33·8

Region	Seats	1885	1886	1892	1895	1900	1906	Jan 1910	Dec 1910
Highlands	12	35·0	38·7	44·0	45·6	48·8	37·9	38·5	40·9
N.E. Scotland	12	28·1	35·6	38·7	41·6	42·9	27·7	33·3	35·7
Forth Valley	15	30·5	41·7	41·7	45·1	46·3	35·3	36·5	38·8
Clyde Valley	18	45·7	50·4	47·9	52·0	53·5	41·0	42·3	43·9
Southern Scotland	13	41·5	50·4	49·8	50·5	52·3	44·0	45·1	45·7
SCOTLAND	70	36·8	44·0	44·7	47·4	49·1	37·8	39·6	41·4
GREAT BRITAIN	560	46·5	52·2	50·2	53·7	54·3	43·1	47·4	48·2

B. *By Type of Constituency* (ENGLAND ONLY)

Type	Seats	1885	1886	1892	1895	1900	1906	Jan 1910	Dec 1910
URBAN									
Predominantly middle-class	48	57·1	65·0	60·3	64·3	65·8	53·6	60·5	61·8
Mixed-class	107	49·7	54·5	52·9	56·0	57·2	45·5	50·2	50·9
Predominantly working-class	124	46·2	50·2	48·5	52·9	54·1	41·0	44·7	45·8
MIXED URBAN/ RURAL	51	51·0	56·2	53·2	56·5	55·3	46·7	52·7	52·7
RURAL	98	49·0	57·4	53·5	56·6	55·9	47·6	53·6	53·3
MINING	28	37·1	42·2	41·6	45·4	46·9	35·9	36·4	38·4
	456								

NOTES

1. University seats excluded from all calculations in this appendix.

2. Figures for 1885 to 1900 calculated by averaging the Unionist percentage of the poll. Figures for 1906 and 1910 based on Appendix IV.

3. For the period from 1885 to 1906 swing is defined simply as the percentage change in the poll of Unionist Party candidates. A slightly different definition is used for the period 1906 to 1910 (see Appendix IV).

4. To avoid distortions arising from regional concentrations of uncontested seats a probable poll has been calculated for uncontested seats. This has been computed on the basis of the poll in the preceding

election and the average swing in contested seats in the same region. January 1910 has been used as the base for calculating probable polls in uncontested seats in both 1906 and December 1910. As there were only six uncontested seats (apart from the University seats) in Great Britain in January 1910, it was considered unnecessary to make any probability calculations for that election.

5. The party proportions in two-member seats are calculated by treating all votes as half votes, except where only one Unionist or one anti-Unionist was standing, in which case that candidate's votes are treated as whole votes. Two-member constituencies are counted twice in determining averages.

6. As the constituency typology is based on material drawn from the 1911 Census, its usefulness for interpreting the results in the early elections of the period might be questioned. In 1910 there were fewer rural seats and more urban seats than in 1885, and within the urban group there had been a relative decline in the number of predominantly middle-class constituencies, and an absolute and relative increase in the number of predominantly working-class seats. However, a check of the 1891 Census suggests that such changes from one category to another were not numerous, and anyhow were unlikely to have any significant impact on the averages.

Results 1910

NOTES

1. A minus sign in the turnout columns indicates a decline in turnout.

2. All votes in two-member seats treated as half-votes except where only one Unionist or one anti-Unionist candidate stood, in which case his votes are treated as whole votes. Details from particular two-member seats and turnout figures in two-member constituencies suggest that, where only one Unionist or one anti-Unionist candidate stood, most of his supporters plumped.

3. Swing is defined as the average of the Unionist percentage gain in the share of the poll and the Liberal *and* Labour percentage loss. A minus sign therefore indicates a swing to the anti-Unionists. This calculation has been adopted as the simplest and most accurate measure of the change of opinion between 1906 and January 1910 and between the two 1910 elections. Despite the different brand names of the anti-Unionists in Great Britain, the Liberal and Labour candidates shared a similar, if not identical, anti-Unionist platform. A comparison between the movement of opinion between 1906 and January 1910, and between the 1910 elections in Labour-held seats and in contiguous Liberal-held seats shows no significant difference in swing. In two-member seats fought together by a Liberal and a Labour candidate there seems to have been only a minimal leakage through plumping or cross-voting with Unionists, except in the special circumstances of Merthyr Tydfil (both elections) and Preston (January election).

It is true that this method causes some distortion of swing in constituencies which at one election had a straight fight and at another a triangular contest. An examination of the following constituencies:
   (a) 17 with only one anti-Unionist candidate in 1906 but two in January 1910,
   (b) 16 with two anti-Unionist candidates in 1906 but only one in January 1910,

(c) and 22 with two anti-Unionist candidates in January 1910 but only one in December 1910,

suggests that, where two anti-Unionist candidates stood, their combined vote averaged about 5 per cent more than the vote of a single anti-Unionist candidate in the same seats.

However the constituencies were few in number and in no case did this factor seem to have affected a sub-regional swing by more than 2 per cent. Swing is only calculated in seats in which at both elections concerned (1906 and January 1910, or January 1910 and December 1910) there was at least one Unionist and one anti-Unionist candidate standing. Swing has not been calculated for Ireland because of the large number of members returned unopposed and the varied types of inter-party and intra-party contests there. Nor because of the high proportion of unopposed returns has swing been calculated for the university seats.

4. Figures in brackets in the tables indicate the number of members returned unopposed.

Regions and Sub-regions	Turnout			Candidates in contested constituencies and votes as % of total votes 1910 Jan				% Swing 1906–1910 Jan	Members elected 1910 Jan					Net Unionist gain 1910 Jan (in seats over) 1906	% Swing 1910 Jan–Dec	Members elected 1910 Dec			
	% change 1906–1910 Jan	% voting 1910 Jan	% change Jan–Dec 1910	Unionist	Liberal	Labour	Other		Total	Unionist	Liberal	Labour	Other			Unionist	Liberal	Labour	Other
A. LONDON																			
1. South of Thames	5·9	85·6	−9·2	19 / 52·6	17 / 41·1	2 / 6·3		6·8	19	11	7		1	6	0·1	8	9		2
2. West End	7·8	80·7	−11·9	15 / 65·0	14 / 34·5		1 / 0·5	7·8	15	15				4	2·0	15 (2)			
3. East End	2·6	83·0	−9·5	11 / 43·9	11 / 50·1	1 / 4·8	1 / 1·1	0·9	11	3	8			1	−1·2	1	9		1
4. Remainder	5·5	85·2	−8·2	14 / 48·9	14 / 51·1			5·6	14	4	10			3	0·7	6	8		
Total	5·6	84·0	−9·6	59 / 53·9	56 / 42·5	3 / 3·3	2 / 0·3	5·7	59	33	25		1	14	0·4	30 (2)	26		3
B. OUTER LONDON																			
1. Middlesex–Essex	8·1	83·5	−8·6	11 / 52·0	10 / 43·5	1 / 4·5		7·5	11	6	4		1	3	−0·8	6 (2)	4	1	
2. Kent–Surrey	4·8	86·1	−4·2	5 / 58·3	5 / 41·7			9·9	5	5				1	−0·7	4 (3)	1		
Total	7·1	84·2	−7·8	16 / 53·7	15 / 43·0	1 / 3·3		8·3	16	11	4		1	4	−0·8	10 (5)	5	1	
C. SOUTH-EAST ENGLAND																			
1. Kent	3·0	86·7	−4·4	13 / 60·4	12 / 33·5	1 / 5·0	1 / 1·1	7·7	13	13				4	−0·9	11 (6)	1		1
2. Surrey–Sussex	2·5	87·3	−7·1	13 / 63·0	13 / 37·0			11·5	13	13				7	−0·1	13 (4)			
Total	2·8	87·0	−5·9	26 / 61·9	25 / 35·5	1 / 2·2	1 / 0·5	9·6	26	26				11	−0·5	24 (10)	1		1

REGIONS AND SUB-REGIONS	TURNOUT % change 1906–1910 Jan	TURNOUT % voting 1910 Jan	TURNOUT % change Jan–Dec 1910	CANDIDATES AND VOTES AS % OF TOTAL VOTES 1910 JAN — Unionist	Liberal	Labour	Other	SWING 1906–1910 JAN	MEMBERS ELECTED 1910 JAN — Total	Unionist	Liberal	Labour	Other	NET UNIONIST GAIN 1910 JAN (in seats over) 1906	SWING 1910 JAN–DEC	MEMBERS ELECTED 1910 DEC — Unionist	Liberal	Labour	Other
D. THAMES VALLEY–ESSEX																			
1. Oxford–Berks Bucks	3·6	90·6	−4·7	12 / 56·6	12 / 43·4			8·1	12	10	2			6	0·2	9 (3)	3		
2. Essex–Herts	3·5	87·5	−5·6	10 / 57·1	10 / 42·9			8·0	10	10				6	−0·6	10 (1)			
Total	3·5	89·0	−5·2	22 / 56·9	22 / 43·1			8·1	22	20	2			12	−0·2	19 (4)	3		
E. WESSEX																			
1. Hampshire Ports	8·9	85·1	−3·3	4 / 52·5	4 / 43·7	1 / 3·8		10·3	4	2	2			2	−1·1	2	2		
2. Rural Wessex	2·8	89·8	−3·5	15 / 57·3	15 / 42·7			8·0	15	14	1			8	0·1	14 (7)	1		
Total	4·1	88·6	−3·4	19 / 56·1	19 / 43·0	1 / 0·9		8·5	19	16	3			10	−0·3	16 (7)	3		
F. EAST ANGLIA																			
1. Norfolk	2·6	88·5	−4·5	10 / 46·2	9 / 47·4	1 / 6·4		4·1	10	2	7	1		1	−0·2	3	6	1	
2. Suffolk	4·8	89·2	−3·3	8 / 51·6	8 / 48·4			7·0	9	6 (1)	3			5	−1·4	4 (2)	5		
3. Bedford–Cambs–Hunts	4·0	90·6	−2·6	9 / 49·7	9 / 50·3			5·7	9	5	4			5	−1·4	3	6		
Total	3·7	89·4	−3·5	27 / 49·0	26 / 48·7	1 / 2·3		5·4	28	13 (1)	14	1		11	−0·9	10 (2)	17	1	

Region	Turnout: % change 1906–1910 Jan	% voting Jan 1910	% change Jan–Dec 1910	Candidates in contested constituencies and votes as % of total votes 1910 Jan — Unionist (n / %)	Liberal (n / %)	Labour (n / %)	Other (n / %)	Swing 1906–1910 Jan %	Members elected 1910 Jan — Total	Unionist	Liberal	Labour	Other	Net Unionist gain 1910 Jan (in seats over) 1906	Swing 1910 Jan–Dec %	Members elected 1910 Dec — Unionist	Liberal	Labour	Other
G. SOUTH-WEST PENINSULA																			
1. Cornwall	5·2	86·2	−5·1	7 / 42·8	7 / 57·2	—	—	3·2	7	1	6	—	—	1	0·5	2	5 (1)	—	—
2. Devonshire	3·1	88·9	−3·7	6 / 49·6	6 / 50·4	—	—	3·1	6	1	5	—	—	—	1·4	2	4	—	—
3. Devon Ports	5·1	86·9	−3·5	4 / 49·8	4 / 50·2	—	—	7·7	4	2	2	—	—	2	1·9	3	1	—	—
Total	4·5	87·5	−4·1	17 / 47·0	17 / 53·0	—	—	4·3	17	4	13	—	—	3	1·1	7	10 (1)	—	—
H. SEVERN																			
1. Somerset–Devon	2·9	91·2	−3·9	13 / 52·8	13 / 47·2	—	—	5·6	13	10	3	—	—	6	0·7	9 (1)	4	—	—
2. Glos.–Wilts	3·3	91·6	−4·2	10 / 49·0	10 / 50·8	1 / 0·2	—	5·9	10	6	4	—	—	5	−1·0	4	6	—	—
3. Bristol	4·3	88·0	−6·5	4 / 44·5	4 / 50·9	2 / 4·6	—	6·2	4	1	3	—	—	—	1·7	1	3	—	—
Total	3·3	90·7	−4·4	27 / 49·8	27 / 49·3	3 / 0·9	—	5·8	27	17	10	—	—	11	0·2	14 (1)	13	—	—
I. WESTERN MIDLANDS																			
1. Birmingham	2·9	77·3	−17·4	7 / 74·3	5 / 14·7	2 / 11·0	—	6·0	8	8 (1)	—	—	—	—	−0·8	8 (5)	—	—	—
2. Black Country	3·3	89·5	−3·8	14 / 54·9	12 / 38·2	2 / 6·9	—	5·1	14	10	3	1	—	6	−0·8	10 (4)	3	1	—
3. Potteries–South Cheshire	4·4	90·0	−6·6	6 / 40·7	4 / 33·9	3 / 25·4	—	2·5	6	—	4	2	—	—	0·5	—	4	2	—
4. Warwicks–Staffs	3·6	90·7	−3·9	7 / 52·8	7 / 47·2	—	—	7·6	8	6 (1)	2	—	—	5	−0·9	5	3	—	—
Total	3·5	87·5	−6·0	34 / 55·1	28 / 33·9	7 / 9·9	—	5·3	36	24 (2)	9	3	—	11	−0·5	23 (9)	10	3	—

REGIONS AND SUB-REGIONS	TURNOUT % change 1906–1910 Jan	TURNOUT % voting Jan 1910	TURNOUT % change Jan–Dec 1910	CANDIDATES IN CONTESTED CONSTITUENCIES AND VOTES AS % OF TOTAL VOTES 1910 JAN — Unionist	Liberal	Labour	Other	SWING 1906–1910 JAN	MEMBERS ELECTED 1910 JAN — Total	Unionist	Liberal	Labour	Other	NET UNIONIST GAIN 1910 JAN (in seats over) 1906	SWING % 1910 JAN–DEC	MEMBERS ELECTED 1910 DEC — Unionist	Liberal	Labour	Other
J. WESTERN MARCHES																			
1. Hereford–Worcs.	2·5	89·9	−5·1	8 / 57·4	8 / 42·6			5·6	8	8				4	−0·2	8 (2)			
2. Cheshire–Salop.	3·6	91·9	−4·1	9 / 52·8	9 / 47·2			4·8	9	7	2			3	0·5	7 (2)	2		
Total	3·1	91·1	−4·6	17 / 54·7	17 / 45·3			5·2	17	15	2			7	0·2	15 (4)	2		
K. EASTERN MIDLANDS																			
1. Derbyshire–Notts.	3·1	88·1	−5·2	9 / 43·0	8 / 50·9	1 / 6·2		3·0	9	3	5	1		1	0·7	4	4	1	
2. Leics.–Northants	3·8	90·6	−3·1	9 / 47·1	9 / 52·9			5·6	9	2	7			2	0·7	3	6		
3. Major Cities	3·6	89·9	−5·9	9 / 43·2	8 / 41·7	3 / 13·3	2 / 1·8	3·3	9	2	5	2		2	0·6	2	5	2	
Total	3·5	89·4	−4·8	27 / 44·4	24 / 49·0	6·1	0·5	4·0	27	7	17	3		5	0·7	9	15	3	
L. LINCOLNSHIRE	3·1	87·2	−3·1	12 / 48·9	12 / 49·2	1 / 1·9		3·1	12	6	6			2	0·9	6 (1)	6		
M. WESTERN LANCASTRIA																			
1. Merseyside	5·0	81·3	−6·4	13 / 52·7	10 / 39·4	2 / 5·3	2 / 2·6	1·5	13	10	2		1	2	3·6	12 (3)			1
2. West Lancashire	2·9	90·3	−3·9	10 / 52·7	7 / 32·3	3 / 13·9	1 / 1·1	4·1	10	6	2	2		3	1·2	9 (2)	1		
Total	4·1	85·5	−5·7	23 / 52·7	17 / 35·9	5 / 9·5	3 / 1·9	2·7	23	16	4	2	1	5	2·5	21 (5)	1		1

Regions and sub-regions	Turnout % change 1906–1910 Jan	Turnout % voting Jan 1910	% change Jan–Dec 1910	Candidates in contested constituencies and votes as % of total votes 1910 Jan — Unionist	Liberal	Labour	Other	% Swing 1906–1910 Jan	Total	Members elected 1910 Jan — Unionist	Liberal	Labour	Other	Net Unionist gain 1910 Jan (in seats over 1906)	% Swing 1910 Jan–Dec	Members elected 1910 Dec — Unionist	Liberal	Labour	Other
N. EASTERN LANCASTRIA																			
1. Manchester Conurbation	3·9	88·6	−5·1	14 / 44·4	10 / 39·2	5 / 14·9	1 / 1·5	5·5	14	1	9	4		1	2·6	2	8 (1)	4	
2. South-East Lancastria	3·4	92·0	−4·3	18 / 41·6	14 / 41·0	7 / 16·5	2 / 0·9	0·5	18	1	13	4			4·4	3	12	3	
3. North-East Lancashire	5·8	94·5	−5·0	7 / 40·1	5 / 35·3	2 / 19·4	2 / 5·2	−0·7	7	1	4	2		−1	2·0	1	4	2	
Total	4·0	91·4	−4·7	39 / 42·2	29 / 39·2	14 / 16·5	5 / 2·1	2·2	39	3	26	10			3·3	6	24 (1)	9	
O. WEST RIDING																			
1. West Yorkshire Conurbation	4·8	88·9	−9·1	20 / 36·5	18 / 50·3	6 / 11·3	2 / 1·9	2·4	21		18	3			1·9		18 (4)	3	
2. South Yorkshire	3·1	84·1	−7·9	16 / 38·6	10 / 37·1	7 / 24·0	1 / 0·3	0·1	16	4	7	5			0·7	3	8 (2)	5 (1)	
Total	3·8	86·8	−8·6	36 / 37·4	28 / 44·5	13 / 16·9	3 / 1·2	1·4	37	4	25	8			1·4	3	26 (6)	8 (1)	
P. NORTH AND EAST RIDINGS																			
1. Counties	2·1	89·5	−3·6	9 / 53·1	9 / 46·9			3·2	9	7	2			2	−0·1	7 (2)	2		
2. Boroughs	5·9	87·9	−3·8	6 / 46·5	6 / 53·5			−1·0	6	2	4				1·2	2 (1)	4 (1)		
Total	3·6	88·9	−3·7	15 / 50·5	15 / 49·5			2·1	15	9	6			2	0·5	9 (3)	6 (1)		
Q. CUMBRIA	3·5	89·0	−4·2	9 / 48·1	8 / 38·7	3 / 12·0	1 / 1·2	2·3	10	7 (1)	2	1		5	1·6	6 (1)	2	2	

REGIONS AND SUB-REGIONS	TURNOUT % change 1906–1910 Jan	TURNOUT % voting 1910 Jan	TURNOUT % change Jan–Dec 1910	CAND. Unionist	CAND. Liberal	CAND. Labour	CAND. Other	% SWING 1906–1910 JAN	MEMBERS ELECTED 1910 JAN Total	Unionist	Liberal	Labour	Other	NET UNIONIST GAIN 1910 JAN (in seats over 1906)	% SWING 1910 JAN–DEC	DEC Unionist	DEC Liberal	DEC Labour	DEC Other
R. NORTH-EAST ENGLAND																			
1. Tyneside	3·1	82·8	−6·4	11 / 39·6	8 / 38·8	5 / 21·6		6·5	11	2	7	2		2	−0·7		8 (2)	3 (1)	
2. Tees-side	1·5	89·3	−5·0	6 / 42·6	6 / 54·1	1 / 3·3	2	−3·5	6		6			−3	2·7	1	5		
3. Remainder	5·9	86·5	−6·3	7 / 35·5	6 / 52·7	2 / 11·8	8	4·3	9	1 (1)	7 (1)	1			0·1	1	7 (3)	1	
Total	3·8	85·3	−6·0	24 / 39·3	20 / 46·0	8 / 14·7		4·2	26	3 (1)	20 (1)	3		−1	0·6	2	20 (5)	4	
ENGLAND	4·0	87·5	−5·8	449 / 49·4	495 / 43·1	62 / 6·9	17 / 0·6	4·9	456	234 (5)	188 (1)	33	1	112	0·6	233 (54)	187 (14)	34 (2)	2
S. INDUSTRIAL WALES																			
1. Glamorgan	7·2	86·1	−11·3	9 / 30·0	6 / 41·5	4 / 26·4	2 / 2·1	2·8	10		6	4			2·7	1	5 (1)	4	
2. Monmouth	0·9	84·7	−5·4	4 / 34·0	3 / 43·0	1 / 23·0		2·4	4		3	1		1	1·9		3	1 (1)	
Total	5·1	85·7	−9·8	13 / 31·1	9 / 41·9	5 / 25·5	2 / 1·5	2·6	14		9	5		1	2·5	1	8 (1)	5 (1)	
T. RURAL WALES																			
1. Counties	0·7	81·8	−5·4	14 / 32·0	14 / 68·0			0·9	14	1	13			1	1·7		14 (8)		
2. Boroughs	1·0	91·8	−3·6	6 / 42·6	6 / 57·4			2·1	6	1	5			1	−0·2	2	4 (1)		
Total	0·8	84·6	−4·6	20 / 34·1	20 / 65·9			1·5	20	2	18			2	0·8	2	18 (9)		
WALES	2·6	84·8	−6·7	33 / 32·3	29 / 51·9	5 / 14·9	2 / 0·9	1·9	34	2	27	5		2	1·5	3	26 (10)	5 (1)	

Regions and sub-regions	Turnout % change 1906–1910 Jan	Turnout % voting Jan 1910	Turnout % change Jan–Dec 1910	Candidates (n / % of total votes 1910 Jan) Unionist	Liberal	Labour	Other	% Swing 1906–1910 Jan	Members elected 1910 Jan Total	Unionist	Liberal	Labour	Other	Net Unionist gain 1910 Jan (in seats over) 1906	% Swing 1910 Jan–Dec	Members elected 1910 Dec Unionist	Liberal	Labour	Other
U. SCOTTISH HIGHLANDS	4·1	79·9	−2·7	12 / 38·5	12 / 61·5			0·6	12	2	10			1	2·4	2	10 (3)		
V. NORTH-EAST SCOTLAND																			
1. Aberdeen–Dundee	7·2	80·8	−6·0	4 / 32·1	3 / 47·1	1 / 14·8	2 / 6·0	10·1	4		3		1		3·7		3		1
2. The Remainder	3·7	82·0	−5·9	8 / 34·0	8 / 62·8		1 / 3·2	3·3	8		8				1·1		8 (4)		
Total	4·9	81·6	−6·0	12 / 33·3	11 / 56·9	1 / 5·5	3 / 4·3	5·6	12		11		1		2·4		11 (4)		1
W. FORTH VALLEY																			
1. Edinburgh	6·4	87·1	−6·2	5 / 40·0	5 / 55·3	1 / 4·7		2·7	5	1	4				2·8	1	4		
2. Remainder	3·2	81·8	−4·0	10 / 34·4	10 / 60·7	1 / 4·9		0·3	10		10			−1	1·9	1	8 (3)		1
Total	4·4	83·8	−4·9	15 / 36·5	15 / 58·7	2 / 4·8		1·2	15	1	14			−1	2·3	2	12 (3)		1
X. CLYDE VALLEY																			
1. Glasgow Conurbation	3·5	86·3	−1·9	10 / 43·6	9 / 45·9	3 / 8·2	1 / 2·3	1·4	10	3	5	1	1		1·6	3	6		1
2. Clydeside	1·7	86·6	−4·1	8 / 40·7	8 / 52·4	3 / 6·9		1·2	8		8			−1	1·6		8		
Total	2·7	86·4	−2·9	18 / 42·3	17 / 48·9	6 / 7·6	1 / 1·2	1·3	18	3	13	1	1	−1	1·6	3	14		1
Y. SOUTHERN SCOTLAND	1·8	87·9	−0·5	13 / 45·1	13 / 53·0	1 / 1·9		1·1	13	3	10				0·6	2 (1)	11 (1)		

REGIONS AND SUB-REGIONS	TURNOUT % change 1906–1910 Jan	TURNOUT % voting Jan 1910	TURNOUT % change Jan–Dec 1910	CANDIDATES IN CONTESTED CONSTITUENCIES AND VOTES AS % OF TOTAL VOTES 1910 JAN Unionist	Liberal	Labour	Other	% SWING 1906–1910 JAN	MEMBERS ELECTED 1910 JAN Total	Unionist	Liberal	Labour	Other	NET UNIONIST GAIN (in seats over) 1906	% SWING 1910 JAN–DEC	MEMBERS ELECTED 1910 DEC Unionist	Liberal	Labour	Other
SCOTLAND	3·5	84·5	−3·4	70 / 39·6	68 / 54·2	10 / 5·1	4 / 1·1	1·8	70	9	58	2	1	−1	1·8	9 (1)	58 (11)	3	
GREAT BRITAIN	3·9	87·0	−5·6	552 / 47·4	502 / 44·8	77 / 7·2	23 / 0·6	4·3	560	245 (5)	273 (1)	40	2	113	0·8	245 (55)	271 (35)	42 (3)	2
UNIVERSITIES	4·1	71·3	1·9	3 / 61·3	2 / 22·3	1 / 16·4			9	9 (6)						9 (8)			

Z. IRELAND

REGIONS AND SUB-REGIONS	TURNOUT			CANDIDATES IN CONTESTED CONSTITUENCIES AND VOTES AS % OF TOTAL VOTES 1910 JAN						MEMBERS ELECTED JAN 1910				
	% change 1906–1910 Jan	% voting 1910 Jan	% change Jan–Dec 1910	Unionist	Liberal and Labour	Nationalist	Ind. Nationalist	Other	Total	Unionist	Liberal	Nationalist	Ind. Nationalist	Other
1. Belfast	2·1	89·5	−5·7	3 / 56·9	1 / 13·9	1 / 16·4	1 / 0·3	1 / 12·5	4	3 (1)		1		
2. Ulster	1·0	90·6	−3·5	13 / 51·7	7 / 26·7	6 / 20·0	1 / 1·6		21	15 (7)	1	5 (1)		
3. Dublin	3·1	78·8	−1·2	3 / 41·3	3	3 / 58·7			6	1		5 (3)		
4. Connaught				2		19	18							
Leinster	6·3	70·5	−0·9	5·0		48·7			70			59 (51)	11	
Munster							46·3							
Total	1·9	80·1	−2·3	21 / 32·7	8 / 11·5	29 / 35·1	20 / 19·0	1 / 1·7	101	19 (8)	1	70 (55)	11	—

<table>
<tr><th rowspan="3">REGIONS AND SUB-REGIONS</th><th>NET UNIONIST GAIN JAN 1910 (over 1906 in seats)</th><th colspan="5">CANDIDATES IN CONTESTED CONSTITUENCIES AND VOTES AS % OF TOTAL VOTES DEC 1910</th><th colspan="5">MEMBERS ELECTED DEC 1910</th></tr>
<tr><th></th><th>Unionist</th><th>Liberal</th><th>Nationalist</th><th>Ind. Nationalist</th><th>Other</th><th>Unionist</th><th>Liberal</th><th>Nationalist</th><th>Ind. Nationalist</th><th>Other</th></tr>
<tr><th></th><th></th><th></th><th></th><th></th><th></th><th></th><th></th><th></th><th></th><th></th></tr>
<tr><td colspan="12">Z. IRELAND</td></tr>
<tr><td>1. Belfast</td><td></td><td>2
57·1</td><td></td><td>1
26·8</td><td></td><td>1
16·1</td><td>3 (2)</td><td></td><td>1</td><td></td><td></td></tr>
<tr><td>2. Ulster</td><td>3</td><td>11
50·4</td><td>7
26·9</td><td>5
21·3</td><td>1
1·4</td><td></td><td>14 (7)</td><td>1</td><td>6 (2)</td><td></td><td></td></tr>
<tr><td>3. Dublin</td><td></td><td>2
38·2</td><td></td><td>3
58·7</td><td>1
3·1</td><td></td><td></td><td></td><td>6 (3)</td><td></td><td></td></tr>
<tr><td>4. Connaught
Leinster
Munster</td><td></td><td>2
3·6</td><td></td><td>22
63·0</td><td>19
33·2</td><td>1
0·2</td><td></td><td></td><td>60 (44)</td><td>10 (4)</td><td></td></tr>
<tr><td>Total</td><td>3</td><td>15
28·6</td><td>7
9·6</td><td>31
44·5</td><td>21
15·8</td><td>2
1·5</td><td>17(9)</td><td>1</td><td>73 (49)</td><td>10 (4)</td><td>—</td></tr>
</table>

Bibliography

A. MANUSCRIPT COLLECTIONS

I. LIBRARY COLLECTIONS

Beaverbrook Library
  Bonar Law Papers
  Lloyd George Papers
  Strachey Papers

Bodleian Library
  Asquith Papers
  Bryce Papers
  Milner Papers

British Library of Political and Economic Science, London School of Economics
  Labour Party Documents (E. R. Pease collection entitled 'The Infancy of the Labour Party')
  Lansbury Papers
  Passfield Papers

British Museum
  Balfour Papers
  Burns Papers
  Robert Cecil Papers
  Dilke Papers
  Herbert Gladstone Papers
  J. A. Spender Papers

National Library of Scotland
  Elibank Papers
  Haldane Papers
  Rosebery Papers

Public Record Office
  Cabinet Papers (Asquith's letters to the King on Cabinet meetings)
  Cromer Papers (typed transcript)

Sheffield Public Library
  H. J. Wilson Papers
Sussex County Archives, Chichester
  L. J. Maxse Papers
University of Birmingham Library
  Austen Chamberlain Papers
University of Edinburgh Library
  Scottish Liberal Association Papers

2. OTHER

Lewis Harcourt Papers, at Stanton Harcourt, Oxon.

Acland-Hood Papers (volume of newspaper cuttings with notes by Acland-Hood), at Fairfield, Stogursey, Bridgwater, Somerset.

Lancashire and Cheshire Liberal Federation Papers, in the office of the Federation, Manchester.

Manchester Liberal Federation Papers, in the office of the Federation, Manchester.

Midland Liberal Federation Papers, in the office of the Federation, Birmingham.

National Liberal Federation Papers, at Liberal Party Headquarters, Smith Square, London.

National Union of Conservative and Unionist Association Papers, at the Conservative Central Office, Smith Square, London.

Northern Liberal Federation Papers, in the office of the Federation, Newcastle upon Tyne.

I am grateful to Dr A. S. King for allowing me to use his transcript of the Carrington Diary, and Dr R. Rempel for his transcript of the Arthur Elliot Papers.

B. OFFICIAL PAPERS

1. The main collection of Parliamentary Papers relating to the elections of 1910 are:

Parl. Papers, 1910, lxxiii 453–705.

Parl. Papers, 1911, lxi 467–865 and *Parl. Papers*, 1911, lxii.

These contain returns on the number of electors, on election expenses, and on the number of illiterate voters. They also contain the minutes of evidence and the judgments on some but not all the election petitions.

2. Other official papers consulted:

Reports, Boundary Commission, *Parl. Papers*, 1884–5, xix.

Report of the Select Committee on Elections (Intervention of Peers, etc.) *Parl. Papers* 1887, ix 207–43.

Census of England and Wales 1911, i, Administrative Areas, *Parl. Papers* 1912–13, cxi 1–679.

Census of England and Wales 1911, x, Occupations and Industries, part i, *Parl. Papers*, 1913, lxxviii 321–1339.

Census of England and Wales 1911, iii, Parliamentary Areas, *Parl. Papers*, 1912–13, cxii 1–42.

Census of England and Wales 1911, General Report, *Parl. Papers* 1917–18, xxxv 483–913.

Report of the Twelfth Decennial Census of Scotland ii, *Parl. Papers* 1913, lxxx.

Census of Ireland 1911, General Report, *Parl. Papers* 1912–13, cxviii.

Report of the Royal Commission on Electoral Systems, *Parl. Papers* 1910, xxvi 295–567.

Report of the Committee of Privileges, *Parl. Papers* 1909, viii 349–55.

Report of the Committee of Privileges, *Parl. Papers* 1911, vii 631–45.

Fourteenth Abstract of Labour Statistics of the United Kingdom 1908–9, *Parl. Papers* 1910, cx 307–636.

Parliamentary Debates

C. PARTY PUBLICATIONS

Constitutional Year Book

Election Addresses Jan, Dec 1910 (4 volumes – National Liberal Club)

Election Petition Reports (Conservative Research Department)

I.L.P., *Annual Conference Reports*

Labour Party, *Annual Conference Reports*

Liberal Magazine

Liberal Year Book

National Union Gleanings

National Union *Leaflets* (Bound in annual volumes – Conservative Research Department)

Pamphlets and Leaflets (Annual volume of Liberal leaflets. Contains also National Liberal Federation, *Annual Conference Reports*)

Photographic Album 1910 elections (Conservative Research Department)

D. NEWSPAPERS AND PERIODICALS

1. Where possible, all newspapers have been read at least for the period Nov 1909–Jan 1910 and Nov–Dec 1910. However there has been extensive bomb damage in the British Museum's collection of English provincial newspapers for this period, and this has not always been possible. All newspapers listed were read at the Colindale Newspaper Library except *Birmingham Daily Post* (Birmingham Public Library) and *Newcastle Daily Chronicle* (*Newcastle Journal* offices, Newcastle upon Tyne).

2. Newspaper political alignment is indicated thus: L = Liberal, U = Unionist, N = Nationalist, I = Independent. A number of newspapers claiming to be independent are classified otherwise here because of their partisan alignment during the elections.

1. LONDON DAILIES

Morning
Daily Chronicle (L)
Daily Express (U)
Daily Graphic (U)
Daily Mail (U)
Daily Mirror (I)
Daily News (L)

Daily Telegraph (U)
Morning Leader (L)
Morning Post (U)
Standard (U)
The Times (U)

Evening
Evening News (U)
Evening Standard (U)
Globe (U)

Pall Mall Gazette (U)
Star (L)
Westminster Gazette (L)

2. LONDON SUNDAY NEWSPAPERS

Lloyds Weekly News (L)
News of the World (I)
Observer (U)
People (U)
Referee (U)

Reynolds News (L)
Sunday Times (U)
Weekly Dispatch (U)
Weekly Times (L)

3. DAILY NEWSPAPERS OUTSIDE LONDON

Birmingham Daily Post (U)
Carlisle Express and Examiner (L)

Lancashire Daily Post (L)
Leeds Mercury (L)

DAILY NEWSPAPERS OUTSIDE LONDON (*continued*)

Liverpool Courier (U)
Liverpool Daily Post (L)
Manchester Courier (U)
Manchester Guardian (L)
Newcastle Daily Chronicle (U)
Newcastle Daily Journal (U)
North Eastern Daily Gazette (L)
North Mail (L)
North Western Daily Mail (L)
Sheffield Daily Independent (L)
Sheffield Daily Telegraph (U)
West Cumberland Times (L)
Western Daily Mercury (L)
Western Morning News (U)

Yorkshire Observer (L)
Yorkshire Post (U)

WALES
South Wales Daily News (L)
South Wales Daily Post (U)

SCOTLAND
Glasgow Herald (U)
Scotsman (U)

IRELAND
Freeman's Journal (N)
Irish Independent (N)
Irish Times (U)

4. WEEKLIES

Baptist Times
British Weekly
The Car
Catholic Times
Christian World
Clarion
Economist
Justice
Labour Leader

Methodist Recorder
Methodist Times
The Motor
Nation
Newspaper Owner
Saturday Review
Spectator
Tablet

5. PERIODICALS

Advertising
Blackwood's Magazine
Contemporary Review
Fortnightly Review
National Review

Nineteenth Century and After
Quarterly Review
Review of Reviews
Westminster Review

E. REFERENCE WORKS

(Place of publication London, unless otherwise indicated)

Annual Register
T. B. Browne's Advertiser's A.B.C.
Burke's Landed Gentry

Burke's Peerage, Baronetage and Knightage

Butler, David, and Freeman, Jennie, *British Political Facts 1900–1960* (1963)

Catholic Directory

Church of England Year Book

Dictionary of National Biography

Dod's Parliamentary Companion

Free Church Year Book

Mitchell's Newspaper Press Directory

Mitchell, B. R. and Deane, Phyllis, *Abstract of British Historical Statistics* (Cambridge 1962)

Pall Mall Gazette House of Commons

Philips's Handy Atlas and Gazetteer of the British Isles. A series of detailed county maps showing local government and parliamentary divisions (n.d.)

Rogers on Elections, 3 vols. 17th ed. (1909)

The Times House of Commons

Willing's Press Guide

Whitaker's Almanack

Who's Who

Who Was Who

Year Book of Social Progress for 1913–14 (1914)

F. OTHER PUBLISHED SOURCES (SELECTED)

(As bibliographical details have been provided in the footnotes, this selection includes only works found generally useful in writing this study, or works used extensively in particular chapters. Place of publication London, unless otherwise indicated.)

1. *Memoirs and Biographies*
(Arranged in order of subjects, by names and titles as in 1910).

Amery, L. S., *My Political Life*, 3 vols. (1953)

Asquith, H. H. (1st Earl of Oxford and Asquith)
  Asquith, by Roy Jenkins (1964)
  Asquith, by R. B. McCallum (1936)
  Life of Lord Oxford and Asquith, by J. A. Spender and Cyril Asquith, 2 vols. (1932)

Balfour, A. J. (1st Earl of Balfour)
  Arthur James, First Earl of Balfour, by Blanche E. C. Dugdale, 2 vols. (1936)

Arthur James Balfour, by Kenneth Young (1963)

Blatchford, Robert, *My Eighty Years* (1931)

Robert Blatchford, Portrait of an Englishman, by Laurence Thompson (1957)

Blunt, W. Scawen, *My Diaries. Being a Personal Narrative of Events 1884–1914* (Single volume ed. 1932)

Burns, John

John Burns: Labour's Lost Leader, by W. R. G. Kent (1950)

Campbell-Bannerman, Sir Henry

The Life of the Rt. Hon. Sir Henry Campbell-Bannerman, by J. A. Spender, 2 vols. (1923)

Chamberlain, Austen, *Politics From Inside* (1936)

The Life and Letters of Sir Austen Chamberlain, by Sir Charles Petrie, 2 vols. (1939)

Chamberlain, Joseph

Joseph Chamberlain. Radicalism and Empire 1868–1914, by Peter Fraser (1966)

Life of Joseph Chamberlain, by J. L. Garvin and Julian Amery, 6 vols. (1932–69)

Churchill, W. S. C.

Winston Churchill as I Knew Him, by Violet Bonham Carter (1965)

Winston S. Churchill, by Randolph S. Churchill, 2 vols. (1966–7), and Companion volumes i and ii (1967–9).

Crewe, Lord

Lord Crewe, by J. Pope-Hennessy (1955)

Davidson, Randall

Randall Davidson Archbishop of Canterbury, by G. K. A. Bell, 2 vols. (1952)

Derby, 17th Earl of

Lord Derby, King of Lancashire, by Randolph Churchill (1960)

Dillon, John

John Dillon, by F. S. L. Lyons (1968)

Edward VII, King

Life of King Edward VII, by Sir Sidney Lee, 2 vols. (1925–7)

King Edward the Seventh, by Sir Philip Magnus (1964)

Elibank, Master of

Master and Brother, by A. C. Murray (1945)

Esher, 2nd Viscount

The Journals and Letters of Reginald, Viscount Esher, eds. M. V. Brett and Oliver, Viscount Esher, 4 vols. (1934–8)

Fisher, Lord
  Fear God and Dread Nought, ii, *Years of Power 1906–14*, by A. J.
    Marder (1956)
Fitzroy, Sir Almeric, *Memoirs*, 2 vols. (1925)
Garvin, J. L.
  The Observer and J. L. Garvin 1908–14, by A. M. Gollin (1960)
George V, King
  King George V, His Life and Reign, by Harold Nicolson (1952)
George, David Lloyd (1st Earl Lloyd-George of Dwyfor)
  My Brother and I, by William George (1958)
  Lloyd George, by Thomas Jones (1949)
  David Lloyd George: Welsh Radical as World Statesman, by Kenneth
    O. Morgan (Cardiff, 1963)
  Tempestuous Journey, Lloyd George His Life and Times, by Frank
    Owen (1954)
  Lloyd George. Rise and Fall, by A. J. P. Taylor (Cambridge, 1961)
  David Lloyd George. The Official Biography, by George Malcolm
    Thomson (1948)
Grey, Sir Edward (1st Viscount Grey of Fallodon)
  Grey of Fallodon, by G. M. Trevelyan (1937)
Haldane, R. B. (1st Viscount Haldane)
  Haldane. The Life of Viscount Haldane of Cloan, by Sir Frederick
    Maurice, 2 vols. (1937–9)
  Haldane of Cloan. His Life and Times 1856–1928, by Dudley Sommer
    (1960)
Hardie, J. Keir,
  J. Keir Hardie: A Biography, by W. Stewart (1925)
Henderson, Arthur
  Arthur Henderson, by Mary Agnes Hamilton (1938)
Hudson, Sir Robert
  Sir Robert Hudson. A Memoir, by J. A. Spender (1930)
Isaacs, Rufus (1st Marquess of Reading)
  Rufus Isaacs, First Marquess of Reading, by the 2nd Marquess, 2 vols.
    (1942–5)
Lang, Cosmo Gordon
  Cosmo Gordon Lang, by J. G. Lockhart (1949)
Lansbury, George, *My Life* (1928)
  Life of George Lansbury, by R. Postgate (1951)
Lansdowne, 5th Marquess of
  Lord Lansdowne: A Biography, by Lord Newton (1929)

Law, Andrew Bonar
   *The Unknown Prime Minister. The Life and Times of Andrew Bonar Law
   1858–1923*, by Robert Blake (1955)
Long, Walter (1st Viscount Long)
   Walter Long and His Times, by Sir Charles Petrie (1936)
MacDonald, James Ramsay
   The Life of James Ramsay MacDonald 1866–1919, by Lord Elton (1939)
McKenna, Reginald
   Reginald McKenna, by Stephen McKenna (1948)
Masterman, C. F. G.
   C. F. G. Masterman, by Lucy Masterman (1939)
Milner, Lord
   Proconsul in Politics, by A. M. Gollin (1964)
Montagu, Edwin
   Edwin Montagu. A Memoir and an Account of his Visits to India, by
   S. D. Waley (Bombay, 1964)
Morley, Lord, *Recollections*, 2 vols. (1917)
Northcliffe, Lord
   Northcliffe, by Reginald Pound and Geoffrey Harmsworth (1959)
O'Brien, William, *An Olive Branch in Ireland and Its Failure* (1910)
Redmond, John
   The Life of John Redmond, by Denis Gwynn (1932)
Riddell, Lord, *More Pages from My Diary 1908–14* (1934)
Robson, Sir William
   A Liberal Attorney General, by George Keeton (1949)
Rosebery, 5th Earl of
   Lord Rosebery, by the Marquess of Crewe, 2 vols. (1931)
   Rosebery. A Biography of Archibald Philip, Fifth Earl of Rosebery, by
   Robert Rhodes James (1963)
St Aldwyn, 1st Earl of
   Sir Michael Hicks Beach, Earl St Aldwyn, by Lady Victoria Hicks
   Beach, 2 vols. (1932)
Salvidge, Sir Archibald
   Salvidge of Liverpool, by Stanley Salvidge (1934)
Smith, F. E. (1st Earl of Birkenhead)
   F. E.: The Life of F. E. Smith, First Earl of Birkenhead, by the 2nd Earl
   of Birkenhead (1959)
Snowden, Philip (1st Viscount Snowden), *An Autobiography*, 2 vols.
   (1934)
Spender, J. A., *Life, Journalism and Politics*, 2 vols. (1927)

Watson, Sir Robert Spence
    The Life of Sir Robert Spence Watson, by Percy Corder (1914)
Webb, Beatrice, *Our Partnership* (1948)
Wolverhampton, 1st Viscount
    Life of Henry Hartley Fowler, First Viscount Wolverhampton, by Edith H. Fowler (1912)
Wyndham, George
    George Wyndham, A Study in Toryism, by John Biggs Davidson (1951)
    Life and Letters of George Wyndham, by J. W. Mackail and Guy Wyndham, 2 vols. (n.d.)

2. *General and Historical*

Allyn, Emily, *Lords versus Commons* (New York, 1931)
Anson, W. R., *The Law and Custom of the Constitution*, part i, *Parliament*, 3rd ed. (Oxford, 1897)
Bealey, Frank and Pelling, Henry, *Labour and Politics 1900-6* (1958)
Blease, W. Lyon, *A Short History of English Liberalism* (1913)
Brand, Carl F., *The British Labour Party, A Short History* (1965)
Butler, D. E., *The Electoral System in Britain, since 1918*, 2nd ed. (1963)
Cambray, P. G., *The Game of Politics. A Study of the Principles of British Political Strategy* (1932)
Campbell, Angus, Converse, Philip E., Miller, Warren E., and Stokes, Donald E., *The American Voter* (New York, 1960)
    Elections and the Political Order (New York, 1966)
Clegg, H. A., Fox, A. and Thompson, A. F., *A History of British Trade Unions since 1889*, i, *1889-1910* (Oxford, 1964)
Cole, G. D. H., *British Working Class Politics 1832-1914* (1941)
Coupland, Sir Reginald, *Welsh and Scottish Nationalism: A Study* (1954)
Craton, Michael and McCready, H. W., *The Great Liberal Revival—1903-6* (1966)
Dangerfield, George, *The Strange Death of Liberal England 1910-14* (New York, 1935)
Ensor, R. C. K., *England 1870-1914* (Oxford 1936)
Fulford, R., *Votes for Women* (1947)
Gollin, A. M., *Balfour's Burden. Arthur Balfour and Imperial Preference* (1965)
Gregory, Roy, *The Miners and British Politics 1906-14* (Oxford, 1968)
Gwyn, William B., *Democracy and the Cost of Politics in Britain* (1962)
Halevy, Elie, *A History of the English People in the Nineteenth Century*, trans. E. I. Watkin, v, *Imperialism and the Rise of Labour* (1895-

1905), 2nd ed. (1951); vi, *The Rule of Democracy* (1905–14), 2 vols. 2nd ed. (1952)

Hanham, H. J., *Elections and Party Management. Politics in the Time of Disraeli and Gladstone* (1959)

Hobhouse, L. T., *Liberalism* (1911)

Hobson, J. A., *The Crisis of Liberalism. New Issues of Democracy* (1909)

Jenkins, Roy, *Mr Balfour's Poodle* (1954)

Jones, Harry, *Liberalism and the House of Lords* (1912)

Kinnear, Michael, *The British Voter* (1968)

Lowell, A. L., *The Government of England*, 2 vols. (1908)

Lloyd, Trevor, *The General Election of 1880* (Oxford, 1968)

Lyons, F. S. L., *The Irish Parliamentary Party 1890–1910* (1951)

McDowell, R. B., *British Conservatism 1832–1914* (1959)

McKenzie, R. T., *British Political Parties* (1955)

Macnamara, T. J., *The Political Situation, Letters to a Working Man* (1909) *Tariff Reform and the Working Man* (1910)

Mallet, B., *British Budgets, 1887–8 to 1912–13* (1913)

Marder, A. J., *From the Dreadnought to Scapa Flow*, i, *The Road to War* (1961)

Masterman, C. F. G., *The Condition of England* (1909)

Matthews, A. H., *Fifty Years of Agricultural Politics: being the History of the Central Chamber of Agriculture* (1915)

Miliband, Ralph, *Parliamentary Socialism* (1961)

Money, L. G. Chiozza, *Riches and Poverty*, 10th ed. (1911) *Money's Fiscal Dictionary 1910* (1910)

Morgan, Kenneth O., *Wales in British Politics 1868–1922* (Cardiff, 1963)

Morris, H. L., *Parliamentary Franchise Reform in England and Wales from 1885–1918* (New York, 1921)

'Nonconformist Minister', *Nonconformity and Politics* (1909)

Nowell-Smith, Simon ed., *Edwardian England 1901–1914* (1964)

O'Leary, Cornelius, *The Elimination of Corrupt Practices in British Elections 1868–1911* (Oxford, 1962)

Ostrogorski, Moisei, *Democracy and the Organisation of Political Parties*, trans. F. Clarke, 2 vols. (1902)

Pelling, Henry, *A Short History of the Labour Party* (1961) *Social Geography of British Elections 1885–1910* (1967) *Popular Politics and Society in Late Victorian Britain* (1968)

Poirier, Philip P., *The Advent of the Labour Party* (1958)

Reid, J. H. Stewart, *The Origins of the British Labour Party* (Minneapolis, 1955)

Rover, Constance, *Women's Suffrage and Party Politics in Britain 1866–1914* (1967)

Rowland, Peter, *The Last Liberal Governments*, i, *The Promised Land 1905–10* (1968)

Semmel, Bernard, *Imperialism and Social Reform* (1960)

Seymour, C. S., *Electoral Reform in England and Wales* (New Haven, 1915)

Smith, Paul, *Disraelian Conservatism and Social Reform* (1967)

Snowden, Philip, *A Few Hints to Loyd George. Where is the Money to Come From? The Question Answered* (1909)

Southgate, Donald, *The Passing of the Whigs* (1962)

Thompson, Paul, *Socialists, Liberals and Labour. The Struggle for London 1885–1914* (1967)

The Times, The History of The Times, iv, *The 150th Anniversary and Beyond*, 2 vols. (1952)

Wallas, Graham, *Human Nature in Politics* (1909)

3. *Theses and articles*

Anonymous, 'Blackbread and Blatchford', *Fortnightly Review*, lxxxvii (Mar 1910) 435–46

'The Elections and Their Moral', *Blackwood's Magazine*, clxxxvii (Mar 1910) 430–42

'The Elections and After', *Blackwood's Magazine*, clxxxix (Jan 1911) 150–60

Barker, J. Ellis, 'How the Unionists Might win the General Election', *Fortnightly Review*, lxxxvi (Nov 1909) 799–812.

Baumann, Arthur A., 'Money and Brains in Politics', *Fortnightly Review*, lxxxvi (Oct 1909), 598–604

Blewett, Neal, 'The Franchise in the United Kingdom 1885–1918', *Past and Present* No. 32 (Dec 1965) 27–56

'Free Fooders, Balfourites, Whole Hoggers. Factionalism within the Unionist Party, 1906–10', *Historical Journal*, xi (1968) 95–124

Brookes, Sydney, 'The British Elections', *North American Review*, cxci (1910) 410–19

Cornford, James, 'The Transformation of Conservatism in the Late Nineteenth Century', *Victorian Studies*, vii (1963–4) 35–66

Dunbabin, J. P. D., 'Parliamentary Elections in Great Britain, 1868–1900: A Psephological Note', *English Historical Review*, lxxxi (1966) 82–9

Glaser, John F., 'English Nonconformity and the Decline of Liberalism', *American Historical Review*, lxxiii (1957-8) 352-63

Hobson, J. A., 'The General Election: A Sociological Interpretation', *Sociological Review*, iii (1910) 105-17.

Jones, R. B., 'Balfour's Reform of Party Organisation', *Bulletin of the Institute of Historical Research*, xxxvii (1965), 94-101

Key, V. O., 'A Theory of Critical Elections', *Journal of Politics*, xvii (1955) 3-18

King, A. S., 'Some Aspects of the Liberal Party 1906-14' (D.Phil. thesis, Oxford, 1962)

Krehbiel, Edward, 'Geographic Influences in British Elections', *The Geographical Review*, ii (1916) 419-32

Mozley, E. N., 'The Political Heptarchy. An Analysis of seven General Elections', *Contemporary Review*, xcv (April 1910) 400-12

Pedder, D. C., 'The Corruption of the Cotter', *Contemporary Review*, xcvi (Dec 1909) 684-90

'Intensive Electioneering', *Contemporary Review*, xcvii (Mar 1910) 273-80

Pomper, Gerald, 'Classification of Presidential Elections', *Journal of Politics*, xxix (1967) 535-66

'Pro-Patria' (J. L. Garvin), 'The General Election and the Next', *National Review*, liv (Feb 1910) 917-33

Russell, A. K., 'The General Election of 1906' (D.Phil. thesis, Oxford, 1962)

Rosenbaum, S., 'The General Election of January 1910, and the Bearing of the Results on Some Problems of Representation', *Journal of the Royal Statistical Society*, lxxiii (1910) 473-528

Urwin, Derek W., 'The Development of the Conservative Party Organisation in Scotland until 1912', *Scottish Historical Review*, xliv (1965) 90-111

Index

Page references in brackets indicate the page location of the relevant note